Encyclopedia of Robust Control: Concepts and Applications

Volume I

Encyclopedia of Robust Control: Concepts and Applications
Volume I

Edited by **Zac Fredericks**

CLANRYE INTERNATIONAL

New Jersey

Published by Clanrye International,
55 Van Reypen Street,
Jersey City, NJ 07306, USA
www.clanryeinternational.com

Encyclopedia of Robust Control: Concepts and Applications
Volume I
Edited by Zac Fredericks

International Standard Book Number: 978-1-63240-200-4 (Hardback)

Printed in the United States of America.

Contents

Preface

The world is advancing at a fast pace like never before. Therefore, the need is to keep up with the latest developments. This book was an idea that came to fruition when the specialists in the area realized the need to coordinate together and document essential themes in the subject. That's when I was requested to be the editor. Editing this book has been an honour as it brings together diverse authors researching on different streams of the field. The book collates essential materials contributed by veterans in the area which can be utilized by students and researchers alike.

This book gives a broad overview of robust control by providing theoretical advances with the help of selected applications. Robust control has been a topic of extensive research in the last three decades culminating in H_2/H_∞ and μ design methods followed by studies on parametric robustness, earlier motivated by Kharitonov's theorem, the extension to non-linear time delay systems, and other recent methods. This book includes contributions of experts in this field from all over the world. While, discussing different theoretical aspects and application areas, it also examines problems in robust control theory and its functioning in electromechanical and robotic systems. It also includes topics on robust control and problem specific solutions. This book serves as a complete guide for researchers, students and other interested individuals in the field of robotics and mechatronics.

Each chapter is a sole-standing publication that reflects each author's interpretation. Thus, the book displays a multi-facetted picture of our current understanding of application, resources and aspects of the field. I would like to thank the contributors of this book and my family for their endless support.

Editor

Part 1

Theoretical Aspects of Robust Control

1

Robustness of Feedback Linear Time-Varying Systems: A Commutant Lifting Approach

Seddik M. Djouadi
Electrical Engineering & Computer Science Department, University of Tennessee, Knoxville, TN 37996-2100 USA

1. Introduction

There have been numerous attempts in the literature to generalize results in robust control theory (42; 45) to linear time-varying (LTV) systems (for e.g. (10–13; 30; 33; 37; 39; 40) and references therein). In (12)(13) and (11) the authors studied the optimal weighted sensitivity minimization problem, the two-block problem, and the model-matching problem for LTV systems using inner-outer factorization for positive operators. Abstract solutions involving the computation of induced operators norms of operators are obtained. However, there is no clear indication on how to compute optimal linear LTV controllers.

In (40) the authors rely on state space techniques which lead to algorithms based on infinite dimensional operator inequalities which are difficult to solve. These methods lead to suboptimal controllers and are restricted to finite dimensional systems. An extension of these results to uncertain systems is reported in (41) relying on uniform stability concepts. In (9) both the sensitivity minimization problem in the presence of plant uncertainty, and robust stability for LTV systems in the ℓ^∞ induced norm is considered. However, their methods could not be extended to the case of systems operating on finite energy signals. In (37) the standard problem of H^∞ control theory for finite-dimensional LTV continuous-time plants is considered. It is shown that a solution to this problem exists if and only if a pair of matrix Riccati differential equations admits positive semidefinite stabilizing solutions. State-space formulae for one solution to the problem are also given.

The gap metric was introduced to study stability robustness of feedback systems. It induces the weakest topology in which feedback stability is robust (6; 7; 31; 32; 38). Extensions of the gap to time-varying systems have been proposed in (33; 34) where a geometric framework was developed. Several results on the gap metric and the gap topology were established, in particular, the concept of a graphable subspace was introduced. In (21) the problem of robust stabilization for LTV systems subject to time-varying normalized coprime factor uncertainty is considered. Operator theoretic results which generalize similar results known to hold for linear time-invariant (infinite-dimensional) systems are developed. In particular, a tight upper bound for the maximal achievable stability margin under TV normalized coprime factor uncertainty in terms of the norm of an operator with a time-varying Hankel structure is computed.

Analysis of time-varying control strategies for optimal disturbance rejection for known time-invariant plants has been studied in (2; 16). A robust version of these problems was considered in (8; 15) in different induced norm topologies. All these references showed that for *time-invariant nominal* plants and weighting functions, time-varying control laws offer no advantage over time-invariant ones.

In this paper, we are interested in optimal disturbance rejection for (*possibly infinite-dimensional*, i.e., systems with an infinite number of states) LTV systems. These systems have been used as models in computational linear algebra and in a variety of computational and communication networks (17). This allows variable number of states which is predominant in networks which can switch on or off certain parts of the system (17), and infinite number of states as in distributed parameter systems.

Using inner-outer factorizations as defined in (3; 11) with respect of the nest algebra of lower triangular (causal) bounded linear operators defined on ℓ^2 we show that the problem reduces to a distance minimization between a special operator and the nest algebra. The inner-outer factorization used here holds under weaker assumptions than (12; 13), and in fact, as pointed in ((3) p. 180), is different from the factorization for positive operators used there.

The optimal disturbance attenuation for LTV systems has been addressed using Banach space duality theory in (20; 28). Its robust version which deals with plant uncertainty is addressed in (4; 5; 19) using also duality theory ideas. Furthermore, using the commutant lifting theorem for nest algebras the optimum is shown to be equal to the norm of a compact time-varying Hankel operator defined on the space of causal Hilbert-Schmidt operators. The latter is the "natural" analogous to the Hankel operator used in the LTI case. An operator identity to compute the optimal TV Youla parameter is also provided.

The results are generalized to the mixed sensitivity problem for TV systems as well, where it is shown that the optimum is equal to the operator induced of a TV mixed Hankel-Toeplitz operator generalizing analogous results known to hold in the linear time-invariant (LTI) case (22; 38; 43).

Our approach is purely input-output and does not use any state space realization, therefore the results derived here apply to *infinite dimensional LTV systems*, i.e., TV systems with an infinite number of state variables (33). Although the theory is developed for causal stable system, it can be extended in a straightforward fashion to the unstable case using coprime factorization techniques for LTV systems discussed in (11; 13).

The rest of the chapter is organized as follows. Section 2 the commutant lifting theorem for nest algebras is introduced. In section 3 the optimal disturbance rejection problem is formulated and solved in terms of a TV Hankel operator. A Generalization to the TV mixed sensitivity problem is carried out in section 4. Section 5 contains some concluding remarks.

Definitions and notation

- $\mathcal{B}(E,F)$ denotes the space of bounded linear operators from a Banach space E to a Banach space F, endowed with the operator norm

$$\|A\| := \sup_{x\in E,\ \|x\|\leq 1} \|Ax\|, \quad A \in \mathcal{B}(E,F)$$

- ℓ^2 denotes the usual Hilbert space of square summable sequences with the standard norm

$$\|x\|_2^2 := \sum_{j=0}^{\infty} |x_j|^2, \quad x := (x_0, x_1, x_2, \cdots) \in \ell^2$$

- P_k the usual truncation operator for some integer k, which sets all outputs after time k to zero.
- An operator $A \in \mathcal{B}(E, F)$ is said to be causal if it satisfies the operator equation:

$$P_k A P_k = P_k A, \ \forall k \ \text{positive integers}$$

- $tr(\cdot)$ denotes the trace of its argument.

The subscript "$_c$" denotes the restriction of a subspace of operators to its intersection with causal (see (11; 29) for the definition) operators. "$\oplus$" denotes for the direct sum of two spaces. "$\star$" stands for the adjoint of an operator.

2. The commutant lifting theorem

The commutant lifting theorem has been proposed by Sz.Nagy and Foias (35; 36). It has been used successfully to solve several interpolation problems including H^∞ control problems for linear time invariant (LTI) systems (31; 32; 43; 44). In this chapter, we rely on a time-varying version of the commutant lifting theorem which corresponds to nest or triangular algebras. Following (3; 18) a nest $\mathcal{N}$ of a Hilbert space $\check{H}$ is a family of closed subspaces of $\check{H}$ ordered by inclusion. The triangular or nest algebra $\mathcal{T}(\mathcal{N})$ is the set of all operators T such that $TN \subseteq N$ for every element N in $\mathcal{N}$. A representation of $\mathcal{T}(\mathcal{N})$ is an algebra homomorphism h from $\mathcal{T}(\mathcal{N})$ into the algebra $\mathcal{B}(\mathcal{H})$ of bounded linear operators on a Hilbert space $\mathcal{H}$. A representation is contractive if $\|h(A)\| \leq \|A\|$, for all $A \in \mathcal{T}(\mathcal{N})$. It is weak* continuous if $h(A_i)$ converges to zero in the weak* topology of $\mathcal{B}(\mathcal{H})$ whenever the net $\{A_i\}$ converges to zero in the weak* topology of $\mathcal{B}(\check{H})$. The representation h is said to be unital if $h(I_{\check{H}}) = I_{\mathcal{H}}$, where $I_{\check{H}}$ is the identity operator on $\check{H}$, and $I_{\mathcal{H}}$ the identity operator on $\mathcal{H}$. The Sz. Nagy Theorem asserts that any such a representation h has a $\mathcal{B}(\check{H})$-dilation, that is, there exists a Hilbert space $\mathcal{K}$ containing $\mathcal{H}$, and a positive representation H of $\mathcal{B}(\check{H})$ such that $P_{\mathcal{H}} H(A) \mid_{\mathcal{H}} = h(A)$, where $P_{\mathcal{H}}$ is the orthogonal projection from $\mathcal{K}$ into $\mathcal{H}$ (3; 18).
We now state the commutant lifting theorem for nest algebras from (3; 18) (see also references therein).

Theorem 1. *(3; 18) Let*

$$h: \ \mathcal{T}(\mathcal{N}) \longmapsto \mathcal{B}(\mathcal{H})$$
$$h^\star: \mathcal{T}(\mathcal{N}) \longmapsto \mathcal{B}(\mathcal{H}')$$

be two unital weak* continuous contractive representations with $\mathcal{B}(\check{H})$-dilations

$$H: \ \mathcal{B}(\check{H}) \longmapsto \mathcal{B}(\mathcal{K})$$
$$H^\star: \mathcal{B}(\check{H}) \longmapsto \mathcal{B}(\mathcal{K}')$$

respectively. Assume that $X: \ \mathcal{H} \longmapsto \mathcal{H}'$ is a linear operator with $\|X\| \leq 1$, such that $Xh(A) = h'(A)X$ for all $A \in \mathcal{T}(\mathcal{N})$, that is, X intertwines h and h'. Then there exists an operator $Y: \ \mathcal{K} \longmapsto \mathcal{K}'$ such that

i) $\|Y\| \leq 1$.

ii) *Y intertwines H and H', that is, $YH(A) = H'(A)Y$ for all $A \in \mathcal{B}(\check{H})$.*

iii) *Y dilates X, that is, $Y : \mathcal{M} \longmapsto \mathcal{M}'$, and $P_{\mathcal{H}'}Y \mid_{\mathcal{M}} = XP_{\mathcal{H}} \mid_{\mathcal{M}}$, where $\mathcal{H} = \mathcal{M} \ominus \mathcal{N}$ is the orthogonal representation of $\mathcal{H}$ as the orthogonal difference of invariant subspaces for $H \mid_{T(\mathcal{N})}$, and similarly for $\mathcal{H}'$.*

In the next section the optimal disturbance rejection problem is formulated and solved using this Theorem in terms of a TV Hankel operator.

3. Time-varying optimal disturbance rejection problem

In this chapter, we first consider the problem of optimizing performance for causal linear time varying systems by considering the standard block diagram for the optimal disturbance attenuation problem represented in Fig. 1, where u represents the control inputs, y the measured outputs, z is the controlled output, w the exogenous perturbations. P denotes a causal stable linear time varying plant, and K denotes a time varying controller. The

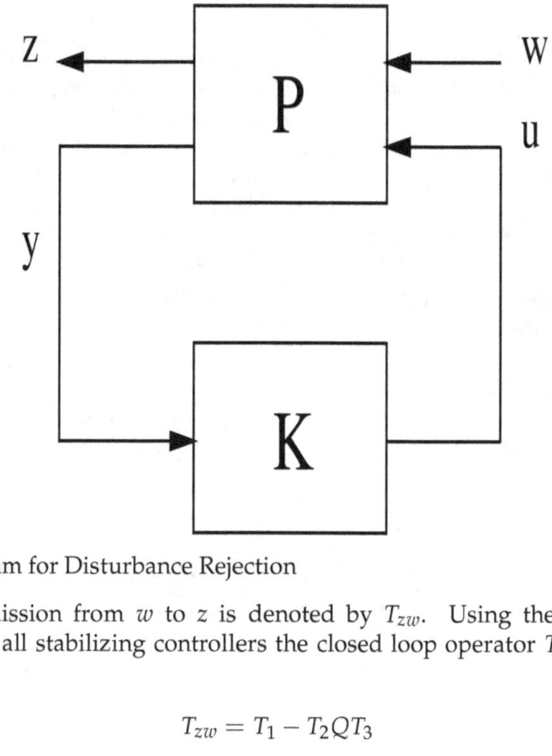

Fig. 1. Block Diagram for Disturbance Rejection

closed-loop transmission from w to z is denoted by T_{zw}. Using the standard TV Youla parametrization of all stabilizing controllers the closed loop operator T_{zw} can be written as (2; 11; 16),

$$T_{zw} = T_1 - T_2 Q T_3 \tag{1}$$

where T_1, T_2 and T_3 are stable causal LTV operators, that is, T_1, T_2 and $T_3 \in B_c(\ell^2, \ell^2)$. Here it is assumed without loss of generality that P is stable, the Youla parameter $Q := K(I + PK)^{-1}$ is then an operator belonging to $B_c(\ell^2, \ell^2)$, and is related in a one-to-one onto fashion to the controller K (29). Note that Q is allowed to be *time-varying*. If P is unstable it suffices to use the coprime factorization techniques in (11; 39) which lead to similar results. The magnitude of the signals w and z is measured in the ℓ^2-norm. The performance index which quantifies optimal disturbance rejection can be written in the following form (20)

$$\mu := \inf\{\|T_{zw}\| : K \text{ being robustly stabilizing linear time} - \text{varying controller}\}$$
$$= \inf_{Q\in\mathcal{B}_c(\ell^2,\ell^2)} \|T_1 - T_2QT_3\| \tag{2}$$

The performance index (2) will be transformed into a shortest distance minimization between a certain bounded linear operator and a subspace to be specified shortly. In order to do so, following (11) define a nest $\mathcal{N}$ as a family of closed subspaces of the Hilbert space ℓ^2 containing $\{0\}$ and ℓ^2 which is closed under intersection and closed span. Let $Q_n := I - P_n$, for $n = -1, 0, 1, \cdots$, where $P_{-1} := 0$ and $P_\infty := I$. Then Q_n is a projection, and we can associate to it the following nest $\mathcal{N} := \{Q_n\ell^2,\ n = -1, 0, 1, \cdots\}$. In this case the triangular or nest algebra $\mathcal{T}(\mathcal{N})$ is the set of all operators T such that $TN \subseteq N$ for every element N in $\mathcal{N}$. That is

$$\mathcal{T}(\mathcal{N}) = \{A \in \mathcal{B}(\ell^2,\ell^2) : P_nA(I - P_n) = 0,\ \forall\, n\}$$
$$= \{A \in \mathcal{B}(\ell^2,\ell^2) : (I - Q_n)AQ_n = 0,\ \forall\, n\} \tag{3}$$

Note that the Banach space $\mathcal{B}_c(\ell^2,\ell^2)$ is identical to the nest algebra $\mathcal{T}(\mathcal{N})$. For N belonging to the nest $\mathcal{N}$, N has the form $Q_n\ell^2$ for some n. Define

$$N^- = \bigvee\{N' \in \mathcal{N} : N' < N\} \tag{4}$$
$$N^+ = \bigwedge\{N' \in \mathcal{N} : N' > N\} \tag{5}$$

where $N' < N$ means $N' \subset N$, and $N' > N$ means $N' \supset N$. The subspaces $N \ominus N^-$ are called the atoms of $\mathcal{N}$. Since in our case the atoms of $\mathcal{N}$ span ℓ^2, then $\mathcal{N}$ is said to be atomic (3).

The early days of H^∞ control theory saw solutions based on the so-called inner-outer factorizations of functions belonging to the Hardy spaces H^2 and H^∞, and their corresponding matrix valued counterparts for multi-input multi-output (MIMO) systems (22; 23). Generalizations in the context of nest algebras have been proposed in (1; 3) as follows: An operator A in $\mathcal{T}(\mathcal{N})$ is called *outer* if the range projection $P(R_A)$, R_A being the range of A and P the orthogonal projection onto R_A, commutes with $\mathcal{N}$ and AN is dense in $N \cap R_A$ for every $N \in \mathcal{N}$. A partial isometry U is called *inner* in $\mathcal{T}(\mathcal{N})$ if $U^\star U$ commutes with $\mathcal{N}$ (1; 3; 11). In our case, $A \in \mathcal{T}(\mathcal{N}) = \mathcal{B}_c(\ell^2,\ell^2)$ is outer if P commutes with each Q_n and $AQ_n\ell^2$ is dense in $Q_n\ell^2 \cap A\ell^2$. $U \in \mathcal{B}_c(\ell^2,\ell^2)$ is inner if U is a partial isometry and $U^\star U$ commutes with every Q_n. Applying these notions to the time-varying operator $T_2 \in \mathcal{B}_c(\ell^2,\ \ell^2)$, we get $T_2 = T_{2i}T_{2o}$, where T_{2i} and T_{2o} are inner outer operators in $\mathcal{B}_c(\ell^2,\ell^2)$, respectively. Similarly, the operator T_3 can be factored as $T_3 = T_{3o}T_{3i}$ where $T_{3i} \in \mathcal{B}_c(\ell^2,\ell^2)$ is inner, $T_{3o} \in \mathcal{B}_c(\ell^2,\ell^2)$ is outer. The performance index μ in (2) can then be written as

$$\mu = \inf_{Q\in\mathcal{B}_c(\ell^2,\ell^2)} \|T_1 - T_{2i}T_{2o}QT_{3o}T_{3i}\| \tag{6}$$

Following the classical H^∞ control theory (22; 23; 45),we assume
(A1) that T_{2o} and T_{3o} are invertible both in $\mathcal{B}_c(\ell^2,\ell^2)$.
Assumption (A1) can be relaxed by assuming instead that the outer operators T_{2o} and T_{3o} are bounded below (see Lemma (1) p. 220). Assumption (A1) guarantees that the map $Q \longrightarrow T_{2o}\mathcal{B}_c(\ell^2,\ell^2)T_{3o}$ is bijective. Under this assumption T_{2i} becomes an isometry and T_{3i}

a co-isometry in which case $T_{2i}^{\star}T_{2i} = I$ and $T_{3i}T_{3i}^{\star} = I$. The operators T_{2o} and T_{3o} can be absorbed into the Youla operator Q, and expression (6) is then equivalent to

$$\mu = \inf_{Q \in \mathcal{B}_c(\ell^2,\ell^2)} \|T_{2i}^{\star}T_1T_{3i}^{\star} - Q\| \tag{7}$$

Expression (7) is the distance from the operator $T_{2i}^{\star}T_1T_{3i}^{\star} \in \mathcal{B}(\ell^2,\ell^2)$ to the nest algebra $\mathcal{B}_c(\ell^2,\ell^2)$. It is the shortest distance from the bounded linear operator $T_{2i}^{\star}T_1T_{3i}^{\star}$ to the space of causal bounded linear operators $\mathcal{B}_c(\ell^2,\ell^2)$, which is a subspace of $\mathcal{B}(\ell^2,\ell^2)$. In the sequel, the commutant lifting theorem is used to solve the minimization (7) in terms of a time varying version of Hankel operators.
First, let $\mathcal{C}_2$ denote the special class of compact operators on ℓ^2 called the Hilbert-Schmidt or Schatten 2-class (3; 14) under the norm,

$$\|A\|_2 := \left(tr(A^{\star}A)\right)^{\frac{1}{2}} \tag{8}$$

Note that $\mathcal{C}_2$ is a Hilbert space under the inner product (3)

$$(A,B) = tr(B^{\star}A), \quad \forall\ A,\ B \in \mathcal{C}_2 \tag{9}$$

Define the space

$$\mathcal{A}_2 := \mathcal{C}_2 \cap \mathcal{B}_c(\ell^2,\ell^2) \tag{10}$$

Then $\mathcal{A}_2$ is the space of causal Hilbert-Schmidt operators. This space can be viewed as the TV counterpart of the standard Hardy space H^2 in the standard H^{∞} theory. Define the orthogonal projection $\mathcal{P}$ of $\mathcal{C}_2$ onto $\mathcal{A}_2$. $\mathcal{P}$ is the lower triangular truncation, and is analogous to the standard positive Riesz projection (for functions on the unit circle) for the LTI case.
Following (27) an operator X in $\mathcal{B}(\ell^2,\ell^2)$ determines a Hankel operator H_X on $\mathcal{A}_2$ if

$$H_X A = (I - \mathcal{P})XA, \quad \text{for } A \in \mathcal{A}_2 \tag{11}$$

We shall show that the shortest distance μ is equal to the norm of a particular LTV Hankel operator using the time varying version of the commutant lifting theorem in Theorem 1, thus generalizing a similar result in the LTI setting. let H_B be the Hankel operator $(I - \mathcal{P})B\mathcal{P}$ associated with the symbol $B := T_{2i}^{\star}T_1T_{3ci}^{\star}$. The Hankel operator H_B belongs to the Banach space of bounded linear operators on $\mathcal{C}_2$, namely, $\mathcal{B}(\mathcal{C}_2,\mathcal{C}_2)$. We have then the following Theorem which relates the optimal distance minimization μ to the induced norm of the Hankel operator $H_{T_{2i}^{\star}T_1T_{3ci}^{\star}}$.

Theorem 2. *Under assumptions (A1) the following holds:*

$$\mu = \|H_{T_{2i}^{\star}T_1T_{3ci}^{\star}}\| = \|(I - \mathcal{P})T_{2i}^{\star}T_1T_{3ci}^{\star}\mathcal{P}\| \tag{12}$$

Proof. Following (3; 18) let $H_1 = \mathcal{A}_2$ and $H_2 = \mathcal{C}_2 \ominus \mathcal{A}_2$ the orthogonal complement of $\mathcal{A}_2$ in $\mathcal{C}_2$. Define the representations h and h' of $\mathcal{A}_2$ by

$$h(A) = R_A\,|_{H_1}, \quad A \in \mathcal{B}_c(\ell^2,\ell^2) \tag{13}$$
$$h'(A) = (I - \mathcal{P})R_{A|H_2}, \quad A \in \mathcal{B}_c(\ell^2,\ell^2) \tag{14}$$

where now R_A denotes the right multiplication associated to the operator A defined on the specified Hilbert space, i.e., $R_A B = BA$, $B \in \mathcal{A}_2$. The representation $h(\cdot)$ and $h'(\cdot)$ have dilations $H = H'$ given by

$$H(A) = H'(A) = R_A \text{ on } \mathcal{C}_2, \; A \in \mathcal{B}_c(\ell^2, \ell^2) \tag{15}$$

(16)

Let $M := \mathcal{B}_c(\ell^2, \ell^2)$, $N = \{0\}$, $M' := \mathcal{C}_2$, $N' := \mathcal{A}_2$, and $H_1 = M \ominus N$, $H_2 = M' \ominus N'$ are orthogonal representations of H_1 and H_2 of invariant subspaces under $H|_{\mathcal{B}_c(\ell^2,\ell^2)}$, that is, $R_A \mathcal{B}_c(\ell^2, \ell^2) \subset \mathcal{B}_c(\ell^2, \ell^2)$. Now we have to show that the operator $H_{T_{2i}^\star T_1 T_{3ci}^\star}$ intertwines h and h', that is, if $B := T_{2i}^\star T_1 T_{3ci}^\star$, then $h'(A)H_B = H_B h(A)$ holds for for all $A \in \mathcal{B}_c(\ell^2, \ell^2)$,

$$h'(A)H_B = (I - \mathcal{P})R_A(I - \mathcal{P})B \,|_{\mathcal{A}_2} = (I - \mathcal{P})R_A B \,|_{\mathcal{A}_2} \tag{17}$$

$$= (I - \mathcal{P})BR_A \,|_{\mathcal{A}_2} = (I - \mathcal{P})B\mathcal{P}R_A \,|_{\mathcal{A}_2} = H_B h(A) \tag{18}$$

Applying the Commutant Lifting Theorem for representations of nest algebras implies that H_B has a dilation $\tilde{H}_B$ that intertwines H and H', i.e., $\tilde{H}_B H(A) = H'(A)\tilde{H}_B$, $\forall A \in \mathcal{B}(\ell^2, \ell^2)$. By Lemma 4.4. in (18) $\tilde{H}_B$ is a left multiplication operator acting from $\mathcal{A}_2$ into $\mathcal{C}_2 \ominus \mathcal{A}_2$. That is, $\tilde{H}_B = L_K$ for some $K \in \mathcal{B}(\ell^2, \ell^2)$, with $\|L_K\| = \|K\| = \|\tilde{H}_X\| = \|H_B\|$ by Lemma 4.5. (18). By Lemma 4.3. (18) $K = B - Q$, $\exists Q \in \mathcal{B}_c(\ell^2, \ell^2)$ with $\|K\| = \|H_B\|$ as required.
By Theorem 2.1. (26) the Hankel operator H_B is a compact operator if and only if B belongs to the space $\mathcal{B}_c(\ell^2, \ell^2) + \mathcal{K}$, where $\mathcal{K}$ is the space of compact operators on the Hilbert space ℓ^2. A basic property of compact operators on Hilbert spaces is that they have maximizing vectors, that is, there exists at least one operator $A^o \in \mathcal{A}_2$, $\|A^o\|_2 = 1$ such that H_B achieves its induced norm at A^o. That is,

$$\|H_B A^o\|_2 = \|H_B\| \|A^o\|_2 = \|H_B\| \tag{19}$$

We can then deduce from (7) and (12) an operator identity for the minimizer, that is, the optimal TV Youla parameter Q_o as follows

$$Q_o A^o = T_{2i}^\star T_1 T_{3ci}^\star A^o - H_{T_{2i}^\star T_1 T_{3ci}^\star} A^o$$

where the unknown is Q_o.
In the next section the mixed sensitivity problems for LTV systems is formulated and solved using the commutant lifting theorem.

4. The time-varying mixed sensitivity problem

The mixed sensitivity problem for stable plants (42; 45) involves the sensitivity operator $T_1 := \begin{pmatrix} W \\ 0 \end{pmatrix}$, the complementary sensitivity operator $T_2 = \begin{pmatrix} W \\ V \end{pmatrix} P$ and $T_3 := I$ which are all assumed to belong to $\mathcal{B}_c(\ell^2, \ell^2 \times \ell^2)$, and is given by the minimization (13; 20; 46)

$$\mu_o = \inf_{Q \in \mathcal{B}_c(\ell^2, \ell^2)} \left\| \begin{pmatrix} W \\ 0 \end{pmatrix} - \begin{pmatrix} W \\ V \end{pmatrix} PQ \right\| \tag{20}$$

where $\|\cdot\|$ stands for the operator norm in $\mathcal{B}(\ell^2, \; \ell^2 \times \ell^2)$ given by

$$\|B\| = \sup_{\|x\|_2 \le 1, \, x \in \ell^2} \left(\|B_1 x\|_2^2 + \|B_2 x\|_2^2 \right)^{\frac{1}{2}}, \; B = \begin{pmatrix} B_1 \\ B_2 \end{pmatrix} \tag{21}$$

The optimization problem (20) can be expressed as a shortest distance problem from the operator T_1 to the subspace $\mathcal{S} = T_2 P\, \mathcal{B}_c(\ell^2, \ell^2)$ of $\mathcal{B}(\ell^2,\ \ell^2 \times \ell^2)$.
To ensure closedness of $\mathcal{S}$, we assume that $W^\star W + V^\star V > 0$, i.e., $W^\star W + V^\star V$ as an operator acting on ℓ^2 is a positive operator. In this case, there exists an outer spectral factorization $\Lambda_1 \in \mathcal{B}_c(\ell^2, \ell^2)$, invertible in $\mathcal{B}_c(\ell^2, \ell^2)$ such that $\Lambda_1^\star \Lambda_1 = W^\star W + V^\star V$ (1; 11). Consequently, $\Lambda_1 P$ as a bounded linear operator in $\mathcal{B}_c(\ell^2, \ell^2)$ has an inner-outer factorization $U_1 G$, where U_1 is inner and G an outer operator defined on ℓ^2 (3).
Next we assume (**A2**) G is invertible, so U_1 is unitary, and the operator G and its inverse $G^{-1} \in \mathcal{B}_c(\ell^2, \ell^2)$. The assumption (A2) is satisfied when, for e.g., the outer factor of the plant is invertible. Let $R := T_2 \Lambda_1^{-1} U_1$, assumption (A2) implies that the operator $R^\star R \in \mathcal{B}(\ell^2, \ell^2)$ has a bounded inverse, this ensures closedness of $\mathcal{S}$. It follows from Corollary 2 (1), that the self-adjoint operator $R^\star R$ has a spectral factorization of the form: $R^\star R = \Lambda^\star \Lambda$, where $\Lambda,\ \Lambda^{-1} \in \mathcal{B}_c(\ell^2, \ell^2)$.
Define the operator $R_2 := R\Lambda^{-1}$, then $R_2^\star R_2 = I$, and $\mathcal{S}$ has the equivalent representation, $\mathcal{S} = R_2 \mathcal{B}_c(\ell^2, \ell^2)$. After "absorbing" Λ into the free parameter Q, the optimization problem (20) is then equivalent to:

$$\mu_o = \inf_{Q \in \mathcal{B}_c(\ell^2, \ell^2)} \|T_1 - R_2 Q\| \tag{22}$$

The minimization problem (22) gives the optimal mixed sensitivity with respect to controller design (as represented by Q). It is solved in terms of a projection of a multiplication operator. If the minimization (22) is achieved by a particular Q_o, we call it optimal.

Theorem 3. *Introduce the orthogonal projection Π as follows*

$$\Pi\ :\ \mathcal{A}_2 \oplus \mathcal{A}_2 \longmapsto (\mathcal{A}_2 \oplus \mathcal{A}_2) \ominus R_2 \mathcal{A}_2$$

Under assumptions (A2) the following holds:

$$\mu_o = \|\Pi T_1\| \tag{23}$$

Proof. Denote by $S := (\mathcal{A}_2 \oplus \mathcal{A}_2) \ominus R_2 \mathcal{A}_2$. That is, S is the orthogonal complement of the subspace $R_2 \mathcal{A}_2$ in $\mathcal{A}_2 \oplus \mathcal{A}_2$, and define the operator

$$\begin{aligned} \Xi\ &:\ \mathcal{A}_2 \longmapsto S \\ \Xi &:= \Pi T_1 \end{aligned} \tag{24}$$

We shall show with the help of the commutant lifting theorem that

$$\mu_o = \|\Xi\| \tag{25}$$

To see this we need, as before, a representation of $\mathcal{B}_c(\ell^2, \ell^2)$, that is, an algebra homomorphism, say, $h(\cdot)$ (respectively $h'(\cdot)$), from $\mathcal{B}_c(\ell^2, \ell^2)$, into the algebra $B(\mathcal{A}_2, \mathcal{A}_2)$ (respectively $\mathcal{B}_c(S, S)$), of bounded linear operators from $\mathcal{A}_2$ into $\mathcal{A}_2$ (respectively from S into S). Define the representations h and h' by

$$\begin{aligned} h:\ \ \mathcal{B}_c(\ell^2, \ell^2) \longmapsto B(\mathcal{A}_2, \mathcal{A}_2),\ \ h' : \mathcal{B}_c(\ell^2, \ell^2)) \longmapsto \mathcal{B}_c(S, S) \\ h(A) := R_A,\ \ A \in \mathcal{B}_c(\ell^2, \ell^2),\ \ h'(A) := \Pi R_A,\ \ A \in \mathcal{B}_c(\ell^2, \ell^2)) \end{aligned} \tag{26}$$

where now R_A denotes the right multiplication associated to the operator A defined on the specified Hilbert space. By the Sz. Nagy dilation Theorem there exist dilations H (respectively H') for h (respectively h') given by

$$H(A) = R_A \text{ on } \mathcal{A}_2 \text{ for } A \in \mathcal{B}_c(\ell^2, \ell^2) \tag{27}$$

$$H'(A) = R_A \text{ on } \mathcal{A}_2 \oplus \mathcal{A}_2 \text{ for } A \in \mathcal{B}_c(\ell^2, \ell^2) \tag{28}$$

The spaces $\mathcal{A}_2$ and S can be written as orthogonal differences of subspaces invariant under H and H', respectively, as

$$\mathcal{A}_2 = \mathcal{A}_2 \ominus \{0\}, \quad S = \mathcal{A}_2 \oplus \mathcal{A}_2 \ominus R_2\mathcal{A}_2 \tag{29}$$

Now we have to show that the operator Ξ intertwines h and h', that is, $h'(A)\Xi = \Xi h(A)$ for all $A \in \mathcal{B}_c(\ell^2, \ell^2)$,

$$\begin{aligned} h'(A)\Xi &= \Pi R_A \Pi T_1 \mid_{\mathcal{A}_2} = \Pi R_A \Pi T_1 \mid_{\mathcal{A}_2} \\ &= \Pi R_A T_1 \mid_{\mathcal{A}_2} = \Pi T_1 R_A \mid_{\mathcal{A}_2} \\ &= \Xi h(A) \end{aligned}$$

Applying the commutant lifting theorem for representations of nest algebras implies that Ξ has a dilation Ξ' that intertwines H and H', i.e., $\Xi' H(A) = H'(A)\Xi'$, $\forall A \in \mathcal{B}(\ell^2, \ell^2)$. By Lemma 4.4. in (18) Ξ' is a left multiplication operator acting from $\mathcal{A}_2$ into $\mathcal{A}_2 \oplus \mathcal{A}_2$, and causal. That is, $\Xi' = L_K$ for some $K \in \mathcal{B}_c(\mathcal{A}_2,\ \mathcal{A}_2 \oplus \mathcal{A}_2)$, with $\|K\| = \|\Xi'\| = \|\Xi\|$. Then $\Xi = \Pi T_1 = \Pi K$, which implies that $\Pi(T_1 - K) = 0$. Hence, $(T_1 - K)f \in R_2\mathcal{A}_2$, for all $f \in \mathcal{A}_2$. That is, $(T_1 - K)f = R_2 g$, $\exists g \in \mathcal{A}_2$, which can be written as $R_2^\star(T_1 - K)f = g \in \mathcal{A}_2$. In particular, $R_2^\star(T_1 - K)f \in \mathcal{B}_c(\ell^2, \ell^2)$, for all $f \in \mathcal{B}_c(\ell^2, \ell^2)$ of finite rank. By Theorem 3.10 (3) there is a sequence F_n of finite rank contractions in $\mathcal{B}_c(\ell^2, \ell^2)$ which converges to the identity operator in the strong *-topology. By an approximation argument it follows that $R_2^\star(T_1 - K) \in \mathcal{B}_c(\ell^2,\ \ell^2)$. Letting $Q := R_2^\star(T_1 - K)$ we have $g = Qf$. We conclude that $T_1 - K = R_2 Q$, that is, $T_1 - R_2 Q = K$, with $\|K\| = \|\Xi\|$, and the Theorem is proved.
The orthogonal projection Π can be computed as

$$\Pi = I - R_2 \mathcal{P} R_2^\star \tag{30}$$

where I is the identity operator on $\mathcal{A}_2 \oplus \mathcal{A}_2$, $R_2^\star$ is the adjoint operator of R_2. To see that (30) holds note that for any $Y \in \mathcal{A}_2 \oplus \mathcal{A}_2$, we have

$$(I - R\mathcal{P}R_2^\star)^2 Y = (I - R\mathcal{P}R_2^\star)(I - R\mathcal{P}R_2^\star)Y \tag{31}$$

$$= (I - R_2\mathcal{P}R_2^\star - R_2\mathcal{P}R_2^\star + R_2\mathcal{P}R_2^\star\mathcal{P}R_2^\star)Y \tag{32}$$

but $R_2^\star R_2 = I$ and $\mathcal{P}^2 = \mathcal{P}$, therefore

$$(I - R\mathcal{P}R_2^\star)^2 Y = (I - R\mathcal{P}R_2^\star)Y \tag{33}$$

This shows that $(I - R\mathcal{P}R_2^\star)$ is a projection. The adjoint of $(I - R\mathcal{P}R_2^\star)$, $(I - R\mathcal{P}R_2^\star)^\star$, is clearly equal to $(I - R\mathcal{P}R_2^\star)$ showing that it is an orthogonal projection. Now we need to show that the null space of $(I - R\mathcal{P}R_2^\star)$ is $R_2\mathcal{A}_2$. Let $Z \in \mathcal{A}_2 \oplus \mathcal{A}_2$ such that $(I - R\mathcal{P}R_2^\star)Z = 0$, so $Z = R_2\mathcal{P}R_2^\star Z$. But $R_2^\star Z \in \mathcal{C}_2$, then $\mathcal{P}R_2^\star Z \in \mathcal{A}_2$, implying that $Z \in R_2\mathcal{A}_2$. We have showed that the null space of the projection $(I - R\mathcal{P}R_2^\star)$ is a subset of $R_2\mathcal{A}_2$. Conversely, let $Z \in \mathcal{A}_2$, then

$$(I - R\mathcal{P}R_2^\star)R_2Z = R_2Z - R_2\mathcal{P}Z = R_2Z - R_2Z = 0 \qquad (34)$$

hence R_2Z belongs to the null space of $(I - R\mathcal{P}R_2^\star)$, and (30) holds.
The operator Ξ has the following explicit form

$$\Xi = (I - R_2\mathcal{P}R_2^\star)T_1 \qquad (35)$$

which leads to the explicit solution

$$\mu_o = \|(I - R_2\mathcal{P}R_2^\star)T_1\| \qquad (36)$$

The expression generalizes the solution of the mixed sensitivity problem in the LTI case (25; 43; 46) to the LTV case. This result also applies to solve the robustness problem of feedback systems in the gap metric (38) in the TV case as outlined in (11; 21; 33), since the latter was shown in (11) to be equivalent to a special version of the mixed sensitivity problem (20).

5. Conclusion

The optimal disturbance rejection and the mixed sensitivity problems for LTV systems involve solving shortest distance minimization problems posed in different spaces of bounded linear operators. LTV causal and stable systems form a nest algebras, this allows the commutant lifting theorem for nest algebras to be applied and solve both problems in term of abstract TV Hankel and a TV version generalization of Hankel-Topelitz operators under fairly weak assumptions. Future work includes investigation of numerical solutions based on finite dimensional approximations, and computation of the corresponding controllers.

Acknowledgement: This work was partially supported by the National Science Foundation under NSF Award No. CMMI-0825921.

6. References

[1] Arveson W. Interpolation problems in nest algebras, *Journal of Functional Analysis*, 4 (1975) pp. 67-71.
[2] Chapellat H., Dahleh M. Analysis of time-varying control strategies for optimal disturbance rejection and robustness, *IEEE Transactions on Automatic Control*, 37 (1992) 1734-1746.
[3] Davidson K.R. *Nest Algebras*, Longman Scientific & Technical, UK, 1988.
[4] Djouadi S.M. Optimal Robust Disturbance Attenuation for Continuous Time-Varying Systems, Proceedings of CDC, vol. 4, (1998) 3819-3824. 1181-1193.
[5] Djouadi S.M. Optimal Robust Disturbance Attenuation for Continuous Time-Varying Systems, International journal of robust and non-linear control, vol. 13, (2003) 1181-1193.
[6] G. Zames and A.K. El-Sakkary, Unstable Systems and Feedback: The Gap Metric, in Proc. of the Allerton Conference, pp. 380-385, 1980.
[7] S.Q. Zhu, M.L.J. Hautus and C. Praagman, Sufficient Conditions for Robust BIBO Stabilisation: Given by the Gap Metric, Systems and Control Letters, vol. 11, pp. 53-59, 1988.

[8] Khammash M., Dahleh M. Time-varying control and the robust performance of systems with structured norm-bounded perturbations, *Proceedings of the IEEE Conference on Decision and Control*, Brighton, UK, 1991.

[9] Khammash M., J.B. Pearson J.B. Performance robustness of discrete-time systems with structured uncertainty, *IEEE Transactions on Automatic Control*, 36 (1991) 398-412.

[10] A. Ichikawa, Quadratic Games and H^{∞}-Type Problems for Time-Varying Systems, Int. J. Control, vol. 54, pp. 1249-1271, 1991.

[11] Feintuch A. *Robust Control Theory in Hilbert Space*, Springer-Verlag, vol. 130, 1998.

[12] Feintuch A., Francis B.A. Uniformly Optimal Control of Linear Time-Varying Systems, Systems & Control Letters, vol. 5, (1984) 67-71.

[13] Feintuch A., Francis B.A. Uniformly Optimal Control of Linear Feedback Systems, Systems & Control Letters, vol. 21, (1985) 563-574.

[14] Schatten R. *Norm Ideals of Completely Continuous Operators*, Springer-Verlag, Berlin, Gottingen, Heidelberg, 1960.

[15] Shamma J.S. Robust stability with time-varying structured uncertainty, *Proceedings of the IEEE Conference on Decision and Control*, 3163-3168, 1992 .

[16] Shamma J.S., Dahleh M.A. Time-varying versus time-invariant compensation for rejection of persistent bounded disturbances and robust stabilization, *IEEE Transactions on automatic Control*, 36 (1991) 838-847.

[17] P. DeWilde A-J. Van der Veen, Time-Varying Systems and Computations, Springer-Verlag, 1998.

[18] J.A. Ball, Commutant Lifting and Interpolation: The Time Varying Case, Intergral Equat. and Operator Theory, vol. 25, pp. 377-405, 1996.

[19] S.M. Djouadi and C.D. Charalambous, Time-Varying Optimal Disturbance Minimization in Presence of Plant Uncertainty, SIAM Journal on Optimization and Control, Vol. 48, No. 5, pp. 3354-3367, 2010

[20] S.M. Djouadi, Disturbance rejection and robustness for LTV Systems, Proceedings of the American Control Conference, pp. 3648-2653-6080, June 14-26, 2006.

[21] S. M. Djouadi, Commutant Lifting for Linear Time-Varying Systems, American Control Conference Proceedings, St. Louis, MO, June 10-12, 2009, pp. 4067-4072.

[22] Francis B.A., Doyle J.C. Linear Control Theory with an H^{∞} Optimality Criterion, SIAM J. Control and Optimization, vol. 25, (1987) 815-844.

[23] Francis B.A. *A Course in H^{∞} Control Theory*, Springer-Verlag, 1987.

[24] Zhou K., Doyle J.C., Glover K. *Robust and Optimal Control*, Prentice Hall, 1996.

[25] M. Verma and E. Jonckheere, L^{∞}-Compensation with Mixed Sensitivity as a Broadband Matching Problem, Systems & Control Letters, vol. 4, pp. 125-129, 1984.

[26] Power S. Commutators with the Triangular Projection and Hankel Forms on Nest Algebras, J. London Math. Soc., vol. 2, (32), (1985) 272-282.

[27] Power S.C. Factorization in Analytic Operator Algebras, J. Func. Anal., vol. 67, (1986) 413-432.

[28] S.M. Djouadi and C.D. Charalambous, On Optimal Performance for Linear-Time Varying Systems, Proc. of the IEEE 43th Conference on Decision and Control, Paradise Island, Bahamas, pp. 875-880, December 14-17, 2004.

[29] Feintuch A., Saeks R. *System Theory: A Hilbert Space Approach*, Academic Press, N.Y., 1982.

[30] Peters M.A. and Iglesias P.A., Minimum Entropy Control for Time-varying Systems, Boston, Birkhäuser, 1997.

[31] T.T. Georgiou and M.C. Smith, Optimal Robustness in the Gap Metric, IEEE Trans. on Automatic Control, vol. 35, No. 6, pp. 673-686, 1990.
[32] Georgiou T., On the Computation of teh Gap Metric, Systems and Control Letters, vol. 11, pp. 253-257, 1988.
[33] Foias C., Georgiou T. and Smith M.C., Robust Stability of Feedback Systems: A Geometric Approach Using The Gap Metric, SIAM J. Control and Optimization, vol. 31, No.6, pp. 1518-1537, 1993.
[34] Foias C., Georgiou T. and Smith M.C., Geometric Techniques for Robust Stabilization of Linear Time-Varying Systems, Proc. of he 29th CDC, pp. 2868-2873, December 1990.
[35] B. Sz. Nagy and C. Foias, Dilatation des commutants des commutateurs d'operateurs, C.R. Academie Sci. paris, Serie A, 266, pp. 493-495, 1968.
[36] B. Sz. Nagy, C. Foias, H. Bercovici, and L. Kerchy, Harmonic Analysis of Operators on Hilbert Space, Springer, 2010.
[37] Ravi R., Nagpal K.M. and Khargonekar P.P., H^∞ Control of Linear Time-Varying Systems: A State Space Approach, SIAM J. Control and Optimization, vol. 29, No.6, pp. 1394-1413, 1991.
[38] T.T. Georgiou and M.C. Smith, Robust Stabilization in the Gap Metric: Controller Design for Distributed Plants, IEEE Trans. on Automatic Control, vol. 37, No. 8, pp. 1133-1143, 1992.
[39] Dale W.N. and Smith M.C., Stabilizability and Existence of System Representation for Discrete-Time-Varying Systems, SIAM J. Control and Optimization, vol. 31, No.6, pp. 1538-1557, 1993.
[40] Dullerud G.E. and Lall S., A new approach for analysis and synthesis of time-varying systems IEEE Trans. on Automatic Control, Vol.: 44 , Issue: 8 , pp. 1486 - 1497, 1999.
[41] C. Pirie and G.E. Dullerud, Robust Controller Synthesis for Uncerttain Time-Varying Systems. SIAM J. Control Optimization., Vol. 40, No. 4, pp. 1312Ű1331, 2002.
[42] J.C. Doyle, B.A. Francis and A.R. Tannenbaum, Feedback Control Theory, Macmillan, NY, 1990.
[43] C. Foias, H. Ozbay and A.R. Tannenbaum, Robust Control of Infinite Dimensional Systems, Springer-Verlag, Berlin, Heidelberg, New York, 1996.
[44] C. Foias, A.E. Frazho, I. Gohberg, and M.A. Kaashoek, Metric constrained interpolation, commutant lifting and systems. Operator Theory: Advances and Applications, 100. Birkhäuser Verlag, Basel, 1998
[45] Zhou K. and Doyle J.C., Essentials of Robust Control, Prentice Hall, 1998.
[46] Djouadi S.M. and Birdwell J.D., On the Optimal Two-Block H^∞ Problem, Proceedings of the American Control Conference, pp. 4289 - 4294, June 2005.

2

Parametric Robust Stability

César Elizondo-González
Facultad de Ingeniería Mecánica y Eléctrica
Universidad Autónoma de Nuevo León
México

1. Introduction

Robust stability of LTI systems with parametric uncertainty is a very interesting topic to study, industrial world is contained in parametric uncertainty. In industrial reality, there is not a particular system to analyze, there is a family of systems to be analyzed because the values of physical parameters are not known, we know only the lower and upper bounds of each parameter involved in the process, this is known as *Parametric Uncertainty* (Ackermann et al., 1993; Barmish, 1994; Bhattacharyya et al., 1995). The set of parameters involved in a system makes a *Parametric Vector*, the set of all vectors that can exists such that each parameter is kept within its lower and upper bounds is called a *Parametric Uncertainty Box*.

The system we are studying is now composed of an infinite number of systems, each system corresponds to a parameter vector contained in the parametric uncertainty box. So as to test the stability of the LTI system with parametric uncertainty we have to prove that all the infinite number of systems are stable, this is called *Parametric Robust Stability*. The parametric robust stability problem is considerably more complicated than determine the stability of an LTI system with fixed parameters. The stability of a LTI system can be analyzed in different ways, this chapter will be analyzed by means of its characteristic polynomial, in the case of parametric uncertainty now exists a set with an infinite number of characteristic polynomials, this is known as a *Family of Polynomials*, and we have to test the stability of the whole family.

The parametric robust stability problem in LTI systems with parametric uncertainty is solved in this chapter by means of two tools, the first is a recent stability criterion for LTI systems (Elizondo, 2001B) and the second is the mathematical tool "Sign Decomposition" (Elizondo, 1999). The recent stability criterion maps the prametric robust stability problem to a robust positivity problem of multivariable polynomic functions, sign decomposition solves this problem in necessary and sufficient conditions.

By means of the recent stability criterion (Elizondo, 2001B) is possible to analyze the characteristic polynomial and determine the number of unstable roots on the right side in the complex plane. This criterion is similar to the Routh criterion although without using the traditional division of the Routh criterion. This small difference makes a big advantage when it is analized the robust stability in LTI systems with parametric uncertainty, the elements of the first column of the table (Elizondo, 2001B) they are multivariable polynomic functions and these must be positive for stability conditions. Robust positivity of a multivariable polynomial function is more easier to prove that in the case of quotients of this class of functions, therefore, the recent criterion (Elizondo, 2001B) is easier to use than Routh criterion. There are other criterions whose its elements are multivariable polynomic functions, such as the Hurwitz criterion and Lienard-Chipart criterion (Gantmacher, 1990), but both use a huge amount of mathematical operations in comparison with the recently stablished stability criterion Elizondo et al. (2005). When industrial cases are analyzed, the difference of mathematical operations is paramount, if the recently stability criterion takes several hours to determine the robust stability, the other criterions take several days. For these reasons the recently stability criterion is used in this chapter instead of other criterions.

Sign Decomposition (Elizondo, 1999) also called by some authors as *Sign definite Decomposition* is a mathematical tool able to determine in necessary and sufficient conditions the robust positivity of multivariable polynomic functions by means of extreme points analysis. Sign Decomposition begun as incipient orthogonal ideas of the author in his PhD research. It was not easy to develop this tool as thus it happens in orthogonal works with respect to the contemporary research line, the orthogonal ideas normally are not well seen. This is a very difficult situation on any research work, there may be many opinions, but we must accept that the world keeps working by the aligned but it changes by the orthogonals.

In LTI systems with parametric uncertainty applications, the multivariable polynomic functions to be analyzed depend on bounded physical parameters and some bounds could be negative. So sign decomposition begins with a coordinates transformation from the physical parameters to a set of mathematical parameters such that all the vectors of the new parameters are contained in a positive convex cone; in other words, all the new parameters are non-negatives. In this way, the multivariable polynomic function is made by non-decreasing terms, some of them are preceded by a positive sign and some by a negative sign. Grouping all the positive terms and grouping all the negative terms, then factorizing the negative sign and defining a "positive part" and a "negative part" of the function we obtain two non-decreasing functions. Now the function can be expressed as the positive part minus the negative part. It is obvious that both parts are independent functions, so they can be taken as a basis in with a graphical representation using two axis, the axis of the negative part and the axis of the positive part. Now, suppose that we have a particular vector contained in the parametric uncertainty box , then evaluating the negative part and the positive part a point on the "negative part, positive part plane" is obtained, this point represents the function evaluated in the particular vector in . The forty five degree line crossing at the origin on the "negative part, positive part plane" represents the set of functions with zero value, a point above this line represents a function with positive value and a point below this line represents a function with negative value.

The decomposition of the function in its negative and positive parts may look very simple and non-transcendent but taking into acount that the negative and positive parts are made by the addition of non-decreasing terms, then the negative and positive parts are nondecreasing functions in a vector space, this implies that the positive part and the negative part are bonded. So, geometrically, any point representing the function evaluated at any parameter vector is contained in a rectangle on the "negative part, positive part plane" and if the lowest right vertex is above the forty five degree line then the function is robust positive, obtaining in this way the basis of the "rectangle theorem". By means of this theorem upper and lower bounds of the multivariable polynomic function in the parametric uncertainty box are obtained. Sign decomposition contains a set of definitions, propositions, facts, lemmas, theorems and corollaries, sign decomposition can be applied to several disciplines; in the case of LTI systems with parametric uncertainty, this mathematical tool can be applied to robust controllability,

obsevability or stability analysis. In this chapter sign decomposition is applied to parametric robust stability.
In this chapter the following topics are studied: recent stability criterion, linear time invariant systems with parametric uncertainty, brief description of sign decomposition and finally a solution for the parametric robust stability problem. All demonstrations of the criterions, theorems, corollaries, lemmas, etc, will be omitted because they are results previously published.

2. A recent stability criterion for LTI systems

The study of stability of the LTI systems begun approximately one and a half century ago with three important criterions: *Hermite* in 1856 (Ackermann et al., 1993), 1854 (Bhattacharyya et al., 1995); *Routh* in 1875 (Ackermann et al., 1993), 1877 (Gantmacher, 1990) and *Hurwitz* in 1895 (Gantmacher, 1990). Routh, using Sturm's theorem and Cauchy Index theory of a real rational function, set up a theorem to determine the number k of roots of polynomial with real coefficients on the right half plane of the complex numbers.

Theorem 1. *(Routh) (Gantmacher, 1990) The number of roots of the real polynomial* $p(s) = c_0 + c_1 s + c_2 s^2 + \cdots + c_n s^n$ *in the right half of the complex plane is equal to the number of variations of sign in the first column of the Routh's table with coefficients:* $a_{i,j} = (a_{i-1,1}a_{i-2,j+1} - a_{i-2,1}a_{i-1,j+1})/a_{i-1,1}$ $\forall i \geq 3$, $a_{i,j} = c_{n+1-i-2(j-1)}$ $\forall i \leq 2$

There are several results related to the Routh criterion, for example (Fuller, 1977; Meinsma, 1995), but they are not appropriate to use in the parametric uncertainty case and they use more mathematical calculations than the Routh criterion.
In this chapter a recent criterion, an arrange similar to the Rouht table, it is presented. The stability in this recent criterion depends on the positivity of a *sign column*. The recent criterion has two advantages: 1) the numerical operations are reduced with respect to above mentioned criterions; 2) the coefficients are multivariable polynomic functions in the case of parametric uncertainty and robust positivity is easier to test than Routh criterion. The criterion is as described below.

Theorem 2. *(Elizondo, 2001B) Given a polynomial* $p(s) = c_0 + c_1 s + c_2 s^2 + \cdots + c_{n-1}s^{n-1} + c_n s^n$ *with real coefficients, the number of roots on the right half of the complex plane is equal to the number of variations of sign in the sign* σ *column on the follow arrange.*

$$\begin{array}{llll} \sigma_1 & c_n & c_{n-2} & c_{n-4} \cdots \\ \sigma_2 & c_{n-1} & c_{n-3} & c_{n-5} \cdots \\ \sigma_3 & e_{3,1} & e_{3,2} & \cdots \\ \vdots & \vdots & \vdots & \end{array}$$

$$e_{i,j} = (e_{i-1,1}e_{i-2,j+1} - e_{i-2,1}e_{i-1,j+1}), \forall 3 \leq i \leq n+1$$
$$e_{i,j} = c_{n+1-i-2(j-1)} \ \forall i \leq 2$$
$$\sigma_i = Sign(e_{i,1}) \ \forall i \leq 2, \qquad \sigma_i = Sign(e_{i,1}) \prod_{j=1}^{(i+1-m)/2} Sign(e_{m+2(j-1),1}) \ \forall i \geq 3$$

The procedure for calculating the elements $(e_{i,j})$ is similar to the Routh table but without using the division. On the other hand, the calculation of an element σ_i is more easier than it looks mathematical expression. We can get the sign σ_i, multiplying the sign of the element $(e_{i,1})$ by the sign of the immediate superior element $(e_{i-1,1})$ and then jumping in pairs. For example $\sigma_6 = Sign(e_{6,1})Sign(e_{5,1})Sign(e_{3,1})Sign(e_{1,1})$. Also $\sigma_1 = Sign(c_n)$ and $\sigma_2 = Sign(c_{n-2})$. So also it is not necessary to calculate the last element $(e_{n+1,1})$, only its sign is necessary to calculate. Each row of $(e_{i,j})$ elements is obtained by means of $(e_{i-1,j})$ and $(e_{i-2,j})$ elements previously calculated and in Hurwitz criterion a principal minor is not calculated from previous, then the Elizondo-González criterion is more advantageous than Hurwitz criterion as shown in table (1)

Remark 3. *a) Given the relation of the above criterion with the Routh criterion, the cases in that one element $e_{i,j}$ is equal to cero or all the elements of a row are cero, they are treated as so as it is done in the Routh criterion. b) The last element $e_{n+1,1}$ is not necessary to calculate, but it is necessary to obtain only its sign*

Mathematical operations in polynomials n degree

grado	Hurwitz		C. Elizondo	
n	$\times$	$+ o -$	$\times$	$+ o -$
3	4	1	2	1
4	9	2	5	2
5	66	18	9	4
6	193	45	14	6
7	780	145	20	9

Table 1. A comparison of stability criterions.

2.1 Examples

Example 1. Given the polynomial $p(s) = s^5 + 2s^4 + 1s^3 + 5s^2 + 2s + 2$ by means of criterion 2 determine the number of roots in the right half of the complex plane and compare the results with the Routh criterion.

Applying 2 criterion we obtain the left table. As an example of the procedure to obtain the elements $e_{i,j}$ and σ_i, we have: $e_{3,1} = 2 \times 1 - 1 \times 5$, $e_{3,2} = 2 \times 2 - 1 \times 2$, $\sigma_6 = Sign(+) \times Sign(-56) \times Sign(-3) \times Sign(1)$, $\sigma_5 = Sign(-56) \times Sign(-19) \times Sign(2)$.

Elizondo-González 2001

$\sigma_1 = +$	1	1	2
$\sigma_2 = +$	2	5	2
$\sigma_3 = -$	-3	2	
$\sigma_4 = +$	-19	-6	
$\sigma_5 = +$	-56		
$\sigma_6 = +$	$+$		

Routh

1	1	2
2	5	2
-1.5	1	
6.3333	2	
1.4737		
$+$		

Table 2. Example 1. Comparison of stability criterions.

The left arrengment shows two sign changes in σ column so the polynomial has two roots on the right half of the complex plane. By means of Routh criterion is obtained the right table, it shows too two sign changes in the first column which is the same previous result. An interesting observation (see table (2)) is that the left table presents a minus sign in the third row of the σ column and the right table presents a minus sign in the same third row but in the first column.

Example 2. Given the polynomial $p(s) = s^5 + 2s^4 + 2s^3 + 2s^2 + s + 3$ by means of criterion 2 determine the number of roots in the right half of the complex plane and compare the results with the Routh criterion.

Elizondo-González 2001

$\sigma_1 = +$	1	2	1
$\sigma_2 = +$	2	2	3
$\sigma_3 = +$	2	-1	
$\sigma_4 = +$	6	6	
$\sigma_5 = -$	-18		
$\sigma_6 = +$	$-$		

Routh

1	2	1
2	2	3
1	-0.5	
3	3	
-1.5		
$+$		

Table 3. Example 2. Comparison of stability criterions.

It is easy to see by means of two criterions that the polynomial has two roots on the right half of the complex plane in accordance to the table (3).
Example 3. Given the polynomial $p(s) = s^5 + 1s^4 + 2s^3 + 2s^2 + 2s + 1$ by means of criterion 2 determine the number of roots in the right half of the complex plane.
When we try to make the table by means of Elizondo-González 2001 criterion or Routh criterion, it is truncated because $e_{3,1} = 0$

σ_1	1	2	2
σ_2	1	2	1
σ_3	0	1	

Table 4. Example 3. Presence of a zero in the first column of elements.

Since the element $e_{3,1}$ is equal zero (see table (4)) then this element is replaced by by an $\epsilon > 0$, thus obtaining the following arrangement.

σ_1	1	2	2
σ_2	1	2	1
σ_3	ϵ	1	
σ_4	$2\epsilon - 1$	ϵ	
σ_5	$2\epsilon - 1 - \epsilon^2$		
σ_6	$(2\epsilon - 1 - \epsilon^2)\epsilon$		

Table 5. Example 3. Solution of the problem of zero in the first column.

Applying the limit $\epsilon \to 0$ in table (5) is obtained the table (6).

$\sigma_1 = +$	1	2	2
$\sigma_2 = +$	1	2	1
$\sigma_3 = +$	ϵ	1	
$\sigma_4 = -$	-1	ϵ	
$\sigma_5 = +$	-1		
$\sigma_6 = +$	$-\epsilon$		

Table 6. Example 3. Final result to the solution of the problem of zero in the first column.

From the table (6) is easy to see that the polynomial has two roots on the right half of the complex plane.

Example 4. Given the polynomial $p(s) = s^5 + 1s^4 + 2s^3 + 2s^2 + 1s + 1$ by means of criterion 2 determine the number of roots in the right half of the complex plane. Applying this criterion we get as following.

σ_1	1	2	1
σ_2	1	2	1
σ_3	0	0	

Table 7. Example 4. A row equal zero.

The table (7) generated, it shows the third row equal zero. Then obtaining the derivative of the polynomial "corresponding" to the immediately superiory row $p(s) = s^4 + 2s^2 + 1$ is obtained $p(s) = 4s^3 + 4s$. Now the coefficients of this polynomial replace the zeros of the third row and the procedure continues, obtaining in this way the follow arrangement.

$\sigma_1 = +$	1	2	1
$\sigma_2 = +$	1	2	1
$\sigma_3 = +$	4	4	
$\sigma_4 = +$	4	4	
$\sigma_5 = +$	ϵ		
$\sigma_6 = +$	4ϵ		

Table 8. Example 4. Solution to the problem of a row equal zero.

We can see in table (8) that there is no sign change in *sigma* column, then there are not roots in the right half complex plane.

3. Linear time invariant systems with parametric uncertainty

3.1 Parametric uncertainty

All phisical systems are dependent on parameters q_i and in the physical world does not know the value of the parameters, only know the lower q_i^- and upper q_i^+ bounds of each parameter, so that $q_i^- \leq q_i \leq q_i^+$, this expression is also written as $q_i \in [q_i^-, q_i^+]$.

For example if we have several electrical resistances with color code of 1,000 ohm, if one measures one of them, the measurement can be: 938, 1,024, or a value close to 1,000 ohm but it is rather difficult that it is exactly 1,000 ohm. By means of tolerance code can be deduced that the resistance will be greater than 900 and less than 1,100 ohm. Another example is the mass of a commercial aircraft, it can fly with few passengers and little baggage or with with many passengers and much baggage, then the mass of the plane is not known until the last passenger to be registered, but not when the plane was designed, however the plane is designed to fly from a minimum mass to a maximum mass.

The set of ℓ parameters involved in a system makes a *Parametric Vector* $q = [q_1, q_2, \cdots, q_\ell]^T$, $q \in \Re^\ell$ and the set of all the possible parameter vectors that may exist makes a *Parametric Uncertainty Box* $Q = \{\ q = [q_1, q_2, \cdots, q_\ell]^T |\ q_i \in [q_i^-, q_i^+]\ \forall i\}$. In the case of $q_i > 0\ \forall i$ then $Q = \{\ q = [q_1, q_2, \cdots, q_\ell]^T |\ q_i > 0,\ q_i \in [q_i^-, q_i^+]\ \forall i\ \}$ and Q is contained in a positive convex cone P, $Q \subset P \subset \Re^\ell$.

For the study of cases involving parametric uncertainty is necessary to define the minimum and maximum vertices of the parametric uncertainty box, so the minimum $v^{\min}$ and maximum $v^{\max}$ Euclidean vertices of Q are defined as so as $\|v^{\min}\|_2 = \min_{q\in Q} \|q\|_2$, $\|v^{\max}\|_2 = \max_{q\in Q} \|q\|_2$.

3.2 Parametric robust stability in LTI systems

In the LTI systems with parametric uncertainty, the characteristic polynomial has coefficients dependent on physical parameters, $p(s,q) = c_0(q) + c_1(q)s + c_2(q)s^2 + \cdots c_n(q)s^n$; so Routh criterion is very difficult to use because it is necessary to test the robust positivity of rational functions dependent on physical parameters. By means of Hurwitz criterion is possible to solve the problem of parametric robust stability by means of robust positivity of principal minors of a matrix dependent on physical parameters, this procedure uses a lot of mathematical calculations. The robust positivity of rational function dependent on physical parameters can be considered as so as a very much difficult problem since only the robust positive test of multivariable polynomic function is very difficult problem (Ackermann et al., 1993) (page 93). So the parametric robust stability problem in LTI systems with parametric uncertainty in the general case is not an easy problem to solve, however in this chapter is presented a solution.

The characteristic polynomials are classified according to its coefficient of maximum complexity; from the simplest structure coefficient to the most complex are: *Interval, Affine, Multilinear and Polynomic*. For example, the coefficients: $c_i(q) = q_i$, $c_i(q) = 2q_1 + 3q_2 + 5q_3 + q_4$, $c_i(q) = 5q_1q_2 + 2q_2q_4 + 5q_3 + q_4$, $c_i(q) = 2q_1^3q_2 + 2q_2^2q_4^5 + q_3$, correspond to classification: Interval, Affine, Multilinear and Polynomic respectively. The number of polynomials $p(s,q)$ that can exist is infinite since the number of vectors that exist is infinite, the collection of all polynomials that exist is a *Family of Polynomials* $P(s,Q) = \{p(s,q) | q \in Q\}$.

The families of polynomials interval and afin are convex sets and these families have subsetting test. This concept, *subsetting test*, means that a family of polynomials is robustly stable if and only if all polynomials contained in the subsetting test are stable.

Kharitonov in (Kharitonov, 1978), by means of his theorem demonstrates that a family of interval polynomials is robust stable if and only if a set of four polynomials are stable. In (Bartlett et al., 1988) by means of their edge theorem, demonstrated that a family of afin polynomials is robustly stable if and only if all the polynomials corresponding to the edges of the parametric uncertainty box are stable. The multilinear an polynomic families are not convex set and they do not have subsetting test. So parametric robust stability of these families can not be resolved by tools based on convexity. In (Elizondo, 1999) was presented a solution for parametric robust stability of any kind of family: Interval, Affine, Multilinear or Polynomic. The solution is based on sign decomposition, and by means of this tool can also solve the problem of robust controllability or robust observability.

3.3 Robust stability mapped to robust positivity

The parametric robust stability problem of LTI systems can be mapped to a problem of robust positivity of polynomial functions for at least three ways.

The first two are: the Hurwitz and Lienard-Chipart criterions, the other is the recently stability criterion (2). By Hurwitz or Lienard-Chipart criterions can do the mapping but as explained these require making a lot of mathematical calculations. The criterion (2) requires much less mathematical calculations that the criterions mentioned as was shown in table (1), (Elizondo et al., 2005)

4. Brief description of sign decomposition

In different areas of sciences the fundamental problem can be mapped to a problem of robust positivity of multivariable polynomic functions. For example the no singularity of a matrix can be analyzed by mean of the robust positivity of its determinant, so it is very useful to have a mathematical tool that solves the problem of robust positivity of multivariable polynomic functions. Practically there are three tools for this purpose: Interval Arithmetic (Moor, 1966); Bernstein Polynomials (Zettler, et all 1998) and Sign Decomposition ((Elizondo, 1999)) whose complete version is developed in (Elizondo, 1999) and its partial versions are presented in (Elizondo, 2000; 2001A;B; 2002A;B), for simplicity only will be mentioned (Elizondo, 1999). Interval arithmetic is very difficult to use because it requires much more calculations than other methods. When robust positivity is analyzed in a very simple function, Bernstein polynomials have advantages over sign decomposition, but when the function is not simple, sign decomposition has advantages over Bernstein polynomials (Graziano et al., 2004). There are several works using sign decomposition instead of Bernstein polynomials, some of them are: (Bhattacharyya et al., 2009; Guerrero, 2006; Keel et al., 2008; 2009; Keel, 2011; Knap et al., 2010; 2011)

4.1 Definition of sign decomposition

The following is a brief description of the more relevant results of Sign Decomposition (Elizondo, 1999). By means of this tool it is possible to determine, in necessary and sufficient conditions, the robust positivity of a multivariable polynomic function depending on ℓ parameters, employing extreme points analysis.
Since mathematically exist the possibility that a parameter $\hat{q}_i$ has negative value , then this tool begins by a "coordinates transformation" from $\hat{q}_i$ to q_i such that the new parameters will be positive $q_i > 0$, then an uncertainty box $Q = \{\ q = [q_1, q_2, \cdots, q_\ell]^T \,|\, q_i > 0,\ q_i \in [q_i^-, q_i^+]\ \}$ is makes, in other words, Q is in a positive convex cone P, $Q \subset P \subset \Re^\ell$ with minimum $v^{\min}$ and maximum $v^{\max}$ Euclidean vertices. The transformation is very easy as shown in the equation (1)

$$q_i = q_i^- + \frac{\hat{q}_i - \hat{q}_i^-}{\hat{q}_i^+ - \hat{q}_i^-}(q_i^+ - q_i^-) \tag{1}$$

From here on we will assume that if necessary, the transformation was made and work with parameters $q_i > 0$. Under this consideration will continue with the rest of this topic.

Definition 4. *(Elizondo, 1999) Let $f : \Re^\ell \rightarrow \Re$ be a continuous function and let $Q \subset P \subset \Re^\ell$ be a box. It is said that $f(q)$ has **Sign Decomposition** in Q if there exist two bounded continuous nondecreasing and nonnegative functions $f_n(\cdot) \geq 0$, $f_p(\cdot) \geq 0$, such that $f(q) = f_p(q) - f_n(q)$ $\forall\ q \in Q$. In this way there are defined the **Positive Part** $f_p(q)$ and **Negative Part** $f_n(q)$ of the function.*

Negative Part is only a name since Negative Part and Positive Part are nonnegative.

4.2 (f_n, f_p) representation

Is obvious that for the general case, $f_n(\cdot)$ and $f_p(\cdot)$ are independent functions then they make a basis in $\Re^2$ with graphical representation in the $(f_n(\cdot), f_p(\cdot))$ plane in accordance with figure (1).

If we take a particular vector $q \in Q$ and evaluated the $f_n(q)$ and $f_p(q)$ parts, we obtain the coordinates $(f_n(q), f_p(q))$ of the function in the (f_n, f_p) plane. The 45° line is the set of points where the function is equal zero because $f_p(q) = f_n(q)$ so $f(q) = f_p(q) - f_n(q) = 0$. If a point is above the 45° line means that $f_p(q) > f_n(q)$ then $f(q) > 0$. If a point is below the 45° line means that $f_p(q) < f_n(q)$ then $f(q) < 0$.

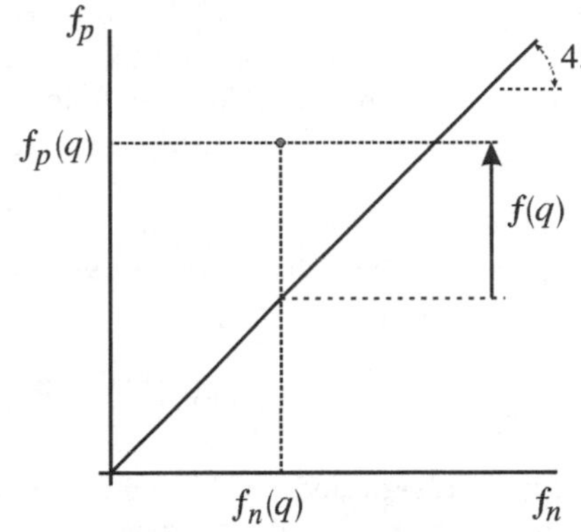

Fig. 1. (f_n, f_p) plane

It should be noted that independently of the number of parameters in which the function depends on, the function will always be represented in $\Re^2$ via $(f_n(q), f_p(q))$. For example, the function $f(q) = 4 - q_2 + q_1q_3 + 8q_1^2q_2 - 9q_1q_2^2q_3^3$ such that $q \in Q \subset P \subset \Re^3$, $Q = \{\ q = [q_1, q_2, q_3]^T |\ q_i \in [0,\ 1]\ \}$. The function has sign decomposition because it is decomposed in two bounded continuous nondecreasing and nonnegative functions $f_p(q) = 4 + q_1q_3 + 8q_1^2q_2$, $f_n(q) = q_2 + 9q_1q_2^2q_3^3$ and $f(q) = f_p(q) - f_n(q)$. The figure (2) was obtained by plotting a hundred lines blue color, (one hundred fifty points per line) of variable q_3 holding (q_1, q_2) constant uniformly distributed in different positions. The process was repeated varying q_2 in green color and finally varying q_1 in red color. According to the position shown in the graph of the function with respect to the 45° line, it appears that the function is robustly positive. But it must be demonstrated mathematically.

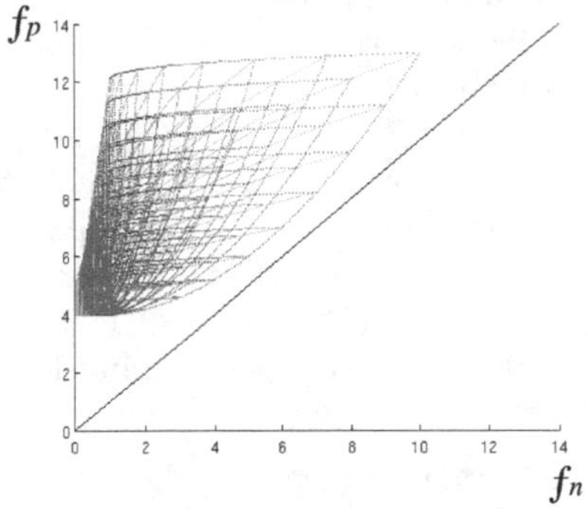

Fig. 2. Function in (f_n, f_p) plane

Some preliminary properties of the continuous functions $f(q)$, $g(q)$, $h(q)$ with sign decomposition in Q and for all $u(q)$ nondecreasing function in Q, are proved in (Elizondo, 1999) as so facts, lemmas and theorems. This properties are employed on the following theorems.
a) $(f_n(q) + u(q), f_p(q) + u(q))$ is a (f_n, f_p) representation of the function $f(q)$ $\forall q \in Q$; **b)** the representation $(f_n(q) + u(q), f_p(q) + u(q))$ of the function is reduced to its minimum expression: $(f_p(q), f_n(q))$; **c)** $f(q) + g(q)$; **d)** $f(q) - g(q)$ and **e)** $f(q)g(q)$ are functions with sign decomposition in Q; **f)** if $f(q) = g(q) + h(q)$, then the positive and negative parts of $f(q) - g(q)$ are reduced to their minimum expressions, as follows: $f(q) - g(q) = (f(q) - g(q))_p - (f(q) - g(q))_n$, $(f(q) - g(q))_n = f_n(q) - g_n(q)$, $(f(q) - g(q))_p = f_p(q) - g_p(q)$.

4.3 The rectangle theorem

Since negative part and positive part are bounded continuous nondecreasing functions, then the following inequalities (2) are fulfilled.

$$\begin{aligned} f_n(v^{min}) \leq f_n(q) \leq f_n(v^{max}) \\ f_p(v^{min}) \leq f_p(q) \leq f_p(v^{max}) \end{aligned} \tag{2}$$

This means that a function $f(q)$ with sign decomposition, evaluated at any vector $q \in Q$, its negative part is contained in a segment and also the positive part is contained in another segment. So, on (f_n, f_p) plane the function is contained in a rectangle as expressed by the following theorem according to figure (3).

Theorem 5. *(Elizondo, 1999)* ***Rectangle Theorem.*** *Let $f : \Re^\ell \rightarrow \Re$ be a continuous function with sign decomposition in a box $Q \subset P \subset \Re^\ell$ with minimum and maximum Euclidean vertices $v^{\min}$, $v^{\max}$, then:* ***a)*** *$f(q)$ is lower and upper bounded by $f_p(v^{\min}) - f_n(v^{\max})$ and $f_p(v^{\max}) - f_n(v^{\min})$ respectively;* ***b)*** *The graphical representation of the function $f(q)$, $\forall q \in Q$ in (f_n, f_p) plane is contained in the rectangle with vertices $(f_n(v^{\min}), f_p(v^{\min}))$, $(f_n(v^{\max}), f_p(v^{\max}))$, $(f_n(v^{\min}), f_p(v^{\max}))$ and $(f_n(v^{\max}), f_p(v^{\min}))$;* ***c)*** *if the lower right vertex $(f_n(v^{\max}), f_p(v^{\min}))$ is over the 45° line then $f(q) > 0$ $\forall q \in Q$;* ***d)*** *if the upper left vertex $(f_n(v^{\min}), f_p(v^{\max}))$ is below the 45° line then $f(q) < 0$ $\forall q \in Q$. In accordance with figure (3).*

The above result seems to be very useful, we can say that the rectangle is the "house" where the multivariable function lives in $\Re^2$. We can know the robust positivity of a function analyzing only one point. It is important to note that this is only sufficient conditions, the lower right vertex can be below the 45° line and the function could be robustly positive or not be. But if the lower right vertex is above the 45° line then the function is robustly positive.
For example, the function $f(q) = 4 - q_2 + q_1q_3 + 8q_1^2q_2 - 9q_3^3q_1q_2^2$ such that $q \in Q \subset P \subset \Re^3$, $Q = \{\ q = [q_1, q_2, q_3]^T |\ q_i \in [0,\ 1]\ \}$, has sign decomposition, its minimum and maximum Euclidean vertices are $v^{min} = [0,\ 0]^T$, $v^{max} = [1,\ 1]^T$, their positive and negative psrtes are: $f_p(q) = 4 + q_1q_3 + 8q_1^2q_2$, $f_n(q) = q_2 + 9q_3^3q_1q_2^2$. Then the lower bound is $f_p(v^{\min}) - f_n(v^{\max})$, $f_p(v^{\min}) = 4 + (0)(0) + 8(0)(0) = 4$, $f_n(v^{\max}) = 1 + 9(1)(1)(1) = 10$, the lower bound is $4 - 10 = -9$. The function could be robustly positive, but for now we do not know, It is necessary see more signs of decomposition items.

Remark 6. *Should be noted three important concepts:*
The graph of the function does not "fills" the whole rectangle, but it is contained in.

The graph of the function always "touches " the rectangle in lower left vertice and upper right vertice. The graph of the function is not necessarily convex.

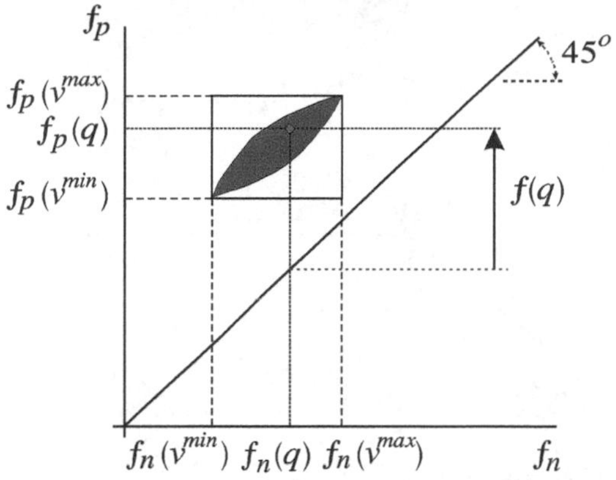

Fig. 3. Rectangle theorem

4.4 The polygon theorem

For the purpose of improving the results shown up to this point, the following proposition is necessary. In some cases it is necessary to analyze the function in a Γ box contained in Q, $\Gamma \subset Q$. The Γ box has Euclidean Vertices $\mu^{\min}$ and $\mu^{\max}$. So, a vector in Γ is expressed as so as $q = \mu^{\min} + \delta$, where δ is a vector in Γ, with origins in $\mu^{\min}$.

Proposition 7. *(Elizondo, 1999) Let $f : \Re^{\ell} \to \Re$ be a continuous function in $Q \subset P \subset \Re^{\ell}$, let $\Gamma^j \subset Q$ be a box with its vertices set $\{\mu^i\}$ with minimum and maximum Euclidean vertices $\mu^{\min}$, $\mu^{\max}$, let $\Delta = \{\delta \mid \delta_i \in [0, \delta_i^{\max}], \delta_i^{\max} = \mu_i^{\max} - \mu_i^{\min}\} \subset P \subset \Re^{\ell}$ be a box with its vertices set $\{\delta^i\}$ with minimum and maximum Euclidean vertices $\mathbf{0}$, $\delta^{\max} = \mu^{\max} - \mu^{\min}$, and let $q \in \Gamma^j$ a vector such that $q = \mu^{\min} + \delta$ where $\delta \in \Delta$. Then the function $f(q)$ is expressed by its: linear, nonlinear and independent parts, in its minimum expression for all $q \in \Gamma^j$.*

$f(q) = f^{\min} + f_L(\delta) + f_N(\delta) \mid \delta \in \Delta \forall q \in \Gamma^j$

$f^{\min} \triangleq Indepent\ Part = f(\mu^{\min})$

$f_L(\delta) \triangleq Linear\ Part = \nabla f(q)|_{\mu^{\min}} \cdot \delta \quad \forall \delta \in \Delta$

$f_N(\delta) \triangleq Nonlinear\ Part = f(\mu^{\min} + \delta) - f^{\min} - f_L(\delta) \ \ \forall \delta \in \Delta$

$$\nabla f(q)|_{\mu^{\min}} \cdot \delta = \left.\frac{\partial f(q)}{q_1}\right|_{\mu^{\min}} \delta_1 + \left.\frac{\partial f(q)}{q_2}\right|_{\mu^{\min}} \delta_2 + \cdots + \left.\frac{\partial f(q)}{q_\ell}\right|_{\mu^{\min}} \delta_\ell$$

Must be noted that $f^{\min} = f(\mu^{\min})$. On other hand, it is clear that we can use the concepts of positive part and negative part in the above proposition, So, $f_p(q) - f_n(q) = f_p^{\min} - f_n^{\min} + f_{Lp}(\delta) - f_{Ln}(\delta) + f_{Np}(\delta) - f_{Nn}(\delta)$ obtaining the following equations (3) where the relation between δ and q can be appreciated in the figure (4).

$$\begin{aligned} f_p(q) &= f_p^{\min} + f_{Lp}(\delta) + f_{Np}(\delta) \\ f_n(q) &= f_n^{\min} + f_{Ln}(\delta) + f_{Nn}(\delta) \end{aligned} \tag{3}$$

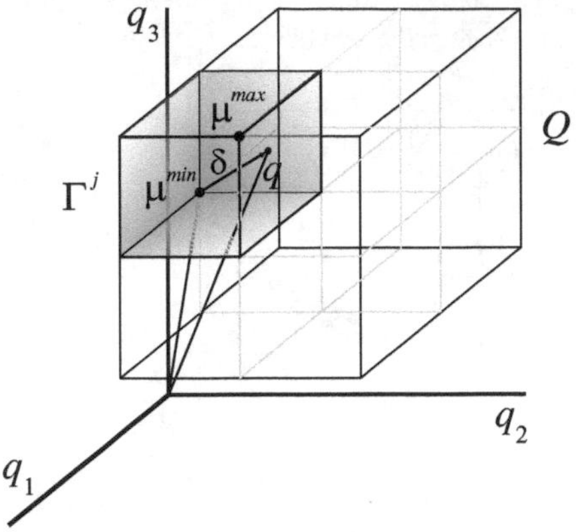

Fig. 4. Gamma box

Theorem 8. ***Polygon Theorem*** *(Elizondo, 1999). Let $f : \Re^\ell \to \Re$ be a continuous function with sign decomposition in Q, let q, δ, Γ^j and Δ in accordance with the proposition (7). Then,* ***a)*** *the lower and upper bounds of the function $f(q)$ are: Lower Bound $= f^{\min} + f_{L\min} - f_{Nn}(\delta^{\max})$ and Upper Bound $= f^{\min} + f_{L\max} + f_{Np}(\delta^{\max})$ $\forall q \in Q$,* ***b)*** *the bounds of incise "a", are contained in the interval defined by the bounds of the rectangle theorem 3. $f_p(\mu^{\min}) - f_n(\mu^{\max}) \leq$ Lower Bound $\leq$ Upper Bound $\leq f_p(\mu^{\max}) - f_n(\mu^{\min})$,* ***c)*** *The graphical representation of the function $f(q)$ $\forall q \in \Gamma$ in the (f_n, f_p) plane is contained in the polygon defined by the intersection of the rectangle of the rectangle theorem (5) and the space between the two 45° lines separated from the origin by the Lower Bound and Upper Bound in accordance with figure (5).*

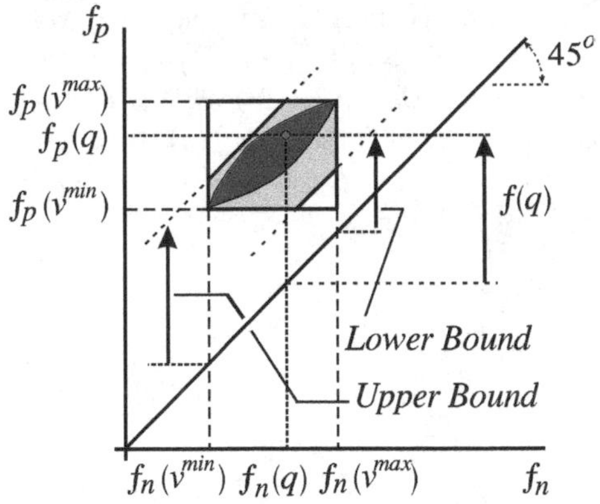

Fig. 5. Bounding of the function

The symbolic expression of the nonlinear part used in the above theorem is not necessary to obtain, because we will use only its numerical value. So, from the equations (3), the nonlinear parts are obtained as so as equations (4).

$$
\begin{aligned}
f_{Np}(\delta) &= f_p(q) - f_p^{min} - f_{Lp}(\delta)\\
f_{Nn}(\delta) &= f_n(q) - f_n^{min} - f_{Ln}(\delta)\\
f_{Lp}(\delta) &= \nabla f_p(q)\big|_{\mu^{\min}} \cdot \delta\\
f_{Ln}(\delta) &= \nabla f_n(q)\big|_{\mu^{\min}} \cdot \delta
\end{aligned} \tag{4}
$$

As an illustration of this theme, by means of rectangle theorem and polygon, we will analyze the lower bound of a function in a gama box. Consider the function corresponding to the figure (2), $f(q) = 4 - q_2 + q_1q_3 + 8q_1^2q_2 - 9q_3^3q_1q_2^2$ such that $q \in Q \subset P \subset \Re^3$, $Q = \{\ q = [q_1, q_2, q_3]^T |\ q_i \in [0,\ 1]\ \}$. Suppose that the function is analyzed into a gamma box $\Gamma \subset Q$, with Euclidean vertices $\mu^{\min} = [0.2\ 0.2\ 0.2\ ]^T$ and $\mu^{\max} = [0.85\ 0.85\ 0.85\ ]^T$.
In accordance with the Rectangle Theorem (3) the lower bound is $f_p(v^{\min}) - f_n(v^{\max}) = -0.1403$. Applying the Polygon Theorem (8) the lower bound is $f^{\min} + f_{L\min} - f_{Nn}(\delta^{\max})$, so it is necessary to obtain each of these expressions, the results are as follows: $f^{\min} = f(\mu^{\min}) = 3.9034$, $f_{L\min} = -0.4457$, $f_{Nn}(\delta^{\max}) = 3.3825$. The last value is obtained of ecuations (4), thus the lower bound is 0.0752. By means of the Rectangle Theorem is obtained $f(q) > -0.1403\ \forall q \in \Gamma$, following the Polygon Theorem is obtained $f(q) > 0.0752\ \forall q \in \Gamma$, so the function is robustly positive in the Γ box.

4.5 The box partition theorem

By means of Rectangle Theorem (3) and Polygon Theorem (8) are obtained sufficient conditions of robust positivity, so to obtain necessary and sufficient conditions is necessary to obtain new results.
When it is not possible to know whether the function is positive or not in $Q = [q_1^-,\ q_1^+] \times [q_2^-,\ q_2^+] \times \cdots \times [q_\ell^-,\ q_\ell^+]$. In this case it is possible to divide each variable $[q_i^-,\ q_i^+]$ in k parts, generating k new intervals: $[q_i^-,\ q_i^1], [q_i^1,\ q_i^2], \cdots, [q_i^j,\ q_i^{j+1}], \cdots\ [q_i^{k-1},\ q_i^+]$, let $[\gamma_i^-,\ \gamma_i^+]$ be a k new interval, giving cause to the generation of k^ℓ new boxes $\Gamma^i = [\gamma_1^-,\ \gamma_1^+] \times [\gamma_2^-,\ \gamma_2^+] \times \cdots \times [\gamma_\ell^-,\ \gamma_\ell^+]$ with $\mu^{\min}, \mu^{\max} \in \Gamma^i$ minimum and maximum Euclidean vertices of Γ^i and $Q = \bigcup_i \Gamma^i$. Through these concepts, the following theorem is obtained.

Theorem 9. ***Box Partition Theorem*** (Elizondo, 1999). *Let $f : \Re^\ell \to \Re$ be a continuous function with sign decomposition in Q such that $Q \subset P \subset \Re^\ell$ is a box with minimum and maximum Euclidean vertices $v^{\min}$, $v^{\max}$. Then the function $f(q)$ is positive (negative) in Q if and only if a Γ boxes set exists, such that $Q = \bigcup_j \Gamma^j$ and Lower Bound $\geq c > 0$ for each Γ^j box (Upper Bound $\leq c < 0$ for each one Γ^j box).*

This theorem can be applied in two ways, one of them we call " **Analytical Partition**" and the other one "**Constant Partition**". In analytical partition, the box where the function has a negative lower bound is subdivided iteratively. In the case of the function is robustly positive is also obtained information about where the function is close to losing positivity. By means of constant partition is only obtained information on whether the function is robustly positive or not.
To illustrate both procedures, we analyze the robust positivity of the function (Elizondo, 1999) $f(q) = (4 + q_1 + 8q_1^2q_2) - (q_2 + 9q_1q_2^2)$, such that $Q = \{\ q = [q_1, q_2]^T |\ q_i \in [0,\ 1]\ \forall i\ \}$. The robust positivity is analized by means of the rectangle theorem because it is more easier to

apply, although it must be said that the bounds of the polygon theorem are better than the rectangle theorem.

Analytical Partition (Elizondo, 1999). In the subfigure 1 of figure (6) shows that the function is robustly positive in boxes Γ^1 and Γ^3 but not in the boxes Γ^2 and Γ^4. So it is necessary apply iteratively the partition box to the boxes where the function is not robust positive, in this way is obtained the subfigure 2 of figure (6). Since there is a set of boxes such that $Q = \bigcup_j \Gamma^j | \ f(q) > 0 \ \forall \Gamma^j$, then the function is robustly positive in Q. The graphs were made to show the procedure in visual way, but for more than two dimensions, using software we can get the coordinates and dimensions of sub boxes where the function is close to losing positivity.

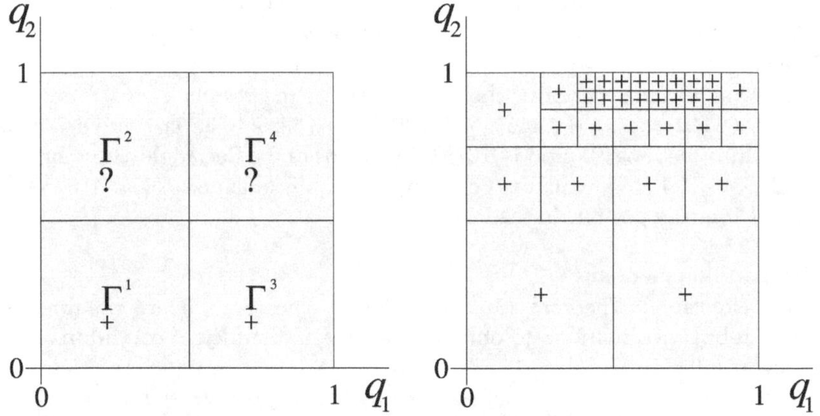

(a) Subfigure 1 (b) Subfigure 2

Fig. 6. Partition box

Constant Partition (Elizondo, 1999). In this procedure the domaine of each one of the ℓ parameters is divide in k equal parts (not necessarily equal), in this way, it is generated a boxes set of k^ℓ sub boxes Γ^i such that $Q = \bigcup_j \Gamma^j$. The robust positivity of each Γ^i box can be analyzed by a computer program so that the computer give us the final result about the robust positivity of the function.

Another way is through a software which plot a $\times$ (blue) mark in the $(f_n, \ f_p)$ plane in each $(f_n(\mu^{\min}), \ f_p(\mu^{\min}))$ and $(f_n(\mu^{\max}), \ f_p(\mu^{\max}))$ coordinates corresponding to the minimum and maximum vertices of each Γ^i box, and plot too a $+$ (red) mark corresponding to the lower bound of each Γ^i box, as can be appreciated in figure (7) that it was obtained with $k = 13$.

If a $\times$ (blue) mark is below the 45° line, means that there is at least one vector for which the function is negative and therefore the function is not robustly positive. If all the $\times$ (blue) marks are above the 45° line, and a $+$ (red) mark is below the 45° line means that it is necessary to increase the k number of partitions up to all the $+$ (red) and $\times$ (blue) marks are above the 45° line. If this is achieved then the function is robustly positive, as shown in figure (7).

In the figure (7) we can see that it is difficult to see that all $+$ (red) marks are above the 45° line, then with purpose to resolve this difficulty is proposed the following representation.

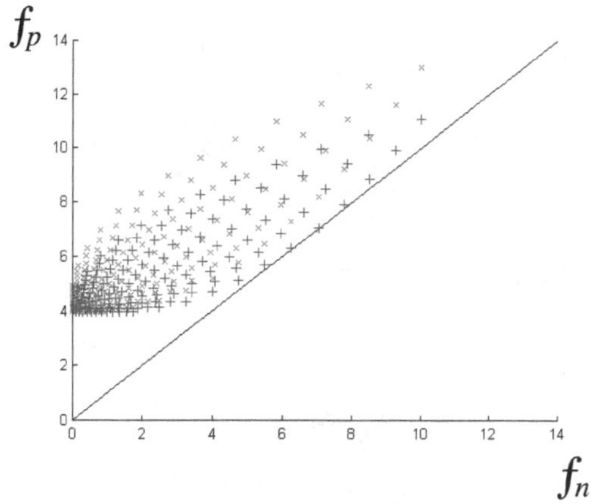

Fig. 7. Function in $(f_n,\ f_p)$ plane

4.6 (α, β) Representation

In some cases as so as figure (7) it is not easy to determine in graphic way whether a point close to the 45° line is over this line or not. So in (Elizondo, 1999) the $(\alpha,\ \beta)$ representation was developed, $\alpha(q) = f_p(q) + f_n(q), \beta(q) = f_p(q) - f_n(q)$, it is similar to rotated 45° the axis with respect to $(f_n,\ f_p)$ representation implying some graphical and algebraic advantages over the negative and positive representation.

Definition 10. *(Elizondo, 1999) Let $f_n(q)$ and $f_p(q)$ be the negative and positive parts of a continuous function $f(q)$ with sign decomposition in Q. Let T be the linear transformation described below such that T^{-1} exists, then it is called a representation of the function $f(q)$, in $(\alpha,\ \beta)$ coordinates, to the linear transformation $(\alpha(q), \beta(q)) = T(f_n(q),\ f_p(q))$ and the inverse transformation of an $(\alpha(q), \beta(q))$ representation is a $(f_n(q),\ f_p(q))$ representation of the function $f(q)$.*

$$T = \begin{bmatrix} 1 & 1 \\ -1 & 1 \end{bmatrix} \qquad T^{-1} = \tfrac{1}{2}\begin{bmatrix} 1 & -1 \\ 1 & 1 \end{bmatrix}$$
$$\begin{bmatrix} \alpha(q) \\ \beta(q) \end{bmatrix} = T\begin{bmatrix} f_n(q) \\ f_p(q) \end{bmatrix} \qquad \begin{bmatrix} f_n(q) \\ f_p(q) \end{bmatrix} = T^{-1}\begin{bmatrix} \alpha(q) \\ \beta(q) \end{bmatrix}$$
$$\alpha(q) = f_p(q) + f_n(q) \qquad f_p(q) = \tfrac{1}{2}(\alpha(q) + \beta(q))$$
$$\beta(q) = f_p(q) - f_n(q) \qquad f_n(q) = \tfrac{1}{2}(\alpha(q) - \beta(q))$$

With the purpose to show the advantages of the $(\alpha,\ \beta)$ representation, by means of the rectangle theorem we analyze the same function in the previous subsection $f(q) = (4 + q_1 + 8q_1^2q_2) - (q_2 + 9q_1q_2^2)$ applying $k = 13$. We can see in the figure (8) beta axis scale is positive implying that all the bounds are positives and consequently the function is robustly positive.

The function $f(q) = 4 - q_2 + q_1q_3 + 8q_1^2q_2 - 9q_3^3q_1q_2^2$ corresponding to the figure (2) is shown in the figure (9) in $(\alpha,\ \beta)$ representation. We can see that beta axis scale is positive implying the function is robustly positive.

The original idea to develop the representation $(\alpha\ ,\ \beta)$ (Elizondo, 1999) was to solve a visual geometric problem, but this representation has interesting algebraic properties on continuous functions $f(q)$, $g(q)$, $h(q)$ with sign decomposition in Q and for all $u(q)$ nondecreasing function in Q, (Elizondo, 1999) as the following:

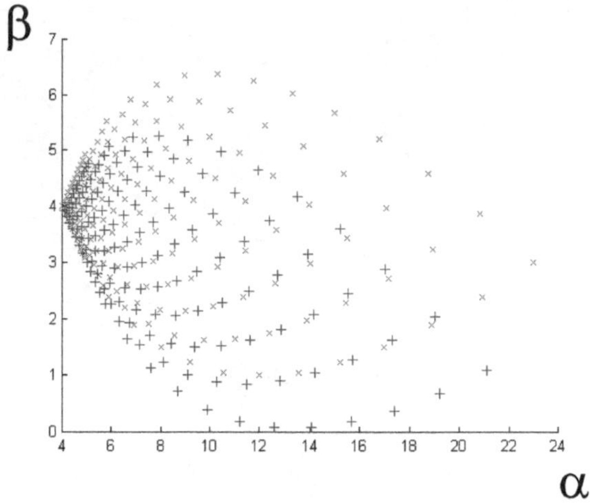

Fig. 8. Function in (α, β) representation

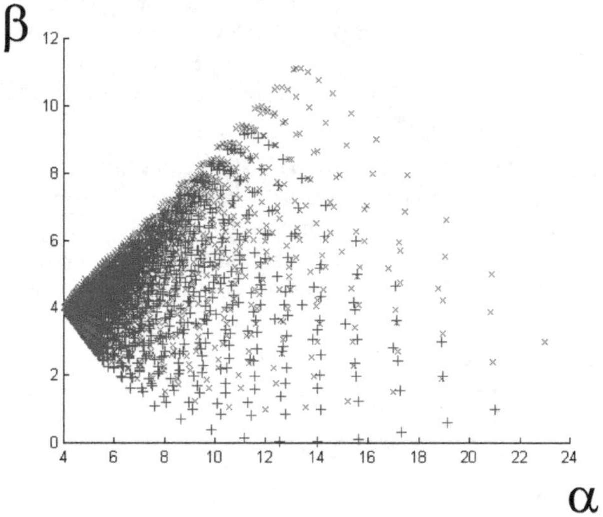

Fig. 9. Function in (α, β) representation

a) $\alpha(q)$ is a non-decreasing and non-negative function in Q; **b)** $\alpha(q) \geq \beta(q)$; **c)** $\beta(q) = f(q)$ $\forall f(q)$, $\forall q \in Q$; **d)** the $(\alpha(q) + u(q),\ \beta(q) + u(q))$ is a α, β representation of $f(q)$; **e)** the $(\alpha(q) + u(q),\ \beta(q))$ representation is reduced to its minimum expression $(\alpha(q),\ \beta(q))$; **f)** *Addition* $f(q) + g(q) : \alpha(q) = \alpha_f(q) + \alpha_g(q), \beta(q) = \beta_f(q) + \beta_g(q)$; **g)** *Subtraction* $f(q) - g(q) : \alpha(q) = \alpha_f(q) + \alpha_g(q), \beta(q) = \beta_f(q) - \beta_g(q)$; **h)** *Product* $f(q)g(q), \alpha(q) = \alpha_f(q)\alpha_g(q)$, $\beta(q) = \beta_f(q)\beta_g(q)$; **i)** the ($\alpha$, β) representation of $-g(q)$ is as follows: $(\alpha_g(q), -\beta_g(q))$; **j)** if $f(q) = g(q) + h(q)$ then the alpha an beta parts of $f(q) - g(q)$ are reduced to its minimum expression as follows $\alpha(q) = \alpha_f(q) - \alpha_g(q), \beta(q) = \beta_f(q) - \beta_g(q)$.

Computationally the (α, β) representation is better than (f_n, f_p) because if the computer does not generate the negative scale in the β axis it is implying that all "marks" are positives.

This is an usful and inetresting property, but above all properties there are three outstanding properties, it would be very useful if they were fulfilled in complex numbers, they are as follows:

$$\begin{array}{llll} \textit{Addition} & f(q)+g(q) & \alpha(q)=\alpha_f(q)+\alpha_g(q) & \beta(q)=\beta_f(q)+\beta_g(q) \\ \textit{Subtraction} & f(q)-g(q) & \alpha(q)=\alpha_f(q)+\alpha_g(q) & \beta(q)=\beta_f(q)-\beta_g(q) \\ \textit{Product} & f(q)g(q) & \alpha(q)=\alpha_f(q)\alpha_g(q) & \beta(q)=\beta_f(q)\beta_g(q) \end{array} \quad (5)$$

Most be noted that the alpha componet of subtraction is correct with $\alpha(q) = \alpha_f(q) + \alpha_g(q)$, it is an "addition" of alphas. It is also important to highlight the simplicity with which made the addition, subtraction and product in alpha beta representation.

4.7 Sign decomposition of the determinant

Sign decomposition of the determinant was developed in (Elizondo, 1999) and it was presented an application in (Elizondo, 2001A; 2002B), by simplicity only will mention (Elizondo, 1999). In parametric robust stability is not very useful the sign decomposition of the determinant, but it is a part of sign decomposition. We can analyze robust stability by means of the Hurwitz criterion means the robust positivity of determinants, but it is so much easier by means of criterion (2), see table (1). Taking account that the reader could work in other areas where the nonsingularity of a matrix dependent in parameters is important, then sign decomposition of the determinant is included in this chapter.

4.7.1 The $(\alpha,\ \beta)$ representation of the determinant

In order to achieve the procedure to determine the robust positivity in necessary and sufficient conditions of a determinant with real coefficients depending on ℓ parameters q_i, the following fact is presented. By means of the $(\alpha,\ \beta)$ properties (5) is obtained the following fact, in the development of the determinant appears the alpha part and beta part, as shown in the following fact.

Fact 1. *(Elizondo, 1999) Let $M(q)$ be a (2×2) matrix with elements $m_{i,j}(q) \in \Re$ with representation $(\alpha_{i,j}(q)\ ,\ \beta_{i,j}(q))$. Then the $(\alpha,\ \beta)$ representation of the determinant of the matrix $M(q)$ is:*

$$(\det(M(q)))_\alpha = (\alpha_{1,1}(q)\alpha_{2,2}(q) + \alpha_{2,1}(q)\alpha_{1,2}(q))$$
$$(\det(M(q)))_\beta = (\beta_{1,1}(q)\beta_{2,2}(q) - \beta_{2,1}(q)\beta_{1,2}(q)).$$

Definition 11. *(Elizondo, 1999) Let $M(q) = \left[m_{i,j}(q)\right]$ be a matrix with elements $m_{i,j}(q) \in \Re$ with $(\alpha_{i,j}(q)\ ,\ \beta_{i,j}(q))$ representation. Then the matrix $M_\alpha(q) = \left[\alpha_{i,j}(q)\right]$ will be called the alpha part of the matrix $M(q)$, and the determinant $\det_\alpha(M(q)) = |M(q)|_\alpha = |M_\alpha(q)|_\alpha$ will be called the alpha part of the determinant $|M(q)|$, which is symilar to the usual determinant changing all the subtractions by additions including the sign rule of Cramer. In a similar way, the matrix $M_\beta(q) = \left[\beta_{i,j}(q)\right]$ will be called the beta part of the matrix $M(q)$, and the determinant $\det_\beta(M(q)) = |M(q)|_\beta = \left|M_\beta(q)\right|$ will be called the beta part of the determinant $|M(q)|$.*

Most be noted that: **a)** $\beta_{i,j}(q) = m_{i,j}(q)$, then, $M_\beta(q) = M(q)$ and $\det_\beta(M(q)) = \det(M(q))$, **b)** In accordance with the above fact, for a (2×2) matrix, the $(\alpha,\ \beta)$ representation of the determinant of the matrix $M(q)$ is $\left(\det_\alpha(M(q)),\ \det_\beta(M(q))\right)$. In the following lemma a generalization of the last expression for a $(n \times n)$ matrix is stablished.

Lemma 12. *(Elizondo, 1999) Let $M(q)$ be a $(n \times n)$ matrix with elements $m_{i,j}(q) \in \Re$ with representation $(\alpha_{i,j}(q)\ ,\ \beta_{i,j}(q)\ )$. Then the $(\alpha,\ \beta)$ representation of the determinant of the matrix $M(q)$ is $\left(\det_\alpha(M(q)),\ \det_\beta(M(q))\right)$. In accordance with definition (11)*

4.7.2 Linear, nonlinear and independent parts of the determinant

When the positivity of the determinant of a matrix with elements $m_{i,j}(q)$ is analyzed via sign decomposition, it is normally necessary to use the box partition and polygon theorems. Then, the independent, linear and nonlinear parts of the determinant need to be obtained. These are obtained in the following theorem.

Theorem 13. *(Elizondo, 1999) (Sign Decomposition of the Determinant Theorem) Let $q \in \Gamma \subseteq Q \mid q = \mu^{\min} + \delta$ be according to the proposition (7). Let $M(q) \in \Re^{n\times n}$ be a matrix with elements $m_{i,j}(q)$ with sign decomposition in Q with representation $(\alpha_{i,j}^{\min} + \alpha_{i,j,L}(\delta) + \alpha_{i,j,N}(\delta),\ \beta_{i,j}^{\min} + \beta_{i,j,L}(\delta) + \beta_{i,j,N}(\delta))$, then the $(\alpha,\ \beta)$ representation of the determinant of the matrix $M(q)$ is as follows:*

$$\begin{aligned}
\alpha(q) &= \alpha^{\min} + \alpha_L(\delta) + \alpha_N(\delta),\\
\beta(q) &= \beta^{\min} + \beta_L(\delta) + \beta_N(\delta)\\
\alpha^{\min} &= det_\alpha\left(\left[\alpha_{i,j}^{\min}\right]\right),\ \beta^{\min} = det\left(\left[\beta_{i,j}^{\min}\right]\right)\\
\alpha_L(q) &= \sum_{k=1}^{k=n} det_\alpha\left(\Phi(k)\left[\alpha_{i,j}^{\min}\right] + [I - \Phi(k)]\left[\alpha_{i,j,L}(\delta)\right]\right)\\
\beta_L(q) &= \sum_{k=1}^{k=n} det\left(\Phi(k)\left[\beta_{i,j}^{\min}\right] + [I - \Phi(k)]\left[\beta_{i,j,L}(\delta)\right]\right)
\end{aligned}$$

$$\begin{aligned}
\Phi(k) &= \left[\varphi_{i,j}(k)\right] \mid\\
\varphi_{1,1}(k) &= |sign(1-k)|\\
\varphi_{2,2}(k) &= |sign(2-k)|\\
&\ \vdots\\
\varphi_{n,n}(k) &= |sign(n-k)|\\
\varphi_{i,j}(k) &= 0\ \forall i \neq j
\end{aligned}$$

$$\alpha_N(\delta) = \alpha(q) - \alpha^{\min} - \alpha_L(\delta),\ \ \beta_N(\delta) = \beta(q) - \beta^{\min} - \beta_L(\delta)$$

4.7.3 Example

(Elizondo, 1999; 2001A). The Frazer and Duncan Theorem is presented in (Ackermann et al., 1993) in the boundary crossing version as follows. Let $P(s,Q) = \{p(s,q) \mid q \in Q \subset P \subset \Re^\ell\}$ be a family of polynomials of invariant degree with parametric uncertainty and real continuous coefficients, then the family $P(s,Q)$ is robust stable if and only if: 1) a stable polynomial $p(s,\hat{q}) \in P(s,Q)$ exists, 2) $\det(H(q)) \neq 0$ for all $q \in Q$.
(Ackermann et al., 1993) Given the family of invariant degree polynomials with parametric uncertainty described by: $p(s,q) = c_0 + c_1 s + c_2 s^2 + c_3 s^3 + c_4 s^4$, with real continuous coefficients: $c_0(q) = 3$, $c_1(q) = 2$, $c_2(q) = 0.25 + 2q_1 + 2q_2$, $c_3(q) = 0.5(q_1 + q_2)$, $c_4(q) = q_1 q_2$, such that $q_i \in [1,\ 5]$. Determine the robust stability of the family by means of the Frazer and Duncan theorem applying in graphical way the sign decomposition of the determinant theorem (13).

The Hurwitz matrix $H(q)$ is obtained, it is proved that the polynomial $p(s,\hat{q})$ is stable for $\hat{q} = [1\,1]^T$ and that the determinant of the Hurwitz matrix $H(\hat{q})$ is positive. Having the first condition of the Frazer and Duncan theorem satisfied, and proving that the determinant is robust positive in Q, the second condition of the Frazer and Duncan theorem will be satisfied too.

$$H(q) = \begin{bmatrix} c_3(q) & c_1(q) & 0 & 0 \\ c_4(q) & c_2(q) & c_0(q) & 0 \\ 0 & c_3(q) & c_1(q) & 0 \\ 0 & c_4(q) & c_2(q) & c_0(q) \end{bmatrix}$$

The robust positivity of the determinant problem is solved by means of: the box partition theorem 9, the polygon theorem 8 in $(\alpha,\ \beta)$ representation and the sign decomposition of the determinant theorem (13). Taking the partition in 9 equal parts in each one of the two variables q_i and applying sign decomposition in constant partition way, the function values in minimum and maximum vertices "×" and lower bound "+" are plotted for each Γ^i box, as it appears in the figure (10). All lower bound marks "+" are above the alpha axis, then all of bounds are positive, therefore the determinant of the Hurwitz matrix $H(q)$ is robust positive implying that the polynomials family is robust stable.

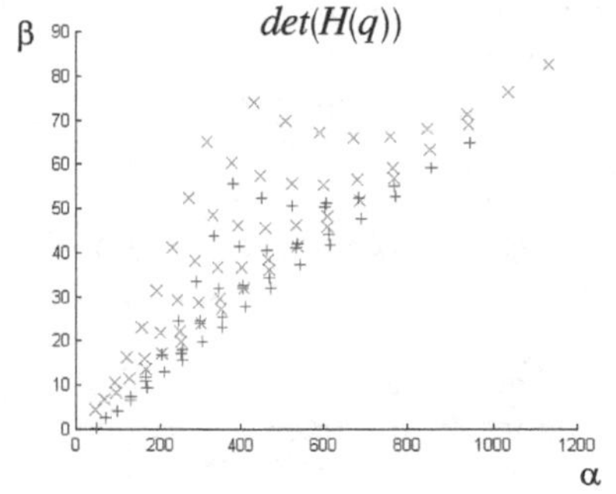

Fig. 10. Positivity of the determinant

5. A solution for the parametric robust stability problem

5.1 Problem identification

In control area, the robust stability of LTI systems with parametric uncertainty problem has been studied in different interesting ways. The problem can be divided in two parts. One of them is that it is not possible to be obtained roots of a polynomial by analytical means for the general case. The second is that we have now a family of polynomials to study instead of a single polynomial.

Since to obtain roots of polynomials for the general case is a difficult problem. Then the extraction of roots of polynomials went mapped firstly to a "position" of roots problem in the complex plane, Routh never tried to extract the roots, his work begun studying the position of the roots. This problem was subjected to a second mapping, it was transferred to mathematical problems of smaller level for example to a positivity problem, as it is the case of: Routh, Hurwitz, Lienard-Chipart and Elizondo-González 2001 criterions.

The objective in this chapter is to study the stability of a family of polynomials with invariant degree (the reder can see poles and zeros canellation cases) and real continuous coefficients dependent on parameters with uncertainty. The essence of the problem is that we have now a set of roots in the the complexes plane, and for stability condition all of them must be in the left half of the complex plane for asymptotic stability. How to obtain that the set of roots remains in the left side of the complex plane?

A well known solution is: a) the family $P(s, Q)$ has at least one element $p(s, q^*)$ stable and b) $\mid H(q) \mid \neq 0 \; \forall q \in Q$. The explanation is because the determinant of a Hurwitz matrix is zero when the polynomial has roots in the imaginary axis, so if there is a $q^* \in Q$ vector such that $p(s, q^*)$ is stable then its roots are at the left half of the complex plane. On other hand, if a vector q slides into Q starting from q^* implies that the coefficients $c_i(q)$ will change in continuous way and the roots of $p(s, q^*)$ will slides too on the complex plane. But if $\mid H(q) \mid \neq 0 \; \forall q \in Q$, it means that does not exist a vector q for which $p(s, q)$ has roots in the imaginary axis, implying that the displacement of the roots never cross the imaginary axis. This solution is very difficult to use because to test the robust positivity of a determinant in the general case is a very difficult problem (Ackermann et al., 1993)(page 93).

Another solution was through the subsetting test, the idea worked well in convex families as interval (Kharitonov, 1978) and affine (Bartlett et al., 1988), but it was not in nonconvex families as multilinear and polynomic.

Then it can be concluded that the solution for robust stability of LTI systems with parametric uncertainty problem for the general case: interval, affine, multilinear, polinomic, cannot be sustained in convexity properties nor subsetting test.

5.2 A proposed solution

In (Elizondo, 1999) it was developed a solution for the general case of robust stability of LTI systems with parametric uncertainty without concerning the convexity of the families, the solution consists of two parts.

A part of the solution was the development of a stability criterion, operating with multivariable polynomic functions in parametric uncertainty case, simpler than Hurwitz and Lienard-Chipart criterions (Elizondo et al., 2005). The mentioned criterion is similar to criterion (Elizondo, 2001B) but without the σ column, therefore it does not determine the number of unstables roots, it only determines whether the polynomial is stable or not. The amount of mathematical operations required in this criterion is equal to the one of (Elizondo, 2001B) but they are much less that the required ones in Hurwitz and Lienard-Chipart criterions (Elizondo et al., 2005).

The other part of the solution was the development of a mathematical tool capable of solving robust positivity problems of multivariable polynomic functions in necessary and sufficient conditions by means of extreme point analysis.The mathematical tool developed in (Elizondo, 1999) was Sign Decomposition.

Then, the solution proposed for robust stability in LTI systems with parametric uncertainty in the general case is supported in two results: the stability criterion for LTI systems (Elizondo, 2001B) and sign decomposition (Elizondo, 1999). Given a polynomial $p(s, q) = c_n(q)s^n + c_{n-1}(q)s^{n-1} + \cdots + c_0(q)$ with real coefficients, where $q \in Q \subset P$, $Q = \{[q_1 \, q_2 \cdots q_\ell]^T | q_i \in [0, \; 1] \; \forall i\}$. The procedure easier to use is by means of the partition box theorem (9) in the modality "Constant Partition", its application could be of the following way.

a) Take the equations of the coefficients $c_i(q)$ and decompose them into positive and negative parts $c_{ip}(q)$ and $c_{in}(q)$. In symbolic way.

b) By means of the positive and negative parts, to obtain the components in alpha and beta representation. $\alpha_i = c_{ip}(q) + c_{in}(q)$, $\beta_i = c_{ip}(q) - c_{in}(q)$.
c) To make a table in accordance to the criterion (2).
d) By means of the rectangle theorem (5) or polygon theorem (8), to analyze the robust positivity in Q of the coefficients $c_n(q)$ and $c_{n-1}(q)$. In case of negative bound in a coefficient, include its graph in the following software.
e) To make a software to develop the table in accordance to the partition box theorem and to graph the wished $e_{i,1}$ element.

Remark 14. *The sigma column in the criterion (2) is not necessary calculate for robust stability*

5.3 Example

Given a LTI system with parametric uncertainty $Q = \{[q_1\ q_2\ q_3]^T | q_i \in [0,\ 1]\ \forall i\}$, its characteristic polynomial of invariant degree is $p(s,q) = c_4(q)s^4 + c_3(q)s^3 + +c_2(q)s^2 + +c_1(q)s + c_0(q)$. To analyze the robust stability of the system.
a) Positive and negative parts $c_{pi}(q)$ and $c_{ni}(q)$.

$$c_0(q) = 2 + q_1q_2q_3^3 - q_2q_3$$
$$c_1(q) = 5 + q_1q_2^3 - q_2q_3$$
$$c_2(q) = 10 + 4q_1q_3 - q_1q_2^2 - q_2^3$$
$$c_3(q) = 5 + q_2^2 - q_1q_2^2$$
$$c_4(q) = 3 + q_1q_2^3 - q_2q_3$$

$$c_{0p}(q) = 2 + q_1q_2q_3^3 \qquad c_{0n}(q) = q_2q_3$$
$$c_{1p}(q) = 5 + q_1q_2^3 \qquad c_{1n}(q) = q_2q_3$$
$$c_{2p}(q) = 10 + 4q_1q_3 \qquad c_{2n}(q) = q_1q_2^2 + q_2^3$$
$$c_{3p}(q) = 5 + q_2^2 \qquad c_{3n}(q) = q_1q_2^2$$
$$c_{4p}(q) = 3 + q_1q_2^3 \qquad c_{4n}(q) = q_2q_3$$

b) The alpha and beta representation of the coefficients is as follows.

$$\alpha_i = c_{pi}(q) + c_{ni}(q), \qquad \beta_i = c_{pi}(q) - c_{ni}(q)$$
$$\alpha_0 = c_{p0}(q) + c_{n0}(q) \qquad \beta_0 = c_{p0}(q) - c_{n0}(q)$$
$$\alpha_1 = c_{p1}(q) + c_{n1}(q) \qquad \beta_1 = c_{p1}(q) - c_{n1}(q)$$
$$\alpha_2 = c_{p2}(q) + c_{n2}(q) \qquad \beta_2 = c_{p2}(q) - c_{n2}(q)$$
$$\alpha_3 = c_{p3}(q) + c_{n3}(q) \qquad \beta_3 = c_{p3}(q) - c_{n3}(q)$$
$$\alpha_4 = c_{p4}(q) + c_{n4}(q) \qquad \beta_4 = c_{p4}(q) - c_{n4}(q)$$

c) To make a table in accordance to the criterion (2).

σ_1	$(\alpha_4,\ \beta_4)$	$(\alpha_2,\ \beta_2)$	$(\alpha_0,\ \beta_0)$
σ_2	$(\alpha_3,\ \beta_3)$	$(\alpha_1,\ \beta_1)$	
σ_3	$\alpha_{3,1} = c_{\alpha 3}c_{\alpha 2} + c_{\alpha 4}c_{\alpha 1}$, $\beta_{3,1} = c_{\beta 3}c_{\beta 2} - c_{\beta 4}c_{\beta 1}$	$\alpha_{3,2} = c_{\alpha 3}c_{\alpha 0}$, $\beta_{3,2} = c_{\beta 3}c_{\beta 0}$	
σ_4	$\alpha_{4,1} = \alpha_{3,1}c_{\alpha 1} + c_{\alpha 3}\alpha_{3,2}$, $\beta_{4,1} = \beta_{3,1}c_{\beta 1} - c_{\beta 3}\beta_{3,2}$		
σ_5	Check robust positivity of $\beta_{4,1}$ and $\beta_{3,2}$		

d) The lower bound of $c_4(q)$ and $c_3(q)$ are as follows.
For $c_4(q)$ is $LB\ c_4 = c_{4p}\left([0\,0\,0]^T\right) - c_{4n}\left([1\,1\,1]^T\right) = 3 + (0)(0)^3 - (1)(1) = 2.$
For $c_3(q)$ is $LB\ c_3 = c_{3p}\left([0\,0\,0]^T\right) - c_{3n}\left([1\,1\,1]^T\right) = 5 + (0)^2 - (1)(1)^2 = 4.$

Then $c_4(q)$ and $c_3(q)$ are robustly positives in Q

e) By means of software applying 8 partitions the graphs $e_{3,1}$, $e_{3,2}$, $e_{4,1}$ were obtained as following.

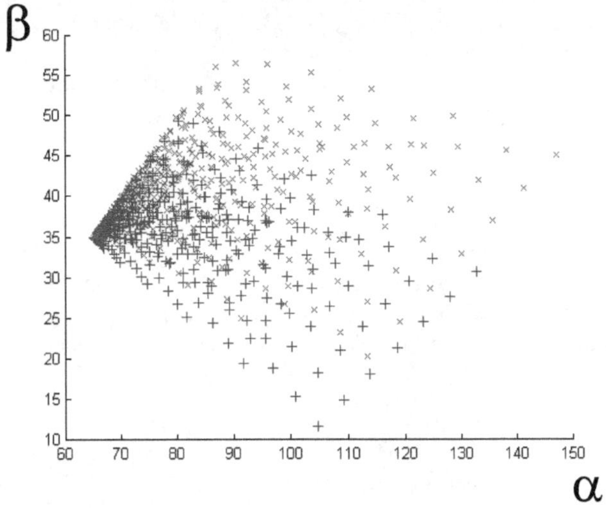

Fig. 11. Element e_{31} in $(\alpha,\ \beta)$ representation

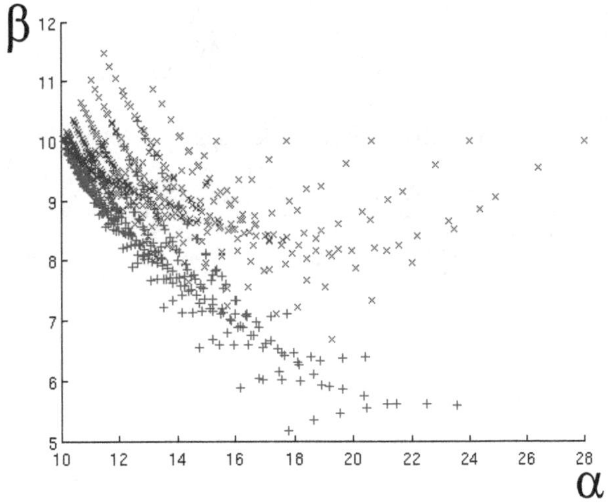

Fig. 12. Element e_{32} in $(\alpha,\ \beta)$ representation

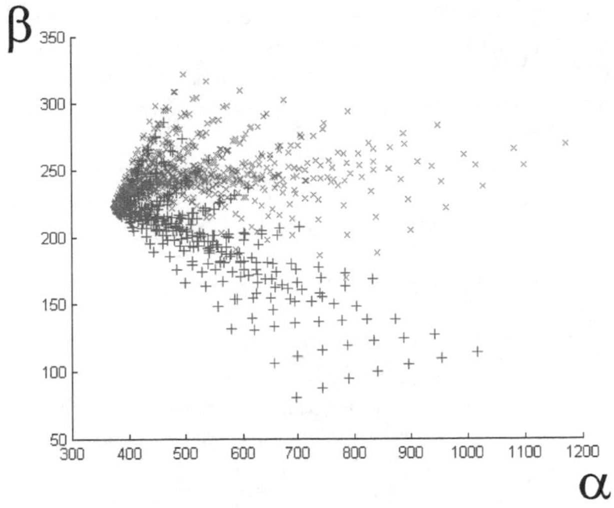

Fig. 13. Element e_{41} in (α, β) representation

Since $c_4(q), c_3(q), e_{31}(q), e_{32}(q), e_{41}(q)$ are robustly positive, then the system is robustly stable.

6. References

Ackermann, J. & Bartlett, A. (1993). *Robust Control Systems with Uncertain Physical Parameters*, Springer, ISBN 978-0387198439.

Barmish, B.R. (1990). *New Tools for Robustness of Linear Systems*, Prentice Hall, ISBN 978-0023060557.

Bartlett, A.C.; Hollot, C.V. & Lin, H. (1988). Root locations of an entire polytope of polynomials: It suffices to check the edges. *Mathematics of Control Signals Systems*, Vol. 1, No. 1, 61-71, DOI: 10.1007/BF02551236.

Bhattacharyya, S.P.; Chapellat, H. & Keel, L.H. (1995). *Robust Control the Parametric Approach*, Prentice Hall, ISBN 0-13-781576-X, NJ, USA.

Bhattacharyya, S.P.;Keel, L.H. & Datta, A. (2009). *Linear Control Theory: Structure, Robustness and Optimization*, CRC Press,ISBN 978-0-8493-4063-5, Boca Raton.

Elizondo-González, C. (1999). Estabilidad y Controlabidad Robusta de Sistemas Lineales con Incertidumbre Multilineal. *Programa Doctoral de la Facultad de Ingeniería Mecánica y Eléctrica de la Universidad Autónoma de Nuevo León.*

Elizondo-González, C. (2000). Necessary and Sufficient Conditions for Robust Positivity of Polynomic Functions Via Sign Decomposition, *3 rd IFAC Symposium on Robust Control Design ROCOND 2000*, pp. 14-17, ISBN-13:9780080432496 , Prague Czech Republic, April, 2000.

Elizondo-González C. (2001). Robust Positivity of the Determinant Via Sign Decomposition, *The 5th World Multi-Conference on Systemics Cybernetics and Informatics SCI 2001*, pp. 14-17, ISBN 980-07-7545-5, Orlando, Florida, USA, July, 2001.

Elizondo-González C. (2001). New Stability Criterion on Space Coefficients, *Conferences on Decision and Control IEEE*, SBN 0-7803-7063-5, Orlando, Florida, USA. Diciembre, 2001.

Elizondo-González, C. (2002). An Application of Recent Reslts on Parametric Robust Stability, *X Congreso Latinoamericano de Control Autmático*, Guadalajara Jalisco, 2002.

Elizondo-González, C. (2002). An Applicaton of Sign Decomposition of the Determinant on Parametric Robust Stability, *X Congreso Latinoamericano de Control Autmático*, Guadalajara Jalisco, 2002.

Elizondo-González, C. & Alcorta-García, E. (2005). Análisis de cotas de raíces de polinomios característicos y nuevo criterio de estabilidad, *Congreso Nacional 2005 de la Asociación de México de Control Automático*, ISBN 970-32-2974-3 Cuernavaca, Morelos, México, Octubre, 2005.

Fuller, A.T. (1977). *On Redundance in Stability Criteria*, Internatinal Journal Control, Vol. 26, No. 2, pp. 207-224.

Gantmacher, F.R. (1990). *The Theory of Matrices*, American Mathematical Society, ISBN-10: 0821813935, ISBN-13: 978-0821813935.

Guerrero, J.; Romero, G.; Mendez, A.; Dominguez, R.; Panduro, M. & Perez, I. (2006). Lecture Notes in Control and Information Sciences, *Robust Absolute Stability Using Polynomial Positivity and Sign Decomposition*, Vol. 341, No. 1, pp. 423-430, 2006. ISSN: 0170-8643.

Graziano-Torres, R.; Elizondo-González, C. (2010). Herramientas para el Análisis de Estabilidad Robusta de Sistemas LTI con Incertidumbre Paramétrica, *Congreso Nacional 2004 de la Asociación de México de Control Automático*, ISBN: 970-32-2137-8 , México D.F., Octubre, 2004.

Keel, L.H. & Bhattacharyya, S.P. (2008). Fixed Order Multivariable Controller Synthesis: A New Algorithm, *Proceedings of the 47th Conference on Decision and Control*, Cancun, Mexico, December, 2008.

Keel, L.H. & Bhattacharyya, S.P. (2009). Fixed Order Multivariable Discrete-Time Control, *Joint 48th IEEE Conference on Decision and Control and 28th Chinese Control Conference*, Shangai, P.R. China, December, 2009.

Keel, L.H. & Bhattacharyya, S.P. (2011). Robust Stability via Sign-Definite Decomposition, *Journal of IEEE Transactions on Automatic Control*, Vol. 56, No. 140 – 155, ISSN: 0018-9286, Jan -2011.

Kharitonov, V. (1978). On a Generalization of a Stability Criterion. *Seria Fizico-matematicheskaia*, Vol.1, pp. 53-57, Izvestiia Akademii Nauk Kazakhskoi SSR.

Knap, M.J.; Keel, L.H. & Bhattacharyya, S.P. (2010). Robust stability of complex systems with applications to performance attainment problems, *American Control Conference.*, Marriot Waterfront, Baltimore, MD, USA, July, 2010.

Knap, M.J.; Keel, L.H. & Bhattacharyya, S.P. (2010). Robust Hurwitz stability via sign-definite decomposition , *Linear Algebra and its Applications.*, Volume 434, Issue 7, pp 1663-1676, 1 April 2011.

Meinsma G. (1995). Elementary Proof of the Routh-Hurwitz Test *Systems & Control Letters 25*, pp. 237-242.

Moore, Ramon E.(1966). *Robust Control the Parametric Approach*, Prentice Hall, NJ, USA.

Zettler M.; Garloff J. (1998). Robustness Analysis of Polynomials with Polynomial Parameter Dependency Using Bernstein Expansion, *IEEE Transactions on Automatic Control* vol. 43 pages 1017-1049, 1998.

3

A Sum of Squares Optimization Approach to Robust Control of Bilinear Systems

Eitaku Nobuyama[1], Takahiko Aoyagi[1] and Yasushi Kami[2]
[1]*Kyushu Institute of Technology*
[2]*Akashi National College of Technology*
Japan

1. Introduction

Robust control problems for nonlinear systems are usually formulated as L_2-induced norm minimization problems and those problems are reduced to the solvability of the so-called "Hamilton-Jacobi equation" (see, for example, van der Schaft (1996) and references therein). However, in the case of bilinear systems the usual L_2-induced norm minimization problem leads to an obvious solution (the zero input is optimal!). To avoid the obvious solution Shimizu et al. (1997) introduced nonlinear weights on the evaluated signal and proposed a design method using linearization of the state-dependent matrix Riccati inequality derived from the Hamilton-Jacobi equation. In contrast to this, the purpose of this paper is to propose a new design method using SOS (Sum-of-Squares) optimization without linearization.
It is known that the Hamilton-Jacobi equality coming from the L_2-induced norm minimization problem is reduced to the solvability of an inequality condition of quadratic form, i.e.,

$$h^T(x)M(x)h(x) \geq 0, \quad \forall x \tag{1}$$

and this inequality is moreover reduced to the following matrix positive semi-definiteness condition:

$$M(x) \succeq 0, \quad \forall x \tag{2}$$

where $M(x)$ is a Riccati-type matrix including the state variables. This matrix inequality is usually called "a state-dependent matrix Riccati inequality" derived from the L_2-induced norm optimization problem. Most papers have tried to find a solution to the matrix inequality (2) so far. See, for example, Ichihara (2009); Prajna et al. (2004) and the references therein. However, it should be noted that the condition (2) is just a sufficient condition for (1) unless $h(x)$ is independent of x, because $M(x)$ includes x. In most L_2-induced norm optimization cases, $h(x)$ includes x (in our case $h(x) = P^{-1}x$ as shown in the later section) and hence the methods of Ichihara (2009); Prajna et al. (2004) and other papers based upon the condition (2) can have significant conservativeness. Note that Ichihara (2009) proposed a redesign method for reducing the conservativeness; however, it has to find a solution to (2) before applying the redesign method. Hence, the redesign method cannot be applied if the matrix inequality (2) does not have a solution.

In the present paper, to avoid the conservativeness we propose a new method for finding a solution to (1) directly without finding a solution to (2). A key idea of our method is to treat the dependency of $h(x)$ with x as an equality condition and formulate the problem to be concerned as an SOS (Sum of Squares) optimization problem with an equality constraint. After that we apply SOS optimization technique to the problem to propose an iterative algorithm for finding a robust feedback controller.

This paper is organized as follows: In Section 2, the plant to be concerned is described and a robust control problem is formulated after introducing nonlinear weights. Moreover, an inequality condition of quadratic form and the corresponding state-dependent matrix Riccati inequality are derived without using the Hamilton-Jacobi equality. In Section 3, some definitions and basic properties of SOS polynomials and SOS matrices are given. In Section 4, a new iterative method is proposed for finding a solution to the inequality condition of quadratic form. In Section 5, a numerical example is demonstrated to show the efficiency of our method, and in Section 6 this paper is concluded.

In this paper, the following notations are used:

$\mathbf{R}$ the set of real numbers.
$\mathbf{Z}$ the set of integers.
$\mathbf{Z}_+$ the set of non-negative integers.
$\mathbf{R}[x]$ the set of polynomials in x. ($\mathbf{R}[x]$ is also written as $\mathbf{R}[x_1 \cdots x_n]$ for $x = [x_1 \cdots x_n]^T$.)
M^T the transpose of the matrix M.
$\otimes$ the Kroneckar product.
Σ the set of SOS polynomials. In particular, Σ_x denotes the set of SOS polynomials in x.
I an identity matrix of appropriate size. In particular, I_r denotes the $r \times r$ identity matrix.

Moreover, for a square matrix M, $M \succ 0$ and $M \succeq 0$ imply that M is positive definite and positive semi-definite, respectively.

2. Problem statement

2.1 Plant and nonlinear weights

Consider the following bilinear systems:

$$\begin{aligned} \dot{x}_p(t) &= A_p x_p(t) + B_{p1} w(t) + \sum_{i=1}^{n_q} B_{p2i} x_p(t) u_i(t) \\ &= A_p x_p(t) + B_{p1} w(t) + B_{p2}(x) u(t) \end{aligned} \tag{3}$$

$$z_p(t) = C_p x_p(t) \tag{4}$$

where $x_p \in \mathbf{R}^{n_p}$ is the state variable, $u := [u_1 \cdots u_{n_q}]^T \in \mathbf{R}^{n_q}$ is the input, $w \in \mathbf{R}^{n_w}$ is the exogenous input, $z_p \in \mathbf{R}^r$ is the output to be evaluated, and the matrices A_p, B_{p1}, B_{p2i} $(i = 1, \ldots, n_q)$ are real matrices of appropriate sizes with

$$B_{p2}(x) := \sum_{i=1}^{n_q} B_{p2i} x.$$

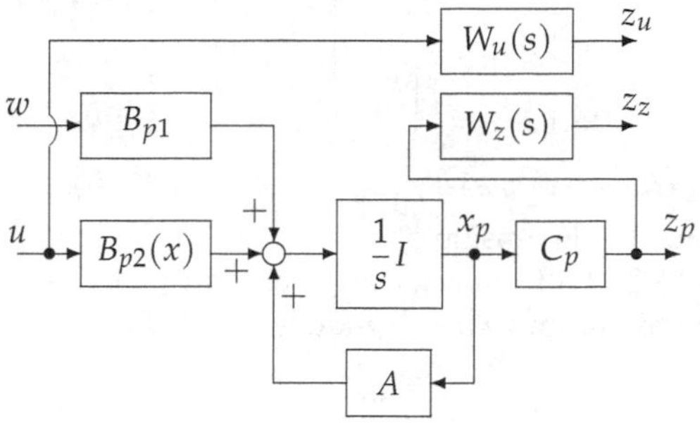

Fig. 1. Plant with frequency weights

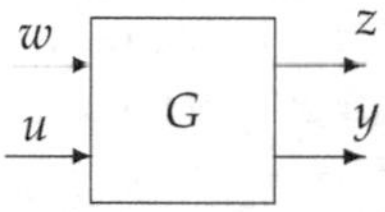

Fig. 2. Generalized plant

In this paper, we consider to evaluate the L_2-induced norm from w to z_p and u with the following frequency weights $W_z(s)$ and $W_u(s)$, respectively (see Fig. 1):

$$W_z(s):\begin{cases}\dot{x}_z(t)=A_zx_z(t)+B_zz_p(t),\\ z_z(t)=C_zx_z(t)+D_zz_p(t),\end{cases} \tag{5}$$

$$W_u(s):\begin{cases}\dot{x}_u(t)=A_ux_u+B_uu(t),\\ z_u(t)=C_ux_u(t)+D_uu(t)\end{cases} \tag{6}$$

where $x_z \subset \mathbf{R}^{n_z}$, $x_u \subset \mathbf{R}^{n_u}$ and the matrices in (5) and (6) are real matrices of appropriate size. Here, we assume that the state variable is available for feedback. Then the plant with the frequency weights in Fig. 1 can be represented as a generalized plant G in Fig. 2 which is given by

$$\dot{x}(t)=Ax(t)+B_1w(t)+B_2(x)u(t) \tag{7}$$

$$z(t)=\begin{bmatrix}C_{11}\\ C_{12}\end{bmatrix}x(t)+\begin{bmatrix}0\\ D_{12}\end{bmatrix}u(t)$$

$$y(t)=x(t) \tag{8}$$

where $y(t)$ is the output for feedback and

$$x(t)=\begin{bmatrix}x_p(t)\\ x_z(t)\\ x_u(t)\end{bmatrix},\ z(t)=\begin{bmatrix}z_z(t)\\ z_u(t)\end{bmatrix}, \tag{9}$$

$$A = \begin{bmatrix} A_p & 0 & 0 \\ B_z C_p & A_z & 0 \\ 0 & 0 & A_u \end{bmatrix}, \; B_1 = \begin{bmatrix} B_{p1} \\ 0 \\ 0 \end{bmatrix}, \; B_2(x) = \begin{bmatrix} B_{p2}(x) \\ 0 \\ B_u \end{bmatrix}, \tag{10}$$

$$C_{11} = \begin{bmatrix} D_z C_p & C_z & 0 \end{bmatrix}, \; C_{12} = \begin{bmatrix} 0 & 0 & C_u \end{bmatrix}, \; D_{12} = D_u. \tag{11}$$

Let n $(:= n_p + n_z + n_u)$ denote the dimension of x.
The purpose of this paper is to find a feedback controller which reduces the effect of w on z. For this purpose, the problem to minimize the L_2-induced norm from w to z defined by

$$\sup_{w \neq 0} \frac{\|z\|_2}{\|w\|_2} \tag{12}$$

is usually considered where $\|\cdot\|_2$ denotes the L_2 norm. However, the bilinear system (3) is uncontrollable for $x = 0$ because of $B_2(0) = 0$, so that the effect of w cannot be reduced around $x = 0$. Moreover, it is known that the zero input $u = 0$ is optimal for the problem of minimizing the L_2-induced norm (12) when the evaluated variable z is affine in x and u. Hence, the minimization problem with respect to the L_2-induced norm (12) is no use for our purpose.
Although the system is uncontrollable at $x = 0$, the system behavior can be improved by some proper controllers except at $x = 0$. To formulate the problem of finding such controllers Shimizu et al. (1997) introduce nonlinear weights on z. It is shown by them that the obvious solution (the zero input) can be avoided by introducing the nonlinear weights.

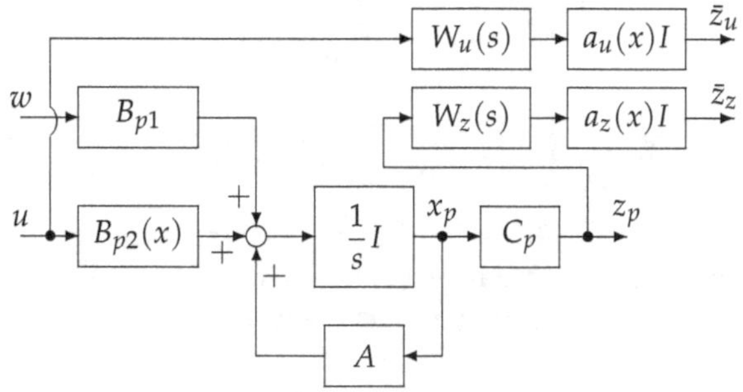

Fig. 3. Plant with nonlinear weights

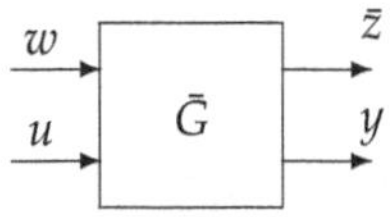

Fig. 4. Generalized plant including nonlinear weights

As in the paper of Shimizu et al. (1997) we will also introduce nonlinear weights on z as shown in Fig. 3 where $a_z(x)$ and $a_u(x)$ are the nonlinear weights which are functions of x.

With the introduction of the nonlinear weights the new generalized plant $\bar{G}$ shown in Fig. 4 is represented as

$$\begin{aligned}\dot{x}(t) &= Ax(t) + B_1 w(t) + B_2(x)u(t),\\ \bar{z}(t) &= \begin{bmatrix} a_z(x)C_{11} \\ a_u(x)C_{12} \end{bmatrix} x(t) + \begin{bmatrix} 0 \\ a_u(x)D_{12} \end{bmatrix} u(t),\\ y(t) &= x(t)\end{aligned} \tag{13}$$

where

$$\begin{aligned}\bar{z}(t) :&= \begin{bmatrix} \bar{z}_z(t) \\ \bar{z}_u(t) \end{bmatrix}\\ &= \begin{bmatrix} a_z(x)z_z(t) \\ a_u(x)z_u(t) \end{bmatrix}.\end{aligned}$$

Then the problem to be considered in this paper is formulated as the one of finding the feedback controller which minimizes the L_2-induced norm from w to $\bar{z}$ defined by

$$\sup_{w \neq 0} \frac{\|\bar{z}\|_2}{\|w\|_2}. \tag{14}$$

The next theorem is shown by Ohsaku et al. (1998); Shimizu et al. (1997) using linealization.

Theorem 1. *Consider the bilinear system* (13) *with* $C_{12} = 0$. *For given* $\gamma > 0$ *suppose that there exits a positive definite symmetric matrix* P *which satisfies*

$$PA + A^T P + \frac{1}{\gamma^2} PB_1 B_1^T P + C_{11}^T C_{11} < 0 \tag{15}$$

and the nonlinear weights $a_z(x)$ *and* $a_u(x)$ *satisfy the condition*

$$\frac{1}{a_u^2(x)} x^T PB_2(x)B_2^T(x)Px + (1 - a_z^2(x))x^T C_{11}^T C_{11} x \geq 0. \tag{16}$$

Then the L_2*-induced norm from* w *to* $\bar{z}$ *is less than or equal to* γ *via the feedback control*

$$u(t) = -\frac{1}{a_u^2(x)} B_2^T(x)Px(t). \tag{17}$$

This theorem gives a method for choosing the nonlinear weights after P is obtained; however, this means that the nonlinear weights cannot be chosen before obtaining P and the condition (16) restricts the choice of the nonlinear weights. In contract to this, in our method given below the nonlinear weights can be chosen a priori and the condition which they have to satisfy is just that $a_z^2(x) \in \mathbf{R}[x]$ and $1/a_u^2(x) \in \mathbf{R}[x]$.

A typical choice of the nonlinear weights is as follows:

$$a_z(x) = \sqrt{1 + x^T R_z x},$$
$$a_u(x) = \frac{1}{\sqrt{1 + x^T R_u x}} \tag{18}$$

where $R_x \succeq 0$ and $R_u \succeq 0$. Fig. 5 shows an example in the case of $x \in \mathbf{R}$. The weight $a_z(x)$ shown in Fig. 5 is utilized for suppressing the effect of w on z_z and $a_u(x)$ is for allowing large input values except at $x = 0$.

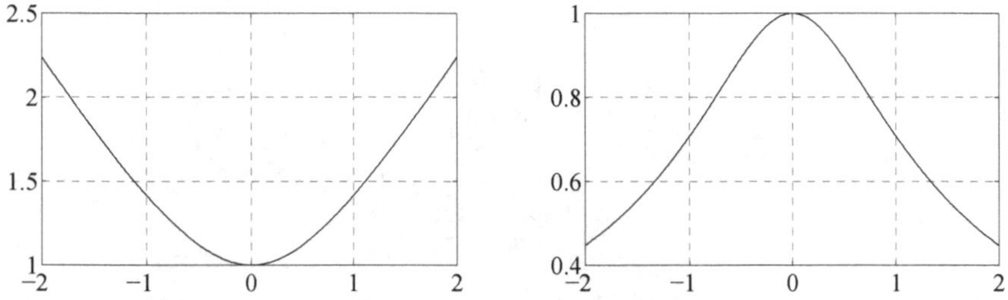

(a) $a_z(x)$ (b) $a_u(x)$

Fig. 5. Example of nonlinear weights

2.2 Derivation of state-dependent inequalities

In the sequel, we assume $D_{12} = I$ for simplicity. Then we have the next theorem.

Theorem 2. *Suppose that for given $\gamma > 0$ there exists a positive definite symmetric matrix P which satisfies the following state-dependent inequality:*

$$\begin{aligned}\phi(x,P) := x^T \Big[& -P^{-1}(A + B_2(x)C_{12}) - (A + B_2(x)C_{12})^T P^{-1} \\ & - P^{-1}\left(\frac{1}{\gamma^2} B_1 B_1^T - \frac{1}{a_u^2(x)} B_2(x) B_2^T(x)\right) P^{-1} - a_z^2(x) C_{11}^T C_{11}\Big] x > 0, \\ & \forall x (\neq 0) \in \mathbf{R}^n \end{aligned} \tag{19}$$

Then by the feedback

$$u(t) = -\left(\frac{1}{a_u^2(x)} B_2^T(x) P^{-1} + C_{12}\right) x(t) \tag{20}$$

the closed-loop system is asymptotically stable and the L_2-induced norm (14) *is less than or equal to γ, i.e.,*

$$\sup_{w \neq 0} \frac{\|z\|_2}{\|w\|_2} \leq \gamma. \tag{21}$$

Proof: First, we will show that the closed-loop system via the feedback (20) with $w(t) = 0$ is stable when (19) holds. To show this we adopt $V(t) = x^T(t)P^{-1}x(t)$ as a Lyapunov function candidate. Then we have

$$
\begin{aligned}
\frac{d}{dt}V(t) =& \dot{x}^T P^{-1}x + x^T P^{-1}\dot{x} \\
=& (Ax + B_2(x)u)^T P^{-1}x + x^T P^{-1}(Ax + B_2(x)u) \\
=& \left[Ax - B_2(x)\left(\frac{1}{a_u^2(x)}B_2^T(x)P^{-1} + C_{12}\right)x\right]^T P^{-1}x \\
& + x^T P^{-1}\left[Ax - B_2(x)\left(\frac{1}{a_u^2(x)}B_2^T(x)P^{-1} + C_{12}\right)x\right] \quad \text{from (20)} \\
=& x^T\left[P^{-1}(A + B_2(x)C_{12}) + (A + B_2(x)C_{12})^T P^{-1} - \frac{2}{a_u^2}P^{-1}B_2(x)B_2^T(x)P^{-1}\right]x \\
<& -x^T\left[\frac{1}{\gamma^2}P^{-1}B_1B_1^T P^{-1} + a_z^2 C_{11}^T C_{11} + \frac{1}{a_u^2}P^{-1}B_2(x)B_2^T(x)P^{-1}\right]x \quad \text{from (19)} \\
\leq& 0, \quad \text{for } x \neq 0.
\end{aligned} \tag{22}
$$

This shows the closed-loop system is asymptotically stable.
Next, from (13) we have

$$
\gamma^2|w|^2 - |z|^2 = \gamma^2|w|^2 - a_z^2 x^T C_{11}^T C_{11}x - a_u^2 x^T C_{12}^T C_{12}x - a_u^2 u^T u - 2a_u^2 x^T C_{12}^T u \tag{23}
$$

and the following identity holds:

$$
\begin{aligned}
0 &= 2x^T P^{-1}\dot{x} - 2x^T P^{-1}\dot{x} \\
&= 2x^T P^{-1}\dot{x} - 2x^T P^{-1}Ax - 2x^T P^{-1}B_1 w - 2x^T P^{-1}B_2(x)u.
\end{aligned} \tag{24}
$$

By adding the both-sides of (24) to (23) and completing the square we have

$$
\begin{aligned}
\gamma^2|w|^2 - |z|^2 =& 2x^T P^{-1}\dot{x} + \gamma^2 w^T w - 2x^T P^{-1}B_1 w \\
& - a_u^2\left[u^T u + 2\left(\frac{1}{a_u^2}x^T P^{-1}B_2(x) + x^T C_{12}^T\right)u\right] \\
& - x^T\left[2P^{-1}A + a_z^2 C_{11}^T C_{11} + a_u^2 C_{12}^T C_{12}\right]x \\
=& 2x^T P^{-1}\dot{x} + \gamma^2\tilde{w}^T\tilde{w} - \frac{1}{\gamma^2}x^T P^{-1}B_1B_1^T P^{-1}x \\
& - a_u^2\tilde{u}^T\tilde{u} + a_u^2 x^T\left(\frac{1}{a_u^2}P^{-1}B_2(x) + C_{12}^T\right)\left(\frac{1}{a_u^2}B_2^T(x)P^{-1} + C_{12}\right)x \\
& - x^T\left[2P^{-1}A + a_z^2 C_{11}^T C_{11} + a_u^2 C_{12}^T C_{12}\right]x \\
=& 2x^T P^{-1}\dot{x} + \gamma^2\tilde{w}^T\tilde{w} - a_u^2\tilde{u}^T\tilde{u} + \phi(x, P)
\end{aligned} \tag{25}
$$

where

$$\tilde{w} = w - \frac{1}{\gamma^2} B_1^T P^{-1} x,$$

$$\tilde{u} = u + \left(\frac{1}{a_u^2} B_2^T(x) P^{-1} + C_{12} \right) x.$$

Then from (19) and (20)

$$\gamma^2 |w|^2 - |z|^2 \geq 2x^T P^{-1} \dot{x} + \gamma^2 \tilde{w}^T \tilde{w},$$

and hence

$$\int_0^\tau (\gamma^2 |w|^2 - |z|^2) dt \geq \int_0^\tau (2x^T P^{-1} \dot{x} + \gamma^2 \tilde{w}^T \tilde{w}) dt$$

$$= x^T(\tau) P^{-1} x(\tau) - x^T(0) P^{-1} x(0) + \int_0^\tau (\gamma^2 \tilde{w}^T \tilde{w}) dt.$$

Here, let $x(0) = 0$ and $\tau \to \infty$ then

$$\gamma^2 \|w\|^2 - \|z\|^2 = \int_0^\infty (\gamma^2 |w|^2 - |z|^2) dt = \int_0^\infty (\gamma^2 \tilde{w}^T \tilde{w}) dt \geq 0, \tag{26}$$

which leads to (21). Note that to derive (26) we use $\lim_{\tau \to \infty} x(\tau) = 0$ which holds because the closed-loop is asymptotically stable. Q.E.D.

Note that $\phi(x, p)$ in (19) can be represented as

$$\phi(x, P) = (P^{-1} x)^T M(x, P) (P^{-1} x) \tag{27}$$

where

$$M(x, P) := -(A + B_2(x) C_{12}) P - P (A + B_2(x) C_{12})^T$$
$$- \left(\frac{1}{\gamma^2} B_1 B_1^T - \frac{1}{a_u^2(x)} B_2(x) B_2^T(x) \right) - a_z^2(x) P C_{11}^T C_{11} P. \tag{28}$$

From this we have the next corollary.

Corollary 1. *Suppose that for given $\gamma > 0$ there exists a positive definite symmetric matrix P which satisfies the following state-dependent inequality:*

$$M(x, P) \succ 0, \quad \forall x \in \mathbf{R}^n \tag{29}$$

Then by the feedback (20) *the closed-loop system is asymptotically stable and the L_2-induced norm* (14) *is less than or equal to γ.*

Proof: It is obvious from (27) that (19) is satisfied if (29) holds. Hence we obtain this corollary from Theorem 2. Q.E.D.

The inequality (29) is called "a state-dependent matrix Riccati inequality" and equivalent to

$$h^T \Big[-(A + B_2(x)C_{12})P - P(A + B_2(x)C_{12}) - \left(\frac{1}{\gamma^2}B_1B_1^T - \frac{1}{a_u^2(x)}B_2(x)B_2^T(x)\right) - a_z^2(x)PC_{11}^TC_{11}P\Big]\, h > 0,$$
$$\forall x \in \mathbf{R}^n,\ h(\neq 0) \in \mathbf{R}^n. \tag{30}$$

Note that h is independent of x in (30), whereas there is a relationship of $h = P^{-1}x$ between h and x in (19). This means that the condition (30) can be very conservative compared with the condition (19). As mentioned in Introduction, most papers have tried to find P which satisfies a matrix state-dependent inequality like (29) (or (30)). In contrary to this, we will try to find P which satisfies (19) (instead of (30)) to reduce the conservativeness.

3. Sum of squares

In this section, we briefly survey the so-called "SOS (Sum of Squares) optimization."

3.1 Definitions and basic properties

A monomial in $x = [x_1 \ \cdots \ x_n]^T$ is represented as $x_1^{\alpha_1} \cdots x_n^{\alpha_n}$ with $\alpha = (\alpha_1, \ldots, \alpha_n) \in \mathbf{Z}_+^n$. This is also written as $x^\alpha = x_1^{\alpha_1} \cdots x_n^{\alpha_n}$. The degree of a monomial x^α, denoted by $\deg(x^\alpha)$, is defined by $\deg(x^\alpha) := \sum_{i=1}^n \alpha_i$ and the degree of a polynomial $f(x) \in \mathbf{R}[x]$, denoted by $\deg(f)$, is defined by the degree of the monomial which has the highest degree among all the monomials included in $f(x)$. For a polynomial matrix $F(x) \in \mathbf{R}^{q\times r}$ the degree of $F(x)$, denoted by $\deg(F)$, is defined by $\deg(F) := max_{ij} \deg(F_{ij})$ where F_{ij} denotes the (i,j) element of $F(x)$.

A real polynomial $f(x) \in \mathbf{R}[x]$ is said to be an *SOS (Sum of Squares) polynomial* if it can be represented as a sum of squares of some polynomials, i.e., there exist some polynomials $g_i(x) \in \mathbf{R}[x]$ $(i = 1, \ldots, p)$ such that

$$f(x) = \sum_{i=1}^{p} g_i^2(x). \tag{31}$$

Moreover, a polynomial symmetric matrix $F(x) \in \mathbf{R}^{r\times r}[x]$ is said to be an *SOS matrix* if it can be represented as

$$F(x) = L^T(x)L(x)$$

for some polynomial matrix $L(x)$ of appropriate size. In this paper, we denote the set of SOS polynomials by Σ, and the set of $r \times r$ SOS matrices by $\Sigma^{r\times r}$.

From the definitions it is obvious that

$$f(x) \in \Sigma \ \Rightarrow f(x) \geq 0 \quad (\forall x \in \mathbf{R}^n), \tag{32}$$
$$F(x) \in \Sigma^{r\times r} \Rightarrow F(x) \succeq 0 \quad (\forall x \in \mathbf{R}^n). \tag{33}$$

Here, for a positive integer d let $v_d(x)$ be a polynomial vector in x of size ${}_{n+d}C_d$ defined by

$$v_d(x) := \left[1 \ x_1 \ \cdots \ x_n \ x_1^2 \ x_1x_2 \ \cdots \ x_n^2 \ \cdots \ x_1^d \ \cdots \ x_n^d\right]^T, \tag{34}$$

which contains all monomials whose degrees are less than or equal to d where ${}_{\alpha}C_{\beta} = \alpha!/(\beta!(\alpha-\beta)!)$ for positive integers α and β with $\alpha \geq \beta$. Then the next lemmas are known.

Lemma 1. *(Parrilo (2003)) Let* $\deg(f) = 2d$ *where* $f(x) \in \mathbf{R}[x]$. *Then the following (i) and (ii) are equivalent:*

(i) $f(x) \in \Sigma$.

(ii) There exists a positive semi-definite symmetric matrix of appropriate size such that $f(x) = v_d^T(x) Q v_d(x)$.

Lemma 2. *(Scherer & Hol (2006)) Let* $\deg(F) = 2d$ *where* $F(x) \in \mathbf{R}[x]^{r \times r}$. *Then the following (i) and (ii) are equivalent:*

(i) $F(x) \in \Sigma^{r \times r}$.

(ii) There exists a positive semi-definite symmetric matrix of appropriate size Q *such that* $F(x) = (v_d(x) \otimes I_r)^T Q (v_d(x) \otimes I_r)$.

Using these lemmas, the problem of determining whether a polynomial $f(x)$ (or a polynomial matrix $F(x)$) is an SOS polynomial (or an SOS matrix) or not is reduced to an SDP (Semi-Definite Programming) problem, which can be solved numerically, of checking the positive semi-definiteness of the corresponding matrix Q.

3.2 SOS polynomials with equality constraints

Let us consider the following equality constraints:

$$f_j(x) = 0, \quad j = 1, \ldots, p \tag{35}$$

where $f_j(x) \in \mathbf{R}[x]$ and their feasible set is defined by

$$S := \{x \in \mathbf{R}^n \mid f_j(x) = 0,\ j = 1, \ldots, p\}. \tag{36}$$

Here we consider the problem of determining whether a given polynomial $f_0(x) \in \mathbf{R}$ is non-negative or not for all $x \in \mathbf{R}$ in the feasible set, i.e., the following condition holds or not:

$$f_0(x) \geq 0, \quad \forall x \in S. \tag{37}$$

For this problem, define a generalized Lagrange function $L(x, \lambda)$ by

$$L(x, \lambda) := f_0(x) - \sum_{j=1}^{p} \lambda_j(x) f_j(x) \tag{38}$$

where $\lambda_j(x) \in \mathbf{R}[x]$ and let

$$\lambda(x) := \begin{bmatrix} \lambda_1(x) & \cdots & \lambda_p(x) \end{bmatrix}^T \in \mathbf{R}[x]^p.$$

Then if for given $\lambda[x] \in \mathbf{R}[x]^p$

$$L(x, \lambda) \geq 0, \quad \forall x \in \mathbf{R}^n \tag{39}$$

holds, the condition (37) is satisfied. In fact, (39) implies

$$f_0(x) \geq \sum_{j=1}^{p} \lambda_j(x) f_j(x) = 0, \quad \forall x \in S. \tag{40}$$

Moreover, if $L(x, \lambda) \in \Sigma$ then (39) holds from Lemma 1 and hence (37) holds. These facts are summarized in the following lemma.

Lemma 3. *If the following (i) or (ii) holds, the condition* (37) *holds.*

(i) There exists $\lambda(x) \in \mathbf{R}[x]^p$ *such that* $L(x, \lambda) \geq 0$ $(\forall x \in \mathbf{R}^n)$.

(ii) There exists $\lambda(x) \in \mathbf{R}[x]^p$ *such that* $L(x, \lambda) \in \Sigma$.

4. Proposed method

Theorem 2 implies that the state feedback (20) will stabilize the closed-loop system and (25) is satisfied if we can obtain a positive definite symmetric matrix P satisfying (19). In this section, we propose an SOS optimization method to find such P.

To this end, let us introduce sufficiently small $\epsilon > 0$ and define

$$\tilde{M}(x, P) := M(x, P) - \epsilon I, \tag{41}$$

$$\tilde{\phi}(x, P) := (P^{-1}x)^T \tilde{M}(x, P)(P^{-1}x). \tag{42}$$

Then it is easy to see

$$\tilde{M}(x, P) \succeq 0, \forall x \in \mathbf{R}^n \quad \Rightarrow \quad M(x, P) \succ 0, \forall x \in \mathbf{R}^n, \tag{43}$$

$$\tilde{\phi}(x, P) \geq 0, \forall x \in \mathbf{R}^n \quad \Rightarrow \quad \phi(x, P) > 0, \forall x (\neq 0) \in \mathbf{R}^n. \tag{44}$$

Hence, for obtaining the feedback (20) it suffices to find $P \succ 0$ such that

$$\tilde{\phi}(x, P) \geq 0, \forall x \in \mathbf{R}^n. \tag{45}$$

From (42), the condition (45) can be written as

$$h^T \tilde{M}(x, P) h \geq 0, \quad \forall (x, h) \in \mathbf{R}^{2n} \quad \text{such that} \quad h = P^{-1}x \tag{46}$$

and moreover this can be written as

$$h^T \tilde{M}(x, P) h \geq 0, \quad \forall (x, h) \in \tilde{S} \tag{47}$$

where

$$\tilde{S} := \{(x, h) \in \mathbf{R}^{2n} \mid x - Ph = 0\}. \tag{48}$$

By this, the condition (45) is represented as the condition (47) including the equality constraint $x - Ph = 0$. For the condition (47) we define a generalized Lagrange function as in Section 3.2 as follows:

$$L(x,h,\lambda;P) := h^T \tilde{M}(x,P)h - \lambda^T(x,h)(x - Ph) \tag{49}$$

where $\lambda(x,h) \in \mathbf{R}[x,h]^n$. Then, from Lemma 3, (47) is satisfied if there exit λ and $P(\succ 0)$ which satisfies

$$L(x,h,\lambda;P) \geq 0, \quad \forall(x,h) \in \mathbf{R}^{2n} \tag{50}$$

Here, suppose the degree of λ is given, say m, then λ can be written as

$$\lambda(x,h) = Hv_m(x,h)$$

where $v_m(x,h)$ is a vector of size ${}_{2n+m}C_m$ which contains all monomials in x and h whose degrees are less than or equal to m, and H is an $n \times ({}_{2n+m}C_m)$ real matrix. From this, (50) is reduced to

$$L_m(x,h;H,P) := h^T \tilde{M}(x,P)h - v_m^T(x,h)H^T(x - Ph) \geq 0, \quad \forall(x,h) \in \mathbf{R}^{2n}, \tag{51}$$

and the problem to be concerned becomes the one for finding matrices P and H which satisfies (51).

Note that $L_m(x,h;H,P)$ includes the product of H and P in the last term. Hence, we consider an iterative algorithm which repeats a step of finding H for fixed P and a step of finding P for fixed H.

First, suppose P is fixed. In this case, $L_m(x,h;H,P)$ can be written as

$$L_m(x,h;H,P) = v_{d_1}^T(x,h)Q_1(H)v_{d_1}(x,h) \tag{52}$$

where $d_1 = \deg(L_m)$, the degree of L_m as a polynomial in x and h, $v_{d_1}(x,h)$ is a vector of size ${}_{2n+d_1}C_{d_1}$ which contains all monomials in x and h whose degrees are less than or equal to d_1, and $Q_1(H)$ is a $({}_{2n+d_1}C_{d_1}) \times ({}_{2n+d_1}C_{d_1})$ symmetric matrix. Then $Q_1(H)$ is affine in H because so is L_m. Hence, in the case of fixed P, the problem to be concerned is reduced to an SDP problem to find H such that $Q_1(H) \succeq 0$, because (51) is satisfied if $L_m \in \Sigma_{(x,h)}$ which is equivalent to the existence of $Q_1(H) \succeq 0$ by Lemma 1.

Next, suppose H is fixed. In this case, L_m is not affine in P, but by Schur complement (51) is equivalent to

$$G(x,h;H,P) := \begin{bmatrix} G_{11}(x,h;H,P) & a_z^2(x)h^T PC_{11}^T \\ a_z^2(x)C_{11}Ph & a_z^2(x)I_{n_z} \end{bmatrix} \succeq 0, \quad \forall(x,h) \in \mathbf{R}^{2n}, \tag{53}$$

which is affine in P, where

$$\begin{aligned} G_{11}(x,h;H,P) :=& h^T \Big[-(A + B_2(x)C_{12})P - P(A + B_2(x)C_{12})^T - \bar{\gamma}B_1B_1^T \\ &+ \bar{a}_u^2(x)B_2(x)B_2^T(x) \Big] h - v_m^T(x,h)H^T(x - Ph) \end{aligned} \tag{54}$$

and

$$\bar{\gamma} := \frac{1}{\gamma^2}, \; \bar{a}_u(x) := \frac{1}{a_u(x)}. \tag{55}$$

Since G is afffine in P, it can be written as

$$G(x,h;H,P) = (v_{d_2}(x,h) \otimes I_{n_z+1})^T Q_2(P)(v_{d_2}(x,h) \otimes I_{n_z+1}) \tag{56}$$

where $d_2 = \deg(G)$, the degree of G as a polynomial matrix in x and h, $v_{d_2}(x,h)$ is a vector of size ${}_{2n+d_2}C_{d_2}$ which contains all monomials in x and h whose degrees are less than or equal to d_2, and $Q_2(P)$ is a real symmetric matrix of appropriate size. Hence, in the case of fixed H, the problem to be concerned is reduced to an SDP problem to find P such that $Q_2(P) \succeq 0$, because (51) is satisfied if $G \in \Sigma_{(x,h)}^{(n_z+1)\times(n_z+1)}$ which is equivalent to the existence of $Q_2(H) \succeq 0$ by Lemma 2.

Note that L_m and G are also affine in $\bar{\gamma}$ and hence we can consider to maximize $\bar{\gamma} = 1/\gamma^2$ (i.e., minimize γ).

Now, let us summarize our method as an algorithm.

Algorithm 1. Step. 0 *Choose an initial value $P_0 \succ 0$ and small ϵ. Let $k := 0$ and $\bar{\gamma}_0 = 0$.*

Step 1 *Let $P = P_k$ and get the optimal value $\bar{\gamma}^*$ and its optimizer H^* by solving numerically the next SDP problem*

$$\max_{\bar{\gamma},H} \bar{\gamma} \quad \text{s.t.} \quad Q_1(H) \succeq 0, \tag{57}$$

and let $H_k := H^*$.

Step 2 *Let $H = H_k$ and get the optimal value $\bar{\gamma}^*$ and its optimizer $P^* \succ 0$ by solving numerically the next SDP problem*

$$\max_{\bar{\gamma},P\succ 0} \bar{\gamma} \quad \text{s.t.} \quad Q_2(P) \succeq 0, \tag{58}$$

and let $\bar{\gamma}_{k+1} := \bar{\gamma}^*$ and $P_{k+1} = P^*$.

Step 3 *If $|\bar{\gamma}_{k+1} - \bar{\gamma}_k|$ is sufficiently small (i.e., $\bar{\gamma}_k$ is convergent), then return P_{k+1} as a solution and exit; otherwise, let $k := k+1$ and go to Step 1.*

Note that a feasible solution to $\tilde{M}(0,P) \succeq 0$ for large γ can be used as an initial value P_0, because $\tilde{M}(0,P) \succeq 0$ is a usual Riccati inequality and has a feasible solution for large γ.

5. Numerical example

In this section, we give a numerical example. The bilinear system to be concerned is the semi-active suspension system for automobiles introduced by Ohsaku et al. (1998); Sampei et al. (1999).

The motion equation of the suspension system is given by

$$M_b\ddot{x}_b = C_s(\dot{x}_w - \dot{x}_b) + C_v(\dot{x}_w - \dot{x}_b) + K_s(x_w - x_b) \tag{59}$$

$$M_w\ddot{x}_w = -C_s(\dot{x}_w - \dot{x}_b) - C_v(\dot{x}_w - \dot{x}_b) - K_s(x_w - x_b) + K_t(x_r - x_w) \tag{60}$$

where

x_b is the displacement of the car body,

x_w is the displacement of the car wheel,

x_r is the displacement of the road,

M_b is the mass of the car body,
M_w is the mass of the car wheel,
K_s is the spring constant of the suspension,
K_t is the elastic coefficient of the tire,
C_s is the fixed damping coefficient of the suspension,
C_v is the variable damping coefficient of the suspension,
and C_v is the input and $\dot{x}_r$ is the disturbance.

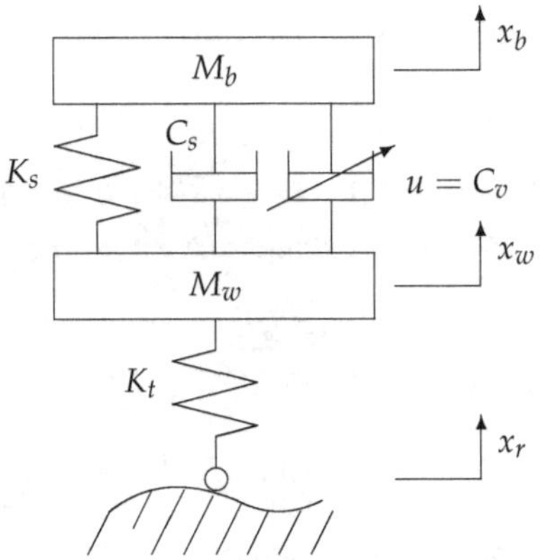

Fig. 6. Semi-active suspension system

Then the state-space representation of the generalized system with $W_z = I$, $W_u = 1$ and nonlinear weights $a_z(x)$, $a_u(x)$ is given by

$$\dot{x}(t) = Ax(t) + B_1 w(t) + B_2(x)u(t) \quad (61)$$

$$z(t) = a_z(x)C_{11}x(t) + a_u(x)u(t) \quad (62)$$

where

$$x(t) = \begin{bmatrix} x_w(t) - x_b(t) \\ \dot{x}_b(t) \\ x_r(t) - x_w(t) \\ \dot{x}_w(t) \end{bmatrix}, \ u(t) = C_v(t), \ w(t) = \dot{x}_r(t)$$

$$A = \begin{bmatrix} 0 & -1 & 0 & 1 \\ \frac{K_s}{M_b} & -\frac{C_s}{M_b} & 0 & \frac{C_s}{M_b} \\ 0 & 0 & 0 & -1 \\ -\frac{K_s}{M_w} & \frac{C_s}{M_w} & \frac{K_t}{M_w} & -\frac{C_s}{M_w} \end{bmatrix}, \ B_1 = \begin{bmatrix} 0 \\ 0 \\ 1 \\ 0 \end{bmatrix}, \ B_2(x) = \begin{bmatrix} 0 \\ \frac{\dot{x}_w - \dot{x}_b}{M_b} \\ 0 \\ -\frac{\dot{x}_w - \dot{x}_b}{M_w} \end{bmatrix},$$

$$C_{11} = [0\ 1\ 0\ 0]$$

and the nonlinear weights are given by

$$\begin{aligned} a_z(x) &= \sqrt{1+x^T R_z x}, \\ a_u(x) &= \frac{1}{\sqrt{1+x^T R_u x}}, \\ R_z &= m_z I, \\ R_u &= m_u I, \end{aligned} \tag{63}$$

with some positive numbers m_z, m_u. Note that this nonlinear weights do not satisfy the condition (16) in Theorem 1 in general. Hence, the method by Ohsaku et al. (1998); Shimizu et al. (1997) cannot be applied to this example with this weights.

The objective of the robust control to be concerned is to minimize the effect of the disturbance (the road roughness) on the velocity of the car body, which is formulated as the problem of minimizing the following L_2-induced norm:

$$\sup_{w \neq 0} \frac{\|\bar{z}\|_2}{\|w\|_2}.$$

Fig. 7 shows the disturbance $w(t) = \dot{x}_r(t)$ and Fig. 8 shows the simulation results where the dashed red line shows the velocity of the car body without feedback control and the solid blue line shows the one with feedback control designed by our method. It can be seen that the amplitude of the body velocity by our method is suppressed compared with that without feedback control. This means that the effect of the disturbance on the body velocity is reduced by our method, which shows the efficiency of our method.

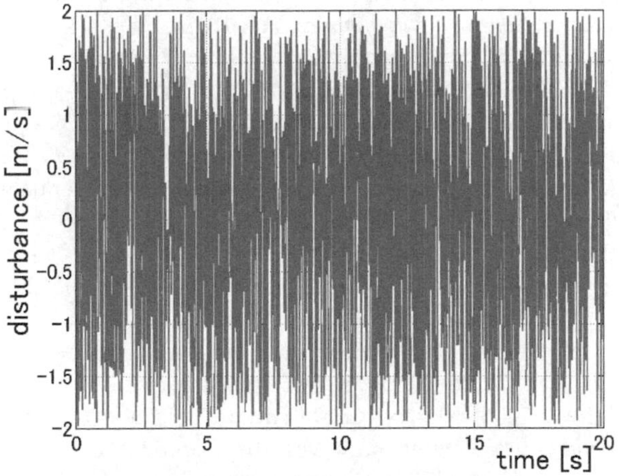

Fig. 7. Disturbance from the road surface

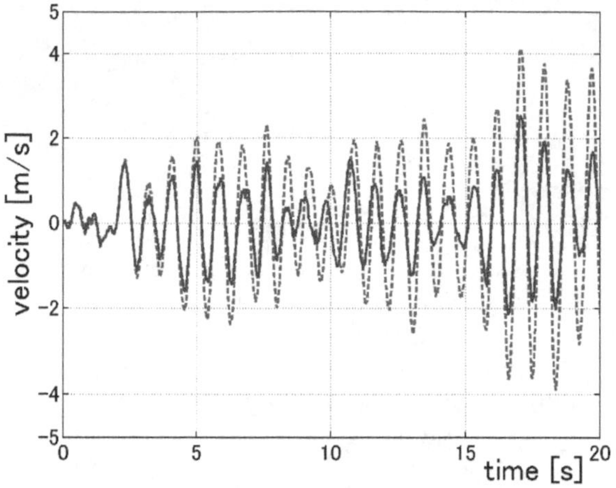

Fig. 8. Velocities of the car body (dashed red: open-loop, solid blue: by our method)

6. Conclusions

In this paper, first we have derived an inequality condition of quadratic form for the robust control problem of bilinear systems with nonlinear weights, and then proposed an iterative method for finding a solution to the inequality condition. Finally, we have given a numerical example to show the effectiveness of our method.

7. References

Huang, J. & Lin, C.-F. (1995). Numerical approach to computing nonlinear H_∞ control laws. *Journal of Guidance, Control and Dynamics*, Vol. 18, pp. 989-994.

Ichihara, H. (2009). Optimal control for polynomial systems using matrix sum of squares relaxations. *IEEE Transactions on Automatic Control*, Vol. 54, No. 5, pp. 1048-1053.

Ohsaku S.; Nakayama T.; Kamimura I. & Motozono, Y. (1998). Nonlinear H_∞ state feedback controller for semi-active controlled suspension. *Proceedings of AVEC '98*, pp. 63-68.

Parrilo, P. A. (2003). Semidefinite programming relaxations for semialgebraic problems. *Mathematical Programming*, Vol. 96, pp. 293-320.

Prajna, S.; Papachristodoulou, A. & Wu, F. (2004). Nonlinear control synthesis by sum of squares optimization. *Proceedings of the Asian Control Conference 2004*, pp. 157-165.

Sampei, M.; Ohsaku S. & Kamimura, I. (1999). Nonlinear H-infinity Control Theory, its Limitation and Possibility - Its Application to Semiactive Suspension. *Systems, Control and Information*, Vol. 43, No. 10, pp. 544-552 (in Japanese).

Scherer, C. W. & Hol, C. W. (2006). Matrix sum-of-squares relaxations for robust semi-definite programs. *Mathematical Programming*, Vol. 107, pp. 189-211.

Shimizu, E.; Sampei M. & Koga M. (1997). Design of a nonlinear H_∞ state feedback controller for bilinear systems with nonlinear weight. *Proceedings of the 36th IEEE Conference on Decision and Control*, pp. 2323-2324.

van der Schaft, A. J. (1996). *L_2-gain and passivity techniques in nonlinear control*, Springer-Verlag.

4

Spatially Sampled Robust Repetitive Control

Cheng-Lun Chen[1] and George T.-C. Chiu[2]
[1]National Chung Hsing University,
[2]Purdue University, West Lafayette,
[1]Taiwan, R.O.C.
[2]USA

1. Introduction

Repetitive control is one control algorithm based on the Internal Model Principle (Francis & Wonham, 1976) and has been widely implemented in various applications. A repetitive control based system has been shown to work well for tracking periodic reference commands or for rejecting periodic disturbances. Although the idea has been verified as early as 1981 (Inoue et al., 1981), a rigorous analysis and synthesis of repetitive controllers for continuous-time systems was not proposed until 1989, by Hara et al. (Hara et al., 1988). Tomizuka et al. (Tomizuka et al., 1989) addressed the analysis and synthesis of discrete-time repetitive controller, considering the fact that digital implementation of a repetitive controller is simpler and more straightforward. Since then, repetitive control has gained popularity in applications where periodic disturbances rejection or repetitive tracking are required, see (Wang et al., 2009; Cuiyan et al., 2004) and the references therein. These include controls of disk drive servo (Tomizuka et al., 1989; Guo, 1997; Moon et al., 1998), hydraulic closed-loop servo for material testing (Srinivasan & Shaw, 1993), vibration suppression (Hillerstrom, 1996), rejection of load disturbances in steel casting process (Manayathara et al., 1996), servo control for a positioning table (Yamada et al., 1999), X-Y table (Tung et al., 1993), noncircular turning process (Alter & Tsao, 1994), motor speed ripple reduction (Godler et al., 1995; Rodriguez et al., 2000), and eccentricity compensation (Garimella & Srinivasan, 1996).
In literatures, repetitive controllers are synthesized and operate in time domain, which is in accordance with the fact that models or differential equations of physical systems are mostly derived using time as the independent variable. One of the key steps for designing a repetitive controller is to determine the period, or equivalently, the number of delay taps (q^{-1}, q is the one step advance operator). This can usually be done by analyzing the periodic tracking or disturbance signal using techniques such as fast Fourier transform (FFT). To ensure effectiveness of the design, an underlying assumption is that the frequency constitutions of the periodic tracking or disturbance signal do not vary with respect to time, which corresponds to a stationary or time-invariant frequency spectrum of the signal. This assumption can be satisfied when the design objective is to track a pre-specified periodic trajectory. However, it might be violated for disturbance rejection problems where the frequency constitutions of the disturbance are time-varying. For a motion system with rotary components such as gear-train, the disturbances due to gear

eccentricity or tooth profile error are inherently angular displacement dependent or spatially periodic. They are periodic with respect to angular displacement, but not necessarily periodic with respect to time. Gear eccentricity induces disturbances with period equal to one revolution and tooth profile error induces disturbances with fundamental frequency equal to the number of teeth per revolution. The spatial periods for these two types of disturbances do not change with the angular velocity. However, the corresponding temporal frequencies will be proportional to the angular velocity and vary accordingly when the system operates at variable speeds. As an example, for a single stage motor/gear transmission system operating an output speed of v revolution per second, the eccentricity error of the final gear will show up as a periodic disturbance with temporal frequency of v Hz. As the operating speed changes, a proportional changes to the temporal frequency of the disturbance will occur whereas its spatial frequency is fixed at 1 cycle per revolution. Suppose that a repetitive controller is implemented using a constant-angular-displacement sampling period (spatially sampled) approach, e.g., m samples per revolution of the final gear, to tackle this disturbance. The number of required delay taps, which reflects the period of the disturbance, will be a constant m regardless of the angular velocity. On the other hand, a repetitive controller synthesized using the conventional approach, i.e., based on the temporal frequency of the disturbance (v Hz), and implemented with constant-time sampling period will not be effective if the number of delay taps for the repetitive controller is not tuned/adapted in real-time in accordance with the angular velocity. If the period fluctuation is small, methods have been shown to improve the robustness of the repetitive controller by increasing the notch width in the frequency domain of the repetitive controller at the cost of reduced attenuation for the periodic disturbance (Onuki & Ishioka, 2001). When the period variation is large, there are two approaches to address the varying period in a repetitive control framework. For situation where the period variation can not be measured or unknown, adaptive control approaches have been shown to be effective in adapting the period of the repetitive controller (Hillerstrom, 1996; Manayathara et al., 1996; Wit & Praly, 2000) at the expense of response time and transient response. When the period variation is known or can be measured, such as the case in gear noise induced disturbance, better trade-off between period adaptability and effectiveness of repetitive control can be made.

Recent researches started studying control problems of rejecting/tracking spatially periodic disturbances/references in spatial domain, i.e., using spatially sampled repetitive controllers. As explained earlier, a spatially sampled repetitive controller has its repetitive kernel (i.e., e^{-st} or z^{-N} with positive feedback) synthesized and operate with respect to angular displacement. Hence its capability for rejecting/tracking spatially periodic disturbances/references will not degrade when the controlled system operates at varying speed. Note that a typical repetitive control system consists of repetitive (i.e., a repetitive kernel) and non-repetitive (e.g., a stabilizing controller) portions. Given a time-domain open-loop system and with the repetitive kernel to be synthesized and implemented in spatial domain, design of the non-repetitive portion that properly interfaces the repetitive kernel and the open-loop system actually poses a challenge. (Nakano et al., 1996) initiated a fundamental design of spatially sampled repetitive controller in 1996. Although the proposed design is rudimentary due to its focus on simple linear time-invariant systems, it has recently motivated several more advanced designs (Mahawan & Luo, 2000; Chen et al., 2006). The design started by transforming a given open-loop system in time domain into one in spatial domain. Specifically, the variable of time is rendered implicit for the transformed system in spatial domain with angular displacement being the new independent variable. This is attained by using the relationship between angular displacement and velocity along with imposing an assumption of bijective mapping between time and angular displacement. The resulting nonlinear system was linearized at a fixed angular velocity and a stabilizing controller with built-in repetitive control action was synthesized. In (Chen et al., 2006), robust control methods were employed to address issues associated with using a linearized plant model in the controller synthesis and actuator saturation. Although effective for small angular velocity fluctuations, the effectiveness of a linearized approach is limited when the application requires a large variation in operating speed. (Mahawan & Luo, 2000) demonstrated the feasibility of augmenting a spatially sampled repetitive controller to a time-sampled stabilizing controller, where no reformulation and linearization of the open-loop plant model is required. However, the complexity of the method lies in the need to solve an optimization problem in real-time to synchronize the hardware and software interrupts associated with time and spatial sampling, respectively. In addition, although reasonable for trajectory tracking, the assumption of a known mapping between time and angular displacement is rarely applicable for disturbance rejection applications. The lack of considerations to modeling uncertainty is another area that can be improved from the methods proposed in (Nakano et al., 1996) and (Mahawan & Luo, 2000). Instead of linearizing the resulting nonlinear plant model, (Chen and Chiu, 2008) shows that the nonlinear plant model can be formulated into a quasi-linear parameter varying (quasi-LPV) system, where the angular speed is one of the measurable varying parameters. Leveraging existing results in controller synthesis for LPV systems (Becker & Packard, 1994; Apkarian et al., 1995; Gahinet, 1996; Gahinet & Apkarian, 1994, 1995) and the robust repetitive design formulation outlined in (Chen et al., 2006; Hanson & Tsao, 2000), an LPV gain-scheduling controller can be obtained that addresses bounded modeling uncertainties, actuator saturation and spatially periodic disturbances.

This book chapter will provide the reader with a review and summary of recent advances in design of spatially sampled repetitive control systems. Specifically, we will elaborate on a few designs which account for the robustness property of the system, i.e., capability in tackling modeling uncertainties and actuator saturation. Current issues and future research directions will also be discussed. The outline of this chapter is as follows:

Section 2 demonstrates how to transform a generic time-domain system into its counterpart in spatial domain. It is also shown that nonlinearity such as actuator saturation may be properly modeled and incorporated into the spatial-domain open-loop system.

Section 3 presents a design of spatially sampled robust repetitive control. A well-known approach for designing controllers for nonlinear systems with a well defined operating point is to first linearize the system around the nominal operating point. Once the linear system is extracted, linear robust design paradigm can be applied to establish a design framework with embedded repetitive controller.

Section 4 presents another design of spatially sampled robust repetitive control. By reformulating the transformed spatial-domain system as a quasi-linear parameter varying (quasi-LPV) system, we gain access to the LPV design framework for gain-scheduling controllers. Hence, an LPV gain-scheduling repetitive control (LPVRC) system can be synthesized by augmenting the repetitive controller with the LPV controller. The LPVRC design is superior to others in the sense that 1) It requires less computation effort when compared to nonlinear design; 2) It is robust to spatially periodic disturbances when

compared to temporal-based design; 3) It allows wider operation range when compared to designs using linearization approaches.
Section 5 concludes the chapter and points out issues and future research directions relevant to spatially sampled robust repetitive control.

2. Problem formulation – Position-invariant rotary systems

In this section, we show how a generic nonlinear time-invariant (NTI) model can be transformed into a nonlinear position-invariant (NPI; as opposed to the definition of time-invariant) model by choosing an alternate independent variable (angular displacement instead of time) and defining a new set of states (or coordinates) with respect to the angular displacement. Note that the transformation described here is equivalent to a nonlinear coordinate transformation or a diffeomorphism. The NPI model will be used for the subsequent design and discussion. In Section 2.1, we further demonstrate this transformation for a typical linear time-invariant (LTI) rotary system with actuator saturation, which will be utilized in subsequent design.
Consider the mathematical model of a single-input single-output (SISO) nth-order NTI system with model uncertainties, and subject to output disturbance, i.e.,

$$\begin{aligned} \dot{x}(t) &= \left[f_t(x(t), f_f) + \Delta f_t(x(t), f_f)\right] + \left[g_t(x(t), f_g) + \Delta g_t(x(t), f_g)\right]u(t) \\ y &= \Psi x(t) + d(t) = x_n(t) + d_y(t) \end{aligned} \tag{1}$$

where $x(t) = \left[x_1(t) \ \cdots \ x_n(t)\right]^T$, $\Psi = \left[0 \ \cdots \ 0 \ 1\right]$, $u(t)$ and $y(t)$ correspond to control input and measured output angular velocity of the system, respectively. $d_y(t)$ represents a class of position-dependent disturbances which constitutes bounded spatially periodic and non-periodic components. Here we refer non-periodic disturbances to signals whose Fourier transform or power spectral density is zero above a certain finite frequency. The only available information of the disturbances is the number of distinctive spatial frequencies and the spectrum distribution for non-periodic disturbance components. $f_t(x(t), \phi_f)$ and $g_t(x(t), \phi_g)$ are known vector-valued functions with unknown but bounded system parameters, i.e., $\phi_f = \left[\phi_{f1} \ \cdots \ \phi_{fk}\right]$ and $\phi_g = \left[\phi_{g1} \ \cdots \ \phi_{gl}\right]$; $\Delta f_t(x(t), \phi_f)$ and $\Delta g_t(x(t), \phi_g)$ represent unstructured modeling inaccuracy, which are also assumed to be bounded. Instead of using time t as the independent variable, consider an alternate independent variable $\theta = \lambda(t)$, i.e., the angular displacement. Since by definition

$$\lambda(t) = \int_0^t \omega(\tau)d\tau + \lambda(0),$$

where $\omega(t)$ is the angular velocity, the following condition

$$\omega(t) = \frac{d\theta}{dt} > 0, \ \forall \ t > 0 \tag{2}$$

will guarantee that $\lambda(t)$ is strictly monotonic such that $t = \lambda^{-1}(\theta)$ exists. Thus all the variables in the time domain can be transformed into their counterparts in the θ-domain, i.e.,

$$\hat{x}(\theta) = x(\lambda^{-1}(\theta)),\ \hat{y}(\theta) = y(\lambda^{-1}(\theta)),$$
$$\hat{u}(\theta) = u(\lambda^{-1}(\theta)),\ \hat{d}(\theta) = d(\lambda^{-1}(\theta)),$$
$$\hat{\omega}(\theta) = \omega(\lambda^{-1}(\theta)),$$

where we denote $\hat{\bullet}$ as the θ-domain representation of $\bullet$. Note that, in practice, (2) can usually be satisfied for most rotary motion system where the rotary component rotates only in one direction. Since

$$\frac{dx(t)}{dt} = \frac{d\theta}{dt}\frac{d\hat{x}(\theta)}{d\theta} = \hat{\omega}(\theta)\frac{d\hat{x}(\theta)}{d\theta}$$

(1) may be rewritten as

$$\begin{aligned} \hat{\omega}(\theta)\frac{d\hat{x}(\theta)}{d\theta} &= \left[f_t\left(\hat{x}(\theta),\phi_f\right)+\Delta f_t\left(\hat{x}(\theta),\phi_f\right)\right]+\left[g_t\left(\hat{x}(\theta),\phi_g\right)+\Delta g_t\left(\hat{x}(\theta),\phi_g\right)\right]\hat{u}(\theta) \\ \hat{y}(\theta) &= \Psi\hat{x}(\theta)+\hat{d}_y(\theta) = \hat{x}_n(\theta)+\hat{d}_y(\theta). \end{aligned} \tag{3}$$

Equation (3) can be regarded as an NPI system with the angular displacement θ as the independent variable. Note that the concept of transfer function is still valid for linear position-invariant systems if we define the Laplace transform of a signal $\hat{g}(\theta)$ in the angular displacement domain as

$$\hat{G}(\tilde{s}) = \int_0^{\infty} \hat{g}(\theta)e^{-\tilde{s}\theta}d\theta\ .$$

This definition will be useful for describing the linear portion of the overall control system.

2.1 Transformation of an LTI rotary system with actuator saturation

Suppose a state space realization of an LTI model for a typical rotary system can be expressed as

$$\begin{bmatrix} \dot{x}(t) \\ z(t) \\ y(t) \end{bmatrix} = \begin{bmatrix} A & B_v & B_u \\ C_z & D_{zv} & D_{zu} \\ C_y & D_{yv} & 0 \end{bmatrix}\begin{bmatrix} x(t) \\ v(t) \\ u(t) \end{bmatrix} \tag{4}$$

where $x(t)$ is the system state vector, $\dot{x}(t)$ denotes the time derivative of the state vector, $v(t)$ is the output disturbance vector that contains spatially periodic components, $z(t)$ denotes the output vector related to system performance, $y(t)$ is the measurement vector, and $u(t)$ is the control input vector. Those signals are linearly related by the matrices shown in (4), i.e., A, B_v, C_z, etc. and all of the matrices and vectors are assumed to have compatible dimensions. If $\Phi(t)$ is a strictly monotonic function of t such that its inverse $t = \Phi^{-1}(t)$ exists and does not vanish, variables in time domain will have a well defined counterpart in the θ-domain, i.e.,

$$\tilde{x}(\theta) \triangleq x(\Phi^{-1}(\theta)),\ \tilde{z}(\theta) \triangleq z(\Phi^{-1}(\theta)),$$
$$\tilde{y}(\theta) \triangleq y(\Phi^{-1}(\theta)),\ \tilde{v}(\theta) \triangleq v(\Phi^{-1}(\theta)),\ \text{and}\ \tilde{u}(\theta) \triangleq u(\Phi^{-1}(\theta)).$$

Suppose the angular velocity can be measured in real-time and written as

$$\tilde{\omega}(\theta) = C_{\omega}\tilde{x}(\theta) + \omega_0 \neq 0, \tag{5}$$

where ω_0 is the nominal angular velocity and C_{ω} is an appropriate output matrix. Applying the aforementioned transformation, substituting (5) into (4), and imposing the saturation function

$$sat(u) = \begin{cases} u_{\max}, & u \geq u_{\max} \\ u, & u_{\min} < u < u_{\max} \\ u_{\min}, & u \leq u_{\min} \end{cases}$$

on $\tilde{u}(\theta)$, we have

$$\begin{bmatrix} \dot{\tilde{x}}(\theta) \\ \tilde{z}(\theta) \\ \tilde{y}(\theta) \end{bmatrix} = \begin{bmatrix} A/(C_{\omega}\tilde{x}+\omega_0) & B_v/(C_{\omega}\tilde{x}+\omega_0) & B_u/(C_{\omega}\tilde{x}+\omega_0) \\ C_z & D_{zv} & D_{zu} \\ C_y & D_{yv} & 0 \end{bmatrix} \begin{bmatrix} \tilde{x}(\theta) \\ \tilde{v}(\theta) \\ sat(\tilde{u}(\theta)) \end{bmatrix}. \tag{6}$$

The system expressed by (6) is an angular displacement reformulated (ADR) system with the angular displacement θ as the independent variable.

3. Linear spatially sampled robust repetitive control

Linear robust controller design is aiming at synthesizing a feedback controller so that stability and performance of the overall (closed-loop) control system is insensitive (i.e., robust) to external disturbances and model uncertainties. There are four popular terms used to characterize the performance of a linear feedback control system, namely nominal stability, nominal performance, robust stability, and robust performance (Zhou & Doyle, 1997). We say that a feedback control system is stable if its output signals are bounded when subject to bounded input signals. A feedback control system meets (steady-state) performance if it is stable and the ratio of the sizes (measured by a mathematical norm, e.g., 2-norm) of its output to input signals is bounded above by certain frequency dependent number. In most cases, stability comes first, and performance comes next in the priority of the design. Nominal stability/performance is to be satisfied by controller design only for a plant, i.e., the model of the to-be-controlled system (free of parameter uncertainty), while robust stability/performance is to be satisfied by more challenged design for a set of plants, which include the nominal one and those due to plant parameter variation. Linear fractional transformation (LFT) is a popular and effective technique to formulate and pose a robust control design problem as will be demonstrated next.

3.1 Synthesis of the robust controller

Start the design by first looking at the LFT representation of the desired closed loop control system depicted in Fig. 1, which incorporate two motors as the actuators. An LFT representation basically consists of three blocks: generalized plant, generalized uncertainty, and the stabilizing controller. Several variables and components need to be explained here. First, the generalized plant $P(z)$ (i.e., discrete-position system with z denoted the variable used in the z-transform) includes the plant, and all linear weighting filters whose magnitude responses are used to specify the frequency-wise bounds on the output signals and modeling uncertainty. All mathematical operations within the generalized plant are either addition of two signals or scalar multiplication of signals, which renders $P(z)$ linear. Note that only motor actuators are considered in the framework and driven by the control input u calculated by the controller $K(z)$. Other type of actuators can also be considered. Second, the inputs to the controller y are output signal measurement, e.g. velocity error from the rotary component. Third, the variable w includes those external signals such as periodic disturbances while the variable z includes those physical quantities which are important to system performance. Furthermore, p and q represent the input and output of the generalized uncertainty which is formed by all the uncertainty blocks from the generalized plant. The uncertainty blocks are usually formed by the modeling error and plant nonlinearity. There exist standard procedures and techniques to 'pull out' uncertainties from the generalized plant (Zhou & Doyle, 1997).

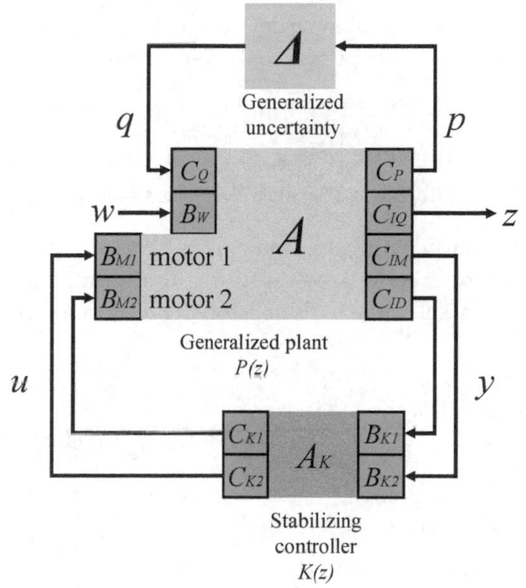

Fig. 1. LFT representation of the EP closed-loop control system using motor actuators.

Based on the LFT representation, a discrete-position state space realization of the to-be-controlled system (the generalized plant plus the generalized uncertainty) can be written as

$$
\begin{aligned}
x_{k+1} &= Ax_k + [B_{M1} \quad B_{M2}]u_k + B_W w_k, \\
y_k &= \begin{bmatrix} C_{IM} \\ C_{ID} \end{bmatrix} x_k + D_{YW} w_k, \\
z_k &= C_{IQ} x_k + D_{ZW} w_k, \\
q &= \Delta p,
\end{aligned} \tag{7}
$$

and the optimal stabilizing controller $K(z)$, parameters of which stabilize the system and also minimize the size of the transfer function from w to z (or the ratio between the sizes of w and z if induced matrix norm is used) in the presence of the generalized uncertainty, can be represented as

$$K(z) = \begin{bmatrix} C_{K1} \\ C_{K2} \end{bmatrix} (zI - A_K)^{-1} [B_{K1} \quad B_{K2}] + D_K. \tag{8}$$

The corresponding optimization (or robust performance) problem can be formulated as

$$\begin{array}{l} \text{minimize } \|H_{wz}(z)\| \\ \text{subject to } K(z) \text{ stabilizes the system,} \end{array}$$

where $H_{wz}(z)$ is the transfer function from w to z, and $\|\bullet\|$ is some induced matrix norm. The decision variables to be found are A_K, $[B_{K1} \quad B_{K2}]$, $[C_{K1} \quad C_{K2}]^T$ and D_K. It has been shown that the above problem is nonconvex and a sophisticated search algorithm (e.g., D-K iteration) needs to be implemented in order to locate the global optimal solution. An alternative way is to consider a suboptimal controller which is the solution to the following problem

$$\begin{array}{l} \text{minimize } \|H_{qw \to pz}(z)\| \\ \text{subject to } K(z) \text{ stabilizes the system,} \end{array}$$

where $H_{qw \to pz}(z)$ is the transfer function from $[q \quad w]$ to $[p \quad z]$, and $\|\bullet\|$ is some induced matrix norm. This is the so-called mixed-sensitivity optimization problem and is convex. There have been standard software tools for solving this type of problems (Gahinet & Nemirovski, 1995).

3.2 Discrete-position model of the system

Suppose that the open-loop LTI system $P(s)$ has a state space realization, i.e.,

$$\begin{aligned} \frac{dx(t)}{dt} &= Ax(t) + B_u u(t) \\ y(t) &= C_y x(t) + D_{yv} v(t), \end{aligned} \tag{9}$$

where $v(t)$ denotes disturbances at the plant output. Equation (9) is basically a simplified version of (4). Instead of using time t as the independent variable, we can pick angular position, $\theta(t)$, as the independent variable, i.e. $\phi = \theta(t)$. Thus in the ϕ-domain Eq. (9) can be expressed as

$$\begin{aligned} \frac{d\phi}{dt} \frac{d\tilde{x}(\phi)}{d\phi} &= A\tilde{x}(\phi) + B_u \tilde{u}(\phi) \\ \tilde{y}(\phi) &= C_y \tilde{x}(\phi) + D_{yv} \tilde{v}(\phi), \end{aligned} \tag{10}$$

where $\tilde{x}(\phi) = x(f^{-1}(\phi))$, $\tilde{u}(\phi) = u(f^{-1}(\phi))$, $\tilde{y}(\phi) = y(f^{-1}(\phi))$, and $\tilde{v}(\phi) = v(f^{-1}(\phi))$. Linearize the equation around the nominal angular velocity ω_0, we have

$$\begin{aligned} \frac{d\tilde{x}(\theta)}{d\phi} &= \frac{A}{\omega_0}\tilde{x}(\theta) + \frac{B_u}{\omega_0}\tilde{u}(\theta) \\ \tilde{y}(\theta) &= C_y\tilde{x}(\theta) + D_{yv}\tilde{v}(\theta). \end{aligned} \tag{11}$$

Equation (11) is a linear position invariant (LPI) system with the angular position $\theta(t)$ as the independent variable. Note that this transformation will render those position-dependent disturbances within $\tilde{v}$ periodic and stationary. The performance of a repetitive controller synthesized in the θ-domain will not be compromised. Properly choosing spatial sampling frequency T_θ (in number of samples per revolution), we can discretize Eq. (11) and acquire a discrete-position model, i.e.

$$\begin{aligned} \tilde{x}_{k+1} &= e^{\frac{A}{\omega_0}T_\theta}\tilde{x}_k + \left(\int_0^{T_\theta} e^{\frac{A}{\omega_0}\tau} d\tau\right)\frac{B_u}{\omega_0}\tilde{u}_k \\ \tilde{y}_k &= C_y\tilde{x}_k + D_{yv}\tilde{v}_k. \end{aligned} \tag{12}$$

The procedures summarized in the literature (Chen & Chiu, 2001) can now be applied to the plant model expressed in Eq. (12) for synthesizing a two degree of freedom (TDOF) discrete-position robust repetitive controller.

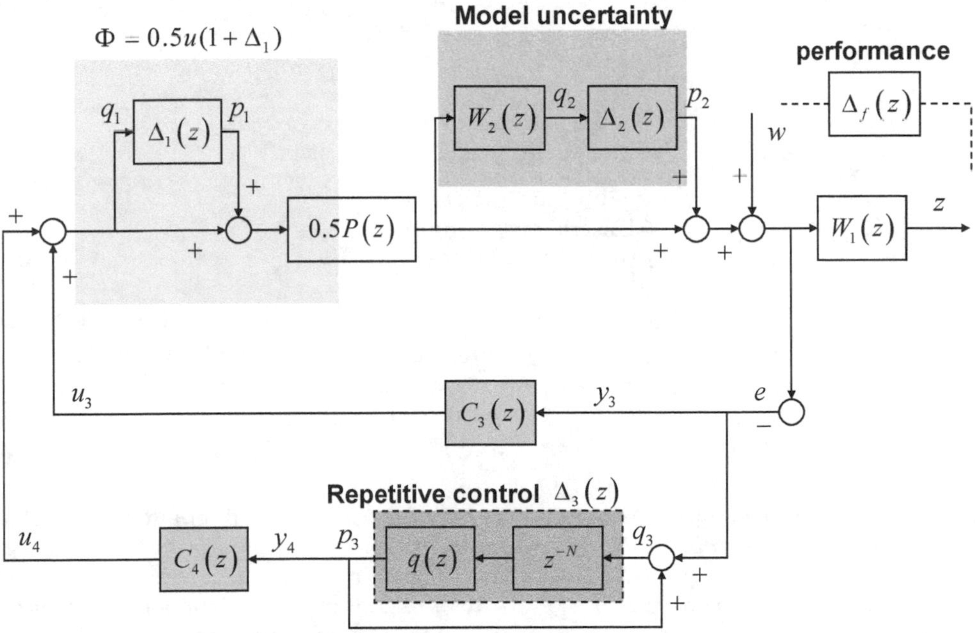

Fig. 2. The proposed TDOF robust repetitive control system.

3.3 TDOF robust repetitive controller

To reduce system sensitivity or increase system robustness to unmodeled dynamics or nonlinearity (i.e. actuator saturation), we can formulate the control problem within a unified linear design framework, i.e. using LFT. The proposed TDOF control structure is depicted in Fig. 2. The actual plant is represented as a saturation element $0.5(1+\Delta_1)$ with $|\Delta_1| \leq 1$ followed by a nominal model $P(z)$ with output multiplicative uncertainties $W_2\Delta_2$. W_2 is the frequency-dependent uncertainty weighting filter such that $\|\Delta_2\|_\infty \leq 1$. It can be picked to be any stable filter with its magnitude upper bounding the multiplicative error between the model and the actual plant, i.e.

$$\left| \frac{\hat{P}(e^{jw}) - P(e^{jw})}{P(e^{jw})} \right| \leq \left| W_2(e^{jw}) \right|, \ \forall w \tag{13}$$

Furthermore, the kernel of the repetitive controller $q(z)z^{-N}$ is replaced by a fictitious uncertainty Δ_3. Also another fictitious uncertainty Δ_f is connected between the disturbance input and plant output. W_1 is the frequency-dependent weighting filter that approximates human contrast sensitivity function (Chen et al., 2003). Thus, a TDOF controller is obtained by solving the following mixed-sensitivity optimization problem given by

$$\gamma_{opt} = \inf_{\text{K stabilizing}} \left\| \begin{matrix} W_1(1+PC_4)^{-1} \\ C_4P(1+C_4P)^{-1} \\ -W_2PC_4(1+PC_4)^{-1} \\ 1-P(1-C_4P)^{-1}C_3 \end{matrix} \right\|_\infty , \tag{14}$$

where

$$\begin{aligned} P &\triangleq \text{Motor/Gear transmission system} \\ W_1 &\triangleq \text{Performance weighting} \\ W_2 &\triangleq \text{Uncertainty weighting} \\ K &\triangleq [C_3 \quad C_4] \ \text{The TDOF controller} \end{aligned}$$

With upper and lower LFT denoted by $F_u(\cdot,\cdot)$ and $F_l(\cdot,\cdot)$, respectively (Zhou & Doyle, 1997), the robust performance of the designed control system can further be evaluated by looking at the structure singular value of $F_l(F_u(M,R),K)$ with respect to the uncertainty block $\Delta = diag(\Delta_1,\Delta_2,\Delta_f)$, i.e. $\mu_\Delta(F_l(F_u(M,R),K))$. Note that $R(z)=q(z)z^{-N}$ is the kernel of the repetitive controller.

3.4 Effect of nominal angular velocity variation on temporal-based repetitive control

A repetitive control system creates comb-like notches in the system sensitivity function at periodic disturbance frequencies. For a motor/gear rotary system where significant disturbance sources come from gear eccentricity or tooth profile error, temporal frequencies of those disturbances will be proportional to the nominal angular velocity. Thus the performance of temporal-based repetitive control systems will deteriorate as the nominal angular velocity varies. The velocity variation can be caused by friction, which is usually time-varying and difficult to be taken into account during design of the controller. Based on the proposed TDOF repetitive controller design, Fig. 3 shows the effect of nominal velocity variation on the performance of the sensitivity reduction. Parameters of the repetitive controller were specified to reject a disturbance located at 16 Hz when the system is operating at a nominal angular velocity of 3.14 rad/s. It can be seen that as the nominal velocity deviates from the desired value, the ability of the repetitive controller to reject the disturbance at 16 Hz degrades significantly. As shown in Fig. 3, a 0.2% variation in the nominal speed has an order of magnitude effect in the effectiveness of disturbance rejection. This high sensitivity to operating velocity is the motivation for pursuing the spatial-based repetitive control.

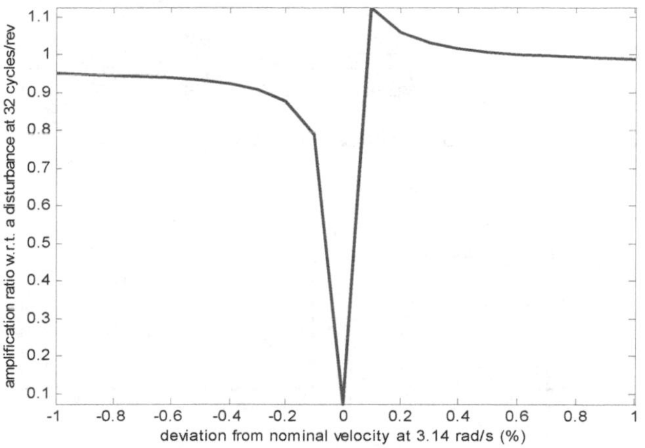

Fig. 3. Effect of nominal angular velocity variation on performance of the repetitive controller.

3.5 Spatial-based repetitive control

The proposed discrete-position repetitive controller was implemented on a typical 600-dpi laser printing system. An optical encoder was mounted on the main rotary component, i.e., an organic photoconductor (OPC) drum. A spatial sampling scheme that uses the encoder pulses (instead of a master clock) to trigger the interrupt of the control algorithm at intervals of equal angular position was implemented. Instead of counting number of pulses within a sampling period, the angular velocity was determined by monitoring the amount of time elapsed for fixed number of encoder pulses. This method actually enables low-cost encoders to achieve high-resolution velocity measurement. The spatial sampling frequency was set at 2000 samples/rev such that the discrete-position repetitive controller has a period of N=2000/16=125. The engine started printing when velocity data of 10 revolutions were collected from the OPC drum for analysis. Fig. 4 shows the measured angular velocity from the OPC drum. Note that as the paper goes through the printing process, it slightly increased the load on the transmission system. This impact decreased the nominal angular velocity from 3.14 rad/s to 3.07 rad/s. However, the frequency spectrums, as shown in Fig. 5, indicated that the performance of the discrete-position repetitive control system was not degraded by this variation in the nominal velocity. Fig. 5 also shows that capability of the temporal-based repetitive controller was compromised due to frequency shifting of those periodic disturbances.

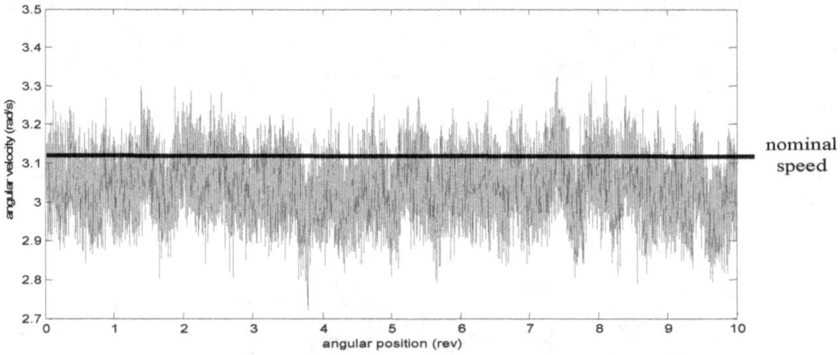

Fig. 4. Measured OPC angular velocity during printing.

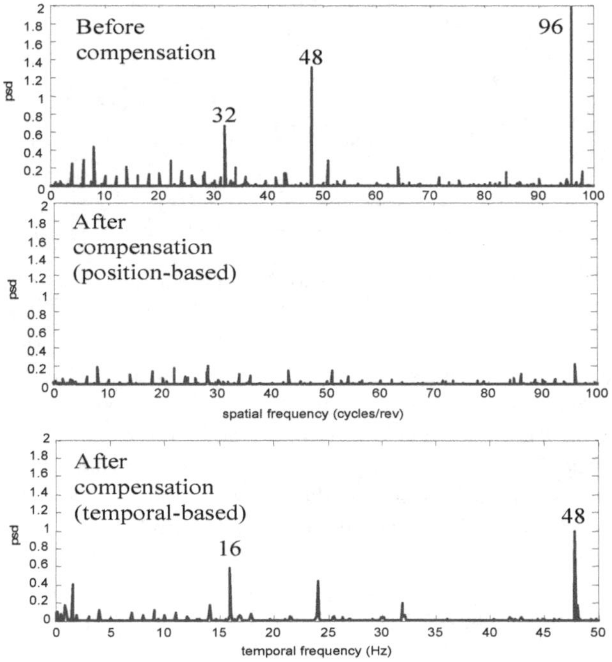

Fig. 5. Experimental PC velocity variation spectrum.

4. Linear parameter varying spatially sampled repetitive control

Several controller design approaches, e.g., design by linearization as shown previously and design for linear periodic system using the lifting technique (Chen & Francis, 1995; Hanson

& Tsao, 2000), can be considered for the ADR system represented in (6). In this section, we first demonstrate that the ADR system with actuator saturation can be formulated into a linear parameter varying (LPV) system. Next, we show that with additional parameterization, LPV gain-scheduling controller synthesis methods (Becker & Packard, 1994; Apkarian et al., 1995) can be applied to the ADR system. Finally, repetitive control and anti-windup (Wu et al., 2000) formulations can be incorporated into the LPV framework to reject spatially periodic disturbances and avoid actuator saturation.

4.1 State-dependent linear parameter varying (LPV) system

Assume that the angular velocity described by (5) can be measured in real-time and the input $\tilde{u}$ and the output $sat(\tilde{u})$ of the actuator saturation is accessible. By defining two varying parameters

$$\rho = \frac{1}{\tilde{\omega}} \text{ and } \phi = \frac{sat(\tilde{u})}{\tilde{u}},$$

we can rewrite (6) as

$$\begin{bmatrix} \dot{\tilde{x}}(\theta) \\ \tilde{z}(\theta) \\ \tilde{y}(\theta) \end{bmatrix} = \left[\begin{array}{c|cc} \tilde{A}(\rho) & \tilde{B}_v(\rho) & \tilde{B}_u(\rho,\phi) \\ \hline C_z & D_{zv} & \tilde{D}_{zu}(\phi) \\ C_y & D_{yv} & 0 \end{array}\right] \begin{bmatrix} \tilde{x}(\theta) \\ \tilde{v}(\theta) \\ \tilde{u}(\theta) \end{bmatrix} \tag{15}$$

where

$$\begin{aligned} &\tilde{A}(\rho) = A\rho, \\ &\tilde{B}_v(\rho) = B_v\rho,\ \tilde{B}_u(\rho,\phi) = B_u\rho\phi, \text{ and} \\ &\tilde{D}_{zu}(\phi) = D_{zu}\phi. \end{aligned}$$

Equation (15) represents a linear parameter-varying (LPV) system with two varying parameters whose values are accessible in real-time. Strictly speaking, (15) represents a quasi-LPV system since one of the varying parameters (ρ) is a function of the system states (Shamma & Athans, 1992).

Without the actuator saturation constraint, i.e. $\phi = 1$, (15) can be written as an affine LPV system,

$$\begin{bmatrix} \dot{\tilde{x}}(\theta) \\ \tilde{z}(\theta) \\ \tilde{y}(\theta) \end{bmatrix} = \left[\begin{array}{c|cc} A\rho & B_v\rho & B_u\rho \\ \hline C_z & D_{zv} & D_{zu} \\ C_y & D_{yv} & 0 \end{array}\right] \begin{bmatrix} \tilde{x}(\theta) \\ \tilde{v}(\theta) \\ \tilde{u}(\theta) \end{bmatrix}. \tag{16}$$

Affine LPV representation has many desirable properties that can facilitate subsequent controller design. For the quasi-LPV system represented by (15), by defining an augmented varying parameter

$$\eta = \rho\phi$$

such that $\tilde{B}_u(\rho,\phi) = B_u\rho\phi = B_u\eta$, (15) can be represented by a pseudo-affine LPV system with three varying parameters (ρ, ϕ, η), i.e.,

$$\begin{bmatrix} \dot{\tilde{x}}(\theta) \\ \tilde{z}(\theta) \\ \tilde{y}(\theta) \end{bmatrix} = \left[\begin{array}{c|cc} \tilde{A}(\rho) & \tilde{B}_v(\rho) & \tilde{B}_u(\eta) \\ \hline C_z & D_{zv} & \tilde{D}_{zu}(\phi) \\ C_y & D_{yv} & 0 \end{array}\right] \begin{bmatrix} \tilde{x}(\theta) \\ \tilde{v}(\theta) \\ \tilde{u}(\theta) \end{bmatrix}. \tag{17}$$

The name pseudo-affine is used since η is not an independent parameter but depends on the other two parameters ρ and ϕ. The impact of over-parameterizing the parameter space will be discussed in later section. Controller synthesis problem for a pseudo-affine LPV system (17) or an affine LPV system (16) can be reduced to solving a finite set of linear matrix inequalities (LMIs) under conditions satisfied by the parameter variation set and the input/output matrices.

The following example demonstrates the process of reformulating a simple 2nd order motor system model to a pseudo-affine LPV system in the angular displacement domain. Consider a transfer function representation of an LTI model for a permanent magnet brushless dc motor,

$$Z(s) = Y(s) + V(s) = \frac{c}{s^2 + as + b}U(s) + V(s), \tag{18}$$

where $U(s)$ is the voltage input to the motor, $V(s)$ is the output disturbance, and $Y(s)$ and $Z(s)$ are the undisturbed and disturbed angular position output, respectively. A state space model for (18) can be obtained by defining a set of state variables $[x_1(t) \quad x_2(t)]^T = [y(t) \quad \dot{y}(t)]^T$, i.e.,

$$\begin{bmatrix} \dot{x}_1(t) \\ \dot{x}_2(t) \\ z(t) \\ y(t) \end{bmatrix} = \left[\begin{array}{cc|cc} 0 & 1 & 0 & 0 \\ -b & -a & 0 & c \\ \hline 1 & 0 & 1 & 0 \\ 1 & 0 & 0 & 0 \end{array}\right] \begin{bmatrix} x_1(t) \\ x_2(t) \\ v(t) \\ sat(u(t)) \end{bmatrix}. \tag{19}$$

Since

$$\begin{bmatrix} \dot{x}_1(t) \\ \dot{x}_2(t) \end{bmatrix} = \frac{d\theta(t)}{dt}\begin{bmatrix} \dot{\tilde{x}}_1(\theta) \\ \dot{\tilde{x}}_2(\theta) \end{bmatrix} = \omega(t)\begin{bmatrix} \dot{\tilde{x}}_1(\theta) \\ \dot{\tilde{x}}_1(\theta) \end{bmatrix},$$

where $\theta(t)$ and $\omega(t)$ are the motor angular position and angular velocity, respectively. We can represent (19) as an ADR pseudo-affine LPV system by defining three varying parameters,

$$\rho = 1/\tilde{\omega}(\theta), \ \phi = sat(\tilde{u})/\tilde{u}, \text{ and } \eta = \rho\phi.$$

From (17), the associated LPV system can be written as

$$\begin{bmatrix} \dot{\tilde{x}}_1(\theta) \\ \dot{\tilde{x}}_2(\theta) \\ \tilde{z}(\theta) \\ \tilde{y}(\theta) \end{bmatrix} = \left[\begin{array}{cc|cc} 0 & \rho & 0 & 0 \\ -\rho b & -\rho a & 0 & \eta c \\ \hline 1 & 0 & 1 & 0 \\ 1 & 0 & 0 & 0 \end{array}\right] \begin{bmatrix} \tilde{x}_1(\theta) \\ \tilde{x}_2(\theta) \\ \tilde{v}(\theta) \\ \tilde{u}(\theta) \end{bmatrix}.$$

4.2 Synthesis of gain-scheduling controller for an affine LPV system

We will briefly summarize the results pertinent to the synthesis of an LPV gain-scheduling controller. Note that these results are originally derived for time-based systems, i.e., using time as the independent variable. However, they are equally applicable for an ADR system using angular displacement as the independent variable.

For the LPV system represented by (17), suppose a parameter-dependent output feedback dynamic controller is to be designed from $\tilde{y}$ to $\tilde{u}$, represented by

$$\begin{bmatrix} \dot{\tilde{x}}_K(\theta) \\ \tilde{u}(\theta) \end{bmatrix} = \begin{bmatrix} \tilde{A}_K(\psi) & \tilde{B}_K(\psi) \\ \tilde{C}_K(\psi) & \tilde{D}_K(\psi) \end{bmatrix} \begin{bmatrix} \tilde{x}_K \\ \tilde{y} \end{bmatrix}, \tag{20}$$

where $\psi = (\rho, \phi, \eta)$ forms a parameter vector. Equation (20) is a full-order design in the sense that $\tilde{x} \in R^n$ implies $\tilde{x}_K \in R^n$. Note that the controller is parameterized by the measurable but varying parameter vector ψ, which explains the gain-scheduling characteristics. Define $\tilde{x}_{cl} = \begin{bmatrix} \tilde{x} & \tilde{x}_K \end{bmatrix}^T$, the closed-loop LPV system with (17) and (20) can be expressed as

$$\begin{bmatrix} \dot{\tilde{x}}_{cl}(\theta) \\ \tilde{z}(\theta) \end{bmatrix} = \begin{bmatrix} \tilde{A}_{cl}(\psi) & \tilde{B}_{cl}(\psi) \\ \tilde{C}_{cl}(\psi) & \tilde{D}_{cl}(\psi) \end{bmatrix} \begin{bmatrix} \tilde{x}_{cl}(\theta) \\ \tilde{v}(\theta) \end{bmatrix},$$

where

$$\begin{bmatrix} \tilde{A}_{cl}(\psi) & \tilde{B}_{cl}(\psi) \\ \tilde{C}_{cl}(\psi) & \tilde{D}_{cl}(\psi) \end{bmatrix} = \left[\begin{array}{cc|c} \tilde{A}(\rho) + \tilde{B}_u(\eta)\tilde{D}_K(\psi)C_y & \tilde{B}_u(\eta)\tilde{C}_K(\psi) & \tilde{B}_v(\rho) + \tilde{B}_u(\eta)\tilde{D}_K(\psi)D_{yv} \\ \tilde{B}_K(\psi)C_y & \tilde{A}_K(\psi) & \tilde{B}_K(\psi)D_{yv} \\ \hline \tilde{C}_z(\rho) + \tilde{D}_{zu}(\phi)\tilde{D}_K(\psi)C_y & \tilde{D}_{zu}(\phi)\tilde{C}_K(\psi) & D_{zv} + \tilde{D}_{zu}(\phi)\tilde{D}_K(\psi)D_{yv} \end{array}\right]$$

$$= \left[\begin{array}{cc|c} \tilde{A}(\rho) & 0 & \tilde{B}_v(\rho) \\ 0 & 0 & 0 \\ \hline \tilde{C}_z(\rho) & 0 & D_{zv} \end{array}\right] + \begin{bmatrix} 0 & \tilde{B}_u(\eta) \\ I & 0 \\ \hline 0 & \tilde{D}_{zu}(\phi) \end{bmatrix} \begin{bmatrix} \tilde{A}_K(\psi) & \tilde{B}_K(\psi) \\ \tilde{C}_K(\psi) & \tilde{D}_K(\psi) \end{bmatrix} \left[\begin{array}{cc|c} 0 & I & 0 \\ C_y & 0 & D_{yv} \end{array}\right].$$

In the above equations, all I's and 0's are identity and zero matrices, respectively, with compatible dimensions for block matrix addition and multiplication. Denote the above LPV closed-loop system as P_{cl}. Define the Laplace transform of a signal $\tilde{g}(\theta)$ in the angular displacement domain to be

$$G(\tilde{s}) = \int_0^\infty \tilde{g}(\theta) e^{-\tilde{s}\theta} d\theta .$$

The quadratic LPV γ-performance problem can be summarized in the following theorem:

Theorem 3.1 The LPV closed-loop system P_{cl} is exponentially stable and the scaled H_∞ norm of the system is less than a scalar $\gamma > 0$, i.e.,

$$\left\| L^{1/2} P_{cl} L^{-1/2} \right\|_\infty = \left\| L^{1/2} \tilde{C}_{cl}(\psi)(\tilde{s}I - \tilde{A}_{cl}(\psi))^{-1} \tilde{B}_{cl}(\psi) + \tilde{D}_{cl}(\psi) L^{-1/2} \right\|_\infty < \gamma, \tag{21}$$

for all ψ belonging to a parameter variation set Ψ, if there exists a symmetric positive definite matrix $X \in \mathbf{R}^{n \times n}$ and a scaling matrix L reflecting certain parameter structure such that

$$\begin{bmatrix} \tilde{A}_{cl}^T(\psi)X + X\tilde{A}_{cl}(\psi) & X\tilde{B}_{cl}(\psi) & \tilde{C}_{cl}^T(\psi) \\ \tilde{B}_{cl}^T(\psi)X & -\gamma L & \tilde{D}_{cl}^T(\psi) \\ \tilde{C}_{cl}(\psi) & \tilde{D}_{cl}(\psi) & -\gamma L^{-1} \end{bmatrix} < 0 \tag{22}$$

Proof: See (Becker & Packard, 1994) or (Gahinet & Apkarian, 1994).

With the help of the projection lemma and the completion lemma, the following theorem can be derived to provide the necessary and sufficient conditions for the solvability of the (quadratic) LPV γ-performance problem stated above.

Theorem 3.2 For a given $\psi \in \Psi$, let $N_R(\psi)$ and $N_S(\psi)$ denote orthonormal bases of the null spaces of $\begin{bmatrix} \tilde{B}_u^T(\psi) & \tilde{D}_{zu}^T(\psi) \end{bmatrix}$ and $\begin{bmatrix} \tilde{C}_y(\psi) & \tilde{D}_{yv}(\psi) \end{bmatrix}$, respectively. The LPV γ-performance problem is solvable if and only if there exist symmetric matrices $(R, S) \in \mathbf{R}^{n \times n}$ and symmetric scaling matrices L and J such that the following matrix inequalities

$$\begin{bmatrix} N_R(\psi) & 0 \\ 0 & I \end{bmatrix}^T \left[\begin{array}{cc|c} \tilde{A}(\psi)R + R\tilde{A}^T(\psi) & R\tilde{C}_z^T(\psi) & \tilde{B}_v(\psi) \\ \tilde{C}_z(\psi)R & -\gamma J & \tilde{D}_{zv}(\psi) \\ \hline \tilde{B}_v^T(\psi) & \tilde{D}_{zv}^T(\psi) & -\gamma L \end{array}\right] \begin{bmatrix} N_R(\psi) & 0 \\ 0 & I \end{bmatrix} < 0, \tag{23}$$

$$\begin{bmatrix} N_S(\psi) & 0 \\ 0 & I \end{bmatrix}^T \left[\begin{array}{cc|c} \tilde{A}^T(\psi)S + S\tilde{A}(\psi) & S\tilde{B}_v(\psi) & \tilde{C}_z^T(\psi) \\ \tilde{B}_v^T(\psi)S & -\gamma J & \tilde{D}_{zv}^T(\psi) \\ \hline \tilde{C}_z(\psi) & \tilde{D}_{zv}(\psi) & -\gamma L \end{array}\right] \begin{bmatrix} N_S(\psi) & 0 \\ 0 & I \end{bmatrix} < 0, \tag{24}$$

$$\begin{bmatrix} R & I \\ I & S \end{bmatrix} \geq 0 \tag{25}$$

$$LJ = I \tag{26}$$

hold for all $\psi \in \Psi$.

Proof: Follows the proof in the appendix of (Gahinet & Apkarian, 1995). The only difference being that most matrices are now parameter dependent.

If the LPV γ-performance problem is solvable, the two symmetric matrices R and S along with the value of γ and the system matrices ($\tilde{A}(\psi)$, $\tilde{B}_v(\psi)$, $\tilde{B}_u(\psi)$, etc.) can be used to synthesize the controller matrices ($\tilde{A}_K(\psi)$, $\tilde{B}_K(\psi)$, $\tilde{C}_K(\psi)$, and $\tilde{D}_K(\psi)$) (Becker & Packard, 1994; Gahinet, 1996).

Remark The scaling matrix L in the above theorems takes into account the structural information on the mapping relating input $\tilde{v}$ and output $\tilde{z}$ in (17), which can include unmodeled dynamics, errors in sensing the varying parameters, and uncertain parameters which can not be measured in real-time. However, the resulting matrix inequalities are nonconvex, mainly due to (26), and computational techniques such as scaling/controller iteration or D/K iteration will be required to solve for matrices R and S.

To simplify the subsequent derivation, we will be conservative and ignore the structural information of the mapping between $\tilde{v}$ and $\tilde{z}$. This is equivalent to setting $L = J = I$ and removing the constraint defined by (26) from the above theorem. The advantage of doing so is that (23)-(25) become LMIs in R and S and the optimization becomes a convex problem that can be solved using numerical solvers based on interior point method, e.g., (Gainet et al., 1995). To check the solvability of the problem for the system given by (17) using Theorem 3.2, the following substitution is used

$$\tilde{A}(\psi) = A\rho,\ \tilde{B}_v(\psi) = B_v\rho,\ \tilde{B}_u(\psi) = B_u\eta,$$
$$\tilde{C}_z(\psi) = C_z,\ \tilde{D}_{zv}(\psi) = D_{zv},\ \tilde{D}_{zu}(\psi) = \tilde{D}_{zu}(\phi),$$
$$\tilde{C}_y(\psi) = C_y,\ \tilde{D}_{yv}(\psi) = D_{yv}.$$

Since Ψ constitutes infinite number of elements, inequalities (23)-(25) pose solvability issue with infinite number of LMI constraints. It was suggested in (Becker & Packard, 1994) that the parameter space be gridded and a controller is synthesized such that it satisfies the solvability conditions at the finite number of parameter values. However, for fixed grid spacing, the number of grid points grows rapidly as the number of parameters increases. Another way to reduce the number of constraints is to take advantage of the properties of polytopic LPV systems.

Definition An LPV system is polytopic if the state-space matrices of the system depend affinely on the varying parameters that lie within a polytope, i.e.,

$$\psi \in \Psi = \left\{ \sum_{i=1}^{r} \alpha_i \psi_i : \sum_{i=1}^{r} \alpha_i = 1,\ \alpha_i \geq 0 \right\},$$

where r is the number of vertices of the polytope and ψ_i is the parameter vector corresponding to a vertex of the polytope.

Proposition Let $f: \Pi \to \mathbf{R}$ be a convex function where Π is a convex set with vertices π_i's, i.e., $\Pi = \left\{ \sum_{i=1}^{r} \alpha_i \pi_i : \sum_{i=1}^{r} \alpha_i = 1,\ \alpha_i \geq 0 \right\}$. Then $f(x) < \gamma$ for all $x \in \Pi$ if and only if $f(\pi_i) < \gamma$ for i=1, 2,…, r (Berkovitz, 2002).

For a polytopic LPV system satisfying the following two assumptions:

i. $\tilde{D}_{yu}(\psi) = 0$; that is, no direct transmission from $\tilde{u}$ to $\tilde{y}$,

ii. $\tilde{B}_u(\psi) = \tilde{B}_u$, $\tilde{C}_y(\psi) = \tilde{C}_y$, $\tilde{D}_{zu}(\psi) = \tilde{D}_{zu}$, and $\tilde{D}_{yv}(\psi) = \tilde{D}_{yv}$; that is, those matrices are constant matrices that are independent of the varying parameters,

it can be easily shown (using the above proposition) that (23) and (24) in Theorem 3.2 hold if and only if they hold for the matrices corresponding to the vertices of the parameter polytope, i.e., $\tilde{A}(\psi_i)$, $\tilde{B}_v(\psi_i)$, $\tilde{C}_z(\psi_i)$, $\tilde{D}_{zv}(\psi_i)$ for i=1, 2,…, r (Apkarian et al., 1995). In other words, only the $2r+1$ LMIs corresponding to the vertices of the parameter polytope need to be formed for solving matrices R and S in Theorem 3.2.

The affine-LPV system represented in (16) qualifies as a polytopic system with matrix $\tilde{D}_{yu}=0$ and the matrices $A\rho$, $B_v\rho$, and $B_u\rho$ depend on the varying parameter ρ. Although the pseudo-affine LPV system represented by (17) has similar structure as (16) with $\tilde{D}_{yu}=0$ and the matrices $\tilde{A}$, $\tilde{B}_v$, $\tilde{B}_u$, and $\tilde{D}_{zu}$ depend on varying parameters, it is not polytopic due to the dependency of the varying parameter η on the two varying parameters ρ and ϕ. In such cases, a polytope can usually be found to bound and replace the parameter variation set. To satisfy the assumption (ii), parameter dependency of the $\tilde{B}_u$ or the $B_u\rho$ matrix can be removed by filtering the input channel, as will be discussed in section 3.3. For systems without direct transmission between $\tilde{u}$ and $\tilde{z}$, e.g. the brushless dc motor system demonstrated in section 3.1, it is easy to verify that $\tilde{D}_{zu}=D_{zu}=0$.

4.3 Incorporating spatial-sampled repetitive control and actuator anti-windup

The overall control structure is summarized in Fig. 6. Here $G(\psi)$ along with the actuator saturation block represents the pseudo-affine LPV system, Δ denotes the modeling uncertainty, and W_1 and W_2 are weighting filters whose frequency-dependent magnitudes are used to bound the performance specifications and model uncertainty. The repetitive controller is denoted by RC and the LPV controller to be designed is denoted by $K(\psi)$. The open-loop LPV system (within the dashed-line block in Fig. 6) can be expressed as

$$\begin{bmatrix} \dot{\tilde{x}}(\theta) \\ \tilde{q}(\theta) \\ \tilde{z}(\theta) \\ \tilde{y}(\theta) \end{bmatrix} = \left[\begin{array}{c|ccc} \tilde{A}(\rho) & \tilde{B}_p(\rho) & \tilde{B}_v(\rho) & \tilde{B}_u(\eta) \\ \hline C_q & D_{qp} & D_{qv} & \tilde{D}_{qu}(\phi) \\ C_z & D_{zp} & D_{zv} & \tilde{D}_{zu}(\phi) \\ C_y & D_{yp} & D_{yv} & 0 \end{array}\right] \begin{bmatrix} \tilde{x}(\theta) \\ \tilde{p}(\theta) \\ \tilde{v}(\theta) \\ \tilde{u}(\theta) \end{bmatrix}, \tag{27}$$

which differs from (17) in that unstructured model uncertainty, connecting output $\tilde{q}$ to input $\tilde{p}$, and weighting filters are also incorporated. The current formulation considers two types of perturbations. One is due to the varying parameters, which is bounded and can be measured in real-time. The other is due to modeling error, which is also bounded but can not be measured in real-time. In (27), without actuator saturation constraint, i.e. $\phi=1$, we have $\eta=\rho$ and the matrices $\tilde{D}_{qu}$ and $\tilde{D}_{zu}$ become constant matrices and independent of varying parameters.

To account for spatially periodic disturbances, we will consider a low-order and attenuated spatial-based repetitive controller that takes the form of

$$RC(\tilde{s})=\frac{1}{\tilde{s}/\omega_r+1}\prod_{i=1}^{k}\frac{\tilde{s}^2+2\zeta_i\omega_{ni}\tilde{s}+\omega_{ni}^2}{\tilde{s}^2+2\xi_i\omega_{ni}\tilde{s}+\omega_{ni}^2}$$

or equivalently in state space representation

$$\begin{aligned}\dot{\tilde{x}}_{rc}&=A_{rc}\tilde{x}_{rc}+B_{rc}\tilde{y}\\ \tilde{y}_2&=C_{rc}\tilde{x}_{rc}\end{aligned},$$

where k is the number of spatially sinusoidal disturbances that is to be compensated. ω_{ni} is the ith disturbance frequency in rad/rev. Damping ratios associated with the poles, ζ_i, and zeros, ξ_i, of the repetitive filter need to satisfy the condition $0 < \xi_i < \zeta_i < 1$, to ensure sensitivity reduction at spatial frequency ω_{ni} rad/rev. The gain of the repetitive controller $RC(\tilde{s})$ can be adjusted by varying ξ_i and ζ_i. A low-pass filter with roll-off frequency ω_r rad/rev is included to attenuate the controller gain in the high frequency region that is similar to the q-filter used in a digital repetitive controller. As shown in Fig. 6, the repetitive controller takes $\tilde{y}$ as input and creates a new input $\tilde{y}_2$ to the 'to-be-designed' LPV controller $K(\psi)$.

To address actuator saturation, an anti-windup scheme as proposed in [36] can be formulated that feeds the difference between the actuator input and output back to the controller. This corresponds to creating a new input for the LPV controller, i.e.,

$$\tilde{y}_1 = (\phi - 1)\tilde{u}.$$

If the control $\tilde{u}$ does not saturate, i.e., $\phi = 1$, then $\tilde{y}_1 = 0$ and this additional input is deactivated. If the control $\tilde{u}$ saturates, i.e., $\phi < 1$, then $\tilde{y}_1 \neq 0$, which provides additional degree of freedom for manipulating the control $\tilde{u}$.

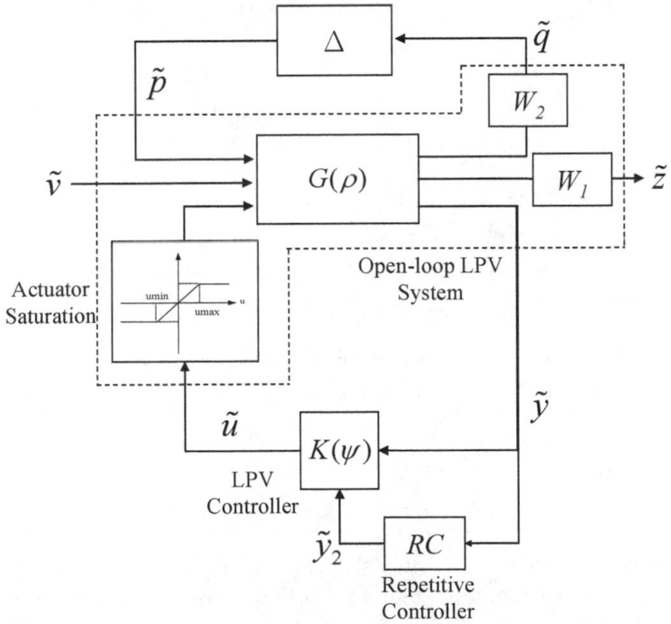

Fig. 6. LPV gain-scheduling control system with repetitive controller.

The open-loop LPV system with repetitive and anti-windup control (within the dashed-line block in Fig. 6) can be shown to have the following state-space representation:

$$\begin{bmatrix} \dot{\tilde{x}}(\theta) \\ \dot{\tilde{x}}_{rc}(\theta) \\ \tilde{q}(\theta) \\ \tilde{z}(\theta) \\ \tilde{y}(\theta) \\ \tilde{y}_1(\theta) \\ \tilde{y}_2(\theta) \end{bmatrix} = \left[\begin{array}{cc|ccc} \tilde{A}(\rho) & 0 & \tilde{B}_p(\rho) & \tilde{B}_v(\rho) & \tilde{B}_u(\eta) \\ B_{rc}C_y & A_{rc} & B_{rc}D_{yp} & B_{rc}D_{yv} & 0 \\ \hline C_q & 0 & D_{qp} & D_{qv} & \tilde{D}_{qu}(\phi) \\ C_z & 0 & D_{zp} & D_{zv} & \tilde{D}_{zu}(\phi) \\ C_y & 0 & D_{yp} & D_{yv} & 0 \\ 0 & 0 & 0 & 0 & \phi-1 \\ 0 & C_{rc} & 0 & 0 & 0 \end{array}\right] \begin{bmatrix} \tilde{x}(\theta) \\ \tilde{x}_{rc}(\theta) \\ \tilde{p}(\theta) \\ \tilde{v}(\theta) \\ \tilde{u}(\theta) \end{bmatrix}. \tag{28}$$

Note that the LPV controller $K(\psi)$ now has three inputs $(\tilde{y},\tilde{y}_1,\tilde{y}_2)$ and one output $\tilde{u}$. The parameter dependency of the input and output matrices (e.g., $\tilde{B}_u$ and C_y), if any, can be removed by considering the dynamics of the sensors and actuators (Apkarian et al., 1995). Let

$$\begin{bmatrix} \dot{\tilde{x}}_{o1} \\ \dot{\tilde{x}}_{o2} \\ \dot{\tilde{x}}_{o3} \end{bmatrix} = \begin{bmatrix} A_{o1} & 0 & 0 \\ 0 & A_{o2} & 0 \\ 0 & 0 & A_{o3} \end{bmatrix} \begin{bmatrix} \tilde{x}_{o1} \\ \tilde{x}_{o2} \\ \tilde{x}_{o3} \end{bmatrix} + \begin{bmatrix} B_{o1} & 0 & 0 \\ 0 & B_{o2} & 0 \\ 0 & 0 & B_{o3} \end{bmatrix} \begin{bmatrix} \tilde{y} \\ \tilde{y}_1 \\ \tilde{y}_2 \end{bmatrix},$$

$$\begin{bmatrix} \hat{y} \\ \hat{y}_1 \\ \hat{y}_2 \end{bmatrix} = \begin{bmatrix} C_{o1} & 0 & 0 \\ 0 & C_{o2} & 0 \\ 0 & 0 & C_{o3} \end{bmatrix} \begin{bmatrix} \tilde{x}_{o1} \\ \tilde{x}_{o2} \\ \tilde{x}_{o3} \end{bmatrix},$$

where $(\hat{y},\hat{y}_1,\hat{y}_2)$ represent the new outputs, and

$$\dot{\tilde{x}}_i = A_i\tilde{x}_i + B_i\hat{u},$$
$$\tilde{u} = C_i\tilde{x}_i,$$

where $\hat{u}$ represent the new input. This action is equivalent to passing each input or output channel of the open-loop LPV system in (28) through a low-pass filter

$$H_j(\tilde{s}) = C_{oj}(\tilde{s}I - A_{oj})^{-1}B_{oj},\ j=1,2,3 \text{ or}$$
$$F(\tilde{s}) = C_i(\tilde{s}I - A_i)^{-1}B_i \qquad ,$$

respectively, before connecting to the LPV controller $K(\psi)$, as depicted in Fig. 7. The bandwidth of the low-pass filters depends on the sensor and actuator dynamics. For negligible senor or actuator dynamics, the bandwidth can be assigned to be much larger than that of the open-loop system to minimize possible interference. With the inclusion of the anti-windup formulation and the input/output filters, the overall open-loop LPV system with parameter-free input-output matrices can be found to be

$$\begin{bmatrix} \dot{\tilde{x}}(\theta) \\ \dot{\tilde{x}}_{rc}(\theta) \\ \dot{\tilde{x}}_{o1}(\theta) \\ \dot{\tilde{x}}_{o2}(\theta) \\ \dot{\tilde{x}}_{o3}(\theta) \\ \dot{\tilde{x}}_{i}(\theta) \\ \tilde{q}(\theta) \\ \tilde{z}(\theta) \\ \hat{y}(\theta) \\ \hat{y}_1(\theta) \\ \hat{y}_2(\theta) \end{bmatrix} = \left[\begin{array}{cccccc|ccc} \tilde{A}(\rho) & 0 & 0 & 0 & 0 & \tilde{B}_u(\eta)C_i & \tilde{B}_p(\rho) & \tilde{B}_v(\rho) & 0 \\ B_{rc}C_y & A_{rc} & 0 & 0 & 0 & 0 & B_{rc}D_{yp} & B_{rc}D_{yv} & 0 \\ B_{o1}C_y & 0 & A_{o1} & 0 & 0 & 0 & B_{o1}D_{yp} & B_{o1}D_{yv} & 0 \\ 0 & 0 & 0 & A_{o2} & 0 & B_{02}(\phi-1)C_i & 0 & 0 & 0 \\ 0 & B_{o3}C_{rc} & 0 & 0 & A_{o3} & 0 & 0 & 0 & 0 \\ 0 & 0 & 0 & 0 & 0 & A_i & 0 & 0 & B_i \\ \hline C_q & 0 & 0 & 0 & 0 & \tilde{D}_{qu}(\phi)C_i & D_{qp} & D_{qv} & 0 \\ C_z & 0 & 0 & 0 & 0 & \tilde{D}_{zu}(\phi)C_i & D_{zp} & D_{zv} & 0 \\ 0 & 0 & C_{o1} & 0 & 0 & 0 & 0 & 0 & 0 \\ 0 & 0 & 0 & C_{o2} & 0 & 0 & 0 & 0 & 0 \\ 0 & 0 & 0 & 0 & C_{o3} & 0 & 0 & 0 & 0 \end{array}\right] \begin{bmatrix} \tilde{x}(\theta) \\ \tilde{x}_{rc}(\theta) \\ \tilde{x}_{o1}(\theta) \\ \tilde{x}_{o2}(\theta) \\ \tilde{x}_{o3}(\theta) \\ \tilde{x}_{i}(\theta) \\ \tilde{p}(\theta) \\ \tilde{v}(\theta) \\ \hat{u}(\theta) \end{bmatrix}. \quad (29)$$

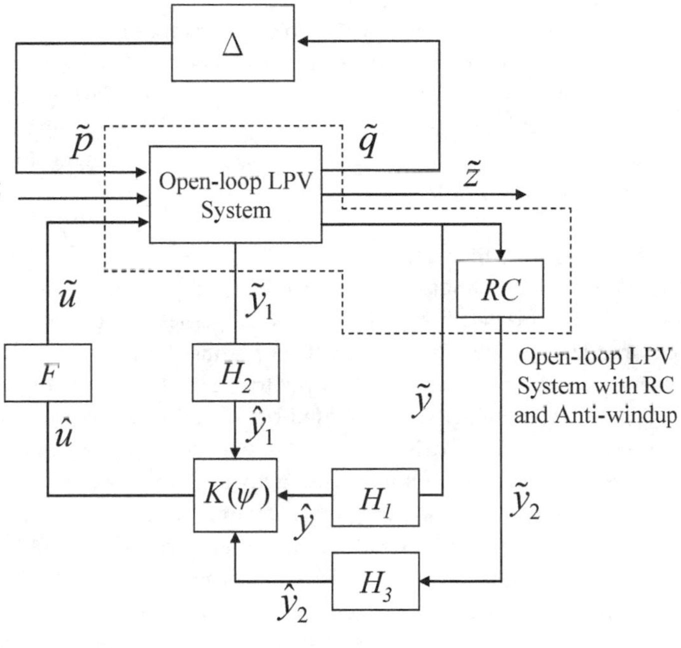

Fig. 7. LPV gain-scheduling control system with repetitive controller, anti-windup scheme, and sensor/actuator dynamics.

By making the following definitions

$$\tilde{X} = \begin{bmatrix} \tilde{x} & \tilde{x}_{rc} & \tilde{x}_{o1} & \tilde{x}_{o2} & \tilde{x}_{o3} & \tilde{x}_i \end{bmatrix}^T,$$

$$\tilde{Z} = \begin{bmatrix} \tilde{q} & \tilde{z} \end{bmatrix}^T, \; \tilde{Y} = \begin{bmatrix} \hat{y} & \hat{y}_1 & \hat{y}_2 \end{bmatrix}^T, \; \tilde{V} = \begin{bmatrix} \tilde{p} & \tilde{v} \end{bmatrix}^T, \; \tilde{U} = \hat{u},$$

we can rewrite the above system as

$$\begin{bmatrix} \dot{\tilde{X}} \\ \tilde{Z} \\ \tilde{Y} \end{bmatrix} = \begin{bmatrix} A(\psi) & B_V(\psi) & B_U \\ C_Z(\psi) & D_{ZV}(\psi) & D_{ZU} \\ C_Y & D_{YV} & 0 \end{bmatrix} \begin{bmatrix} \tilde{X} \\ \tilde{V} \\ \tilde{U} \end{bmatrix}, \tag{30}$$

where the system and input/output matrices are of appropriate dimensions and can be identified from (2). Note that the matrices B_U and C_Y are free of varying parameters.

4.4 Discretization of angular displacement reformulated systems

A spatial sampling scheme that uses the output pulses of an optical shaft encoder (instead of a clock signal) to trigger the interrupt of the control algorithm at intervals of equal angular displacement was implemented. The constant angular displacement based sampling effectively discretized the control system in the angular displacement domain. Note that an ADR system, see (15), without varying parameters can be viewed as an LTI system with angular displacement θ as the independent variable as compared with time t. Theorems or methods used to derive the discrete equivalent of LTI systems, e.g., z-transform (impulse invariant), zero-order hold (step invariant), and bilinear or trapezoid rule, can be applied to ADR systems with slightest modification. What needs to be kept in mind is that the sampling behavior has changed from equal time interval (in sec) to equal angular displacement interval (in revolution).

4.5 Experimental setup and validation

Rotational velocity regulation in a laser printer will be used to verify the effectiveness of the proposed spatially sampled repetitive control in rejecting spatially periodic disturbances. A 600-dpi monochrome laser printer is used as the experimental platform that comprised of one brushless dc motor, with a set of gear and a photosensitive drum. The hardware setup is depicted in Fig. 8. The motor velocity is regulated by adjusting the voltage input to a pulse width modulated (PWM) power drive. A digital encoder with a resolution of 50,000 pulses/rev is mounted on the photosensitive drum to measurement of angular displacement and velocity. To maintain the desired dot placement accuracy, the photosensitive drum is expected to rotate at a nominal angular velocity of 0.5 rev/sec. This corresponds to a motor voltage input of 2.56 volts. The saturation limits for the input voltage are identified to be ±0.5 volts around the nominal value, i.e., $u_{\max} = 3.06$ and $u_{\min} = 2.06$. According to the frequency spectrum of the measured speed fluctuations, spatially periodic components at spaitial frequencies of 32, 48, and 96 cycles/rev need to be reduced, since they caused visible bands in printed images. A 2nd order transfer function from the motor voltage input to the drum angular velocity output is obtained to approximate the actual frequency response of the experimental platform, i.e.

$$P_{yu}(s) = \frac{4.184 \times 10^5}{s^2 + 2246s + 8.932 \times 10^4}.$$

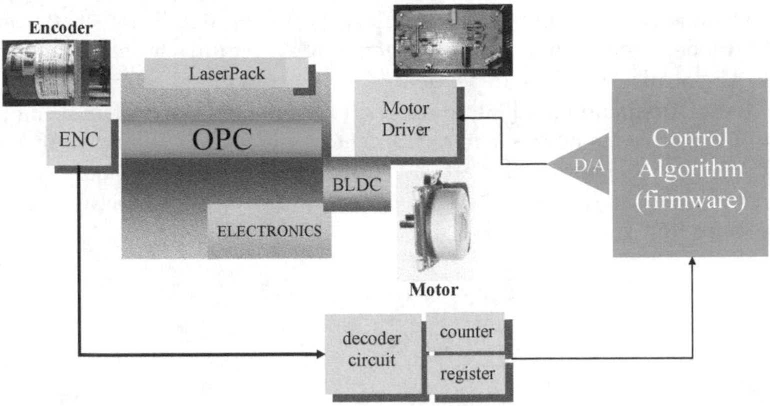

Fig. 8. Experimental setup for the closed-loop control of a typical 600-dpi monochrome laser printer.

The output multiplicative modeling errors are obtained by comparing the frequency responses of the plant model and the experimental platform, as shown in Fig. 9. Note that the spatial frequency response shown in Fig. 9 is obtained from the temporal frequency response where the spatial frequency in cycle per revolution is scaled by the nominal angular velocity. A stable 1st order filter that upper bounds the multiplicative model uncertainty can be found to be

$$W_2(\tilde{s}) = 0.03\frac{\tilde{s}/16+1}{\tilde{s}/700+1}.$$

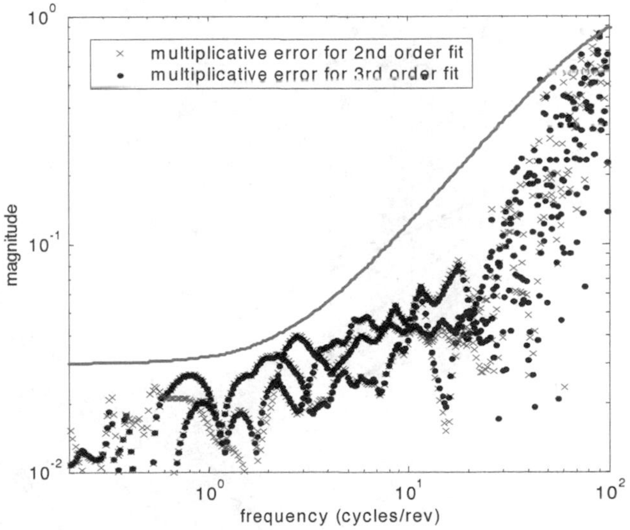

Fig. 9. Output multiplicative uncertainties for the experimental platform approximated using a 2nd or 3rd order transfer function. The solid line is the magnitude of a 1st order filter that upper bounds the uncertainties.

Note that the affine nature of the open-loop LPV system (29) will be intact after inclusion of the parameter independent filter, W_2. The selection of W_1 requires more considerations. First of all, the LPV controller will be independent of the saturation indicator ϕ if the performance weighting does not depend on ϕ [36]. In other words, the design problem using parameter-free W_1 will degenerate to one without actuator saturation. Secondly, if a parameter dependent W_1 filter is chosen, the affine nature of the LPV open-loop system will be preserved after incorporating the filter. Thus, a feasible W_1 filter can assume the following state space realization

$$\dot{\tilde{x}}_{w1} = -(\omega_b\phi + b)\tilde{x}_{w1} + \sqrt{e}\tilde{z},$$
$$\hat{z} = \sqrt{e}\phi\tilde{x}_{w1} + k\tilde{z},$$

which has the transfer function

$$W_1(\tilde{s}) = k + \frac{e\phi}{\tilde{s} + \omega_b\phi + b}.$$

Note that the magnitude curve of W_1 can be specified by tuning the constant values of ω_b, b, e, and k. Specifically, k can be used to specify the lower bound for the W_1 magnitude at high frequencies (i.e., as $\tilde{s} \to \infty$); the coefficient b can be used to specify the lower bound of the corner frequencies; coefficients ω_b and e can be used to specify the exact corner frequencies and the W_1 magnitude at low frequencies (i.e., as $\tilde{s} \to 0$). The parameter variation set $\bar{\Psi}$ is determined to be

$$\bar{\Psi} = \{(\rho,\phi,\eta):\ 1 \le \rho \le 10,\ 0.1 \le \phi \le 1,\ \eta = \rho\phi\}.$$

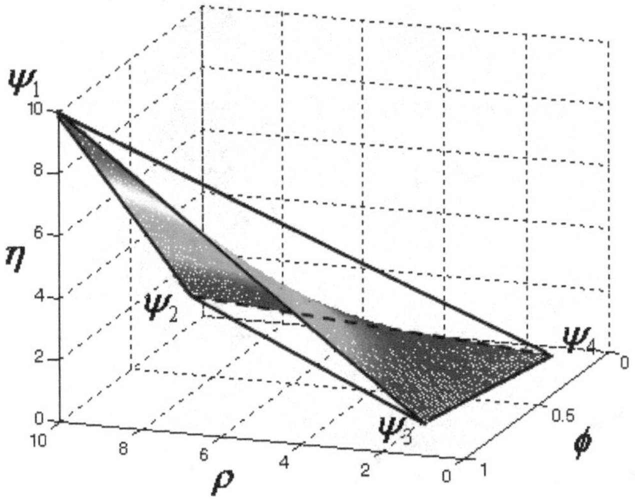

Fig. 10. Parameter variation set $\bar{\Psi}$ and the selected (convex) polytope Ψ which bounds the set.

The upper and lower bounds of ρ and ϕ are empirically determined based on a velocity variation from -80 % to +100% around the nominal value of 0.5 rev/sec and a 10-to-1 saturation limit, respectively. The parameter variation set $\overline{\Psi}$ is not convex but can be shown to lie within a polytope Ψ with four vertices located at $\psi_1 = (10,1,10)$, $\psi_2 = (10,0.1,1)$, $\psi_3 = (1,1,1)$, and $\psi_4 = (1,0.1,0.1)$ (see Fig. 10). The polytope Ψ will be used for the following design. Given that $\phi \in [0.1, 1]$ in Ψ, the parameters of the weighting filter W_1 can be properly determined to reflect the different performance requirement for the unsaturated ($\phi = 1$) and saturated ($\phi < 1$) system. Fig. 11 shows the magnitude curves of W_1 with $k = 0.03$, $\omega_b = 2\pi \times 12$, $b = 0.1\omega_b$ and $e = 5/3 \times \omega_b$ as $\phi \in [0.1, 1]$. The magnitude curve of W_2 is also shown in the figure. The low-pass filters $H_j(\tilde{s})$ and $F(\tilde{s})$ are selected as

$$H_1(\tilde{s}) = H_2(\tilde{s}) = H_3(\tilde{s}) = F(\tilde{s}) = \frac{1}{\tilde{s}/(2\pi \times 1000) + 1}$$

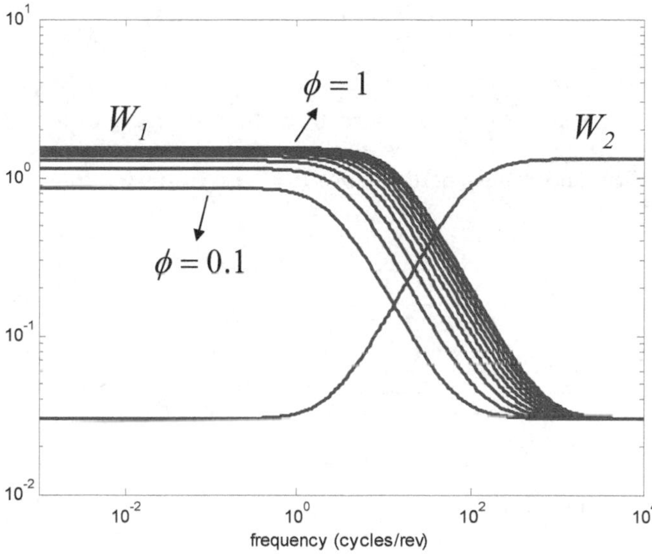

Fig. 11. The parameter-dependent performance weighting W_1 and uncertainty weighting W_2.

where the frequency value of 1000 cycles/rev is specified to reflect the negligible sensor and actuator dynamics. The low-order attenuated repetitive controller can be expressed as

$$RC(\tilde{s}) = \frac{1}{\tilde{s}/(2\pi \times 200) + 1} \prod_{\substack{\omega_n = 32,48,96 \\ \xi_n = 0.002,0.002,0.001}} \frac{\tilde{s}^2 + 2 \times 0.1 \times \omega_n \tilde{s} + \omega_n^2}{\tilde{s}^2 + 2 \times \xi_n \omega_n \tilde{s} + \omega_n^2},$$

where the periodic disturbances are at 32, 48 and 96 cycles/rev. A feasible LPV controller is determined based on the above parameters, which attains $\gamma = 1.1669$. The controller can be written as

$$\begin{bmatrix} \dot{\tilde{x}}_K \\ \dot{\tilde{x}}_{rc} \end{bmatrix} = \begin{bmatrix} A_K(\psi) & 0 \\ 0 & A_{rc} \end{bmatrix} \begin{bmatrix} \tilde{x}_K \\ \tilde{x}_{rc} \end{bmatrix} + \begin{bmatrix} B_{K1}(\psi) & B_{K2}(\psi) & B_{K3}(\psi) & 0 \\ 0 & 0 & 0 & B_{rc} \end{bmatrix} \begin{bmatrix} \hat{y}_1 \\ \hat{y} \\ \hat{y}_2 \\ \tilde{y} \end{bmatrix}, \tag{31}$$

$$\begin{bmatrix} \hat{u} \\ \tilde{y}_2 \end{bmatrix} = \begin{bmatrix} C_K(\psi) & 0 \\ 0 & C_{rc} \end{bmatrix} \begin{bmatrix} \tilde{x}_K \\ \tilde{x}_{rc} \end{bmatrix} + \begin{bmatrix} D_{K1}(\psi) & D_{K2}(\psi) & D_{K3}(\psi) & 0 \\ 0 & 0 & 0 & 0 \end{bmatrix} \begin{bmatrix} \hat{y}_1 \\ \hat{y} \\ \hat{y}_2 \\ \tilde{y} \end{bmatrix}, \tag{32}$$

where

$$B_K(\psi) = [B_{K1}(\psi) \quad B_{K2}(\psi) \quad B_{K3}(\psi)],$$
$$D_K(\psi) = [D_{K1}(\psi) \quad D_{K2}(\psi) \quad D_{K3}(\psi)].$$
$$\psi = \{\sum_{i=1}^{4} \alpha_i \psi_i : \alpha_i \geq 0, \ \sum_{i=1}^{4} \alpha_i = 1\}$$

We can view (31) and (32) as an LPV repetitive controller (LPVRC). For practical implementation, the vertex controllers need to be transformed into their discrete-position invariant counterparts, e.g., using bilinear transformation. The nominal performance (NP), robust stability (RS), and robust performance (RP) curves for the four vertex systems are shown in Fig. 12.

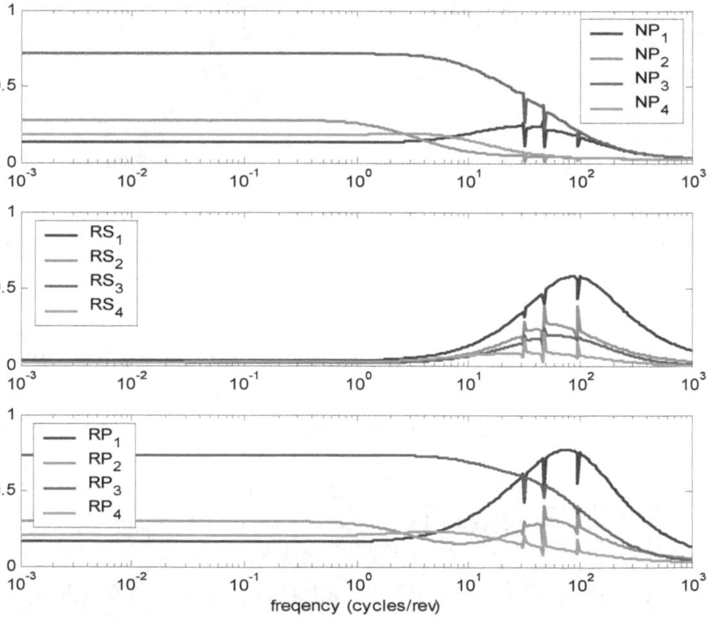

Fig. 12. NP, RS and RP curves for the four vertex closed-loop systems.

The experiment was performed by activating the LPVRC controller and rotating the photosensitive drum for 40 revolutions with step change in nominal velocity. During the operation, the nominal motor input voltage was changed at the 10th, 20th and 30th revolution, which shifted the nominal drum angular velocity. This can be seen in Fig. 13, which depicts the histories of drum angular velocity, motor input voltage and the three varying parameters with respect to the drum angular position. Fig. 14 compares the spatial frequency spectrum of the velocity signals within each 10-revolution interval to that of the uncompensated system. We can see that the performance of the LPVRC controlled system is insensitive to changes in nominal drum angular velocity. Note that the magnitude increases near dc frequency are due to the transient responses. As a comparison, Fig. 15 shows the responses when the system is under the control of a fixed temporal repetitive controller. As expected, a fixed-period repetitive controller operating in the time domain is unable to effectively compensate for the disturbances whose temporal periods change with the rotational speed of the system.

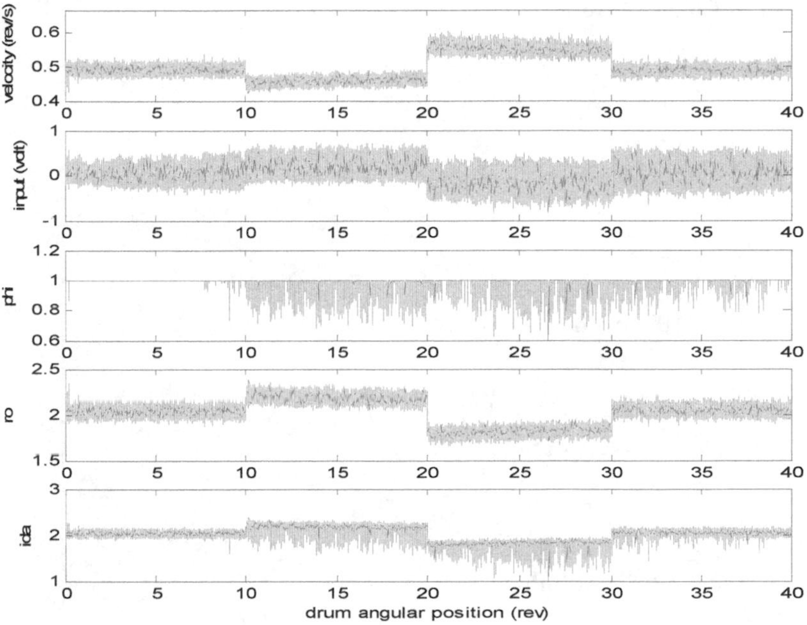

Fig. 13. Histories of drum angular velocity, motor input voltage and the three varying parameters with respect to drum angular position.

The spatial sampling scheme proposed in this section raises a practical issue when synthesizing digital full-order repetitive controllers. The available sampling frequencies when conducting the scheme depends on the encoder resolution. For example, if the resolution of an encoder is 5000 pulses/rev, the highest sampling frequency achievable using the scheme will be 5000 cycles/rev. Other available sampling frequencies, depending on implementable divide-by-N circuits, might be 2500 (when the pulses are divided by 2), 500 (divided by 10), etc. Due to limited choices of sampling frequencies, the number of delay taps N for the repetitive kernel (i.e. q^{-N}), which is the ratio of the sampling frequency and the disturbance frequency, might end up being non-integral when tackling certain disturbance frequencies.

Other nonlinear control design approaches (e.g., sliding mode and adaptive control) can also be employed. However, it is not clear if frequency-wise tradeoff between performance and stability can be easily performed within those nonlinear design frameworks.

It is also worth mentioning that the LPV gain-scheduling design may encounter the following implementation issues:

i. The state-dependent varying parameters may leave the parameter variation set.
ii. The measurement of the varying parameters may be contaminated by noise.
iii. There may be delay induced in the measurement of the varying parameters.

A feasible solution for the first issue is to setup the parameter variation set more accurately. Note that (22) implies that $\tilde{A}_{cl}^T(\psi)X + X\tilde{A}_{cl}(\psi) < 0$, and we can pick a Lyapunov function $V(\tilde{x}_{cl}(\theta)) = \tilde{x}_{cl}^T(\theta)X\tilde{x}_{cl}(\theta)$ for the closed-loop system such that $dV/d\theta < 0$. Thus, the state of the closed-loop system starting from $\tilde{x}_{cl}(\theta_0)$ will stay within an ellipsoid ε centered at the equilibrium point and defined by

$$\varepsilon = \left\{ \tilde{x}_{cl}(\theta) \middle| \tilde{x}_{cl}^T(\theta)X\tilde{x}_{cl}(\theta) \le \tilde{x}_{cl}^T(\theta_0)X\tilde{x}_{cl}(\theta_0) \right\}.$$

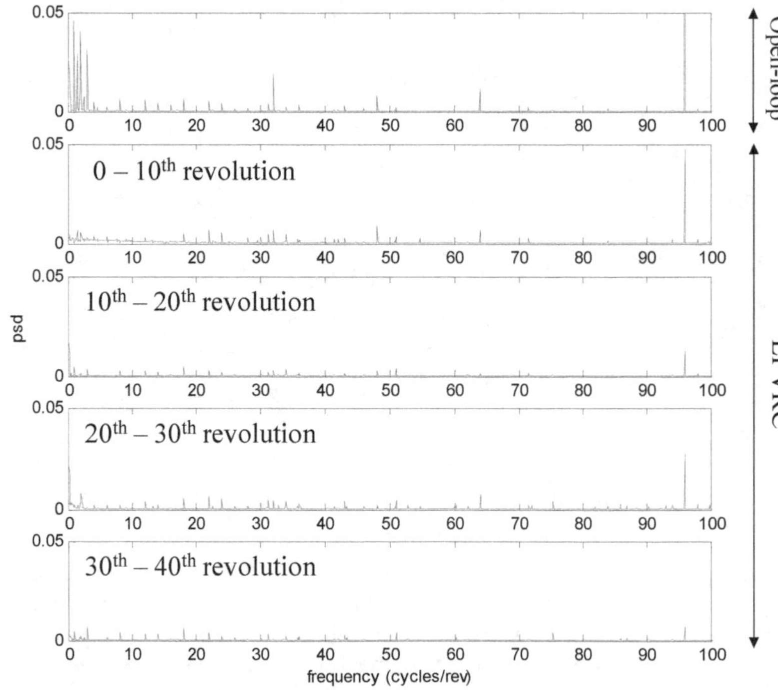

Fig. 14. Frequency spectra of the velocity signals for the open-loop and closed-loop systems. Spectra for the closed-loop system are divided into four, with each corresponding to signals measured from each 10-revolution interval (psd is abbreviation for power spectrum density)

The ellipsoid ε provides a bound for the state-dependent varying parameters, e.g., ρ. If a bound for the initial states can be established or estimated, a bound for the state-dependent varying parameters can be estimated, and the polytope Ψ which contains the parameter variation set $\bar{\Psi}$ can be determined more accurately. Since the proposed LPV control system has the property of being robust to unstructured but bounded uncertainty (specified by W_2 and Δ), the issues of measurement noise and uncertainty can be accounted for in the proposed formulation if they can be incorporated into the W_2 filter and the Δ block.

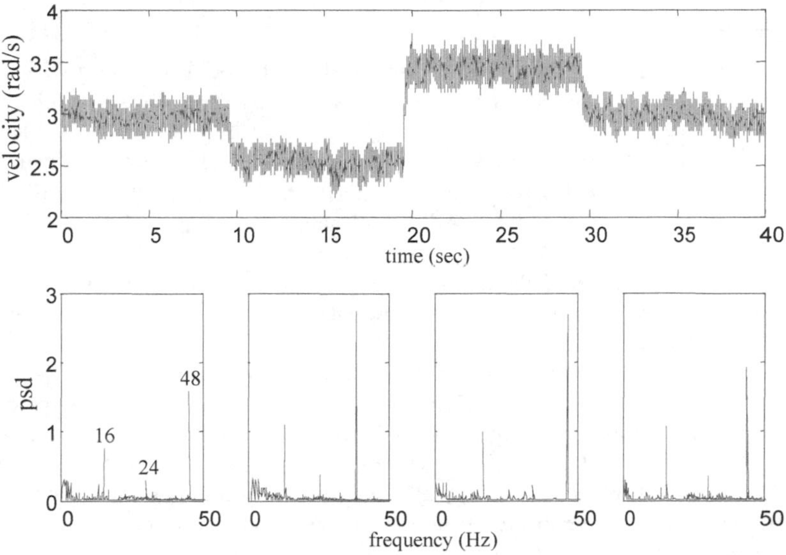

Fig. 15. Frequency spectra of the velocity signals for the closed-loop system using fixed period temporal repetitive control.

5. Conclusion

In this chapter, the notion of spatial-based repetitive control system and its historical development were introduced. Two designs, which were experimentally verified on a rotary motion system, representative of recent advancement in this field were presented. The designs, which are applicable to a generic class of LTI systems, address important practical issues such as actuator saturation and modelling uncertainty. However, several drawbacks and limitations are worth notice. First of all, the designs resorted to linear robust control paradigm and account for only unstructured uncertainty. It is well known that such control approach might lead to limited performance if information regarding the uncertainty (e.g., structure) is not properly utilized. Second, the LPVRC design relies on a common Lyapunov function, which also results in conservative design. The design is further degraded if the number of varying parameters increases or the varying parameter space is nonconvex. Finally, both designs along with other exiting ones are applicable only to rotary systems operating unidirectionally. The LPVRC design can improve by employing parameter varying Lyapunov function (Apkarian & Adams, 1998). On the other hand, since the open-loop spatial-based system, i.e., (3) or (6), is nonlinear, we may apply nonlinear control paradigm to directly approach the nonlinearities. Existing nonlinear robust control schemes are capable of tackling various types of modelling uncertainty. Some have built-in parametric adaptation mechanism or can integrate with an existing parametric identification scheme to improve the performance of the design. Theoretical results (with numerical simulation) of several designs based on adaptive feedback linearization, adaptive backstepping, and adaptive iterative learning control have been reported (Chen & Yang, 2007, 2008, 2009; Yang & Chen, 2008, 2011).

6. References

Alter, D. M. & Tsao, T.-C. (1994). Two-dimensional exact model matching with application to repetitive control. *ASME Journal of Dynamic, Systems, Measurements and Control,* Vol. 116, pp. 2-9.

Apkarian, P., Gahinet, P., & Becker, G. (1995). Self-scheduled H^∞ control of linear parameter varying systems: a design example. *Automatica,* Vol. 31, No. 9, pp. 1251-1261.

Apkarian, P., & Adams, R. J. (1998). Advanced gain-scheduling techniques for uncertain systems. *IEEE Transactions on Control Systems Technology,* Vol. 6, No. 1, pp. 21-32.

Becker, G., & Packard, A. K. (1994). Robust performance of linear parametrically varying systems using parametrically-dependent linear feedback. *Systems and Control Letters,* Vol. 23, No. 3, pp. 205-215.

Berkovitz, L. D. (2002). *Convexity and Optimization in* R^n , John Wiley & Sons, New York.

Chen, C.-L., & Chiu, G. T. C. (2001). Disturbance Rejection Using Two Degree of Freedom Repetitive Control Through Mixed Sensitivity Optimization. *Proceedings of 2001 ASME International Mechanical Engineering Congress and Exposition*, New York, NY.

Chen, C.-L., Chiu, G. T. C., & Allebach, J. P. (2003). Banding reduction in EP processes using human contrast sensitivity function shaped photoconductor velocity control. *J. Imaging Science and Technology,* Vol. 47, No. 3, pp. 209-223.

Chen, C.-L., Chiu, G. T. C.,& Allebach, J. P. (2006). Robust spatial-sampling controller design for banding reduction in electrophotographic process. *Journal of Imaging Science and Technology,* Vol. 50, No. 6, pp. 1-7.

Chen, C.-L., & Yang, Y.-H. (2007). Spatially periodic disturbance rejection for uncertain rotational motion systems using spatial domain adaptive backstepping repetitive control. *33rd Annual Conference of the IEEE Industrial Electronics Society,* Taipei, Taiwan, pp. 638-643.

Chen, C.-L., & Chiu, G. T. C. (2008). Spatially periodic disturbance rejection with spatially sampled robust repetitive control. *ASME Journal of Dynamic Systems, Measurement and Control,* Vol. 130, No. 2, pp. 11-21.

Chen, C.-L., & Yang, Y.-H. (2008). Spatial-based output feedback adaptive feedback linearization repetitive control of uncertain rotational motion systems subject to spatially periodic disturbances. *17th IFAC World Congress on Automatic Control,* Seoul, Korea, pp. 13151-13156.

Chen, C.-L., & Yang, Y.-H. (2009). Position-dependent disturbance rejection using spatial-based adaptive feedback linearization repetitive control. *International Journal of Robust and Nonlinear Control,* Vol. 19, pp. 1337-1363.

Chen, T., & Francis, B. (1995). *Optimal Sampled-Data Control Systems,* Springer, London, NY.

Cuiyan, L., & et al.. (2004). A survey of repetitive control. *Proceedings of IEEE International Conference on Intelligent Robots and Systems,* Sendai, Japan.

Francis, B. A., & Wonham, W. M. (1976). The internal model principle of control theory. *Automatica,* Vol. 12, No. 5, pp. 457-465.

Godler, I., Kobayashi, K., & Yamashita, T. (1995). Reduction of speed ripple due to transmission error of strain wave gearing by repetitive control. *International Journal of the Japan Society for Precision Engineering,* Vol. 29, No. 4, pp. 325-330.

Guo, L. (1997). Reducing the manufacturing costs associated with hard disk drives - A new disturbance rejection control scheme. *IEEE Transactions on Mechatronics,* Vol. 2, No. 2, pp. 77-85.

Gahinet, P., & Apkarian, P. (1994). A linear matrix inequality approach to H^{∞} control. *International Journal of Robust and Nonlinear Control,* Vol. 4, pp. 421-448.

Gahinet, P., & Apkarian, P. (1995). A convex characterization of gain-scheduled H^{∞} controllers. *IEEE Transactions on Automatic Control,* Vol. 40, No. 5, pp. 853-864.

Gahinet, P., Nemirovski, A., Laub, A. J., & Chilali. M. (1995). MATLAB LMI Control Toolbox, Mathworks.

Gahinet, P.,& et al. (1995). MATLAB LMI Control Toolbox, Mathworks, Natick, MA.

Gahinet, P. (1996). Explicit controller formulas for LMI-based H^{∞} synthesis. *Automatica,* Vol. 32, No. 7, pp.1007-1014

Garimella, S. S., & Srinivasan, K. (1996). Application of repetitive control to eccentricity compensation in rolling. *ASME Journal of Dynamic, Systems, Measurements and Control,* Vol. 118, pp. 657-664.

Hanson, R. D.,& Tsao, T. C. (2000). Periodic sampling interval repetitive control and its application to variable spindle speed noncircular turning process. *ASME Journal of Dynamic Systems, Measurements and Control,* Vol. 122, pp. 560-566.

Hara, S., Yamamoto, Y., Omata, T., & Nakano, M. (1988). Repetitive control system: A new type servo system for periodic exogenous signals. *IEEE Transactions on Automatic Control,* Vol. 33, No. 7, pp. 659-668.

Hillerstrom, G. (1996). Adaptive suppression of vibrations - A repetitive control approach. *IEEE Transactions on Control Systems Technology,* Vol. 4, No. 1, pp. 72-78.

Inoue,T., Nakano, M., & Iwai, S. (1981). High accuracy control of servomechanism for repeated contouring, *Proceeding of the 10th Annual Symposium on Incremental Motion Control Systems and Devices,* pp. 258-262.

Mahawan, B., & Luo, Z.-H. (2000). Repetitive control of tracking systems with time-varying periodic references. *International Journal of Control,* Vol. 73, No. 1, pp. 1-10.

Manayathara, T. J., Tsao, T. C., Bentsman, J., & Ross, D. (1996). Rejection of unknown periodic load disturbances in continuous steel casting process using learning repetitive control approach. *IEEE Transactions on Control Systems Technology,* Vol. 4, No. 3, pp. 259-265.

Moon, J. H., Lee, M. N., & Chung, M. J. (1998). Repetitive control for the track-following servo system of an optical disk drive. *IEEE Transactions on Control Systems Technology,* Vol. 6, No. 5, pp. 663-670.

Nakano, M., She, J. H., Mastuo, Y., & Hino, T. (1996). Elimination of position-dependent disturbances in constant-speed-rotation control systems. *Control Engineering Practice,* Vol. 4, pp. 1241-1248.

Onuki, Y., & Ishioka, H. (2001). Compensation for repeatable tracking errors in hard drives using discrete-time repetitive controllers. *IEEE/ASME Transactions on Mechatronics,* Vol. 6, No. 2, pp. 132-136

Rodriguez, H., Pons, J. L., & Ceres, R. (2000). A ZPET-repetitive speed controller for ultrasonic motors. *Proceeding of the 2000 IEEE International Conference on Robotics and Automation*, pp. 3654-3659.

Srinivasan, K., & Shaw, F. R. (1993). Discrete-time repetitive control system design using the regeneration spectrum. *ASME Journal of Dynamic Systems, Measurements and Control*, Vol. 115, No. 2A, pp. 228-237.

Tomizuka, M., Tsao, T. C., & Chew, K. K. (1989). Analysis and synthesis of discrete-time repetitive controllers. *ASME Journal of Dynamic Systems, Measurements and Control*, Vol. 111, No. 3, pp. 353-358.

Tung, E. D., Anwar, G., & Tomizuka, M. (1993). Low velocity friction compensation and feedforward solution based on repetitive control. *ASME Journal of Dynamic, Systems, Measurements and Control*, Vol. 115, pp. 279-284.

Wang, Y., & et al. (2009). Survey on iterative learning control, repetitive control, and run-to-run control. *Journal of Process Control*, Vol. 19, pp. 1589-1600.

Wit, C. C., & Praly, L. (2000). Adaptive eccentricity compensation. *IEEE Transactions on Control Systems Technology*, Vol. 8, No. 5, pp. 757-766.

Wu, F., Grigoriadis, K. M., & Packard, A. (2000). Anti-windup controller design using linear parameter-varying control methods. *International Journal of Control*, Vol. 73, No. 12, pp. 1104-1114.

Yamada, M., Riadh, Z., & Funahashi, Y. (1999). Design of discrete-time repetitive control system for pole placement and application. *IEEE Transactions on Mechatronics*, Vol. 4, No. 2, pp. 110-118.

Yang, Y.-H., & Chen, C.-L. (2008). Spatially periodic disturbance rejection using spatial-based output feedback adaptive backstepping repetitive control. *2008 American Control Conference*, Seattle, WA, pp. 4117-4122.

Yang, Y.-H., & Chen, C.-L. (2011). Spatial-based adaptive iterative learning control of nonlinear rotary systems with spatially periodic parametric variation. *International Journal of Innovative Computing, Information and Control*, Vol. x, pp. ????-????.

Zhou, K., & Doyle, J. (1997). *Essentials of Robust Control*, Prentice Hall.

5

Optimizing the Tracking Performance in Robust Control Systems

Hossein Oloomi[1] and Bahram Shafai[2]
[1]*Department of Electrical & Computer Engineering, Purdue University at Fort Wayne*
[2]*Department of Electrical & Computer Engineering, Northeastern University*
USA

1. Introduction

A typical control engineering problem deals with the design of a control system subject to closed-loop stability and certain performance requirements. The requirements may include the figures of merit such as gain/phase margin, bandwidth, and tracking error to a reference command. The control system is required to achieve the design objectives against unknown or unmeasurable disturbances. The difficulty arises since the plant is often poorly modeled and the set of performance requirements is typically stringent. The robust control theory attempts to address the question of stability and performance of multivariable systems in the face of modeling errors and unknown disturbances (Zhou et al., 1996).

In robust control theory, the question concerning the achievable performance limits is generally posed as an optimization problem in an appropriate mathematical setting. A major benefit of this approach is that it provides a means to optimize the system performance by trading off various stringent, and often conflicting, specifications against each other. In the last three decades, H_∞ control theory has evolved as the primary multivariable optimization and synthesis tool that can effectively deal with the modeling errors and unknown disturbances (Skogesttad & Postlethwaite, 2007).

In a tracking problem, the reference command is usually specified as a step or ramp signal. Accordingly, the tracking error is also specified in terms of such signals. This class of signals, however, does not model all command signals of interest. For example, a servo control system may be required to track a periodic signal of a fixed period. For this class of applications, the tracking performance must instead be specified in terms of a periodic command signal. Since every periodic signal can be represented by its Fourier series for all time, the steady state tracking performance of a linear feedback system with a periodic command signal can be studied in terms of the steady state tracking performance of each of its sinusoidal components. Design of the control systems that can track periodic reference signals falls in the category of repetitive control (Hara et al., 1998; Lee & Smith, 1998; Sugimoto & Washida, 1997). This has been an active area of research in the last three decades where many successful applications have been reported in the literature. However, applications of the results to certain high performance positioning systems have proved to be more challenging. For example, in (Broberg & Molyet, 1994) a robust repetitive control system is designed to improve the turn-around sinusoidal tracking performance of the imaging mirror system of a weather satellite in face of stringent tracking error specifications. A similar situation has been investigated recently by (Aphale et al., 2008; Salapaka et. al, 2002) who considered a robust control design for a high bandwidth nano-positioning system.

An important step in studying the tracking performance of a control system to a sinusoidal reference signal is to investigate the inherent limitations of a feedback system. These limitations provide a deeper understanding of the problem and help a designer to evaluate his/her design against the best attainable tracking error obtained over all possible controller design. The topic been investigated thoroughly in (Su et al., 2003; 2005). The results show that the best achievable performance can be characterized in terms of the inherent properties, mainly the nonminimum phase zeros of the plant and the frequency of the reference signal.

After gaining the necessary insight into the fundamental limitations on the best achievable tracking performance, the next step is to pose the problem as an H_∞ robust performance problem. Among the various approaches reported in the literature, the mixed-sensitivity H_∞ control (Kwakernaak H., 2002), signal-based H_∞ control (Skogesttad & Postlethwaite, 2007), and H_∞ loop-shaping design (Balas et al., 998) have perhaps gained more popularity with designers. The mixed-sensitivity H_∞ design is particularly attractive as it gives the designer the ability to directly shape the sensitivity and complementary sensitivity functions. This, in turn, greatly facilitates the trade-off study among several competing performance objectives. The mixed sensitivity design is a conceptually attractive method, but how easily does it lend itself in practical applications? To apply the design, the designer starts by selecting certain weights such that the H_∞ optimal controller can provide a good trade-off between conflicting objectives in various frequency ranges. After several iterations, the designer is in a position to assess the design to see if all objectives have been met by the controller. If not, the next logical step is to go back and change the weights and repeat the process until a satisfactory result is obtained. Evidently, this is a tedious and often a long process, especially when the system dimension is high. To shorten the design cycle, it is of great interest to have a set of guidelines that can help the designer in selecting the appropriate weights in the optimization process.

The selection of optimal weights for the H_∞ control has received attention only very recently (Chiang & Hadaegh, 1994; Lanzon, 2001). In (Lanzon, 2000), the problem is formulated in such a way that the controller and the weights are obtained simultaneously and in an iterative manner. However, the question of the suitability of the weights and the complexity of the algorithm employed are yet to be judged. As an alternative, a new set of simple guidelines have been developed recently that can greatly facilitate the selection of appropriate weights (Oloomi & Shafai, 2003). These guidelines are derived using elementary arguments based on phasors and straight-line approximation of the magnitude response, and in the same spirit as what is usually done in the classical control theory. These results are simple to interpret and provide insights into the interplay among various design parameters including the peaks of the sensitivity and complementary sensitivity functions and the system bandwidth.

The chapter is outlines as follows. In Section 2, we briefly discuss the general guidelines used for the selection of the weighting functions in the mixed S/T sensitivity design. In Section 3, we study the problem of the weights selection for tracking sinusoidal reference signals and obtain certain expressions which relate the parameters of the weights to the steady state tracking error specifications. We then outline a procedure for the selection of the parameters of the weighting functions using the derived expressions. The approximate formulae obtained in this chapter are derived using elementary arguments from phasors and straight-line approximation of the magnitude response, in the same spirit as what is usually done in the classical control theory. The results obtained are simple to interpret and provide insights into the interplay among various design parameters including the peaks of the sensitivity and complementary sensitivity functions and the system bandwidth. In Section 4, we briefly demonstrate how these results can be used to obtain the weights in a robust control mixed sensitivity design of a high bandwidth nano-positioning system. We conclude the chapter in Section 4.

2. Weights selection in general mixed sensitivity design

We initiate the discussion by considering the feedback system shown in Figure 1. Let $S(s) = 1 + G(s)K(s)$ and $T(s) = 1 - S(s)$ be the sensitivity and complementary sensitivity transfer functions, respectively. In the S/T mixed sensitivity design, the objective is to minimize the infinity norm

$$\left\| \begin{matrix} W_P S \\ W_T T \end{matrix} \right\|_\infty$$

where $W_P(s)$ and $W_T(s)$ are the performance and the stability weights, respectively (Skogesttad and Postlethwaite, 2000; Zhou *et al.*, 1996). These weights are often taken to be

$$W_P(s) = \left(\frac{s/\sqrt[m]{M_S} + \omega_B^\star}{s + \omega_B^\star \sqrt[m]{A_S}} \right)^m, \qquad W_T(s) = \left(\frac{s/\omega_{BT}^\star + 1/\sqrt[n]{M_T}}{\sqrt[n]{A_T} s/\omega_{BT}^\star + 1} \right)^n.$$

The amplitude responses of these weights and their inverses are shown in Figure 2.

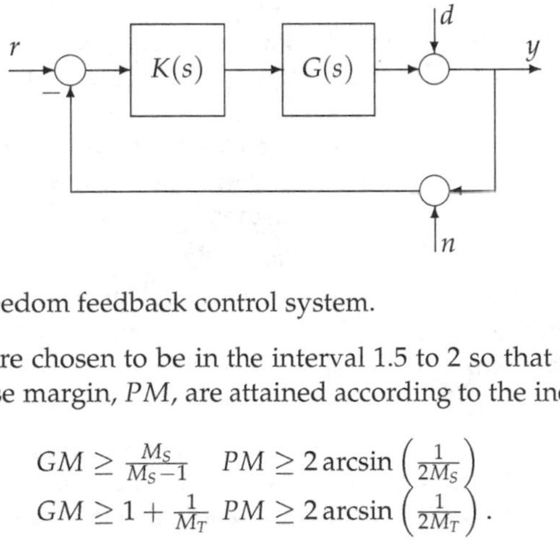

Fig. 1. One degree of freedom feedback control system.

Typically M_S and M_T are chosen to be in the interval 1.5 to 2 so that sufficient gain margin, GM, and sufficient phase margin, PM, are attained according to the inequalities

$$\begin{matrix} GM \geq \frac{M_S}{M_S - 1} & PM \geq 2\arcsin\left(\frac{1}{2M_S}\right) \\ GM \geq 1 + \frac{1}{M_T} & PM \geq 2\arcsin\left(\frac{1}{2M_T}\right). \end{matrix}$$

However, larger values of M_S and M_T are unavoidable for nonminimum phase systems. Ideally, $A_S = A_T = 0$ so that $1/|W_P|$ and $1/|W_T|$ have the desirable Butterworth highpass and Butterworth lowpass characteristics. This ensures that the frequency responses of $1/|W_P|$ and $1/|W_T|$ are maximally flat in the high and low frequency ranges respectively, where they take the general shapes of the sensitivity and the complementary sensitivity functions. Although, due to the numerical difficulties (Balas *et al.*, 1998), one is often forced to set the parameters

A_S and A_T to some small non-zero values, the forgoing observations still hold true in the frequency ranges of interest. Keeping this into consideration, A_S and A_T are chosen to be sufficiently small so that poles of $1/W_P(s)$ are at least two decades above the zeros of $1/W_P(s)$, and zeros of $1/W_T(s)$ are at least two decades above the poles of $1/W_T(s)$. In general, it is required to have $A_S \ll M_S$ and $A_T \ll M_T$. Assuming that M_S, A_S, M_T, and A_T are chosen based on these observations, we now concentrate on selecting the remaining parameters of the weighting functions, namely, m, $\omega_{BT}^{\star}$, n, and $\omega_{BT}^{\star}$. General guidelines for selecting these parameters are given below (Skogesttad and Postlethwaite, 2000).

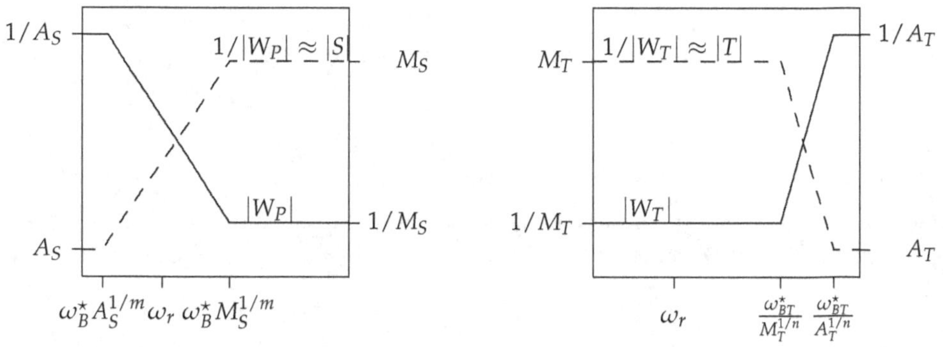

Fig. 2. Stability and performance weighting functions and their inverses.

2.1 General guidelines

1. For systems with $PM \leq 90^{\circ}$, it is well known that $\omega_B \leq \omega_c \leq \omega_{BT}$ where ω_B, ω_{BT}, and ω_c are the closed loop bandwidth measured on the basis of S, the closed loop bandwidth measured on the basis of T, and the gain crossover frequency, respectively. Therefore, it is required that $\omega_B^{\star} \leq \omega_{BT}^{\star}$. It should be noted that the presence of nonminimum phase zeros places restriction on the achievable bandwidth. Moreover, for high performance tracking applications with noticeable measurement noise it often becomes necessary to make a compromise and instead choose $\omega_{BT}^{\star} < \omega_B^{\star}$.
2. When disturbance attenuation is the control objective, the general rule is to increase $\omega_B^{\star}$ as much as possible. However, increasing $\omega_B^{\star}$ more than necessary causes the appearance of a peak in the sensitivity curve. This implies that the system will have less stability margins which manifests itself in an increased overshoot in the step response.
3. When the control objective is to reduce the effect of the measurement noise, the general rule is to decrease $\omega_{BT}^{\star}$ as much as possible. However, decreasing $\omega_{BT}^{\star}$ more than necessary causes a reduction in the system bandwidth and this manifests itself in a poor tracking performance.
4. Increasing m and n can improve the disturbance rejection and measurement noise attenuation, respectively. However, m and n should be kept as low as possible since large values of these parameters adversely affect the stability margins, and the controller order becomes unnecessarily high. (Controller order is $N + n + m$ where N is the order of the plant.)

3. Weights selection for sinusoidal tracking performance

In this section, we study the tracking performance of the feedback system in Figure 1 to a sinusoidal command signal. Tracking of other periodic command waveforms can be reduced to this case since every periodic signal can be represented by its Fourier series and ω_r can be chosen to represent the highest frequency component of $r(t)$ beyond which all other components are negligible. For example, when tracking a triangular waveform, ω_r can represent the frequency of the third harmonic of $r(t)$ since higher frequency harmonics have negligible amplitudes for this signal. Thus, let us assume that $d = n = 0$ in Figure 1 and consider the sinusoidal reference command

$$r(t) = A_r \cos \omega_r t, \quad \omega_r \ll \omega_B^\star.$$

Then the sinusoidal steady state output is

$$\begin{aligned} y_{ss}(t) &= A_r |T(j\omega_r)| \cos(\omega_r t + \angle T(j\omega_r)) \\ &= A_r |T(j\omega_r)| \cos \left[\omega_r \left(t + \frac{\angle T(j\omega_r)}{\omega_r} \right) \right] \\ &= A_r |T(j\omega_r)| \cos \left[\omega_r (t - \tau_e) \right], \end{aligned}$$

where the tracking delay is given by

$$\tau_e = -\frac{\angle T(j\omega_r)}{\omega_r}.$$

This delay is an increasing function of the tracking frequency.
In tracking applications, the complementary sensitivity function is shaped so that at least up to the tracking frequency the system behaves as an all-pass filter with negligible phase shift, that is $|T(j\omega_r)| \approx 1$ and $\angle T(j\omega_r) \approx 0$. This ensures that the peak steady state error and delay are small so that $y_{ss}(t) \approx r(t)$. However, as was mentioned earlier, for high performance applications even small deviation of $y_{ss}(t)$ from the reference signal $r(t)$ may exceed the performance requirements. Thus, our objective in this chapter is to address this issue by outlining a procedure for selecting the parameters m, $\omega_B^\star$, n, and $\omega_{BT}^\star$. To this end, we first define what we mean by the steady state tracking errors.
Using basic results from trigonometry, it is readily seen that the steady state error signal

$$e_{ss}(t) = A_r \cos \omega_r t - A_r |T(j\omega_r)| \cos \left[\omega_r (t - \tau_e) \right]$$

can be written in the compact form

$$e_{ss}(t) = R_e \cos(\omega_r t + \phi_e)$$

where

$$R_e = A_r \sqrt{1 + |T(j\omega_r)|^2 - 2|T(j\omega_r)| \cos \omega_r \tau_e}, \tag{1}$$

$$\phi_e = \arctan \left(\frac{|T(j\omega_r)| \sin \omega_r \tau_e}{1 - |T(j\omega_r)| \cos \omega_r \tau_e} \right). \tag{2}$$

The result is depicted in Figure 3 where the sinusoidal components of the steady state error signal are represented as phasors in the quadrature plane with the reference axis taken as $\cos\omega_r t$. It is seen that the steady state error phasor is rotated by an angle of ϕ_e in the counter-clockwise direction due to the presence of the tracking delay τ_e, and that the peak amplitude of the steady state tracking error, namely R_e, is influenced by this rotation as well as the gain of the closed loop system at the tracking frequency ω_r. It should be noted that when $|T(j\omega_r)|\cos\omega_r\tau_e \leq 1$, this phasor resides in the first quadrant so that $\tan\phi_e > 0$. However, when $|T(j\omega_r)|\cos\omega_r\tau_e > 1$, the steady state error phasor moves to the second quadrant for which $\tan\phi_e < 0$. Therefore, in obtaining ϕ_e from $\tan\phi_e$ in the latter case, we must interpret ϕ_e as being in the second quadrant ant not in the fourth. Typical sinusoidal tracking waveforms with small peak steady state error and small delay are also shown in Figure 4 where the lead property of the steady state error signal is cleanly seen.

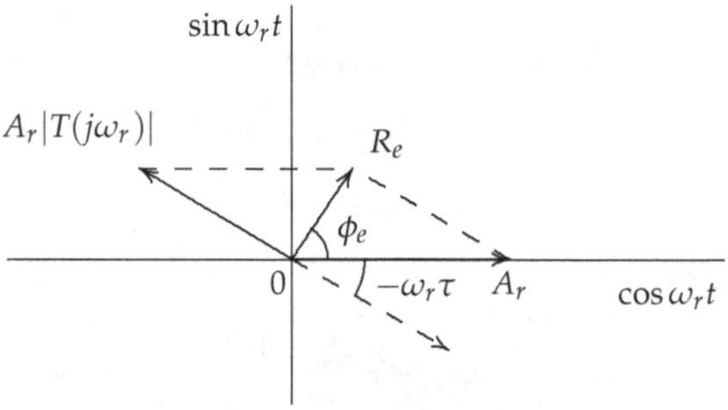

Fig. 3. Phasor diagram for the steady state sinusoidal tracking error.

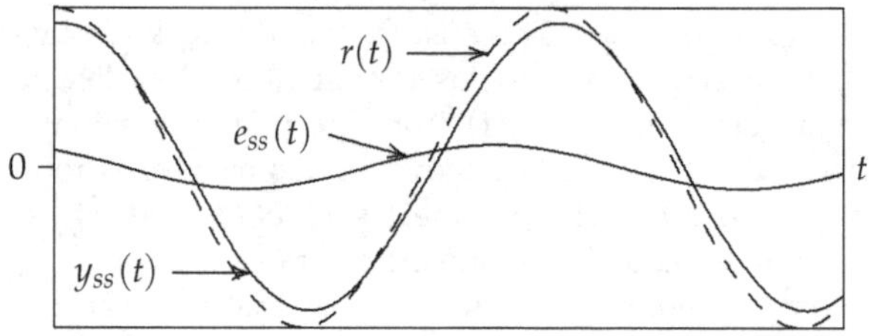

Fig. 4. Steady state sinusoidal tracking error signal.

We now derive expressions for the parameters of the weighting functions in terms of the tracking error parameters R_e and τ_e. To this end, recall from (Skogesttad and Postlethwaite, 2000) that in the mixed sensitivity design the weighting functions W_P and W_T are used to scale the closed loop transfer functions S and T, respectively in order to satisfy the performance and stability requirements, and that the inverse of these weighting functions are upper bounds, up to constant scaling factors, on the transfer functions they are used to scale. These constant factors can be absorbed in the weighting functions themselves so that the approximations $W_P S \approx 1$ and $W_T T \approx 1$ are reasonable for appropriate weights. However, the discrepancies can become noticeable if the controller is not designed properly or when the nonminimum

phase zeros are located near the origin for which large peaks appear in the sensitivity and complementary sensitivity response curves.
We first derive an expression for the tracking delay. To simplify notation, let

$$\alpha := \frac{\omega_r}{\omega_B^\star}, \qquad \beta := \frac{\omega_r}{\omega_{BT}^\star} \tag{3}$$

and note that $0 < \alpha, \beta \ll 1$. Using the approximation $W_T T \approx 1$, we have

$$|T(j\omega_r)| \approx \frac{1}{|W_T(j\omega_r)|}, \qquad \angle T(j\omega_r) \approx -\angle W_T(j\omega_r).$$

Therefore, using the straight line approximation

$$\begin{aligned} |T(j\omega_r)| &\approx \frac{1}{|W_T(j\omega_r)|} \\ &= M_T \left| \frac{1 + j\beta\sqrt[n]{A_T}}{1 + j\beta\sqrt[n]{M_T}} \right|^n \\ &\approx M_T, \qquad \text{for } \beta \ll \frac{1}{\sqrt[n]{M_T}}, \end{aligned} \tag{4}$$

and

$$\begin{aligned} \tau_e &\approx \frac{\angle W_T(j\omega_r)}{\omega_r} \\ &\approx \frac{n}{\omega_r}\left[\arctan\left(\beta\sqrt[n]{M_T}\right) - \arctan\left(\beta\sqrt[n]{A_T}\right)\right]. \end{aligned} \tag{5}$$

Next, we derive an expression for the peak steady state error. Since $W_P S \approx 1$, we have

$$|S(j\omega_r)| \approx \frac{1}{|W_P(j\omega_r)|}, \qquad \angle S(j\omega_r) \approx -\angle W_P(j\omega_r).$$

Therefore,

$$\begin{aligned} |S(j\omega_r)| &\approx \frac{1}{|W_P(j\omega_r)|} \\ &= A_S \left| \frac{1 + j\frac{\alpha}{\sqrt[m]{A_S}}}{1 + j\frac{\alpha}{\sqrt[m]{M_S}}} \right|^m \\ &\approx \alpha^m, \qquad \text{for } \sqrt[m]{A_S} \ll \alpha \ll \sqrt[m]{M_S}. \end{aligned}$$

On the other hand, $E(s) = S(s)R(s)$ so that at the steady state we also have

$$R_e \approx A_r \alpha^m. \tag{6}$$

Therefore, by equating (1) and (6) and using (4) we obtain

$$\alpha^m \approx \sqrt{1 + M_T^2 - 2M_T \cos\omega_r\tau_e}. \tag{7}$$

An expression relating (5) to (7) can now be derived noting that

$$\angle W_P(j\omega_r) \approx m\left[\arctan\left(\frac{\alpha}{\sqrt[m]{M_S}}\right) - \arctan\left(\frac{\alpha}{\sqrt[m]{A_S}}\right)\right]. \tag{8}$$

Since

$$\begin{aligned}\angle E(j\omega_r) &= \angle S(j\omega_r) + \angle R(j\omega_r)\\ &= \angle S(j\omega_r)\\ &= -\angle W_P(j\omega_r),\end{aligned} \tag{9}$$

from (2), (4), (8), and (9) we obtain

$$\arctan\left(\frac{M_T \sin\omega_r\tau_e}{1 - M_T\cos\omega_r\tau_e}\right) \approx m\left[\arctan\left(\frac{\alpha}{\sqrt[m]{A_S}}\right) - \arctan\left(\frac{\alpha}{\sqrt[m]{M_S}}\right)\right]. \tag{10}$$

Expressions (5), (6), (7), and (10) are the basic expressions to be used in the selection of the weighting functions. In order to gain insight into the relationships among various parameters involved in these equations, we make further simplifications by noting that A_S, A_T, α and β are small positive numbers. Thus, by neglecting appropriate terms, these equations reduce to

$$\omega_B^\star \approx \omega_r\left(\frac{A_r}{R_e}\right)^{\frac{1}{m}}, \tag{11}$$

$$M_T \approx \cos\omega_r\tau_e + \sqrt{\left(\frac{\omega_B^\star}{\omega_r}\right)^{2m} - \sin^2\omega_r\tau_e}, \tag{12}$$

$$\omega_{BT}^\star \approx \frac{\omega_r\sqrt[n]{M_T}}{\tan\left(\frac{\omega_r\tau_e}{n}\right)}, \tag{13}$$

$$M_S \approx \left[\frac{\omega_r}{\omega_B^\star\left|\tan\left(\frac{m\pi}{2} - \gamma\right)\right|}\right]^m, \qquad (\gamma \neq m\pi/2) \tag{14}$$

where

$$\gamma = \arctan\left(\frac{M_T\sin\omega_r\tau_e}{1 - M_T\cos\omega_r\tau_e}\right). \tag{15}$$

Note that $\omega_B^\star \gg \omega_r$ so that (12) is well defined. For (13), we have used the trigonometric identity $\tan(x-y) = (\tan x - \tan y)/(1 + \tan x \tan y)$ to obtain the quadratic equation

$$\sqrt[n]{M_T A_T}\tan\left(\frac{\omega_r\tau_e}{n}\right)\beta^2 + \left(\sqrt[n]{A_T} - \sqrt[n]{M_T}\right)\beta + \tan\left(\frac{\omega_r\tau_e}{n}\right) = 0,$$

and then have set $A_T \approx 0$. Derivation of the remaining equations is straightforward. When $m = 1$, (14) and (15) can be combined using the trigonometric identity $\tan(x-y) = (\tan x - \tan y)/(1 + \tan x \tan y)$ resulting in

$$M_S \approx \frac{\omega_r M_T \sin\omega_r\tau_e}{\omega_B^\star|1 - M_T\cos\omega_r\tau_e|}, \qquad (M_T\cos\omega_r\tau_e \neq 1). \tag{16}$$

3.1 Guidelines for sinusoidal tracking performance

Assume that A_r, ω_r, and the upper bounds on the tracking errors R_e and τ_e are specified. Further, assume that the parameters A_S and A_T are chosen to be some small positive numbers on the basis of our earlier guidelines. A procedure for selecting the remaining parameters of the weighting functions $W_P(s)$ and $W_T(s)$ are given below assuming that R_e and τ_e are the only specifications to be dealt with.

1. Initially, let $m = 1$ and calculate $\omega_B^\star$ from (11). If this value is too large, increase m and re-calculate $\omega_B^\star$.
2. Calculate M_T from (12) using the values of m and $\omega_B^\star$ obtained in Step 1.
3. Let $n = 1$ and calculate $\omega_{BT}^\star$ from (13) with the values of m, $\omega_B^\star$, and M_T calculated in Steps 1 and 2. If $\omega_{BT}^\star$ is not large enough, increase n and recalculate $\omega_{BT}^\star$ from (13) till a satisfactory result is obtained.
4. Finally, calculate M_S from (14) and (15), or from (16) if $m = 1$, using the values of $\omega_B^\star$, m, and M_T calculated in Steps 1 and 2.

4. Application

The importance of nanotechnology has been brought to full attention by the scanning probe microscopy and is the result of new techniques used to explore the properties of near atomic-scale structure (Aphale et al., 2008; Barrett & Quate, 1991; Teoh et al., 2008). However, most schemes of nanotechnology impose severe specifications on positioning systems, making the control system design more challenging. For example, micro/nano positioning systems are essential in auto focus systems, fast mirror scanners, image steering devices in optics; disk spin stands and vibration cancelation in disk drives; wafer and mask positioning in microelectronics; micropumps, needle valve actuation, linear drives, and piezo hammers in precision mechanics; and cell penetration and microdispensing devices in medicine and biology (Daniele et al., 1999; Salapaka et. al, 2002; Tamer & Dahleh, 1994).

In (Salapaka et. al, 2002), a mixed sensitivity robust control has been successfully applied to a noano-poistioning device, suited to biological samples as part of an atomic force microscope, where it is shown that substantial improvement in the positioning and precision is attainable over the conventional PI control. The improvement reported in this chapter is judged on the basis of the system ability to track a "high frequency" triangular reference waveform with a small peak error (in order of micro-meter) and a small delay (in order of milli-seconds). However, it is notable that the success of the design reported in (Salapaka et. al, 2002), as well as other mixed sensitivity designs, depends largely on the appropriate selection of the weights used in the optimization process. While for typical applications appropriate weights are often easily chosen after several trials and errors, the stringent performance requirements imposed for the ultra-high performance applications makes the selection of appropriate weights difficult, or at least time-consuming.

In the last section, we derived certain approximate expressions in terms of the tracking performance specifications and provided a guideline for the selection of the weights in the mixed sensitivity design. These expressions should prove valuable to the designer as they expedite the weights selection process in the simulation/design cycle. In order to demonstrate the usefulness of the guideline, consider the mixed sensitivity robust control design for a high bandwidth nano-positioning system as discussed in (Salapaka et. al, 2002). A model of the device obtained experimentally is a fourth order nonminimum phase transfer function

$$G(s) = \frac{9.7 \times 10^4 (s - (7.2 \pm 7.4j) \times 10^3)}{(s + (1.9 \pm 4.5j) \times 10^3)(s + (1.2 \pm 15.2j) \times 10^2)}.$$

The design considered is a mixed S/T/KS design where the weight on the controller transfer function KS is chosen to be $W_u = 0.1$ in order to restrict the magnitude of the input signal within the saturation limit. The other weights chosen are

$$W_P(s) = \frac{0.1667s + 2827}{s + 2.827}, \qquad W_T(s) = \frac{s + 235.6}{0.01s + 1414}.$$

A simulation result presented in this chapter which shows a sinusoidal tracking response with $R_e \approx 1(\mu m)$ and $\tau_e \approx 2$ [msec] when system is subjected to a 100 [Hz] command signal with peak value of 5 $[\mu m]$. From the selected weights, it is seen that

$$\begin{array}{l} m = 1,\ \omega_B^\star = 2827,\ \ M_S \approx 36,\ A_S = 10^{-6}, \\ n = 1,\ \omega_{BT}^\star = 1414,\ M_T \approx 36,\ A_T = 10^{-4}. \end{array}$$

We like to demonstrate how the initial weights can be obtained using the expressions derived earlier. Starting with $m = 1$, $A_r/R_e = 5$, and $\omega_r \approx 628$ [rad/sec], we obtain $\omega_B^\star \approx 3142$ [rad/sec] which is not too far from the given value of 2827 [rad/sec]. Since $\omega_r\tau_e \approx 70.4$ and $\omega_B^\star/\omega_r \approx 5$, equation (12) gives $M_T \approx 5.245$ which is better than the one chosen in (Salapaka et. al, 2002). With the calculated values and from (13) we next obtain $\omega_{BT}^\star \approx 1176$ [rad/sec] which is again not too far from the given value in (Salapaka et. al, 2002). Finally, from (16) we obtain $M_S \approx 1.5$ which is lower than what is considered in that chapter. Therefore, we see that while $\omega_B^\star$ and $\omega_{BT}^\star$ are fairly close in the first try, the values of M_S and M_T are considerably lower. This is however expected since large values of M_S and M_T are unavoidable here due to the presence of a complex pair of RHP zeros (Su et al., 2003; 2005).
In conclusion, we see that using the expressions derived in this chapter, a designer can start off with a fairly reasonable set of parameters and further adjust these parameters for the desired performance. Additionally, if larger values of M_T and M_S are to be allowed, the derived expressions can be used to see how these changes affect the remaining parameters like $\omega_B^\star$ and $\omega_{BT}^\star$. For example, it is seen from (12) that a larger M_T is obtained at the expense of a larger value for $\omega_B^\star$. From (13), this in turn implies a larger value for $\omega_{BT}^\star$ as well, and the same can be said for M_S form (14) and (15). In summary, the values obtain from the derived expressions in this chapter can form the basis of the first try in the simulation and as such should prove valuable to the designers.

5. Conclusion

In this chapter, the mixed sensitivity robust tracking problem of a feedback system with sinusoidal command waveforms is studied. Approximate expressions relating the tracking errors specifications to various parameters of the weighting functions used in the mixed S/T sensitivity design are derived. The derivation presented in this chapter uses simple arguments using phasors and straight line approximation of magnitude response. We have outlined guidelines for the selection of the weighting functions parameters using the derived expressions. Application of the results in minimizing the tracking errors of a nano-positioning system is demonstrated.

6. References

Aphale, S. S.; Devasia, S. & Moheimani, S. O. R. (2008). Achieving High-Bandwidth Nanopositioning In Presence of Plant Uncertainties, *Proc. of the IEEE/ASME Int. Conf. on Advanced Intelligent Mechatronics*, pp. 943-948, Xian, China.

Balas, G. J.; Doyle, J. C., Glover, K., Packard A. & and Smith, R. (1998). *μ-Analysis and Synthesis Toolbox*, Mathworks Inc, Natick, MA.

Barrett, R. C. & Quate, C. F. (1991). Optical Scan Correction System Applied to Atomic Force Microscopy. *Rev. Sci. Instruments*, Vol. 62, No. 6, pp. 1393-1399.

Broberg, H. L. & Molyet, R. G. (1994). A New Approach to Phase Cancellation in Repetitive Control, *Conf. Record of the 1994 IEEE Annual Meeting of the Industry Applications Society*, Vol. 3, pp. 1766-1770.

Chiang R. Y. & Hadaegh F. Y. (1994). Theory and Weighting Strategies of Mixed Sensitivity H^{∞} Synthesis on a Class of Aerospace Applications, *JFAC Symp. on Automat. Contr. in Aerospace*, pp. 12-16, Palo Alto, CA.

Daniele, A.; Salapaka, S., Salapaka, M. V. & Dahleh, M. (1999). Piezoelectric Scanners for Atomic Force Microscopes: Design of Lateral Sensors, Identification and Control, *Proc. of the American Contr. Conf.*, pp. 253-257, San Diego, CA.

Hara, S.; Yamamoto, Y., Omata T. & and Nakano M. (1998). Repetitive Control System: A New Type Servo System for Periodic Exogenous Signals. *IEEE Trans. on Automat. Contr.*, Vol. 33, No. 7, pp. 659-668.

Kwakernaak H. (2002). Mixed Sensitivity Design, *15th IFAC Triennial World Congress*, Barcelona, Spain.

Lee, R. C. H. & Smith, M. C. (1998). Robustness and Trade-offs in Repetitive Control. *Automatica*, Vol. 34, pp. 889-896.

Lanzon, A. (2000). Weight Selection in Robust Control: An Optimization Approach. *PhD Thesis*, Cambridge University.

Lanzon, A. (2001). Simultaneous Synthesis of Weights and Controllers in H_{∞} Loop-Shaping, *Proc. of Conf. on Decision and Contr.*, pp. 670-675, Orlando, FL.

Lanzon, A. (2005). Weight Optimization in H_{∞} Loop-Shaping. *Automatica*, Vol. 41, No. 7, pp. 1201-1208.

Oloomi, H. & Shafai, B. (2003). Weight Selection in Mixed Sensitivity Robust Control for Improving the Sinusoidal Tracking Performance, *Proc. of the IEEE Conf. on Decision and Control*, pp. 300-305, Maui, HI.

Salapaka, S.; Sebastian, A., Cleveland, J. P. & and Salapaka, M. V. (2002). High Bandwidth Nano-Positioner: A Robust Control Approach. *Rev. Sci. Instruments*, Vol. 73, No. 9, pp. 3232-3241.

Skogesttad, S. & Postlethwaite, I. (2007). *Multivariable Feedback Control*, John Wiley & Sons, ISBN 978-0-470-01168-3, New York.

Su W.; Qiu L. & Chen J. (2003). Fundamental Performance Limitations in Tracking Sinusoidal Signals. *IEEE Trans. on Automat. Contr.*, Vol. 48, No. 8, pp. 1371-1380.

Su W.; Qiu L. & Chen J. (2005). On Performance Limitation in Tracking a Sinusoid. *IEEE Trans. on Automat. Contr.*, Vol. 51, No. 8, pp. 1320-1325.

Sugimoto, H. & Washida, K. (1997). A Proposition of Design Method for Modified Repetitive Control System with Corrected Dead Time Using Sensitivity Function Shaping and its Application to Motor Control System, *Proc. of the Power Conversion Conf.*, Vol. 2, pp. 619-624, Nagaoka.

Tamer, N. & Dahleh, M. (1994). Feedback Control of Piezoelectric Tube Scanners, *Proc. of the American Contr. Conf.*, pp. 1826-1831, Lake Buena Vista, FL.

Teoh J. N.; Du, C. & Xie, L. (2008). Combined H_2 and KYP Lemma Based Control for Positioning Error Minimization and Specific Narrowband Disturbance Rejections, *IEEE Int. Conf. on Control Applications (IEEE Multi-Conference on System and Control)*, pp. 828-833.

Zhou, K.; Doyle, J. C. & and Glover, K. (1996). *Robust and Optimal Control*, Prentice Hall, ISBN 0-13-456567-3, New Jersey.

6

An Iterative Approach to the Fixed-Order Robust H_∞ Control Problem Using a Sequence of Infeasible Controllers

Yasushi Kami and Eitaku Nobuyama
Akashi National College of Technology
and Kyushu Institute of Technology
Japan

1. Introduction

It is well known that the robust disturbance attenuation against uncertainties can be achieved by the robust H_∞ controllers and some practical situations make us use the fixed-order controllers. These facts imply that the fixed-order robust H_∞ controllers are important for practical control problems. However it is difficult to design such robust controllers, because the robust H_∞ control problems include an infinite number of matrix inequality constraints, in other words, they are described by Robust Semi-Definite Programming (RSDP) problems. For obtaining a feasible solution of the RSDP problems coming from the robust control problems with state feedback controllers or full-order controllers, many numerical methods have been proposed. Classically, the quadratic stability theory, i.e. a common constant Lyapunov function for the entire uncertain set is used for reducing the infinite constraints to the finite ones at the expense of conservatism (Boyd et al. 1994). Recently, parameter dependent Lyapunov functions are used to improve the conservatism (Chesi et al. 2005) - (Ichihara et al. 2003), (Kami et al. 2009) - (Shaked 2001), (Xie 2008) and some one-shot type approaches using extended LMI conditions, which allows to use the affine parameter dependent Lyapunov functions, have been proposed (Pipeleers et al. 2009), (Shaked 2001), (Xie 2008). However these methods can not always produce the robust controller, because common additional variables are required and these methods can not be used for designing fixed-order controllers. In this sense, an iterative type approach may be useful to the problems such that these one-shot type approaches can not be applied.
In the field of the numerical optimization, there are two types of iterative approaches for finding feasible or locally optimal solutions of the optimization problems: one is an interior-point approach which needs an initial feasible solution to be carried out and the other is an exterior-point approach which does not need it. From these facts, exterior-point approach can be efficient for obtaining the solutions of the problems such that feasible solutions are difficult to be found. However, there are no exterior-point approaches except those in (Iwasaki & Skelton 1995), (Kami & Nobuyama 2004), (Kami et al. 2009), (Vanbierviet 2009) for control problems to our knowledge.

In this paper, we deal with the fixed-order robust H_∞ controller synthesis problem against time invariant polytopic uncertainties, which can be described by parameter dependent bilinear matrix inequality (PDBMI) problems. The purpose of this paper is to propose an iterative approach which is like an exterior-point one. To do that, we introduce an `axis-shifted system' which is obtained by shifting the imaginary axis of the complex plane so that all perturbing closed-poles are included in the LHS of the shifted imaginary axis. Our approach constructs a sequence of infeasible controller variables on which the shifted imaginary axis returns to the original position while the H_∞ norm of the axis-shifted system is less than the prescribed H_∞ norm bound. The advantage of our approach is to be able to use any controller variables as an initial point. The efficiency of our approach is shown by a numerical example.

In this paper, the following notations are used. $\mathbf{R}$, $\mathbf{R}^{n\times m}$ and $\mathbf{S}^n$ are the sets of real scalars, $n\times m$ real matrices and $n\times n$ real symmetric matrices, respectively. He$\{Z\}$, $\begin{bmatrix} A & * \\ B^T & C \end{bmatrix}$ and $\sigma(\cdot)$ denote $Z+Z^T$, the block symmetric matrix $\begin{bmatrix} A & B \\ B^T & C \end{bmatrix}$ and a set of eigenvalues, respectively. Moreover, Ω denotes a hyper-rectangle and vert Ω indicates the set of vertices of Ω.

2. Problem formulation

In this paper, we consider the following plant $P(\theta)$ with a time invariant uncertain parameter $\theta := [\theta_1 \ \cdots \ \theta_N]$:

$$P(\theta) := \begin{cases} \dot{x}(t) = A(\theta)x(t) + Bu(t) + B_w w(t) \\ z(t) = Cx(t) + Du(t) \\ y(t) = Ex(t) \end{cases} \tag{1}$$

$$A(\theta) := A_0 + \sum_{i=1}^{N} \theta_i A_i \tag{2}$$

where $x(t)$ is the plant state, $w(t)$ is any exogenous input, $u(t)$ is the control input, $z(t)$ is the performance output, $y(t)$ is the measurement output and $\theta := [\theta_1 \ \cdots \ \theta_N] \in \Omega$ is an uncertain parameter vector whose elements satisfy

$$\theta_i \in [\underline{\theta}_i \ \ \overline{\theta}_i], i = 1, \cdots, N. \tag{3}$$

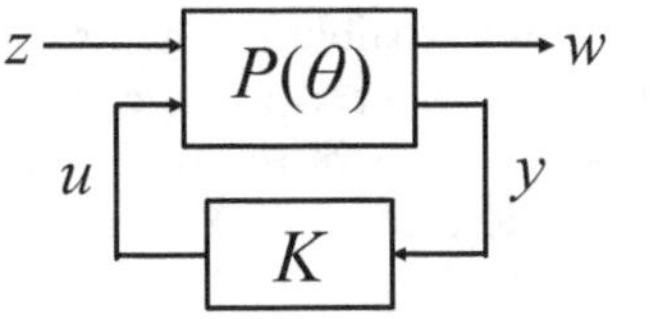

Fig. 1. Control system.

Moreover, we have the following assumptions:

1. $(A(\theta), B)$ is controllable for all $\theta \in \Omega$.
2. $(A(\theta), B_w, C)$ is controllable and observable for all $\theta \in \Omega$.

For this system let us consider the following fixed-order controller Σ_d or the static state feedback controller Σ_s:

$$\Sigma_d : \begin{cases} \dot{x}_c(t) = A_c x_c(t) + B_c y(t) \\ u(t) = C_c x_c(t) + D_c y(t) \end{cases} \tag{4}$$

$$\Sigma_s : u(t) = Kx(t) \tag{5}$$

where $x_c(t) \in \mathbf{R}^r$ is the controller state and r is the prescribed integer which achieves $0 < r < n$. Note that Σ_d and Σ_s become state feedback controllers in the case that $E = I$ holds.

Via the controller Σ_d and Σ_s the closed-loop system can be described by

$$\begin{cases} \dot{x}_{cl}(t) = A_{cl}(\overline{K},\theta)x_{cl}(t) + B_{clw}w(t) \\ z(t) = C_{cl}(\overline{K})x_{cl}(t) \end{cases}. \tag{6}$$

$$A_{cl}(\overline{K},\theta) := \overline{A}(\theta) + \overline{B}\overline{K}\overline{E}, C(\overline{K}) := \overline{C} + \overline{D}\overline{K}\overline{E} \tag{7}$$

For the controller Σ_d $x_{cl}(t)$ and the coefficient matrices in (7) are given by

$$x_{cl}(t) = \begin{bmatrix} x(t) \\ x_{cl}(t) \end{bmatrix}, \overline{A}(\theta) = \overline{A}_0 + \sum_{i=1}^{N} \theta_i \overline{A}_i, \overline{A}_i = \begin{bmatrix} A_i & 0 \\ 0 & 0 \end{bmatrix} (i = 0,1,\cdots,N), \tag{8}$$

$$\overline{B} = \begin{bmatrix} B & 0 \\ 0 & I \end{bmatrix}, \overline{E} = \begin{bmatrix} E & 0 \\ 0 & I \end{bmatrix}, \overline{C} = \begin{bmatrix} C & 0 \end{bmatrix}, \overline{D} = \begin{bmatrix} D & 0 \end{bmatrix}, \overline{K} = \begin{bmatrix} D_c & C_c \\ B_c & A_c \end{bmatrix}. \tag{9}$$

For the controller Σ_s $x_{cl}(t)$ and the coefficient matrices are given by

$$x_{cl}(t) = x(t), \overline{A}(\theta) = A(\theta), \overline{B} = B, \overline{E} = E, \overline{C} = C, \overline{D} = D, \overline{K} = K \tag{10}$$

For the closed-loop system (6) the control problem to be solved in this paper is defined as follows:

Robust H_∞ synthesis problem:

Given an H_∞ norm bound γ_p, find $\overline{K}$ which achieves

$$\left\| T_{zw}(\overline{K},\theta) \right\|_\infty < \gamma_p \tag{11}$$

where $T_{zw}(\overline{K},\theta)$ is the transfer function from w to z of the closed-loop system (6) and $\|\cdot\|_\infty$ denotes the H_∞ norm.

For the control problem (11) the following lemma holds (Boyd et al. 1994):

Lemma 1 $\left\|T_{zw}(\bar{K},\theta)\right\|_\infty < \gamma_p$ holds if there exists a parameter dependent Lyapunov function

$$P^\infty(\theta) := P_0^\infty + \sum_{i=1}^{N} \theta_i P_i^\infty > 0 \tag{12}$$

which satisfies

$$\begin{bmatrix} P^\infty(\theta)A_{cl}(\bar{K},\theta) + A_{cl}(\bar{K},\theta)^T P^\infty(\theta) & * & * \\ B_{clw}^T P^\infty(\theta) & -\gamma_p I & * \\ C_{cl}(\bar{K}) & 0 & -\gamma_p I \end{bmatrix} < 0. \tag{13}$$

This lemma implies that the robust H_∞ synthesis problem (11) can be described as PDBMI problem, which has an infinite number of BMI constraints corresponding to all points on Ω. Hence it is difficult to obtain the feasible controller variables $\bar{K}$ achieving (13). One well known classical method for obtaining Σ_s in the case that $E = I$ is to use quadratic (parameter independent constant) Lyapunov functions (Boyd et al. 1994). i.e., defining

$$P^\infty(\theta)^{-1} := X \,,\ W := KX \tag{14}$$

to get the controller variables from

$$K = WX^{-1} \tag{15}$$

where X and W are the solutions of the next inequalities:

$$\begin{bmatrix} A(\theta)X + XA(\theta)^T + BW + W^T B^T & * & * \\ B_w^T & -\gamma_p I & * \\ CX + DW & 0 & -\gamma_p I \end{bmatrix} < 0, \forall \theta \in \mathrm{vert}\,\Omega \tag{16}$$

However the quadratic Lyapunov functions X do not always exist and even if they exist the obtained controller includes a high conservatism. Moreover, this method can be only used in the case that $E = I$.

Recently, various studies with parameter dependent Lyapunov functions have been reported to reduce the conservatism (Chesi et al. 2005) - (Ichihara et al. 2003), (Kami et al. 2009) - (Shaked 2001), (Xie 2008). Especially, some interesting one-shot type approaches for designing static state feedback controllers or full-order controllers with extended matrix inequality conditions have been proposed (Pipeleers et. al., 2009), (Shaked 2001), (Xie 2008). However these methods do not always produce the feasible controllers in some cases, because some additional common matrix variables are required and this method can not be used in the case that $E \neq I$. In this paper, we propose an iterative approach to the fixed-order robust H_∞ synthesis problem, which can be used if $E \neq I$. The features of our approach are to constructs a controller sequence from the infeasible region to the feasible one and to be able to use any matrix as an initial point.

3. Multi-convex relaxation method

In this section, let us consider the next PDMI problem

$$\text{find } z \text{ s.t. } M(z,\theta) := M_0(z) + \sum_{i=1}^{N} \theta_i M_i(z) + \sum_{i=1}^{N}\sum_{j=i}^{N} \theta_i\theta_j M_{ij}(z) < 0, \forall \theta \in \Omega \tag{17}$$

where $z := \begin{bmatrix} z_1 & \cdots & z_N \end{bmatrix}^T$ $(z_i \in \mathbf{R})$ is a vector of decision variables, $\theta := \begin{bmatrix} \theta_1 & \cdots & \theta_N \end{bmatrix}^T \in \Omega$ is a parameter vector whose elements $\theta_i \in \mathbf{R}$ are in the given range $\theta_i \in \begin{bmatrix} \underline{\theta}_i & \overline{\theta}_i \end{bmatrix}$ and $M_0(z)$, $M_i(z)$ and $M_{ij}(z)$ are symmetric matrices with appropriate sizes. It is well known that feasible solutions of the PDMI problem (17) are difficult to be obtained, because this problem has an infinite number of constraints corresponding to all points on Ω. In this section, we show the multi-convex relaxation method (Ichihara et al. 2003) which is used for reducing the infinitely constrained problem to a finitely constrained one for obtaining a feasible solution of (17).

3.1 Multi-convex function

In this subsection, we review the definition and the properties of the multi-convex function.

Definition 1: If the function $f(\theta), \theta = \begin{bmatrix} \theta_1 & \cdots & \theta_N \end{bmatrix}$ becomes a multi-convex function with respect to any θ_j in the case that $\theta_i (i = 1, \cdots, j-1, j+1, \cdots, N)$ are fixed then the function $f(\theta)$ is said as a multi-convex function.

From the definition the multi-convex function has the next properties:

Lemma 2 The next statements hold:

1. The function $f(\theta)$ is the multi-convex function if and only if $\frac{\partial f(\theta)}{\partial \theta_i} \geq 0$ hold $\forall i = 1, \cdots, N$.
2. The maximum of the multi-convex function $f(\theta)$ on $\theta \in \Omega$ is on the vertex of Ω (See Fig. 2).

Using these properties the relaxation method for obtaining the feasible solution of (17) is shown in the next subsection.

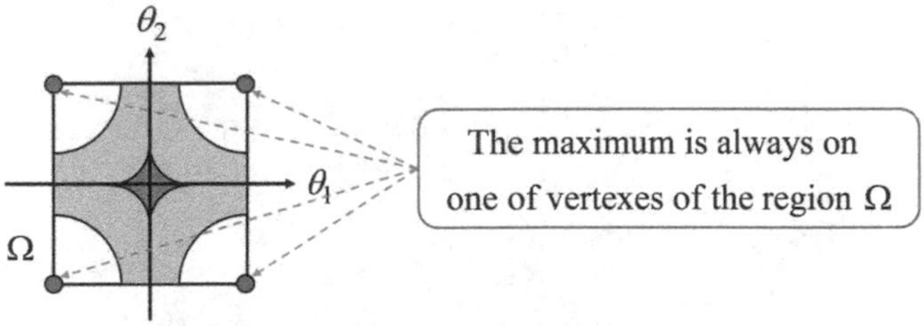

Fig. 2. The concept of the multi-convex functions.

3.2 Multi-convex relaxation

In this subsection, we show a relaxation method with multi-convex function (Ichihara et al. 2003) which is needed to derive our approach. The key idea of this method is to make the multi-convex upper bound of $M(z,\theta)$.

The multi-convex relaxation method can be described as the next lemma:

Lemma 3 z is a feasible solution of the PDMI problem (17) if there exist z, $Q_i \in \mathbf{R}^{n\times n}$ and $R_i \in \mathbf{S}^n (i = 1,\cdots,N)$ which achieve

$$\begin{bmatrix} M(z,\theta) & * & * & * \\ Q_1 - \theta_1 R_1 & -R_1 & * & * \\ \vdots & 0 & \ddots & * \\ Q_N - \theta_N R_N & 0 & 0 & -R_N \end{bmatrix} < 0, \forall \theta \in \text{vert}\,\Omega \tag{18}$$

$$M_{ii}(z) + R_i \geq 0 (i = 1,\cdots N). \tag{19}$$

Proof $M(z,\theta) < 0, \forall \theta \in \Omega$ holds iff we have

$$f(z,\theta) := x^T M(z,\theta)x < 0, \forall \theta \in \Omega, \forall x (\neq 0) \in \mathbf{R}^n . \tag{20}$$

Now, let us define $f_1(z,\theta)$ and $f_2(\theta)$ as

$$f_1(z,\theta) := x^T M(z,\theta)x + \sum_{i=1}^{N} \theta_i^2 x^T R_i x, \tag{21}$$

$$f_2(\theta) := \sum_{i=1}^{N} \theta_i^2 x^T R_i x, \tag{22}$$

respectively, where $R_i \in \mathbf{S}^n$ achieve

$$x^T (M_{ii}(z) + R_i)x \geq 0, i := 1,\cdots N \tag{23}$$

which is the necessary and sufficient condition for $f_1(z,\theta)$ to be multi-convex function with respect to θ. Then the function $\overline{f}(z,\theta)$ given by (24) becomes a multi-convex upper bound function of $f(z,\theta)(= f_1(z,\theta) - f_2(\theta))$:

$$\overline{f}(z,\theta) := f_1(z,\theta) - \overline{f}_2(\theta) , \tag{24}$$

$$\overline{f}_2(\theta) := \sum_{i=1}^{N} \left(\theta_i \mathrm{B}_i^T R_i + \theta_i R_i \mathrm{B}_i - \mathrm{B}_i^T R_i \mathrm{B}_i \right). \tag{25}$$

This is because $-f_2(\theta) \leq -\overline{f}_2(\theta)$ holds from

$$-\theta_i^2 R_i \leq -(\theta_i \mathrm{B}_i^T R_i + \theta_i R_i \mathrm{B}_i - \mathrm{B}_i^T R_i \mathrm{B}_i), \forall \mathrm{B}_i \in \mathbf{R}^{n\times n} . \tag{26}$$

Then, from the property of the multi-convex functions $\overline{f}(z,\theta) < 0$ holds iff we have

$$M(z,\theta) + \sum_{i=1}^{N} (\theta_i I - \mathrm{B}_i)^T R_i (\theta_i I - \mathrm{B}_i) < 0, \forall \theta \in \text{vert}\,\Omega \tag{27}$$

and the inequality (27) can be transformed into

$$\begin{bmatrix} M(z,\theta) & * & * & * \\ R_1 B_1 - \theta_1 R_1 & -R_1 & * & * \\ \vdots & 0 & \ddots & * \\ R_N B_N - \theta_N R_N & 0 & 0 & -R_N \end{bmatrix} < 0, \forall \theta \in \text{vert}\,\Omega. \tag{28}$$

Therefore, z is a feasible solution of $M(\theta,z)<0$ if there exist z, B_i and R_i which achieve (28) for all $\theta \in \text{vert}\,\Omega$ and replacing $R_i B_i$ by Q_i in (28) we have (18).
Using this lemma the problem (17) with an infinite number of constraints can be reduced into that with a finite number of constraints.

4. Iterative approach to the robust H_∞ synthesis problems

In this section, we propose an iterative approach to the robust H_∞ control problem (11) using Lemma 3. To do that, we introduce an `axis-shifted system' which is obtained by shifting the imaginary axis so that all perturbing poles are located in the LHS of the imaginary axis. The key idea of our approach is to return the shifted imaginary axis to the original position while the H_∞ norm of the axis-shifted system is less than γ_p. The feature of our approach is to be able to use any controller variables as an initial point.
Firstly, we add the practical assumption for the closed-loop system (6) such that the poles of the system (6) do not exist infinitely far from the imaginary axis on the RHS of the complex plane, i.e., there always exists a finite scalar β which achieves:

$$\max_{\lambda \in \sigma(A_{cl}(\bar{K},\theta))} \text{Re}[\lambda] < \beta, \forall \theta \in \Omega \tag{29}$$

and we introduce the following system using β, which is needed to derive our iterative approach:

$$\begin{cases} \dot{x}_{cl}(t) = (A_{cl}(\bar{K},\theta) - \beta I)x_{cl}(t) + B_{clw}w(t) \\ z(t) = C_{cl}(\bar{K})x_{cl}(t) \end{cases}. \tag{30}$$

This system has the next property.
Lemma 4 The system (30) is robustly stable for the parameter $\theta \in \Omega$.
Proof It is obvious from (29).
Remark 1. In this paper, we interpret the meaning of " $A_{cl}(\bar{K},\theta) - \beta I$ " as shifting the imaginary axis of the complex plane to the right by β (See Fig. 3). In this sense, the system (30) is called as `axis-shifted system' in this paper.
Now, letting $\bar{T}_{zw}(\bar{K},\theta,\beta)$ be a transfer function of the system (30) from w to z the next lemma holds for the H_∞ norm condition

$$\left\|\bar{T}_{zw}(\bar{K},\theta,\beta)\right\|_\infty < \gamma_p. \tag{31}$$

Lemma 5 (31) holds if there exists a parameter dependent Lyapunov function

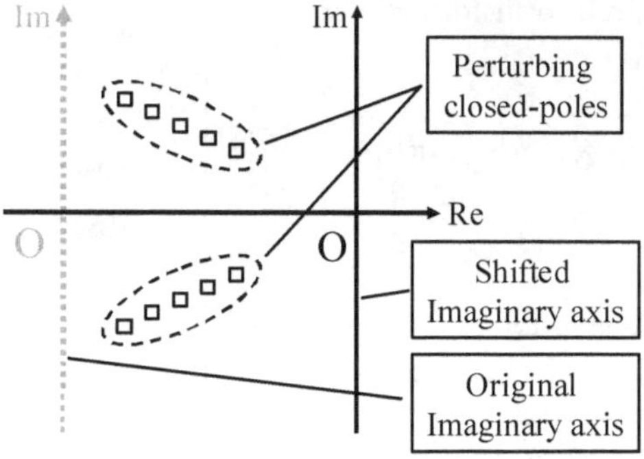

Fig. 3. Concept of complex plane of the axis-shifted system.

$$P(\theta) := P_0^\infty + \sum_{i=1}^{N} \theta_i P_i^\infty > 0 \tag{32}$$

which achieves

$$M^\infty(P^\infty(\theta), \overline{K}, \beta, \theta, \gamma_p) < 0 \tag{33}$$

where

$$M^\infty(P^\infty(\theta), \overline{K}, \beta, \theta, \gamma_p) := \begin{bmatrix} P^\infty(\theta)(A_{cl}(\overline{K},\theta) - \beta I) + (A_{cl}(\overline{K},\theta) - \beta I)^T P^\infty(\theta) & * & * \\ B_{clw}^T P^\infty(\theta) & -\gamma_p I & * \\ C_{cl}(\overline{K}) & 0 & -\gamma_p I \end{bmatrix}. \tag{34}$$

Proof It is obvious from Lemma 1.

Remark 2. If $A_{cl}(\overline{K},\theta)$ is robustly stable $\forall \theta \in \Omega$ we can let $\beta = 0$ and in this case $\|\overline{T}_{zw}(\overline{K},\theta,0)\|_\infty = \|T_{zw}(\overline{K},\theta)\|_\infty$ holds.

Now, the inequality (33) can be described as

$$M_0^\infty + \sum_{i=1}^{N} \theta_i M_i^\infty + \sum_{i=1}^{N} \sum_{j=i}^{N} \theta_i \theta_j M_{ij}^\infty < 0 \tag{35}$$

$$M_0^\infty = \begin{bmatrix} P_0^\infty(\overline{A}_0 + \overline{B}\overline{K}\overline{E}) + (\overline{A}_0 + \overline{B}\overline{K}\overline{E})^T P_0^\infty & * & * \\ B_{clw}^T P_0^\infty & -\gamma_p I & * \\ \overline{C} + \overline{D}\overline{K}\overline{E} & 0 & -\gamma_p I \end{bmatrix} \tag{36}$$

$$M_i^\infty = \begin{bmatrix} P_0^\infty \overline{A}_i + \overline{A}_i^T P_0^\infty + P_i^\infty(\overline{A}_0 + \overline{B}\overline{K}\overline{E}) + (\overline{A}_0 + \overline{B}\overline{K}\overline{E})^T P_i^\infty & * & * \\ B_{clw}^T P_i^\infty & 0 & * \\ 0 & 0 & 0 \end{bmatrix} \tag{37}$$

$$M_{ij}=\begin{cases}\begin{bmatrix}P_i^\infty A_j+A_j^T P_i^\infty+P_j^\infty A_i+A_i^T P_j^\infty & * & * \\ 0 & 0 & * \\ 0 & 0 & 0\end{bmatrix} & i=j \\ \begin{bmatrix}P_i^\infty A_i+A_i^T P_i^\infty & * & * \\ 0 & 0 & * \\ 0 & 0 & 0\end{bmatrix} & i\neq j\end{cases} \tag{38}$$

Then we can get the next the next lemma with Lemma 3 which is needed to derive our iterative approach.

Lemma 6 $\bar{K}$ and P_i^∞ achieve the H_∞ norm constraint (31) if there exist Q_i and $R_i (i:=1,\cdots,N), \forall\theta\in \text{vert}\,\Omega$, which achieve

$$\bar{M}^\infty(P^\infty(\theta),\bar{K},\beta,\gamma_p,\theta):=\begin{bmatrix}M^\infty(P^\infty(\theta),\bar{K},\beta,\gamma_p,\theta) & * & \cdots & * \\ Q_1^\infty-\theta_1 R_1^\infty & -R_1 & & * \\ \vdots & & \ddots & \vdots \\ Q_N^\infty-\theta_N R_N^\infty & 0 & \cdots & -R_N\end{bmatrix}<0, \tag{39}$$

$$M_{ii}^\infty+R_i\geq 0,\forall i. \tag{40}$$

Moreover, we have the next lemma with respect to the existence of β which achieves $\|\bar{T}_{zw}(\bar{K},\theta,\beta)\|_\infty<\gamma_p,\forall\theta\in\Omega$ for given controller variables $\bar{K}_k$.

Lemma 7 For a given $\bar{K}_k$ achieving the condition (29) there always exists β achieving

$$\|\bar{T}_{zw}(\bar{K},\theta,\beta)\|_\infty<\gamma_p,\forall\theta\in\Omega \tag{41}$$

Proof: Let us consider the next matrix:

$$A_{cl}(\bar{K}_k,\theta)+A_{cl}(\bar{K}_k,\theta)^T+\begin{bmatrix}B_{clw} & C_{cl}(\bar{K})^T\end{bmatrix}\begin{bmatrix}\gamma_p & 0 \\ 0 & \gamma_p\end{bmatrix}^{-1}\begin{bmatrix}B_{clw}^T \\ C_{cl}(\bar{K})\end{bmatrix} \tag{42}$$

Then, from (29), we can choose β which is larger than the maximum eigenvalue of the next symmetric matrix:

$$\frac{1}{2}\left(A_{cl}(\bar{K}_k,\theta)+A_{cl}(\bar{K}_k,\theta)^T+\begin{bmatrix}B_{clw} & C_{cl}(\bar{K})^T\end{bmatrix}\begin{bmatrix}\gamma_p & 0 \\ 0 & \gamma_p\end{bmatrix}^{-1}\begin{bmatrix}B_{clw}^T \\ C_{cl}(\bar{K})\end{bmatrix}\right), \tag{43}$$

which implies that there exists β which achieves

$$2\beta I>A_{cl}(\bar{K}_k,\theta)+A_{cl}(\bar{K}_k,\theta)^T+\begin{bmatrix}B_{clw} & C_{cl}(\bar{K})^T\end{bmatrix}\begin{bmatrix}\gamma_p & 0 \\ 0 & \gamma_p\end{bmatrix}^{-1}\begin{bmatrix}B_{clw}^T \\ C_{cl}(\bar{K})\end{bmatrix},\theta\in\text{vert}\,\Omega. \tag{44}$$

This inequality can be transformed into the next inequality:

$$\begin{bmatrix} A_{cl}(\bar{K},\theta)-\beta I+(A_{cl}(\bar{K},\theta)-\beta I)^T & * & * \\ B_{clw}^T & -\gamma_p I & * \\ C_{cl}(\bar{K}) & 0 & -\gamma_p I \end{bmatrix} < 0, \theta \in \text{vert}\,\Omega \tag{45}$$

and this inequality can be obtained by substituting the common constant Lyapunov function $P^{\infty}(\theta) = I$ into (33). Hence $\left\|\bar{T}_{zw}(\bar{K},\theta,\beta)\right\|_{\infty} < \gamma_{p,} \forall\theta \in \Omega$ holds.

Using Lemmas 6 and 7, we propose the following iterative approach to obtain a feasible solution of the problem (11):

Algorithm

Step 1: Find any $\bar{K}_1$ and let β_1 and μ_1 be scalars which achieve

$$\beta_1 > \max_{\lambda \in \sigma(A_{cl}(\bar{K}_1,\theta))} \text{Re}[\lambda],\ \left\|\bar{T}_{zw}(\bar{K}_1,\theta,\mu_1)\right\|_{\infty} < \gamma_p,\ \beta_1 \le \mu_1 \tag{46}$$

respectively, for $\theta \in \text{vert}\,\Omega$. For example, let $\mu_1 = \beta_1$ where μ_1 can be chosen as the solution of the LMI's (45). Let $k := 1$ and choose ω from 0 to 1.

Step 2: If $\beta_k \le 0$ then let $K^* := K_k$ and exit. Otherwise let

$$\mu_{k+1} := \omega\beta_k + (1-\omega)\mu_k \tag{47}$$

and go to the next step.

Step 3: Find $P_i^{\infty}(i := 0,\cdots,N)$ which satisfy

$$\bar{M}^{\infty}(P^{\infty}(\theta), K_k, \mu_{k+1}, \gamma_p, \theta) < 0, \forall\theta \in \text{vert}\,\Omega \tag{48}$$

and let them be P_{ik}^{∞} and define

$$P_k^{\infty}(\theta) := P_{0k}^{\infty} + \sum_{i=1}^{N} \theta_i P_{ik}^{\infty} \tag{49}$$

Step 4: Find K and β_t which are the solutions of

$$\min_{K,\beta_t} \beta_t \text{ s.t. } \beta_t < \mu_{k+1}, \tag{50}$$

$$\bar{M}^{\infty}(P_k^{\infty}(\theta), K, \beta_t, \gamma_p, \theta) < 0, \forall\theta \in \text{vert}\,\Omega \tag{51}$$

and let $K_{k+1} := K, \beta_{k+1} := \beta_t$ and $k := k+1$ and go to Step 2.

Theorem 1 The next statements hold for our algorithm.

1. μ_k is an upper bound of β_k, i.e., $\mu_k \ge \beta_k$ holds.
2. μ_k is monotonically decreasing, i.e., $\mu_k > \mu_{k+1}$ holds.
3. $\left\|\bar{T}_{zw}(\bar{K}_k,\theta,\mu_k)\right\|_{\infty} < \gamma_{p,} \forall\theta \in \Omega$ holds for all k.

Proof 1. and 2. From (46) and (50), $\mu_k \geq \beta_k$ holds. Moreover, from (47) we have

$$\beta_k < \mu_{k+1} < \mu_k . \tag{52}$$

3. From Step 4 of the algorithm and the fact that $\mu_k \geq \beta_k$ holds, we have

$$\begin{aligned} 0 &> \bar{M}^{\infty}(P_{k-1}^{\infty}(\theta), K_k, \beta_k, \gamma_p, \theta) \\ &\geq \bar{M}^{\infty}(P_{k-1}^{\infty}(\theta), K_k, \mu_k, \gamma_p, \theta) \\ &\geq M^{\infty}(P_{k-1}^{\infty}(\theta), K_k, \mu_k, \gamma_p, \theta) , \end{aligned} \tag{53}$$

which implies K_k achieves $\left\|\bar{T}_{zw}(\bar{K}_k, \theta, \mu_k)\right\|_{\infty} < \gamma_p, \forall \theta \in \Omega$. Hence Theorem 1 holds.

Remark 1: The key idea of our approach is to decrease μ_k so as to approach β_k to 0, i.e., the shifted imaginary axis approach the original position while the H_{∞} norm constraint $\left\|\bar{T}_{zw}(\bar{K}_k, \theta, \mu_k)\right\|_{\infty} < \gamma_p, \forall \theta \in \Omega$ is achieved(See Fig.4). This fact implies that the controller K_k is updated from a non robust H_{∞} controller for the original system to a robust H_{∞} one as k increases. In this sense, this approach can be an exterior-point approach.

Remark 2: Unfortunately, our approach can not always produce a robust H_{∞} controller, in other words, there does not exist the efficient ways of choices of K_1, β_1, μ_1 and ω so that a feasible robust controller is always obtained. Hence a condition for detecting an infeasibility for obtaining a robust feasible H_{∞} controller may be needed. Moreover, $\beta_k \leq 0$ is a sufficient condition for $\left\|T_{zw}(\bar{K}_k, \theta)\right\|_{\infty} < \gamma_p, \forall \theta \in \Omega$. Hence we may also need a efficient criterion for K_k to be a feasible solution of the problem (11).

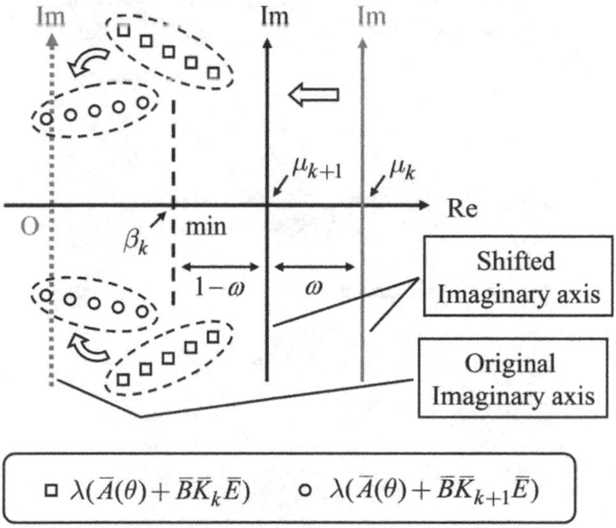

Fig. 4. Concept of our exterior-point approach.

5. Numerical example

To demonstrate the efficiency of our approach let us consider the following matrices:

$$A_0 = \begin{bmatrix} -9 & 1 & 2 \\ 6 & -8 & -11 \\ -1 & 4 & -7 \end{bmatrix}, A_1 = \begin{bmatrix} 0 & 0 & 1 \\ -5 & 1 & 4 \\ 0 & -1 & 1 \end{bmatrix}, A_2 = \begin{bmatrix} -2 & -3 & -2 \\ 0 & -1 & 5 \\ -3 & 2 & 0 \end{bmatrix}, B = \begin{bmatrix} 0 \\ 0 \\ -3 \end{bmatrix}, B_w = \begin{bmatrix} 0 \\ 1 \\ 0 \end{bmatrix} \quad (54)$$

$$C = \begin{bmatrix} 1 & 0 & 0 \end{bmatrix}, D = 0.1, E = \begin{bmatrix} 1 & 0 & 0 \\ 0 & 1 & 0 \end{bmatrix}, \gamma_p = 0.1 \quad (55)$$

Note that the one-shot type methods (Pipeleers et al. 2009), (Shaked 2001), (Xie 2008) can not use for designing the robust H_∞ controller because of $E \neq I$.
For this numerical example, we set the initial condition for carrying out our approach as follows:

$$K_1 = \left[\begin{array}{cc|cc} 0 & 0 & 1 & 0 \\ \hline 1 & 0 & 0 & 0 \\ 0 & 1 & 0 & 0 \end{array}\right], \omega = 0.3, \beta_1 = \mu_1 = 8.1027 \quad (56)$$

where $\beta_1 (= \mu_1)$ is given as the solution of the LMI's (45).
Fig. 5 shows locations of eigenvalues of $\overline{A}(\theta) + \overline{B}\overline{K}_1\overline{E}$, i.e., the perturbations of poles of the uncertain closed-loop system via initial controller variables $\overline{K}_1$. This figure shows that $\overline{K}_1$ is not a robust stabilizing controller.
After 10 iterations the next controller variables are given from our approach:

$$\overline{K}^* = \left[\begin{array}{cc|cc} -1.5195 & -3.6942 & -8.3794 & -2.6309 \\ \hline 35.6459 & -43.3047 & -270.7538 & 85.3833 \\ -40.8834 & -1.7382 & 131.5127 & -91.5248 \end{array}\right]. \quad (57)$$

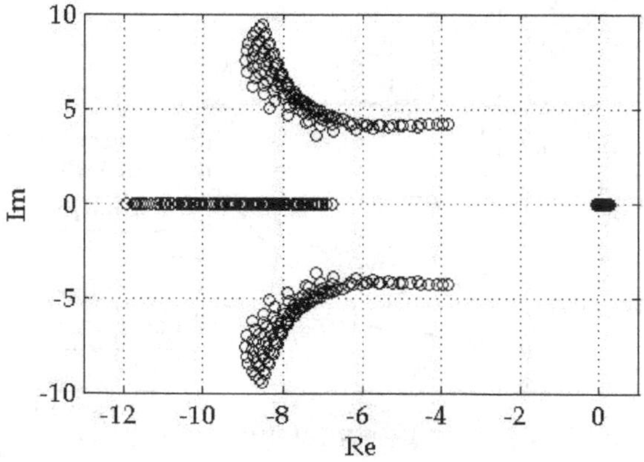

Fig. 5. Placement of the closed-poles via $\overline{K}_1$.

Fig. 6 and 7 show locations of eigenvalues of $\overline{A}(\theta)+\overline{B}\overline{K}^{*}\overline{E}$, i.e., the perturbations of poles of the uncertain closed-loop system via controller variables $\overline{K}^{*}$ and the contour plot of $\left\|T_{zw}(\overline{K}^{*},\theta)\right\|_{\infty}$ on Ω, respectively. From these figures, K^{*} is a feasible solution of the problem (11).

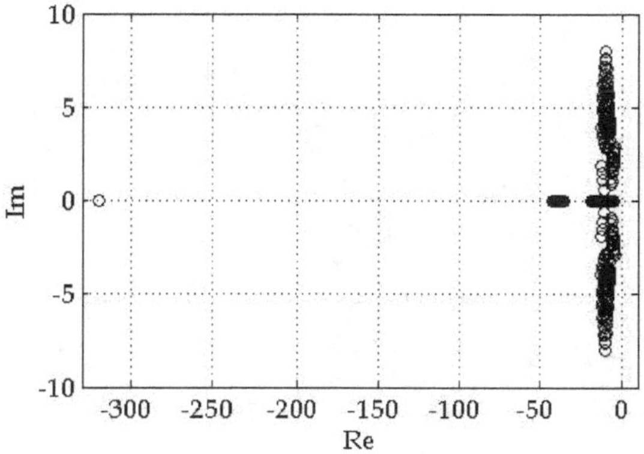

Fig. 6. Placement of the closed-poles via $\overline{K}^{*}$.

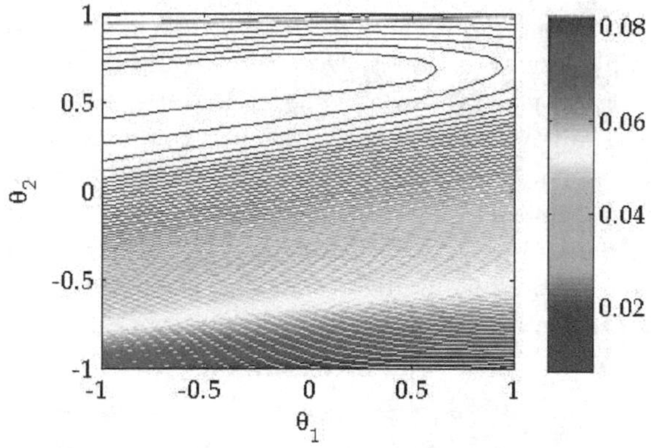

Fig. 7. The contour plot of $\left\|T_{zw}(\overline{K}^{*},\theta)\right\|_{\infty}$ on Ω.

Fig. 8 shows behaviours of μ_k and β_k as a function of iteration number k. This figure shows that μ_k is an upper bound of β_k and monotonically decreasing, which implies that the controller variables $\bar{K}_k$ is updated from a non robust stabilizing controller to a robust H_∞ controller.

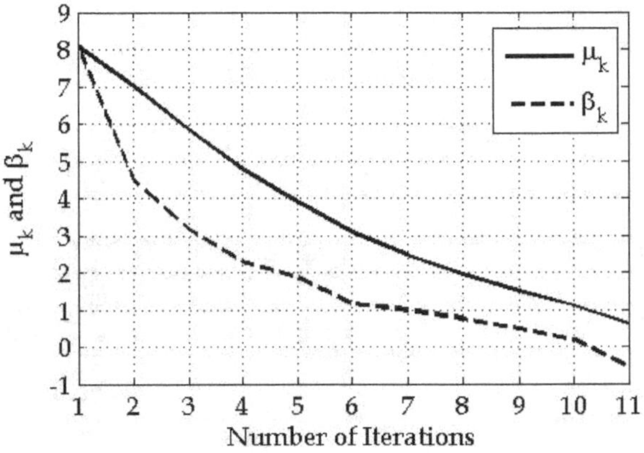

Fig. 8. Behaviours of μ_k and β_k.

6. Conclusions

In this paper, we have considered the robust H_∞ control problem against time invariant uncertainties. Firstly, we show the relaxation method for obtaining a feasible solution of the PDMI problem with multi-convex functions. Secondly, we introduce the axis-shifted system and show that this system can be constructed so as to achieve the H_∞ norm constraint. Next, we propose an iterative approach using the axis-shifted system and multi-convex relaxation method for obtaining the robust H_∞ controllers. The property of our approach is to construct a controller sequence on which the shifted imaginary axis approaches the original position with the H_∞ norm constraint achieved and to be able to choose any controller variables as an initial point. Finally we have given a numerical example which shows the efficiency of our approach.

7. References

Boyd, S.; Ghaoui, L. E.; Feron, E. & Balakrishnan, V. (1994). *Linear matrix inequalities in system and control theory*, Society for Industrial and Applied Mathematics, ISBN 978-0898714852, Philadelphia

Chesi, G.; Garulli, A.; Tesi, A. & Vicino, A. (2005) Polynomially parameter-dependent Lyapunov functions for robust stability of polytopic systems: an LMI approach, *IEEE Trans. Automatic Contr.*, Vol. 50, No. 3, pp. 365-370, ISSN 0018-9286

Gahinet, P.; Apkarian, P. & Chilali, M. (1996) Affine Parameter-Dependent Lyapunov Functions and Real Parametric Uncertainty, *IEEE Trans. Automatic Contr.*, Vol. 41, No. 3, pp. 436-442, ISSN 0018-9286

Geromel, J. C & Korogui R. H. (2006) Analysis and Synthesis of Robust Control Systems Using Linear Parameter Dependent Lyapunov Functions, *IEEE Trans. Automatic Contr.*, Vol. 51, No. 12, pp. 1984-1989, ISSN 0018-9286

Ichihara, H.; Nobuyama, E. & Ishii, T. (2003) Stability analysis and control synthesis with D.C. relaxation of parameterized LMIs, *Proceedings of European Control Conference '03*, 4 pages, Cambridge, UK, September, 2003

Ichihara, H. & Nobuyama, E. (2005) Minimax Polynomial Optimization by using Sum of Squares Relaxation and its Application to Robust Stability Analysis of Parameter-dependent Systems, *Proceedings of American Control Conference*, pp. 3433-3434, Oregon, USA, June, 2005

Iwasaki, T. & Skelton, R. E (1995) The XY-centering algorithm for the dual LMI problem: a new approach to fixed order control design, *International Journal of Control*, Vol. 62, pp. 1257-1272, ISSN 0020-7179

Kami, Y & E. Nobuyama (2004) A Mixed H_∞ / D-stability Controller Design Using an Exterior-point Approach, *Proceedings of Conference of Decision and Control*, pp. 790-795, Bahama, (2004)

Kami, Y.; Tanaka, H. & Nobuyama, E. An Exterior-point Approach to the Robust D-stability Control Problem, *Proceedings of the IEEE Conference of Decision and Control*, pp. 2204-2209, Shanghai, China, December, 2009

Leite, V. J. S. & Peres, P. L. D. (2003) An improved LMI condition for robust D-stability of uncertain polytopic systems, *IEEE Trans. Automatic Contr.*, Vol. 48, No. 3, pp. 500-504, ISSN 0018-9286

Oliveira, R. C. L. F. & Peres, P. L. D. (2005) Stability of polytopes of matrices via affine parameter-dependent Lyapunov functions: Asymptotically exact LMI conditions, *Linear Algebra and Its Applications*, Vol. 405, pp. 209-228, ISSN 0024-3795

Pipeleers, G.; Demeulenaere, B.; Swevers, J. & Vandenberghe, L. (2009) Extended LMI characterizations for stability and performance of linear systems, *System & Control letters*, Vol. 58, No. 7, pp. 510-518, ISSN 0167-6911

Peaucelle, D.; Arzelier, D.; Bachelier, O. & Bernussou, J. (2000) A new robust D-stability condition for real convex polytopic uncertainty, *System & Control letters*, Vol. 40, No. 1, pp.21-30, ISSN 0167-6911

Shaked, U. (2001) Improved LMI representations for the analysis and the design of continuous-time systems with polytopic type uncertainty *IEEE Trans. Automatic Contr.*, Vol. 46, No. 4, pp. 652-656, ISSN 0018-9286

Vanbierviet, J.; Michiels, W. & S. Vandewalle, (2009) Smooth stabilization and optimal H_2 design, *Proceedings of IFAC Workshop on Control Applications of Optimisation*, 6pages, ISBN 978-3-902661-42-5

Xie, W. (2008) An equivalent LMI representation of bounded real lemma for continuous-time systems *Journal of Inequalities and Applications*, art. No. 672905, ISSN 1025-5834

Part 2

Robust Control of Robotic Systems

7

Robust Adaptive Position/Force Control of Mobile Manipulators

Tatsuo Narikiyo and Michihiro Kawanishi
Toyota Technological Institute
Japan

1. Introduction

A mobile manipulator is a class of mobile robot on which the multi-link manipulator is mounted. This system is expected to play an important role both in the production process of factory and in the medical care system of welfare business. To come up to this expectation, a mobile manipulator is required to simultaneously track to both the desired position trajectory and force trajectory. However, these tracking performances are subject to nonholonomic and holonomic constraints. Furthermore, mobile manipulators possess complex and strongly coupled dynamics of mobile bases and manipulators. Then, there are very few studies on the problems of stabilization position/force control for mobile manipulators.

In (Chang & Chen, 2002; Oya et al., 2003; Su et al., 1999), position and force control methods for mobile robot without manipulators have been addressed. Since in these studies holonomic constraints representing the interaction between end-effector of the manipulator and environment have not been considered, those approaches could not be applied to the position/force control problems of the mobile manipulators. In (Dong, 2002; Li et al., 2007; 2008), adaptive and robust control approaches have been applied to the position/force control problems of the mobile manipulators. In these approaches, since the chained form transforms are required, synthesis methods of the control torques and adaptation laws of these approaches are too complicated to apply. On the other hand, we have derived the stabilizing controllers for a class of mobile manipulators(Narikiyo et al., 2008). In (Narikiyo et al., 2008) we have proposed robust adaptive control scheme for the system with dynamic uncertainties and external disturbances directly from the reduced order dynamics subject to both the holonomic and nonholonomic constraints. Furthermore, in (Narikiyo et al., 2009) we have developed this control scheme to control the system with both kinematic and dynamic uncertainties. In these studies usefulness of these control schemes have been demonstrated by numerical examples. However, proof of the closed loop stability has not been completed under an inadequate assumption(Narikiyo et al., 2009).

In this study we complete the proof and relax the assumptions of (Narikiyo et al., 2009). Then we implement these control schemes (Narikiyo et al., 2008; 2009) experimentally and apply to the prototype shown in Fig.1 to demonstrate the effectiveness of these proposed control schemes. It is also guaranteed theoretically that the tracking position and force errors to the desired trajectories are asymptotically converged to zero by the proposed control schemes.

2. Modeling of mobile manipulator

Fig. 1. Mobile manipulator

Fig.1 shows the prototype of mobile manipulator employed in experiments. Let $q_B \in R^n$, $q_M \in R^m$ and $q = [q_B^T \ \ q_M^T]^T \in R^{n+m}$ be the generalized coordinates of the mobile base, manipulator and whole system, respectively. Then the equations of nonholonomic constraints imposed on the mobile base are written as

$$J_B(q_B)\dot{q}_B = 0, \tag{1}$$

where $q_B = [q_{B1}^T \ q_{B2}^T]^T$ and $J_B(q_B) = [J_{B1} \ J_{B2}] \in R^{(n-k)\times n}, det J_{B1} \neq 0$. The equations of holonomic constraints imposed on the manipulator are given by

$$\Phi(q) = 0, \tag{2}$$

where $\Phi(q) \in R^{m-h}$. Let $J_M(q) = \partial\Phi/\partial q \in R^{(m-h)\times(n+m)}, rank J_M = m - h$. Then (2) can be rewritten as

$$J_M(q)\dot{q} = 0. \tag{3}$$

Furthermore, let

$$J_M(q) = \left[\frac{\partial\Phi}{\partial q_B} \ \frac{\partial\Phi}{\partial q_{M1}} \ \frac{\partial\Phi}{\partial q_{M2}}\right] = [J_{M0} \ J_{M1} \ J_{M2}],$$

$q_M = [q_{M1}^T \ q_{M2}^T]^T, q_{M1} \in R^h, q_{M2} \in R^{m-h}$ and $det J_{M2} \neq 0$. Then the equations of motion of the mobile manipulator is written as

$$M(q)\ddot{q} + C(q,\dot{q})\dot{q} + G(q) + d(q,t) = J^T(q)\lambda + B(q)\tau, \tag{4}$$

$$J(q)\dot{q} = 0, \tag{5}$$

where

$$M(q) = \begin{bmatrix} M_{11}(q) & M_{12}(q) \\ M_{21}(q) & M_{22}(q) \end{bmatrix}, G(q) = \begin{bmatrix} G_{11}(q) \\ G_{21}(q) \end{bmatrix}, C(q,\dot{q}) = \begin{bmatrix} C_{11}(q,\dot{q}) \\ C_{21}(q,\dot{q}) \end{bmatrix},$$

$$B(q) = \begin{bmatrix} B_{11}(q_B) & 0 \\ 0 & I_m \end{bmatrix}, d(q,t) = \begin{bmatrix} d_{11}(q,t) \\ d_{21}(q,t) \end{bmatrix},$$

$$J(q) = \begin{bmatrix} J_B & 0 & 0 \\ J_{M0} & J_{M1} & J_{M2} \end{bmatrix}, \tau = \begin{bmatrix} \tau_B \\ \tau_M \end{bmatrix}, \lambda = \begin{bmatrix} \lambda_B \\ \lambda_M \end{bmatrix}.$$

Indices $\{i, j = 1, 2\}$ correspond to decompositions of q_B, q_M. $d(t)$ denotes uncertain disturbance. For $\lambda = [\lambda_B^T \ \lambda_M^T]^T$, $\lambda_B \in R^{n-k}$ denote reaction forces acted on the wheels from the floor and $\lambda_M \in R^{m-h}$ denote reaction forces acted on the end-effector from the environment. The equation (4) has following properties(Slotine & Li, 1991).
Property 1:$\dot{M} - 2C$ is skew symmetric.
Property 2:For any ξ

$$M(q)\dot{\xi} + C(q, \dot{q})\xi + G(q) = Y(q, \dot{q}, \xi, \dot{\xi})p_0,$$

where $p_0 \in R^{s_0}$ denotes unknown parameter vector and $Y \in R^{(n+m)\times s_0}$ is called regressor matrix whose elements consist of known functions.
Let $f_B(q_B) = [f_1(q_B), ..., f_k(q_B)]$ be the bases of null space of $J_B(q_B)$, then there exists $\eta = [\eta_1, ..., \eta_k]^T$ such that (1) is equivalent to

$$\dot{q}_B = f_B(q_B)\eta. \tag{6}$$

Using the suitable selection of $f_B(q_B)$, η can be specified to be equal to forward linear velocity u and angular velocity ω of the mobile base, that is, $k = 2$ and $\eta = [\eta_1 \ \eta_2]^T = [u \ \omega]^T$, without loss of generality. Since η corresponds to angular velocity of wheels ν_B, there exists φ such that $\nu_B = \varphi\eta$. Therefore (6) is rewritten as

$$\dot{q}_B = S_B(q_B)\nu_B, \tag{7}$$

where

$$S_B(q_B) = f_B(q_B)\varphi^{-1} = \begin{bmatrix} -J_{B1}^{-1}J_{B2} \\ I_k \end{bmatrix}.$$

Furthermore, let

$$S(q_B) = Blockdiag\{S_B(q_B), I_m\} \in R^{(n+m)\times(k+m)},$$

$$\nu = \left[\nu_B^T, \dot{q}_{M1}^T, -\left\{J_{M2}^{-1}\left(J_{M0}f_B\varphi^{-1}\nu_B + J_{M1}\dot{q}_{M1}\right)\right\}^T\right]^T \in R^{k+m},$$

then we have

$$\dot{q} = S(q_B)\nu. \tag{8}$$

Differentiating (8), substituting it into (4) and multiplying both sides by $S^T(q_B)$ from the left, we have(Yamamoto & Yun, 1996)

$$M_1(q)\dot{\nu} + C_1(q, \dot{q})\nu + G_1(q) + d_1(q, t) = B_1(q)\tau + \bar{J}_M^T(q)\lambda_M, \tag{9}$$

where

$$\begin{aligned} M_1(q) &= S^T(q_B)M(q)S(q_B), \\ C_1(q, \dot{q}) &= S^T(q_B)\left\{M(q)\dot{S}(q_B) + C(q, \dot{q})S(q_B)\right\}, \\ G_1(q) &= S^T(q_B)G(q), d_1(q, t) = S^T(q_B)d(q, t), \\ B_1(q) &= S^T(q_B)B(q), \bar{J}_M = \left[J_{M0}f_B\varphi^{-1} \ J_{M1} \ J_{M2}\right]. \end{aligned}$$

It is well known that Property 1 and 2 are invariant under changes of coordinates(Murray et al., 1993). Then (9) has following properties similarly to (4).

Property 3:$\dot{M}_1 - 2C_1$ is skew-symmetric.
Property 4:For any $\bar{\xi}$

$$M_1(q)\dot{\bar{\xi}} + C_1(q,\dot{q})\bar{\xi} + G_1(q) = Y_1(q,\dot{q},\bar{\xi},\dot{\bar{\xi}})p_1,$$

where $p_1 \in R^{s_1}$ denotes unknown parameter vector and $Y_1 \in R^{(k+m)\times s_1}$ is called the regressor matrix whose elements consist of known functions. Furthermore, kinematic uncertainties of the system give the following properties(Cheah et al., 2003; Fukao et al., 2000).
Property 5:$S_B(q_B)v_B$ in (7) can be written as

$$S_B(q_B)v_B = \sum_{i=1}^{k}\left(\sigma_{i0}(q_B) + \sum_{j=1}^{h_i}\theta_{ij}\sigma_{ij}(q_B)\right)v_{Bi}.$$

Property 6:$\bar{J}_M^T(q)\lambda_M$ in (9) can be written as

$$\bar{J}_M^T(q)\lambda_M = Z_1(q,\lambda_M)\psi,$$

where θ_{ij} is unknown parameter which consists of unknown parameters of mobile base, and σ_{ij} is known functions which consists of the coordinate q_B, $(i = 1,...,k,\ j = 1,...,h_i)$. $\psi \in R^c$ is unknown parameter vector of the whole system and $Z_1(q,\lambda_M) \in R^{(k+m)\times c}$ is known matrix function of the position/force coordinate q and λ_M , respectively.
Following assumptions are required to synthesize the control scheme.
Assump.1:There are no unknown parameters in $B_1(q)$ and $detB_1(q) \neq 0$ for all q. d_1 and its derivative are bounded and $||d_1|| \leq D$. Where D is unknown.
Assump.2:$J_B, J_M, J_{B1}^{-1}, J_{M2}^{-1} \in L_\infty$ and these matrices are all continuously differentiable with respect to q and kinematic parameters, and these derivatives are bounded.

3. Hybrid position/force control scheme

Let q^* be the desired position trajectory, then there exist desired velocity input $v^* = [v_1^*,...,v_k^*,v_M^{*T}]^T$ such that

$$\dot{q}^* = S(q_B^*)v^*. \tag{10}$$

Since $[v_1^*,...,v_k^*]^T$ are desired velocities of the mobile base, we can set $[v_1^*\ \ v_2^*]^T = \varphi[u^*\ \ \omega^*]^T$ and $k = 2$ without loss of generality. Where desired forward linear velocity u^* and desired angular velocity ω^* of the mobile base. Using the relations such as $v_{M1}^* = \dot{q}_{M1}^*$ and $v_{M2}^* = \dot{q}_{M2}^*$, $v_{M2}^*(= \dot{q}_{M2}^*)$ can be determined by v_{M1}^* and u^*,ω^*. For these values following assumptions are required.
Assump.3:q^*, $u^*,\omega^*,\dot{q}^*$, $\dot{u}^*,\dot{\omega}^*,\ddot{q}^*,\ddot{u}^*,\ddot{\omega}^*$ and $\dddot{q}^*$ are bounded globally. And $u^* \neq 0$.

3.1 Reference robot

To specify error dynamics of trajectory tracking system we introduce the reference robot shown in Fig.1. Trajectory error e_B for base coordinates $q_B = [x\ \ y\ \ \phi]^T$, trajectory error e_{M1} for manipulator coordinates q_{M1} and trajectory error $\tilde{\lambda}_M$ for constrained forces are given

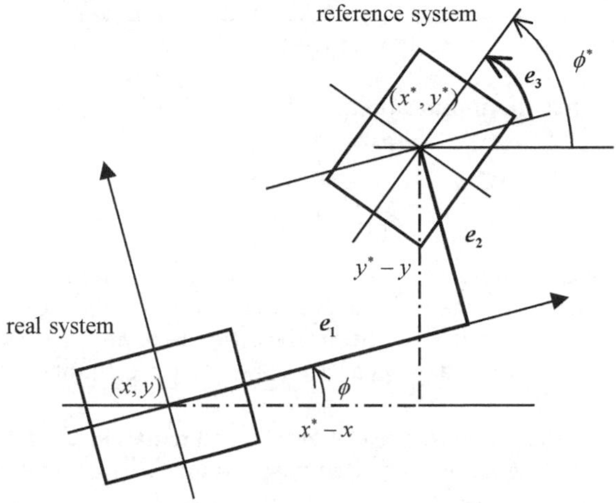

Fig. 2. Reference robot and tracking errors

by

$$e_B = \begin{bmatrix} e_1 \\ e_2 \\ e_3 \end{bmatrix} = \begin{bmatrix} (x^* - x)\cos\phi + (y^* - y)\sin\phi \\ -(x^* - x)\sin\phi + (y^* - y)\cos\phi \\ \phi^* - \phi \end{bmatrix}$$
$$e_{M1} = q^*_{M1} - q_{M1}, \ \tilde{\lambda}_M = \lambda_M - \lambda^*_M \tag{11}$$

Using the results in (Fukao et al., 2000), desired velocity inputs $v_c = [v_{Bc}^T \ v_{M1c}^T \ v_{M2c}^T]^T$ for trajectory tracking are written as the following.

$$\begin{aligned} v_{Bc} &= \varphi u_{Bc}, \ u_{Bc} = \begin{bmatrix} u_c \\ \omega_c \end{bmatrix} \\ &= \begin{bmatrix} u^* \cos e_3 + K_1 e_1 \\ \omega^* + u^* K_2 e_2 + K_3 \sin e_3 \end{bmatrix} \\ v_{M1c} &= \dot{q}^*_{M1} + K_{M1} e_{M1} \\ v_{M2c} &= -J_{M2}^{-1}\left(J_{M0} f_B \varphi^{-1} v_{Bc} + J_{M1} v_{M1c}\right) \end{aligned} \tag{12}$$

Where $K_i > 0, i = 1, 2, 3$ and K_{M1} are arbitrarily assigned.
For the system (7) the following Lemma is shown in (Fukao et al., 2000).

Lemma 1. *If $v_B = v_{Bc}$ is applied to (7), then the first derivatives of trajectory error coordinates are given by the following equations.*

$$\begin{aligned} \dot{e}_1 &= -K_1 e_1 + (\omega^* + u^* K_2 e_2 + K_3 \sin e_3) e_2 \\ \dot{e}_2 &= -(\omega^* + u^* K_2 e_2 + K_3 \sin e_3) e_1 + u^* \sin e_3 \\ \dot{e}_3 &= -u^* K_2 e_2 - K_3 \sin e_3 \end{aligned} \tag{13}$$

Then, $\lim_{t\to\infty} e_B = 0$.

However, since Lemma1 has not considered kinematic parameter uncertainties, ν_{Bc} cannot be applied to our problem. Therefore, we give the following assumption similar manner to (Fukao et al., 2000).

Assump.4:There exist velocity inputs and adaptive laws:

$$\nu_B = \nu_{Bc}(q_B, q_B^*, \hat{a})$$

$$\dot{\hat{a}}_i = T_i(q_B, q_B^*, \hat{a}) \tag{14}$$

such that the closed loop system of (7) is stable at q_B^*. Furthermore, there exists Lyapunov function $V_1(q_B, q_B^*, \tilde{a})$ such that the time derivative of V_1 along the closed loop system of (7) with (14) is negative semi-definite. Where $\hat{a}$ is the estimate of an unknown parameter vector $a = [a_1, ..., a_k]^T$, which is composed of θ_{ij}, and $\tilde{a} = \hat{a} - a$ is the estimated error.

3.2 Control laws for the system with both kinematic and dynamic uncertainties

In this section we propose the robust and adaptive position/force control scheme of the mobile manipulators with both the kinematic and dynamic uncertainties. To begin with, we introduce filter coordinates in a similar way to (Yuan, 1997) as follows. For any constant α_1 we set $\beta_M \in R^m$ as

$$\dot{\beta}_M = -\alpha_1 \beta_M - \alpha_1 \left[\hat{\bar{J}}_{M1}\ \hat{\bar{J}}_{M2}\right]^T \tilde{\lambda}_M, \tag{15}$$

where $\hat{\bar{J}}_M(q, \hat{\psi})$ denotes the Jacobian matrix which is replaced ψ with estimate $\hat{\psi}$ and

$$\hat{\bar{J}}_M(q, \hat{\psi}) = \left[\hat{J}_{M0}(q, \hat{\psi}) f_B(q_B) \hat{\varphi}^{-1}\ \hat{J}_{M1}(q, \hat{\psi})\ \hat{J}_{M2}(q, \hat{\psi})\right]$$

$$= \left[\hat{\bar{J}}_{M0}(q, \hat{\psi})\ \hat{\bar{J}}_{M1}(q, \hat{\psi})\ \hat{\bar{J}}_{M2}(q, \hat{\psi})\right].$$

Secondly, we set

$$\tilde{\nu} = \nu - \nu_c, \beta = [0_k^T\ \beta_M^T]^T, \tilde{\nu} = R\tilde{s}, \delta = \tilde{\nu} + \beta,$$

$$\chi = \nu_c - \beta, \tilde{s} = [\tilde{\nu}_B^T\ \tilde{\nu}_{M1}^T]^T, e = [e_B^T\ e_M^T]^T, \tag{16}$$

where

$$R = \begin{bmatrix} I_k & 0 \\ 0 & I_l \\ -\hat{\bar{J}}_{M2}^{-1}\hat{\bar{J}}_{M0} & -\hat{\bar{J}}_{M2}^{-1}\hat{\bar{J}}_{M1} \end{bmatrix}.$$

Finally we introduce variable $\rho(t)$ which satisfies following conditions (Li et al., 2008).

$$(1)\quad \rho(t) > 0,\ \ \forall t \in [0, \infty)$$

$$(2)\quad \lim_{t \to \infty} \rho(t) = 0$$

$$(3)\quad \lim_{t \to \infty} \int_0^t \rho(\tau) d\tau = \rho_0 < \infty$$

Under assumptions from Assump.1 to Assump.4, following theorem is derived.

Theorem 1. *Applying the following control law and adaptive laws to the mobile manipulator (4) and (5),*

$$\tau = B_1^{-1}\left[-K_d\delta - F + Y_1(q,\dot{q},\chi,\dot{\chi})\hat{p}_1 - \left(\frac{\partial V_1}{\partial q}\hat{S}(q_B,\hat{\theta})\right)^T\right.$$
$$\left.+\alpha_2\hat{\bar{J}}_M^T(q,\hat{\psi}\tilde{\lambda}_M) - Z_1(q,\lambda_M)\hat{\psi}\right]$$
$$\dot{\hat{p}}_1 = -\Gamma_1 Y_1^T(q,\dot{q},\chi,\dot{\chi})\delta \tag{17}$$
$$\dot{\hat{\psi}} = \Gamma_2 Z_1^T(q,\lambda_M)\delta$$
$$\dot{\hat{a}}_i = T_i(q_B,q_B^*,\hat{a})$$
$$\dot{\hat{\theta}}_i = \Lambda_i\left(\frac{\partial V_1}{\partial q}\sigma_i\right)^T\tilde{v}_i$$
$$\dot{\hat{D}} = \gamma\|\delta\|$$

then all internal signals are bounded and

$$\lim_{t\to\infty} e = 0, \lim_{t\to\infty}\tilde{\lambda}_M = 0, \tag{18}$$

where $\hat{\theta}_i$ is estimate of θ_i, $\sigma_i = [\sigma_{i1},\cdots,\sigma_{ih_i}], 1 \le i \le k$, and $K_d, \Gamma_1, \Gamma_2, \Lambda_i$ are positive definite matrix with appropriate dimensions, α_2 is arbitrary constant and

$$F(t) = \frac{\delta\hat{D}^2}{\|\delta\|\hat{D} + \rho(t)}.$$

Letting parameter estimation errors be $\tilde{p} = \hat{p} - p$ and $\tilde{D} = \hat{D} - D$, closed loop system can be written as follows.

$$M_1\dot{\delta} = -(C_1 + K_d)\delta + Y_1(q,\dot{q},\chi,\dot{\chi})\tilde{p}_1 - \left(\frac{\partial V_1}{\partial q}\hat{S}(q_B,\hat{\theta})\right)^T$$
$$+\alpha_2\hat{\bar{J}}_M^T\tilde{\lambda}_M - Z_1\tilde{\psi} - (F + d_1) \tag{19}$$

Proof of this theorem is shown by the following Lemmas.

Lemma 2. *For the closed loop system, $\delta, \beta \in L_2$, and $\tilde{v}, \hat{p}, e_{M1}, \dot{e}_{M1}, v_c, \chi, q, \dot{q}, \hat{\theta}, \hat{\psi}, \hat{a}, \hat{D} \in L_\infty$.*

(Proof)

We set V_2 as

$$V_2 = V_1 + \frac{1}{2}\delta^T M_1\delta + \frac{1}{2}\alpha_2\alpha_1^{-1}\beta^T\beta + \frac{1}{2}\tilde{p}_1^T\Gamma^{-1}\tilde{p}_1$$
$$+\frac{1}{2}\sum_{i=1}^{k}\tilde{\theta}_i^T\Lambda_i^{-1}\tilde{\theta}_i + \frac{1}{2}\tilde{\psi}^T\Gamma_2^{-1}\tilde{\psi} + \frac{1}{2\gamma}\tilde{D}^2. \tag{20}$$

Differentiating V_2 along (19), we have

$$\dot{V}_2 = \frac{\partial V_1}{\partial q}S(q_B)(v_c + \tilde{v}) + \frac{\partial V_1}{\partial q^*}S(q_B^*)v^* + \sum_{i=1}^{g}\frac{\partial V_1}{\partial \hat{a}_i}T_i - \delta^T K_d\delta$$
$$-\frac{\partial V_1}{\partial q}\hat{S}(q_B)\tilde{v} - \alpha_2\beta^T\beta + \sum_{i=1}^{k}\tilde{\theta}_i^T\Lambda_i^{-1}\dot{\hat{\theta}}_i - \delta^T(F + d_1) + \frac{\tilde{D}\dot{\hat{D}}}{\gamma}.$$

In this computation, we used the relations $\frac{\partial V_1}{\partial q}\hat{S}\beta = 0$ and:

$$\hat{\bar{J}}_M R = \left[\hat{\bar{J}}_{M0}\ \hat{\bar{J}}_{M1}\ \hat{\bar{J}}_{M2}\right]\begin{bmatrix} I_k & 0 \\ 0 & I_l \\ -\hat{\bar{J}}_{M2}^{-1}\hat{\bar{J}}_{M0} & -\hat{\bar{J}}_{M2}^{-1}\hat{\bar{J}}_{M1} \end{bmatrix} = \left[0_{(m-l)\times k}\ 0_{(m-l)\times l}\right].$$

Furthermore, by using the relation

$$\frac{\partial V_1}{\partial q}\tilde{S}(q_B)\tilde{\nu} = \frac{\partial V_1}{\partial q}(\hat{S}-S)\tilde{\nu} = \frac{\partial V_1}{\partial q}\left[\sum_{i=1}^{k}\left(\sigma_{i0}(q_B) + \sum_{j=1}^{l_i}\hat{\theta}_{ij}\sigma_{ij}(q_B)\right) - \sum_{i=1}^{k}\left(\sigma_{i0}(q_B) + \sum_{j=1}^{l_i}\theta_{ij}\sigma_{ij}(q_B)\right)\right]\nu_{Bi} = \frac{\partial V_1}{\partial q}\sum_{i=1}^{k}\sigma_i\tilde{\theta}_i\tilde{\nu}_i$$

we have

$$\dot{V}_2 = \dot{V}_1^{\nu_B=\nu_{BC}} - \delta^T K_d\delta - \alpha_2\beta^T\beta - \delta^T(F+d_1) + \frac{\tilde{D}\dot{\hat{D}}}{\gamma}, \tag{21}$$

where

$$\dot{V}_1^{\nu_B=\nu_{BC}} = \frac{\partial V_1}{\partial q}S(q_B)\nu_c + \frac{\partial V_1}{\partial q^*}S(q_B^*)\nu^* + \sum_{i=1}^{g}\frac{\partial V_1}{\partial \hat{a}_i}T_i \leq 0.$$

Last inequality sign $\leq$ is given by Assump.4. From the definition of $F(t)$ and adaptive law of $\hat{D}$ following inequality is derived.

$$\begin{aligned} -\delta^T(F+d_1) + \frac{\tilde{D}\dot{\hat{D}}}{\gamma} &= -\delta^T\frac{\delta\hat{D}^2}{\|\delta\|\hat{D}+\rho(t)} - \delta^T d_1 + \frac{\hat{D}\dot{\hat{D}}}{\gamma} - \frac{D\dot{\hat{D}}}{\gamma} \\ &< -\frac{\|\delta\|^2\hat{D}^2}{\|\delta\|\hat{D}+\rho(t)} + \|\delta\|D + \frac{\hat{D}\dot{\hat{D}}}{\gamma} - \frac{D\dot{\hat{D}}}{\gamma} \\ &= -\frac{\|\delta\|^2\hat{D}^2}{\|\delta\|\hat{D}+\rho(t)} + \frac{\hat{D}(\gamma\|\delta\|)}{\gamma} + \frac{D}{\gamma}\left(\gamma\|\delta\| - \dot{\hat{D}}\right) \\ &= \frac{\rho(t)\|\delta\|\hat{D}}{\|\delta\|\hat{D}+\rho(t)} < \rho(t) \end{aligned}$$

These inequalities lead the right hand of (32) to

$$\dot{V}_2 < -\delta^T K_d\delta - \alpha_2\beta^T\beta + \rho(t). \tag{22}$$

Integrating both sides of this inequality and using definition of $\rho(t)$, we have

$$V_2(t) - V_2(0) < -\int_0^t \delta^T K_d\delta d\tau - \alpha_2\int_0^t \beta^T\beta d\tau + \rho_0 < \infty. \tag{23}$$

This shows

$$V_2(t) < V_2(0) + \rho_0 < \infty. \tag{24}$$

Therefore, $V_2(t)$ is bounded, that is, $q_B, \tilde{a}, \delta, \beta, \tilde{p}_1, \tilde{D}, \tilde{\theta}, \tilde{\psi} \in L_\infty$, and $\delta, \beta \in L_2$. From definition of variable $\tilde{v}$, we have $\tilde{v} \in L_\infty$. Since unknown parameters are constant and bounded, $\hat{p}, \hat{D}, \hat{a}, \hat{\theta}, \hat{\psi} \in L_\infty$. From (12) and definitions of v and v_c, $\tilde{v}_{M1} = -\dot{e}_{M1} - K_{M1}e_{M1} \in L_\infty$. Then $e_{M1}, \dot{e}_{M1} \in L_\infty$. From (12), Assump.3 and Assump.4, we have $v_c, \chi \in L_\infty$. From Assump.2 and Assump.3, we have $q_M, \dot{q}_M \in L_\infty$. Similarly from $\tilde{v}, v_c \in L_\infty$ and Assump.2, we have $\dot{q}_B, \dot{e}_B \in L_\infty$. Therefore $q, \dot{q} \in L_\infty$.

Lemma 3. *Let* $\hat{M}_1 = M_1(\hat{p}_1)$ *and*

$$\Delta(\psi, \hat{\psi}) = \bar{J}_M^T \left(\hat{\bar{J}}_M \hat{\bar{J}}_M^T \right)^{-1} \hat{\bar{J}}_M + \left(\hat{\bar{J}}_M^T \right)^\dagger - I_{k+m},$$

where $\left(\hat{\bar{J}}_M^T \right)^\dagger$ *is left annihilator of* $\hat{\bar{J}}_M^T$. *If there exist* α_1 *and* α_2 *such that*

$$\left\{ \alpha_1 \hat{M}_1 Blockdiag(0_k, I_m) + \alpha_2 I_{k+m} + \Delta(\psi, \hat{\psi}) \right\}$$

is nonsingular, then $\tilde{\lambda}_M \in L_\infty$.

(Proof)

Substituting (15) and (16) into (19), we have

$$\begin{aligned}
&\left\{ \alpha_1 \hat{M}_1 Blockdiag(0_k, I_m) + \alpha_2 I_{k+m} + \Delta(\psi, \hat{\psi}) \right\} \hat{\bar{J}}_M^T \tilde{\lambda}_M \\
&= M_1(R\dot{\tilde{s}} + \dot{R}\tilde{s}) + (C_1 + K_d)\delta - Y_1(q, \dot{q}, \chi, \dot{\chi} + \dot{\beta})\tilde{p}_1 - \alpha_1 \hat{M}_1 \beta \\
&+ \left(\frac{\partial V_1}{\partial q} \hat{S}(q_B, \hat{\theta}) \right)^T + \Delta(\psi, \hat{\psi}) \hat{\bar{J}}_M^T \lambda_M^* + (F + d_1).
\end{aligned} \tag{25}$$

In this calculation, following relations are used.

$$\begin{aligned}
Y_1(q, \dot{q}, \chi, \dot{\chi})\tilde{p}_1 &= Y_1(q, \dot{q}, \chi, \dot{\chi} + \dot{\beta})\tilde{p}_1 - \left\{ \hat{M}_1(q) - M_1(q) \right\} \dot{\beta} \\
Z_1 \tilde{\psi} &= \left(\hat{\bar{J}}_M^T - \bar{J}_M^T \right) \tilde{\lambda}_M + \left(\hat{\bar{J}}_M^T - \bar{J}_M^T \right) \lambda_M^* \\
&= -\Delta(\psi, \hat{\psi}) \hat{\bar{J}}_M^T \tilde{\lambda}_M - \Delta(\psi, \hat{\psi}) \hat{\bar{J}}_M^T \lambda_M^*
\end{aligned}$$

Multiplying (25) by $\hat{\bar{J}}_M M_1^{-1}$ from left, we have

$$\begin{aligned}
&\hat{\bar{J}}_M M_1^{-1} \left\{ \alpha_1 \hat{M}_1 Blockdiag(0_k, I_m) + \alpha_2 I_{k+m} + \Delta(\psi, \hat{\psi}) \right\} \\
&\times \hat{\bar{J}}_M^T \tilde{\lambda}_M = \hat{\bar{J}}_M \left[\dot{R}\tilde{s} + M_1^{-1} \{ (C_1 + K_d)\delta \right. \\
&- Y_1(q, \dot{q}, \chi, \dot{\chi} + \dot{\beta})\tilde{p}_1 + \alpha_1 \hat{M}_1 \beta \\
&\left. + \left(\frac{\partial V_1}{\partial q} \hat{S}(q_B, \hat{\theta}) \right)^T + \Delta(\psi, \hat{\psi}) \hat{\bar{J}}_M^T \lambda_M^* + (F + d_1) \right\} \Bigg].
\end{aligned} \tag{26}$$

By definition and Assump.3 $\dot{\nu}_c \in L_\infty$ and $\dot{\chi} + \dot{\beta} = \dot{\nu}_c$, we have

$$Y_1(q, \dot{q}, \chi, \dot{\chi} + \dot{\beta}) \in L_\infty.$$

Therefore, if α_1 and α_2 are selected such that

$$\{\alpha_1 \hat{M}_1 Blockdiag(0_k, I_m) + \alpha_2 I_{k+m} + \Delta(\psi, \hat{\psi})\}$$

is nonsingular, then $\tilde{\lambda}_M \in L_\infty$.

Lemma 4. $Z_1, \dot{\nu}_c, \dot{\beta}, \dot{\chi}, Y_1(q, \dot{q}, \chi, \dot{\chi}), F(t) \in L_\infty$.

(Proof)

$Z_1 \in L_\infty$ is derived from Lemma 2 and 3. $\dot{\nu}_c \in L_\infty$ is derived from definition of ν_c, Assump.2 and adaptive laws of $\hat{a}, \hat{\psi}$. $\dot{\beta} \in L_\infty$ is derived directly from (15). Then $\dot{\chi} = \dot{\nu}_c - \dot{\beta} \in L_\infty$. These relations imply $Y_1(q, \dot{q}, \chi, \dot{\chi}) \in L_\infty$. And finally,

$$\|F(t)\| = \|\frac{\delta \hat{D}^2}{\|\delta\| \hat{D} + \rho(t)}\| < \|\frac{\delta \hat{D}^2}{\|\delta\| \hat{D}}\| = \hat{D} \in L_\infty.$$

Lemma 5.

$$\lim_{t \to \infty} e = 0$$

(Proof)

From definitions and Lemma 4, we have $\dot{\delta} \in L_\infty$. Since $\delta, \beta \in L_2$, by Barbalatat's Lemma(Kristic et al., 1995; Slotine & Li, 1991) we have $\lim_{t\to\infty} \delta = 0$ and $\lim_{t\to\infty} \beta = 0$. This means $\lim_{t\to\infty} \tilde{\nu} = 0$. By Lemma1 $\lim_{t\to\infty} e_B = 0$. Since $\lim_{t\to\infty} \tilde{\nu} = 0$ and

$$\tilde{\nu}_{M1} = -\dot{e}_{M1} - K_{M1} e_{M1},$$

$\lim_{t\to\infty} e_{M1} = 0$. Then $\lim_{t\to\infty} e = 0$.
From above 5 Lemmas and next Lemma the proof of Theorem 1 is completed.

Lemma 6.

$$\lim_{t \to \infty} \lambda_M = \lambda_M^*$$

(Proof)

From (19), Lemma 3 and Lemma 4, $\dot{\delta} \in L_\infty$. And from definitions, $\dot{\beta} \in L_\infty, \dot{\tilde{\nu}} \in L_\infty$. Then $\ddot{q} \in L_\infty, \ddot{R}$ and $\ddot{\nu}_c \in L_\infty$. These lead us to $\dot{Y}_1(q, \dot{q}, \chi, \dot{\chi} + \dot{\beta}) \in L_\infty$.

Differentiating both sides of (26), we have $\dot{\tilde{\lambda}}_M \in L_\infty$, that is $\dot{\lambda}_M \in L_\infty$.Then, by above Lemmas and definition of β_M, $\ddot{\beta}_M \in L_\infty$. This shows that $\dot{\beta}_M$ is uniformly continuous. And $\beta_M \to 0$ is shown in previous Lemma. Therefore from Barbalat's Lemma(Kristic et al., 1995; Slotine & Li, 1991) we have $\lim_{t\to\infty} \dot{\beta}_M = 0$. Since $[\hat{\bar{J}}_{M1}\ \hat{\bar{J}}_{M2}]^T$ in (15) is full column rank, we have

$$\lim_{t \to \infty} \tilde{\lambda}_M = 0.$$

3.3 Control laws for the system only with the dynamic uncertainties

In this section we propose the robust and adaptive position/force control scheme of the mobile manipulators with only the dynamic uncertainties. Since kinetic parameters are known, the Jacobian matrix $\hat{\bar{J}}_M(q,\hat{\psi})$ has no uncertainties. Therefore (15) and $\hat{R}$ are replaced with

$$\dot{\beta}_M = -\alpha_1\beta_M - \alpha_1\left[J_{M1}\ J_{M2}\right]^T\tilde{\lambda}_M, \tag{27}$$

$$R = \begin{bmatrix} I_k & 0 \\ 0 & I_l \\ -J_{M2}^{-1}J_{M0}f_B\varphi^{-1} & -J_{M2}^{-1}J_{M1} \end{bmatrix}.$$

Then the robust adaptive control scheme proposed in (Narikiyo et al., 2008) can be applied to the system with dynamic uncertainties. This control scheme is shown in the following theorem.

Theorem 2. *Let the kinematic parameters be known. Applying the following control law and adaptive laws to the mobile manipulator (4) and (5),*

$$\begin{aligned} \tau &= B_1^{-1}[-K_d\delta - F + Y_1(q,\dot{q},\chi,\dot{\chi})\hat{p} \\ &\quad -\left(\frac{\partial V_1}{\partial q}S(q_B)\right)^T + \bar{J}_M^T(-\lambda_M^* + \alpha_2\tilde{\lambda}_M)] \\ \dot{\hat{p}} &= -\Gamma Y_1^T(q,\dot{q},\chi,\dot{\chi})\delta \\ \dot{\hat{D}} &= \gamma\|\delta\| \end{aligned} \tag{28}$$

then internal signals are bounded and

$$\lim_{t\to\infty} e = 0,\ \lim_{t\to\infty}\tilde{\lambda}_M = 0, \tag{29}$$

where

$$F(t) = \frac{\delta\hat{D}^2}{\|\delta\|\hat{D} + \rho(t)}.$$

Substituting (28) into (4), we can obtain the following closed loop system.

$$\begin{aligned} M_1\dot{\delta} &= -(C_1 + K_d)\delta + Y_1(q,\dot{q},\chi,\dot{\chi})\tilde{p} - \left(\frac{\partial V_1}{\partial q}S(q_B)\right)^T \\ &\quad +(1+\alpha_2)\bar{J}_M^T\tilde{\lambda}_M - (F + d_1) \\ \dot{\hat{p}} &= -\Gamma Y_1(q,\dot{q},\chi,\dot{\chi})\delta \\ \dot{\hat{D}} &= \gamma\|\delta\| \\ \dot{\beta}_M &= -\alpha_1\beta_M - \alpha_1[J_{M1}\ \ J_{M2}]^T\tilde{\lambda}_M \end{aligned} \tag{30}$$

Proof of the theorem 2 is completed by the following Lemmas as similar to the proof of Theorem 1.

Lemma 7. *For the closed loop system, $\delta, \beta \in L_2, \tilde{v}, R\tilde{s}, \hat{p}, e_{M1}, \dot{e}_{M1}, v_c, \chi, q, \dot{q} \in L_\infty$ and*

$$\lim_{t\to\infty} e_1 = 0,\ \lim_{t\to\infty} e_3 = 0.$$

(Proof)
We set V_2 as

$$V_2 = V_1 + \frac{1}{2}\delta^T M_1 \delta + \frac{1+\alpha_2}{2\alpha_1}\beta^T\beta + \frac{1}{2}\tilde{p}^T\Gamma^{-1}\tilde{p} + \frac{1}{2\gamma}\tilde{D}^2. \tag{31}$$

Differentiating V_2 along (30), we have

$$\begin{aligned}\dot{V}_2 &= \frac{\partial V_1}{\partial q}S(q_B)(\nu_c+\tilde{\nu}) + \frac{\partial V_1}{\partial q^*}S(q_B^*)\nu^* \\ &-\delta^T K_d\delta - (1+\alpha_2)\beta^T\beta - \delta^T S^T(q_B)\left(\frac{\partial V_1}{\partial q}\right)^T \\ &+(1+\alpha_2)\tilde{\lambda}_M \bar{J}_M R\tilde{s} - \delta^T(F+d_1).\end{aligned}$$

Furthermore, by using definitions of $V_1 = V_1(q_B, q_B^*)$ and δ,

$$\frac{\partial V_1}{\partial q}S(q_B)\tilde{\nu} = \frac{\partial V_1}{\partial q}S(q_B)\delta$$

is derived and by using the relation

$$\begin{aligned}\bar{J}_M R &= \begin{bmatrix} J_{M0}f_B\varphi^{-1} & J_{M1} & J_{M2}\end{bmatrix}\begin{bmatrix} I_k & 0 \\ 0 & I_l \\ -J_{M2}^{-1}J_{M0}f_B\varphi^{-1} & -J_{M2}^{-1}J_{M1}\end{bmatrix} \\ &= \begin{bmatrix} 0_{(m-l)\times k} & 0_{(m-l)\times l}\end{bmatrix},\end{aligned}$$

we have

$$\dot{V}_2 = -K_1 e_1^2 - \frac{K_3}{K_2}\sin^2 e_3 - \delta^T K_d \delta - (1+\alpha_2)\beta^T\beta - \delta^T(F+d_1). \tag{32}$$

$F(t)$ and adaptive laws lead the right hand of (32) to

$$\dot{V}_2 < -K_1 e_1^2 - \frac{K_3}{K_2}\sin^2 e_3 - \delta^T K_d\delta - (1+\alpha_2)\beta^T\beta + \rho(t). \tag{33}$$

Integrating both side of this inequality and using definition of $\rho(t)$, we have

$$\begin{aligned}V_2(t) - V_2(0) &< -K_1\int_0^t e_1^2 d\tau - \frac{K_3}{K_2}\int_0^t \sin^2 e_3 d\tau \\ &- \int_0^t \delta^T K_d \delta d\tau - (1+\alpha_2)\int_0^t \beta^T\beta d\tau + a < \infty.\end{aligned} \tag{34}$$

This shows

$$V_2(t) < V_2(0) + a < \infty. \tag{35}$$

Therefore, $V_2(t)$ is bounded, that is, $e_1, e_2, \delta, \beta, \tilde{p}, \tilde{D} \in L_\infty$, and $e_1, \sin e_3, \delta, \beta \in L_2$. From definitions of variables $\tilde{\nu}$, we have $R\tilde{s}, \hat{p}, \hat{D} \in L_\infty$. From (12) and definitions of ν and ν_c,

$\tilde{v}_{M1} = -\dot{e}_{M1} - K_{M1}e_{M1} \in L_\infty$. Then $e_{M1}, \dot{e}_{M1} \in L_\infty$. Furthermore, from (12) and Assump.3, we have $v_c, \chi \in L_\infty$ and $e_{M1}, \dot{e}_{M1} \in L_\infty$. From Assump.2, we have $q_M, \dot{q}_M \in L_\infty$. Similarly from $\tilde{v}, v_c \in L_\infty$ and Assump.2, we have $\dot{q}_B, \dot{e}_B \in L_\infty$. Therefore $q, \dot{q} \in L_\infty$. Finally, from $e_1, \sin e_3 \in L_2$ and Barbalat's Lemma(Slotine & Li, 1991), we have

$$\lim_{t\to\infty} e_1 = 0, \lim_{t\to\infty} e_3 = 0.$$

Lemma 8. *Let $\hat{M}_1 = M_1(\hat{p})$. If there exist α_1, α_2 such that*

$$\{\alpha_1 \hat{M}_1 Blockdiag(0_k, I_m) + (1+\alpha_2) I_{k+m}\}$$

is nonsingular, then $\tilde{\lambda}_M \in L_\infty$.

(Proof)

From (30) we have

$$(1+\alpha_2)\bar{J}_M^T \tilde{\lambda}_M = M_1(R\dot{\tilde{s}} + \dot{R}\tilde{s}) + M_1\dot{\beta} + (C_1 + K_d)\delta$$
$$-Y_1(q, \dot{q}, \chi, \dot{\chi})\tilde{p} + (F + d_1).$$

By using the relation

$$Y_1(q, \dot{q}, \chi, \dot{\chi})\tilde{p} = Y_1(q, \dot{q}, \chi, \dot{\chi} + \dot{\beta})\tilde{p}$$
$$-\{\hat{M}_1(q) - M_1(q)\}\dot{\beta},$$

above equation is converted into

$$\{\alpha_1 \hat{M}_1 Blockdiag(0_k, I_m) + (1+\alpha_2) I_{k+m}\}\bar{J}_M^T \tilde{\lambda}_M$$
$$= M_1(R\dot{\tilde{s}} + \dot{R}\tilde{s}) + (C_1 + K_d)\delta$$
$$-Y_1(q, \dot{q}, \chi, \dot{\chi} + \dot{\beta})\tilde{p} - \alpha_1 \hat{M}_1 \beta + (F + d_1). \tag{36}$$

Multiplying (36) by $\bar{J}_M M_1^{-1}$ from left, we have

$$\bar{J}_M M_1^{-1}\{\alpha_1 \hat{M}_1 Blockdiag(0_k, I_m) + (1+\alpha_2) I_{k+m}\}$$
$$\times \bar{J}_M^T \tilde{\lambda}_M = \bar{J}_M \left[\dot{R}\tilde{s} + M_1^{-1}\{(C_1 + K_d)\delta\right.$$
$$\left.-Y_1(q, \dot{q}, \chi, \dot{\chi} + \dot{\beta})\tilde{p} - \alpha_1 \hat{M}_1 \beta + (F + d_1)\}\right]. \tag{37}$$

Furthermore, since (12) and Assump.3 lead to $\dot{v}_c \in L_\infty$ and $\dot{\chi} + \dot{\beta} = \dot{v}_c$, we have

$$Y_1(q, \dot{q}, \chi, \dot{\chi} + \dot{\beta}) \in L_\infty.$$

Therefore, if $\alpha_1 and \alpha_2$ are selected such that

$$\{\alpha_1 \hat{M}_1 Blockdiag(0_k, I_m) + (1+\alpha_2) I_{k+m}\}$$

is nonsingular, then $\tilde{\lambda}_M \in L_\infty$.

Since from these Lemmas and Barbalat's Lemma(Slotine & Li, 1991) we have

$$\lim_{t\to\infty} e = 0, \quad \lim_{t\to\infty} \tilde{\lambda}_M = 0,$$

proof of the theorem is completed.

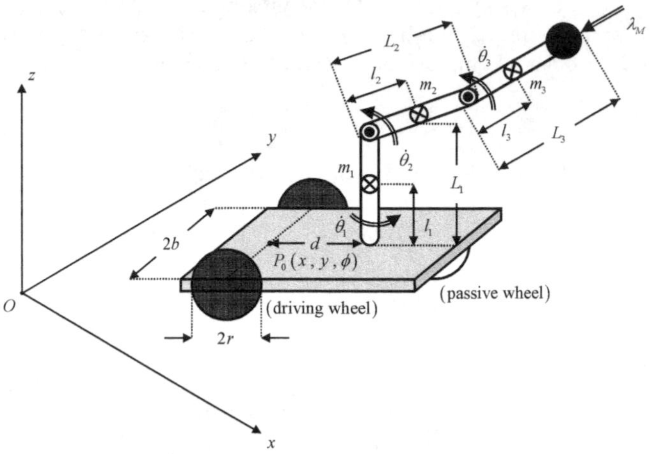

Fig. 3. Mobile manipulator used for simulations and experiments

4. Simulations and experiments

4.1 Mobile manipulator

Schematic model of mobile manipulator used for simulations and experiments is shown in Fig.3. This mobile manipulator consists of 3 wheel mobile base and 3 link manipulator. m_B, m_W and m_1, m_2, m_3 denote masses of base, wheels and manipulator links, respectively. I_B,I_W,I_m and I_1, I_2, I_3 denote moment of inertia of base, wheel axis, wheel and manipulator links, respectively. These dynamic parameters are unknown. Kinematic parameters are denoted in Fig.3. Numerical values of kinematic parameters are estimated as follows. $2b = 0.316, r = 0.098, d = 0.11, L_1 = 0.143, L_2 = 0.19, L_3 = 0.342, l_1 = 0.0715, l_2 = 0.095, l_3 = 0.171$. On the other hand, dynamic parameters are hardly identified. However, in simulations we use following estimates; $m_B = 5.0, m_W = 1.25, I_B = 0.137, I_W = 0.00313, I_m = 0.00582, 2b = 0.316, m_1 = 1.25, m_2 = 0.5, m_3 = 0.75, I_1 = 0.00259, I_2 = 0.00173, I_3 = 0.00201$. Unknown parameter vector $p_1 \in R^{26}$ is consisting of these parameters and is given by

$$p_1 = [p_1^1, p_2^1, \cdots, p_{26}^1]^T,$$

where

$$p_1^1 = \frac{r^2}{4}(m_B + m_1 + m_2 + m_3),$$
$$p_2^1 = \frac{r^2 d}{2b}(m_B + m_1 + m_2 + m_3),$$
$$p_3^1 = \frac{r^2}{4b^2}\left\{(m_B + m_1 + m_2 + m_3)d^2 + I_B + 2I_W\right\},$$
$$p_4^1 = m_W r^2 + I_m, p_5^1 = (m_2 l_2 + m_3 L_2)g,$$
$$p_6^1 = \frac{r}{2}(m_2 l_2 + m_3 L_2), p_7^1 = \frac{1}{2}(m_2 l_2^2 + m_3 L_2^2),$$

$$
\begin{aligned}
p_8^1 &= \frac{r^2}{4b}(m_2 l_2 + m_3 L_2), p_9^1 = \frac{rd}{2b}(m_2 l_2 + m_3 L_2),\\
p_{10}^1 &= \frac{r}{4b}(m_2 l_2^2 + m_3 L_2^2), p_{11}^1 = \frac{r^2 d}{4b^2}(m_2 l_2 + m_3 L_2),\\
p_{12}^1 &= \frac{r^2}{8b^2}(m_2 l_2^2 + m_3 L_2^2), p_{13}^1 = m_3 l_3 g, p_{14}^1 = \frac{1}{2} m_3 r l_3,\\
p_{15}^1 &= m_3 L_2 l_3, p_{16}^1 = \frac{1}{2} m_3 l_3^2, p_{17}^1 = \frac{1}{4b} m_3 r^2 l_3,\\
p_{18}^1 &= \frac{1}{2} m_3 r d l_3, p_{19}^1 = \frac{1}{2b} m_3 r l_3 L_2, p_{20}^1 = \frac{1}{4b} m_3 r l_3^2,\\
p_{21}^1 &= \frac{1}{4b^2} m_3 r^2 d l_3, p_{22}^1 = \frac{1}{4b^2} m_3 r^2 L_2 l_3,\\
p_{23}^1 &= \frac{1}{8b^2} m_3 r^2 l_3^2, p_{24}^1 = I_1, p_{25}^1 = I_2, p_{26}^1 = I_3.
\end{aligned}
$$

Generalized coordinates are also shown in this Figure. Base coordinates (x, y, ϕ) can be detected by 3D camera system and others can be detected by encoders. Nonholonomic constraints imposed on this system are written as follows.

$$
\begin{aligned}
\dot{x}\sin\phi - \dot{y}\cos\phi &= 0\\
\dot{x}\cos\phi + \dot{y}\sin\phi + b\dot{\phi} &= r\dot{\theta}_r\\
\dot{x}\cos\phi + \dot{y}\sin\phi - b\dot{\phi} &= r\dot{\theta}_r
\end{aligned}
$$

Coordinates (θ_r, θ_l) are related with forward velocity u and angular velocity ω as

$$
\begin{bmatrix} \dot{\theta}_r \\ \dot{\theta}_l \end{bmatrix} = \begin{bmatrix} \frac{1}{r} & \frac{b}{r} \\ \frac{1}{r} & -\frac{b}{r} \end{bmatrix} \begin{bmatrix} u \\ \omega \end{bmatrix}.
$$

Then (θ_r, θ_l) can be eliminated from the equations of motion by using (u, ω) as generalized velocities. Therefore, kinematic equations (8) are given by

$$
\begin{bmatrix} \dot{x} \\ \dot{y} \\ \dot{\phi} \\ \dot{\theta}_1 \end{bmatrix} = \begin{bmatrix} \frac{r}{2}\cos\phi & \frac{r}{2}\cos\phi & 0 \\ \frac{r}{2}\sin\phi & \frac{r}{2}\sin\phi & 0 \\ \frac{r}{2b} & -\frac{r}{2b} & 0 \\ 0 & 0 & 1 \end{bmatrix} \begin{bmatrix} v_r \\ v_l \\ v_{M1} \end{bmatrix}. \tag{38}
$$

4.2 Simulation for the system with both the kinetic and dynamic uncertainties

Mobile manipulator used for simulation is shown in Fig.3. In this simulation both the kinematic and dynamic parameters are all unknown.

In this simulation, the mobile base is controlled to track to the desired position/orientation trajectory on the floor and the end-effector of the manipulator is controlled to be constrained on the ceiling with desired reaction force. Then, nonholonomic constraints imposed on this system are same as shown before. On the other hand, holonomic constarint imposed on this system is

$$
\Phi(q) = L_1 + L_2\sin\theta_2 + L_3\sin(\theta_2 + \theta_3) - L = 0.
$$

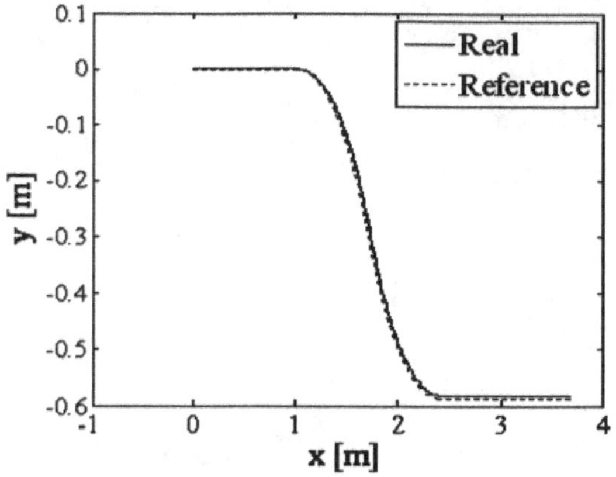

Fig. 4. Trajectory on (x, y) plane

This holonomic constraint represents that the end-effector of manipulator is constrained on the ceiling.
Desired trajectory of the manipulator is given by

$$\theta_1^* = 1.2(1 - \cos 0.25t),\ \theta_2^* = \frac{\pi}{4}$$

and desired force trajectory λ_M^* is 10. Desired position trajectories of the base $q_B^* = [x^*\ y^*\ \phi^*]^T$ are generated by the reference robot given by

$$\dot{q}^* = f_B(q_B^*)\eta^*. \tag{39}$$

To obtain the mixed straight and curved line, desired velocities $\eta^* = [u^*\ \omega^*]^T$ are defined as follows.

$$\begin{cases} u^* = & 0.1\left(1 - \cos \frac{\pi}{2.5}t\right) \\ \omega^* = 0 & (0 \le t < 2.5) \end{cases} \quad \begin{cases} u^* = & 0.2 \\ \omega^* = 0 & (2.5 \le t < 5) \end{cases}$$

$$\begin{cases} u^* = & 0.1\left(1 + \cos \frac{\pi}{2.5}t\right) \\ \omega^* = 0 & (5 \le t < 7.5) \end{cases} \quad \begin{cases} u^* = & 0.1\pi\left(1 - \cos \frac{2\pi}{2.5}t\right) \\ \omega^* = -u^* & (7.5 \le t < 10) \end{cases}$$

$$\begin{cases} u^* = & 0.1\pi\left(1 - \cos \frac{2\pi}{2.5}t\right) \\ \omega^* = u^* & (10 \le t < 12.5) \end{cases} \quad \begin{cases} u^* = & 0.1\left(1 + \cos \frac{\pi}{2.5}t\right) \\ \omega^* = 0 & (12.5 \le t < 15) \end{cases}$$

$$\begin{cases} u^* = & 0.2 \\ \omega^* = 0 & (15 \le t) \end{cases}$$

Initial conditions are $\dot{q}(0) = 0$, $q(0) = [0\ 0\ -\pi/20\ 0; \pi/4, \pi/3]^T$ and $\hat{p}_1(0) = 0, \hat{a}_i(0) = 0, \hat{\theta}_i(0) = 0, \hat{D}(0) = 0, \hat{\psi}(0) = [0.1\ 0.1]^T$. Disturbance vector is $d_1(q) = [1\ 1\ 0.5\ 0.5\ 0.5]^T$. For this system design parameters are asigned as $K_d = 10 \times I_4, \Gamma_1 = \Gamma_2 = \gamma = \Lambda_1 = \Lambda_2 = 1, \alpha_1 = 5 \times I_3, \alpha_2 = 25, \gamma_1 = \gamma_2 = 100, K_1 = K_2 = K_3 = K_{M11} = K_{M12} = 10$ and

$$\rho(t) = \frac{1}{(1 + \frac{t}{10})^2}.$$

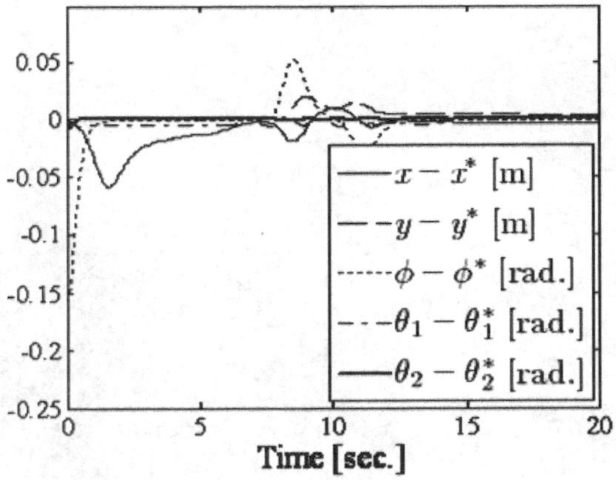

Fig. 5. Position tracking errors

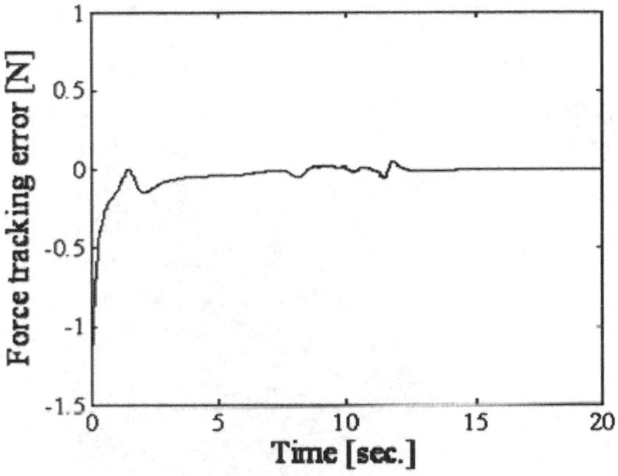

Fig. 6. Force tracking error

Fig.4 shows a desired trajectory and a tracking trajectory. Broken line shows a desired trajectory generated by the reference robot and solid line shows a tracking trajectory of the mobile manipulator. In spite of quite a large initial tracking error, tracking error is converged sufficiently small. Fig.5 and Fig.6 show the trajectory tracking errors of each coordinate and force tracking error, respectively.

4.3 Experiments

Fig.7 and 8 show a snapshot of experiments and the end-effector of the mobile manipulator respectively. In order to reduce the adverse effects of friction from the wall rolling ball is mounted on the top of the end-effector and to detect the reaction force from the wall force sensor is equipped under the rolling ball. In experiments mobile manipulator is controlled to move on the straight line parallel to the wall with assigned speed and simultaneously end-effector is controlled to press against the wall with assigned force. Since the end-effector

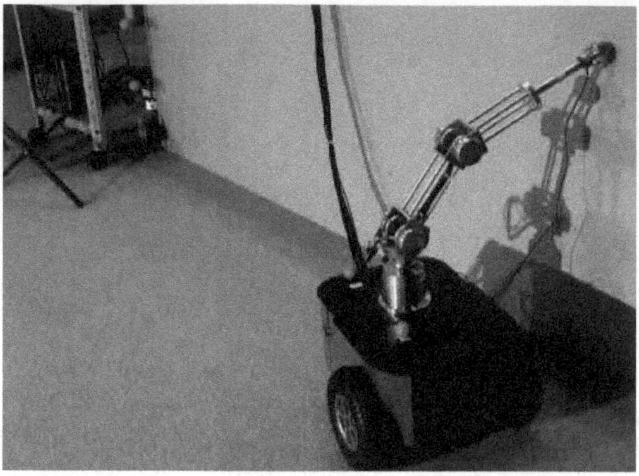

Fig. 7. Snapshot of experiments

is constrained on the wall, following holonomic constraint $\Phi(q)$ is imposed.

$$\Phi(q) = y + d\sin\phi + \{L_2\cos\theta_2 + L_3\cos(\theta_2+\theta_3)\} \\ \times \sin(\phi+\theta_1) - L = 0,$$

where L denotes distance between the wall and P_0 which is center of wheel axis. Then θ_2 is also eliminated by using the holonomic constraint.

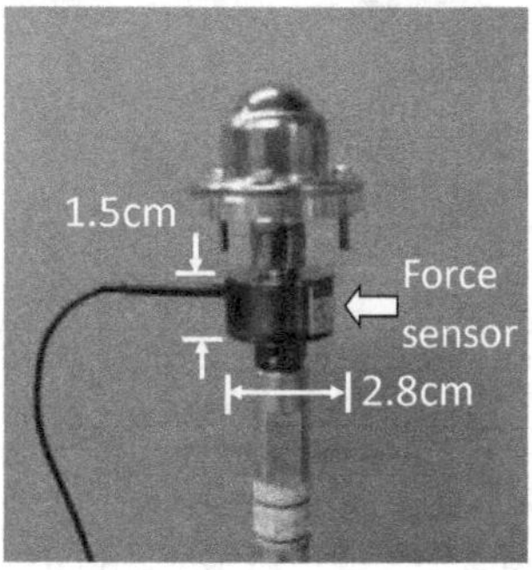

Fig. 8. End-effector

4.3.1 Application to the system only with the dynamic uncertainties

In case when kinetic parameters are known, we can apply control laws given in Theorem 2 and we can use estimates of kinematic parameters shown in Subsection 4.1. Control parameters are give as follows. $K_d = 5, K_1 = 5, K_2 = 50, K_3 = 10, K_{M1} = [10\ 10], \alpha_1 = 5, \alpha_2 = 5, \Gamma = 0.2, \gamma = 1$. $\rho(t)$ is given as

$$\rho(t) = \frac{1}{(t/K_\rho + 1)^2},$$

where K_ρ is constant and is assigned 500 in this experiments.
Experimental situation is shown in Fig.7. Mobile manipulator is controlled to move on the straight line with constant speed $5cm/sec$. End-effector is controlled to press against the wall

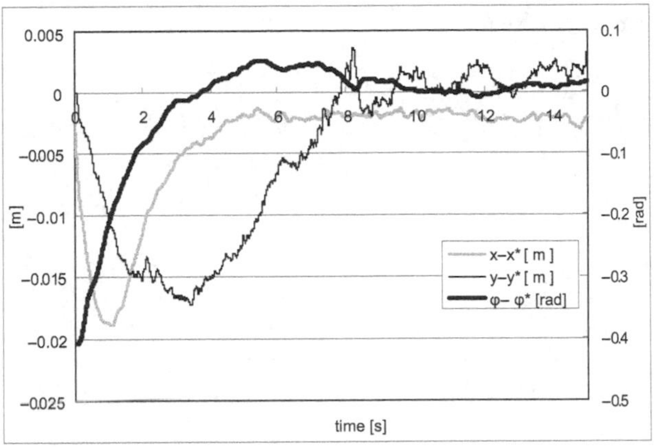

Fig. 9. Position error trajectories

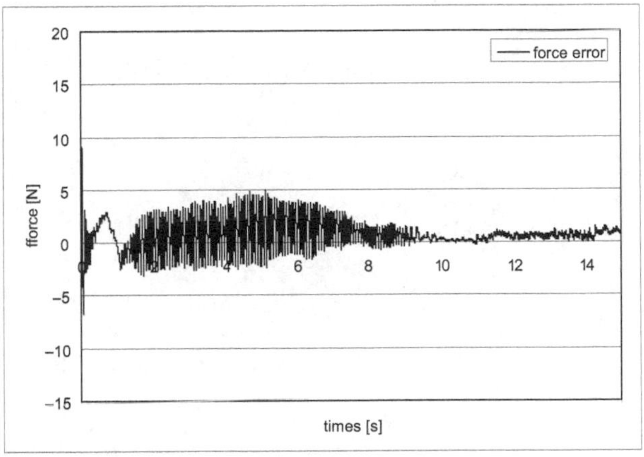

Fig. 10. Force error trajectory

with constant force $2N$. Fig.9 shows position error trajectories of the mobile base. Even though the mobile base is declined about 20 degrees parallel to the wall initially, position errors are settled to the neighbourhood of origin. Fig.10 shows force error. Also the force error is settled similarly to the position error trajectories.

4.3.2 Application to the system with both the kinetic and dynamic uncertainties

In this experiment we assume that not only dynamic parameters but also kinematic parameters are unknown. Then we apply control laws given in Theorem 1. In these control laws, unknown parameters are defined as follows.

$$a_1 = \frac{1}{r}, a_2 = \frac{b}{r},$$
$$\theta_{p1} = \begin{bmatrix} \frac{r}{2} \\ \frac{r}{2b} \end{bmatrix}, \theta_{p2} = \begin{bmatrix} \frac{r}{2} \\ \frac{r}{2b} \end{bmatrix}.$$

Furthermore, from Property 6

$$
\begin{aligned}
\bar{J}_M^T(q)\lambda_M &= Z_1(q,\lambda_M)\psi \\
&= \begin{bmatrix}
\lambda_M \sin\phi & \lambda_M \cos\phi & \lambda_M \cos(\phi+\theta_1)\cos\theta_2 & \lambda_M \cos(\phi+\theta_1)\cos(\theta_2+\theta_3) & 0 & 0 \\
\lambda_M \sin\phi & -\lambda_M \cos\phi & -\lambda_M \cos(\phi+\theta_1)\cos\theta_2 & -\lambda_M \cos(\phi+\theta_1)\cos(\theta_2+\theta_3) & 0 & 0 \\
0 & 0 & 0 & 0 & \lambda_M \cos(\phi+\theta_1)\cos\theta_2 & 0 \\
0 & 0 & 0 & 0 & -\lambda_M \sin(\phi+\theta_1)\sin\theta_2 & -\lambda_M \sin(\phi+\theta_1)\sin(\theta_2+\theta_3) \\
0 & 0 & 0 & 0 & 0 & -\lambda_M \sin(\phi+\theta_1)\sin(\theta_2+\theta_3)
\end{bmatrix}
\begin{bmatrix} \psi_1 \\ \psi_2 \\ \psi_3 \\ \psi_4 \\ \psi_5 \\ \psi_6 \end{bmatrix},
\end{aligned}
$$

then we have

$$
\begin{aligned}
\psi_1 &= \frac{1}{2}r, \psi_2 = \frac{1}{2}\frac{rd}{b}, \psi_3 = \frac{1}{2}\frac{L_2 d}{b}, \\
\psi_4 &= \frac{1}{2}\frac{L_3 d}{b}, \psi_5 = L_2, \psi_6 = L_3.
\end{aligned}
$$

Therefore control scheme given in Theorem 1 is overparameterized scheme. Control

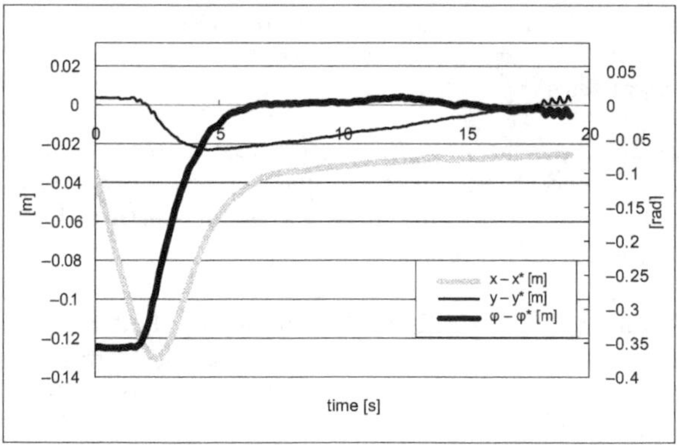

Fig. 11. Position error trajectories

parameters are as follows. $K_d = 5, K_1 = 5, K_2 = 50, K_3 = 10, K_{M1} = [10\ 10], \alpha_1 = 5, \alpha_2 = 5, \Gamma_1 = 0.01, \Gamma_2 = 0.01, \gamma = 0.01, \gamma_1 = 10, \gamma_2 = 10, \Lambda_1 = 1, \Lambda_2 = 1$. $\rho(t)$ is same as that given in case when kinetic parameters are known.

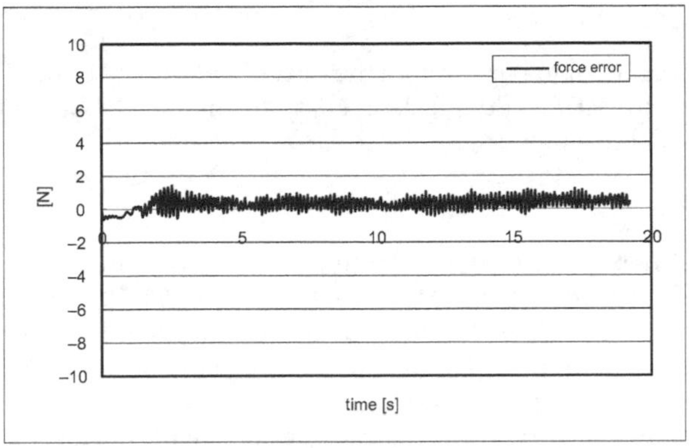

Fig. 12. Force error trajectory

As similar in case when kinetic parameters are known, mobile manipulator is controlled to move on the straight line with constant speed $5cm/sec$. End-effector is controlled to presss against the wall with constant force $2N$. Fig.11 shows position error trajectories of the mobile base. Similarly to the previous experiment, even though the mobile base is declined about 20 degrees to the wall initially, position errors are settled to the neighbourhood of origin. Fig.12 shows force error. Also the force error is settled similarly to the position error trajectories.

5. Concluding remark

In this study robust adaptive hybrid position/force control problems have been investigated. Proposed control schemes can be applied to the system which has not only dynamic uncertainties but also both the kinematic and dynamic uncertainties. Furthermore unknown disturbances have been considered. It is guaranteed theoretically that the tracking position errors and force errors are asymptotically converged to zero and all internal signals are bounded. This means that all estimated parameters are also bounded and still remained to be small. However, some estimated parameters are monotonically increasing, especially $\hat{D}$. Since $\hat{D}$ is updated by

$$\dot{\hat{D}} = \gamma\|\delta\|,$$

$\hat{D}$ is increased in so far as $\delta \neq 0$. Furthermore in this experiments sensor noise and unmodeled nonlinearities hinder the proposed control schemes from achievement of the perfect regulation $\delta = 0$. These lead us to the fact that the estimate $\hat{D}$ becomes large with the passage of time. Therefore, in the practical situation to avoid the numerical difficulties of $\hat{D}$ resulted from the long-term control, $\hat{D}$ should be set constant value when the estimate $\hat{D}$ exceeds the designated threshold or $\|\delta\|$ should be set 0 in the computation of the adaptive laws if $\|\delta\| < \epsilon$, where ϵ is specified small number.

Usefulness of the proposed control schemes has been demonstrated by experiments. Especially, since environmental uncertainties can be considered as the kinematic uncertainties, the proposed control scheme given by Theorem 1 can be applied to the case when environmental uncertainties arise.

6. Acknowledgements

This study was supported in part by both the scientific Research Fund (B)19360110 and Hitech Research Center, Project for Private University from the Ministry of Education, Culture, Sports, Science and Technology.

7. References

Chang, Y. C. & Chen, B. S. (2002). Adaptive tracking control for nonholonomic Caplygin systems. *IEEE Trans. Control Systems Technology*, Vol. 10, No. 1, pp. 96-104

Cheah, C. C.;Kawamura, S. & Arimoto, S. (2003). Stability of Hybrid Position and Force Control for Robotic Manipulator with Kinamatic and Dynamics Uncertainties. *Automatica*, Vol.39, pp.847-855

Dong, W. (2002). On trajectory and force tracking control of constrained mobile manipulators with parameter uncertainty. *Automatica*, Vol. 32, pp. 1475-1484

Fukao, T.;Hasegawa, H. & Adachi, H. (2000). Adaptive Tracking Control of a Nonholonomic Mobile Robot. *IEEE Trans. Robotics and Automation*, Vol. 16, No. 5, pp. 609-615

Kristic, M.;Kanellakopoulos, I. & Kokotovic, P. (1995). *Nonlinear and Adaptive Control Design*, John Wiley and Sons

Li, Z.;Yang, J.;Luo, J.;Wang, Z. & Ming, A. (2007). Robust motion/force control of nonholonomic mobile manipulators using hybrid joints. *Advanced Robotics*, Vol. 21, No. 11, pp. 1231-1252

Li, Z.;Adams, M. & Wijesoma, W. S. (2008). Robust Adaptive control of uncertain force/motion constrained nonholonomic mobile manipulators. *Automatica*, Vol. 44, pp. 776-784

Murray, R. M.; Li, Z. & Sastry, S. S. (1993). *An Introduction to Robotic Manipulation*, CRC Press

Narikiyo, T.; Kawanishi, M. & Nakagawa, M. (2008). Robust Adaptive Position/Force Control of Mobile Manipulators with Dynamic Uncertainties, *Proceedings of IASTED CA2009*, pp. 264-269, ISBN, Cambridge, UK

Narikiyo, T.; Kawanishi, M. & Mizuno, T. (2009). Robust Adaptive Position/Force Control of Mobile Manipulators with Kinematic and Dynamic Uncertainties, *Proceedings of ICROS-SICE International Joint Conference*, pp. 4704–4709, Fukuoka, Japan

Oya, M.;Su, C. Y.& Katoh, R. (2003). Robust Adaptive Motion/Force Tracking Control of Uncertain Nonholonomic Mechanical Systems. *IEEE Trans. Robotics and Automation*, Vol. 19, No. 1, pp. 175-181

Slotine, J-J. E. & Li, W. (1991). *Applied Nonlinear Control*, Prentice Hall

Su, C. Y.;Stepanenko, Y. & Goldenberg, A. A. (1999). Reduced Order Model and Robust Control Architecture for Mechanical Systems with Nonholonomic Pfaffian Constraints. *IEEE Trans. Systems, Man, and Cybernetics-Part A*, Vol. 29, No. 3, pp. 307-313

Yamamoto, Y. & Yun, X. (1996). Effect of the Dynamic Interaction on Coordinated Control of Mobile Manipulators. *IEEE Trans. Robotics and Automation*, Vol. 12, No. 5, pp.816-824

Yuan, J. (1997). Adaptive Control of a Constrained Robot-Ensuring Zero Tracking and Zero Force Errors. *IEEE Trans. Automatic Control*, Vol. 42, No. 12, pp. 1709-1714

8

Robust Visual Servoing of Robot Manipulators Based on Passivity

A. Luis Rodríguez and Yu Tang
National University of Mexico
Mexico

1. Introduction

Servo applications (regulation and tracking) are an important class of tasks for robots. Robustness in a servo controller must be guaranteed when the robot manipulator operates in an uncertain environment to ensure the stability and performance in the presence of uncertain robot manipulator dynamics, objects to be manipulated by the robot, and obstacles to be avoid. Also, robots must have sensing capability to adapt to the new tasks without reprogramming. Servoing based on visual measurements, also referred to as *visual servoing* (Hutchinson et al. (1996)), provided an alternative solution to these applications. Commonly used schemes include position-based and image-based visual servoing, being the main difference how to use the visual measurements: if the visual measurements are used to infer the end-effector pose to implement a cartesian control, we get a position-based visual servoing (PBVS) (see, *e.g.*, Fujita et al. (2007)); if the visual measurements are used directly to calculate the control torque to the manipulator, we get an image-based visual servoing (IBVS) (see, *e.g.*, Espiau et al. (1992) and Kelly (1996)). It is generally recognized that IBVS has the advantages of having less on-line computation burden, being more accurate, while the PBVS is more flexible for its implementation.

Dynamic visual servoing was proposed by Weiss et al. (1987). A key point in this approach is to view the visual measurements as the output of a dynamic system. By adopting this point of view, Dickmanns & Graefe (1988) set up a dynamic model of curvature evolution of the road in a driving application. However, stability and robustness issues were not addressed . To address these important questions and to investigate further the applications of IBVS for general scenarios, Hashimoto et al. (1996) and Ma et al. (1999) studied the image dynamics, *i.e.*, how the image feature of an object moving in a 3-D space evolutes in the 2-D image plane. The visual system in a robotics application is linearized in Hashimoto et al. (1996) at the desired point yielding a linear-time-invariant (LTI) multi-input-multi-output (MIMO) model. Ma et al. (1999) proposed a curve dynamic model in vision guided navigation application and based on it designed a linearizing control law that controls the curvature dynamics in the image plane using only perspective projection thanks to a state-observer. By combining passivity of the visual feedback system and the manipulator dynamics, Fujita et al. (2007) addressed the PBVS to track a 3-D object in a camera-in-hand configuration. However, the resulting control law was more complicated than that obtained with the transposed jacobian approach

(Kelly et al. (2000)) and had to be restricted to consider a steady object in order to establish the stability of the control system.
Motivated by these works, we consider in this chapter the servo problem in a robot manipulator based only on the visual measurements by following the dynamic visual servoing approach to design an IBVS with a fixed camera configuration. To model the whole visual servoing system, we "lift" the manipulator dynamics up to the image space, reconstructed based on the perspective projection of the robot space in the image plane, and model it with the lagrangian formalism by formulating the kinetic and potential energy in the image space. The resulting motion equation has the same structure as that obtained in the joint space using the lagrangian modeling (Spong et al. (2006)), and therefore inheriting the passivity property. Robust control schemes based on the passivity of the motion equation are then designed for visual servoing. The main features of this robust control law are (1) No image derivative is required as it uses only the image position for feedback, (2) no camera parameters and robot inertia parameters are needed for the implementation, making it robust to the parameter uncertainties in both the camera and robot manipulator, (3) no other measurements as from optical encoders are needed but the visual measurements from a single fixed camera.
The rest of this chapter is organized as follows: Section 2 presents the robot image dynamics obtained by gathering together manipulator dynamics, manipulator kinematics and the camera model into a single dynamic system, and its experimental validation in a laboratory set. Section 3 gives the controller design and the main results. Experiments results are shown in Section 4 to illustrate the performance of the proposed IBVS. Concluding remarks and future works are given in Section 5.

2. Robot image dynamics

2.1 Robot joint dynamics

Consider a 3-DOF articulated (RRR) manipulator moving in a (robot) space, whose motion equation in the joint space is

$$M(q)\ddot{q} + C(q,\dot{q})\dot{q} + g(q) = \tau, \tag{1}$$

where $\tau(t) \in \Re^3$ is the control torque and $q(t) \in \Re^3$, the joint position of the manipulator. $M(q) \in \Re^{3\times 3}$ represents the inertia matrix, and $C(q,\dot{q})\dot{q} \in \Re^3$ and $g(q) \in \Re^3$ are Coriolis/centrifugal and gravity torques, respectively. This equation can be obtained by modeling the manipulator in the joint space using the lagragian formalism (Spong et al. (2006)) with kinetic energy $K(q,\dot{q}) = \frac{1}{2}\dot{q}^T M(q)\dot{q}$ and potential energy $P(q)$. The motion equation (1) has the following properties:
Property 1 : The inertia matrix $M(q)$ is positive definite, i.e.,

$$\underline{\mathrm{m}} \le q^T M(q) q \le \overline{m}, \;\; \forall q \in \Re^3, \; q \neq 0, \; 0 < \underline{\mathrm{m}} \le \overline{m}. \tag{2}$$

Property 2: The matrix $\dot{M}(q) - 2C(q,\dot{q})$ is skew-symmetric, i.e.,

$$x^T[\dot{M}(q) - 2C(q,\dot{q})]x = 0, \;\; \forall x \in \Re^3. \tag{3}$$

Property 3: The dynamics of (1) is linearly parameterizable:

$$M(q)\ddot{q} + C(q,\dot{q})\dot{q} + g(q) = Y(q,\dot{q},\ddot{q})a = \tau, \tag{4}$$

where the regressor $Y(q,\dot{q},\ddot{q}) \in \Re^{3\times n_a}$, contains known functions of q, $\dot{q}$, $\ddot{q}$, and $a \in \Re^{n_a}$ is the vector of manipulator parameters, n_a the number of parameters.
Property 4: The gravity torque satisfies

$$\| \frac{\partial g(q)}{\partial q} \| \leq c_g, \text{ for some } c_g > 0 \text{ and } \forall q \in \Re^3. \tag{5}$$

Passivity of the mapping $\tau \rightarrow \dot{q}$ in the the manipulator dynamics (1) follows from Property 2 by considering the stored energy $V(q,\dot{q}) = \frac{1}{2}\dot{q}^T M(q)\dot{q} + P(q)$ and its time derivatives along (1) $\dot{V} = \tau^T \dot{q}$ (Ortega & Spong (1989)). Based on the passivity, simple and robust control laws have been proposed (see, *e.g.*, Slotine & Li (1987); Takegaki & Arimoto (1981)) for robot control.

2.2 Robot forward kinematics

The forward kinematics $f : \Re^3 \rightarrow \Re^3$ gives the cartesian position X of a feature point in the robot coordinate frame in terms of the joint position q

$$X = f(q), \tag{6}$$

and the velocity kinematics $J(q) = \partial f(q)/\partial q \in \Re^{3\times 3}$ relates the feature point velocity $\dot{X}$ with the joint velocity $\dot{q}$

$$\dot{X} = J(q)\dot{q}. \tag{7}$$

2.3 Camera model

The pin-hole model of a CCD camera (Hutchinson et al. (1996)) is considered. In this model, a point in the robot space seen in the camera frame $X = [X_1\ X_2\ X_3]$ (meter) is transformed into the image position $x \in \Re^2$ (pixel) in the image plane by perspective projection (Fig. 1)

$$x = HR(\theta)[X - X_0], \tag{8}$$

where $R(\theta) \in SO(3)$ is the rotation matrix generated by clockwise rotating the camera about its optical axis by θ radians,

$$R(\theta) = \begin{bmatrix} \cos(\theta) & -\sin(\theta) & 0 \\ \sin(\theta) & \cos(\theta) & 0 \\ 0 & 0 & 1 \end{bmatrix},$$

H is the magnification matrix,

$$H = \frac{\lambda}{\lambda - X_3} \begin{bmatrix} \alpha_1 & 0 & 0 \\ 0 & \alpha_2 & 0 \end{bmatrix},$$

with λ the focus length, X_3 the depth (the distance from the lens to the image plane), α_1 and α_2 (pixels/m) the scale factors of length units in the image plane, X_0 the intersection point of the optical axis at the robot plane.

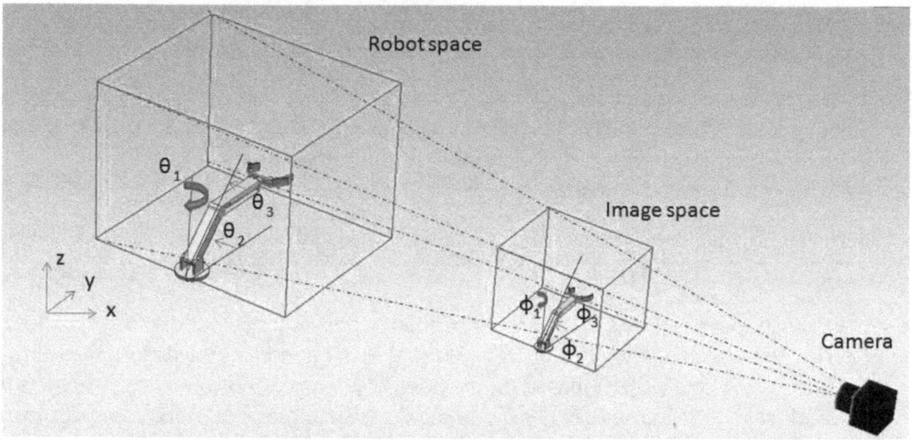

Fig. 1. The robot plane (Y-Z) is the plane perpendicular to the camera optical axis and containing the origin of the robot coordinate frame. The image-plane (y-z) is its perspective projection.

2.4 Robot image dynamics

By robot image dynamics we refer to the dynamics of the robot image evolving in the image space (defined below) when the robot moves in the robot space.

Let the robot plane (Y-Z) be the plane perpendicular to the camera optical axis and containing the origin of the robot coordinate frame. The robot manipulator moves in the robot space defined by the robot coordinate frame (X-Y-Z) (Fig. 1). The image-plane (y-z) is the perspective projection of the robot plane (Y-Z), and the image space (x-y-z) is the space reconstructed based on the perspective projection of the robot space in the image plane (y-z). Common methods used for this reconstruction include range identification (Chen & Kano (2002); Dixon et al. (2003); Karagiannis & Astolfi (2005)), utilization of multiple feature points attached to the end effector as well as to the target (Kelly et al. (2006); Yuan (1989)). In this work, we use the feature points attached to the links to reconstruct the joint angles of the robot image in the image space needed for the controller implementation.

The robot image dynamics we consider in this chapter is obtained by lumping together manipulator dynamics, forward kinematics and the camera transformation into a single dynamics (Fig. 2). Consider the kinetic energy $K_\phi(\phi,\dot{\phi}) = \frac{1}{2}\dot{\phi}^T M_\phi(\phi)\dot{\phi}$ and potential energy $P_\phi(\phi)$ in the image space, where, similar to modeling the manipulator in the joint space, ϕ is the joint image position (rad)[1], $M_\phi(\phi)$ the inertia matrix seen in the image space. The motion equation as seen in the image space is obtained by modeling the visual servo system (manipulator and camera) with lagragian formalism:

$$M_\phi(\phi)\ddot{\phi} + C_\phi(\phi,\dot{\phi})\dot{\phi} + g_\phi(\phi) = \tau. \tag{9}$$

As in the joint-space model, this motion equation has the following properties:

Property 1′: The inertia matrix $M_\phi(\phi)$ is positive definite, i.e.,

$$\underline{m}_\phi \le \phi^T M_\phi(\phi)\phi \le \overline{m}_\phi, \ \forall \phi \in \Re^3, \ \phi \ne 0, \ 0 < \underline{m}_\phi \le \overline{m}_\phi. \tag{10}$$

[1] Joint image position is meant here the joint position in the image space.

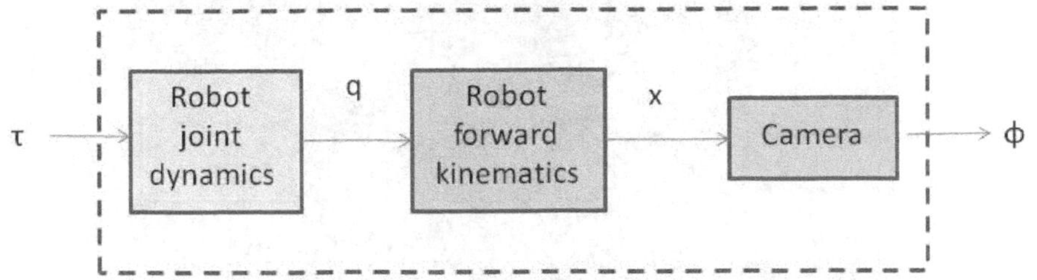

Fig. 2. Graphic representation of the robot image dynamics (9).

Property 2′: The matrix $\dot{M}_\phi(\phi) - 2C_\phi(\phi,\dot{\phi})$ is skew-symmetric, i.e.,

$$x^T[\dot{M}_\phi(\phi) - 2C_\phi(\phi,\dot{\phi})]x = 0, \ \ \forall x \in \Re^3. \tag{11}$$

Property 3′: The dynamics of (9) is linearly parameterizable:

$$M_\phi(\phi)\ddot{\phi} + C_\phi(\phi,\dot{\phi})\dot{\phi} + g_\phi(\phi) = Y_\phi(\phi,\dot{\phi},\ddot{\phi})a_\phi = \tau, \tag{12}$$

For this 3-DOF articulated robot manipulator, a parametrization with a_ϕ, $Y_\phi(\phi,\dot{\phi},\ddot{\phi}) \in \Re^{15}$ may be obtained (Spong et al. (2006)).
Property 4′: The gravity torque satisfies

$$\| \frac{\partial g_\phi(\phi)}{\partial \phi} \| \leq c_{g_\phi}, \text{ for some } c_{g_\phi} > 0 \text{ and } \forall \phi \in \Re^3. \tag{13}$$

Remark 1: As a consequence of this paradigm, the parameters of the manipulator dynamics, forward kinematics and camera transformation are all lumped together into the parameters of the model (9). The passivity property followed from Property 2′ will simplify significantly the control design based on visual measurements.
Remark 2: The aforementioned robot plane (Y-Z) and the image-plane (y-z) in Fig.1 are uniquely defined once the camera position and orientation are set, and are parallel from perspective projection (8). In the experiments, X_0 will be defined as the anti-image of the principal point in the image plane determined using the method in Grammatikopoulos et al. (2004).
Before moving to consider the control design, we validate our point of view through experiments. The validation was carried out by first identifying the robot image dynamics using an off-line least-square algorithm, and then by comparing the output of the robot image system in Fig. 2 with that of the model (9).
The experiment platform is shown in Fig 3. It consists of a three-link manipulator (made in the laboratory) moving in the (robot) space, and a fixed IEEE 1394 digital camera from Basler (model A601 FC). The camera has focus length $\lambda = 0.9091$ (cm), and scaling factors $\alpha_1 = \alpha_2 = 4.6$ (pixels/cm). The rotation angle of the camera about its optical axis was set to $\theta = 0$ (rad). The image plane has a resolution of (horizontal x vertical) 320×240 pixels.
Before the experiments, the feature point corresponding to the robot base point (origin of the robot coordinate frame) and length of the link 1, link 2 and link 3 are determined in the

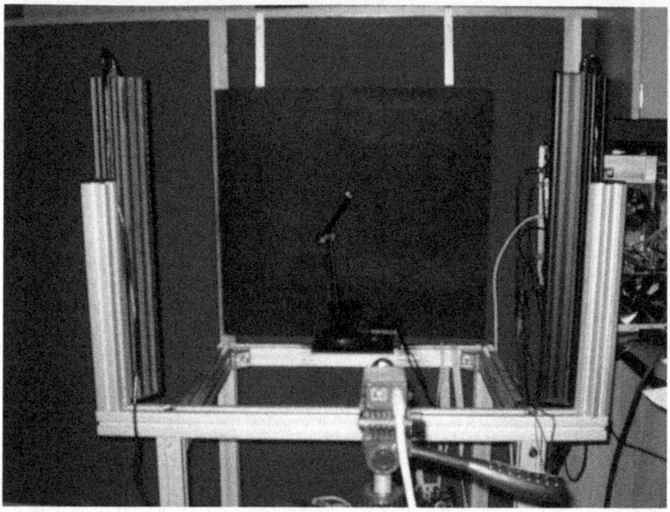

Fig. 3. Experiment platform.

image plane. Using this information, the joint image position (ϕ) is obtained by measuring two feature points at the second and the third joint (end-effector).
To attenuate the noise in the image measurements image thresholding was first applied to the images of the feature points, then the centroid of each feature point image was calculated, which was used as the image positions of the feature points to calculate the joint image position.
The applied voltage, which is proportional to the applied torque, is fed through a D/A converter (AI-1608AY card from CONTEC) to the power amplification unit. A PC Pentium D running at 3 GHz was used in the experiments. The sampling time was set to 50 (frames/sec). The joint image position together with the applied voltage is shown in Fig. 4.
First the robot image dynamics (9) is identified using an off-line least square algorithm and the parametrization (12). In order to avoid from using the image acceleration, a first order low-pass filter is applied to both sides of the parametrization (12) to get a filtered version of the parametrization (12):

$$Y_f(\phi, \dot{\phi})a_\phi = \tau_f, \tag{14}$$

where

$$\tau_f = \frac{\beta}{s+\beta}\tau, \; Y_f = \frac{\beta}{s+\beta}Y_\phi$$

are the filtered regressor and the filtered input torque, respectively, and $\beta/(s+\beta)$, with $\beta = 0.9$ and s the Laplace transform variable, the filter transfer function. In order to further avoid from using the derivatives of the joint image position, $\dot{\phi}$ is substituted by its approximate derivative $\dot{\phi} = \frac{s}{1+\epsilon_f s}\phi$, with $\epsilon_f = 0.001$. 900 samples were used. The estimated parameters are shown in Table 1.
After the parameter vector of the robot image dynamics (12) is obtained, this dynamical model is validated by comparing the output of the robot image dynamics (Fig. 2) and the output of the identified robot image dynamics (9). The applied torques and the measured joint image positions and the outputs of the identified robot image dynamics are shown in Fig. 5.

Parameter	a_{ϕ_1}	a_{ϕ_2}	a_{ϕ_3}	a_{ϕ_4}	a_{ϕ_5}	a_{ϕ_6}	a_{ϕ_7}	a_{ϕ_8}
Value	0.0036	0.0537	0.0389	0.0021	0.0914	0.0596	0.0225	0.0402
Parameter	a_{ϕ_9}	$a_{\phi_{10}}$	$a_{\phi_{11}}$	$a_{\phi_{12}}$	$a_{\phi_{13}}$	$a_{\phi_{14}}$	$a_{\phi_{15}}$	
Value	0.0758	0.0463	0.0073	0.0052	0.0641	0.0598	0.0047	

Table 1. Estimated parameters of the robot image dynamics (12).

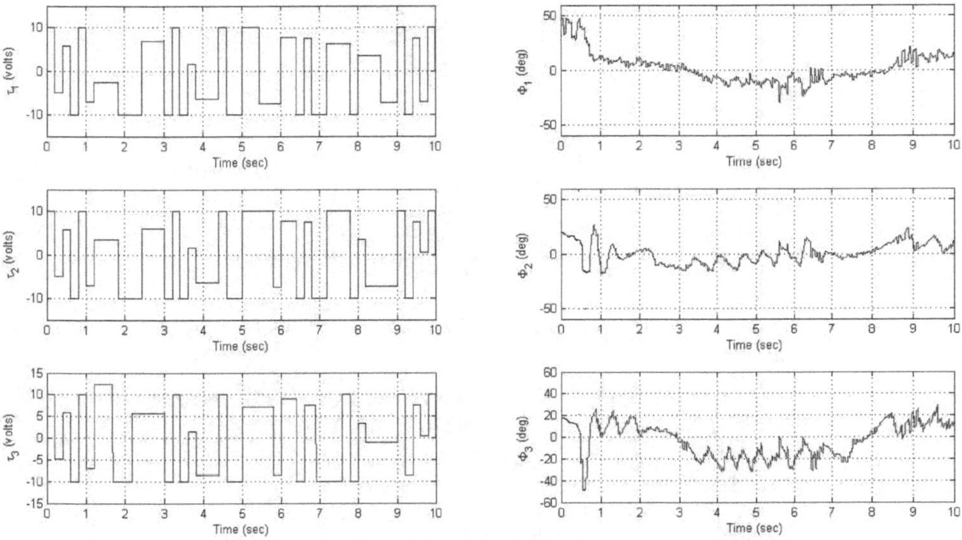

Fig. 4. Identification of the robot image dynamics: Left column shows the torque inputs, right column shows the joint image position for Link 1 (up), 2 (middle) and 3 (down).

3. Controller design for IBVS

In this section, motivated from joint space control in Escobar et al. (1999); Kelly (1999); Tomei (1991) we design an output feedback control law with bounded control action and desired gravity compensation to regulate the joint image position. The results are summarized in the following.

Theorem 1: Consider the robot image dynamics (9) and the control law

$$\tau = -\psi_1(\tilde{\phi}) - \psi_2(z) + g_\phi(\phi_d), \tag{15}$$

where

$$g_\phi(\phi_d) = [0 \quad a_{\phi 4} g \cos(\phi_{d2}) + a_{\phi 5} g \cos(\phi_{d2} + \phi_{d3})$$
$$a_{\phi 5} g \cos(\phi_{d2} + \phi_{d3})],$$

is the desired gravity compensation term, $\tilde{\phi} = \phi - \phi_d$ the image position error, $\phi_d \in \Re^3$ the desired joint image position, $\psi_i^T(x) = [\psi_{i1}(x_1)\ \psi_{i2}(x_2)\ \psi_{i3}(x_3)] : \Re^3 \to \Re^3$, $i = 1, 2$, are

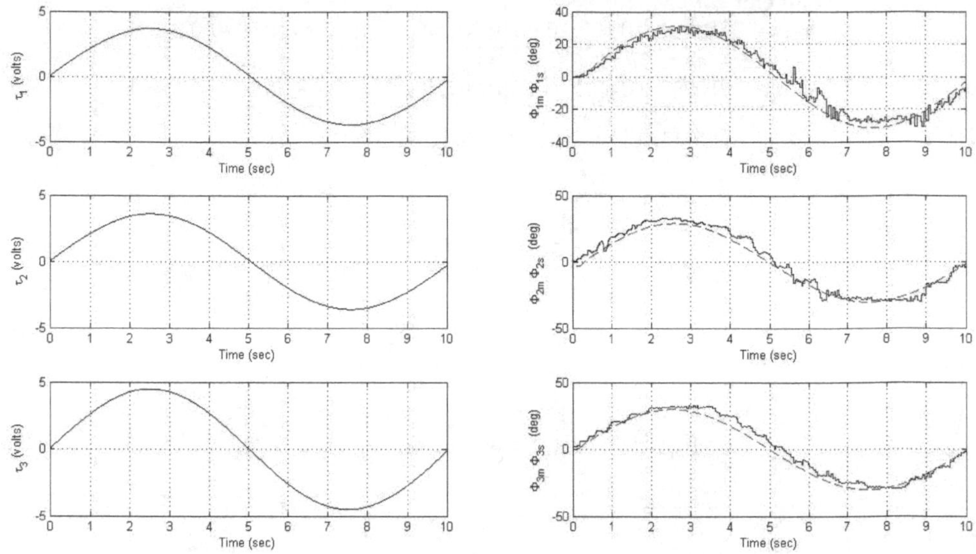

Fig. 5. Validation of the robot image dynamics: Left column shows the torque inputs, right column shows the joint image position measured from the robot image dynamics (Fig. 2) (solid line) and the joint image position from the model (9) (dashed line) for Link 1 (up), 2 (middle) and 3 (down).

continuous functions satisfying

$$x\psi_{ij}(x) > 0, \ \forall x \in \Re, \ \psi_{ij}(0) = 0, \ i = 1,2, \ j = 1,2,3, \tag{16}$$

$$\frac{\partial \psi_1}{\partial x} = diag[\frac{\partial \psi_{11}}{\partial x_1} \ \frac{\partial \psi_{12}}{\partial x_2} \ \frac{\partial \psi_{13}}{\partial x_3}] \geq c_{g_\phi} I, \tag{17}$$

where c_{g_ϕ} is given in Property 4′ and

$$\dot{w} = -\alpha(w + \phi), \ \alpha > 0,$$

$$z = w + \phi. \tag{18}$$

Then all the signals in the control loop are bounded and $\tilde{\phi} \to 0$ asymptotically.

Proof. Substituting the control law (15) into the robot image dynamics (9) gets the closed-loop equation

$$M_\phi(\phi)\ddot{\phi} + C_\phi(\phi, \dot{\phi})\dot{\phi} + g_\phi(\phi) = -\psi_1(\tilde{\phi}) - \psi_2(z) + g_\phi(\phi_d). \tag{19}$$

First, we show that $(\tilde{\phi}, \ \dot{\phi}, \ z)$ has a unique equilibrium at the origin, and then using the Lyapunov analysis to show this equilibrium is asymptotically stable.
In fact, at the equilibria we have

$$\psi_1(\tilde{\phi}) = g_\phi(\phi_d) - g_\phi(\phi). \tag{20}$$

On the other hand, it follows from Property 4′ and (17) that

$$\| g_\phi(\phi_d) - g_\phi(\phi) \| \leq c_{g_\phi} \| \phi_d - \phi \| \leq \| \psi_1(\tilde{\phi}) \| .$$

The above two expressions imply that $\phi = \phi_d$.
Rewriting the observer dynamics (18) as

$$\dot{z} = -\alpha z + \dot{\phi}. \tag{21}$$

Therefore, $(\tilde{\phi},\ \dot{\phi},\ z) = (0,\ 0,\ 0)$ is the unique equilibrium of the closed-loop system.
Consider the following potential energy-like function for the closed-loop system

$$\begin{aligned} P_1 &= \int_0^\phi \left[\psi_1(\tilde{\phi}) - g_\phi(\phi_d) + g_\phi(\phi)\right] d\phi \\ &= \phi^T \psi_1(\tilde{\phi}) - \phi^T g_\phi(\phi_d) + P_\phi(\phi). \end{aligned} \tag{22}$$

Then $\phi = \phi_d$ is the global minimum of $P_1(\phi)$ since $\frac{\partial P_1}{\partial \phi} = 0 \Rightarrow \phi = \phi_d$ and $\frac{\partial^2 P_1}{\partial \phi^2} = \frac{\partial \psi_1(\tilde{\phi})}{\partial \phi} + \frac{\partial g_\phi(\phi)}{\partial \phi} > 0$.
Consider the Lyapunov function candidate

$$V(\tilde{\phi}, \dot{\phi}, z) = \frac{1}{2}\dot{\phi}^T M_\phi(\phi)\dot{\phi} + P_1(\phi) - P_1(\phi_d) + \int_0^z \psi_2(z)dz. \tag{23}$$

Its time derivative along the error dynamics (19) is

$$\begin{aligned} \dot{V} &= -\dot{\phi}^T \psi_2(z) + \dot{z}^T \psi_2(z) \\ &= -\psi_2^T(z)[-\dot{z} + \dot{\phi}] \\ &= -\alpha z^T \psi_2(z) \leq 0. \end{aligned} \tag{24}$$

In order to conclude the asymptotic stability of the equilibrium, we invoke LaSalle theorem (Khalil (2002)) by considering the invariant set

$$\Omega = \{(\tilde{\phi}\ \dot{\phi}\ z) \in \Re^3 \times \Re^3 \times \Re^3 : \dot{V}(\tilde{\phi}, \dot{\phi}, z) = 0\}, \tag{25}$$

which contains only the equilibrium. Therefore the asymptotic stability of the equilibrium follows. □

Remark 3: Since the control law is developed based on the robot image dynamics, no other measurements than the joint image positions are need for its implementation. This is important because taking time derivative of image measurements are in general not acceptable given noisy image measurements. Also, notice that the only parameters in the control law are the gravity term of the robot image dynamics, which may be also tuned on-line as in Tomei (1991).
Remark 4: Due to the occlusion effect in a single fixed camera configuration, it is impossible to determine uniquely the joint image positions for certain poses of the manipulator by the

geometrical method used here. For practical purposes, the given desired image joint position ϕ_{d1} must be restricted away ± 20 (deg) away from the camera optical axis.
Remark 5: Typically, $\psi_i^T(x) = [\psi_{i1}(x_1)\ \psi_{i2}(x_2)\ \psi_{i3}(x_3)]$ is taken a sigmoid function, *e.g.*, $\frac{2k_1}{\pi} atan(\frac{x}{k_2})$ with k_1, $k_2 > 0$ determining the magnitude and shape of the sigmoid function, to avoid the control signal from saturating (Escobar et al. (1999)).

4. Experiments results

In order to evaluate the robustness of the proposed control in the presence of quantization errors in camera transformation, lens distortion, possible misalignment of the camera rotation angle about its optical axis, laboratory experiments were carried out.
The control law (15) with gravity compensation term $g_\phi(\phi_d)$ was applied to the robot the experiment platform in Fig.3. The sigmoid function as in Remark 5 was used with $k_1 =$ 7.65, 2.25, 1.75 and $k_2 = 4.35$, 1.98, 1.15 for the joint 1, 2 3, respectively, and $\alpha = 5$ in (18).
Fig. 6 depicts the regulation of the joint image position to its desired position, which corresponds to moving the end-effector from an initial position corresponding to $\phi(0) =$ [10 -100 -110] (deg) to a desired position $\phi_d(0) = [-30\ -30\ -30]$ (deg) at $t = 0$ (sec.) and $\phi_d(5) = [30\ 40\ 40]$ (deg) at $t = 5$ (sec.). Although not established in theory here, the results of tracking a desired image trajectory, which corresponds to drawing a figure in the image space shown in Fig. 7, with the proposed control law are shown in Fig. 8 and Fig. 9.

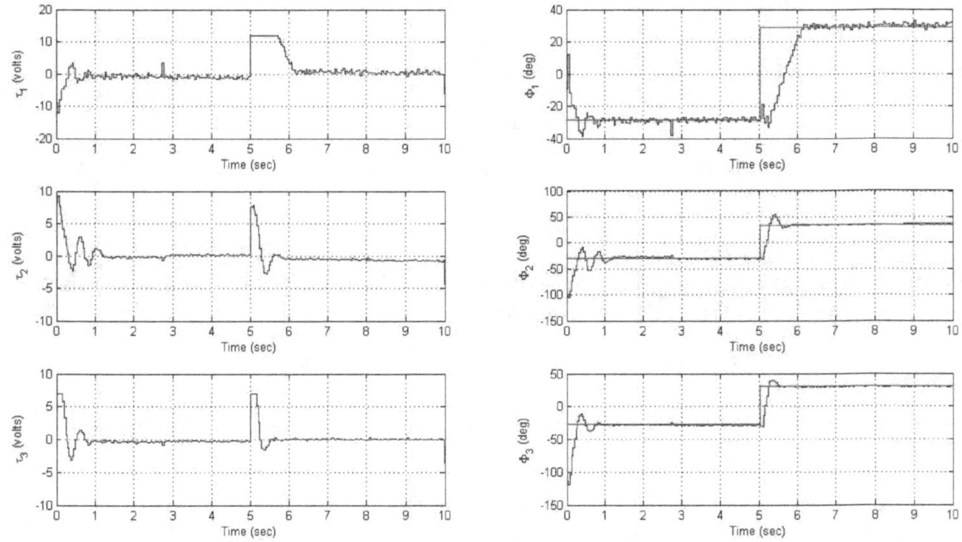

Fig. 6. Experiments of the visual servoing: regulation of the joint image position for joint 1 (up), 2 (middle) and 3 (down). Left column shows the torque inputs, right column shows the joint image position and the desired position.

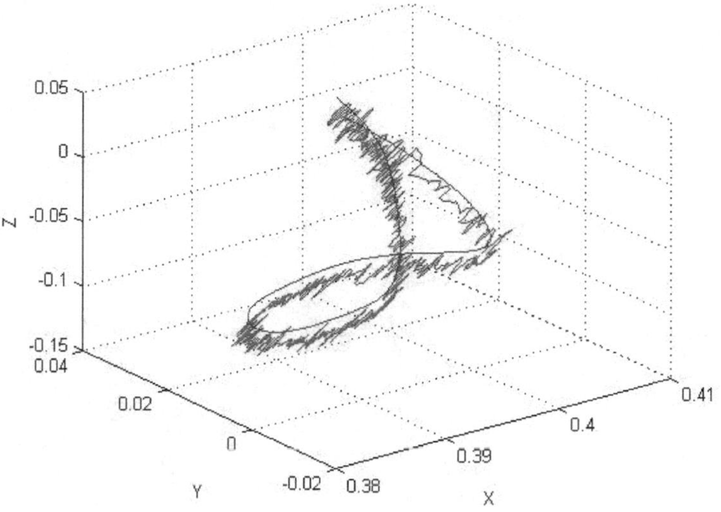

Fig. 7. Experiments of the visual servoing: tracking of the joint image trajectory in the image space.

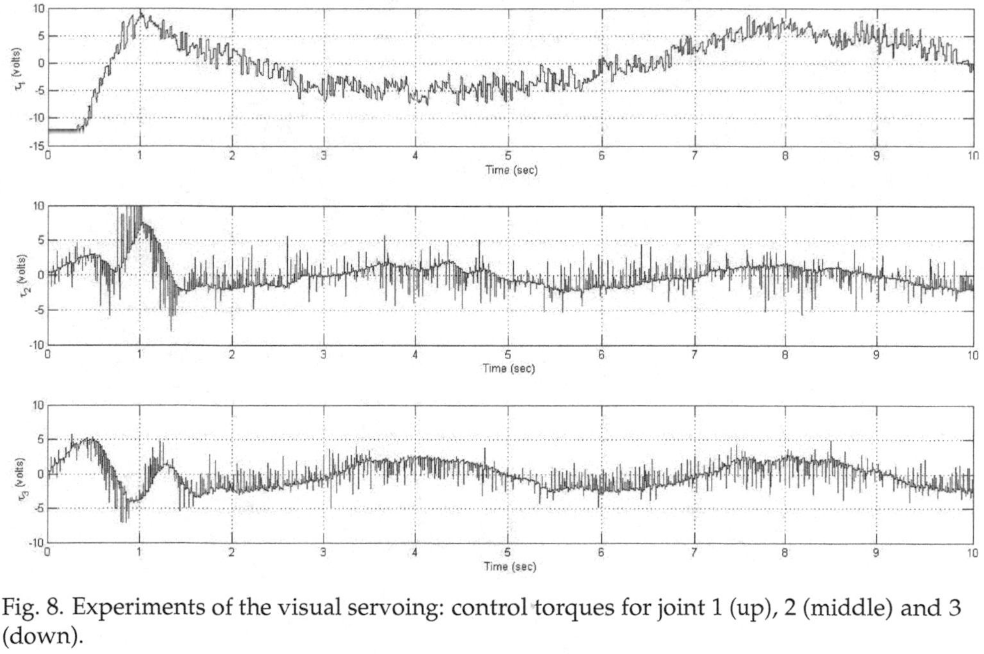

Fig. 8. Experiments of the visual servoing: control torques for joint 1 (up), 2 (middle) and 3 (down).

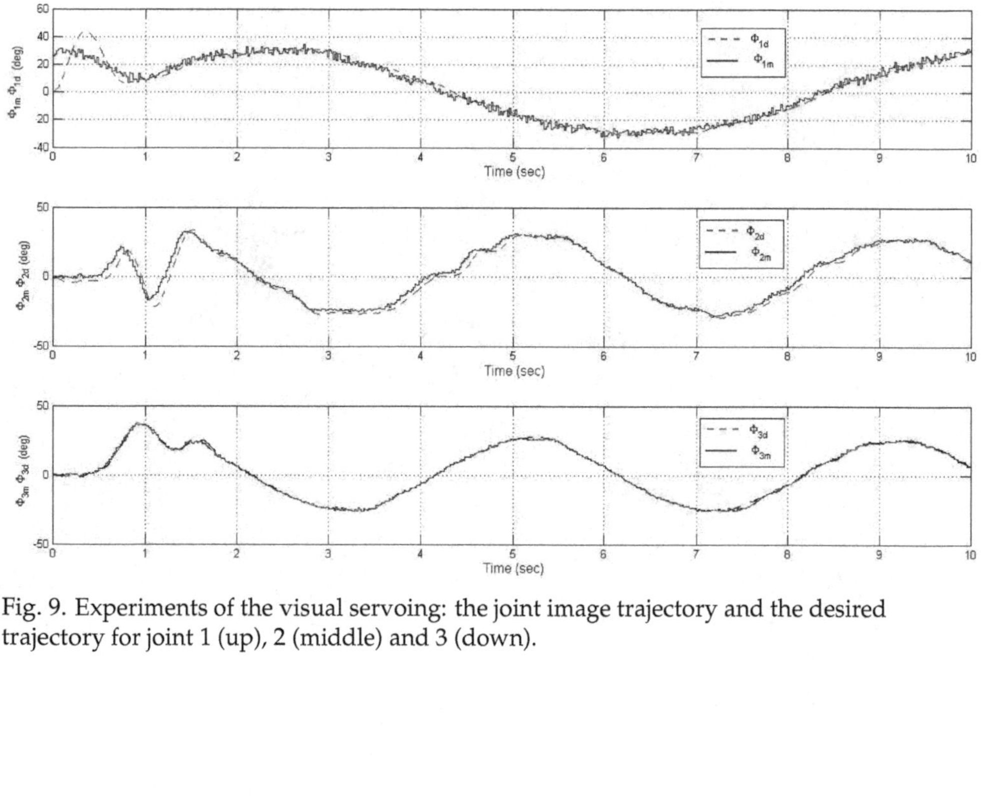

Fig. 9. Experiments of the visual servoing: the joint image trajectory and the desired trajectory for joint 1 (up), 2 (middle) and 3 (down).

5. Conclusions

This chapter has presented an IBVS based on passivity of the robot image dynamics obtained by lumping together the manipulator dynamics, forward kinematics and perspective projection the camera. Using the passivity, controller design was considerably simplified. Regulation and tracking performances were illustrated through laboratory experiments.
Although the general basic idea presented in this chapter is applicable to n-DOF scenarios, much research works related to more precise state observation of the robot image dynamics in the image space using its perspective projection, and analysis of the robustness issues remain to be done. Further works in these directions are undergoing.

6. Acknowledgement

The authors acknowledge the financial support from CONACyT-Mexico through Project 129800 and PAPIIT-UNAM Project IN120009.

7. References

Chen, X. & Kano, H. (2002). A new state observer for perspective systems, *IEEE Transactions on Automatic Control* 47(4): 658–663.

Dickmanns, E. & Graefe, V. (1988). Dynamic monocular machine vision, *Machine Vision and Applications* 1(4): 223–240.

Dixon, W., Fang, Y., Dawson, D. & Flynn, T. (2003). Range identification for perspective vision systems, *IEEE Transactions on Automatic Control* 48(12): 2232–2238.

Escobar, G., Ortega, R. & Sira-Ramirez, H. (1999). Output-feedback global stabilization of a nonlinear benchmarksystem using a saturated passivity-based controller, *IEEE Transactions on Control Systems Technology* 7(2): 289–293.

Espiau, B., Chaumette, B. & Rives, P. (1992). A New Approach to Visual Servoing in Robotics, *IEEE Trans. Robotics and Automation* 8(3): 313–326.

Fujita, M., Kawai, H. & Spong, M. (2007). Passivity Based Dynamic Visual Feedback Control for Three-Dimensional Target Tracking: Stability and L_2-Gain Performance Analysis, *IEEE Transactions on Control Tech.* 15(1): 40.

Grammatikopoulos, L., Karras, G. & Petsa, E. (2004). Camera calibration combining images with two vanishing points, *International Archives of the Photogrammetry, Remote Sensing & Spatial Information Sciences* 35(5): 99–104.

Hashimoto, K., Ebine, T. & Kimura, H. (1996). Visual servoing with hand-eye manipulator-optimal control approach, *IEEE Transactions on Robotics and Automation* 12(5): 766–774.

Hutchinson, S., Hager, G. D. & Corke, P. I. (1996). A tutorial on visual servo control, *IEEE Trans. Robot. Autom.* 12(9): 651.

Karagiannis, D. & Astolfi, A. (2005). A new solution to the problem of range identification in perspective vision systems, *IEEE Transactions on Automatic Control* 50(12): 2074–2077.

Kelly, R. (1999). Regulation of manipulators in generic task space: an energy shapingplus damping injection approach, *IEEE Transactions on Robotics and Automation* 15(2): 381–386.

Kelly, R., Bugarin, E., Cervantes, I. & Alvarez-Ramirez, J. (2006). Monocular direct visual servoing for regulation of manipulators moving in the 3d cartesian space, *Decision and Control, 2006 45th IEEE Conference on*, pp. 1782–1787.

Kelly, R., Carelli, R., Nasisi, O., Kuchen, B. & Reyes, F. (2000). Stable visual servoing of camera-in-hand robotic systems, *Mechatronics, IEEE/ASME Transactions on* 5(1): 39–48.

Khalil, H. K. (2002). *Nonlinear Systems*, Prentice-Hall, New Jersey.

Ma, Y., Kosecka, J. & Sastry, S. (1999). Vision guided navigation for a nonholonomic mobile robot, *Robotics and Automation, IEEE Transactions on* 15(3): 521–536.

Ortega, R. & Spong, M. (1989). Adaptive motion control of rigid robots: A tutorial, *Automatica* 25(6): 877–888.

Slotine, J. & Li, W. (1987). On the Adaptive Control of Robot Manipulators, *The International Journal of Robotics Research* 6(3): 49.

Spong, M., Hutchinson, S. & Vidyasagar, M. (2006). *Robot modeling and control*, John Wiley & Sons.

Takegaki, M. & Arimoto, S. (1981). A new feedback method for dynamic control of manipulators, *ASME, Transactions, Journal of Dynamic Systems, Measurement and Control* 103: 119–125.

Tomei, P. (1991). Adaptive PD controller for robot manipulators, *IEEE Transactions on Robotics and Automation* 7(4): 565–570.

Weiss, L., Sanderson, A. & Neuman, C. (1987). Dynamic sensor-based control of robots with visual feedback, *Robotics and Automation, IEEE Journal of* 3(5): 404–417.

Yuan, J. (1989). A general photogrammetric method for determining object positionand orientation, *IEEE Transactions on Robotics and Automation* 5(2): 129–142.

9

Robust Modeling and Control Issues of Parallel Manipulators with Actuation Redundancy

Andreas Mueller *
University Duisburg-Essen, Chair of Mechanics and Robotics
Germany

1. Introduction

Parallel manipulators, often called parallel kinematics machines (PKM), are controlled non-linear dynamical systems. From a mechanical point of view PKM are (holonomically) constrained mechanical systems characterized by a power transmission between input and output. A so-called end-effector (EE), representing the mechanical output, is connected to a fixed platform by several (often identical) serial linkages, and the constraints reflect the existence of closed loops formed by these chains. Each chain is equipped with one or more actuators, representing the mechanical inputs. The modeling, identification, and control of PKM have advanced in the last decades culminating in successful industrial implementations. Yet the acceptance of PKM is far beyond that of the well-established serial manipulators. This is mainly due to the limited workspace, drastically varying static and dynamic properties, the abundance of singularities within the workspace, and the seemingly complex control.

Traditionally the number of mechanical inputs of a PKM equals its mechanical degree-of-freedom (DOF) so that the PKM is non-redundantly actuated. A means to overcome the aforementioned mechanical limitations is the inclusion of additional actuators, commonly by adding further limbs to the moving platform without increasing the DOF of the PKM. As a simple example consider the PKM in figure 1. The EE can be positioned in the plane thus possesses 2 degrees of freedom. Also the PKM as a whole has the DOF 2 so that two actuators would be sufficient for controlling this PKM. Yet the PKM is actuated by 3 actuators, which gives rise to actuation redundancy in the sense that the actuator forces are not independent. Such actuation redundancy has the potential to increase the EE-acceleration, to homogenize stiffness and manipulability, and to eliminate input singularities (where the motion of the moving platform is not controllable by the actuators), and thus to increase the usable workspace. The design of RA-PKM, and the possible dexterity improvement were addressed in several publications as for instance Garg et al. (2009); Gogu (2007); Krut et al. (2004); Kurtz & Hayward (1992); Lee et al. (1998); Nahon & Angeles (1989); O'Brien & Wen (1999); Shin et al. (2011); Wu et al. (2009).

The existence of redundant actuators allows for control forces that have no effect on the PKM motion but rather lead to mechanical prestress within the PKM. This effect can be exploited for different second-level control tasks such as backlash avoidance and stiffness control. In

*All control concepts proposed in this chapter were implemented by Timo Hufnagel at the Heilbronn University.

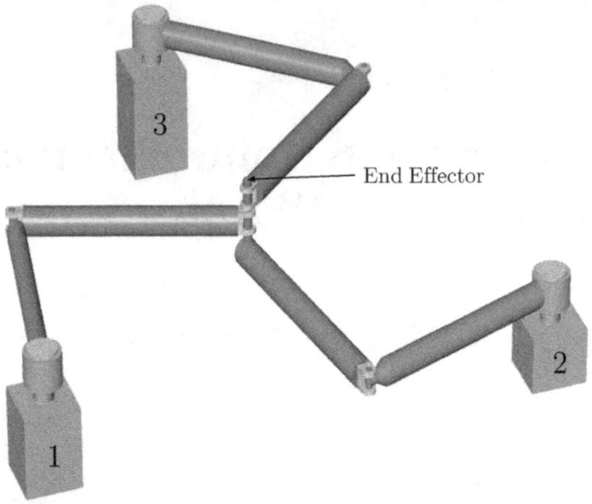

Fig. 1. Multibody model of a 2 DOF planar RA-PKM.

a power port representation of the PKM control system this means that control forces are possible without a (mechanical) power inflow into the system. This also means that in the non-linear control system there are more control vector fields than the dimension of the state space manifold, and that the control forces are not unique. Several strategies for redundancy resolution were proposed exploiting redundancy for second-level control tasks, see Lee et al. (2005); Müller (2005; 2006).

While the described advantages make the redundant actuation scheme attractive its implementation raises several challenges, however. These challenges are due to model uncertainties, synchronization errors in decentralized control schemes, as well to the lack of a globally valid dynamics model. The effect of uncertainties has been analyzed in Müller (2008) and Müller (2010) and it was show that geometric imperfections cause a qualitative change of the way in which actuation forces act upon the PKM. This is in sharp contrast to non-redundantly actuated manipulators where geometric uncertainties simply cause quantitative control errors and so impair the control performance. Moreover, geometric uncertainties of redundantly actuated PKM (RA-PKM) lead to antagonistic control forces proportional to the linear feedback gains. It turns out that this can severely deteriorate the integrity of the controlled RA-PKM.

Although model-based control concepts have been proposed for a long time and implemented recently, robotic manipulators are dominantly controlled by means of decentralized control schemes in practice. Now the indiscriminate application of decentralized control methods to RA-PKM leads again to the problem of antagonistic control forces. In contrast to intentionally generated counteracting control forces, generating desired prestresses, the latter are uncontrolled parasitic control forces. This is an inherent problem of the decentralized control of RA-PKM that can be observed even for a perfect matching of model and plant. To eliminate such antagonistic control forces a so-called antagonism filter (AF) was proposed in Müller & Hufnagel (2011).

The motion equations governing the PKM dynamics form the basis for any model-based control. Aiming on an efficient formulation, the motion equations are usually derived in terms of a minimal number of generalized coordinates that constitute a local parameterization of the configuration space. A well-known problem of this formulation is that such minimal

coordinates are not globally valid on the entire configuration space. Configurations where these coordinates become invalid are called parameterization singularities. That is, it is not possible to uniquely determine any PKM configuration by one specific set of minimal coordinates. The most natural and practicable choice of minimal coordinates is to use the actuator (input) coordinates as they can be measured. Then, the parameterization singularities are also input singularities. An ad hoc method to cope with this phenomenon is to switch between different minimal coordinates as proposed in Hufnagel & Müller (2011). This is a computationally expensive approach since it requires monitoring the numerical conditioning of the constraint equations, and the entire set of motion equation must be changed accordingly. To avoid such switching a novel formulation of motion equations that does use minimal coordinates was proposed in Müller (2011). This formulation is robust with respect to input respectively parameterization singularities and hence does not require switching between different parameterizations. Exponentially stable trajectory tracking can be shown when this formulation is employed in a computed torque and augmented PD control scheme.
These observations call for robust modeling and control concepts. This chapter reports some recent developments in modeling and control of RA-PKM.

2. The PKM control problem

2.1 Manipulator dynamics

Aiming for efficient real-time implementations model-based control schemes for PKM are based on a dynamic model in terms of minimal coordinates as pursued in Cheng et al. (2003); Müller (2005); Nakamura & Ghodoussi (1989); Thanh et al. (2009). A PKM is a force-controlled mechanism with kinematic loops. Following the standard approach in multibody dynamics the Lagrangian motion equations of first kind are first derived for the unconstrained system (opening kinematic loops), and the Lagrange multipliers are eliminated by projecting these equations to the configuration space defined by the (holonomic) geometric constraints. This approach is know as the coordinate partitioning method, see Wehage & Haug (1982).
Denote with $\mathbf{q} \in \mathbb{V}^n$ the vector of joint variables $q^a, a = 1, \ldots, n$ of the unconstrained system, obtained by opening the kinematic loops, where in each kinematic loop one joint is removed. The loop closure is enforced by the corresponding loop constraints giving rise to a set of r geometric and kinematic loop constraints

$$\begin{aligned} \mathbf{0} &= \mathbf{h}(\mathbf{q}),\ \mathbf{h}(\mathbf{q}) \in \mathbb{R}^r \\ \mathbf{0} &= \mathbf{J}(\mathbf{q})\,\dot{\mathbf{q}},\ \mathbf{J}(\mathbf{q}) \in \mathbb{R}^{r,n}. \end{aligned} \tag{1}$$

The PKM in figure 1, for instance, comprises two independent kinematic loops that can be opened by removing the two joints at the EE connecting the kinematic chain formed by joints 2 and 5 with that formed by joints 1 and 4, and joints 3 and 6, respectively. The resulting unconstrained tree-system in figure 2 has $n = 6$ generalized coordinates $q^a, a = 1, \ldots, 6$.
With the constraints (1) the Lagrangian motion equations of the PKM are

$$\mathbf{G}(\mathbf{q})\,\ddot{\mathbf{q}} + \mathbf{C}(\mathbf{q}, \dot{\mathbf{q}})\,\dot{\mathbf{q}} + \mathbf{Q}(\mathbf{q}, \dot{\mathbf{q}}, t) + \mathbf{J}^T(\mathbf{q})\,\boldsymbol{\lambda} = \mathbf{u}. \tag{2}$$

$\mathbf{G}$ is the generalized mass matrix of the tree-system, $\mathbf{C}\dot{\mathbf{q}}$ represents generalized Coriolis and centrifugal forces, $\mathbf{Q}$ represents all remaining forces, including EE loads, and $\mathbf{u}$ are the generalized control forces. The Lagrange multipliers $\boldsymbol{\lambda}$ can be identified with the

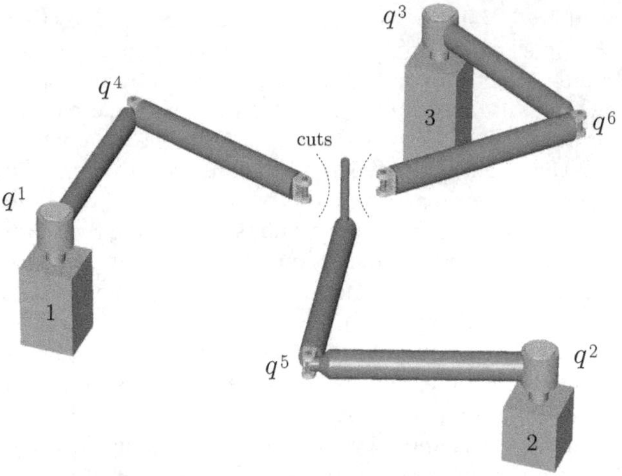

Fig. 2. Definition of loop constraints for the planar 2 DOF RA-PKM.

constraint reactions in cut-joints. The vector $\mathbf{q} \in \mathbb{V}^n$ represents the PKM configuration. The configuration space (c-space) of the PKM model is defined by the geometric constraints:

$$V := \{\mathbf{q} \in \mathbb{V}^n | \mathbf{h}(\mathbf{q}) = \mathbf{0}\}. \tag{3}$$

If $\mathbf{J}$ has locally full rank r, one can select $\delta := n - r$ joint variables, called independent coordinates, such that the admissible configurations $\mathbf{q} \in V$ are functions of these independent coordinates. This induces a coordinate partitioning. If the rank of $\mathbf{J}$ is constant, the c-space is smooth δ-dimensional manifold and δ is the DOF of the PKM, see Müller (2009). A configuration $\mathbf{q}$ where the rank of $\mathbf{J}$ changes is called a c-space singularity since then V is not a smooth manifold in $\mathbf{q}$.
Denote with $\mathbf{q}_1$ and $\mathbf{q}_2$ respectively the vector of dependent and independent coordinates, the velocity constraints can be written as

$$\mathbf{J}_1\dot{\mathbf{q}}_1 + \mathbf{J}_2\dot{\mathbf{q}}_2 = \mathbf{0}, \tag{4}$$

where $\mathbf{J} = (\mathbf{J}_1, \mathbf{J}_2)$, with $\mathbf{J}_1(\mathbf{q}) \in \mathbb{R}^{r,r}$, $\mathbf{J}_2(\mathbf{q}) \in \mathbb{R}^{r,\delta}$. By definition of independent coordinates $\mathbf{J}_1$ has full rank, and the generalized velocities can be expressed as

$$\dot{\mathbf{q}} = \mathbf{F}\dot{\mathbf{q}}_2, \text{ where } \mathbf{F} := \begin{pmatrix} -\mathbf{J}_1^{-1}\mathbf{J}_2 \\ \mathbf{I}_\delta \end{pmatrix}. \tag{5}$$

where the matrix $\mathbf{F}$ is an orthogonal complement of $\mathbf{J}$ because $\mathbf{JF} \equiv \mathbf{0}$. The time derivative of (5) yields the accelerations $\ddot{\mathbf{q}} = \mathbf{F}\ddot{\mathbf{q}}_2 + \dot{\mathbf{F}}\dot{\mathbf{q}}_2$.
Due to the existence of kinematic loops, PKM comprise passive joints and only the m control forces corresponding to the active joints are present in $\mathbf{u}$. Denote with $\mathbf{c} \equiv (c_1, \ldots, c_m)$ the vector of generalized control forces in the actuated joints, and let $\mathbf{A}$ be that part of $\mathbf{F}$ so that $\mathbf{F}^T\mathbf{u} = \mathbf{A}^T\mathbf{c}$. This means that if $\mathbf{q}_a$ denote the vector of m actuator coordinates, then $\dot{\mathbf{q}}_a = \mathbf{A}\dot{\mathbf{q}}_2$.

Projecting the motion equations (2) of the tree-system to the configuration space V, with the help of the orthogonal complement $\mathbf{F}$, and with (5), yields

$$\overline{\mathbf{G}}(\mathbf{q})\,\ddot{\mathbf{q}}_2 + \overline{\mathbf{C}}\,(\mathbf{q},\dot{\mathbf{q}})\,\dot{\mathbf{q}}_2 + \overline{\mathbf{Q}}(\mathbf{q},\dot{\mathbf{q}},t) = \mathbf{A}^T(\mathbf{q})\,\mathbf{c} \tag{6}$$

where

$$\overline{\mathbf{G}} := \mathbf{F}^T\mathbf{G}\mathbf{F},\ \overline{\mathbf{C}} := \mathbf{F}^T(\mathbf{C}\mathbf{F} + \mathbf{G}\dot{\mathbf{F}}),\ \overline{\mathbf{Q}} := \mathbf{F}^T\mathbf{Q}. \tag{7}$$

The $\delta = n - m$ equations (6) together with the r dynamic constraints $\mathbf{J}\ddot{\mathbf{q}} + \dot{\mathbf{J}}\dot{\mathbf{q}} = \mathbf{0}$ yield a system of n ODE's in the n generalized coordinates $\mathbf{q}$ that govern the PKM dynamics when controlled via the generalized control forces $\mathbf{c}$. The equations (6) have been first proposed by Voronets (1901) and are a special kind of Maggi's equations, Maggi (1901). They have been proposed for use in multibody dynamics in Angles & Lee (1988); Wehage & Haug (1982), and were put forward for PKM modeling in Cheng et al. (2003); Müller (2005); Thanh et al. (2009). The PKM control problem can now be represented as the control-affine control system

$$\dot{\mathbf{x}} = \mathbf{f}\,(\mathbf{x}) + \sum_{i=1}^{m} \mathbf{g}^i\,(\mathbf{x})\,c_i \tag{8}$$

with state vector $\mathbf{x} := (\mathbf{q}_2, \dot{\mathbf{q}}_2)$, where

$$\mathbf{f} := \begin{pmatrix} \dot{\mathbf{q}}_2 \\ -\overline{\mathbf{G}}^{-1}(\overline{\mathbf{C}}\dot{\mathbf{q}}_2 + \overline{\mathbf{Q}}) \end{pmatrix},\quad \mathbf{g} := \begin{pmatrix} \mathbf{0} \\ \overline{\mathbf{G}}^{-1}\mathbf{A}^T \end{pmatrix}. \tag{9}$$

$\mathbf{f}$ is the drift vector field, and the columns $\mathbf{g}^i, i = 1,\ldots,m$ are the control vector fields that determine how the control forces affect the system's state.

2.2 Actuation concepts

Based on the control system (8) different actuation schemes can be distinguished. Actuation refers to the immediate effect of control forces in a given state of the PKM. Apparently the degree of actuation has to do with the number of independent control vector fields. The degree of actuation (DOA) can be defined as the number of independent input vector fields $\mathbf{g}^i$ in the control system (8). With regular $\overline{G}$ the DOA is

$$\alpha\,(q) := \operatorname{rank} \overline{M}\,(q)\,. \tag{10}$$

If $\alpha\,(q) < \delta$, the system is called *underactuated*, and if $\alpha\,(q) = \delta$, it is called *full-actuated* at q. The system is called *redundantly actuated* at q, if $m - \alpha\,(q) > 0$ and *non-redundantly actuated* at q, if $m = \alpha\,(q)$. Apparently a system can be redundantly underactuated. Configurations q where the DOA changes, i.e. when α is not constant in a neighborhood of q, are called *input singularities*, see Müller (2009); Zlatanov & Fenton (1998).

2.3 Inverse dynamics solution

The inverse dynamics problem is to find the control forces $\mathbf{c}$ required for controlling the PKM along a prescribed target trajectory $\mathbf{q}\,(t)$. The system (6) has no unique solution for $\mathbf{c}$. Moreover, it is clear that only those $\mathbf{c}$ in the range of the control matrix $\mathbf{A}^T$ are effective control forces, and that arbitrary forces $\mathbf{c}^0$ (prestress) in the null-space of $\mathbf{A}^T$ can be superposed. If $\mathbf{c}^0$ is the vector of desired prestress, for given $\mathbf{q}, \dot{\mathbf{q}}, \ddot{\mathbf{q}}$, a solution such that

$\left(\mathbf{c}-\mathbf{c}^0\right)^T \mathbf{W}\left(\mathbf{c}-\mathbf{c}^0\right) \rightarrow \min$ is given by

$$\begin{aligned}\mathbf{c} &= \left(\mathbf{A}^T\right)^+_{\mathbf{W}} \mathbf{F}^T(\mathbf{G}(\mathbf{q})\ddot{\mathbf{q}}+\mathbf{C}(\mathbf{q},\dot{\mathbf{q}})\dot{\mathbf{q}}+\mathbf{Q}(\mathbf{q},\dot{\mathbf{q}}))+\mathbf{N}_{\mathbf{A}^T,\mathbf{W}}\mathbf{c}^0 \\ &= \left(\mathbf{A}^T\right)^+_{\mathbf{W}} (\overline{\mathbf{G}}(\mathbf{q})\ddot{\mathbf{q}}_2+\overline{\mathbf{C}}(\mathbf{q},\dot{\mathbf{q}})\dot{\mathbf{q}}_2+\overline{\mathbf{Q}}(\mathbf{q},\dot{\mathbf{q}}))+\mathbf{N}_{\mathbf{A}^T,\mathbf{W}}\mathbf{c}^0 \end{aligned} \tag{11}$$

where $\left(\mathbf{A}^T\right)^+_{\mathbf{W}} := \mathbf{W}^{-1}\mathbf{A}\left(\mathbf{A}^T\mathbf{W}^{-1}\mathbf{A}\right)^{-1}$ is the weighted right pseudoinverse, and $\mathbf{N}_{\mathbf{A}^T,\mathbf{W}} := \left(\mathbf{I}_m - \left(\mathbf{A}^T\right)^+_{\mathbf{W}}\mathbf{A}^T\right)$ is a projector to the null-space of $\mathbf{A}^T$. $\mathbf{W}$ is a symmetric positive definite weighting matrix for the drive forces in accordance with the drive capabilities. The pseudoinverse solution in (11) delivers the controls that produce the desired motion, where the drive load is balanced between the individual drives according to the weights. The second part of the control vector $\mathbf{c}$ is the null-space component generating prestress that is closest to the desired $\mathbf{c}^0$. The possibility of generating control forces in the null-space has been used for backlash avoidance and stiffness control Müller (2005; 2006); Valasek et al. (2002); Yi et al. (1989).

3. Decentralized control schemes

3.1 Peculiarities of PKM with actuation redundancy

Decentralized control of individual actuators without taking into account the dynamics of the controlled system is still the standard control method in industrial applications. Moreover the majority of contemporary robotic manipulators are controlled by a decentralized PD law in favor of its simple computation and low-cost setup. In contrast to model-based control, the actuators are controlled independently, without reference to the dynamics of the non-linear control system, exclusively upon the individual commands obtained from motion planning and inverse kinematics. In other words, it is assumed that all actuators can be independently controlled without mutual interference. This applies to serial manipulators as well as to PKM without actuation redundancy as summarized in Paccot et al. (2009) and Thanh et al. (2009). However, since in case of RA-PKM more actuators are activated than required, decentralized control of RA-PKM naturally leads to conflicting control forces, reflected by undesired prestresses and an increased power consumption as observed in Saglia et al. (2009),Valasek et al. (2005), Wang et al. (2009). Hence antagonistic control forces cannot be attributed to model uncertainties alone, as analyzed in Müller (2010), which could be minimized using model identification methods. Even more such counteraction is inherent to the decentralized control method. In order to eliminate contradicting control forces the actuation redundancy must be resolved also within decentralized control, which requires a kinematic model. In the following the interplay of measurement errors and decentralized control is discussed.

As above denote with $\mathbf{q}$ and $\mathbf{q}_{\mathrm{a}}$ the actual generalized coordinates of the plant (which is unknown). Further a measurement error is assumed caused by a constant (calibration) offset $\Delta\mathbf{q}_{\mathrm{a}}$. The vector of measured actuator coordinates is then introduced as $\widetilde{\mathbf{q}}_{\mathrm{a}} := \mathbf{q}_{\mathrm{a}} + \Delta\mathbf{q}_{\mathrm{a}}$. If $\mathbf{q}^{\mathrm{d}}_{\mathrm{a}}(t)$ denotes the desired actuator motion, $\mathbf{e}_{\mathrm{a}} := \mathbf{q}_{\mathrm{a}} - \mathbf{q}^{\mathrm{d}}_{\mathrm{a}}$ is the actual tracking error. Due to the calibration offset the measured tracking error is $\widetilde{\mathbf{e}}_{\mathrm{a}} = \widetilde{\mathbf{q}}_{\mathrm{a}} - \mathbf{q}^{\mathrm{d}}_{\mathrm{a}} = \mathbf{e}_{\mathrm{a}} + \Delta\mathbf{q}_{\mathrm{a}}$.

The simple PD control law that independently regulates the m actuator positions upon these measurements is

$$\mathbf{c} = -\mathbf{K}_{\mathrm{P}}\widetilde{\mathbf{e}}_{\mathrm{a}} - \mathbf{K}_{\mathrm{D}}\dot{\widetilde{\mathbf{e}}}_{\mathrm{a}}. \tag{12}$$

$\mathbf{K}_\text{P}$ and $\mathbf{K}_\text{D}$ are diagonal positive definite gain matrices. The effect of measurement errors can be understood considering the pose $\widetilde{\mathbf{q}}_\text{a}$ that is attained as result of a constant setpoint command $\mathbf{q}_\text{a}^\text{d}$. The stationary control forces, not producing any motion, are those $\mathbf{c}^0$ in the null-space of $\mathbf{A}^T(\mathbf{q})$, i.e.

$$\mathbf{0} = \mathbf{A}^T(\mathbf{q})\,\mathbf{c}^0 = -\mathbf{A}^T(\mathbf{q})\,\mathbf{K}_\text{P}\widetilde{\mathbf{e}}_\text{a} = -\mathbf{A}^T(\mathbf{q})\,\mathbf{K}_\text{P}\left(\mathbf{e}_\text{a} + \Delta\mathbf{q}_\text{a}\right). \tag{13}$$

If there are no measurement errors (and no model uncertainties) it is $\Delta\mathbf{q}_\text{a} = \mathbf{0}$, and the PKM converges to $\mathbf{e}_\text{a} = 0$ since $\mathbf{q}_\text{a}$ and $\mathbf{q}_\text{a}^\text{d}$ satisfy the geometric constraints. Since generally $\Delta\mathbf{q}_\text{a}$ do not comply with the geometric constraints the PKM converges to a $\mathbf{q}_\text{a}$ such that $\mathbf{e}_\text{a} + \Delta\mathbf{q}_\text{a}$ is in the null-space of $\mathbf{A}^T\mathbf{K}_\text{P}$. The exact value of $\mathbf{q}$ depends on external forces, e.g. gravity and process loads. The attained steady state error is

$$\mathbf{e}_\text{a} = -\mathbf{K}_\text{P}^{-1}\left(\mathbf{A}^T\right)^+\mathbf{K}_\text{P}\Delta\mathbf{q}_\text{a} \tag{14}$$

with the right pseudoinverse $\left(\mathbf{A}^T\right)^+ = \mathbf{A}\left(\mathbf{A}^T\mathbf{A}\right)^{-1}$ of $\mathbf{A}^T$. In this equilibrium configuration the PD controllers yield the steady state actuator forces $\mathbf{c}^0 = \mathbf{K}_\text{P}\left(\mathbf{e}_\text{a} + \Delta\mathbf{q}_\text{a}\right)$. Since they are in the null-space of $\mathbf{A}^T$ the RA-PKM stays at rest.

The consideration so far applies to constant calibration offsets. A further source of systematic measurement errors is the encoder resolution within the actuators. Assuming exact calibration, for simplicity, the error measurement, and thus $\Delta\mathbf{q}_\text{a}$, change discontinuously according to the resolution. Then the solution for the steady state error (14) is only piecewise valid and may not be unique. Moreover the interplay of antagonistic forces and the quantization of $\widetilde{\mathbf{q}}_\text{a}$ can cause alternating control forces, and hence excited vibrations. This is clear by noting that $\Delta\mathbf{q}_\text{a}$ changes in discrete steps so that during the settling process the components of $\mathbf{e}_\text{a} + \Delta\mathbf{q}_\text{a}$ in the null-space of $\mathbf{A}^T\mathbf{K}_\text{P}$ are changing discontinuously and thus cause discontinuous control forces.

The crucial point is that the decentralized control scheme (13) is not restricted to the range of $\mathbf{A}^T$, and so yields antagonistic control forces in the null-space of $\mathbf{A}^T$. Such contradictory control forces are on the one hand due to measurement errors but are on the other hand inevitably caused by the uncoordinated control of individual actuators with (12). In the decentralized PD control the individual controller for each kinematic chain, connecting the EE to the base, acts independently without respecting the coordination within the closed kinematic loops of the RA-PKM. Consider this phenomenon for the 2 DOF RA-PKM in figure 1. The manipulator can be viewed as the cooperation of two (virtually independent) non-redundantly actuated 5-bar linkages as shown in figure 3. Consider the situation when the EE is to follow a straight line depicted in figure 3. The three base joints, with coordinates q^1, q^2, and q^3, are actuated. Two of these actuators are sufficient for this 2 DOF system, however. For instance, the PKM can be controlled by joints 1 and 2, or joints 2 and 3. Consequently the motion control of the 5-bar loop consisting of joints 1 and 2, and the other 5-bar loop with joints 2 and 3 must be synchronized. Controlling the loops independently, the control commands for steering the EE along the straight line, determined from (12), drive either 5-bar loop along a straight line in the $q^1 - q^2$ and $q^2 - q^3$ joint subspace, respectively. The latter correspond to EE-curves depicted in figure 3. It is apparent that the control commands of the 5-bar linkages are contradicting due to the missing synchronization of the two loops. This is an inherent problem of the decentralized control, which does exist for the model-based control schemes that a priori respects such interdependencies.

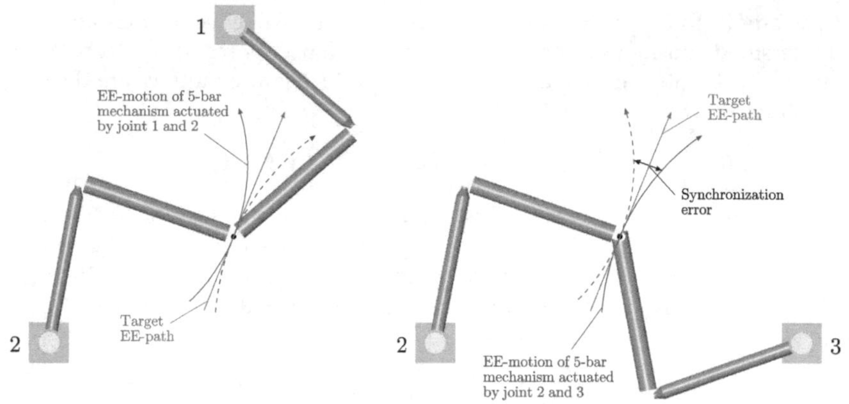

Fig. 3. Explanation of the synchronization error in decentralized control.

3.2 Antagonism filter - a method for reducing counteraction

Apparently the antagonistic actuator forces are those control commands that are (unintentionally) in the null-space of $\mathbf{A}^T$. Elimination of these antagonistic control forces is hence equivalent to the removal of those components of the control forces $\mathbf{c}$ that are in the null-space of $\mathbf{A}^T$. This is readily achieved using the projector

$$\mathbf{R}_{\mathbf{A}^T} := \mathbf{I} - \mathbf{N}_{\mathbf{A}^T} = \left(\mathbf{A}^T\right)^+ \mathbf{A}^T \tag{15}$$

onto the range of $\mathbf{A}^T$, where $\mathbf{N}_{\mathbf{A}^T}$ is the null-space projector. This projector can be applied to any actuator force commands (not necessarily computed from (12)), and return the effective control forces

$$\mathbf{c}_{\text{eff}} = \mathbf{R}_{\mathbf{A}^T}\mathbf{c}. \tag{16}$$

These control forces can be applied to the PKM without changing the drive action since $\mathbf{A}^T\mathbf{R}_{\mathbf{A}^T} = \mathbf{A}^T$. Because $\mathbf{R}_{\mathbf{A}^T}$ eliminates the antagonistic actuator forces it is called the *antagonism filter* (AF) in Müller & Hufnagel (2011).

In practice the individual actuators are position/velocity controlled rather than force controlled. Since this splitting concerns the actuator forces it needs to be transformed to the position and velocity command. Therefore the error vector in (12) is projected to the range of $\mathbf{A}^T\mathbf{K}_{\text{P}}$ and $\mathbf{A}^T\mathbf{K}_{\text{D}}$, respectively, so that

$$\mathbf{e}_{\text{eff}} = \mathbf{R}_{\mathbf{A}^T\mathbf{K}_{\text{P}}}\widetilde{\mathbf{e}}_{\text{a}}, \quad \dot{\mathbf{e}}_{\text{eff}} = \mathbf{R}_{\mathbf{A}^T\mathbf{K}_{\text{D}}}\dot{\widetilde{\mathbf{e}}}_{\text{a}}. \tag{17}$$

Then the corrected command sent to the individual PD controllers is

$$\mathbf{q}^{\text{d}}_{\text{eff}} = \mathbf{q}_{\text{a}} - \mathbf{e}_{\text{eff}}, \quad \dot{\mathbf{q}}^{\text{d}}_{\text{eff}} = \dot{\mathbf{q}}_{\text{a}} - \dot{\mathbf{e}}_{\text{eff}}. \tag{18}$$

3.3 Case study: Planar 2 DOF RA-PKM

The AF has been applied to decentralized control of the planar 2 DOF redundantly full-actuated PKM in figure 1. The testbed was developed at the Heilbronn University as reported in Hufnagel & Müller (2011) and Müller & Hufnagel (2011), where all experiments were carried out. The prototype consists of arm segments with a length of 200 mm. The three revolute joints are located at an equilateral triangle with lateral length 400 mm. The base joints are actuated with DC motors (Maxon Re30). The RA-PKM can be controlled either with individual PD controllers or a model-base control scheme (see section 4.5). The PD controllers are designed for a load corresponding to the weight of one arm (134 g). In the following results for the PD controller are reported.

As example the PKM is controlled within 5 s along the triangular EE trajectory in figure 4. The trajectory is planned according to the maximal acceleration of about 0.5 $\frac{m}{s^2}$. The required actuator motions are determined from the inverse kinematics that are the target trajectories of the PD controllers. The manipulator was calibrated manually in order to reduce calibration errors. The required joint torques are shown in figure 5 and the joint errors in figure 6. The

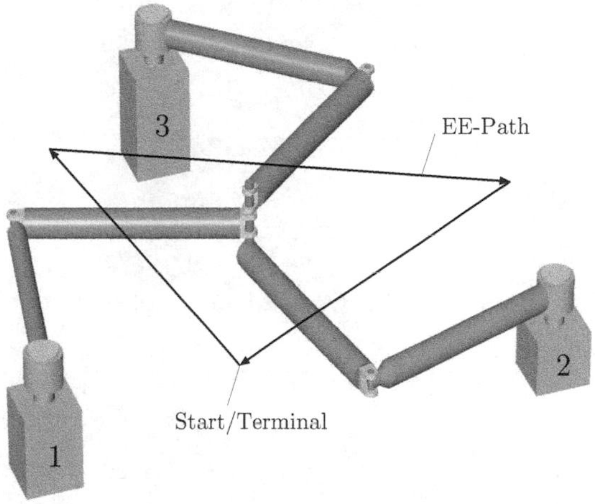

Fig. 4. Triangular EE-path along which the RA-PKM is controlled with the CTC.

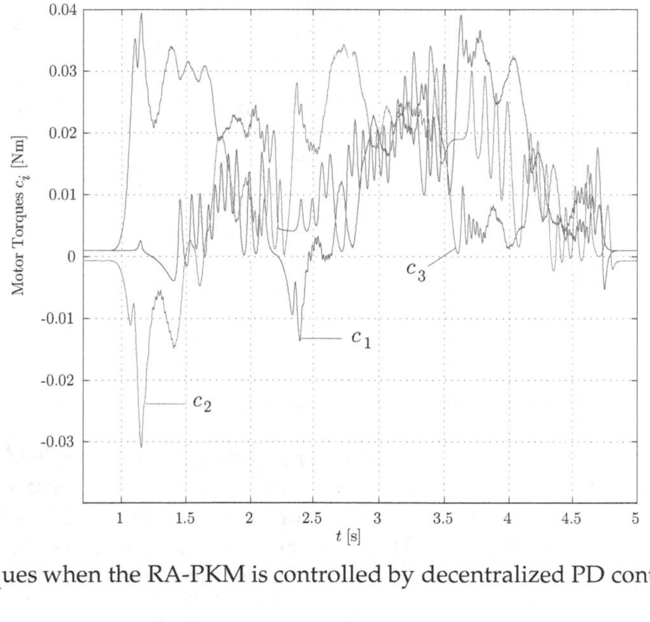

Fig. 5. Joint torques when the RA-PKM is controlled by decentralized PD controllers.

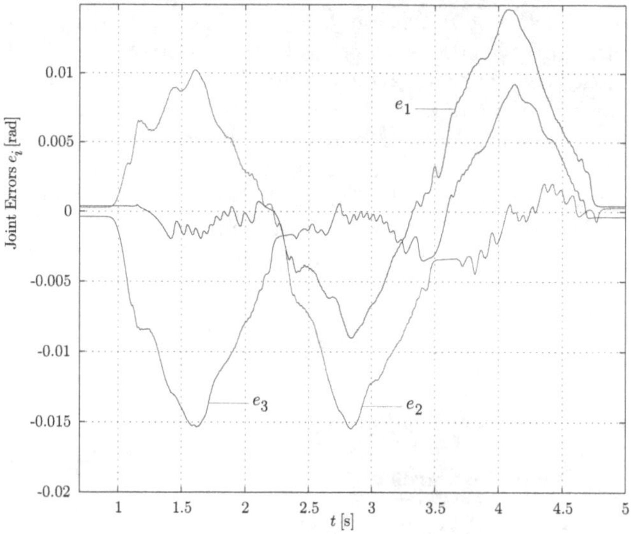

Fig. 6. Actuator tracking errors when the RA-PKM is controlled by decentralized PD controllers.

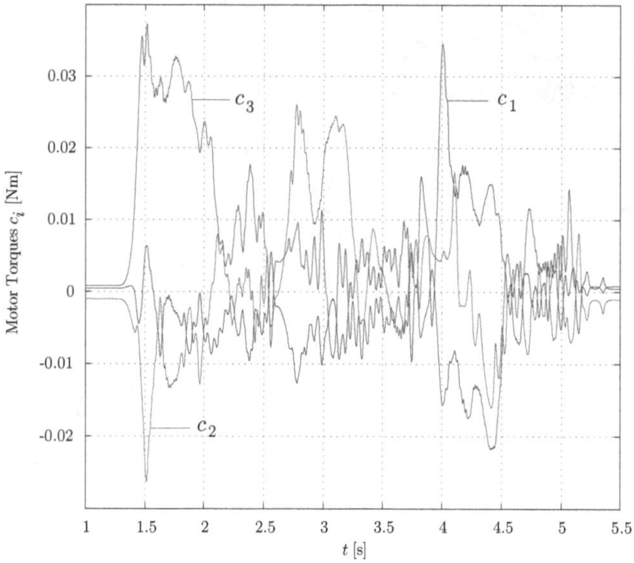

Fig. 7. Joint torques when the AF is applied to decentralized PD control of the RA-PKM.

initial and final torques and errors in the actuator joint angles when the PKM is at rest are due to the remaining calibration uncertainty and encoder quantization. These steady state drive torques are in accordance with (13) and (14). Application of the AF (15) reduces the overall drive torques as shown in figure 7. The antagonistic actuator torques are almost removed by the AF. A small part of the constant initial and final actuator torques remain, however.

Motor i	Electric Energy Consumption E_i^{el}	
	without AF	with AF
1	1.3347 Ws	0.4574 Ws
2	1.5414 Ws	0.7010 Ws
3	1.6844 Ws	1.0801 Ws

Table 1. Energy consumption if the PKM is manually recalibrated.

This can be explained by noting that the control matrix $\mathbf{A}^T$ and the AF are computed upon the measurement $\widetilde{\mathbf{q}}_a$, and that there are always model imperfections. A reduction of electric energy translates directly to the reduction of actuator torques, and the reduced actuator torques are reflected by a reduced electrical power consumption E_i^{el} of motor i. Table 1 shows the energy consumptions when the RA-PKM is controlled with and without application of the AF. A significant reduction of electrical energy consumption and thus of the drive torques is apparent. The performed mechanical work is indeed not altered by AF.

4. Model-based control schemes

4.1 Augmented PD and computed torque controller

Two accepted methods for the model-based control of robotic manipulators are the augmented PD (APD) and computed torque control (CTC) schemes Asada & Slotine (1986); Murray et al. (1993). Both schemes consist of a non-linear feedforward term, that delivers the control forces required for steering the PKM along the desired trajectory, and a linear feedback term to compensate drifts from the desired motion. Now the feedforward term requires the inverse dynamics solution (11). These control methods, originally derived for non-redundantly actuated systems, can be directly adopted for RA-PKM as in Cheng et al. (2003); Müller (2005); Paccot et al. (2009). The APD can be used in the form (omitting null-space components)

$$\mathbf{c} = \left(\mathbf{A}^T(\mathbf{q})\right)^+ \left[\overline{\mathbf{G}}(\mathbf{q})\, \ddot{\mathbf{q}}_2^{\mathrm{d}} + \overline{\mathbf{C}}(\mathbf{q},\dot{\mathbf{q}})\, \dot{\mathbf{q}}_2^{\mathrm{d}} + \overline{\mathbf{Q}}(\mathbf{q},\dot{\mathbf{q}}) - \mathbf{K}_{\mathrm{D}}\dot{\mathbf{e}}_2 - \mathbf{K}_{\mathrm{P}}\mathbf{e}_2\right], \tag{19}$$

wherein $\mathbf{q}^{\mathrm{d}}(t)$ is the desired path, and $\mathbf{e}_2(t) := \mathbf{q}_2(t) - \mathbf{q}_2^{\mathrm{d}}(t)$ is the tracking error of the independent coordinates. The gain matrices $\mathbf{K}_{\mathrm{D}}$ and $\mathbf{K}_{\mathrm{P}}$ are diagonal and positive definite. An adopted form of the CTC law for RA-PKM is

$$\mathbf{c} = \left(\mathbf{A}^T(\mathbf{q})\right)^+ \left[\overline{\mathbf{G}}(\mathbf{q})\, \mathbf{v}_2 + \overline{\mathbf{C}}(\mathbf{q},\dot{\mathbf{q}})\, \dot{\mathbf{q}}_2 + \overline{\mathbf{Q}}(\mathbf{q},\dot{\mathbf{q}})\right], \tag{20}$$

with $\mathbf{v}_2 := \ddot{\mathbf{q}}_2^{\mathrm{d}} - \mathbf{K}_{\mathrm{D}}\dot{\mathbf{e}}_2 - \mathbf{K}_{\mathrm{P}}\mathbf{e}_2$. Perfect matching of model and plant presumed, both control laws applied to (6) result in exponentially stable trajectory tracking for sufficiently large gains $\mathbf{K}_{\mathrm{D}}$ and $\mathbf{K}_{\mathrm{P}}$, provided $\overline{\mathbf{G}}$ is regular. The latter assumption only fails in configuration space singularities of the PKM and in singularities of the parameterization of the model. This is in particular critical for RA-PKM as explained in the next section.

4.2 Parameterization-singularities of the dynamic model

It is well-known that there is generally no choice of minimal coordinates that is valid for the entire motion range of the manipulator. Parameterization-singularities refer to configurations where a selected set of independent coordinates becomes invalid. This problem is usually solved ad-hoc by switching between different mathematical models as proposed in Hufnagel & Müller (2011). There is, however, no general approach to cope with this problem. While this is essentially a numerical problem of the particular PKM model it does have a great significance for PKM control. In particular the improper selection of generalized coordinates can severely deteriorate the stability of model-based control schemes.

The inherent problem of the minimal coordinate formulation is the need for selecting independent minimal coordinates $\mathbf{q}_2$. Since they are local coordinates on the c-space V the PKM configuration cannot be expressed globally in terms of these minimal coordinates. That is, any such minimal coordinates are only valid in a limited range of motion, and a collection of different sets of minimal coordinates is necessary to cover the entire c-space. The switching method proposed in Hufnagel & Müller (2011) switches between such local coordinates.

From a practical point of view it makes sense to use δ actuator coordinates as independent coordinates in the motion equations (6). That is, $\mathbf{q}_2$ is a subset of $\mathbf{q}_a$. In other words the PKM is considered as non-redundantly actuated and its motion equations are parameterized in terms of δ actuator coordinates. Consequently, parameterization-singularities are exactly the input-singularities of the non-redundantly actuated PKM. For example, the planar 2 DOF RA-PKM in figure 1 is naturally parameterized in terms of $\delta = 2$ out of the $m = 3$ actuator coordinates. This leads to parameterization-singularities shown in figure 8. Figure 8 a) shows two configurations where the actuator coordinates q^1 and q^2 are not valid as independent coordinates for the PKM model. In these configurations the PKM configuration is not uniquely determined by the motion joints of 1 and 2 so that q^1 and q^2 fail as independent coordinates. Alternatively joints 1 and 3 could be used to control the PKM. That is, q^1 and q^3 would constitute independent coordinates of the minimal coordinate model (6). This parameterization exhibits the singular configurations in figure 8 b), however. Similar singularities exist when q^2 and q^3 are used as independent, and moreover there are parameterization-singularities for any choice of two actuator angles.

Now it is important to notice that any switching to different independent coordinates $\mathbf{q}_2$ causes a complete change of the motion equations (6). Such a switching method is thus computationally rather complex and accompanied by a high implementation effort. Its application to general RA-PKM requires monitoring the numerical conditioning of the orthogonal complement $\mathbf{F}$ in (5) in order to detect switching points. Only for simple mechanisms, such as the reported 2 DOF RA-PKM in figure 1, the switching points can be determined explicitly giving rise to a switching map.

4.3 A robust formulation of the dynamic model in redundant coordinates

The minimal coordinate formulation (6) is prone to parameterization-singularities. Coordinate switching methods, introduced to cope with this problem, are computationally rather complex for general PKM. An approach that completely avoids the use of independent coordinates was proposed in Müller (2011) where the motion equations are expressed in terms of n redundant coordinates. The idea is to eliminate the Lagrange multipliers from (2) by means of a projector to the null-space of $\mathbf{J}$. That is, instead of premultiplication with $\mathbf{F}^T$, (2) is premultiplied with a null-space projector determined from the pseudoinverse of $\mathbf{J}$. As long as the PKM does not encounter c-space singularities, where rank $\mathbf{J}$ drops, the constraint Jacobian $\mathbf{J}$ is always full rank r, and its right pseudoinverse is given by $\mathbf{J}^+ = \mathbf{J}^T(\mathbf{J}\mathbf{J}^T)^{-1}$. The corresponding projector to the null-space of $\mathbf{J}$ is then $\mathbf{N}_\mathbf{J} = \mathbf{I}_n - \mathbf{J}^+\mathbf{J}$. This projector does not

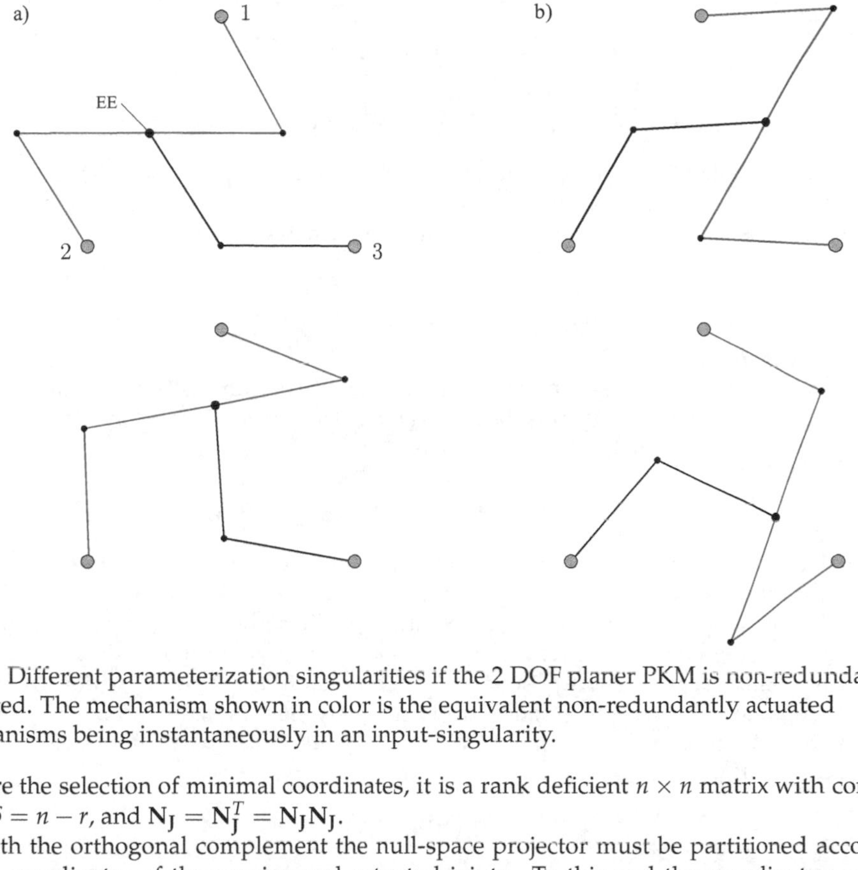

Fig. 8. Different parameterization singularities if the 2 DOF planer PKM is non-redundantly actuated. The mechanism shown in color is the equivalent non-redundantly actuated mechanisms being instantaneously in an input-singularity.

require the selection of minimal coordinates, it is a rank deficient $n \times n$ matrix with constant rank $\delta = n - r$, and $\mathbf{N}_\mathrm{J} = \mathbf{N}_\mathrm{J}^T = \mathbf{N}_\mathrm{J}\mathbf{N}_\mathrm{J}$.
As with the orthogonal complement the null-space projector must be partitioned according to the coordinates of the passive and actuated joints. To this end the coordinate vector is rearranged as $\mathbf{q} = (\mathbf{q}_\mathrm{p}, \mathbf{q}_\mathrm{a})$, Denote with $\mathbf{q}_\mathrm{p}$ and $\mathbf{q}_\mathrm{a}$ the vector consisting of the m coordinates of passive joints and δ coordinates of actuator joints, respectively. With the assumption that the PKM configuration is determined by the m actuator coordinates, δ actuator coordinates serve as minimal coordinates, so that $\mathbf{q}_\mathrm{a} = (..., \mathbf{q}_2)$. Then the projector can be partitioned as

$$\mathbf{N}_\mathrm{J} = \begin{pmatrix} \widetilde{\mathbf{P}} \\ \widetilde{\mathbf{A}} \end{pmatrix} \begin{matrix} -\ (n-m) \times n \\ -\ m \times n \end{matrix} \tag{21}$$

where $\widetilde{\mathbf{A}}$ corresponds to the actuator coordinates so that $\dot{\mathbf{q}}_\mathrm{a} = \widetilde{\mathbf{A}}\dot{\mathbf{q}}$. Premultiplication of the motion equations (2) with $\mathbf{N}_\mathrm{J}^T = \mathbf{N}_\mathrm{J}$ and $\mathbf{J}\mathbf{N}_\mathrm{J} = \mathbf{0}$ yields a system of n motion equations

$$\mathbf{N}_\mathrm{J}(\mathbf{G}(\mathbf{q})\ddot{\mathbf{q}} + \mathbf{C}(\mathbf{q}, \dot{\mathbf{q}})\dot{\mathbf{q}} + \mathbf{Q}(\mathbf{q}, \dot{\mathbf{q}}, t)) = \widetilde{\mathbf{A}}^T\mathbf{c}. \tag{22}$$

Only $\delta = n - r$ of these n equations are independent, however. The $\dot{\mathbf{q}}$ and $\ddot{\mathbf{q}}$ in (22) must satisfy the constraints. If this cannot be ensured, in particular if $\mathbf{q}$ are determined from measured values, they must be projected according to $\dot{\mathbf{q}}_\mathrm{proj} = \mathbf{N}_\mathrm{J}\dot{\mathbf{q}}$ and $\ddot{\mathbf{q}}_\mathrm{proj} = \mathbf{N}_\mathrm{J}\ddot{\mathbf{q}} + \dot{\mathbf{N}}_\mathrm{J}\dot{\mathbf{q}}$. This leads to

$$\widetilde{\mathbf{G}}(\mathbf{q})\,\ddot{\mathbf{q}}+\widetilde{\mathbf{C}}(\mathbf{q},\dot{\mathbf{q}})\,\dot{\mathbf{q}}+\widetilde{\mathbf{Q}}(\mathbf{q})=\widetilde{\mathbf{A}}^{T}\mathbf{c} \tag{23}$$

with

$$\widetilde{\mathbf{G}}{:=}\mathbf{N}_{\mathrm{J}}^{T}\mathbf{G}\mathbf{N}_{\mathrm{J}},\;\widetilde{\mathbf{C}}:=\mathbf{N}_{\mathrm{J}}^{T}(\mathbf{C}\mathbf{N}_{\mathrm{J}}+\mathbf{G}\dot{\mathbf{N}}_{\mathrm{J}}),\;\widetilde{\mathbf{Q}}{:=}\mathbf{N}_{\mathrm{J}}^{T}\mathbf{Q}. \tag{24}$$

The time derivative in (21) is readily found to be $\dot{\mathbf{N}}_{\mathrm{J}}=-\left(\mathbf{B}^{+}\dot{\mathbf{B}}\mathbf{N}_{\mathrm{J}}\right)-\left(\mathbf{B}^{+}\dot{\mathbf{B}}\mathbf{N}_{\mathrm{J}}\right)^{T}$.
The dynamics model (22) in redundant coordinates is globally valid in all regular configurations as it does not involve any minimal coordinates.

4.4 Model-based control in redundant coordinates

4.4.1 Inverse dynamics

In order to use the dynamics formulation in redundant coordinates within a model-based controller (22), respectively (23), must be solved for $\mathbf{c}$. The general inverse dynamics solution (neglecting prestress forces) is

$$\mathbf{c}=\left(\widetilde{\mathbf{A}}^{T}\right)^{+}\mathbf{N}_{\mathrm{J}}(\mathbf{G}(\mathbf{q})\,\ddot{\mathbf{q}}+\mathbf{C}(\mathbf{q},\dot{\mathbf{q}})\,\dot{\mathbf{q}}+\mathbf{Q}(\mathbf{q},\dot{\mathbf{q}},t)). \tag{25}$$

The crucial point here is the computation of the pseudoinverse. The $n\times m$ matrix $\widetilde{\mathbf{A}}^{T}$ is not regular since rank $\widetilde{\mathbf{A}}^{T}=\delta<m<n$. Hence the closed form Moore-Penrose pseudoinverse is not applicable. The singular value decomposition (SVD) can always be used to iteratively determine the pseudoinverse. This is generally not applicable for real-time applications due to its numerical complexity. Now if the redundantly actuated PKM does not poses input-singularities, the PKM configuration is uniquely determined by the $m>\delta$ input coordinates. Hence at any time rank $\widetilde{\mathbf{A}}=\delta$, and a full-rank $\delta\times n$ submatrix $\widetilde{\mathbf{A}}_1$ can be separated so that

$$\widetilde{\mathbf{A}}=\begin{pmatrix}\widetilde{\mathbf{A}}_1\\ \widetilde{\mathbf{A}}_2\end{pmatrix} \tag{26}$$

with the remaining $(m-\delta)\times n$ matrix $\widetilde{\mathbf{A}}_2$. Upon this partitioning the following explicit expression for the pseudoinverse was presented in Müller (2011):

$$\left(\widetilde{\mathbf{A}}^{T}\right)^{+}=\begin{pmatrix}\left(\widetilde{\mathbf{A}}_1^{T}\right)^{+}\left(\mathbf{I}_n-\widetilde{\mathbf{A}}_2^{T}\left(\mathbf{I}_{m-\delta}+\mathbf{B}^{T}\mathbf{B}\right)^{-1}\mathbf{B}^{T}\left(\widetilde{\mathbf{A}}_1^{T}\right)^{+}\right)\\ \left(\mathbf{I}_{m-\delta}+\mathbf{B}^{T}\mathbf{B}\right)^{-1}\mathbf{B}^{T}\left(\widetilde{\mathbf{A}}_1^{T}\right)^{+}\end{pmatrix} \tag{27}$$

with $\mathbf{B}=\left(\widetilde{\mathbf{A}}_1^{T}\right)^{+}\widetilde{\mathbf{A}}_2^{T}$ and the left pseudoinverse $\left(\widetilde{\mathbf{A}}_1^{T}\right)^{+}=\left(\widetilde{\mathbf{A}}_1\widetilde{\mathbf{A}}_1^{T}\right)^{-1}\widetilde{\mathbf{A}}_1$.
The partitioning (26) is equivalent to selecting δ independent coordinates. As already discussed such a selection, and thus the submatrix $\widetilde{\mathbf{A}}_1$, is not unique, which rises again the problem of selecting δ independent coordinates out of the m actuator coordinates. Consequently the full-rank $\delta\times n$ matrix $\widetilde{\mathbf{A}}_1$ must be selected depending on the actual PKM pose. The important difference to the minimal coordinate formulation is that only the submatrix $\widetilde{\mathbf{A}}$ must be selected whereas the motion equations (22) and (23) are globally valid and remain unaltered in the entire motion range. Switching is only performed within the pseudoinverse computation for $\widetilde{\mathbf{A}}^{T}$. The selection of a proper submatrix requires monitoring the rank of the $\delta\times\delta$ matrix $\widetilde{\mathbf{A}}_1\widetilde{\mathbf{A}}_1^{T}$.

4.4.2 Augmented PD control

The control task is to minimize the tracking error of the actuator coordinates given a target trajectory with $\mathbf{q}_a^d(t)$. With the above formulation it is straightforward to introduce the following APD control scheme

$$\begin{aligned}\mathbf{c} &= (\widetilde{\mathbf{A}}^T)^+ \left(\widetilde{\mathbf{G}}(\mathbf{q})\ddot{\mathbf{q}}^d + \widetilde{\mathbf{C}}(\dot{\mathbf{q}},\mathbf{q})\dot{\mathbf{q}}^d + \widetilde{\mathbf{Q}}(\mathbf{q},\dot{\mathbf{q}},t) - \mathbf{K}_P\mathbf{e} - \mathbf{K}_D\dot{\mathbf{e}}\right) \\ &= (\widetilde{\mathbf{A}}^T)^+ \mathbf{N}_J(\mathbf{G}(\mathbf{q})\ddot{\mathbf{q}}^d + \mathbf{C}(\mathbf{q},\dot{\mathbf{q}})\dot{\mathbf{q}}^d + \mathbf{Q}(\mathbf{q},\dot{\mathbf{q}},t) - \mathbf{K}_P\mathbf{e} - \mathbf{K}_D\dot{\mathbf{e}})\end{aligned} \tag{28}$$

with error vector $\mathbf{e} := \mathbf{q} - \mathbf{q}^d$. Now the gain matrices measure the errors in the m actuator coordinates. That is, assuming the coordinate partitioning $\mathbf{q} \equiv (\mathbf{q}_p, \mathbf{q}_a)$, they have the form

$$\mathbf{K} = \mathrm{diag}\,(0,\ldots,0,K_1,\ldots,K_m)\,. \tag{29}$$

The closed loop dynamics, when (28) is applied to the model (23), is governed by

$$\widetilde{\mathbf{G}}\ddot{\mathbf{q}} - \mathbf{D}\widetilde{\mathbf{G}}\ddot{\mathbf{q}}^d + \widetilde{\mathbf{C}}\dot{\mathbf{q}} - \mathbf{D}\widetilde{\mathbf{C}}\dot{\mathbf{q}}^d + \widetilde{\mathbf{Q}} - \mathbf{D}\widetilde{\mathbf{Q}} + \mathbf{D}\mathbf{K}_D\dot{\mathbf{e}} + \mathbf{D}\mathbf{K}_P\mathbf{e} = \mathbf{0} \tag{30}$$

with $\mathbf{D} = \widetilde{\mathbf{A}}^T(\widetilde{\mathbf{A}}^T)^+ \neq \mathbf{I}_n$. The rank deficiency of $\widetilde{\mathbf{A}}$ implies that $\mathbf{D} \neq \mathbf{I}_n$.
It can be shown that the APD control scheme (28) achieves exponential trajectory tracking on the c-space V using the Lyapunov function

$$\mathcal{V}(\dot{\mathbf{e}},\mathbf{e},t) = \frac{1}{2}\dot{\mathbf{e}}^T\widetilde{\mathbf{G}}(\mathbf{q})\dot{\mathbf{e}} + \frac{1}{2}\mathbf{e}^T\mathbf{K}_P\mathbf{e} + \frac{1}{2}\varepsilon\mathbf{e}^T\widetilde{\mathbf{G}}(\mathbf{q})\dot{\mathbf{e}} \tag{31}$$

with $\varepsilon > 0$. $\mathcal{V}(\dot{\mathbf{e}},\mathbf{e},t)$ is positive definite, and $\dot{\mathcal{V}}$ is negative definite for all trajectories in V. These properties are directly inherited from the minimal coordinate formulation via the projection onto V with the projector $\mathbf{N}_J$.

4.4.3 Computed torque control

The standard CTC scheme is easily adapted to the redundant coordinate formulation as

$$\begin{aligned}\mathbf{c} &= (\widetilde{\mathbf{A}}^T)^+ \left(\widetilde{\mathbf{G}}(\mathbf{q})\mathbf{v} + \widetilde{\mathbf{C}}(\dot{\mathbf{q}},\mathbf{q})\dot{\mathbf{q}} + \widetilde{\mathbf{Q}}(\mathbf{q},\dot{\mathbf{q}},t)\right) \\ &= (\widetilde{\mathbf{A}}^T)^+ \mathbf{N}_J(\mathbf{G}(\mathbf{q})\mathbf{v} + \mathbf{C}(\mathbf{q},\dot{\mathbf{q}})\dot{\mathbf{q}} + \mathbf{Q}(\mathbf{q},\dot{\mathbf{q}},t))\end{aligned} \tag{32}$$

with $\mathbf{v} = \ddot{\mathbf{q}} - \mathbf{K}_P\mathbf{e} - \mathbf{K}_D\dot{\mathbf{e}}$ and the gain matrices in (29). It is readily shown that the CTC (32) achieves exponential trajectory tracking on V. Choose local coordinates $\mathbf{q}_2$ on V, and let $\mathbf{P}_1$ be a projector to the vector space of dependent velocities $\dot{\mathbf{q}}_1$, and $\mathbf{P}_2$ a projector to the vector space of independent velocities $\dot{\mathbf{q}}_2$. Then the dynamics of the closed loop splits into

$$\mathbf{P}_1\left(\widetilde{\mathbf{G}}\ddot{\mathbf{q}} + \widetilde{\mathbf{C}}\dot{\mathbf{q}} + \widetilde{\mathbf{Q}}\right) = \mathbf{0} \tag{33}$$

$$\mathbf{P}_2\widetilde{\mathbf{G}}(\ddot{\mathbf{e}} + \mathbf{K}_D\dot{\mathbf{e}} + \mathbf{K}_P\mathbf{e}) = \mathbf{0}. \tag{34}$$

The first $n - \delta$ equations are automatically satisfied for trajectories in V if the second system is satisfied. The second system, consisting of δ equations, governs the error dynamics in term of independent coordinates. For trajectories in V this is equivalent to the system of δ equations

$$\overline{\mathbf{G}}\left(\ddot{\mathbf{e}}_2 + \mathbf{F}^T\mathbf{K}_{\mathrm{D}}\mathbf{F}\dot{\mathbf{e}}_2 + \mathbf{F}^T\mathbf{K}_{\mathrm{P}}\mathbf{F}\mathbf{e}_2\right) = \mathbf{0} \tag{35}$$

with positive definite $\overline{\mathbf{G}} = \mathbf{F}^T\widetilde{\mathbf{G}}\mathbf{F}$ in (7). The stability of the controller is ensured with positive definite gains.

4.5 Case study: Planar 2 DOF RA-PKM

The proposed CTC control scheme in redundant coordinates was implemented in a prototype of the planar 2 DOF PKM in figure 1, which is briefly described in section 3.3. As discussed in section 2.1 the dynamic model is given in terms of $n = 6$ joint angles, giving rise to a system of $n = 6$ motion equations (22). The projected 6×3 control matrix $\widetilde{M}$ has rank 2.

The manipulator is controlled along the EE-path in figure 4. If two actuator joint angles are used as independent coordinates the minimal coordinate model (6) exhibits parameterization singularities as described in section 4.2. Moreover the EE-path passes such singularities several times and the minimal coordinate model is not valid. The redundant coordinate formulation does not suffer from such singularities.

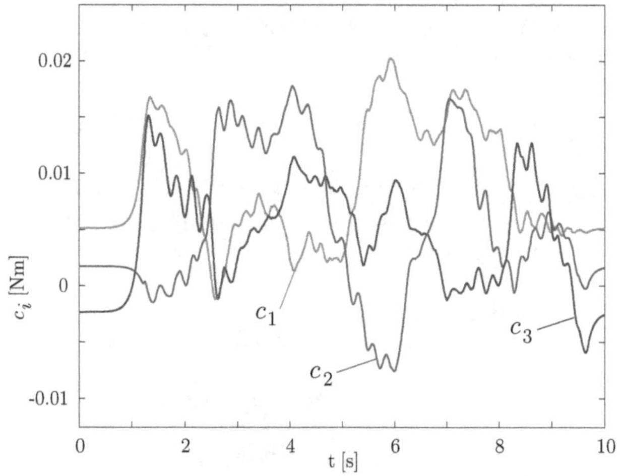

Fig. 9. Actuator torques when the RA-PKM is controlled along the EE-path of figure 4 by a CTC model in terms of redundant coordinates.

Figure 9 shows the actuator torques when the RA-PKM is controlled by the CTC scheme (32). Figure 10 shows the corresponding actuator tracking errors. Apparently the motion and the torque evolution is smooth and unaffected by any singularities thanks to the redundant coordinate formulation. Notice that also for this CTC method there are non-zero drive torques even if the RA-PKM is at rest. This is again due to measurement errors in conjunction with actuation redundancy. The crucial point in the inverse dynamics formulation (25) is the computation of the pseudoinverse (27). This requires identification of a full rank submatrix $\widetilde{\mathbf{A}}_1$, i.e. δ actuator coordinates representing valid local coordinates on V. A straightforward implementation is to select one of the three combinations $\mathbf{q}_2^{(1)} = (q^1, q^2)$, $\mathbf{q}_2^{(2)} = (q^1, q^3)$, and

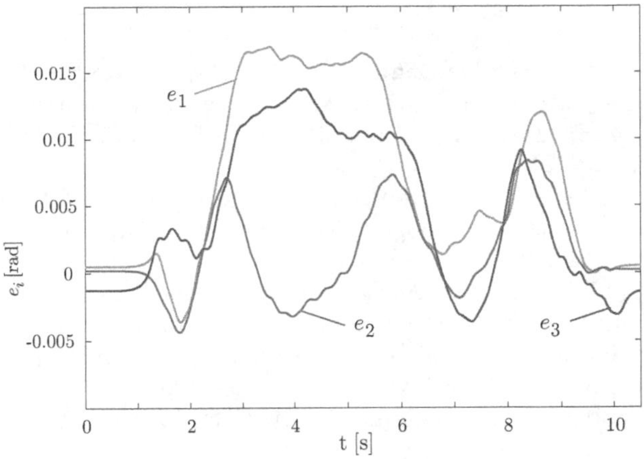

Fig. 10. Joint tracking error when the RA-PKM is controlled by a CTC model in redundant coordinates.

$\mathbf{q}_2^{(3)} = (q^2, q^3)$ based on the infinity norm of the corresponding $\widetilde{\mathbf{A}}_1$. That is, the submatrix $\widetilde{\mathbf{A}}_1$, corresponding to a certain $\mathbf{q}_2^{(i)}$, is selected for which $||\widetilde{\mathbf{A}}_1||_\infty$ is minimal.

5. Summary

Redundant actuation has the potential to improve the kinematic and dynamic performance of PKM. This redundancy is easily taken into account within the design process so to optimize dexterity. It turns out, however, that the control of RA-PKM poses several challenges. A problem that is peculiar to RA-PKM is the existence of antagonistic control forces. Such forces can be employed purposefully to avoid backlash or to modulate the EE stiffness, but impair the performance and stability of decentralized control schemes for RA-PKM. In this chapter the applicability of decentralized control schemes is analyzed, and it is shown that they inherently cause antagonistic control forces. As remedy a so-called antagonism filter is proposed that eliminates antagonistic control forces. Another problem arises in the model-based control of RA-PKM. Since the dynamics model is commonly formulated in terms of a set of independent actuator coordinates the model of the RA-PKM becomes invalid at the input singularities of the non-redundantly actuated PKM. This would limit the controllable motion range to that of the non-redundant PKM. To overcome this problem a formulation in redundant coordinates was presented that does not require the selection of independent actuator coordinates. This formulation is valid in the entire motion range. Thereupon an augmented PD and computed torque controller was proposed. Experimental results are reported for the planar 2 DOF RA-PKM that confirmed the robustness of these control schemes.

6. Acknowledgment

The author is indebted to Timo Hufnagel from Heilbronn University who implemented the proposed control methods. Support from the company Schunk GmbH is gratefully acknowledged.

7. References

Abdellatif, H.; Grotjahn, M.; Heimann, B. (2005). High Efficient Dynamics Calculation Approach for Computed-Force Control of Robots with Parallel Structures, *IEEE Conference on Decision and Control and European Control Conference (CDC-ECC)*, 12-15 Dec. 2005, pp. 2024-2029

Angles, J.; Lee, S. (1988). The formulation of dynamical equations of holonomic mechanical systems using a natural orthogonal complement, *ASME J. of Applied Mechanics*, Vol. 55, 1988, pp. 243-244

Asada, H.; Slotine, J.J.E. (1986). *Robot Analysis ad Control*, John Wiley and Sons, 1986

Cheng, H.; Yiu, Y.-K.; Li, Z.(2003). Dynamics and Control of Redundantly Actuated Parallel Manipulators, *IEEE/ASME Trans. on Mechatronics*, Vol. 8, no. 4, 2003, pp. 483-491

Garg, V.; Noklely, S.B.; Carretero, J.A. (2009). Wrench capability analysis of redundantly actuated spatial parallel manipulators, *Mech. Mach. Theory*, Vol. 44, No. 5, 2009, pp: 1070-1081

Gogu, G. (2007). Fully-isotropic redundantly-actuated parallel wrists with three degrees of freedom, *Proc. ASME Int. Design Eng. Tech. Conf. (IDETC)*, Las Vegas, NV, 2007, DETC2007-34237

Hufnagel, T.; Müller, A. (2011). A Realtime Coordinate Switching Method for Model-Based Control of Parallel Manipulators, *Proc. ECCOMAS Thematic Conference on Multibody Dynamics*, Brussels, Belgium, Juli 4-7, 2011

Krut, S.; Company, O.; Pierrot, F. (2004). Velocity performance indicies for parallel mechanisms with actuation redundancy, *Robotica*, Vol. 22, 2004, pp. 129-139

Kurtz, R.; Hayward, V. (1992). Multiple-goal kinematic optimization of a parallel spherical mechanism with actuator redundancy, *IEEE Trans. on Robotics Automation*, Vol. 8. no. 5, 1992, pp. 644-651

Lee, J.H.; Li, B.J.; Suh, H. (1998). Optimal design of a five-bar finger with redundant actuation, *Proc. IEEE Int. Conf. Rob. Aut. (ICRA)*, Leuven, 1998, pp. 2068-2074

Lee, S.H.; Lee J.H.; Yi, B.J.; Kim, S.H., Kwak, Y.K., (2005). Optimization and experimental verification for the antagonistic stiffness in redundantly actuated mechanisms: a five-bar example, *Mechatronics*, Vol. 15, No. 2, 2005, pp. 213-238

Maggi, G.A. (1901). Da alcune nuove forma della equazioni della dinamica applicabile ai sistemi anolonomi, *Atti della Reale Acad. Naz. dei Lincei. Rend. Cl. fis. e math*, Ser. 5 1901. Vol. 10, No. 2, pp. 287-291

Müller, A. (2005). Internal Prestress Control of redundantly actuated Parallel Manipulators - Its Application to Backlash avoiding Control, *IEEE Trans. on Rob.*, Vol. 21, No. 4, 2005, pp. 668 - 677

Müller, A. (2006). Stiffness Control of redundantly actuated Parallel Manipulators, *Proc. IEEE Int. Conf. Rob. Automat. (ICRA)*, pp. 1153 - 1158, Orlando, 15.-19. May, 2006,

Müller, A. (2008). Consequences of Kinematic Imperfections for the Control of Redundantly Actuated Parallel Manipulators, *Second International Workshop on Fundamental Issues and Future Research Directions for Parallel Mechanisms and Manipulators*, Montpellier, France, September 21-22, 2008

Müller, A. (2009). On the Concept of Mobility used in Robotics, *33rd Mechanisms & Robotics Conference, ASME Int. Design Eng. Tech. Conf. (IDETC)*, August 30 - September 2, 2009, San Diego, CA, USA

Müller, A. (2010). Consequences of Geometric Imperfections for the Control of Redundantly Actuated Parallel Manipulators, *IEEE Trans. Robotics*, Vol. 26, No. 1, 2010, pp. 21-31

Müller, A.; T. Hufnagel (2011). A Projection Method for the Elimination of Contradicting Control Forces in Redundantly Actuated PKM, *Proc. IEEE Int. Conf. Rob. Automat. (ICRA)*, pp. 668 - 677, Shanghai, China, May 9-13, 2011

Müller, A. (2011). A Robust Inverse Dynamics Formulation for Redundantly Actuated PKM, *Proc. 13th World Congress in Mechanism and Machine Science*, Guanajuato, Mexico, 19-25 June 2011

Murray, R.M.; Li, Z.; Sastry, S.S. (1993). *A mathematical Introduction to robotic Manipulation*, CRC Press, 1993

Nakamura, Y.; Ghodoussi, M. (1989). Dynamics Computation of Closed-Link Robot Mechanisms with Nonredundant and Redundant Actuators, *IEEE Tran. Rob. and Aut.*, Vol. 5, No. 3, 1989, 294-302

Nahon, M.A.; Angeles, J. (1989). Force optimization in redundantly-actuated closed kinematic chains, *Proc. IEEE Int. Conf. Rob. Automat. (ICRA)*, Scottsdale, USA, May 14-19, 1989, pp. 951-956

O'Brien, J.F.; Wen, J.T. (1999). Redundant actuation for improving kinematic manipulability, *Proc. IEEE Int. Conf. Robotics Automation*, 1999, pp. 1520-1525

Paccot, F.; Andreff, N.; Martinet, P. (2009). A Review on the Dynamic Control of Parallel Kinematic Machines: Theory and Experiments, *Int. J. Rob. Res.*, Vol. 28, No. 3, 2009, 395-416

Saglia, J.A.; Tsagarakis, N.G.; Dai, J.S.; Caldwell, D.G. (2009). Inverse-kinematics-based control of a redundantly actuated platform for rehabilitation, *Proc. IMechE*, Vol. 223 Part I: J. Systems and Control Engineering

Shin, H.; Lee, S.; In, W., Jeong, J.I.; Kim, J. (2011). Kinematic Optimization of a Redundantly Actuated Parallel Mechanism for Maximizing Stiffness and Workspace Using Taguchi Method, *J. Comput. Nonlinear Dynam.*, Vol. 6, 2011

Thanh, T.D.; Kotlarski, J.; Heimann, B.; Ortmaier, T. (2009). On the Inverse Dynamics Problem of General Parallel Robots, *Proc. IEEE Int. Conf. Mechatronics*, Malaga, Spain, April 2009

Valasek, M.; Bauma, V.; Sika, Z.; Vampola, T. (2002). Redundantly actuated parallel structures - principle, examples, advantages, *Proc. 3rd Parallel Kinematics Seminar Chemnitz*, 2002, pp. 993-1009

Valasek, M.; Bauma, V.; Sika, Z.; Belda, K.; Pisa, P. (2005). Design-by-Optimization and Control of Redundantly Actuated Parallel Kinematics Sliding Star, *Multibody System Dynamics*, Vol. 14, no. 3-4, 2005, 251-267

Voronets, P.V. (1901). Equations of motion for nonholonomic systems, Matem. Sbornik, 22, No. 4, 1901

Wang, L.; Wu, J.; Wang, J.; You, Z. (2009). An Experimental Study of a Redundantly Actuated Parallel Manipulator for a 5-DOF Hybrid Machine Tool, *Mechatronics*, Vol. 14, No. 1, 2009, pp. 72 - 81

Wehage, R.A.; Haug, E.J. (1982). Generalized coordinates partitioning for dimension reduction in analysis of constrained dynamic systems, *J. Mech. Design*, Vol. 104, 1982, pp. 247-255

Wu, J.; Wang, J.S.; Wang, L.P.; Li, T.M. (2009). Dynamics and control of a planar 3-DOF parallel manipulator with actuation redundancy, *Mech. Mach. Theory*, Vol. 44, 2009, pp. 835-849.

Yi, B.Y.; Freeman, R.A.; Tesar, D. (1989). Open-loop stiffness control of overconstrained mechanisms/robot linkage systems, *Proc. IEEE Int. Conf. Robotics Automation*, Scottsdale, 1989, pp. 1340-1345

Zlatanov, D.; Fenton, R.G.; Benhabib, B. (1998). Identification and classification of the singular configurations of mechanisms, *Mech. Mach. Theory*, Vol. 33, No. 6, 1998, pp. 743-760

10

Positioning Control of One Link Arm with Parametric Uncertainty Using the QFT Method

Takayuki Kuwashima, Jun Imai and Masami Konishi
Okayama University
Japan

1. Introduction

Many manufacturing robots are currently operated in various factories, with the aim of saving labor and cost. In particular, automatic sorting robots for products in assortment lines are used to improve productivity. In case of having the robots operate in such ways, the manipulators are demanded to have positioning performance of high precision to the target position. But in condition that products of various weights are handled, control performance such as positioning precision and settling time would be deteriorated if the controller is designed based on a fixed mathematical model; and they include parameters such as weights of grabbing product with their robot hands. So the controller needs to have robust control performance against parameter uncertainty in plant dynamics. It means that a control system should maintain its performance even if there exists uncertainty. In decades, control problems under plant uncertainty have been much studied because conventional control theory is based on the assumption that the dynamics of plant is fully well-known and certain, and that the mathematical model accurately reflects behavior of controlled plant in the real world. Nowadays, robust control theory is developed in order to cope with such problems. H_∞ control theory, among robust control theories, has been applied to many control systems and can handle unstructured uncertainty of plant, but it can not directly deal with structured uncertainty such as parameter variation.

In this chapter, a robust controller design using Quantitative Feedback Theory(QFT) (Houpis et al., 2006) is presented for one link arm with parametric uncertainty. QFT is a robust control theory developed based mainly on classical control. QFT can cope with parametric uncertainty in a plant(Khodabakhshian & Golbon, 2005; Barve & Nataraj, 1998; Zolotas & Halikias, 1999; Ryoo et al., 2002). In design procedure, the region where the plant can exists in accordance with parameter variation is illustrated on Nichols chart for each frequency, which is called template. By using templates, the controller is designed in order to satisfy performance specification for all possible plants.

2. Model of one link arm

Let us consider the one link arm as shown in Fig.1. It simulates the sorting robot in manufacturing facility. It consists of a Direct-Drive (DD) motor as an actuator, a rigid arm and a payload mass at free end of the arm, simulating a carried product. The arm is driven by the DD motor and rotates in the horizontal plane. The DD motor is actuated by input torque τ[Nm]. The specification of the motor is as shown in Table. 1 and the arm is made of stainless

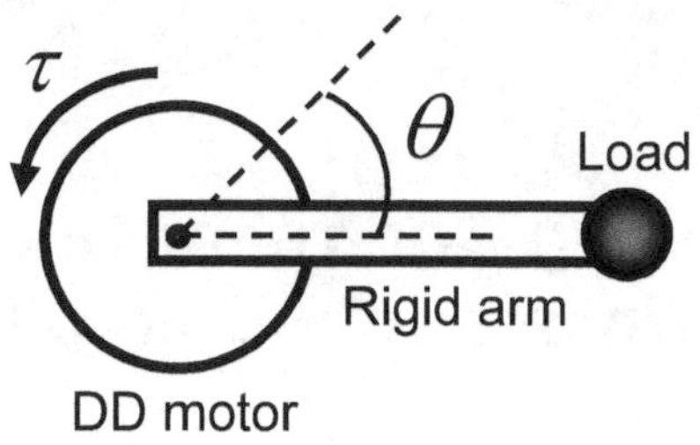

Fig. 1. One link arm

Rated voltage[V]	200
Rated torque[N·m]	25
Rated current[A]	2.7
Rated velocity[min^{-1}]	150
Inertia moment J_0[kg·m^2]	0.0909

Table 1. Specification of the DD motor

steel with length of L=0.3m, line density ρ=0.79 Kg/m and cross-section 1cm^2. Now, let $\theta(t)$ be the angle of rotation from the initial position, an equation of motion describing this system is

$$J\ddot{\theta} + D\dot{\theta} = \tau. \tag{1}$$

The Laplace transform of Eq.(1) gives the transfer function from τ to θ as

$$P(s) = \frac{1}{Js^2 + Ds}. \tag{2}$$

Here, J donates rotating inertia of the whole arm system, and is represented as

$$J = J_0 + \frac{\rho L^3}{3} + ML^3. \tag{3}$$

D is the friction coefficient around the motor rotary axis. From Eq.(3), it is found that value of J varies depending on weight of product. This time, we considered 6 samples of products, and their weights are from 0.5 through 3.0 at 0.5kg intervals. On the other hand, D varies with time. So observation experiment of D using step response method has been performed for 200 times. The variation ranges for J and D are as

$$J \in (0.098,\ 0.368),\ D \in (0.475,\ 0.814). \tag{4}$$

Then, we consider 7 samples of J and 10 samples of D as parameters of $P(s)$, and let $\mathcal{P}$ donates the set of the plant transfer functions, that is

$$\mathcal{P} = \{P_l\} \quad \text{where } l = 1, 2, ..., 70. \tag{5}$$

3. Effect of parameter variation

In this section, the effect of plat parameter variation on control performance of the one link arm system is studied. As described in Section 2, values of J and D vary in a certain range. We employ average values

$$\bar{J} = 0.233\text{kg} \cdot \text{m}^2, \quad \bar{D} = 0.644\text{N} \cdot \text{m} \cdot \text{s} \tag{6}$$

for each parameter as the nominal parameter. Let $\bar{P}(s)$ donates the nominal plant. A PD controller has been designed for $\bar{P}(s)$ in order to satisfy following performance specifications:

$$\text{Overshoot}: \ O_s < 10\% \tag{7}$$

$$\text{Peak time}: \ t_p < 1.0\text{sec.} \tag{8}$$

Designed controller is

$$C(s) = 3.0 + \frac{0.5}{1 + 0.001s}. \tag{9}$$

Numerical experiment has been done on the control system shown in Fig. 2. The target rotary angle $\theta_r(t)$ is aimed at 1 rad and computational interval is 0.005s. Simulation result to control $\bar{P}(s)$ is shown in Fig. 3. On the other hand, J and D can take various values. Control results for $\mathcal{P}$ are shown in Fig. 4, and it is found that the responses of output $\theta(t)$ are scattered and some responses violate performance specifications. From these results, it can be seen that the controller designed for $\bar{P}(s)$ does not always ensure the desired performance with variation in parameters of $\bar{P}(s)$.

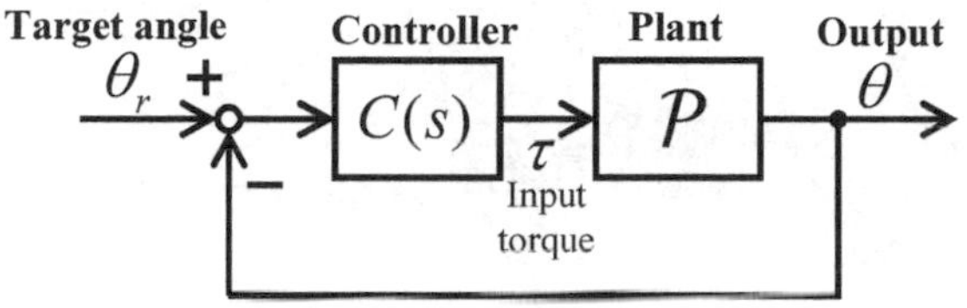

Fig. 2. Feedback Control System

4. Control system design using QFT

In control systems, it is desirable for controlled output of plant $\theta(t)$ to satisfy performance specification in spite of parameter uncertainty in a plant. In QFT design procedure, designer can determine the performance specifications that response of $\theta(t)$ should lie in. It has certain width as tolerance in time and frequency domains. Controller is designed on Nichols Chart (NC) so that all $\theta(t)$ lie between these specifications. These specifications are described on NC as boundary.

Consider feedback control system shown in Fig.5. Control objective is to control angular position of arm. We design $C(s)$ and $F(s)$ in order to satisfy performance specifications.

QFT design procedure is as follows:

STEP1. Determine performance specification in time and frequency domains.

STEP2. Gain the area where varying plant can exist on NC, called template.

STEP3. Construct performance specification on NC as bounds.

STEP4. Form the open loop transfer function $C(s)P(s)$ to satisfy bounds.

STEP5. Design the filter $F(s)$.

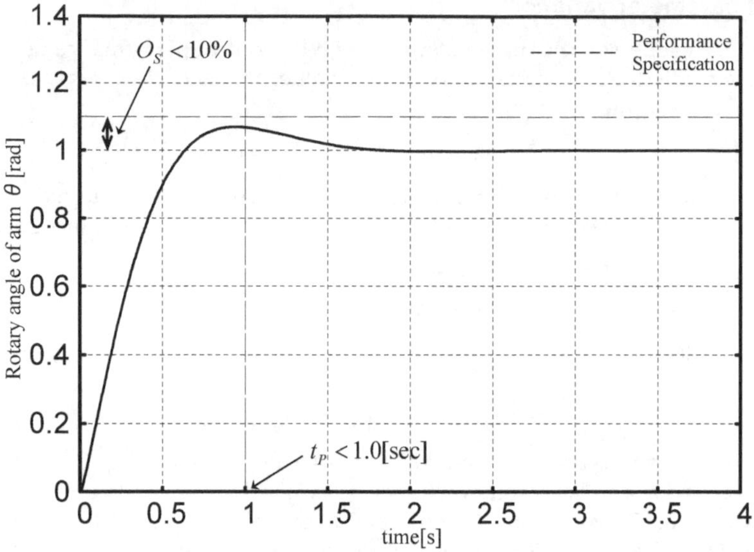

Fig. 3. Simulation result for $\bar{P}(s)$

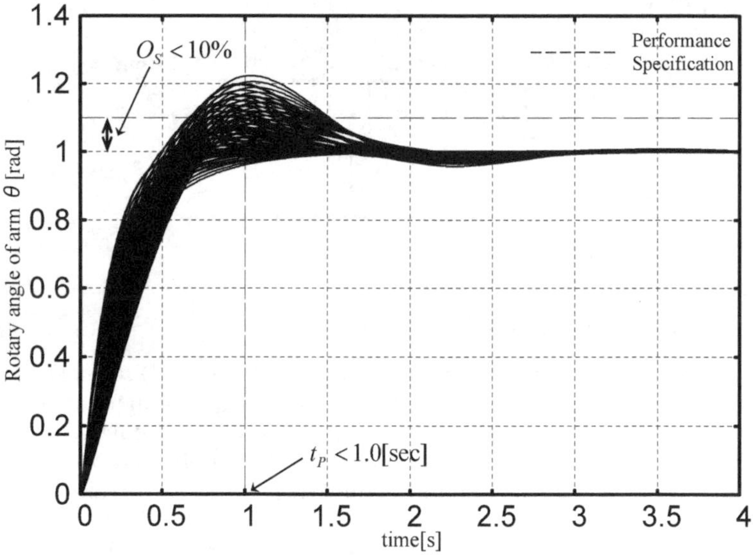

Fig. 4. Simulation result for $\mathcal{P}(s)$

4.1 Performance specification

Here, performance specifications in time domain is determined as

$$\text{Overshoot}: \ O_s = 0 \sim 10\%, \tag{10}$$

$$\text{Settling time}: \ t_s < 2.0\text{sec}. \tag{11}$$

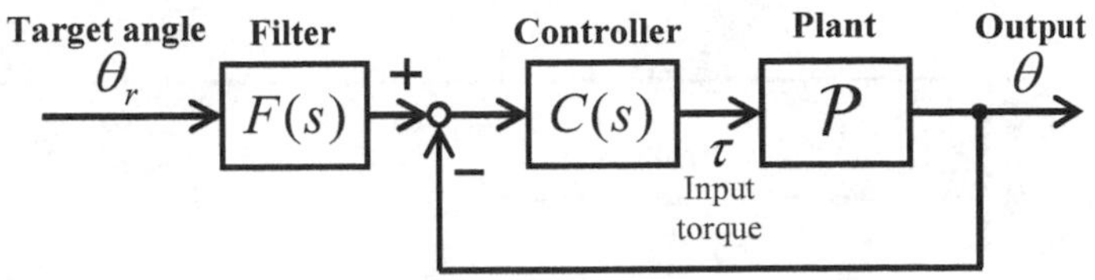

Fig. 5. QFT Control System

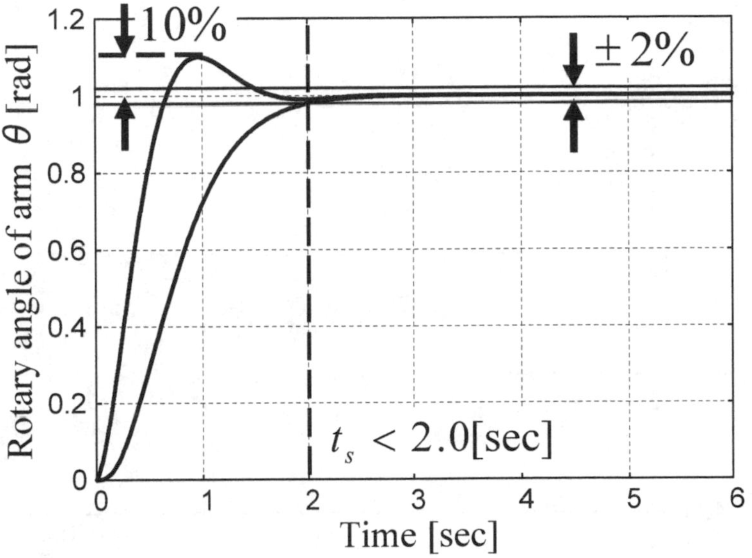

Fig. 6. Time domain performance specification

In QFT, more concrete specification is constructed so as to have certain width by determining upper and lower bounds according to Eqs.(10) and (11). Transfer function T_{R_U} and T_{R_L} that represents upper and lower bounds respectively, is designed as follows:

$$T_{R_U}(s) = \frac{0.5(s+30)}{s^2 + 4.6148s + 15.2}, \tag{12}$$

$$T_{R_L}(s) = \frac{52.8}{(s+3.3)(s+4)^2}. \tag{13}$$

The time and frequency responses of these functions are shown in Figs.6 and 7.

4.2 Template

One of the features of QFT is to describe the plant as a contour. On NC, a plant is expressed as a point at certain frequency. If parameters of the plant model vary, the plant is expressed on NC as contour for each frequency. It is referred to as a *template*. Therefore the template represents the region where the plant can exist. So the designer can recognize uncertainty in plant visually from templates. Fig.8 shows templates of $P(s)$ with variations of J and D at each frequency.

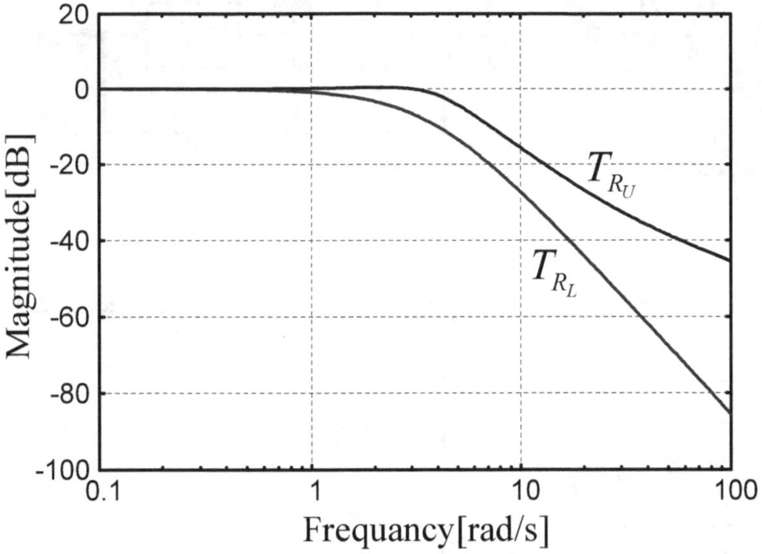

Fig. 7. Frequency domain performance specification

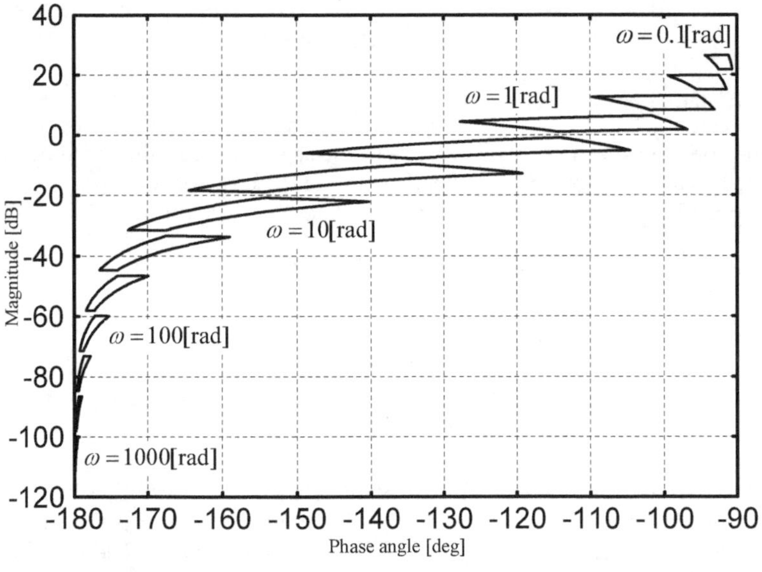

Fig. 8. Plant's template on NC

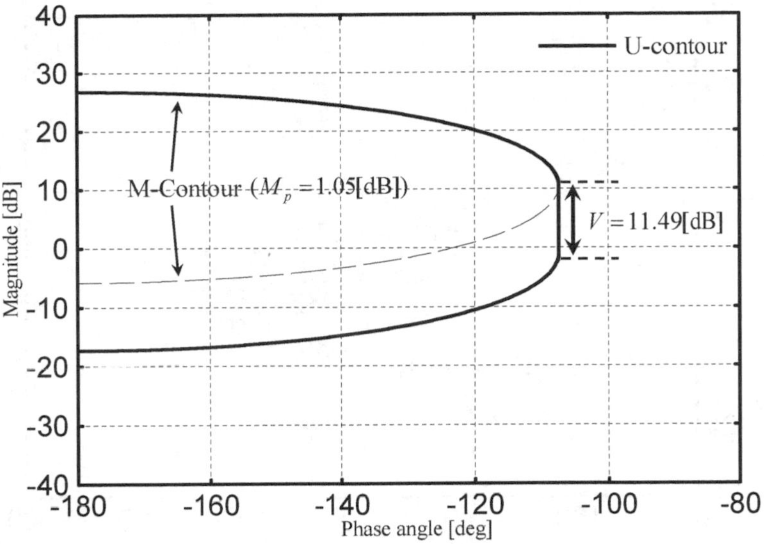

Fig. 9. U-contour on NC

4.3 Bound on NC

Let us determine performance specification on NC. As one of the features of NC, we can obtain a peak gain of a closed loop system by plotting gain-phase curve of open loop transfer function on NC. This peak gain is given by constant M curve to which gain-phase curve is tangent, called M-contour. Therefore, if peak gain M_p(dB) of performance specification in frequency domain is given, M-contour representing M_p can be obtained on NC, which indicate performance specification about the peak gain. So this specification can be satisfied unless gain-phase curve of open loop transfer function $C(s)P(s)$ does not enter this M-contour. However, gain-phase curve of $C(s)P(s)$ is represented as certain region if plant model $P(s)$ has parametric uncertainty, as stated in former section. So consider that we take down lower half of M-contour by V(dB), which is maximum variation of templates in bandwidth frequency, to make gain margin. The region constructed by M-contour and gain margin is called *U-contour*. If gain-phase curve of $C(s)P(s)$ does not enter U-contour, it means that performance specification about the peak gain is satisfied for all varying plant $\mathcal{P}$.
This time, peak gain of frequency domain performance specification, M_p, and maximum variation of templates, V(dB) take the values

$$M_p = 1.05\text{dB}, V = 11.49\text{dB}. \tag{14}$$

Then, U-contour has form as shown in Fig.9.

4.4 Loop shaping

From upper specification in Eq.(12), the main object of controller design is written as

$$\left| \frac{CP}{1+CP} \right| < M_p = 1.05\text{dB}. \tag{15}$$

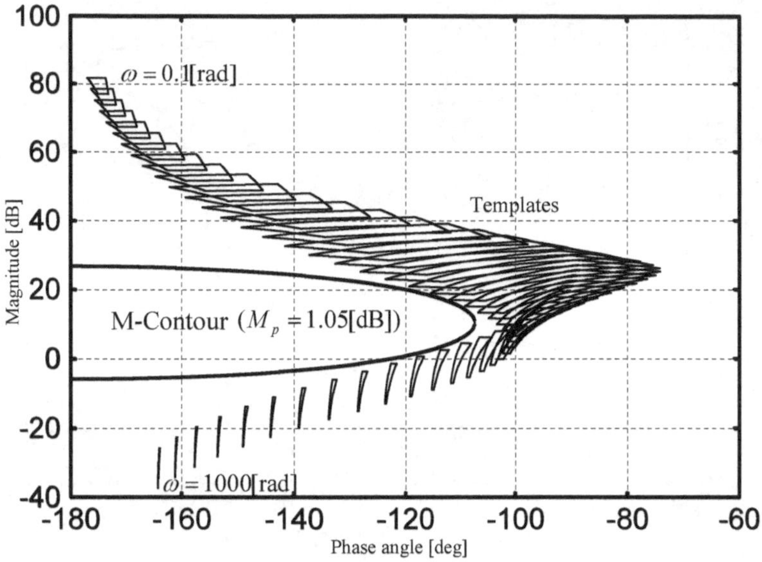

Fig. 10. M-contour and templates on NC

M_p is a peak magnitude of closed loop transfer function. This specification is described on NC as bound, called as U-contour (See Fig.9). As stated in Sec.4.3, this bound means the region that the gain-phase curve of open loop transfer function $C(s)P(s)$ must not enter to satisfy Eq.(15) for all possible plant. $C(s)$ is designed by trial and error in order not to penetrate U-contour. This time, $C(s)$ is consist of integrator and phase-delay compensator. Then, $C(s)$ has been decided as

$$C(s) = 5.2 \cdot 10^3 \frac{(s+1)(s+3.2)}{s(s+285)}. \tag{16}$$

Fig.10 shows templates of $C(s)\mathcal{P}(s)$ and M-contour representing M_p. From this figure, it is found that all templates do not enter the M-contour. It means that the system including $\mathcal{P}(s)$ satisfies Eq.(15).

4.5 Design of $F(s)$

In the final step, filter $F(s)$ is designed so that transfer function from input to output

$$\frac{F(s)C(s)\mathcal{P}(s)}{1+C(s)\mathcal{P}(s)}$$

lies between performance specifications T_{R_U} and T_{R_L}. Then, $F(s)$ was decided as

$$F(s) = \frac{(s/25+1)^2}{(s/3+1)(s/4+1)}. \tag{17}$$

5. Simulation

In this section, based on numerical simulation, control performance of QFT control system designed in former section are compared with conventional PID control system. We consider 70 samples of set of J and D in plant dynamics. As a conventional controller to be compared, the following PID controller

$$C_P(s) = 1.3 + \frac{0.001}{s} + \frac{0.8}{1 + 0.001s} \tag{18}$$

is adopted. The target rotary angle $\theta_r(t)$ is 1 rad and computational time step is 0.005s. The simulation results for two control system are shown in Figs.11 and 12. We found that scattering of the output $\theta(t)$ due to the parametric uncertainty are suppressed, and all $\theta(t)$ lies between upper and lower performance specifications, while the PID controller can not cope with parametric uncertainty. Now let us consider settling time t_s[s] and overshoot O_s[rad] as performance indices and use standard deviation to assess the scattering of these indices. The results are shown in Table 2. From this table, it is found that standard deviation of t_s[s] is reduced to 1/80 and that of O_s[s] is decreased to 1/7, compared with PID.

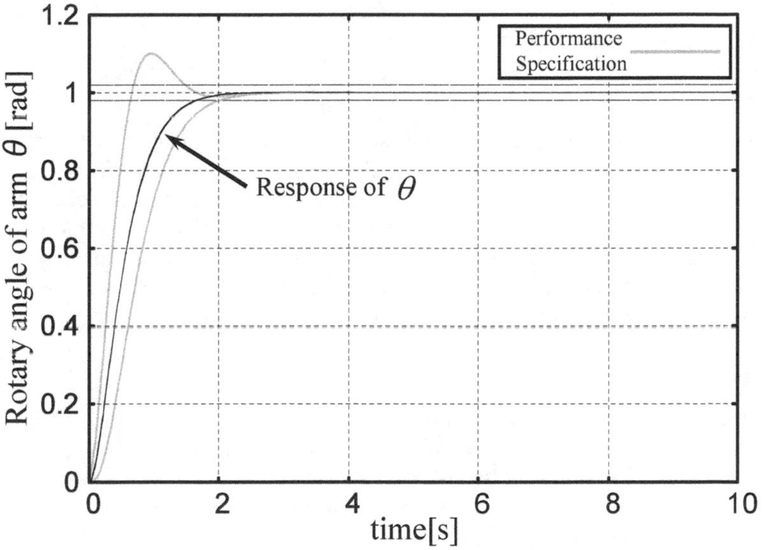

Fig. 11. Simulation result with QFT

	PID	QFT
t_s[s]	64.0×10^{-2}	0.875×10^{-2}
O_s[rad]	1.95×10^{-3}	0.278×10^{-3}

Table 2. Standard deviation of t_s and O_s

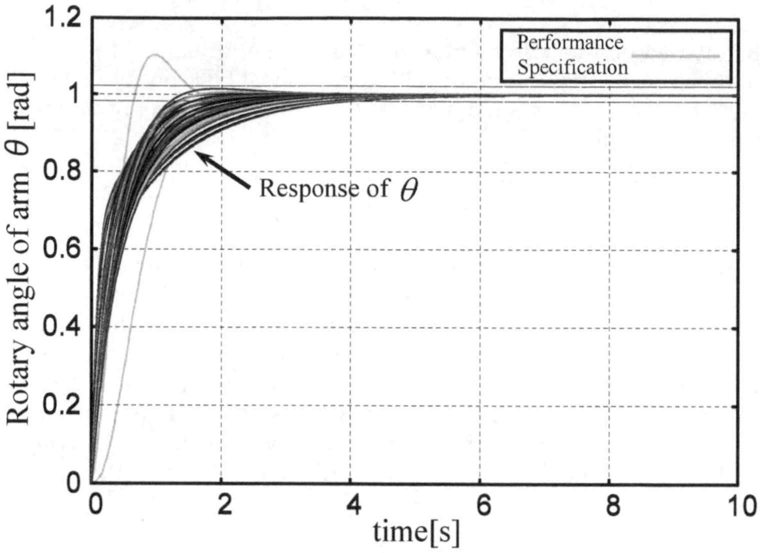

Fig. 12. Simulation result with PID

6. Conclusion

We presented a controller design for a one link arm with parametric uncertainty. In condition that there is uncertainty in plant's dynamics, the desirable control performance may not be obtained because the controller is designed based on only nominal model of plant. In this chapter, robust controller based on QFT is designed for plant with parametric uncertainty. By numerical experiments, systems designed by using QFT and conventional method are compared. It is found that the control system designed by QFT shows robust performance and can suppress the undesirable output due to parametric uncertainty.

7. References

Houpis, C. H.; Rasmussen, S. J. & Garcia-Sanz, M. (2006). *Quantitative Feedback Theory: Fundamentals and Applications*, pp.22-99,Taylor & Francis.

Khodabakhshian, A. & Golbon, N. (2005). Design of a New Load Frequency PID Controller using QFT, *Proceedings of the 13th Mediterranean Conference on Control and Automation*, pp. 970-975, Limassol, Cyprus.

Barve, J. J. & Nataraj, P. S. V. (1998). Synthesis of a robust pH controller using QFT, *Proceedings of IEEE TENCON '98. IEEE Region 10 International Conference on Global Connectivity in Energy, Computer, Communication and Control*, pp. 214-217, vol.1, New Delhi.

Zolotas, A. C. & Halikias, G. D. (1999). Optimal design of PID controllers using the QFT method, *IEE Proceedings-Control Theory and Applications.*, Vol. 146, Issue 6, pp. 585-589.

Ryoo, J. R.; Doh, T. & Chung, Y. M. J. (2002). A QFT Design of Disturbance Observer for the Track-following Control System of an Optical Disk Drive, *7th International Workshop on Advanced Motion Control. 2002. Proceedings*, pp. 209 - 214, Slovenia.

11

Modelling of Bound Estimation Laws and Robust Controllers for Robot Manipulators Using Functions and Integration Techniques

Recep Burkan
Istanbul University, Faculty of Engineering, Mechanical Engineering Department, Istanbul Turkey

1. Introduction

Some robust control methods have been developed in the past in order to increase tracking performance in the presence of parametric uncertainties. In the presence of parametric uncertainty, unmodelled dynamics and other sources of uncertainties, robust control laws are used. Corless-Leitmann [1] approach is a popular approach used for designing robust controllers for robot manipulators. In early application of Corless-Leitmann [1] approach to robot manipulators [2, 3], it is difficult to compute uncertainty bound precisely. Because, uncertainty bound on parameters depends on the inertia parameters, the reference trajectory and manipulator state vector. Spong [4] proposed a new robust controller for robot manipulators using the Lyapunov theory that guaranties stability of uncertain systems. In this approach, Leithmann [5] or Corless-Leithman [1] approach is used for designing the robust controller. One of the advantage of Spong's approach [4] is that uncertainty on parameter is needed to derive robust controller and uncertainty bound parameters depends only on the inertia parameters of the robots. Yaz [6] proposed a robust control law based on Spong's study [4] and global exponential stability of uncertain system is guaranteed. However, disturbance and unmodelled dynamics are not considered in algorithm of [4, 6]. Danesh at al [7] develop Spong's approach [4] in such a manner that control scheme is made robust not only to uncertain inertia parameters but also to robust unmodelled dynamics and disturbances. Koo and Kim [8] introduce adaptive scheme of uncertainty bound on parameters for robust control of robot manipulators. In [8], upper uncertainty bound is not known as would be in robust controller [4] and uncertainty bound is estimated with estimation law in order to control the uncertain system. A new robust control approach is proposed by Liu and Goldenerg [9] for robot manipulators based on a decomposition of model uncertainty. Parameterized uncertainty is distinguished from unparameterized uncertainty and a compensator is designed for parameterized and unparameterized uncertainty. A decomposition-based control design framework for mechanical systems with model uncertainties is proposed by Liu [10].

In order to increases tracking performance of uncertain systems, design of uncertainty bound estimation functions are considered. For this purpose, some uncertainty bound estimation functions are developed [11-15] based on a Lyapunov function, thus, stability of

uncertain system is guaranteed. In early derivation of uncertainty bound estimation laws [11-13], only a single derivation is possible because selection of variable function is difficult for other derivation and first order differential equation is used. Only exponential function and logarithmic functions are used for derivations because it is diffucut to define variable functions for other derivations.
In previous studies, some robust control laws are introduced, however, a method for derivation of adaptive bound estimation law for robust controllers is not proposed. Recently, a new approach for derivation of bound estimation laws for robust control of robot manipulators is proposed [14, 15]. A general equation is developed based on the Lyapunov theory in order to derive adaptive bound estimation laws and stability of uncertain system is guaranteed. In the approach [15], some functions depending on robot kinematics and control parameters and proper integration techniques can be used for derivation of new bound estimation laws. Then, new bound estimation laws are derived and this derivations also show how the general rule can be used for derivation of different bound estimation laws. After that, four new robust controllers are designed based on each bound estimation law. Lyapunov theory based on Corless-Leitmann [1] approach is used and uniform boundedness error convergence is achieved. This study also shows that bound estimation laws for robust control input do not only include these derivations but also allows derivation of other bound estimation laws for robust controllers provided that appropriate function and proper integration techniques are chosen. In this work, based on the study [15], some appropriate functions are developed and proper integration techniques are chosen. As results, new uncertainty bound estimation laws for robust control input are developed and new robust controllers are proposed. In derivations, some functions and integration techniques are used.

2. A method for derivation of bound estimation laws

In the absence of friction or other disturbances, the dynamic model of an n-link manipulator can be written as [16]

$$M(q)\ddot{q} + C(q,\dot{q})\dot{q} + G(q) = \tau \tag{1}$$

where q denotes generalised coordinates, τ is the n-dimensional vector of applied torques (or forces), $M(q)$ is a positive definite mass matrix, $C(q,\dot{q})\dot{q}$ is the n-dimensional vector of centripetal and Coriolis terms and G(q) is the n-dimensional vector of gravitational terms. Equation (1) can also be expressed in the following form.

$$\tau = Y(q,\dot{q},\ddot{q})\pi \tag{2}$$

where π is a p-dimensional vector of robot inertia parameters and Y is an nxp matrix which is a function of joint position, velocity and acceleration. For any specific trajectory, the desired position, velocity and acceleration vectors are q_d, $\dot{q}_d$ and $\ddot{q}_d$. The measured actual position and velocity errors are $\tilde{q} = q - q_d$, and $\dot{\tilde{q}} = \dot{q} - \dot{q}_d$. Using the above information, the corrected desired velocity and acceleration vectors for nonlinearities and decoupling effects are proposed as:

$$\dot{q}_r = \dot{q}_d - \Lambda\tilde{q}\ ;\ \ddot{q}_r = \ddot{q}_d - \Lambda\dot{\tilde{q}} \tag{3}$$

where Λ is a positive definite matrix. Then the following nominal control law is considered:

$$\begin{aligned}\tau_0 &= M_0(q)\ddot{q}_r + C_0(q,\dot{q})\dot{q}_r + G_0(q) - K\sigma \\ &= Y(q,\dot{q},\dot{q}_r,\ddot{q}_r)\pi_0 - K\sigma\end{aligned} \tag{4}$$

where $\pi_0 \in R^p$ represents the fixed parameters in dynamic model and $K\sigma$ is the vector of PD action. The corrected velocity error σ is given as

$$\sigma = \dot{q} - \dot{q}_r = \dot{\tilde{q}} + \Lambda\tilde{q} \tag{5}$$

The control input τ is defined in terms of the nominal control vector τ_0 as

$$\tau = \tau_0 + Y(q,\dot{q},\dot{q}_r,\ddot{q}_r)u(t) = Y(q,\dot{q},\dot{q}_r,\ddot{q}_r)(\pi_0 + u(t)) - K\sigma \tag{6}$$

Where u(t) is the additional robust control input. It is assumed that there exists an unknown bound on parametric uncertainty such that

$$\tilde{\pi} = \pi_0 - \pi \leq \rho \tag{7}$$

Since $\rho \in R^{+p}$ is assumed to be unknown, ρ should be estimated with the estimation law to control the system properly. $\hat{\rho}(t)$ shows the estimate of ρ and $\tilde{\rho}(t)$ is

$$\tilde{\rho}(t) = \rho - \hat{\rho}(t) \tag{8}$$

Substituting (6) into (1) and after some algebra yields

$$M(q)\dot{\sigma} + C(q,\dot{q})\sigma + K\sigma = Y(q,\dot{q},\dot{q}_r,\ddot{q}_r)(\tilde{\pi} + u(t)) \tag{9}$$

By taking into account above parameters and control algorithm, the Lyapunov function candidate is defined as [15, 16].

$$V(\sigma,q,\tilde{\rho}(t)) = \frac{1}{2}\sigma^T M(q)\sigma + \frac{1}{2}\tilde{q}^T B\tilde{q} + \frac{1}{2}\tilde{\rho}(t)^T \Phi(t)^2 \tilde{\rho}(t) \tag{10}$$

where $B \in R^{nxn}$ is a positive diagonal matrix, $\Phi(t)$ is chosen as a pxp dimensional diagonal matrix changes in time. The time derivative of V along the trajectories is

$$\dot{V} = \sigma^T M(q)\dot{\sigma} + \frac{1}{2}\sigma^T \dot{M}(q)\sigma + \tilde{q}^T B\dot{\tilde{q}} + \tilde{\rho}(t)^T \Phi(t)\dot{\Phi}(t)\tilde{\rho}(t) + \tilde{\rho}(t)^T \Phi(t)^2 \dot{\tilde{\rho}}(t) \tag{11}$$

Taking $B = 2\Lambda K$, using the property $\sigma^T[\dot{M}(q) - 2C(q,\dot{q})]\sigma = 0 \ \forall \sigma \in R^n$ [17, 18], and taking time derivative of V of system (9) is

$$\dot{V} = -\dot{\tilde{q}}^T K\dot{\tilde{q}} - \tilde{q}^T \Lambda K \Lambda \tilde{q} + \sigma^T Y u(t) + \sigma^T Y\tilde{\pi} + \tilde{\rho}(t)^T \Phi(t)\dot{\Phi}(t)\tilde{\rho}(t) + \tilde{\rho}(t)^T \Phi(t)^2 \dot{\tilde{\rho}}(t) \tag{12}$$

Equation (12) is arranged as

$$\begin{aligned}\dot{V} = &-\dot{\tilde{q}}^T K\dot{\tilde{q}} - \tilde{q}^T \Lambda K \Lambda\, \tilde{q} + \sigma^T Y u(t) + \sigma^T Y\tilde{\pi} \\ &+ (\rho - \hat{\rho}(t))^T \Phi(t)\dot{\Phi}(t)(\rho - \hat{\rho}(t)) - (\rho - \hat{\rho}(t))^T \Phi(t)^2 \dot{\hat{\rho}}(t) \leq 0\end{aligned} \tag{13}$$

$\dot{\hat{\rho}}(t) = -\dot{\hat{\rho}}(t)$ (since ρ is a constant). Remembering that $\rho \geq \tilde{\pi}$ and if u(t) is taken as the estimated term of uncertainty bound, that is $u(t) = -\hat{\rho}(t)$ then Equation (13 is written as

$$\begin{aligned}\dot{V} = &-\dot{\tilde{q}}^T K\dot{\tilde{q}} - \tilde{q}^T \Lambda K \Lambda \tilde{q} + \sigma^T Y(-\hat{\rho}(t)) + \sigma^T Y\rho \\ &+ [\rho - \hat{\rho}(t)]^T \Phi(t)\dot{\Phi}(t)[\rho - \hat{\rho}(t)] - (\rho - \hat{\rho}(t))^T \Phi(t)^2 \dot{\hat{\rho}}(t)] \leq 0\end{aligned} \tag{14}$$

Equation (14) can be arranged as

$$\begin{aligned}\dot{V} = &-\dot{\tilde{q}}^T K\dot{\tilde{q}} - \tilde{q}^T \Lambda K \Lambda \tilde{q} + \sigma^T Y[\rho - \hat{\rho}(t)] \\ &+ [\rho - \hat{\rho}(t)]^T \Phi(t)\dot{\Phi}(t)[\rho - \hat{\rho}(t)] - (\rho - \hat{\rho}(t))^T \Phi(t)^2 \dot{\hat{\rho}}(t)] \leq 0\end{aligned} \tag{15}$$

Consequently, a suitable expression for the time derivative of V is obtained.

$$\dot{V} = -\dot{\tilde{q}}^T K\dot{\tilde{q}} - \tilde{q}^T \Lambda K \Lambda \tilde{q} + [(\rho - \hat{\rho}(t)]^T [Y^T\sigma + \Phi(t)\dot{\Phi}(t)(\rho - \hat{\rho}(t)) - \Phi(t)^2 \dot{\hat{\rho}}(t)] \leq 0 \tag{16}$$

where $-\dot{\tilde{q}}^T K\dot{\tilde{q}} - \tilde{q}^T \Lambda K \Lambda \tilde{q} \leq 0$. If the rest of Equation (16) is zero, system will be stable. Remaining terms in Equation (16) are

$$[(\rho - \hat{\rho}(t)]^T [Y^T\sigma + \Phi(t)\dot{\Phi}(t)(\rho - \hat{\rho}(t)) - \Phi(t)^2 \dot{\hat{\rho}}(t)] = 0 \tag{17}$$

$[(\rho - \hat{\rho}(t)]$ is considered as a common multiplier then

$$Y^T\sigma + \Phi(t)\dot{\Phi}(t)(\rho - \hat{\rho}(t)) - \Phi(t)^2 \dot{\hat{\rho}}(t) = 0 \tag{18}$$

Hence, we look for the conditions for which the equation

$$Y^T\sigma + \Phi(t)\dot{\Phi}(t)(\rho - \hat{\rho}(t)) - \Phi(t)^2 \dot{\hat{\rho}}(t) = 0$$

is satisfied. Equation (18) can be written as

$$\Phi(t)\dot{\Phi}(t)(\rho - \hat{\rho}(t)) - \Phi(t)\Phi(t)\dot{\hat{\rho}}(t) = -Y^T\sigma \tag{19}$$

Then

$$\Phi(t)\dot{\hat{\rho}}(t) + \dot{\Phi}(t)\hat{\rho}(t) = \Phi(t)^{-1} Y^T\sigma + \dot{\Phi}(t)\rho \tag{20}$$

Equation (20) is arranged as

$$\frac{d}{dt}(\Phi(t)\hat{\rho}(t)) = \Phi(t)^{-1} Y^T\sigma + \dot{\Phi}(t)\rho \tag{21}$$

Integration both side of Equation (21) yields

$$\Phi(t)\hat{\rho}(t) = \int \Phi(t)^{-1} Y^T\sigma dt + \int \dot{\Phi}(t)\rho dt + C \tag{22}$$

Then, a general equation for derivation derivation of bound estimation law is developed as [14, 15]

$$\hat{\rho}(t) = \Phi(t)^{-1} [\int \Phi(t)^{-1} Y^T\sigma dt] + \rho + \Phi(t)^{-1} C \tag{23}$$

The Equation (23) is a general equation for derivation of the bound estimation law and it is derived from Lyapunov function. As a result, $\hat{\rho}(t)$ all derived from Equation (23) guarantess stability of uncertain system. However, $\Phi(t)^{-1}$ and $\hat{\rho}(t)$ are unknown and $\hat{\rho}(t)$ is derived depending on the function $\Phi(t)^{-1}$. For derivation, selection of $\Phi(t)^{-1}$ and integration techniques are very important. There is no certain rule for selection of $\Phi(t)^{-1}$ and integration techniques for this systems. System state parameters and mathematical insight are used to search for appropriate function of $\Phi(t)^{-1}$ as a solution of the Equation (23).

2.1 First choice of $\Phi(t)^{-1}$

For the first derivation of $\hat{\rho}(t)$, $\Phi(t)^{-1}$ is chosen as a time varying function such that

$$\Phi(t)^{-1} = diag(\beta_i e^{(\alpha_i \int Y^T \sigma dt)_i} sin(e^{(\alpha_i \int Y^T \sigma dt)_i})) \tag{24}$$

Substituting Equation (24) into (23) yields

$$\begin{bmatrix} \hat{\rho}(t)_1 \\ \hat{\rho}(t)_2 \\ ..... \\ \hat{\rho}(t)_p \end{bmatrix} = \Phi(t)^{-1}[\int \begin{bmatrix} \beta_1 e^{(\alpha_1 \int Y^T \sigma dt)_1} sin(e^{(\alpha_1 \int Y^T \sigma dt)_1})(Y^T\sigma)_1 \\ \beta_2 e^{(\alpha_2 \int Y^T \sigma dt)_2} sin(e^{(\alpha_2 \int Y^T \sigma dt)_2})(Y^T\sigma)_2 \\ .... \\ \beta_p e^{(\alpha_p \int Y^T \sigma dt)_p} sin(e^{(\alpha_p \int Y^T \sigma dt)_p})(Y^T\sigma)_p \end{bmatrix} dt] + \begin{bmatrix} \rho_1 \\ \rho_2 \\ ..... \\ \rho_p \end{bmatrix} + \Phi(t)^{-1} \begin{bmatrix} 1 \\ 1 \\ ..... \\ 1 \end{bmatrix} \tag{25}$$

After integration, the result is

$$\begin{bmatrix} \hat{\rho}(t)_1 \\ \hat{\rho}(t)_2 \\ ..... \\ \hat{\rho}(t)_p \end{bmatrix} = \Phi(t)^{-1} \begin{bmatrix} -(\beta_1/\alpha_1)cos(e^{(\alpha_1 \int Y^T \sigma dt)_1}) \\ -(\beta_2/\alpha_2)cos(e^{(\alpha_2 \int Y^T \sigma dt)_2}) \\ .... \\ -(\beta_p/\alpha_p)cos(e^{(\alpha_p \int Y^T \sigma dt)_p}) \end{bmatrix} + \begin{bmatrix} \rho_1 \\ \rho_2 \\ ..... \\ \rho_p \end{bmatrix} + \Phi(t)C^{-1} \begin{bmatrix} 1 \\ 1 \\ ..... \\ 1 \end{bmatrix} \tag{26}$$

Then

$$\begin{bmatrix} \hat{\rho}(t)_1 \\ \hat{\rho}(t)_2 \\ ..... \\ \hat{\rho}(t)_p \end{bmatrix} = \begin{bmatrix} -(\beta_1^2/\alpha_1)e^{(\alpha_1 \int Y^T \sigma dt)_1} sin(e^{(\alpha_1 \int Y^T \sigma dt)_1})cos(e^{(\alpha_1 \int Y^T \sigma dt)_1}) \\ -(\beta_2^2/\alpha_2)e^{(\alpha_2 \int Y^T \sigma dt)_2} sin(e^{(\alpha_2 \int Y^T \sigma dt)_2})cos(e^{(\alpha_2 \int Y^T \sigma dt)_2}) \\ .... \\ -(\beta_p^2/\alpha_p)e^{(\alpha_p \int Y^T \sigma dt)_p} sin(e^{(\alpha_p \int Y^T \sigma dt)_p})cos(e^{(\alpha_p \int Y^T \sigma dt)_p}) \end{bmatrix} + \begin{bmatrix} \rho_1 \\ \rho_2 \\ ..... \\ \rho_p \end{bmatrix} + C \begin{bmatrix} \beta_1 e^{(\alpha_1 \int Y^T \sigma dt)_1} sin(e^{(\alpha_1 \int Y^T \sigma dt)_1}) \\ \beta_2 e^{(\alpha_2 \int Y^T \sigma dt)_2} sin(e^{(\alpha_2 \int Y^T \sigma dt)_2}) \\ ..... \\ \beta_p e^{(\alpha_p \int Y^T \sigma dt)_p} sin(e^{(\alpha_p \int Y^T \sigma dt)_p}) \end{bmatrix} \tag{27}$$

If $\hat{\rho}(0)=\rho$ is taken as initial condition, constant C is equivalent to Cos(1). So, the estimation law for the uncertainty bound is derived as.

$$\begin{bmatrix}\hat{\rho}(t)_1\\ \hat{\rho}(t)_2\\ \cdots\\ \hat{\rho}(t)_p\end{bmatrix}=\begin{bmatrix}-(\beta_1^2/\alpha_1)\mathrm{e}^{(\alpha_1\int Y^T\sigma dt)_1} sin(\mathrm{e}^{(\alpha_1\int Y^T\sigma dt)_1})cos(\mathrm{e}^{(\alpha_1\int Y^T\sigma dt)_1})\\ -(\beta_2^2/\alpha_2)\mathrm{e}^{(\alpha_2\int Y^T\sigma dt)_2} sin(\mathrm{e}^{(\alpha_2\int Y^T\sigma dt)_2})cos(\mathrm{e}^{(\alpha_2\int Y^T\sigma dt)_2})\\ \cdots\cdots\\ -(\beta_p^2/\alpha_p)\mathrm{e}^{(\alpha_p\int Y^T\sigma dt)_p} sin(\mathrm{e}^{(\alpha_p\int Y^T\sigma dt)_p})cos(\mathrm{e}^{(\alpha_p\int Y^T\sigma dt)_p})\end{bmatrix}+\begin{bmatrix}\rho_1\\ \rho_2\\ \cdots\\ \rho_p\end{bmatrix}$$
$$+Cos(1)\begin{bmatrix}\beta_1\mathrm{e}^{(\alpha_1\int Y^T\sigma dt)_1} sin(\mathrm{e}^{(\alpha_1\int Y^T\sigma dt)_1})\\ \beta_2\mathrm{e}^{(\alpha_2\int Y^T\sigma dt)_2} sin(\mathrm{e}^{(\alpha_2\int Y^T\sigma dt)_2})\\ \cdots\\ \beta_p\mathrm{e}^{(\alpha_p\int Y^T\sigma dt)_p} sin(\mathrm{e}^{(\alpha_p\int Y^T\sigma dt)_p})\end{bmatrix} \tag{28}$$

2.2 Second choice of $\Phi(t)^{-1}$

For the second derivation of $\hat{\rho}(t)$, $\Phi(t)^{-1}$ is defined as

$$\Phi(t)^{-1}=diag(\beta_i\frac{\mathrm{e}^{\int(\alpha_i Y^T\sigma dt)_i}}{1+\mathrm{e}^{(\int 2\alpha_i Y^T\sigma dt)_i}}) \tag{29}$$

Substituting Equation (29) into (23) yields

$$\begin{bmatrix}\hat{\rho}(t)_1\\ \hat{\rho}(t)_2\\ \cdots\\ \hat{\rho}(t)_p\end{bmatrix}=\Phi(t)^{-1}[\int\begin{bmatrix}\beta_1\frac{\mathrm{e}^{\int(\alpha_1 Y^T\sigma dt)_1}}{1+\mathrm{e}^{(2\alpha_1\int Y^T\sigma dt)_1}}(Y^T\sigma)_1\\ \beta_2\frac{\mathrm{e}^{\int(\alpha_2 Y^T\sigma dt)_2}}{1+\mathrm{e}^{(2\alpha_2\int Y^T\sigma dt)_2}}(Y^T\sigma)_2\\ \cdots\\ \beta_p\frac{\mathrm{e}^{\int(\alpha_p Y^T\sigma dt)_p}}{1+\mathrm{e}^{(2\alpha_p\int Y^T\sigma dt)_p}}(Y^T\sigma)_p\end{bmatrix}dt]+\begin{bmatrix}\rho_1\\ \rho_2\\ \cdots\\ \rho_p\end{bmatrix}+\Phi(t)^{-1}C\begin{bmatrix}1\\ 1\\ \cdots\\ 1\end{bmatrix} \tag{30}$$

After integration, the result is

$$\begin{bmatrix}\hat{\rho}(t)_1\\ \hat{\rho}(t)_2\\ \cdots\\ \hat{\rho}(t)_p\end{bmatrix}=\Phi(t)^{-1}\begin{bmatrix}(\beta_1/\alpha_1)arctan(\mathrm{e}^{\int(\alpha_1 Y^T\sigma dt)_1})\\ (\beta_2/\alpha_2)arctan(\mathrm{e}^{\int(\alpha_2 Y^T\sigma dt)_2})\\ \cdots\\ (\beta_p/\alpha_p)arctan(\mathrm{e}^{\int(\alpha_p Y^T\sigma dt)_p})\end{bmatrix}+\Phi(t)\begin{bmatrix}\rho_1\\ \rho_2\\ \cdots\\ \rho_p\end{bmatrix}+C\begin{bmatrix}1\\ 1\\ \cdots\\ 1\end{bmatrix} \tag{31}$$

After multiplication by $\Phi(t)^{-1}$, the result will be

$$\begin{bmatrix} \hat{\rho}(t)_1 \\ \hat{\rho}(t)_2 \\ \cdots \\ \hat{\rho}(t)_p \end{bmatrix} = \begin{bmatrix} (\beta_1^2/\alpha_1)\dfrac{e^{\int(\alpha_1 Y^T\sigma dt)_1}}{1+e^{(2\alpha_1\int Y^T\sigma dt)_1}} arctan(e^{\int(\alpha_1 Y^T\sigma dt)_1}) \\ (\beta_2^2/\alpha_2)\dfrac{e^{\int(\alpha_2 Y^T\sigma dt)_2}}{1+e^{(2\alpha_2\int Y^T\sigma dt)_2}} arctan(e^{\int(\alpha_2 Y^T\sigma dt)_2}) \\ \cdots \\ (\beta_p^2/\alpha_p)\dfrac{e^{\int(\alpha_p Y^T\sigma dt)_p}}{1+e^{(2\alpha_p\int Y^T\sigma dt)_p}} arctan(e^{\int(\alpha_p Y^T\sigma dt)_p}) \end{bmatrix} + \begin{bmatrix} \rho_1 \\ \rho_2 \\ \cdots \\ \rho_p \end{bmatrix} + C \begin{bmatrix} \beta_1\dfrac{e^{\int(\alpha_1 Y^T\sigma dt)_1}}{1+e^{(2\alpha_1\int Y^T\sigma dt)_1}} \\ \beta_2\dfrac{e^{\int(\alpha_2 Y^T\sigma dt)_2}}{1+e^{(2\alpha_2\int Y^T\sigma dt)_2}} \\ \cdots \\ \beta_p\dfrac{e^{\int(\alpha_p Y^T\sigma dt)_p}}{1+e^{(2\alpha_p\int Y^T\sigma dt)_p}} \end{bmatrix} \quad (32)$$

If $\hat{\rho}(0)=\rho$ is taken as initial condition, constant C is equivalent to -arctan(1). So, the estimation law for the uncertainty bound is derived as.

$$\begin{bmatrix} \hat{\rho}(t)_1 \\ \hat{\rho}(t)_2 \\ \cdots \\ \hat{\rho}(t)_p \end{bmatrix} = \begin{bmatrix} (\beta_1^2/\alpha_1)\dfrac{e^{\int(\alpha_1 Y^T\sigma dt)_1}}{1+e^{(2\alpha_1\int Y^T\sigma dt)_1}} arctan(e^{\int(\alpha_1 Y^T\sigma dt)_1}) \\ (\beta_2^2/\alpha_2)\dfrac{e^{\int(\alpha_2 Y^T\sigma dt)_2}}{1+e^{(2\alpha_2\int Y^T\sigma dt)_2}} arctan(e^{\int(\alpha_2 Y^T\sigma dt)_2}) \\ \cdots \\ (\beta_p^2/\alpha_p)\dfrac{e^{\int(\alpha_p Y^T\sigma dt)_p}}{1+e^{(2\alpha_p\int Y^T\sigma dt)_p}} arctan(e^{\int(\alpha_p Y^T\sigma dt)_p}) \end{bmatrix} + \begin{bmatrix} \rho_1 \\ \rho_2 \\ \cdots \\ \rho_p \end{bmatrix} - arctan(1) \begin{bmatrix} \beta_1\dfrac{e^{\int(\alpha_1 Y^T\sigma dt)_1}}{1+e^{(2\alpha_1\int Y^T\sigma dt)_1}} \\ \beta_2\dfrac{e^{\int(\alpha_2 Y^T\sigma dt)_2}}{1+e^{(2\alpha_2\int Y^T\sigma dt)_2}} \\ \cdots \\ \beta_p\dfrac{e^{\int(\alpha_p Y^T\sigma dt)_p}}{1+e^{(2\alpha_p\int Y^T\sigma dt)_p}} \end{bmatrix} \quad (33)$$

2.3 Third choice of $\Phi(t)^{-1}$

For the third derivation of $\hat{\rho}(t)$, $\Phi(t)^{-1}$ is defined as

$$\Phi(t)^{-1} = diag(\beta_i \mathrm{Sin}^2(\alpha_i\int Y^T\sigma dt)_i \mathrm{Cos}(\alpha_i\int Y^T\sigma dt)_i) \quad (34)$$

Substitution of Equation (34) into Equation (23) yields

$$\begin{bmatrix} \hat{\rho}(t)_1 \\ \hat{\rho}(t)_2 \\ \cdots \\ \hat{\rho}(t)_p \end{bmatrix} = \Phi(t)^{-1}[\int \begin{bmatrix} \beta_1 \mathrm{Sin}^2(\alpha_1\int Y^T\sigma dt)_1 \mathrm{Cos}(\alpha_1\int Y^T\sigma dt)_1 (Y^T\sigma)_1 \\ \beta_2 \mathrm{Sin}^2(\alpha_2\int Y^T\sigma dt)_2 \mathrm{Cos}(\alpha_2\int Y^T\sigma dt)_2 (Y^T\sigma)_2 \\ \cdots \\ \beta_p \mathrm{Sin}^2(\alpha_p\int Y^T\sigma dt)_p \mathrm{Cos}(\alpha_p\int Y^T\sigma dt)_p (Y^T\sigma)_p \end{bmatrix} dt] + \begin{bmatrix} \rho_1 \\ \rho_2 \\ \cdots \\ \rho_p \end{bmatrix} + \Phi(t)^{-1} C \begin{bmatrix} 1 \\ 1 \\ \cdots \\ 1 \end{bmatrix} \quad (35)$$

After integration, the result is

$$\begin{bmatrix} \hat{\rho}(t)_1 \\ \hat{\rho}(t)_2 \\ \cdots\cdots \\ \hat{\rho}(t)_p \end{bmatrix} = \Phi(t)^{-1} \begin{bmatrix} (\beta_1 / \alpha_1)\dfrac{\mathrm{Sin}^3(\alpha_1 \int \mathrm{Y}^{\mathrm{T}}\sigma \mathrm{dt})_1}{3} \\ (\beta_2 / \alpha_2)\dfrac{\mathrm{Sin}^3(\alpha_2 \int \mathrm{Y}^{\mathrm{T}}\sigma \mathrm{dt})_2}{3} \\ \cdots\cdots\cdots \\ (\beta_p / \alpha_p)\dfrac{\mathrm{Sin}^3(\alpha_p \int \mathrm{Y}^{\mathrm{T}}\sigma \mathrm{dt})_p}{3} \end{bmatrix} + \begin{bmatrix} \rho_1 \\ \rho_2 \\ \cdots\cdots \\ \rho_p \end{bmatrix} + \Phi(t)^{-1} C \begin{bmatrix} 1 \\ 1 \\ \cdots\cdots \\ 1 \end{bmatrix} \tag{36}$$

If $\hat{\rho}(0) = \rho$ is taken as initial condition, constant C is equivalent to zero. So, the estimation law for the uncertainty bound is derived as .

$$\begin{bmatrix} \hat{\rho}(t)_1 \\ \hat{\rho}(t)_2 \\ \cdots\cdots \\ \hat{\rho}(t)_p \end{bmatrix} = \begin{bmatrix} (\beta_1^2 / \alpha_1)\dfrac{\mathrm{Sin}^5(\alpha_1 \int \mathrm{Y}^{\mathrm{T}}\sigma \mathrm{dt})_1 \mathrm{Cos}(\alpha_1 \int \mathrm{Y}^{\mathrm{T}}\sigma \mathrm{dt})_1}{3} \\ (\beta_2^2 / \alpha_2)\dfrac{\mathrm{Sin}^5(\alpha_2 \int \mathrm{Y}^{\mathrm{T}}\sigma \mathrm{dt})_2 \mathrm{Cos}(\alpha_2 \int \mathrm{Y}^{\mathrm{T}}\sigma \mathrm{dt})_2}{3} \\ \cdots\cdots\cdots \\ (\beta_p^2 / \alpha_p)\dfrac{\mathrm{Sin}^5(\alpha_p \int \mathrm{Y}^{\mathrm{T}}\sigma \mathrm{dt})_p \mathrm{Cos}(\alpha_p \int \mathrm{Y}^{\mathrm{T}}\sigma \mathrm{dt})_p}{3} \end{bmatrix} + \begin{bmatrix} \rho_1 \\ \rho_2 \\ \cdots\cdots \\ \rho_p \end{bmatrix} \tag{37}$$

If we substitute Φ, $\dot{\Phi}$, and $\dot{\hat{\rho}}(t)$ into Equation (16), the right terms of Equation (16) $[(\rho\text{-}\hat{\rho}(t)]^{\mathrm{T}}[\mathrm{Y}^{\mathrm{T}}\sigma + \Phi(t)\dot{\Phi}(t)(\rho - \hat{\rho}(t)) - \Phi(t)^2\dot{\hat{\rho}}(t)] = 0$ will be always zero and the derivation of the Lyapunov function will become a negative semidefinite function such that

$$\dot{\mathrm{V}} = -\dot{\tilde{\mathrm{q}}}^{\mathrm{T}}\mathrm{K}\dot{\tilde{\mathrm{q}}} - \tilde{\mathrm{q}}^{\mathrm{T}}\Lambda\mathrm{K}\Lambda\tilde{\mathrm{q}} \le 0 \tag{38}$$

So, the system is stable for all $\hat{\rho}(t)$ derived from Equation (23).

3. Design of robust contol laws

Based on the uncertainty bound estimation laws derived in section 2, and in [15], it is possible to develop robust control inputs.

3.1 Robust control law 1

In order to define first robust control input, the following theorem is proposed.

Theorem:

Additional control input in control law (6) is

$$(u(t))_i = \begin{cases} -\dfrac{(Y^T\sigma)_i}{\left|(Y^T\sigma)_i\right|}\hat{\rho}(t)_i & if\ \left|(Y^T\sigma)_i\right| > \varepsilon_i \\ -\dfrac{(Y^T\sigma)_i}{\varepsilon_i}\hat{\rho}(t)_i & if\ \left|(Y^T\sigma)_i\right| \le \varepsilon_i \end{cases} \tag{39}$$

Where $\varepsilon>0$. If the control input (39) is substituted into the control law (6) for the control of the model manipulator, then, the control law (6) is continuous and the closed-loop system is uniformly ultimate bounded.

Proof

It is assumed that there exists an unknown bound on parametric uncertainty such that

$$\pi_0 - \pi \leq \rho \quad \text{and} \quad \|\pi_0 - \pi\| \leq \delta \tag{40}$$

If Φ, $\hat{\rho}(t)$, $\dot{\Phi}$ and $\dot{\hat{\rho}}(t)$ are substituded into (13), the time derivative of the Lyapunov function (13) is written as [14, 15].

$$\begin{aligned}\dot{V} &= -\dot{\tilde{q}}^T K \dot{\tilde{q}} - \tilde{q}^T \Lambda K \Lambda \tilde{q} + \sigma^T Y u(t) + \sigma^T Y \tilde{\pi} + \sigma^T Y \tilde{\rho} \\ &= -\dot{\tilde{q}}^T K \dot{\tilde{q}} - \tilde{q}^T \Lambda K \Lambda \tilde{q} + \sigma^T Y u(t) + \sigma^T Y \tilde{\pi} - \sigma^T Y (\rho - \hat{\rho}(t) \\ &=\leq -x^T Q x + \sigma^T Y u(t) + \sigma^T Y \hat{\rho}(t)\end{aligned} \tag{41}$$

Where $x^T = [\tilde{q}^T, \dot{\tilde{q}}^T]$ and $Q=\text{diag}[\Lambda^T K \Lambda, K]$. Based on the Leitman [1], we can show that $\dot{V} \leq 0$ for $||x||>w$ where

$$w^2 = \hat{\rho}(t)/2\lambda_{\min}(Q) \tag{42}$$

Where $\lambda_{\min}(Q)$ denotes the minimum eigenvalue of Q. Second term in Equation (41), if $||Y^T\sigma||>\varepsilon$ then

$$\leq -x^T Q x + \sigma^T Y \hat{\rho}(t) - \sigma^T Y \begin{bmatrix} \dfrac{(Y^T\sigma)_1}{|(Y^T\sigma)_1|}\hat{\rho}(t)_1 \\ \dots\dots\dots\dots\dots \\ \dfrac{(Y^T\sigma)_p}{|(Y^T\sigma)_p|} + \hat{\rho}(t)_p \end{bmatrix} \tag{43}$$

$$\leq -x^T Q x + \sigma^T Y (\hat{\rho}(t)) - \hat{\rho}(t)) \leq 0$$

From the Cauchy-Schawartz inequality and our assumption on . If $||Y^T \sigma||<\varepsilon$ then

$$\begin{aligned}\sigma^T Y u(t) + \sigma^T Y(\hat{\rho}(t)) &\leq (Y^T\sigma)^T \left(\|\hat{\rho}(t)\| \frac{Y^T\sigma}{\|Y^T\sigma\|} + u(t) \right) \\ &\leq (Y^T\sigma)^T \left(\|\hat{\rho}(t)\| \frac{Y^T\sigma}{\|Y^T\sigma\|} - \frac{Y^T\sigma}{\varepsilon}\|\hat{\rho}(t)\| \right)\end{aligned} \tag{44}$$

This last term achieves a maximum value of $\varepsilon\|\hat{\rho}(t)\|/4$ when $||Y^T \sigma||=\varepsilon/2$. We have that

$$\dot{V} \leq -x^T Q x + \varepsilon \|\hat{\rho}(t)\| / 4 \tag{45}$$

Note that $\hat{\rho}(t)$ is bounded. The rest of the proof can be seen in [4, 8].

3.2 Robust control law 2

Based on the bound estimation law $\hat{\rho}(t)$ derived from general Equation (23), additional control input u(t) are defined [15]. The additional control input in control law (6) is defined as [15]

$$u(t) = \begin{bmatrix} -\hat{\rho}(t)_1 \operatorname{sgn}(Y^T\sigma)_1 \\ -\hat{\rho}(t)_2 \operatorname{sgn}(Y^T\sigma)_2 \\ \cdots\cdots\cdots \\ -\hat{\rho}(t)_p \operatorname{sgn}(Y^T\sigma)_p \end{bmatrix} \tag{46}$$

3.3 Robust control law 3

υ_i denote the ith component of the vector $Y^T\sigma$, ε_i choose as the ith component of ε. Then, considering the $\hat{\rho}(t)$ derived from Equation (23), u(t) for each $\hat{\rho}(t)$ is defined as as follows: For Equation (28), $u(t)_i$ is

$$u(t)_i = \begin{cases} -\dfrac{\upsilon_i}{|\upsilon_i|}\left[-(\beta_i^2/\alpha_i)e^{\alpha_i\left|\int v_i dt\right|} sin(e^{\alpha_i\left|\int v_i dt\right|}) cos(e^{\alpha_i\left|\int v_i dt\right|} + Cos(1)e^{\alpha_i\left|\int v_i dt\right|} sin(e^{\alpha_i\left|\int v_i dt\right|}) + \rho_i\right] & \text{if } |\upsilon_i| > \varepsilon_i \\ -\dfrac{\upsilon_i}{\varepsilon_i}\left[-(\beta_i^2/\alpha_i)e^{\alpha_i\left|\int v_i dt\right|} sin(e^{\alpha_i\left|\int v_i dt\right|}) cos(e^{\alpha_i\left|\int v_i dt\right|} + Cos(1)e^{\alpha_i\left|\int v_i dt\right|} sin(e^{\alpha_i\left|\int v_i dt\right|}) + \rho_i\right] & \text{if } |\upsilon_i| \le \varepsilon_i \end{cases} \tag{47}$$

For Equation (33),

$$u(t)_i = \begin{cases} -\dfrac{\upsilon_i}{|\upsilon_i|}\left[(\beta_i^2/\alpha_i)\dfrac{e^{\alpha_i\left|\int v_i dt\right|}}{1+e^{2\alpha_i\left|\int v_i dt\right|}} arctan(e^{\alpha_i\left|\int v_i dt\right|}) - arctan(1)\dfrac{e^{\alpha_i\left|\int v_i dt\right|}}{1+e^{2\left|\int v_i dt\right|}} + \rho_i)\right] & \text{if } |\upsilon_i| > \varepsilon_i \\ -\dfrac{\upsilon_i}{\varepsilon_i}\left[(\beta_i^2/\alpha_i)\dfrac{e^{\alpha_i\left|\int v_i dt\right|}}{1+e^{2\alpha_i\left|\int v_i dt\right|}} arctan(e^{\alpha_i\left|\int v_i dt\right|}) - arctan(1)\dfrac{e^{\alpha_i\left|\int v_i dt\right|}}{1+e^{2\left|\int v_i dt\right|}} + \rho_i)\right] & \text{if } |\upsilon_i| \le \varepsilon_i \end{cases} \tag{48}$$

For Equation (36):

$$u(t)_i = \begin{cases} -\dfrac{\upsilon_i}{|\upsilon_i|}\left[(\beta_i^2/\alpha_i)\dfrac{sin^5(\alpha_i\left|\int v_i dt\right|) Cos(\alpha_i\left|\int v_i dt\right|)}{3} + \rho_i\right] & \text{if } |\upsilon_i| > \varepsilon_i \\ -\dfrac{\upsilon_i}{\varepsilon_i}\left[(\beta_i^2/\alpha_i)\dfrac{sin^5(\alpha_i\left|\int v_i dt\right|) Cos(\alpha_i\left|\int v_i dt\right|)}{3} + \rho_i\right] & \text{if } |\upsilon_i| \le \varepsilon_i \end{cases} \tag{49}$$

3.4 Robust control law 4

From Equations (43) and (44), it is ease to define the following control law.

$$u(t) = \begin{cases} -\dfrac{Y^T\sigma}{\left\|(Y^T\sigma)\right\|}\left\|\hat{\rho}(t)\right\| & if \ \left\|(Y^T\sigma)\right\| > \varepsilon \\ -\dfrac{Y^T\sigma}{\varepsilon}\left\|\hat{\rho}(t)\right\| & if \ \left\|(Y^T\sigma)\right\| \le \varepsilon \end{cases} \tag{50}$$

4. Simulation results

For illustration, a two-link robot manipulator is given in Figure 1 [4]. Parameterisation of this robot is given by

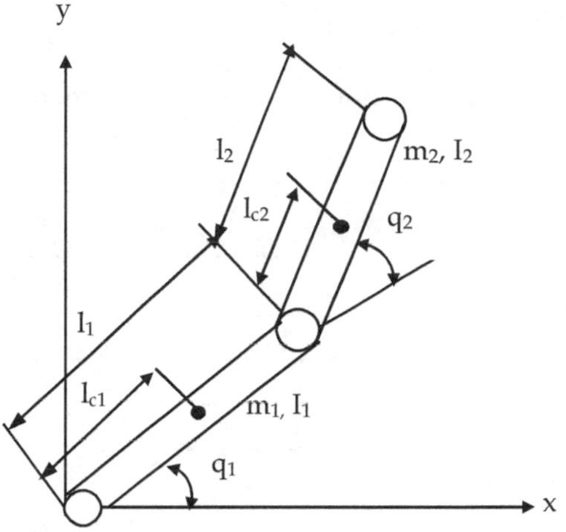

Fig. 1. Two-link planar robot [4].

$$\pi_1 = m_1 l_{c1}^2 + m_2 l_1^2 + I_1, \qquad \pi_2 = m_2 l_{c2}^2 + I_2, \qquad \pi_3 = m_2 l_1 l_{c2},$$

$$\pi_4 = m_1 l_{c1}, \qquad \pi_5 = m_2 l_1, \qquad \pi_6 = m_2 l_{c2}, \tag{51}$$

With this parameterisation, the component y_{ij} of $Y(q,\dot{q},\ddot{q})$ in Equation 2 are given as

$$y_{11} = \ddot{q}_1; \quad y_{12} = \ddot{q}_1 + \ddot{q}_2; \quad y_{13} = \cos(q_2)(2\ddot{q}_1 + \ddot{q}_2) - \sin(q_2)(\dot{q}_2^{\,2} + 2\dot{q}_1\dot{q}_2);$$

$$y_{14} = g_c\cos(q_1); \quad y_{15} = g_c\cos(q_1); \quad y_{16} = g_c\cos(q_1+q_2);$$

$$y_{21} = 0; \quad y_{22} = \ddot{q}_1 + \ddot{q}_2; \quad y_{23} = \cos(q_2)\ddot{q}_1 + \sin(q_2)(\dot{q}_1^{\,2});$$

$$y_{24} = 0; \quad y_{25} = 0; \quad y_{26} = g_c\cos(q_1+q_2). \tag{52}$$

$Y(q,\dot{q},\dot{q}_r,\ddot{q}_r)$ in Equation (4) have the components

$$y_{11} = \ddot{q}_{r1}; \; y_{12} = \ddot{q}_{r1} + \ddot{q}_{r2};$$

$$y_{13} = \cos(q_2)(2\ddot{q}_{r1} + \ddot{q}_{r2}) - \sin(q_2)(\dot{q}_1\dot{q}_{r2} + \dot{q}_1\dot{q}_{r2} + \dot{q}_2\dot{q}_{r2});$$

$$y_{14} = g_c\cos(q_1); \quad y_{15} = g_c\cos(q_1); \quad y_{16} = g_c\cos(q_1+q_2)$$

$$y_{21} = 0; \quad y_{22} = \ddot{q}_{r1} + \ddot{q}_{r2}; \quad ; y_{23} = \cos(q_2)\ddot{q}_{r1} + \sin(q_2)(\dot{q}_1\dot{q}_{r1})$$

$$y_{24} = 0; \quad y_{25} = 0; \quad y_{26} = g_c\cos(q_1+q_2). \tag{53}$$

For illustrated purposes let us assume that the parameters of the unloaded manipulator are known and are given by Table 1. Using these values in Table 1, the ith component of π obtained by means of Equation (51) are given in Table 2. It is assumed that the parameters m_2, l_{c2} and I_2 are changed in the intervals

$$0 \le \Delta m_2 \le 10 \ ; \quad 0 \le \Delta l_{c2} \le 0.5 \ ; \quad 0 \le I_2 \le \frac{15}{12} \tag{54}$$

Choosing the mean value for the range of possible π_i in Equation (54) yields the nominal parameter vector and the computed values for ith component of π_0 is shown in Table 3 [4].

m_1	m_2	l_1	l_2	l_{c1}	l_{c2}	I_1	I_2
10	5	1	1	0.5	0.5	10/12	5/12

Table 1. Parameters of the unloaded arm [4].

π_1	π_2	π_3	π_4	π_5	π_6
8.33	1.67	2.5	5	5	2.5

Table 2. π_i for the unloaded arm [4]

π_{01}	π_{02}	π_{03}	π_{04}	π_{05}	π_{06}
13.33	8.96	8.75	5	10	8.75

Table 3. Nominal parameter vector π_0 [4].

With this choice of nominal parameter vector π_0 and uncertainty range given by (54), it is an easy matter to calculate the uncertainty bound ρ as follows:

$$\|\tilde{\pi}\|^2 = \sum_{i=1}^{6} (\pi_{i0} - \pi_i)^2 \le 181.26 \tag{55}$$

and thus $\delta = \sqrt{181.26} = 13.46$.
For explanation, Spong's algorithms are given.

$$u(t) = \begin{cases} -\delta \dfrac{Y^T\sigma}{\|Y^T\sigma\|} & \text{if } \|Y^T\sigma\| > \varepsilon \\ -\delta \dfrac{Y^T\sigma}{\varepsilon} & \text{if } \|Y^T\sigma\| \le \varepsilon \end{cases} \tag{56}$$

As a measure of parameter uncertainty on which the additional control input is based, ρ can be defined as

$$\delta = \left(\sum_{i=1}^{p} \rho_i^2 \right)^{1/2} \tag{57}$$

Having a single number ρ to measure the parameter uncertainty may lead to overly conservative design, higher than necessary gains, etc. For this purpose, different "weights" or gains to the components of u may be assigned. This can be done as follows: Supposing that a measure of uncertainty for each parameter $\tilde{\pi}_i$ can be defined separately as:

$$\lfloor \tilde{\pi}_i \rfloor \le \rho_i \qquad I=1,2,.........,p \tag{58}$$

Let υ_i denote the *i*tch component of the vector $Y^T\sigma$, ε_i choose as the itch component of ε, and consequently the *i*tch component of the control input u_p is defined as [4].

$$u_i = \begin{cases} -\rho_i\upsilon_i/|\upsilon_i| & \text{if } |\upsilon_i| > \varepsilon_i \\ -(\rho_i/\varepsilon_i)\upsilon_i & \text{if } |\upsilon_i| \le \varepsilon_i \end{cases} \tag{59}$$

Since extended algorithm (56) is used, the uncertainty bounds for each parameter are shown separately in Table 4. The uncertainty bounds ρ_i in Table 4 are simply the difference between values given in Table 3 and Table 2, and the value of ρ is the Euclidean norm of the vector with components ρ_i [4].

ρ_1	ρ_2	ρ_3	ρ_4	ρ_5	ρ_6
5	7.29	6. 25	0	5	6.25

Table 4. Uncertainty bound [4].

For computer simulation, a fifth order polynomial function is used as a reference trajectory for both joints. In order to analyse performance of the proposed controllers, each control law with the same control parameters K and Λ is applied to the same model system using same trajectory. The control matrices Λ and K are chosen to be identical as Λ=diag(10 10) and K=diag(30 30) for all controllers. The obtained results are plotted in Figures 2-4.

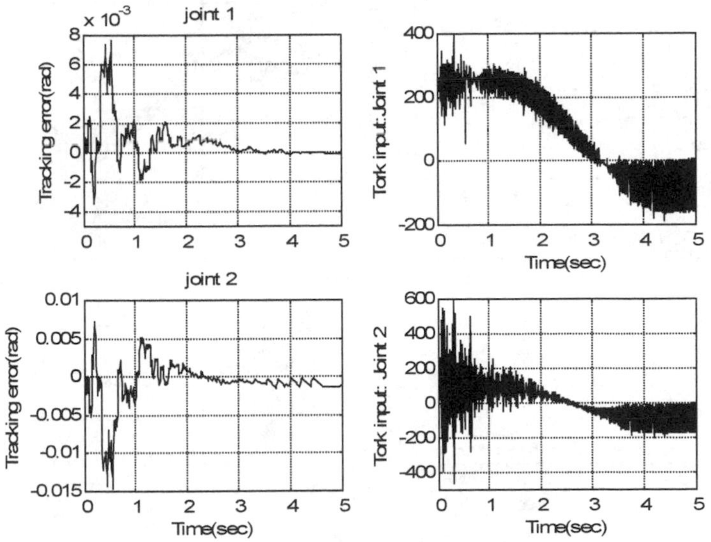

Fig. 2. Response using the robust control law (39) with uncertainty bound estimation law (28) when Λ=diag(10 10), K=diag(30 30), α=1, β=1.

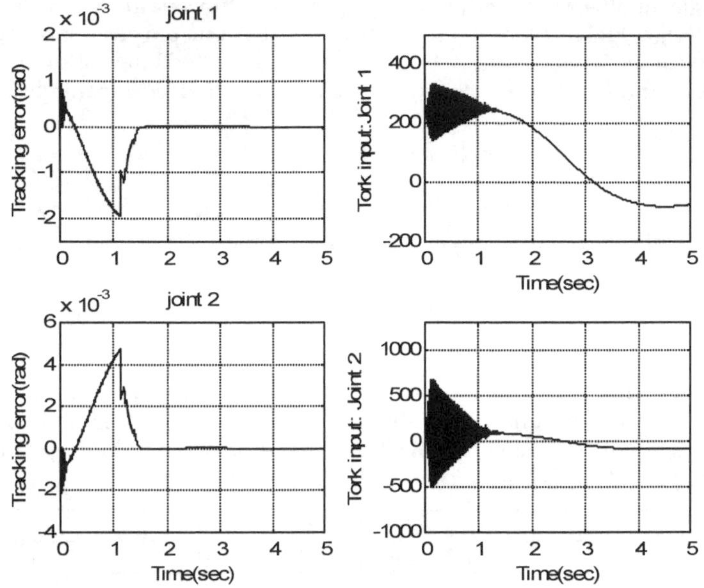

Fig. 3. Response using the robust control law (39) with uncertainty bound estimation law (35) when Λ=diag(10 10), K=diag(30 30), α=0.8, β=0.4.

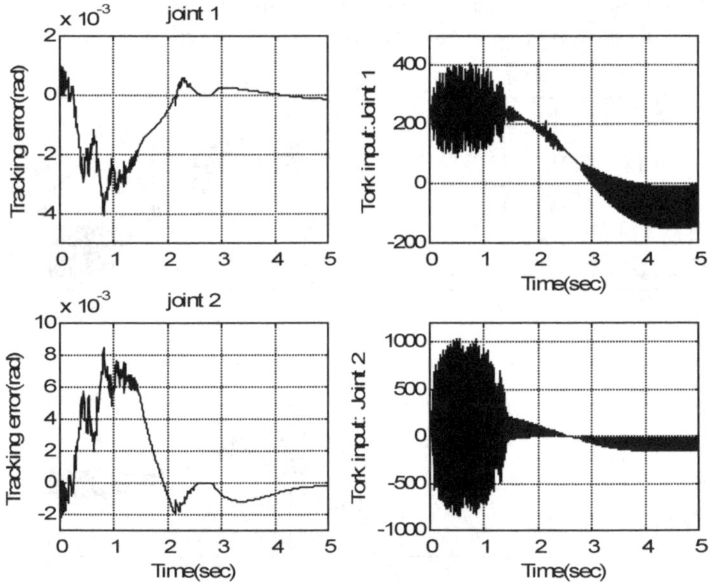

Fig. 4. Response using the robust control law (39) with uncertainty bound estimation law (37) when Λ=diag(10 10), K=diag(30 30), α=0.5, β=2.

As shown in Figures 2-4, tracking error is small and tracking performance changes according to uncertainty bound estimation laws.

5. Conclusion

In the past, some robust controllers are developed for robot manipulators. Corless-Leitmann [1] approach is a popular approach used for designing robust controllers for robot manipulators. Spong [4] proposed a new robust controller for robot manipulators and Leithmann [5] or Corless-Leithman [1] approach is used for designing the robust controller. In [4], uncertainty bound on parameter is needed to derive robust controller and uncertainty bound parameters depends only on the inertia parameters of the robots. However, constant uncertainty bound parameters cause pure tracking performances. In order to increase tracking performance of the uncetain system, uncertainty bound estimation laws are developed [11-13]. Uncertainty bound estimation laws are updated as a function of exponential [11, 12], logarithmic [13] and trigonometric [14] functions depending on robot kinematics parameters and tracking error. A first order differential equation function is developed for derivation of control parameters and only a single derivation of uncertainty bound estimation law is possible. A new method for derivation of a bound estimation law is not proposed in [11-13], because, definition of a new variable function for other derivation is diffucult.

In the study [14], a general equation is developed from Lyapunov function and uncertainty bound estimation laws depending on trigonometric functions are developed. However, a general method for derivation of uncertainty bound estimation laws is not proposed. In a recent study [15], a general method for derivation of bound estimation laws based on the Lyapunov theory is proposed. In this method, functions and integration techniques are used for derivation of uncertainty bound estimation laws. Then, relations between the bound estimation laws and robust control inputs are established and four new robust control inputs are designed depending on each bound estimation law. It is possible to derive other different uncertainty bound estimation laws from general equation (23) if appropriate functions and integration techniques are defined. In this work, three different variable functions are defined and integration techniques are used in order to derive $\hat{\rho}(t)$ and relations between the uncertainty bouns and robust control laws are established. There is no distinct rule for definition of the $\Phi(t)$ and integration techniques in order to derive $\hat{\rho}(t)$. We use system state parameters and mathematical insight to search for appropriate function of $\Phi(t)$ as a derivtion of $\hat{\rho}(t)$. This study also shows that robust controllers are not limited with these derivations. It will be also possible to derive another bound estimation laws from Equation (23) if appropriate function $\Phi(t)$ and integration techniques are chosen.

6. References

[1] M. Corless, G. Leitmann, "Continuous feedback guaranteeing uniform ultimate boundedness for uncertain dynamic systems", IEEE Transactions Automatic Control Vol.26, pp. 1139-1144, 1981.

[2] M. Corless, "Tracking controllers for uncertain systems: Applications to a manutec R3 robot. Journal of Dynamic Systems Measurement and Control", Vol.111, pp. 609-618, 1989.

[3] M.W. Spong, M. Vidyasagar, "Robust linear compensator design for nonlinear robotic control", IEEE Journal of Robotic and Automation, Vol.3(4), pp. 345-350, 1987.

[4] M.W. Spong, "On the robust control of robot manipulators", IEEE Transactions on Automatic Control, Vol.37, pp.1782-1786, 1992.

[5] G. Leitmann, "On the efficiency of nonlinear control in uncertain linear system", Journal of Dynamic Systems Measurement and Control, Vol.102, pp. 95-102, 1981.

[6] E. Yaz, "Comments on the robust control of robot manipulators", IEEE Transactions on Automatic Control, Vol. 38(38), pp. 511-512, 1993.

[7] M. Danesh, M. Keshmiri and F. Sheikholeslam, "Developing a robust control scheme robust to uncertain model parameters and unmodeled dynamics" Proceeding of IEEE Conference on Industrial Electronics and Applications (ICIEA), May 24-26, 2006, Singapore.

[8] K.M. Koo, J.H. Kim, "Robust control of robot manipulators with parametric uncertainty", IEEE Transactions Automatic Control, Vol.39(6), pp. 1230-1233, 1994.

[9] G. Liu, A.A. Goldenberg, "Uncertainty decomposition-based robust control of robot manipulators", IEEE Transactions on Control Systems Technology, Vol.4, pp. 384-393, 1996.

[10]. G. Liu, Decomposition-based control of mechanical systems Electrical and Computer Engineering, 2000 Canadian Conference on Volume: 2 Publication Year: 2000 , Page(s): 966 - 970 vol.2

[11] R. Burkan, New approaches in controlling robot manipulators with parametric uncertainty, Ph.D. Thesis, Erciyes University, Institute of Science, Turkey, 2002.

[12] R. Burkan, İ. Uzmay, "Upper bounding estimation for robustness to the parameter uncertainty in trajectory control of robot arm", Robotics and Autonomous Systems Vol.45, pp.99-110, 2003.

[13] R. Burkan, İ. Uzmay, "Logarithmic based robust approach to parametric uncertainty for control of robot manipulators", International Journal of Robust and Nonlinear Control, Vol.15, pp. 427-436, 2005.

[14] R. Burkan, "Upper bounding estimation for robustness to the parameter uncertainty with trigonometric function in trajectory control of robot arms". Journal of Intelligent & Robotic Systems, Vol.46, pp.263-283, 2006.

[15] R. Burkan, "Modelling of bound estimation laws and robust controllers for robustness to parametric uncertainty for control of robot manipulators", Journal of Intelligent and Robotic Systems, Vol.60, pp. 365-394, 2010.

[16] M.W. Spong, S. Hutchinson, M. Vidyasagar, Robot Dynamics and Control, John Willey&Sons, Inc., 2006.

[17] J.J. Slotine, W. Li, "On the adaptive control of robotic manipulator", The International Journal of Robotics Research, Vol.6(3), pp. 49-59, 1987.

[18] L. Sciavicco, B. Siciliano, Modeling and Control of Robot Manipulators, The McGraw-Hill Companies, 1996.

12

Missile Cooperative Engagement Formation Configuration Control Method

Changzhu Wei[1,2], Yi Shen[1], Xiaoxiao Ma[3],
Naigang Cui[1] and Jifeng Guo[1]
[1]*Harbin Institute of Technology, Harbin,*
[2]*Yonsei University Observatory, Seoul,*
[3]*Xuzhou Air Force College, Xuzhou,*
[1,3]*China*
[2]*Republic of Korea*

1. Introduction

In traditional engagement model, there is only one single weapon or platform which resists to another single one, and the connections between members are few, so the complete and global information in engagement space can't be utilized sufficiently, which directly results in traditional model is confronting with more and more disadvantages especially as the high-tech and information-tech are developing faster and faster. In view of those issues, the concepts and technology of missile formation cooperative are presented, developed and expanded recently(Cui et al., 2009). Compared to traditional model, weapon or platform with cooperative manner manifests great advantages in aspects of ability of penetration, electronic countermeasures and ability of searching moving targets etc, furthermore the synthetical engagement efficacy is developed greatly.

Many new cooperative weapon systems are established and developed fast recently, such as Cooperative Engagement Capability (CEC) system, Net Fire System and LOw Cost Autonomous Attack System (LOCAAS) etc, wherein the LOCAAS is most relevant to our topic, so we will introduce it more detailed.

In order to meet the requirements of future aerial warfare, United States Force has developed a series of high technical and high accurate airborne guided weapon systems, such as Joint Common Missile (JCM), Joint Direct Attack Missile (JDAM), Wind Corrected Munitions Dispenser (WCMD) and LOw Cost Autonomous Attack System (LOCAAS). These weapons are paid much attention because their great capabilities of high-precision, all-weather engagement and attacking beyond defence area etc. Especially, LOCAAS also has other great advantages besides those aspects mentioned above, such as low cost, general utilization and attacking multi-targets simultaneously, so it is paid more attention than other weapons, and it becomes an outstanding representative of high-tech weapon and new engagement model.

LOCAAS is developed from an previous weapon named as Low Cost Anti-Armor Sub-munitions (also called LOCAAS for short) which was a kind of short-range unpowered airborne and air-to-ground guided weapon developed in 1998. At a later time, researchers added thrust system to this old LOCAAS, so it had capability of launching beyond defence area and searching moving targets within large scope. This weapon was added bidirectional data link once again in 2003, so it can implement Man-in-the-Loop control and command, which meant that this weapon system can attack targets autonomously and manifest a kind of smart engagement capability. After those improvements, this old anti-armor weapon was re-named to LOw Cost Autonomous Attack System (LOCAAS). LOCAAS adopts INS and mid-course guidance, and it also equips a smart fuze and a sensor that can be used to search moving targets, so LOCAAS can not only monitor targets within large range but also can re-locate, recognize and aim at them autonomously. The most outstanding character is that LOCAAS can also make intelligent decision for choosing the optimal orientation and sequence to achieve optimal attack, and it also has the capability of on-line planning mission.

At present, United State Force sets the engagement schemes for LOCAAS as: there will be some LOCAASs flying in the battle field to cruise or put on standby, and they can connect with each other by data link. While one of them finding the targets and can't destroy them alone, it will send out the signals to require for cooperative attacking, however if it can destroy the targets by itself, this LOCAAS will attack the targets and the other LOCAASs will continue searching targets after receiving the instruction signals from the mentioned LOCAAS which has gone into the battle. The sketch map Fig.1 shows the main concepts of how LOCAASs take part in engagement cooperatively. Authors who are interested in LOCAAS can get more detailed information in the website of Lockheed Martin.

Fig. 1. The sketch map of LOCAAS engagement.

The background and significance were presented first, and then the technique frame of missile formation cooperative control system is showed, which can clearly elaborate how missiles in a formation work together in a cooperative manner. The specific relationships between each loop are analyzed, which are very necessary to clearly explain how to design missile formation control system. Followed are the main contents of this chapter, which are the detailed processes of establishing and designing missile formation control system. In this part, we will only consider the external loop of missile formation control system because the design method on individual missile inner controller is easy to be found in many literatures, and then we just assumed it is closed-loop and stable. The detailed process is divided into two steps, first is using proportion-differential control method to design missile formation keeping controller, the other explains how to design optimal keeping controller of missile formation. Some simulations are made to compare these two formation control systems proposed in this chapter at last.

2. Frame of missile formation control system

The missile formation control system mentioned in this chapter only has one leader missile (showed as Fig.2), and it mainly consists of the following subsystems: cooperative engagement mission planning subsystem, formation configuration describing subsystem, leader inner-loop control subsystem, follower inner-loop control subsystem and formation configuration control subsystem. The sketch map illustrates relationships between each subsystem in one missile formation system is showed in Fig.3.

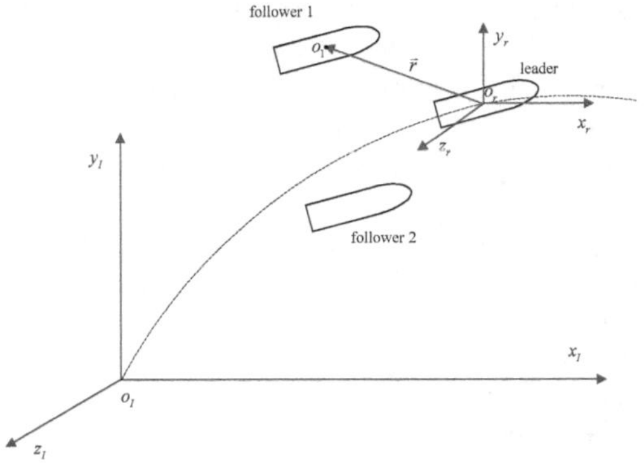

Fig. 2. Sketch map of missile formation consisted of two followers and only one leader.

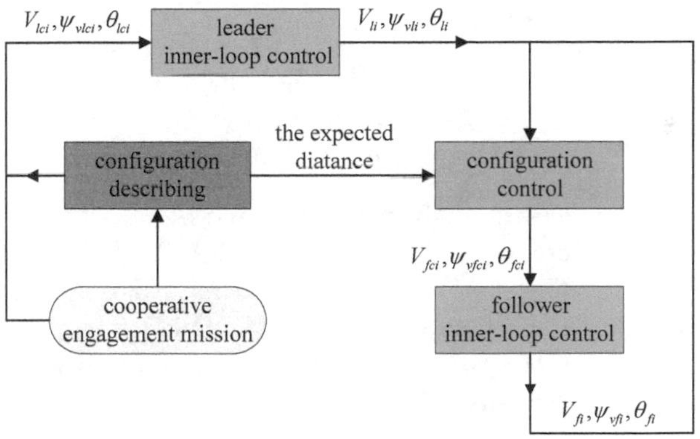

Fig. 3. Relationships between subsystems of missile formation control system.

The cooperative mission planning subsystem supplies real-time status of mission space and distribution situation of targets, and restricts the flight status of leader at the same time; the formation configuration describing system receives the information supplied by cooperative engagement subsystem and establishes associated function of engagement efficacy according to different missile formation configurations, and then makes the decision set about formation configurations based on the returned value of this efficacy function. After optimizing the values of efficacy function according to the specific mission space, the optimal formation configuration can be calculated within this decision set. The optimal formation configuration will be different when the missile formation is flying in different segments of mission space, that is, the optimal formation configuration will be decided by specific engagement requirement. The formation configuration describing subsystem will also restrict flight status of leader together with cooperative mission planning subsystem at the same time; The leader inner-loop control subsystem receives the information sent from the cooperative engagement planning subsystem and controls the leader to fly stably, and then the real flight states of leader can be obtained; The required states of follower missile can be calculated through the states in relative spatial dimension i.e. the distance between missiles which is obtained from formation configuration describing subsystem; The follower inner-loop control subsystem receives the command states, which is similar to that of leader mentioned above, and then control follower to fly stably. The actual flight states of follower missiles are fed back to the formation configuration control subsystem and used to achieve the expected formation configuration which is decided by the specific cooperative engagement mission.

This chapter focus on missile formation keeping control problems. First, we consider the actual flight states of leader as perturbation variables acting on the controller, and assume the follower inner-controller is closed and stable loop, that is, followers can track the required commands of velocity, flight path angle and flight deflection angle rapidly and stably. We will make further assumption that those three channels referred above are one-order systems expressed as (Wei et al., 2010):

$$\begin{aligned} \dot{V}_f &= -\frac{1}{\tau_{vf}}(V_f - V_{fc}) \\ \dot{\theta}_f &= -\frac{1}{\tau_{\theta f}}(\theta_f - \theta_{fc}) \\ \dot{\psi}_{vf} &= -\frac{1}{\tau_{\psi_{vf}}}(\psi_{vf} - \psi_{vfc}) \end{aligned} \tag{1}$$

where V_f, θ_f and ψ_{vf} is the velocity, flight path angle and flight deflection angle of follower respectively; V_{fc}, θ_{fc} and ψ_{vfc} are commands of velocity, flight path angle and flight deflection angle of follower respectively; $\tau_{vf}, \tau_{\theta f}$ and $\tau_{\psi_{vf}}$ are the inertial time constants of velocity, flight path angle and flight deflection angle channel of follower respectively. These values can be calculated by analyzing four-dimensional guidance and control system referrd in the literature of Cui et al., 2010, they are:

$$\begin{aligned} \tau_v &= 3.51\text{s} \\ \tau_\theta &= 2.25\text{s} \\ \tau_{\psi_v} &= 2.37\text{s} \end{aligned} \tag{2}$$

These inertial time constants will be used in the subsequent sections for designing and simulating missile formation keeping controller.

After missile formation achieving four-dimensionally rendezvous, this formation should carry out some subsequent missions, such as relative navigation and location, cooperative searching targets, locating and recognizing targets and cooperative penetration etc., however, these missions require missile formation keeping its configuration or relative dimensional states for some periods of time. Next sections will present some further and detailed researches on how to keep missile formation optimally and robustly.

The main thought of the following parts is showed as below: basing on the kinematics relationships between missiles in inertial coordinate frame, the missile formation proportional-derivative (PD) controller via feeding back full states will be present firstly; Second, the relative motion will be established in relative coordinates frame, which can indicate the characteristics of relative motion directly. Based on this direct relative motion, the optimal controller that has non-zero given point and restrains slowly variant perturbations is designed in the third part.

3. PD controller of missile formation keeping

3.1 Definition of coordinate frame system

1. Relative coordinate frame $o_r - x_r y_r z_r$

The origin o_r of this coordinate coincides with the mass centre of leader, and axis $o_r x_r$ points to the velocity direction of leader, $o_r y_r$ is perpendicular to $o_r x_r$ and points to up direction, $o_r z_r$ composes right-hand coordinate frame together with other two axes mentioned above.

2. Inertial coordinate frame system $O_I - X_I Y_I Z_I$

The origin O_I of this coordinate frame is fixed to an arbitrary point on ground, axis $O_I X_I$ lies in horizontal plane and points to target, axis $O_I Y_I$ is perpendicular to $O_I X_I$ and points to up direction, the last axis $O_I Z_I$ also composes right-hand coordinate frame system together with those two axes mentioned above.

The relationship between these two coordinate frames is showed in Fig.4.

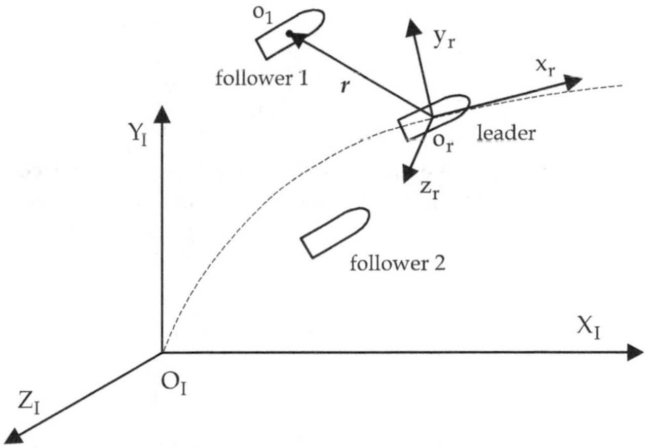

Fig. 4. Relationship between relative and inertial coordinate frame.

3. Trajectory coordinate frame system $o_1 - x_2 y_2 z_2$

The origin of this coordinate o_1 coincides with the mass centre of missile, and axis $o_1 x_2$ points to the velocity direction of missile, $o_1 y_2$ is perpendicular to $o_1 x_2$ and points to up direction, o_1z_2 composes right-hand coordinate frame together with other two axes mentioned above. The spatial directions are parallel to those in relative coordinate frame system.

3.2 Model of relative motion between missiles

3.2.1 Basic assumptions

It is assumed that the control system of missile self is closed-loop and stable, that is, missile can track the required velocity, flight path angle and flight deflection angle rapidly and stably. Further, we consider these tracking channels are one-order inertial loops described as section 2. In order to express the relationships conveniently, we will change the one-order inertial loops showed in Equ.(1) to the following forms:

$$\begin{cases} \dot{V}_i = -\lambda_v(V_i - V_{ic}) \\ \dot{\theta}_i = -\lambda_\theta(\theta_i - \theta_{ic}) \\ \dot{\psi}_{vi} = -\lambda_{\psi_v}(\psi_{vi} - \psi_{vic}) \end{cases} \tag{3}$$

where i is the number of missile, V_i, θ_i and ψ_{vi} represent the actual velocity, flight path angle and flight deflection angle of ith missile respectively; V_{ic}, θ_{ic} and ψ_{vic} are desired velocity, desired flight path angle and desired flight deflection angle of ith missile respectively; λ_v, λ_θ and λ_{ψ_v} are the reciprocals of inertial time constants τ_v, τ_θ and τ_{ψ_v} in channels of veloctiy, flight path angle and flight deflection angle respectively.

3.2.2 Establishing the control model

The kinematics equations of missile in inertial coordinate frame can be expressed as:

$$\begin{cases} \dot{X}_i = V_i \cos\theta_i \cos\psi_{vi} \\ \dot{Y}_i = V_i \sin\theta_i \\ \dot{Z} = -V_i \cos\theta_i \sin\psi_{vi} \end{cases} \tag{4}$$

The kinematics relationship of two missiles in inertial and relative coordinate frame is showed in Fig.5, so the relative positions of two missiles can be obtained from these sketch maps:

$$\begin{bmatrix} X_2 \\ Y_2 \\ Z_2 \end{bmatrix} = \begin{bmatrix} X_1 \\ Y_1 \\ Z_1 \end{bmatrix} + \boldsymbol{T}_2(\psi_{v1})\boldsymbol{T}_1(\theta_1)\begin{bmatrix} x^* \\ y^* \\ z^* \end{bmatrix} \tag{5}$$

where x^*, y^* and z^* are the distances relative to leader in relative coordinate frame, and the transformation matrices in Equ.(5) are:

$$\boldsymbol{T}_1(.) = \begin{bmatrix} \cos(.) & -\sin(.) & 0 \\ \sin(.) & \cos(.) & 0 \\ 0 & 0 & 1 \end{bmatrix}, \ \boldsymbol{T}_2(.) = \begin{bmatrix} \cos(.) & 0 & \sin(.) \\ 0 & 1 & 0 \\ -\sin(.) & 0 & \cos(.) \end{bmatrix}$$

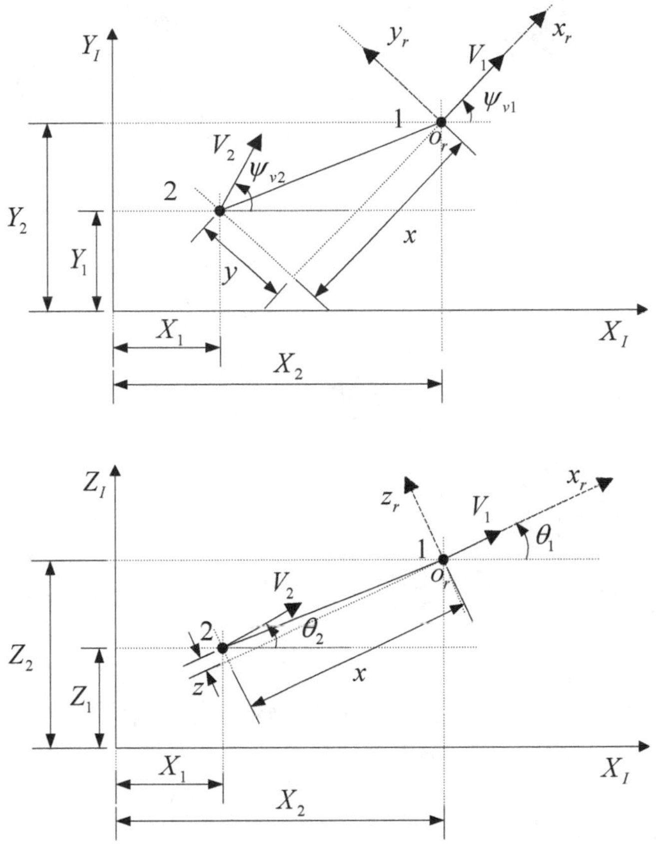

Fig. 5. Relative position relations between two missiles.

Further, the deviations of relative positions can be expressed from Equ.(5) to:

$$\boldsymbol{e} = \begin{bmatrix} X_2 - X_1 \\ Y_2 - Y_1 \\ Z_2 - Z_1 \end{bmatrix} - \boldsymbol{T}_2(\psi_{v1})\boldsymbol{T}_1(\theta_1)\begin{bmatrix} x^* \\ y^* \\ z^* \end{bmatrix} \tag{6}$$

and making derivatives to last equation yields:

$$\dot{\boldsymbol{e}} = \begin{bmatrix} \dot{X}_2 - \dot{X}_1 \\ \dot{Y}_2 - \dot{Y}_1 \\ \dot{Z}_2 - \dot{Z}_1 \end{bmatrix} - \frac{d\boldsymbol{T}_2(\psi_{v1})}{d\psi_{v1}}\dot{\psi}_{v1}\boldsymbol{T}_1(\theta_1)\begin{bmatrix} x^* \\ y^* \\ z^* \end{bmatrix} - \boldsymbol{T}_2(\psi_{v1})\frac{d\boldsymbol{T}_1(\theta_1)}{d\theta_1}\dot{\theta}_1\begin{bmatrix} x^* \\ y^* \\ z^* \end{bmatrix} \tag{7}$$

making further derivatives gets:

$$\ddot{\boldsymbol{e}}=\begin{bmatrix}\ddot{X}_2-\ddot{X}_1\\ \ddot{Y}_2-\ddot{Y}_1\\ \ddot{Z}_2-\ddot{Z}_1\end{bmatrix}-\frac{d\boldsymbol{T}_2^2(\psi_{v1})}{d\psi_{v1}^2}\dot{\psi}_{v1}^2\boldsymbol{T}_1(\theta_1)\begin{bmatrix}x^*\\ y^*\\ z^*\end{bmatrix}-\frac{d\boldsymbol{T}_2(\psi_{v1})}{d\psi_{v1}}\ddot{\psi}_{v1}\boldsymbol{T}_1(\theta_1)\begin{bmatrix}x^*\\ y^*\\ z^*\end{bmatrix}$$

$$-2\frac{d\boldsymbol{T}_2(\psi_{v1})}{d\psi_{v1}}\dot{\psi}_{v1}\frac{d\boldsymbol{T}_1(\theta_1)}{d\theta_1}\dot{\theta}_1\begin{bmatrix}x^*\\ y^*\\ z^*\end{bmatrix}-\boldsymbol{T}_2(\psi_{v1})\frac{d\boldsymbol{T}_1^{\,2}(\theta_1)}{d\theta_1^2}\dot{\theta}_1^2\begin{bmatrix}x^*\\ y^*\\ z^*\end{bmatrix}-\boldsymbol{T}_2(\psi_{v1})\frac{d\boldsymbol{T}_1(\theta_1)}{d\theta_1}\ddot{\theta}_1\begin{bmatrix}x^*\\ y^*\\ z^*\end{bmatrix} \quad (8)$$

where

$$\ddot{\theta}_1=-\lambda_\theta(\dot{\theta}_1-\dot{\theta}_{1c}),\quad \ddot{\psi}_{v1}=-\lambda_{\psi_v}(\dot{\psi}_{v1}-\dot{\psi}_{v1c})$$

$$\frac{d\boldsymbol{T}_1(.)}{d(.)}=\begin{bmatrix}-\sin(.) & -\cos(.) & 0\\ \cos(.) & -\sin(.) & 0\\ 0 & 0 & 0\end{bmatrix},\quad \frac{d\boldsymbol{T}_2(.)}{d(.)}=\begin{bmatrix}-\sin(.) & 0 & \cos(.)\\ 0 & 0 & 0\\ -\cos(.) & 0 & -\sin(.)\end{bmatrix}$$

$$\frac{d^2\boldsymbol{T}_1(.)}{d^2(.)}=\begin{bmatrix}-\cos(.) & \sin(.) & 0\\ -\sin(.) & -\cos(.) & 0\\ 0 & 0 & 0\end{bmatrix},\quad \frac{d^2\boldsymbol{T}_2(.)}{d^2(.)}=\begin{bmatrix}-\cos(.) & 0 & -\sin(.)\\ 0 & 0 & 0\\ \sin(.) & 0 & -\cos(.)\end{bmatrix}$$

besides, there is:

$$\begin{aligned}\ddot{X}_i&=\dot{V}_i\cos\theta_i\cos\psi_{vi}-V_i\sin\theta_i\dot{\theta}_i\cos\psi_{vi}-V_i\cos\theta_i\sin\psi_{vi}\dot{\psi}_{vi}\\ \ddot{Y}_i&=\dot{V}_i\sin\theta_i+V_i\cos\theta_i\dot{\theta}_i\\ \ddot{Z}_i&=-\dot{V}_i\cos\theta_i\sin\psi_{vi}+V_i\sin\theta_i\dot{\theta}_i\sin\psi_{vi}-V_i\cos\theta_i\cos\psi_{vi}\dot{\psi}_{vi}\end{aligned} \quad (9)$$

so we can get the following vector equation:

$$\ddot{\boldsymbol{e}}=\boldsymbol{f}_1+\boldsymbol{G}_r\boldsymbol{u} \quad (10)$$

where

$$\boldsymbol{f}_1=-\begin{bmatrix}\ddot{X}_1\\ \ddot{Y}_1\\ \ddot{Z}_1\end{bmatrix}-\boldsymbol{G}_r\begin{bmatrix}V_2\\ \theta_2\\ \psi_{v2}\end{bmatrix}-\frac{d\boldsymbol{T}_2^2(\psi_{v1})}{d\psi_{v1}^2}\dot{\psi}_{v1}^2\boldsymbol{T}_1(\theta_1)\begin{bmatrix}x^*\\ y^*\\ z^*\end{bmatrix}-\frac{d\boldsymbol{T}_2(\psi_{v1})}{d\psi_{v1}}\ddot{\psi}_{v1}\boldsymbol{T}_1(\theta_1)\begin{bmatrix}x^*\\ y^*\\ z^*\end{bmatrix}$$

$$-2\frac{d\boldsymbol{T}_2(\psi_{v1})}{d\psi_{v1}}\dot{\psi}_{v1}\frac{d\boldsymbol{T}_1(\theta_1)}{d\theta_1}\dot{\theta}_1\begin{bmatrix}x^*\\ y^*\\ z^*\end{bmatrix}-\boldsymbol{T}_2(\psi_{v1})\frac{d\boldsymbol{T}_1^{\,2}(\theta_1)}{d\theta_1^2}\dot{\theta}_1^2\begin{bmatrix}x^*\\ y^*\\ z^*\end{bmatrix}-\boldsymbol{T}_2(\psi_{v1})\frac{d\boldsymbol{T}_1(\theta_1)}{d\theta_1}\ddot{\theta}_1\begin{bmatrix}x^*\\ y^*\\ z^*\end{bmatrix}$$

$$G_r = \begin{bmatrix} \lambda_v \cos\theta_2 \cos\psi_{v2} & -\lambda_\theta V_2 \sin\theta_2 \cos\psi_{v2} & -\lambda_{\psi_v} V_2 \cos\theta_2 \sin\psi_{v2} \\ \lambda_v \sin\theta_2 & \lambda_\theta V_2 \cos\theta_2 & 0 \\ -\lambda_v \cos\theta_2 \sin\psi_{v2} & \lambda_\theta V_2 \sin\theta_2 \sin\psi_{v2} & -\lambda_{\psi_v} V_2 \cos\theta_2 \cos\psi_{v2} \end{bmatrix} \tag{11}$$

The control variables of follower are:

$$\boldsymbol{u} = \begin{bmatrix} V_{2c} \\ \theta_{2c} \\ \psi_{v2c} \end{bmatrix} \tag{12}$$

As for the expression of $\boldsymbol{f}_1$, we also need to know:

$$\begin{bmatrix} \ddot{X}_1 \\ \ddot{Y}_1 \\ \ddot{Z}_1 \end{bmatrix} = \begin{bmatrix} \dot{V}_1 \cos\theta_1 \cos\psi_{v1} - V_1 \sin\theta_1 \dot{\theta}_1 \cos\psi_{v1} - V_1 \cos\theta_1 \sin\psi_{v1} \dot{\psi}_{v1} \\ \dot{V}_1 \sin\theta_1 + V_1 \cos\theta_1 \dot{\theta}_1 \\ -\dot{V}_1 \cos\theta_1 \sin\psi_{v1} + V_1 \sin\theta_1 \dot{\theta}_1 \sin\psi_{v1} - V_1 \cos\theta_1 \cos\psi_{v1} \dot{\psi}_{v1} \end{bmatrix}$$

In order to eliminate the deviations of relative positions, that is, make the deviation $\boldsymbol{e}$ be asymptotically equivalent to zero, we will choose the following PD control laws:

$$\ddot{\boldsymbol{e}} + k_1 \dot{\boldsymbol{e}} + k_2 \boldsymbol{e} = \boldsymbol{0} \tag{13}$$

so there will be:

$$-k_1 \dot{\boldsymbol{e}} - k_2 \boldsymbol{e} = \boldsymbol{f}_1 + \boldsymbol{G}_r \boldsymbol{u}$$

further, the required control quantity can be expressed as below:

$$\boldsymbol{u} = \boldsymbol{G}_r^{-1}(-\boldsymbol{f}_1 - k_1 \dot{\boldsymbol{e}} - k_2 \boldsymbol{e}) \tag{14}$$

What should be done next is to analyze the existence conditions of expression (14). The condition is: iff matrix $\boldsymbol{G}_r$ is non-singular, the control quantity exists. The determinant of $\boldsymbol{G}_r$ can be calculated by Equ.(11), it is:

$$\det \boldsymbol{G}_r = -\lambda_\theta \lambda_{\psi_v} \lambda_v V_2^2 \cos\theta \tag{15}$$

Through checking this expression, it is obvious that $\boldsymbol{G}_r$ is non-singular when the missile formation is flying, that is, $V_2 \neq 0$, so we can choose proper coefficients k_1, k_2 to guarantee expression (13) to be converged, which is $\lim_{t\to\infty} \boldsymbol{e} = \boldsymbol{0}$.

4. Optimal controller of missile formation keeping

4.1 Establishing model of relative motion

Because relative coordinate frame is rotating, the relationship between relative derivative and absolute derivative should be considered during the process of establishing relative motion equations in relative coordinate frame. The relationship between these two derivatives is:

$$\boldsymbol{V}_{fr} - \boldsymbol{V}_{lr} = \boldsymbol{V}_r + \boldsymbol{\omega} \times \boldsymbol{r} \tag{16}$$

where $\boldsymbol{V}_{fr}$ and $\boldsymbol{V}_{lr}$ are the absolute velocities of follower and leader in relative coordinate frame respectively; $\boldsymbol{V}_r$ is the relative velocity from follower to leader in relative coordinate frame; $\boldsymbol{\omega}$ represents the rotating angular velocity of relative coordinate frame relative with respect to inertial space, and it is described in relative coordinate frame; $\boldsymbol{r}$ is the position vector of follower relative to leader in relative coordinate frame.
We can get the absolute velocities of follower and leader in relative coordinate frame by the transformations as below:

$$\boldsymbol{V}_{fr} = \boldsymbol{\Phi}_I^r \boldsymbol{\Phi}_2^I \boldsymbol{V}_{f2}$$
$$\boldsymbol{V}_{lr} = \boldsymbol{V}_{l2}$$

where $\boldsymbol{\Phi}_I^r$ is the transformation matrix from inertial coordinate frame to relative coordinate frame:

$$\boldsymbol{\Phi}_I^r = \begin{bmatrix} \cos\theta_l \cos\psi_{vl} & \sin\theta_l & -\cos\theta_l \sin\psi_{vl} \\ -\sin\theta_l \cos\psi_{vl} & \cos\theta_l & \sin\theta_l \sin\psi_{vl} \\ \sin\psi_{vl} & 0 & \cos\psi_{vl} \end{bmatrix}$$

$\boldsymbol{\Phi}_2^I$ is the transformation matrix from trajectory coordinate frame of follower $O_{1f} - x_2 y_2 z_2$ to inertial coordinate frame:

$$\boldsymbol{\Phi}_2^I = \begin{bmatrix} \cos\theta_f \cos\psi_{vf} & -\sin\theta_f \cos\psi_{vf} & \sin\psi_{vf} \\ \sin\theta_f & \cos\theta_f & 0 \\ -\cos\theta_f \sin\psi_{vf} & \sin\theta_f \sin\psi_{vf} & \cos\psi_{vf} \end{bmatrix}$$

$\boldsymbol{V}_{f2}$ and $\boldsymbol{V}_{l2}$ represent the velocity vectors of follower and leader in themselves trajectory coordinate frames respectively, and the components of them are:

$$\boldsymbol{V}_{f2} = \begin{bmatrix} V_f \\ 0 \\ 0 \end{bmatrix}, \boldsymbol{V}_{l2} = \begin{bmatrix} V_l \\ 0 \\ 0 \end{bmatrix}$$

Besides, V_l is the velocity of leader in inertial coordinate frame; θ_l is the flight path angle of leader; ψ_{vl} is flight deflection angle of leader.
Further, the difference of absolute velocities between two missiles in the relative coordinate frame is:

$$\boldsymbol{V}_{fr} - \boldsymbol{V}_{lr} = \begin{bmatrix} V_f \cos\theta_f \cos\theta_l \cos(\psi_{vl} - \psi_{vf}) + V_f \sin\theta_f \sin\theta_l - V_l \\ -V_f \cos\theta_f \sin\theta_l \cos(\psi_{vl} - \psi_{vf}) + V_f \sin\theta_f \cos\theta_l \\ V_f \cos\theta_f \sin(\psi_{vl} - \psi_{vf}) \end{bmatrix} \tag{17}$$

at the same time, the relative velocity between two missiles in relative coordinate frame:

$$V_r = [\dot{x}, \dot{y}, \dot{z}]^T \quad (18)$$

where x, y and z are components of relative position vector $\boldsymbol{r}$ in relative coordinate frame, and the rotating angular velocity of relative coordinate frame with respect to inertial space can be expressed as:

$$\boldsymbol{\omega} = \begin{bmatrix} \dot{\psi}_{vl} \sin\theta_l \\ \dot{\psi}_{vl} \cos\theta_l \\ \dot{\theta}_l \end{bmatrix} \quad (19)$$

so, as for the expression $\boldsymbol{\omega} \times \boldsymbol{r}$, there will be:

$$\boldsymbol{\omega} \times \boldsymbol{r} = \begin{bmatrix} z\dot{\psi}_{vl} \cos\theta_l - y\dot{\theta}_l \\ x\dot{\theta}_l - z\dot{\psi}_{vl} \sin\theta_l \\ y\dot{\psi}_{vl} \sin\theta_l - x\dot{\psi}_{vl} \cos\theta_l \end{bmatrix} \quad (20)$$

further, we can get the following expression directly from equation (16):

$$\boldsymbol{V}_r = (\boldsymbol{V}_{fr} - \boldsymbol{V}_{lr}) - \boldsymbol{\omega} \times \boldsymbol{r} \quad (21)$$

After expanding all the terms from Equ.(17) to Equ.(20) finally, we can obtain the missile relative kinematics model in 3-dimension space:

$$\begin{cases} \dot{x} = V_f \cos\theta_f \cos\theta_l \cos\psi_e + V_f \sin\theta_f \sin\theta_l - V_l - z\dot{\psi}_{vl} \cos\theta_l + y\dot{\theta}_l \\ \dot{y} = -V_f \cos\theta_f \sin\theta_l \cos\psi_e + V_f \sin\theta_f \cos\theta_l - x\dot{\theta}_l + z\dot{\psi}_{vl} \sin\theta_l \\ \dot{z} = V_f \cos\theta_f \sin\psi_e - y\dot{\psi}_{vl} \sin\theta_l + x\dot{\psi}_{vl} \cos\theta_l \\ \psi_e = \psi_{vl} - \psi_{vf} \end{cases} \quad (22)$$

4.2 Establishing the optimal control model of missile formation keeping

4.2.1 Linearized method

The formation motion equations (22) are nonlinear, we can treat them by linearized method to get linear forms that can be utilized and analyzed more conveniently. During the process of missile formation flight, some variables can be considered as small quantities, such as θ_f, θ_l and $\psi_e = \psi_l - \psi_f$, and the states of leader can be considered as inputs, then Equ.(22) can be transformed to:

$$\begin{cases} \dot{x} = V_f + V_f\theta_f\theta_l - V_l - z\dot{\psi}_{vl} + y\dot{\theta}_l \\ \dot{y} = -V_f\theta_l + V_f\theta_f - x\dot{\theta}_l + z\dot{\psi}_{vl}\theta_l \\ \dot{z} = V_f(\psi_{vl} - \psi_{vf}) - y\dot{\psi}_{vl}\theta_l + x\dot{\psi}_{vl} \end{cases}$$

Dealing with this expression by small perturbation linearized method yields:

$$\begin{cases} \dot{x} = \dot{\theta}_l y - \dot{\psi}_{vl} z + (1 + \theta_{fb}\theta_l)V_f + V_{fb}\theta_l\theta_f - V_l \\ \dot{y} = -\dot{\theta}_l x + \theta_l\dot{\psi}_{vl} z + (\theta_{fb} - \theta_l)V_f + V_{fb}\theta_f \\ \dot{z} = \dot{\psi}_{vl} x - \dot{\psi}_{vl}\theta_l y + (\psi_{vl} - \psi_{vfb})V_f - V_{fb}\psi_{vf} \end{cases} \quad (23)$$

where V_{fb}, θ_{fb} and ψ_{vfb} are feature points of linearized equations. We can describe this model by the following states space form:

$$\begin{aligned} \dot{\boldsymbol{X}} &= \boldsymbol{AX} + \boldsymbol{BU} + \tilde{\boldsymbol{B}}\boldsymbol{W} \\ \boldsymbol{Y} &= \boldsymbol{CX} \end{aligned} \tag{24}$$

where $\boldsymbol{X} = [x, y, z]^T$ are the state variables; the control variables of formation controller are motion states of follower, that is, $\boldsymbol{U} = [V_f, \theta_f, \psi_{vf}]^T$; outputs are $\boldsymbol{Y} = [x, y, z]^T$; perturbation variables are the velocities of leader $\boldsymbol{W} = [V_l, 0, 0]^T$, which can be considered as slowly variant variables; the system matrix $\boldsymbol{A}$ is described as:

$$\boldsymbol{A} = \begin{bmatrix} 0 & \dot{\theta}_l & -\dot{\psi}_{vl} \\ -\dot{\theta}_l & 0 & \theta_l \dot{\psi}_{vl} \\ \dot{\psi}_{vl} & -\dot{\psi}_{vl}\theta_l & 0 \end{bmatrix}$$

control matrix $\boldsymbol{B}$ is:

$$\boldsymbol{B} = \begin{bmatrix} 1 + \theta_{f0}\theta_l & V_{f0}\theta_l & 0 \\ \theta_{f0} - \theta_l & V_{f0} & 0 \\ \psi_{vl} - \psi_{vf0} & 0 & -V_{f0} \end{bmatrix}$$

and output matrix $\boldsymbol{C}$ is:

$$\boldsymbol{C} = \begin{bmatrix} 1 & 0 & 0 \\ 0 & 1 & 0 \\ 0 & 0 & 1 \end{bmatrix}$$

effect matrix of perturbations $\tilde{\boldsymbol{B}}$ is:

$$\tilde{\boldsymbol{B}} = \begin{bmatrix} -1 \\ 0 \\ 0 \end{bmatrix}$$

4.2.2 Method of substituting variables

As analyzed in last section, we can get linear control model showed as Equ.(24) via small perturbation linearized method, however, this linear model requires the actual flight path is closely around feature points. Although we can design the missile formation keeping controller at those points within the whole flight scope by gain-scheduled method, it will increase amount of work greatly. Next we will re-deal with the nonlinear equations of relative kinematics showed in Equ.(22). If we transform the control variables from $\boldsymbol{U} = [V_f, \theta_f, \psi_{vf}]^T$ to $\bar{\boldsymbol{U}}$ with the following form:

$$\bar{\boldsymbol{U}} = \begin{bmatrix} u_1 \\ u_2 \\ u_3 \end{bmatrix} = \begin{bmatrix} V_f \cos\theta_f \cos\psi_{vf} \\ V_f \sin\theta_f \\ V_f \cos\theta_f \sin\psi_{vf} \end{bmatrix} \tag{25}$$

then an indirectly linear control model of relation motion can be obtained:

$$\begin{cases} \dot{x} = \dot{\theta}_l y - \dot{\psi}_{vl} \cos\theta_l z + \cos\theta_l \cos\psi_{vl} u_1 + \sin\theta_l u_2 + \cos\theta_l \sin\psi_{vl} u_3 - V_l \\ \dot{y} = -\dot{\theta}_l x + \dot{\psi}_{vl} \sin\theta_l z - \sin\theta_l \cos\psi_{vl} u_1 + \cos\theta_l u_2 - \sin\theta_l \sin\psi_{vl} u_3 \\ \dot{z} = \dot{\psi}_{vl} \cos\theta_l x - \dot{\psi}_{vl} \sin\theta_l y + \sin\psi_{vl} u_1 - \cos\psi_{vl} u_3 \end{cases} \tag{26}$$

further, the direct control variables $\boldsymbol{U}$ which act on followers can be calculated by the following expressions:

$$\psi_{vf} = \arctan\left(\frac{u_3}{u_1}\right), \theta_f = \arctan\left[\frac{u_2 \cos(\psi_{vf})}{u_1}\right], V_f = \frac{u_2}{\sin\theta_f}$$

at last, we can tranform equation (26) to the states space form showed as below:

$$\begin{aligned} \dot{\boldsymbol{X}} &= \boldsymbol{A}\boldsymbol{X} + \boldsymbol{B}\bar{\boldsymbol{U}} + \tilde{\boldsymbol{B}}\boldsymbol{W} \\ \boldsymbol{Y} &= \boldsymbol{C}\boldsymbol{X} \end{aligned} \tag{27}$$

where system matrix $\boldsymbol{A}$ is:

$$\boldsymbol{A} = \begin{bmatrix} 0 & \dot{\theta}_l & -\dot{\psi}_{vl} \cos\theta_l \\ -\dot{\theta}_l & 0 & \dot{\psi}_{vl} \sin\theta_l \\ \dot{\psi}_{vl} \cos\theta_l & -\dot{\psi}_{vl} \sin\theta_l & 0 \end{bmatrix}$$

control matrix $\boldsymbol{B}$ is:

$$\boldsymbol{B} = \begin{bmatrix} \cos\theta_l \cos\psi_{vl} & \sin\theta_l & \cos\theta_l \sin\psi_{vl} \\ -\sin\theta_l \cos\psi_{vl} & \cos\theta_l & -\sin\theta_l \sin\psi_{vl} \\ \sin\psi_{vl} & 0 & -\cos\psi_{vl} \end{bmatrix}$$

the meanings of other variables are same as those in Equ.(24).

It can be stated through analyzing this section that the indirect control model of relative motion based on the relationships of relative motion between missiles has a direct mapping relationship between inputs and outputs. However, this mapping just can be indicated by a mathematical form rather than some intuitive physical meanings, so we can't give the linear expressions just through modelling directly. As mentioned above, we should transform the coordinate space of input variables and then establish the indirect linear model (27).

After the missile formation controller system is described by the Equ.(27), we also need to consider the completely controllable ability of those indirect variables $\bar{\boldsymbol{U}}$, that is, we should analyze the relationships between rank of $[\boldsymbol{B} \vdots \boldsymbol{AB} \vdots \boldsymbol{A}^2\boldsymbol{B}]$ and the dimensions of this system. Because matrix $\boldsymbol{B}$ is full rank in the feasible flight scope, that is, $\text{rank}[\boldsymbol{B} \vdots \boldsymbol{AB} \vdots \boldsymbol{A}^2\boldsymbol{B}]=3$, system(27) should be completely controllable.

4.3 Establishing the optimal control model of missile formation keeping

As for the missile formation keeping control problem, the aim is to keep the distances between members within one formation on a non-zero states. After considering equation (27), we can further describe this formation keeping problem to another problem that how to regulate non-zero given value of output affected by slowly variant perturbations. So we can design this optimal controller by two steps: first, we need to design an optimal output regulator that can overcome slowly variant perturbations; second, we should further design optimal controller based on the first step which can maintain the missile formation on a non-zero desired relative states.

4.3.1 Optimal proportional-integral (PI) controller of missile formation

As for the system with invariant or slowly variant perturbations showed in expression (27), we can choose PI control law to overcome these perturbations, which is similar to classical control method.

In order to clearly explain the principle of how this integral feed-back controller eliminates stable errors, we will make a hypothesis that the stable outputs of system are zeros. Because there has an integrator in the controller, outputs can be constants although inputs are zeros, if these values are just rightly equivalent to the perturbations that are effecting on the input points but the signs are inverse, then the inputs of this control system will be eliminated to zeros, so the final outputs of system can be kept to zeros (Xie, 1986).

First, we transform the perturbations of system to control inputting ports, and then system (27) can be changed to:

$$\dot{\boldsymbol{X}} = \boldsymbol{A}\boldsymbol{X} + \boldsymbol{B}(\boldsymbol{U} + \tilde{\boldsymbol{W}}) \tag{28}$$

where $\tilde{\boldsymbol{W}}$ is transformation of initial perturbations, it has following form after comparing to the Equ.(27):

$$\tilde{\boldsymbol{W}} = \boldsymbol{B}^{-1}\tilde{\boldsymbol{B}}\boldsymbol{W}$$

Until now, the problem has been transformed to how to design PI optimal controller for system(28). This new system is augmented to:

$$\begin{aligned} &\dot{\boldsymbol{X}} = \boldsymbol{A}\boldsymbol{X} + \boldsymbol{B}(\boldsymbol{U} + \tilde{\boldsymbol{W}}) \\ &\dot{\boldsymbol{U}} + \dot{\tilde{\boldsymbol{W}}} = \boldsymbol{U}_1 \qquad \boldsymbol{U}(\mathrm{t}_0) + \tilde{\boldsymbol{W}}(\mathrm{t}_0) \text{is given} \end{aligned} \tag{29}$$

This augmented system can be further marked as:

$$\begin{aligned} &\dot{\boldsymbol{X}}_1 = \boldsymbol{A}_1\boldsymbol{X}_1 + \boldsymbol{B}_1\boldsymbol{U}_1 \\ &\boldsymbol{Y} = \boldsymbol{C}_1\boldsymbol{X}_1 \end{aligned} \tag{30}$$

where states variables of augmented system are $\boldsymbol{X}_1 = [\boldsymbol{X}, \boldsymbol{U} + \tilde{\boldsymbol{W}}]^{\mathrm{T}}$; system matrix $\boldsymbol{A}_1$ of this augmented system is:

$$\boldsymbol{A}_1 = \begin{bmatrix} \boldsymbol{A} & \boldsymbol{B} \\ \boldsymbol{0}_{3\times 3} & \boldsymbol{0}_{3\times 3} \end{bmatrix}$$

control matrix of this augmented system is $\boldsymbol{B}_1 = [\boldsymbol{0}_{3\times3}, \boldsymbol{I}_{3\times3}]^T$, and output matrix is $\boldsymbol{C}_1 = [\boldsymbol{I}_{3\times3}, \boldsymbol{0}_{3\times3}]$.
The quadratic optimal performance index for system (30) is appointed to:

$$J = \int_{t_0}^{t_f} [\boldsymbol{X}_1^T \boldsymbol{Q}_1 \boldsymbol{X}_1 + \boldsymbol{U}_1^T \boldsymbol{R}_1 \boldsymbol{U}_1] dt \tag{31}$$

where $\boldsymbol{Q}_1$ is state regulating weight matrix of augmented system; $\boldsymbol{R}_1$ is control energy weight matrix of augmented system. When augmented system (30) is controllable, the optimal control quantities for minimizing the performance index (31) should be:

$$\boldsymbol{U}_1^* = -\boldsymbol{R}_1^{-1} \boldsymbol{B}_1^T \bar{\boldsymbol{P}} \boldsymbol{X}_1 \tag{32}$$

where $\bar{\boldsymbol{P}}$ is the solution of Riccati Equation:

$$\dot{\bar{\boldsymbol{P}}} = -\bar{\boldsymbol{P}} A_1 - A_1^T \bar{\boldsymbol{P}} + \bar{\boldsymbol{P}} \boldsymbol{B}_1 \boldsymbol{R}_1^{-1} \boldsymbol{B}_1^T \bar{\boldsymbol{P}} - \boldsymbol{Q}_1$$

Here we have to make further analysis on performance index expression(31). $\boldsymbol{Q}_1$ can be decomposed to the following form based on the expansions of state variables $\boldsymbol{X}_1$:

$$\boldsymbol{Q}_1 = \begin{bmatrix} \boldsymbol{Q} & 0 \\ 0 & \boldsymbol{R} \end{bmatrix}$$

and then, there will be:

$$\boldsymbol{X}_1^T \boldsymbol{Q}_1 \boldsymbol{X}_1 = \boldsymbol{X}^T \boldsymbol{Q} \boldsymbol{X} + (\boldsymbol{U} + \tilde{\boldsymbol{W}})^T \boldsymbol{R} (\boldsymbol{U} + \tilde{\boldsymbol{W}}) \tag{33}$$

where $\boldsymbol{Q}$ is the states regulating weight matrix of original system(27), $\boldsymbol{R}$ is the control energy weight matrix of original system. From original system(27), there will be expression showed as below:

$$\boldsymbol{X}^T \boldsymbol{Q} \boldsymbol{X} = \boldsymbol{X}^T \boldsymbol{C}^T \boldsymbol{Q}_Y \boldsymbol{C} \boldsymbol{X} = \boldsymbol{Y}^T \boldsymbol{Q}_Y \boldsymbol{Y}$$

where $\boldsymbol{Q}_Y$ is the outputs regulating weight matrix, then expression(31) that describes the problem of quadratic optimal states regulating can be transformed to the problem of quadratic optimal output regulating, which is:

$$J = \int_{t_0}^{t_f} [\boldsymbol{Y}^T \boldsymbol{Q}_Y \boldsymbol{Y} + (\boldsymbol{U} + \tilde{\boldsymbol{W}})^T \boldsymbol{R} (\boldsymbol{U} + \tilde{\boldsymbol{W}}) + \boldsymbol{U}_1^T \boldsymbol{R}_1 \boldsymbol{U}_1] dt \tag{34}$$

besides, because perturbations $\tilde{\boldsymbol{W}}$ is slowly variant variables, following expression can be noted:

$$\dot{\tilde{\boldsymbol{W}}} = 0$$

and then

$$\boldsymbol{U}_1 = \dot{\tilde{\boldsymbol{U}}} \tag{35}$$

At last the quadratic optimal performance index of outputs regulating can be expressed as:

$$\mathrm{J} = \int_{t_0}^{t_f} [\boldsymbol{Y}^{\mathrm{T}} \boldsymbol{Q}_{\mathrm{Y}} \boldsymbol{Y} + (\tilde{\boldsymbol{U}} + \tilde{\boldsymbol{W}})^{\mathrm{T}} \boldsymbol{R} (\tilde{\boldsymbol{U}} + \tilde{\boldsymbol{W}}) + \dot{\tilde{\boldsymbol{U}}}^{\mathrm{T}} \boldsymbol{R}_1 \dot{\tilde{\boldsymbol{U}}}] \mathrm{d}t \tag{36}$$

As for the optimal control variables(32), it can be transformed from Equ.(35) to:

$$\boldsymbol{U}_1^* = \dot{\tilde{\boldsymbol{U}}}^* = -\boldsymbol{R}_1^{-1} \boldsymbol{B}_1^{\mathrm{T}} \overline{\boldsymbol{P}} \boldsymbol{X}_1 \tag{37}$$

Expanding equation(37) yields:

$$\begin{aligned} \dot{\tilde{\boldsymbol{U}}}^* &= -\boldsymbol{R}_1^{-1} \begin{bmatrix} \boldsymbol{0} \\ \boldsymbol{I} \end{bmatrix} \begin{bmatrix} \overline{\boldsymbol{P}}_{11} & \overline{\boldsymbol{P}}_{12} \\ \overline{\boldsymbol{P}}_{21} & \overline{\boldsymbol{P}}_{22} \end{bmatrix} \begin{bmatrix} \boldsymbol{X} \\ \dot{\tilde{\boldsymbol{U}}}^* + \tilde{\boldsymbol{W}} \end{bmatrix} \\ &= -\boldsymbol{R}_1^{-1} \overline{\boldsymbol{P}}_{21} \boldsymbol{X} - \boldsymbol{R}_1^{-1} \overline{\boldsymbol{P}}_{22} (\tilde{\boldsymbol{U}}^* + \tilde{\boldsymbol{W}}) \end{aligned} \tag{38}$$

which is the expression of optimal control quantities that can minimize the performance index (34) for zero-given points.

4.3.2 Optimal controller for non-zero given points

In order to keep the output variables $\boldsymbol{Y} = [x, y, z]^T$ on non-zero points, the final system states and control inputs should also be non-zero, and then the optimal control quantities will be transformed from Equ.(37) to the following form:

$$\dot{\tilde{\boldsymbol{U}}}^* = -\boldsymbol{R}_1^{-1} \boldsymbol{B}_1^T \overline{\boldsymbol{P}} \boldsymbol{X}_1 + \boldsymbol{U}_0' = -\boldsymbol{K} \boldsymbol{X}_1 + \boldsymbol{U}_0' \tag{39}$$

where $\boldsymbol{U}_0'$ is additional control quantities for non-zero states.
Considering the output equations of augmented system:

$$\boldsymbol{Y} = \boldsymbol{C}_1 \boldsymbol{X}_1 \tag{40}$$

and the expansions of augmented states $\boldsymbol{X}_1$:

$$\boldsymbol{X}_1 = [x, y, z, V_f + \tilde{\boldsymbol{W}}(1), \theta_f + \tilde{\boldsymbol{W}}(2), \psi_{vf} + \tilde{\boldsymbol{W}}(3)]^T$$

we should choose the following output matrix of augmented system to make sure the outputs of augmented system accord with those of original system:

$$\boldsymbol{C}_1 = \begin{bmatrix} 1 & 0 & 0 & 0 & 0 & 0 \\ 0 & 1 & 0 & 0 & 0 & 0 \\ 0 & 0 & 1 & 0 & 0 & 0 \end{bmatrix}$$

Substituting the control values(39) into the state equation(30) of augmented system yields:

$$\dot{\boldsymbol{X}}_1 = (\boldsymbol{A}_1 - \boldsymbol{B}_1 \boldsymbol{K}) \boldsymbol{X}_1 + \boldsymbol{B}_1 \boldsymbol{U}_0' \tag{41}$$

Because the closed-loop system(41) is asymptotically stable, there will be:

$$\lim_{t\to\infty} \dot{X}_1(t) = 0$$

and then the asymptotically stable system can be expressed as:

$$\mathbf{0} = (A_1 - B_1K)X_{10} + B_1U_0' \tag{42}$$

where X_{10} is the stable value of state X_1. If all the eigenvalues of matrix $A_1 - B_1K$ lie in the left complex plane, then matrix is $A_1 - B_1K$ non-singular, and further we can get the expression showed as below from Equ.(42):

$$X_{10} = -(A_1 - B_1K)^{-1}B_1U_0' \tag{43}$$

and the relationship between non-zero points and stable value of states will meet:

$$Y_{10}^* = C_1X_{10}$$

further the relationship required between non-zero states Y_{10}^* and the stable value X_{10} of state X_1 should be expressed as:

$$U_0' = [C_1(B_1K - A_1)^{-1}B_1]^{-1}Y_{10}^* \tag{44}$$

At last we can implement optimal control to system(27) that describes the relative kinematics of missiles by the following optimal control quantity:

$$\dot{U}^* = -R_1^{-1}B_1^T\bar{P}X_1 + [C_1(-B_1R_1^{-1}B_1^T\bar{P} - A_1)^{-1}B_1]^{-1}Y_{10}^* \tag{45}$$

and this control quantity can keep missile formation on the desired relative dimensional states.

4.4 Stability analysis

In order to analyze the stability of optimal controller of missile formation, we need to transform the model of missile formation relative motion to tracking error model. The tracking error of state is chosen by state equation(27) as:

$$\hat{X} = X - X_d \tag{46}$$

where is X the actual flight states of missile formation; X_d is the expected states. Substituting last equation into Equ.(27) obtains the error state equation:

$$\dot{\hat{X}} = A\hat{X} + BU + \hat{W} \tag{47}$$

where $\hat{W}$ is the invariant perturbations of tracking error state equation, the value of this term is:

$$\hat{W} = W + AX_d$$

Because invariant perturbations do not affect the dynamic performance of control system no more than affect the stable tracking performance of this system, we can ignore this term when just analyzing the stability of control system, that is, we can just analyze the following control system:

$$\dot{\hat{X}} = A\hat{X} + BU \tag{48}$$

Taking Lyapunov function to this system gets:

$$\Phi = \frac{1}{2}(\hat{x}^2 + \hat{y}^2 + \hat{z}^2) \tag{49}$$

The derivative of this Lyapunov function is:

$$\dot{\Phi} = \hat{x}\dot{\hat{x}} + \hat{y}\dot{\hat{y}} + \hat{z}\dot{\hat{z}} \tag{50}$$

Substituting Equ.(26) to expression(50) yields:

$$\dot{\Phi} = (BU)^T \hat{X} \tag{51}$$

and the optimal control quantity U for this error state equation is:

$$U = -R^{-1}B^T P\hat{X}$$

substituting it into Equ.(50) gets:

$$\dot{\Phi} = (-BR^{-1}B^T P\hat{X})^T \hat{X}$$

Because the control energy weight matrix R in this chapter is unit matrix, there should have:

$$BR^{-1}B^T P\hat{X} = P\hat{X}$$

and then the derivative of Lyapunov function can be changed to:

$$\dot{\Phi} = -\hat{X}^T P^T \hat{X} \tag{52}$$

where P is the solution of Riccati Equation, which has the following characters (Xie, 1986):

1. for every $t \in [t_0, T]$, P is symmetrical matrix;
2. for every $t \in [t_0, T]$, P is non-negative matrix.

So Equ.(52) is non-negative, and it also states that we can't get the conclusion that this system is asymptotical until now, and need some more stronger conditions. Original system is time-variant system, so we can complement the stability conditions of system(48) through Barbalat Lemma.

The contents of Barbalat Lemma are: if a scalar function $\Theta(x,t)$ is satisfied with the following series of conditions:

1. $\Theta(x,t)$ has lower bounded;
2. $\dot{\Theta}(x,t)$ is semi-negative;
3. $\dot{\Theta}(x,t)$ is uniformly continuous with respect to time.

then $\dot{\Theta}(x,t) \to 0$ when $t \to \infty$ (Slotine et al, 1991).

After analyzing that Lyapunov function appointed in the previous section, we can find that this function satisfies the former two aspects of Barbalat Lemma. If we want to prove expression(52) also satisfies the third point, we just need to prove $\ddot{\Phi}$ exists and is bounded. The expression of $\ddot{\Phi}$ is:

$$\ddot{\Phi} = -\dot{\hat{\boldsymbol{X}}}^T \boldsymbol{P}^T \hat{\boldsymbol{X}} - \hat{\boldsymbol{X}}^T \boldsymbol{P}^T \dot{\hat{\boldsymbol{X}}}$$

at the same time, from Equ.(52) we can know:

$$\dot{\Phi} \le 0$$

so, according to Equ.(49), it can be concluded that system state $\hat{\boldsymbol{X}}$ is bounded, further $\ddot{\Phi}$ exists and is bounded, and then Lyapunov function meets Barbalat Lamme, that is, when $t \to \infty$,there will be $\dot{\Phi}(x,t) \to 0$,and then further $\hat{\boldsymbol{X}} \to \boldsymbol{0}$, which indicates that the system(48) is asymptotically stable.

5. Simulations

5.1 Simulations for PD controller of missile formation keeping

5.1.1 Initial conditions

We will choose the following conditions for the simulations of PD controller:

1. missile formation is consisted of three missiles;
2. flight time of missile formation is 150s ;
3. three inertial time constants of each channel of follower are $\tau_v = 3.51\text{s}$, $\tau_\theta = 2.25\text{s}$ and $\tau_{\psi_v} = 2.37\text{s}$;
4. the flight states of leader are:
   - initial positions in inertial coordinate frame are: $X_{l0} = 500\text{m}$, $Y_{l0} = 800\text{m}$ and $Z_{l0} = 0\text{m}$; intial velocitiy is $V_{l0} = 240\text{m/s}$; initial flight path angle is $\theta_0 = 10^\circ$;initial flight deflection angle is $\psi_{v0} = 20^\circ$.
   - the change rules of veloctity, fligh path angle and flight deflection angle of leader are:

$$V_l = 240 + 20\sin(0.15t)$$
$$\theta_l = 0.2\sin(0.05t + 0.4515)$$
$$\psi_{vl} = 0.4\sin(0.06t + 0.5511)$$

initial distances between leader and follower 1 and follower 2 are:

$$\begin{bmatrix} x_{f1} \\ y_{f1} \\ z_{f1} \end{bmatrix} = \begin{bmatrix} -500 \\ -550 \\ -350 \end{bmatrix}\text{m}, \begin{bmatrix} x_{f2} \\ y_{f2} \\ z_{f2} \end{bmatrix} = \begin{bmatrix} -400 \\ -450 \\ 350 \end{bmatrix}\text{m}$$

desired distances between leader and follower 1 and follower 2 are:

$$\begin{bmatrix} x_{f1}^* \\ y_{f1}^* \\ z_{f1}^* \end{bmatrix} = \begin{bmatrix} -450 \\ -500 \\ -400 \end{bmatrix} \text{m}, \begin{bmatrix} x_{f2}^* \\ y_{f2}^* \\ z_{f2}^* \end{bmatrix} = \begin{bmatrix} -450 \\ -500 \\ 400 \end{bmatrix} \text{m}$$

intial states of follower 1 and follower 2 are:

- velocity: $V_{f10} = 180\text{m/s}$, $V_{f20} = 240\text{m/s}$;
- flight path angle: $\theta_{f10} = 5^\circ$, $\theta_{f20} = -5^\circ$;
- flight deflection angle: $\psi_{vf10} = -10^\circ$, $\psi_{vf20} = 10^\circ$.

satuaration of control quantities

Considering the feasible fight scope of missile formation, we should limit the control quantities of formation controller, that is, the command states of follower should be limilted. Here we set the satuatations are:

$$150\text{m/s} \le V_{fc} \le 300\text{m/s} \text{ , -}15^\circ \le \theta_{fc} \le 35^\circ \text{ , -}40^\circ \le \psi_{vfc} \le 40^\circ$$

5.1.2 Simulation results and analysis

After simulating, we can get the result curves Fig.6-Fig.12, where Fig.6 is the 3-dimensional motions of missile formation; Fig.7 and Fig.8 are the position components of follower 1 and follower 2 in relative coordinate frame respectively; Fig.9 is the distances between members in missile formation; Fig.10-Fig.11 are the control quantities in velocity, flight path angle and flight deflection angle channels of followers respectively.

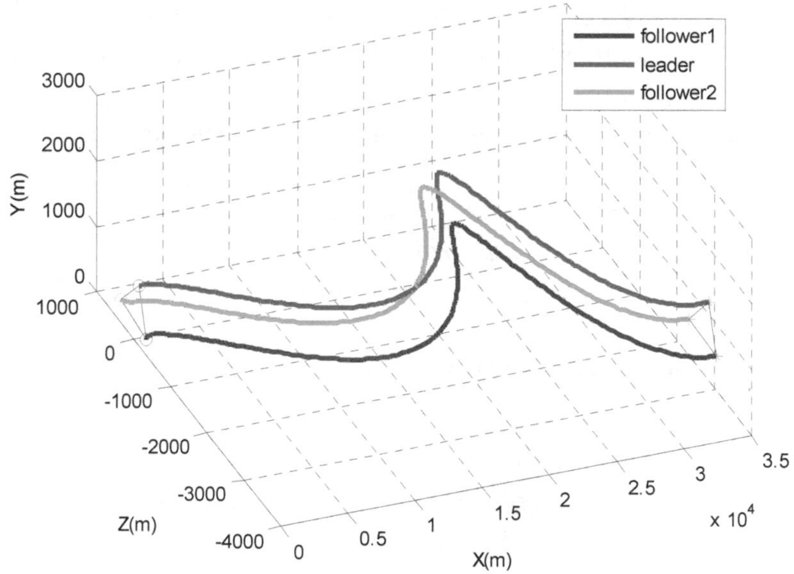

Fig. 6. Three-dimensional trajectories of missile formation under PD controlling.

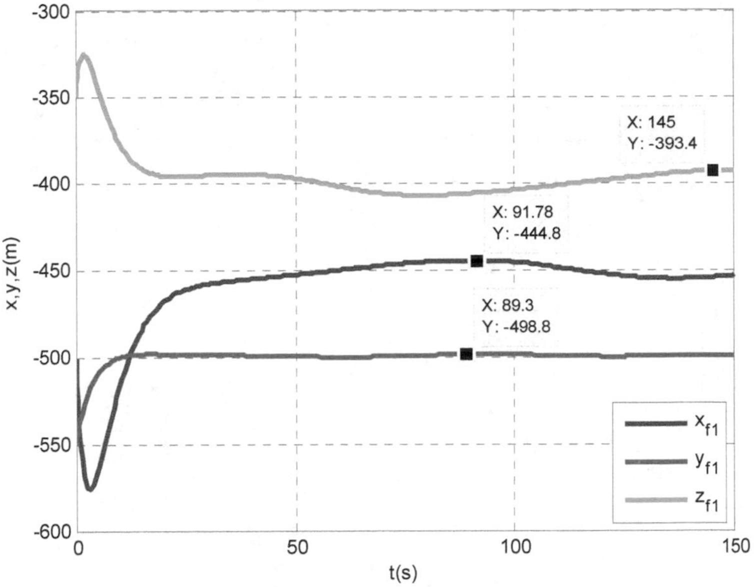

Fig. 7. Distances between follower 1 and leader in relative coordinate frame.

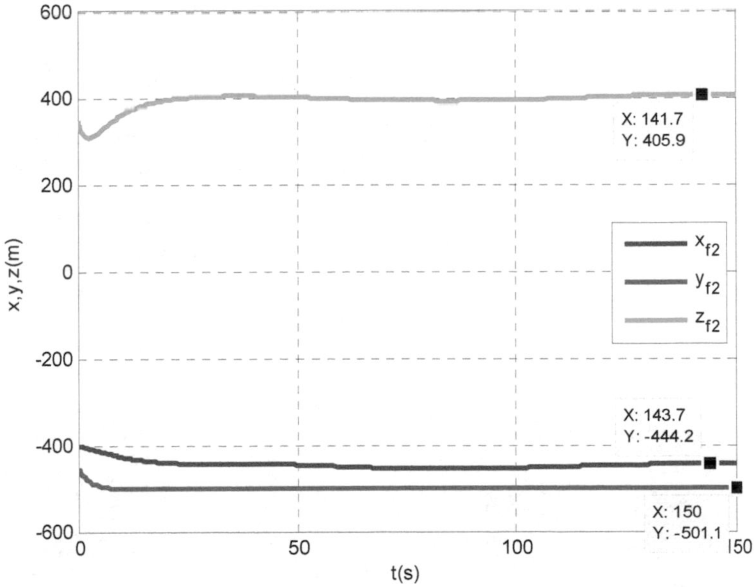

Fig. 8. Distances between follower 2 and leader in relative coordinate frame.

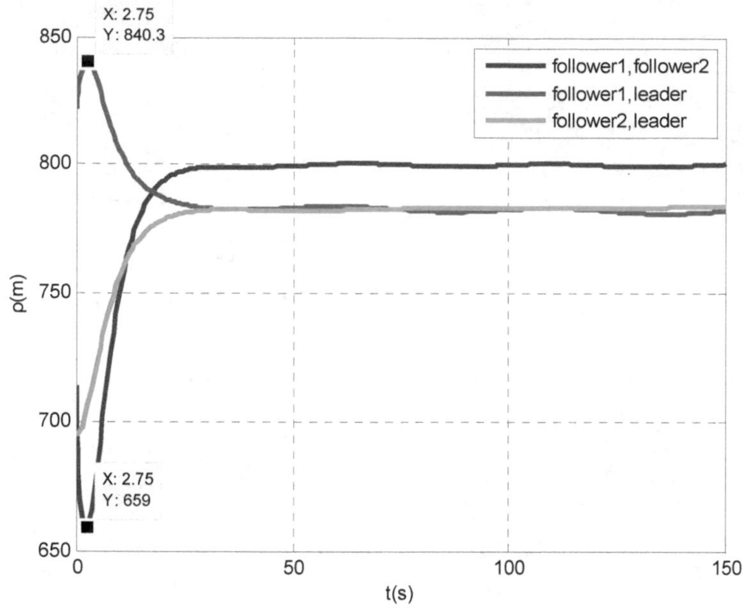

Fig. 9. Distances between members of missile formation in relative coordinate frame.

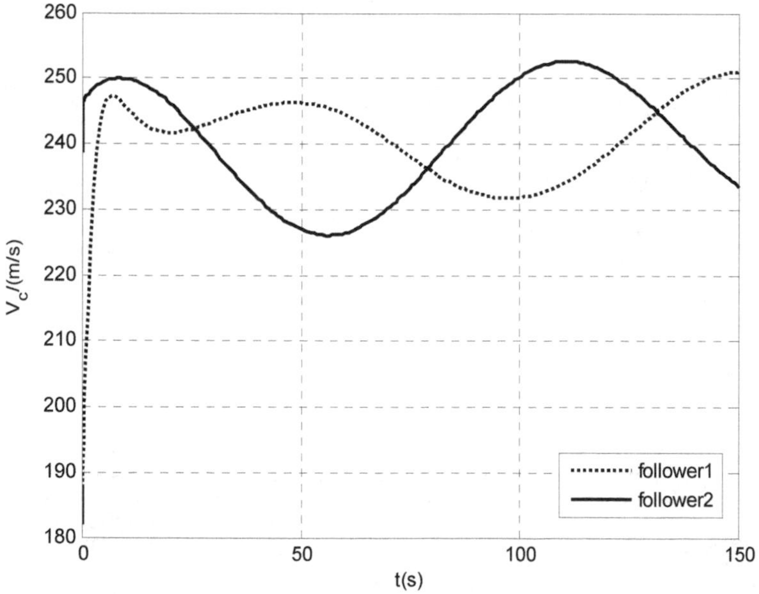

Fig. 10. Velocity commands of followers.

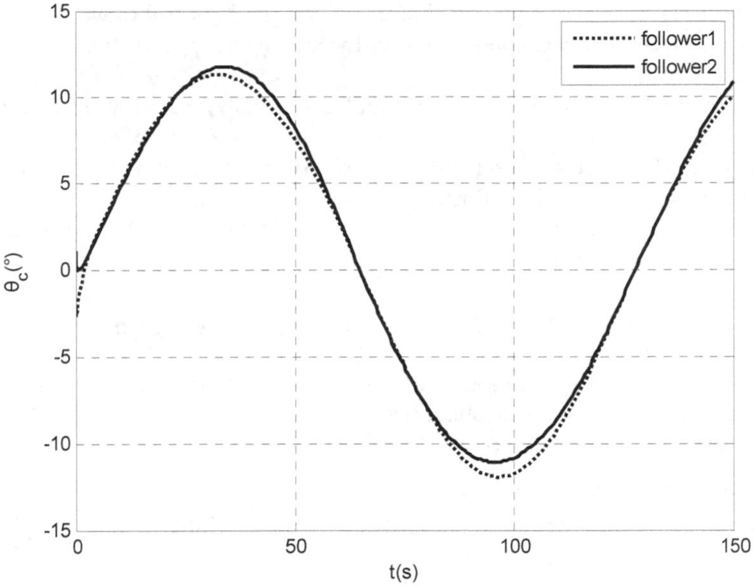

Fig. 11. Flight path angle commands of followers.

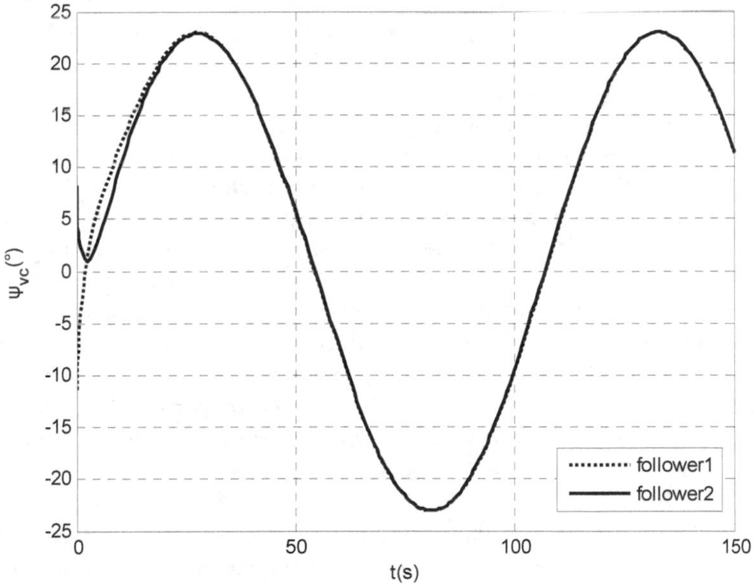

Fig. 12. Flight deflection angle commands of followers.

It can be found from those result curves showed above that PD keeping controller of missile formation can implement keeping control at about 25s, and control quantities are feasible; the stable error in x_r direction is about 5m, and those in y_r and z_r directions are 1m and 6m respectively.

Because three channels of PD controller are coupled seriously, it is very difficult to find the obvious relationships between the inertial time constants of each channel and control performance; From the change of each curve, we can find that the maneuver of leader affect the formation keeping control distinctly; Besides, we can find that there are evident regulating processes from initial states to expected states, and the maximum control quantity exists in two followers, its value is about 60m.

5.2 Simulations for Optimal Controller of missile formation keeping

5.2.1 Initial Conditions

We will choose the following conditions for the simulations to optimal controller:

1. weight matrices of optimal controller are:

- output regulating weight matrix: $\boldsymbol{Q}_y = \text{diag}(4.0,6.0,6.0)$;
- control energy weight matrix: $\boldsymbol{R} = \text{diag}(1.0,1.0,1.0)$;
- weight matrix of control energy changing: $\boldsymbol{R}_1 = \text{diag}(1.0,1.0,1.0)$.

2. other conditions are same as section 5.1.

5.2.2 Simulation results and analysis

After simulating, we can get the result curves Fig.13-Fig.18, where Fig.13 is the 3-dimensional motion of missile formation; Fig.14 and Fig.15 are the position components of follower 1 and follower 2 in relative coordinate frame respectively; Fig.16-Fig.18 are the control quantities in velocity, flight path angle and flight deflection angle channels of followers respectively.

There are following conclusions after analyzing above result curves:

1. Optimal keeping controller of missile formation can implement keeping on desired relative states at about 20s, it has faster response speed than PD controller;
2. The maneuver motion of leader also disturbs missile formation keeping control, and there also exists regulation process when the states of missile formation changing from initial states to final states, but the disturbance amplitude is smaller that of PD controller;
3. The stable error of relative motion in x_r direction is about 0.5m, and those in other two directions are 3m and 4m respectively, which are decreased by comparing to PD controller. Especially the improvement in x_r direction is more evident, which is because the velocity of leader is considered as slowly variant perturbation that will affect evidently to the relative motion in x_r direction, however, the optimal controller designed in this chapter can restrict this perturbation well, so there will be more higher tracking precision;
4. We can further decrease the stable errors by enhancing output regulating weight matrix $\boldsymbol{Q}_y$, but this manner will increase the changing rate at the same time, so we should coordinate the values of weight matrix $\boldsymbol{Q}_y$, $\boldsymbol{R}$ and $\boldsymbol{R}_1$ to obtain proper control quantities, and achieve the minimum stable tracking error.

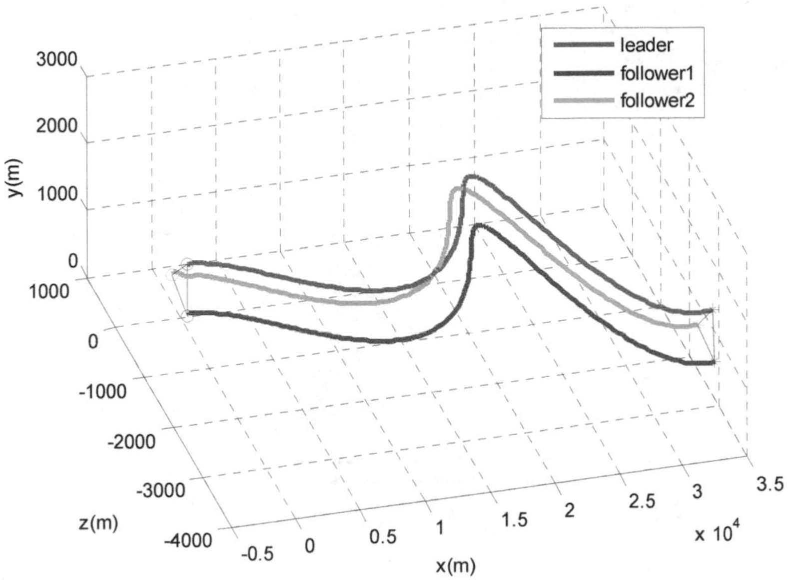

Fig. 13. Three-dimensional trajectories of missile formation under optimal controlling.

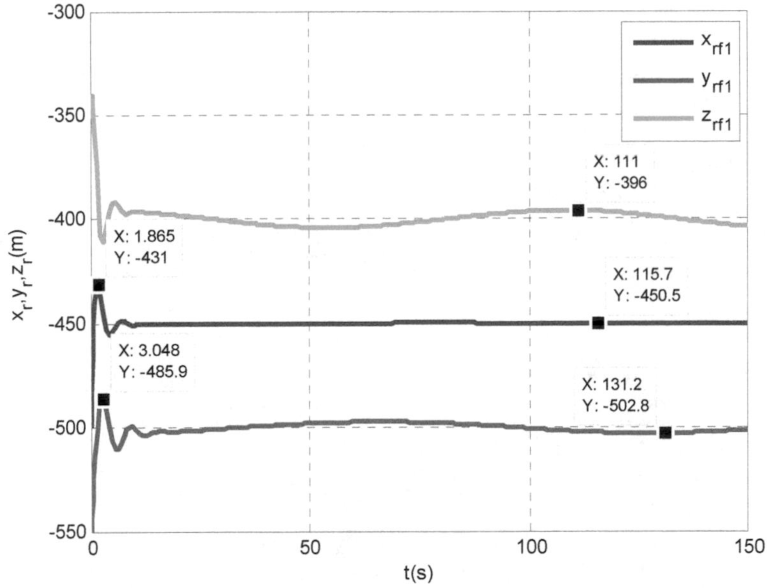

Fig. 14. Distances between follower 1 and leader in relative coordinate frame.

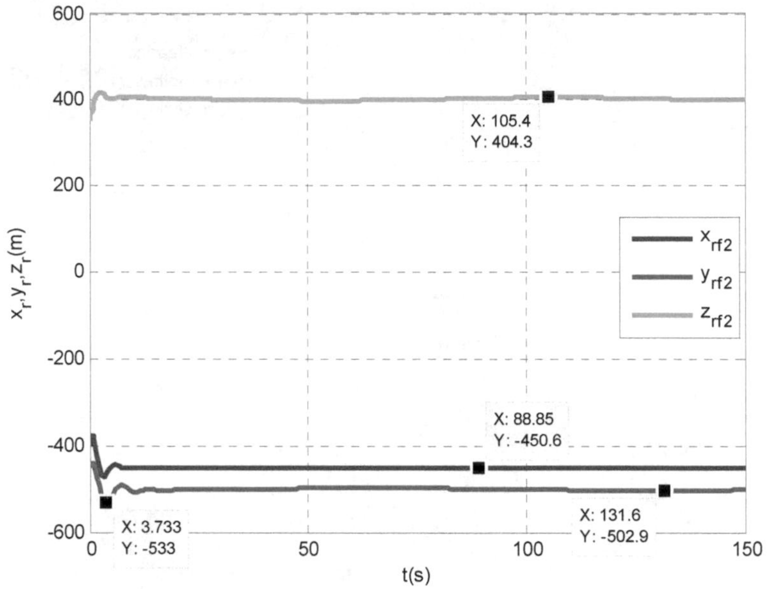

Fig. 15. Distances between follower 2 and leader in relative coordinate frame.

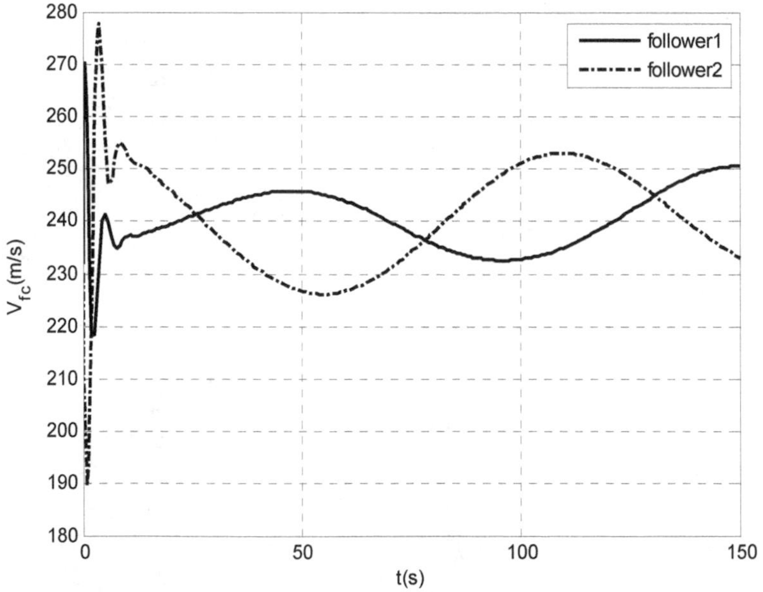

Fig. 16. Velocity commands of followers.

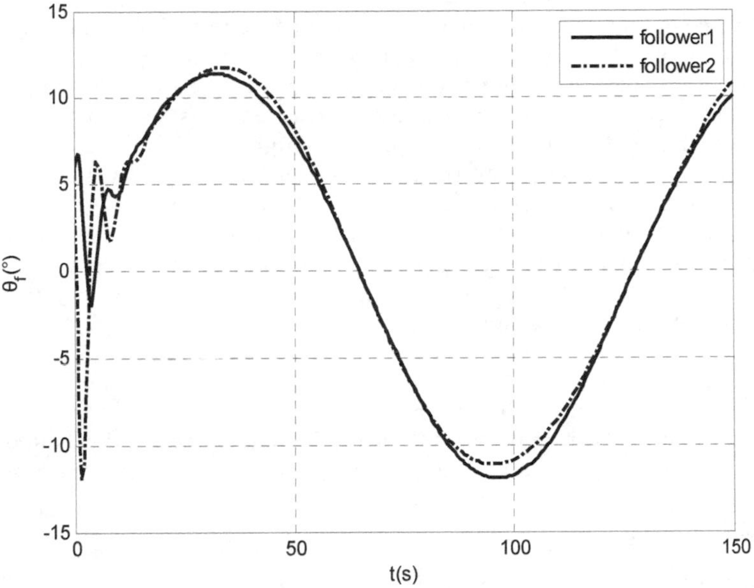

Fig. 17. Flight path angle commands of followers.

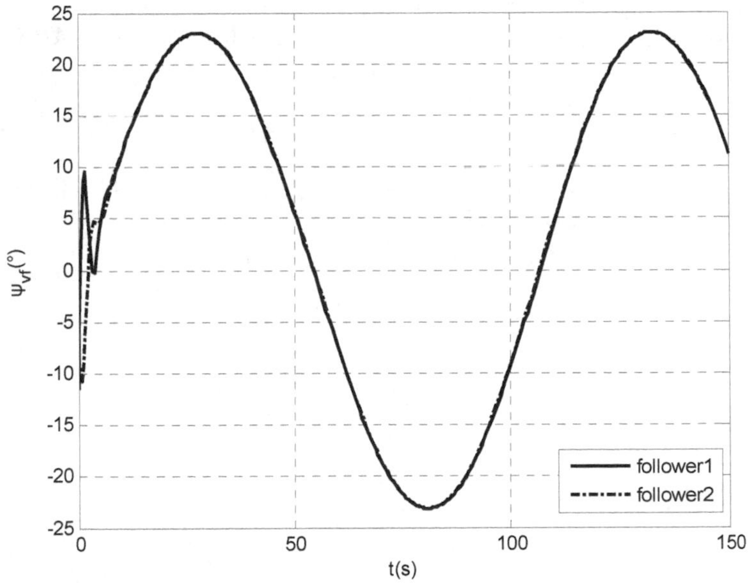

Fig. 18. Flight deflection angle commands of followers.

6. Conclusion

In this chapter, we mainly focus on some control problems of missile formation engagement. Significance of cooperative engagement was first presented by taking LOCAAS as instance, which showed the synthetical efficacy can be greatly increased by adopting cooperative engagement manner. Following the significance was analysis of frame of cooperative engagement system, which supplied the train of thought of how to research on missile formation control problem. Missile formation keeping control system design is the main content of this chapter. In this part, we established the model of relative motion in two ways firstly, and then designed missile formation control system based on PD control law and optimal control method respectively. Finally, the comparisons were made by a series of simulations, the conclusion that optimal controller is better from the points of view of stability and rapidity can be obtained from the result curves.

7. Acknowledgment

Thank Prof. Sang-Young Park and Korean Industry-Academic Cooperation Foundation very much. They supply plenteous financial support and good working conditions.

8. References

Cui, Naigang ; Wei, Changzhu; Guo, Jifeng & Zhao, Biao (2010). Research on the missile formation control system. *Proceeding of the 2009 IEEE International Conference on Mechatronics and Automation*, pp. 4197-4198, Changchun, China, August 9-12, 2009

Wei, Changzhu; Guo, Jifeng & Cui, Naigang (2010). Research on the missile formation keeping optimal control for cooerative engagement. *Journal of Astronautics*, Vol.31, No.4, (2010), pp. 1043-1044, ISBN 1000-1328

Cui, Naigang; Wei, Changzhu & Guo, Jifeng (2010). Research on four-dimensional guidance and control for missile cooperative engagement. *Flight Dynamics*, Vol.28, No.2, (2010), pp. 63-66, ISBN 1002-0853

Xie, Xueshu (1986). *Optimal control theroty and application* (1St edition), Tsinghua University Press, Beijing

Slotine, Jean Jacques & Li, Weiping (1991). *Applied nonlinear control* (1St edition), Prentice-Hall International (UK) Limited, London, ISBN: 0130408905

Part 3

Robust Control of Electromechanical Systems

13

Robust High Order Sliding Mode Control of Permanent Magnet Synchronous Motors

Huangfu Yigeng[1], S. Laghrouche[2], Liu Weiguo[1] and A. Miraoui[2]
[1]*Northwestern Polytechnical University*
[2]*University of Technology of Belfort-Montbéliard*
[1]*China*
[2]*France*

1. Introduction

Nonlinear system control has been widely concern of the research. At present, the nonlinear system decoupling control and static feedback linearization that based on the theory of differential geometry brought the research getting rid of limitation for local linearization and small scale motion. However, differential geometry control must depend on precise mathematical model. As a matter of fact, the control system usually is with parameters uncertainties and output disturbance. Considering sliding mode variable structure control with good robust, which was not sensitive for parameters perturbation and external disturbance, the combination idea of nonlinear system and sliding mode controls was obtained by reference to the large number of documents. Thus, it not only can improve system robustness but solve the difficulties problem of nonlinear sliding mode surface structure. As known to all, traditional sliding mode had a defect that is chattering phenomenon. A plenty of research papers focus on elimination/avoidance chattering by using different methods. By comparing, the chapter is concerned with novel design method for high order sliding mode control, which can eliminate chattering fundamentally. Especially, the approach and realization of nonlinear system high order sliding mode control is presented.

High order sliding mode technique is the latest study. This chapter from the theory analysis to the simulation and experiment deeply study high order sliding mode control principle and its applications. The arbitrary order sliding mode controller is employed, whose relative degree can equal any values instead of one.

In addition, the control systems design is very often to differentiate the variables. Through the derivation of sliding mode, the expression of sliding mode differential value is obtained. At the same time, the differentiator for arbitrary sliding mode is given to avoiding complex numerical calculation. It not only remains the precision of variables differential value, but also obtains the robustness.

Due to its inherent advantages, the permanent magnet synchronous motor (PMSM) deserves attention and is the most used drive in machine tool servos and modern speed control applications. For improving performance, this chapter will apply nonlinear high order sliding mode research achievement to MIMO permanent magnet synchronous motor. It changes the coupling nonlinear PMSM to single input single output (SISO) linear subsystem control problem instead of near equilibrium point linearization. Thereby, the problem of nonlinear and coupling for PMSM has been solved. In addition, Uncertainty nonlinear robust control system has been well-received study of attention. Because the robust control theory is essentially at the expense of certain performance. This kind of robust control strategy often limits bandwidth of closed loop, so that system tracking performance and robustness will be decreased. So, sliding mode control is an effective approach for improving system robust. This chapter first proposed a robust high order sliding mode controller for PMSM. The system has good position servo tracking precision in spite of parameters uncertainties and external torque disturbance.

On this basis, according to the principle of high order sliding mode, as well as differentiator, the state variables of PMSM are identified online firstly and successfully. The results of simulation indicate observe value has high precision when sliding mode variable and its differentials are convergent into zero. The same theory is used in external unknown torque disturbance estimation online for PMSM. As if, load torque will no longer be unknown disturbance. System performance can be improved greatly. It establishes theoretical foundation for the future applications.

At the end of chapter, using advanced half-physical platform controller dSPACE to drive a PMSM, hardware experiment implement is structured completely. The experiment results illustrate that PMSM adopting precious feedback linearization decoupling and high order sliding mode controller can realize system servo tracking control with good dynamic and steady character.

2. Robust high order sliding mode control

As known to all, the sliding mode control with the strong robustness for the internal parameters and external disturbances. In addition, the appropriate sliding surface can be selected to reduce order for control system. However, due to the chattering phenomena of sliding mode control, the high frequency oscillation of control system brings challenge for the application of sliding mode control. On the other hand, the choice of sliding surface strictly requires system relative degree to equal to 1, which limits the choice of sliding surface.

In order to solve the above problems, this chapter focuses on a new type of sliding mode control, that is, higher order sliding mode control. The technology not only retains advantage of strong robustness in the traditional sliding mode control, but also enables discontinuous items transmit into the first order or higher order sliding mode derivative to eliminate the chattering. Besides, the design of the controller no longer must require relative degree to be 1. Therefore, it is greatly simplified to design parameters of sliding mode surface.

Emelyanov and others first time propose the concept of high order differentiation of sliding mode variable, but also provide a second order sliding mode twisting algorithm, and prove its convergence (Emelyanov et al., 1996). Another algorithm is super twisting, which can completely eliminate chattering (Emelyanov et al., 1990), although the relative degree of sliding mode variable is required to equal to 1. In the second order sliding mode control, Levant proved sliding mode accuracy is proportional to $o(\tau^2)$ the square of the switching delay time. It has also become one of the merits of high order sliding mode control (Levant, 1993). Since then, the high order sliding mode controller has been developed and applied rapidly. For example, Bartolini and others propose a second order sliding mode control applied the sub-optimal algorithm (Bartolini et al., 1997, 1999). After the concept of high order sliding mode control was applied to bound operator in (Bartolini et al., 2000). Levant used high order sliding mode control in aircraft pitch control (Levant, 2000) as well as the exact robust differentiator (Levant, 1998). About the summary of high order sliding mode control is also described in the literature (Fridman & Levant, 2002).

2.1 Review of high order sliding mode control

In recent years, because arbitrary order sliding mode control technique not only retains the traditional sliding mode control simple structure with strong robustness, but also eliminates the chattering phenomenon in the traditional sliding mode, at the same time, gets rid of the constraints of system relative degree. Therefore theoretical research and engineering applications has caused widespread concern and has been constant development.
Without losing generality, considering a state equation of single input nonlinear system as

$$\begin{aligned} \dot{x} &= f(x) + g(x)u \\ y &= s(x,t) \end{aligned} \tag{1}$$

Where, $x \in R^n$ is system state variable, t is time, y is output, u is control input. Here, $f(x)$, $g(x)$ and $s(x)$ are smooth functions. The control objective is making output function $s \equiv 0$. Differentiate the output variables continuously, we can get every order derivative of s. According to the conception of system relative degree, there are two conditions.

i. Relative degree $r = 1$, if and only if $\partial\dot{s}/\partial u \neq 0$
ii. Relative degree $r \geq 2$, if $\partial s^{(i)}/\partial u = 0$ $(i = 1,2,\cdots r-1)$, and $\partial s^{(r)}/\partial u \neq 0$

In arbitrary order sliding mode control, its core idea is the discrete function acts on a higher order sliding mode surface, making

$$s(x,t) = \dot{s}(x,t) = \ddot{s}(x,t) = \cdots s^{(r-1)}(x,t) = 0 \tag{2}$$

Suppose the relative degree of system (1) equals to r, generally speaking, when the control input u first time appears in r-order derivative of s, that is $ds^{(r)}/du \neq 0$, then we take r-order derivative of s for the output of system (1), $s,\dot{s},\ddot{s},\cdots s^{(r-1)}$ can be obtained. They are continuous function for all the x and t. However, corresponding discrete control law u acts on $s^{(r)}$. Selecting a new local coordinate, then

$$y = (y_1, y_2, \cdots y_r) = (s, \dot{s}, \cdots s^{(r-1)}) \tag{3}$$

So, the following expression can be obtained

$$s^{(r)} = a(y,t) + b(y,t)u, \quad b(y,t) \neq 0 \tag{4}$$

Therefore, high order sliding mode control is transformed to stability of r order dynamic system (2), (4). Through the Lie derivative calculation, it is very easy to verify that

$$\begin{aligned} b &= L_g L_f^{r-1} s = ds^{(r)}/du \\ a &= L_f^r s \end{aligned} \tag{5}$$

Suppose $\eta = (y_{r+1}, y_{r+2}, \cdots y_n)$, then

$$\eta = \xi(t,s,\dot{s},\cdots,s^{(r-1)},\eta) + \chi(t,s,\dot{s},\cdots,s^{(r-1)},\eta)u \tag{6}$$

Now, equation (3), (4) and (6) are transformed to Isidori-Brunowsky canonical form. The sliding mode equivalent control is $u_{eq} = -a(y,t)/b(y,t)$ (Utkin,1992). At present, the aim of control is to design a discrete feedback control $u = U(x,t)$, so that new system converge into origin on the r order sliding mode surface within limited time. Therefore, in equation (4), both $a(y,t)$ and $b(y,t)$ are bounded function. There are positive constants K_m, K_M and C so that

$$\begin{aligned} &0 < K_m \le b(y,t) \le K_M \\ &|a(y,t)| \le C \end{aligned} \tag{7}$$

Theorem 1: (Levant, 1998, 2003) Suppose the relative degree of nonlinear system (1) to output function $s(x,t)$ is r, and satisfying the condition (7), the arbitrary order sliding mode controller has following expression

$$u = -\alpha \ \mathrm{sgn}(\psi_{r-1,r}(s,\dot{s},\cdots,s^{(r-1)})) \tag{8}$$

Where,

$$\begin{aligned} \psi_{0,r} &= s \\ \psi_{1,r} &= \dot{s} + \beta_1 N_{1,r}\,\mathrm{sgn}(s) \\ \psi_{i,r} &= s^{(r)} + \beta_i N_{i,r}\,\mathrm{sgn}(\psi_{i-1,r}), \qquad i = 1,\cdots,r-1 \\ N_{1,r} &= \ |s|^{(r-1)/r} \\ N_{i,r} &= (|s|^{p/r} + |\dot{s}|^{p/(r-1)} \cdots + |s^{(i-1)}|^{p/(r-i+1)})^{(r-i)/p} \qquad i = 1,\cdots,r-1 \\ N_{r-1,r} &= (|s|^{p/r} + |\dot{s}|^{p/(r-1)} \cdots + |s^{(r-2)}|^{p/2})^{1/p} \end{aligned} \tag{9}$$

Properly choose positive parameters $\beta_1, \beta_2, \cdots \beta_{r-1}$, the system converge into origin on the r order sliding mode surface within limited time. Finally, when $s \equiv 0$, it achieves control object. The choice of positive parameters $\beta_1, \beta_2, \cdots \beta_{r-1}$ is not unique. Here, $r \le 4$ order sliding mode controller is given, which is also tested.

$$\begin{aligned} &1.\ u = -\alpha \ \mathrm{sgn}(s) \\ &2.\ u = -\alpha \ \mathrm{sgn}(\dot{s} + |s|^{1/2}\,\mathrm{sgn}(s)) \\ &3.\ u = -\alpha \ \mathrm{sgn}(\ddot{s} + 2(|\dot{s}|^3 + |s|^2)^{1/6}\,\mathrm{sgn}(\dot{s} + |s|^{2/3}\,\mathrm{sgn}(s))) \\ &4.\ u = -\alpha \ \mathrm{sgn}\{\dddot{s} + 3[(\ddot{s})^6 + (\dot{s})^4 + |s|^3]^{1/12}\,\mathrm{sgn}[\ddot{s} + ((\dot{s})^4 \\ &\quad + |s|^3)^{1/6}\,\mathrm{sgn}(\dot{s} + 0.5|s|^{3/4}\,\mathrm{sgn}(s))]\} \\ &\quad \vdots \end{aligned} \tag{10}$$

From the above equation (10) we can also see that, when $r = 1$, the controller is traditional relay sliding mode control; when $r = 2$, in fact, the controller is super twisting algorithm of second order sliding mode.

To get the differentiation of a given signal is always essential in automatic control systems. We often need derivative a variable or function. So there are a lot of numerical algorithms for this issue. The same situation also appears in the design of high order sliding mode controller (10) that needs to calculate the derivative values of sliding mode variable. In order to be able to accurately calculate, at the same time simplifying the algorithm, this chapter directly uses own advantages of high order sliding mode control due to high accuracy and robustness. We can design a high order sliding mode differentiator used to calculate the numerical derivative of the variables.

Presentation above in the previous has been explained in detail the principles of high order sliding mode control and sliding mode controller design method. This part focuses on how to take use of high order sliding mode technique to solve the differentiation of a given signal or variable function. And their simulation results are verified

Suppose given signal is $f(t)$, now set a dynamic system as

$$\dot{x} = u \tag{11}$$

The control object is to make the variable x follow given signal $f(t)$, that is

$$x = f(t) \tag{12}$$

Therefore, sliding mode surface is selected as

$$s = x - f(t) \tag{13}$$

At this moment, according to the principle of sliding mode control, a proper controller is designed. When the system enter into sliding mode, $s = x - f(t) = 0$. Derivative of sliding mode surface (13),

$$\dot{s} = \dot{x} - \dot{f}(t) = u - \dot{f}(t) \tag{14}$$

Because control input u first time appears in the derivative of sliding mode surface s, the relative degree of system is $r = 1$. It satisfies the requirement about relative degree of second order sliding mode. So the super twisting algorithm (Fridman & Levant, 2002) is adopted. Thus,

$$\begin{aligned} u &= -\lambda |x - f(t)|^{1/2} \operatorname{sgn}(x - f(t)) + u_1 \\ \dot{u}_1 &= -\alpha \ \operatorname{sgn}(x - f(t)) \end{aligned} \tag{15}$$

Where, $\lambda > 0$, $\alpha > 0$ are positive constant. Definite a function as $\Theta(\alpha, \lambda, C) = |\Psi(t)|$, C is Lipschitz constant about derivative of $f(x)$. $(\Sigma(t), \Psi(t))$ is the solution of equation of (16), the initial value are $\Sigma(0) = 0$, $\Psi(0) = 1$

$$\begin{aligned} \dot{\Sigma} &= -|\Sigma|^{1/2} + \Psi \\ \dot{\Psi} &= \begin{cases} -\dfrac{1}{\lambda^2}(\alpha - C), & -|\Sigma|^{1/2} + \Psi > 0 \\ -\dfrac{1}{\lambda^2}(\alpha + C), & -|\Sigma|^{1/2} + \Psi \le 0 \end{cases} \end{aligned} \tag{16}$$

Theorem 2: (Levant, 1998) Let $\alpha > C > 0$, $\lambda > 0$, function $\Theta(\alpha,\lambda,C) < 1$. Then, provided $f(t)$ has a derivative with Lipschitz's constant C, the equality $u = \dot{f}(t)$ is fulfilled identically after finite time transient process. And the smaller value of Θ, faster convergence; If $\Theta(\alpha,\lambda,C) > 1$, control input u will not converge into $\dot{f}(t)$. Observer parameters should meet the following sufficient condition for convergence of the second-order sliding mode control,

$$\begin{aligned} &\alpha > C \\ &\lambda^2 \geq 4C\frac{\alpha + C}{\alpha - C} \end{aligned} \tag{17}$$

According to the principle of second order sliding mode, after a finite time, the system will converge into the origin, that is,

$$s(x,t) = \dot{s}(x,t) = 0 \tag{18}$$

Then,

$$u = \dot{f}(t) \tag{19}$$

Now, observer input u is the estimation of derivative of given signal $f(t)$. Using a sliding mode controller achieve differentiation of variable function.

Let input signal be presented in the form $f(t) = f_0(t) + n(t)$, where $f_0(t)$ is a differentiable base signal, $f_0(t)$ has a derivative with Lipschitz's constant $C > 0$, and $n(t)$ is a noise, $|n(t)| < \varepsilon$. Then, there exists such a constant $b > 0$ depend on $(\alpha - C)/\lambda^2$ and $(\alpha + C)/\lambda^2$ that after a finite time, the inequality $|u(t) - \dot{f}_0(t)| < \lambda b \varepsilon^{1/2}$ holds. (Levant, 1998)

Through the first order sliding mode differentiator description of the working principle, it will naturally think, whether can design a sliding mode differentiator to obtain the arbitrary order derivative of given signal. Well, the design of high order sliding mode controller (10) needs to know all sliding mode variables and their corresponding differentiation.

Theorem 3: Design an arbitrary order sliding mode differentiator, which can be used to estimate the derivative value of sliding mode variables, so as to achieve a simplified numerical differential purposes as following.

$$\begin{aligned} \dot{z}_0 &= v_0 \\ v_0 &= -\lambda_0 |z_0 - f(t)|^{n/(n+1)} \operatorname{sgn}(z_0 - f(t)) + z_1, \\ \dot{z}_1 &= v_1 \\ v_1 &= -\lambda_1 |z_1 - v_0|^{(n-1)/n} \operatorname{sgn}(z_1 - v_0) + z_2, \\ &\vdots \\ \dot{z}_{n-1} &= v_{n-1} \\ v_{n-1} &= -\lambda_{n-1} |z_{n-1} - v_{n-2}|^{1/2} \operatorname{sgn}(z_{n-1} - v_{n-2}) + z_n, \\ \dot{z}_n &= -\lambda_n \operatorname{sgn}(z_n - v_{n-1}) \end{aligned} \tag{20}$$

The same with first order sliding mode differentiator, suppose given signal is $f(t)$, $t \in [0,\infty)$. It has been known that the n order derivative of $f(t)$ has Lipschitz constant,

recorded as $L > 0$. Now, the object of sliding mode differentiator is estimating the value of $f'(t), f''(t), \cdots, f^{(n)}(t)$ in real time.
Arbitrary order sliding mode differentiator has the following recursive form as equation (20).
It can be verified, When $n = 1$, it is first order differentiator. Suppose $f_0(t)$ is basic value of given signal $f(t)$, $\delta(t)$ is uncertain part, but bounded, satisfying $|\delta(t)| < \varepsilon$, then $f(t) = f_0(t) + \delta(t)$.
Theorem 4: (Levant, 2003) If properly choose parameter $\lambda_i (0 \le i \le n)$, the following equalities are true in the absence of input noise after a finite time of a transient process.

$$\begin{aligned} z_0 &= f_0(t) \\ z_i &= v_i = f_0^{(i)}(t), \quad i = 1, \cdots, n \end{aligned} \tag{21}$$

The theorem 4 illustrates that arbitrary order sliding mode differentiator can use differentiation $z_i (0 \le i \le n)$ to estimate any order derivative of input function $f(t)$ online within limited time.
Theorem 5: (Levant, 2003) Let the input noise satisfy the inequality $\delta(t) = | f(t) - f_0(t) | \le \varepsilon$. Then the following inequality are established in finite time for some positive constants μ_i, τ_i depending exclusively on the parameters of the differentiator.

$$\begin{aligned} | z_i - f_0^{(i)}(t) | &\le \mu_i \varepsilon^{(n-i+1)/(n+1)} \quad & i = 0, \cdots, n \\ | v_i - f_0^{(i+1)}(t) | &\le \tau_i \varepsilon^{(n-i)/(n+1)} \quad & i = 0, \cdots, n-1 \end{aligned} \tag{22}$$

By Theorem 5, we can see that the arbitrary order sliding mode differentiator has robustness.
The arbitrary order sliding mode differentiator can accurately estimate any order derivative of a given input. If this differentiator can be used in high order sliding mode controller (10), any order derivative of sliding mode variable s can be accurately estimated avoiding the complicated calculation, which greatly simplifies the controller design. Adopting the differentiator, consider $s(t)$ in high order sliding mode controller as given input for differentiator. Then the output of differentiator $z_i (0 \le i \le n)$ can substitute any order derivative of $s(t)$, that is

$$\begin{aligned} z_0 &= s \\ z_i &= s^{(i)} \quad i = 1, \cdots n \end{aligned} \tag{23}$$

The sliding mode controller (8) can be rewritten by

$$u = -\alpha \ \mathrm{sgn}(\psi_{r-1,r}(z_0, z_1, \cdots, z_{(r-1)})) \tag{24}$$

The expression from this controller can also be clearly seen, with high order sliding mode differentiator, the differentiation of arbitrary order sliding mode variable will not be difficult to solve, which makes the high order sliding mode controller design has been simplified greatly.

2.2 Applications for permanent magnet synchronous motor

Permanent magnet synchronous motors (PMSM) are receiving increased attention for electric drive applications due to their high power density, large torque to inertia ratio and high efficiency over other kinds of motors (Glumineau et al, 1993; Ziribi et al, 2001; Caravani et al, 1998).

But the dynamic model of a PMSM is highly nonlinear because of the coupling between the motor speed and the electrical quantities, such as the d, q axis currents. In last years, many different control algorithms have been used to improve the performance of the magnet motor. For example, as the dynamic model of the machine is nonlinear, a natural approach is the exact feedback linearization control method, by which the original nonlinear model can be transformed into a linear model through proper coordinate transformation. However, in general, the dynamics of the synchronous motors may not be fully known, since some of parameters appearing in the equations will vary. For instance, the resistance and inductance will be changed when the temperature alters. As a consequence, nonlinearities can only be partially cancelled by the feedback linearization technique, and parameters uncertainties act on the equations of the motion. Then an important aim of the control design is to develop a robust controller which ensures good dynamic performances in spite of parameters uncertainties and perturbation.

The sliding mode control is known to be a robust approach to solve the control problems of nonlinear systems. Robustness properties against various kinds of uncertainties such as parameter perturbations and external disturbances can be guaranteed. However, this control strategy has a main drawback: the well known chattering phenomenon. In order to reduce the chattering, the sign function can be replaced by a smooth approximation. However, this technique induces deterioration in accuracy and robustness. In last decade, another approach called higher order sliding mode (HOSM) has been proposed and developed. It is the generalization of classical sliding mode control and can be applied to control systems with arbitrary relative degree r respecting to the considered output. In HOSM control, the main objective is to obtain a finite time convergence in the non empty manifold $S = \{x \in X \mid s = \dot{s} = \ddot{s} = \cdots = s^{(r-1)} = 0\}$ by acting discontinuously on r order derivatives of the sliding variable s. Advantageous properties of HOSM are: the chattering effect is eliminated, higher order precision is provided whereas all the qualities of standard sliding mode are kept, and control law is not limited by relative degree of the output.

The common analysis of permanent magnet synchronous motor is d-q axis mathematical model. It can be used to analyze not only the permanent magnet synchronous motor steady state operating characteristics, but also can be used to analyze the transient performance motor. In order to establish sinusoidal PMSM d-q axis mathematical model, firstly assume:

i. Motor core saturation neglected;
ii. Excluding the eddy current and magnetic hysteresis loss of motor;
iii. The motor current is symmetrical three phase sine wave current.

Thereby, the following voltage, flux linkage, electromagnetic torque and mechanical motion equations can be obtained, where all the values in equations are transient.

The voltage equation:

$$\begin{aligned} u_d &= \frac{d\psi_d}{dt} - \omega\psi_q + Ri_d \\ u_q &= \frac{d\psi_q}{dt} + \omega\psi_d + Ri_q \end{aligned} \tag{25}$$

The flux linkage equation:

$$\begin{aligned} \psi_d &= L_d i_d + \psi_f \\ \psi_q &= L_q i_q \end{aligned} \tag{26}$$

The electromagnetic torque equation:

$$T_{em} = P(\psi_d i_q - \psi_q i_d) = P[(L_d - L_q) i_d i_q + \psi_f i_q] \tag{27}$$

The motor motion equation:

$$J\frac{d\Omega}{dt} = T_{em} - T_l - B\Omega \tag{28}$$

Where: u_d, u_q are d-q axis stator voltage; i_d, i_q are d-q axis stator current; L_d, L_q are d-q axis stator inductance, as $L_d = L_q$, motor is non-salient pole; as $L_d < L_q$, motor is salient pole; ψ_d, ψ_q are d-q axis stator flux linkage; ψ_f is magnetic potential generated by permanent magnet rotor; ω is motor's electrical angular velocity; R is stator phase resistance; P is number of motor pole pairs; T_{em} is electromagnetic torque; T_l is load torque; Ω is motor's mechanical angular velocity, with $\Omega = P\omega$; J is total inertia of rotor and load; B is viscous friction coefficient.
Set of equations (25), (26), (27) and (28), we can get the state equation expression of PMSM as following.

$$\begin{bmatrix} \frac{d\omega}{dt} \\ \frac{di_d}{dt} \\ \frac{di_q}{dt} \end{bmatrix} = \begin{bmatrix} \frac{P}{J}[(L_d - L_q)i_d + \psi_f]i_q - \frac{B}{J}\omega - \frac{T_l}{J} \\ -\frac{R}{L_d}i_d + P\frac{L_q}{L_d}\omega i_q + \frac{1}{L_d}u_d \\ -P\frac{\psi_f}{L_q}\omega - P\frac{L_d}{L_q}\omega i_d - \frac{R}{L_q}i_q + \frac{1}{L_q}u_q \end{bmatrix} \tag{29}$$

Suppose θ_e is the electrical angle between rotor axis and stator A phase axis, θ is mechanical angular position of motor, with $\theta = P\theta_e$, and following equality is set up.

$$\theta = \int \Omega dt + \theta_0 \tag{30}$$

Where, θ_0 is rotor initial angular position. Considering position control, equation (29) can be rewritten by

$$\begin{bmatrix} \frac{d\theta}{dt} \\ \frac{d\omega}{dt} \\ \frac{di_d}{dt} \\ \frac{di_q}{dt} \end{bmatrix} = \begin{bmatrix} P\omega \\ \frac{P}{J}[(L_d - L_q)i_d + \psi_f]i_q - \frac{B}{J}\omega - \frac{T_l}{J} \\ -\frac{R}{L_d}i_d + P\frac{L_q}{L_d}\omega i_q + \frac{1}{L_d}u_d \\ -P\frac{\psi_f}{L_q}\omega - P\frac{L_d}{L_q}\omega i_d - \frac{R}{L_q}i_q + \frac{1}{L_q}u_q \end{bmatrix} \tag{31}$$

From the equation (31) we can see that PMSM is a multi-variable, coupling, nonlinear time varying systems. In addition, the variables in d-q axis can be changed to three phase *abc* axis by coordinate transformation.

2.2.1 Robust control for PMSM

This section will use the high order sliding mode control algorithm with differentiator, in spite of system parameter uncertainties, external disturbances and other factors, to design a robust controller for nonlinear multi-input multi-output permanent magnet synchronous motor. The advantage of this controller is the elimination of the chattering in standard sliding mode. At the same time, it is still with precision and robustness of the standard sliding mode control. And its control law no longer subjects to relative degree constraints.
Firstly, let x denotes the motor state variable $x=[x_1,x_2,x_3,x_4]^T=[\theta,\Omega,i_d,i_q]^T$, and control input $u=[u_1,u_2]^T=[u_d,u_q]^T$. The parameters R, L_d, L_q and B are considered as uncertain parameters, such as R will change with the temperature rise of the synchronous motor. Therefore, use R_0, L_{d0}, L_{q0} and B_0 to express their nominal value part of R, L_d, L_q and B respectively.

$$\begin{aligned}
k_1 &= k_{01}+\delta k_1 = P(L_d-L_q)/J \\
k_2 &= k_{02}+\delta k_2 = P\psi_f/J \\
k_3 &= k_{03}+\delta k_3 = -B/J \\
k_4 &= k_{04}+\delta k_4 = -R/L_d \\
k_5 &= k_{05}+\delta k_5 = PL_q/L_d \\
k_6 &= k_{06}+\delta k_6 = 1/L_d \\
k_7 &= k_{07}+\delta k_7 = -P\psi_f/L_q \\
k_8 &= k_{08}+\delta k_8 = -PL_d/L_q \\
k_9 &= k_{09}+\delta k_9 = -R/L_q \\
k_{10} &= k_{010}+\delta k_{10} = 1/L_q
\end{aligned} \tag{32}$$

In order to facilitate the calculation, the coefficient $k_i(1\le i\le 10)$ is used to plan these variable expressions, Where, $k_{0i}(1\le i\le 10)$ is the nominal value of the concerned parameter, δk_i is the uncertainty on the concerned parameter such that $|\delta k_i|\le \delta k_{0i}\le|k_{0i}|$, with δk_{0i} a known positive bound. The state variable $x\in R^4$, such that $|x_i|\le x_{iMAX}(2\le i\le 4)$, x_{2MAX} is the maximum values of the angular velocity, x_{3MAX} and x_{4MAX} are the maximum values of the current i_d and i_q respectively. And control input $u\in R^2$ such that $|u_i|\le u_{iMAX},(1\le i\le 2)$. Where, u_{1MAX} and u_{2MAX} are the maximum values of the voltage input v_d and v_q respectively.
Then the state space model of the synchronous motor can be changed as following nonlinear system.

$$\begin{bmatrix}\dot{x}_1\\ \dot{x}_2\\ \dot{x}_3\\ \dot{x}_4\end{bmatrix} = \underbrace{\begin{bmatrix} x_2 \\ (k_1x_3+k_2)x_4+k_3x_2-T_l/J \\ k_4x_3+k_5x_2x_4 \\ k_7x_2+k_8x_2x_3+k_9x_4\end{bmatrix}}_{f(x,t)} + \underbrace{\begin{bmatrix} 0 & 0\\ 0 & 0\\ k_6 & 0\\ 0 & k_{10}\end{bmatrix}}_{g(x,t)}\begin{bmatrix}u_1\\ u_2\end{bmatrix} \tag{33}$$

The aim is to design an appropriate control which guarantees robust performance in presence of parameters and load variations. The control objective is double aspect. First, the rotor angular position $x_1 = \theta$ must track a reference trajectory angular position x_{1ref}. Second, the nonlinear electromagnetic torque must be linearized to avoid reluctance effects and torque ripple. This objective is equivalent to constrain $x_3 = i_d$ to track a constant direct current reference $x_{3ref} = 0$.
As we known that PMSM is a multi-input multi-output nonlinear dynamic system. It is assumed that the position and current are available for measurement. A first sliding variable s for the tracking of direct current x_3 towards its equilibrium point x_{3ref} f is defined from the direct current error. So, the first sliding mode variable is

$$s_1 = h_1(x) = x_3 - x_{3ref} \tag{34}$$

Derivative of s_1, we can see that the relative degree of sliding mode variable s_1 equals 1, that is

$$\begin{aligned} \dot{s}_1 &= \dot{x}_3 - \dot{x}_{3ref} \\ &= k_4 x_3 + k_5 x_2 x_4 + k_6 u_1 - \dot{x}_{3ref} \end{aligned} \tag{35}$$

To track the angular position $x_1 = \theta$, another sliding manifold is proposed so that the error dynamics follows a desired third order dynamic. Denoting x_{1ref} the desired trajectory, following form can be obtained.

$$s_2 = h_2(x) = x_1 - x_{1ref} \tag{36}$$

Considering load torque as external disturbance, derivative of s_2 continuously until control input appears.

$$\begin{aligned} \dot{s}_2 &= \dot{x}_1 - \dot{x}_{1ref} = x_2 - \dot{x}_{1ref} \\ \ddot{s}_2 &= \dot{x}_2 - \ddot{x}_{1ref} = (k_1 x_3 + k_2) x_4 + k_3 x_2 - \ddot{x}_{1ref} \\ \dddot{s}_2 &= k_1 x_4 (k_3 x_3 + k_5 x_2 x_4) + k_1 k_6 x_4 u_1 + k_3[(k_1 x_3 + k_2) x_4 + k_3 x_2] \\ &\quad + (k_1 x_3 + k_2)(k_7 x_2 + k_8 x_2 x_3 + k_9 x_4) + (k_1 x_3 + k_2) k_{10} u_2 - \dddot{x}_{1ref} \end{aligned} \tag{37}$$

The control input u appears in the 3 order derivative of s_2, so the relative degree of s_2 equals 3. Considering sliding mode variable $s = [\dot{s}_1, \dddot{s}_2]^T$ as a new dynamci system, the space state express can be writtern by

$$\begin{bmatrix} \dot{s}_1 \\ \dddot{s}_2 \end{bmatrix} = \begin{bmatrix} A_1 \\ A_2 \end{bmatrix} + \begin{bmatrix} B_{11} & 0 \\ B_{21} & B_{22} \end{bmatrix} \begin{bmatrix} u_1 \\ u_2 \end{bmatrix} \tag{38}$$

Where,

$$A_1 = k_4 x_3 + k_5 x_2 x_4 =: A_{10} + \delta A_1$$

$$A_2 = (k_1 x_3 + k_2)(k_7 x_2 + k_8 x_2 x_3 + k_9 x_4) + k_3[(k_1 x_3 + k_2) x_4 + k_3 x_2] + k_1 x_4 (k_3 x_3 + k_5 x_2 x_4) - \dddot{x}_{1ref} =: A_{20} + \delta A_2$$

$$B_{11} = k_6 =: B_{110} + \delta B_{11}$$

$$B_{21} = k_1 k_6 x_4 =: B_{210} + \delta B_{21}$$

$$B_{22} = (k_1 x_3 + k_2) k_{10} =: B_{220} + \delta B_{22}$$

A_{10}, A_{20}, B_{110}, B_{210} and B_{220} are the known nominal expressions whereas the expressions of δA_1, δA_2, δB_{11}, δB_{21} and δB_{22} contain all the uncertainties due to parameters and load torque variations.

Next, controller should be designed so that sliding mode variable s_1 achieves to zero in finite time. Another sliding mode variable s_2 and its first and second derivative likewise achieve to zero in finite time. When the sliding mode happens, then

$$\begin{aligned} S_1 &= \{x \in X \mid s_1(x,t) = 0\} \\ S_2 &= \{x \in X \mid s_2(x,t) = \dot{s}_2(x,t) = \ddot{s}_2(x,t) = 0\} \end{aligned} \tag{39}$$

The control problem is equivalent to the finite time stabilization of the following MIMO system.

$$\begin{bmatrix} \dot{s}_1 \\ \dddot{s}_2 \end{bmatrix} = A + B \begin{bmatrix} u_1 \\ u_2 \end{bmatrix} \tag{40}$$

Where,

$$A = \begin{bmatrix} A_{10} \\ A_{20} \end{bmatrix} + \begin{bmatrix} \delta A_1 \\ \delta A_2 \end{bmatrix} =: A_0 + \delta A \tag{41}$$

$$B = \begin{bmatrix} B_{110} & 0 \\ B_{210} & B_{220} \end{bmatrix} + \begin{bmatrix} \delta B_{11} & 0 \\ \delta B_{21} & \delta B_{22} \end{bmatrix} =: B_0 + \delta B \tag{42}$$

From the equation (37), the outputs of this MIMO system are coupled since $\dddot{s}_2$ is affected by u_1 and u_2. So an input-output feedback linearization technique can be used, here w is new control input.

$$u = B_0^{-1} \cdot [-A_0 + w] \tag{43}$$

Now, if considering influence of external disturbance and parameter uncertainties, equation (40) can be rewritten by

$$\begin{aligned} s &= A + Bu \\ &= A_0 + \delta A + (B_0 + \delta B)u \\ &= A_0 + \delta A + (B_0 + \delta B)[B_0^{-1}(-A_0 + w)] \end{aligned} \tag{44}$$

Evolution and ordinate, then

$$\Rightarrow \begin{bmatrix} \dot{s}_1 \\ \dddot{s}_2 \end{bmatrix} = \begin{bmatrix} \hat{A}_1 \\ \hat{A}_2 \end{bmatrix} + \begin{bmatrix} \hat{B}_{11} & 0 \\ \hat{B}_{21} & \hat{B}_{22} \end{bmatrix} \begin{bmatrix} w_1 \\ w_2 \end{bmatrix} \tag{45}$$

Where,

$$\hat{A}_1 = \delta A_1 - \frac{\delta B_{11}}{B_{110}} A_{10}$$

$$\hat{A}_2 = \delta A_2 - [\frac{\delta B_{21}}{B_{110}} - \frac{\delta B_{22} B_{210}}{B_{110} B_{220}}] A_{10} - \frac{\delta B_{22}}{B_{220}} A_{20}$$

$$\hat{B}_{11} = 1 + \frac{\delta B_{11}}{B_{110}}$$

$$\hat{B}_{21} = \frac{\delta B_{21}}{B_{110}} - \frac{\delta B_{22} B_{210}}{B_{110} B_{220}}$$

$$\hat{B}_{22} = 1 + \frac{\delta B_{22}}{B_{220}}$$

In the new dynamic system with $w = [w_1, w_2]^T$, it leads to s_1 equals integrator of w_1 and s_2 equals three time integrators of w_2, if the part of uncertainties $\delta A = 0$ and $\delta B = 0$. Then w_1 and w_2 are designed to stabilize in this new system.

In fact, the term $-B_0^{-1} A_0$ of (43) is the so-called equivalent control in the sliding mode context. In this new system, due to state variable $x_i (2 \le x \le 4)$, there exist three positive constants C_1, C_2, K_{11m}, K_{22m}, K_{11M}, K_{22M} and K_{21}, so that

$$\begin{aligned} & |\hat{A}_1| \le C_1, \quad 0 < K_{11m} \le \hat{B}_{11} \le K_{11M} \\ & |\hat{A}_2| \le C_2, \quad 0 < K_{22m} \le \hat{B}_{22} \le K_{22M} \\ & |\hat{B}_{21}| \le K_{21} \end{aligned} \tag{46}$$

Then, owing to the relative degree of s_1 equals 1, the first order sliding mode algorithm previously presented with control law

$$w_1 = -\alpha_1 \operatorname{sgn}(s_1) \tag{47}$$

Where α_1 is positive constant. In the actual system, due to all the state variables have the bound, selecting parameter α_1 properly to satisfy convergence. For the motor angular position control, a 3 order sliding mode control law is used. In this case, only a single scalar parameter α_2 is to be adjusted. Actually, the control input w_2 can be chosen as following.

$$w_2 = -\alpha_2 \operatorname{sgn}(\ddot{s}_2 + 2(|\dot{s}_2|^3 + |s_2|^2)^{1/6} \operatorname{sgn}(\dot{s}_2 + |s_2|^{2/3} \operatorname{sgn}(s_2))) \tag{48}$$

According to the principle of sliding mode differentiator, the arbitrary order derivative of s_2 can be estimated by the output of differentiator z_0, z_1 and z_2.

$$\begin{aligned} & \dot{z}_0 = v_0, \; v_0 = -150 |z_0 - s|^{2/3} \operatorname{sgn}(z_0 - s) + z_1 \\ & \dot{z}_1 = v_1, \; v_1 = -160 |z_1 - v_0|^{1/2} \operatorname{sgn}(z_1 - v_0) + z_2 \\ & \dot{z}_2 = -400 |z_2 - v_1| \end{aligned} \tag{49}$$

Then, substituting z_0, z_1 and z_2 for s_2, $\dot{s}_2$ and $\ddot{s}_2$ respectively in equation (48), that is

$$w_2 = -\alpha_2 \operatorname{sgn}(z_2 + 2(|z_1|^3 + |z_0|^2)^{1/6} \operatorname{sgn}(z_1 + |z_0|^{2/3} \operatorname{sgn}(z_0))) \tag{50}$$

The figure 1 is the block graph of control system. The first sliding mode variable s_1 is given by the error between direct axis current reference and feedback. And the second variable s_2 is identified by the error between the motor reference position and actual feedback. According to the Theorem 4 after finite time, z_0, z_1 and z_2 can be used to estimate s_2, $\dot{s}_2$ and $\ddot{s}_2$. In system, the state variable speed of motor w_2 is obtained by differentiator of angle position signal θ. Finally, the nonlinear dynamic system must be linearized by input-output feedback linearization, then the control input u_1 and u_2 are used to drive the synchronous motor.

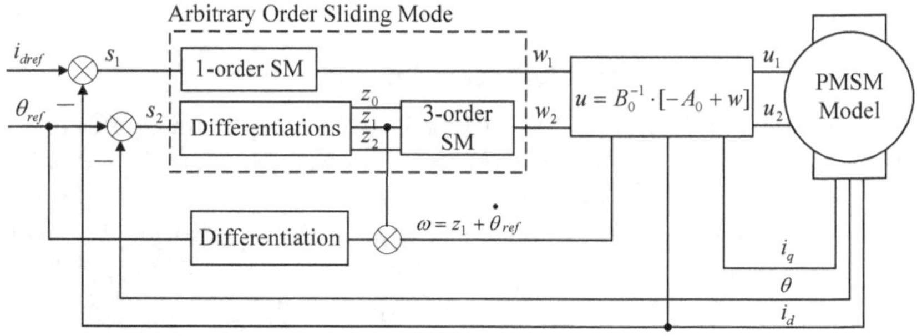

Fig. 1. The block graph of dynamic system structure.

In the simulation, The PMSM is a DutymAx 95DSC060300 (Leroy Somer Co.) drive. Two sensors give measurements of phase currents, a optical encoder is used to measure the position of the motor. The parameters of synchronous motor are $P = 3$, $R = 3.3\Omega$, $L_d = 0.027H$, $L_q = 0.0034H$, $B = 0.0034N \cdot m \cdot s$, $\psi_f = 0.341Wb$, $J = 0.00037kg \cdot m^2$. A phase current of the maximum accepted value is $6.0A$, the load torque maximum value is $6N \cdot m$, and angular velocity is $3000rpm$ .To achieve the efficiency of controller, the parameter in (47) and (50) are chosen by $\alpha_1 = 5$, $\alpha_2 = 3300$. In the differentiator, the coefficient of (49) are selected by $\lambda_0 = 150$, $\lambda_1 = 160$, $\lambda_2 = 400$ in order to allow the convergence of the differentiator. The system sampling frequency is $8000Hz$. To show the system robustness of the controller, consider permanent magnet synchronous motor parameters uncertainties (with $\delta R = \pm 50\% R$, with $\delta L_{d0} = \pm 25\% L_d$ and $\delta L_{q0} = \pm 25\% L_q$ and with $\pm 20\% B$).
The trajectory of motor angular position reference and feedback are shown in figure 2 above in spit of PMSM parameters uncertainty. From this figure, we can see that the servo system track trajectory has good performance. The precision can achieve 10^{-3}. In addition, using high order sliding mode control, the chattering is eliminated in lower sliding mode surface so that the track trajectory becomes smoother.
Figure 2 below shows position tracking error, which does not exceed 0.09 rad. It means that the controller has high robust capability versus the parameters variations.
The figure 3 shows the curve of input u_d and u_q for PMSM using the high order sliding mode observer.

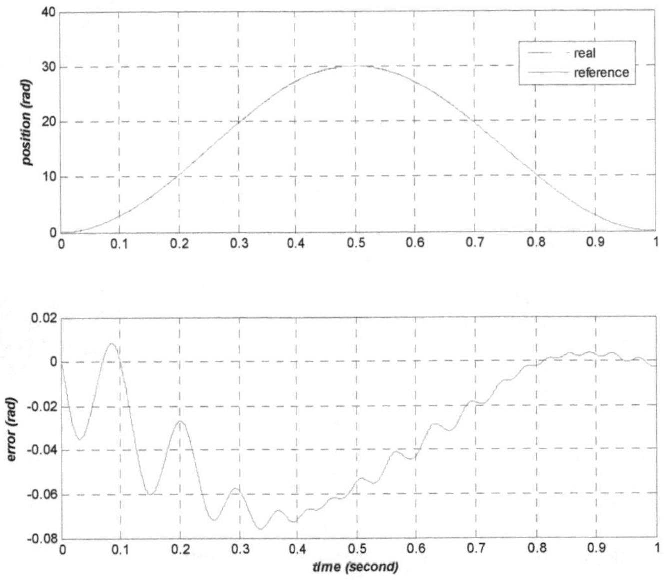

Fig. 2. Reference angle positon and actual angle position.

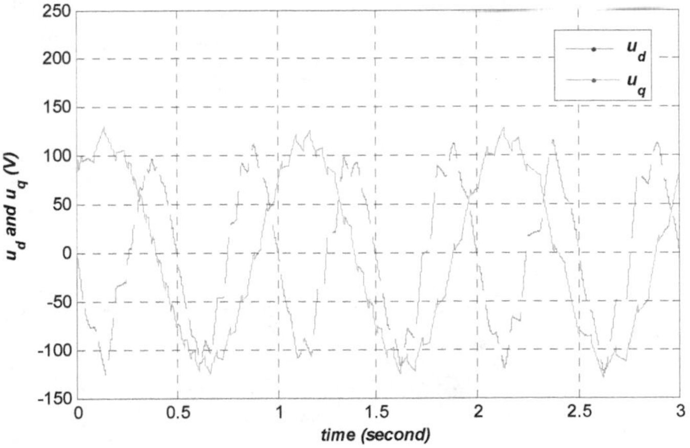

Fig. 3. The curve of input u_d and u_q .

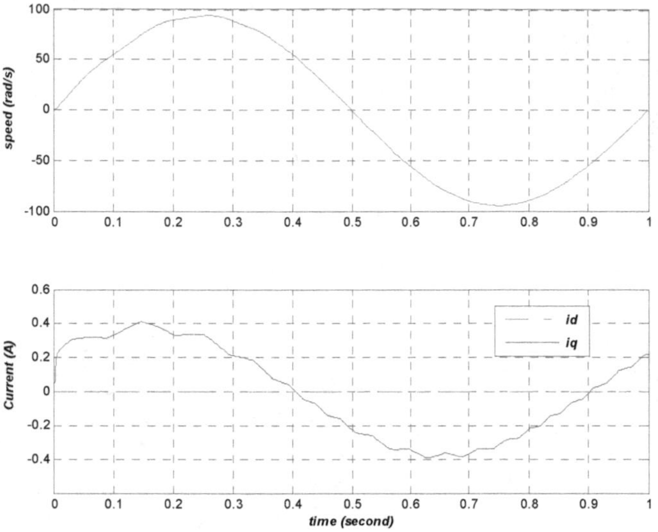

Fig. 4. Four quadrant run and quadrature/direct axis currents.

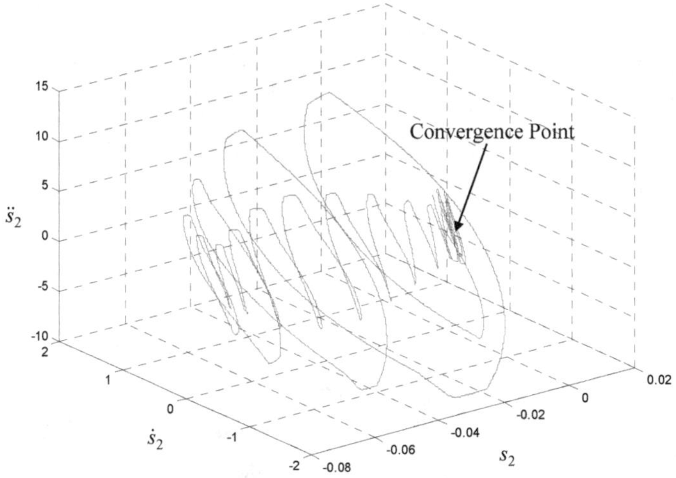

Fig. 5. Sliding mode variables s_2, $\dot{s}_2$ and $\ddot{s}_2$.

The figure 4 is the speed and d-q axis current of synchronous motor. The motor in the four-quadrant operation, with acceleration, deceleration, has good dynamic performance. In this figure, direct axis current i_d is very near reference $i_{dref} = 0$.
The figure 5 shows that sliding mode variable s_2 converge into origin in three dimensional surface within limited time.

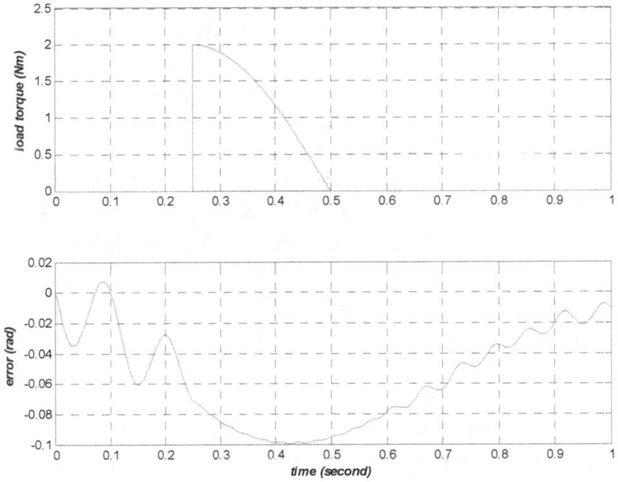

Fig. 6. Tracking error of motor with the load torque disturbance.

The Figure 6 shows the controller is strong robustness versus the load torque variations. The error of angular position does not exceed 0.1 rad even though the load perturbation.
To sum up, this section takes the multiple-input multiple-output nonlinear permanent magnet synchronous motor as control object, and designs a robust high order sliding mode controller with differentiator, through the state feedback linearization to decouple the system. The simulation results show that, despite the existence of parameter uncertainties and external disturbances, the system still has a better dynamic performance and robustness, which is due to higher order sliding mode control converge within limited time. Comparing with the traditional sliding mode control, high order sliding mode control eliminates the chattering phenomenon. And the better test results prove the feasibility of the theory.

2.2.2 States estimation

The parameters and state estimation of permanent magnet synchronous motor has been more concerned in motor control. As the motor itself is a typical nonlinear, multivariable system with strong coupling, there are a lot algorithms to improve the motor control performance in recent years. Earlier off-line estimation of the static dynamic system can not satisfy the control requirements; the use of extended Kalman filter (EKF) usually have a group of high order nonlinear equations, which is not conducive to the calculation (Yan, 2006), and its stability is also a local stable; In least squares procedure, the matrix forgotten factor (Poznyak et al, 1999; Poznyak, 1999) is used to solve non-static parameter identification; as a result of sliding mode control with strong robustness and global convergence, In recent years, sliding mode observer (Floret-Pontet, 2001; Koshkouei, 2002) has been used for dynamic system state and parameter estimation, but the observer feedback gain is usually not easy to choose.

With the development of nonlinear theory, in order to enhance the performance of permanent magnet synchronous motor, many advanced control strategies have been proposed and used in motor control, which requires the state of motor can be measured, such as mechanical angular position, rotational speed, the electrical current and so on. Hence mechanical, electromagnetic or photoelectric sensor are needed, as well known to all, the sensors have many other shortcomings such as drift, friction, high costs, as well as electromagnetic interference caused by additional conductors. Therefore, the control system should be as possible as release the use of sensors to ensure the reliability and stability, which requires the system observer to precisely estimate the value of the state.

The high order sliding mode control is widely used in last decade, which take high order derivetives of sliding mode variables to substitute original discrete control, so that the chattering disappears in the high order differentiation. This section uses a high order sliding mode observer with differentiator algorithm to estimates the value of state variables. In this case, it removes the speed and current sensors of motor, and a better control precision and accurate state estimation are obtained.

In this section, the mathematical model of PMSM is the same with above section (33). In order to make control effectiveness more smooth, the relative order is raised artificially. Considering control input $\dot{u}$ as a new input, original sliding mode variable (35) and (37) are transformed into

$$\begin{aligned} \ddot{s}_1 &= A_1{}' + B_{11}{}'\dot{u}_1 \\ s_2^{(4)} &= A_2{}' + B_{21}{}'\dot{u}_1 + B_{22}{}'\dot{u}_2 \end{aligned} \tag{51}$$

Then, the coefficient matrix of original system A_1, A_2, B_{11}, B_{21} and B_{22} become new matrixes $A_1{}'$, $A_2{}'$, $B_{11}{}'$, $B_{21}{}'$ and $B_{22}{}'$. Where,

$$\begin{aligned} A_1{}' = {} & k_4(k_4x_3 + k_5x_2x_4 + k_6u_1) + k_5[(k_1x_3 + k_2)x_4 + k_3x_2]x_4 \\ & + k_5x_2(k_7x_2 + k_8x_2x_3 + k_9x_4 + k_{10}u_2) - \ddot{x}_{3ref} \end{aligned}$$

$$\begin{aligned} A_2{}' = {} & (k_1k_5x_4^2 + k_1k_7x_3 + k_1k_8x_3^2 + k_2k_7 + k_2k_8x_3 + k_3^2)[(k_1x_3 + k_2)x_4 + k_3x_2] \\ & + (k_1k_4x_4 + k_1k_7x_2 + 2k_1k_8x_2x_3 + k_1k_9x_4 + k_2k_8x_2 + k_1k_{10}u_2 + k_1k_3x_4)(k_4x_3 \\ & + k_5x_2x_4 + k_6u_1) + 2k_1k_5x_2x_4 + k_1k_6u_1 + k_1k_9x_3 + k_2k_9 + k_1k_3x_3 + (k_1k_4x_3 \\ & + k_2k_3)(k_7x_2 + k_8x_2x_3 + k_9x_4 + k_{10}u_2) - x_{3ref}^{(4)} \end{aligned}$$

$$B_{11}{}' = k_6 \ ;$$

$$B_{21}{}' = k_1k_6x_4 \ ;$$

$$B_{22}{}' = (k_1x_3 + k_2)k_{10} \ ;$$

Next, it still is high order sliding mode controller design that make the sliding mode variables converge into origin within limited time in the sliding mode surface. In another word, it should satisfy following conditions.

$$\begin{aligned} S_1 &= \{x \in X \mid s_1(x,t) = \dot{s}_1(x,t) = 0\} \\ S_2 &= \{x \in X \mid s_2(x,t) = \dot{s}_2(x,t) = \ddot{s}_2(x,t) = \dddot{s}_2(x,t) = 0\} \end{aligned} \tag{52}$$

Let $s = [\ddot{s}_1, s_2^{(4)}]^T$, $u = [\dot{u}_1, \dot{u}_2]$, this control object is equivalent to stable of following multi-input multi-output system in limited time.

$$s = A' + B'u \tag{53}$$

Due to $s_2^{(4)}$ effected by $\dot{u}_1$ and $\dot{u}_2$, the output of this system are coupled. Here, input-output feedback linearization technology is used to decouple system.

$$u = \frac{1}{L_g L_f^{r-1} h(x)} (w - L_f^r h(x)) = B'^{-1} \cdot [-A' + w] \tag{54}$$

After decoupling, the relative degree of s_1 equals 2, so 2 order sliding mode control law is adopted

$$w_1 = -\alpha_1 \operatorname{sgn}(\dot{s}_1 + |s_1|^{1/2} \operatorname{sgn}(s_1)) \tag{55}$$

Where, α_1 is a positive constant. Now, we use the output of sliding mode differentiator z_{01} and z_{11} to estimate the value of s_1 and $\dot{s}_1$.

$$\begin{aligned} &\dot{z}_{01} = v_{01}, \quad v_{01} = -\lambda_{01} |z_{01} - s_1|^{1/2} \operatorname{sgn}(z_{01} - s_1) + z_{11} \\ &\dot{z}_{11} = -\lambda_{11} \operatorname{sgn}(z_{11} - v_{01}) \end{aligned} \tag{56}$$

For the motor's angular position control, 4 order sliding mode control law is used. In this case, we only adjust a single parameter α_2 to make the system converge within limited time.

$$\begin{aligned} w_2 = -\alpha_2 \operatorname{sgn}\{\dddot{s}_2 + 3[(\ddot{s}_2)^6 + (\dot{s}_2)^4 + |s_2|^3]^{1/12} \operatorname{sgn}[\ddot{s}_2 + (|\dot{s}_2|^4 \\ + |s_2|^3)^{1/6} \operatorname{sgn}(\dot{s}_2 + 0.5|s_2|^{3/4} \operatorname{sgn}(s_2))]\} \end{aligned} \tag{57}$$

Similarly, the output z_{02}, z_{12}, z_{22} of 3 order differentiator is used to estimated sliding mode variables $s_2, \dot{s}_2, \ddot{s}_2$.

$$\begin{aligned} &\dot{z}_{02} = v_{02}, \quad v_{02} = -\lambda_{02} |z_{02} - s_2|^{3/4} \operatorname{sgn}(z_{02} - s_2) + z_{12}; \\ &\dot{z}_{12} = v_{12}, \quad v_{12} = -\lambda_{12} |z_{12} - v_{02}|^{2/3} \operatorname{sgn}(z_{12} - v_{02}) + z_{22}; \\ &\dot{z}_{22} = v_{22}, \quad v_{22} = -\lambda_{22} |z_{22} - v_{12}|^{1/2} \operatorname{sgn}(z_{22} - v_{12}) + z_{32} \\ &\dot{z}_{32} = -\lambda_{32} \operatorname{sgn}(z_{32} - v_{22}) \end{aligned} \tag{58}$$

Generally speaking, in the actual system not all the state variables is measurable. Sometimes, due to the limitation of condition, some state variables can not be measured. Therefore, it requires the controller can estimate state variables of system as possible as accurate.
PMSM only uses the position sensors, taking the use of high order sliding mode control techniques, so that its speed and the current state variable are estimated online. In this way, it avoids the use of other sensors, at the same time ensures the motor position tracking progress.
In the design of controller, we have obtained that

$$\dot{s}_1 = k_4 x_3 + k_5 x_2 x_4 + k_6 u_2 - x_{3ref}$$

$$\dot{s}_2 = x_2 - \dot{x}_{1ref}$$

$$\ddot{s}_2 = \ddot{x}_1 - \ddot{x}_{1ref} = (k_1 x_3 + k_2) x_4 + k_3 x_2 - \ddot{x}_{1ref} \tag{59}$$

From the above equations, we can calculate the speed estimation of synchronous motor $\tilde{x}_2 = \dot{s}_2 + \dot{x}_{1ref}$, so the current estimation expressed by

$$\begin{aligned} \tilde{x}_3 &= \frac{1}{k_4}[\dot{s}_1 - k_5 \tilde{x}_4 (\dot{s}_2 + \dot{x}_{1ref}) - k_6 u_2] \\ \tilde{x}_4 &= \frac{\ddot{s}_2 - k_3(\dot{s}_2 + \dot{x}_{1ref}) + \ddot{x}_{1ref}}{k_1 \tilde{x}_3 + k_2} \end{aligned} \tag{60}$$

For calculating $\tilde{x}_3$ and $\tilde{x}_4$, considering sliding mode variables $\dot{s}_1$, $\dot{s}_2$, $\ddot{s}_2$ and u_2 as known value, adopt recursive algorithm to get

$$\begin{aligned} \tilde{x}_{3(j+1)} &= \frac{1}{k_4}[\dot{s}_{1(j)} - k_5 \tilde{x}_{4(j)} (\dot{s}_{2(j)} + \dot{x}_{1ref}) - k_6 u_{2(j)}] \\ \tilde{x}_{4(j+1)} &= \frac{\ddot{s}_{2(j)} - k_3(\dot{s}_{2(j)} + \dot{x}_{1ref}) + \ddot{x}_{1ref}}{k_1 \tilde{x}_{3(j)} + k_2} \quad j = 1, 2, \cdots \end{aligned} \tag{61}$$

Where, j is the j-th sample point of system, $j+1$ is the next sample point. Through the above recursive equation, current estimation $\tilde{x}_3$ and $\tilde{x}_4$ are obtained. Take these estimation into the control system so that save the sensors. Thereby, system become more simple and reliability.
In the simulation, we use the DutyMAX95-BSC060300 permanent magnetic synchronous motor. The parameters of motor are $P = 3$, $R = 3.3\Omega$, $L_d = 0.027H$, $L_q = 0.0034H$, $\psi_f = 0.341Wb$, $B = 0.0034N \cdot m \cdot s$, $J = 0.0037kg \cdot m^2$. A phase current of the maximum accepted value is $6.0A$, the load torque maximum value is $6N \cdot m$, and angular velocity is $3000rpm$.
The parameter of controller are $\alpha_1 = 5$ and $\alpha_2 = 50$; the parameter of sliding mode differentiator are $\lambda_{01} = 2$, $\lambda_{11} = 1.5$, $\lambda_{02} = 25$, $\lambda_{12} = 25$, $\lambda_{22} = 33$ and $\lambda_{32} = 500$.

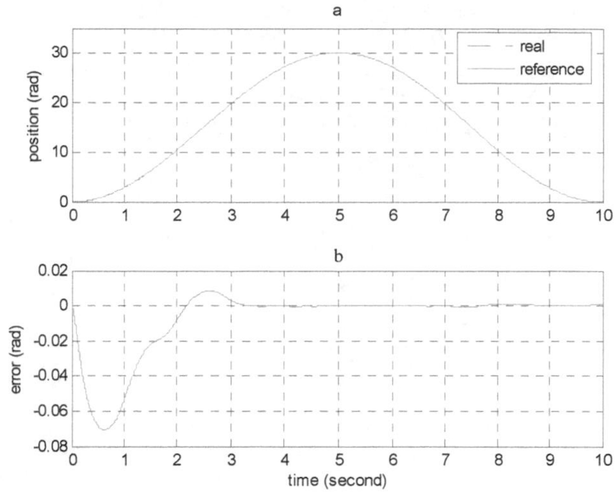

Fig. 7. Position tracking and error curve of PMSM.

From the figure 7 above, it can be seen that the permanent magnet synchronous motor control system has good performance. This figure shows the permanent magnet synchronous motor can precisely track the given position. And the error between reference and the actual position feedback is shown in Figure 7 below. The maximal error does not exceed to 0.08 rad.

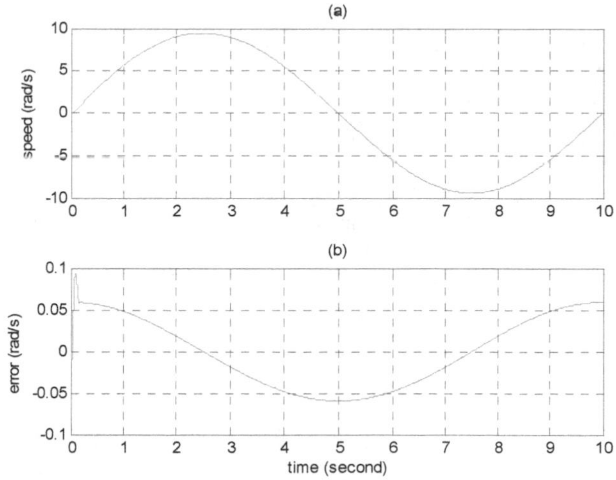

Fig. 8. Speed estimation and error curve of PMSM.

The figure 8 above shows the motor angular speed by derivative of the motor's angular position. The figure 8 below shows the error between the estimation of the electrical angular speed.

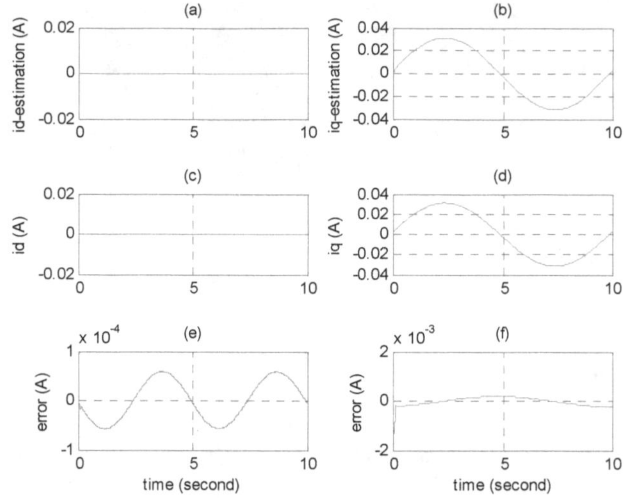

Fig. 9. The direct/quadrature axis currents and their estimations.

For permanent magnet synchronous motor, its angular position, speed and current are system state values. The figure 9(a), (b), (c), (d) shows that the estimated value and actual current value of direct axis and quadrature axis respectively. The figure 9(e), (f) are the error between actual current value and the estimated value. In this figure, the error of direct axis current is between $\pm 1.0\times 10^{-4}(A)$, and the error of quadrature axis is between $\pm 1.0\times 10^{-3}(A)$.

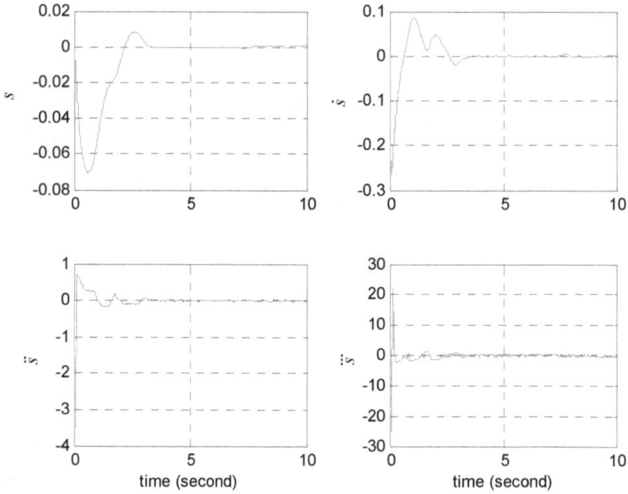

Fig. 10. System sliding mode variables curve.

The figure 10 is the convergence curve of sliding mode variable and its high order derivatives. From the figure we can clearly see that the discrete control law acts on the high

order sliding mode surface, which makes the lower sliding mode surface smooth. That is the reason why high order sliding mode control can eliminate the chattering.
This subsection focuses on a state estimation of PMSM online. In the practical systems, not all the state variables are measurable, or because of objective reasons they are often not easy to measure. In this section, we just use the motor position sensor, through the high order sliding mode control with differentiator, to achieve the state variables of motor estimation online. The simulation results show that the PMSM control system has good dynamic performance, while the electrical angular speed and d-q axis current are estimated precisely.

2.2.3 Torque disturbance identification

In high precious servo control, the disturbance load will impact servo control. Therefore, the estimation of the disturbance load is very necessary to reduce its influence. Usually in the actual system, the disturbance load torque is often random and uncertain. So, this requires the controller can estimate the value of state variables as accurately as possible. This section will use the arbitrary order sliding mode differentiator, to calculate the high order derivative of sliding mode variables online, so as to avoid the complexity of differential calculation. Then, through the expression of the unknown disturbance load torque, it is estimated. Take the estimation as system input, thereby enhancing the system performance. In the simulation, the position and current sensors of PMSM are used. Adopt high order sliding mode control, its disturbance torque is estimated online. Then, the unknown uncertain external disturbance torque can be entered as a known value so that improve the motor position tracking accuracy.
In order to facilitate the description, the mathematical model of motor still use system state equation (31) in d-q axis coordinate. The meaning of the parameters remains unchanged. Then, from the mathematical model of PMSM, the following solution can easily get

$$\tilde{T}_l = p[(L_d - L_q)x_3 + \psi_f]x_4 - B\tilde{x}_2 - J\tilde{\dot{x}}_2 \tag{62}$$

In equation (62), $\tilde{T}_l$ is the estimation of external torque. $\tilde{x}_2$ and $\tilde{\dot{x}}_2$ are the estimation of angular speed and angular acceleration respectively.
From the controller of previous section, the following expression can be obtained

$$\begin{aligned} \dot{s}_2 &= x_2 - \dot{x}_{1ref} \\ \ddot{s}_2 &= \ddot{x}_1 - \ddot{x}_{1ref} = \dot{x}_2 - \ddot{x}_{1ref} \end{aligned} \tag{63}$$

Therefore, the above equation (63) can solve the estimation of angular speed and angular acceleration.

$$\begin{aligned} \tilde{x}_2 &= \dot{s}_2 + \dot{x}_{1ref} \\ \tilde{\dot{x}}_2 &= \ddot{s}_2 + \ddot{x}_{1ref} \end{aligned} \tag{64}$$

Until now, if we can get the 1 and 2 order derivative of sliding mode variable s_2, the estimation of state variable $\tilde{x}_2$ and its differentiation $\tilde{\dot{x}}_2$ can be solved. According to the principle of high order sliding mode differentiator, $\dot{s}_2$ and $\ddot{s}_2$ in equation (64) can be estimated by the output of differentiator z_{12} and z_{22}.

$$\begin{aligned} \dot{z}_{02} &= v_0, \quad v_0 = -130\,|\,z_{02} - s_2\,|^{2/3}\,\mathrm{sgn}(z_{02} - s_2) + z_{12} \\ \dot{z}_{12} &= v_1, \quad v_1 = -150\,|\,z_{12} - v_0\,|^{1/2}\,\mathrm{sgn}(z_{12} - v_0) + z_{22} \\ \dot{z}_{22} &= -500\,|\,z_{22} - v_1\,| \end{aligned} \tag{65}$$

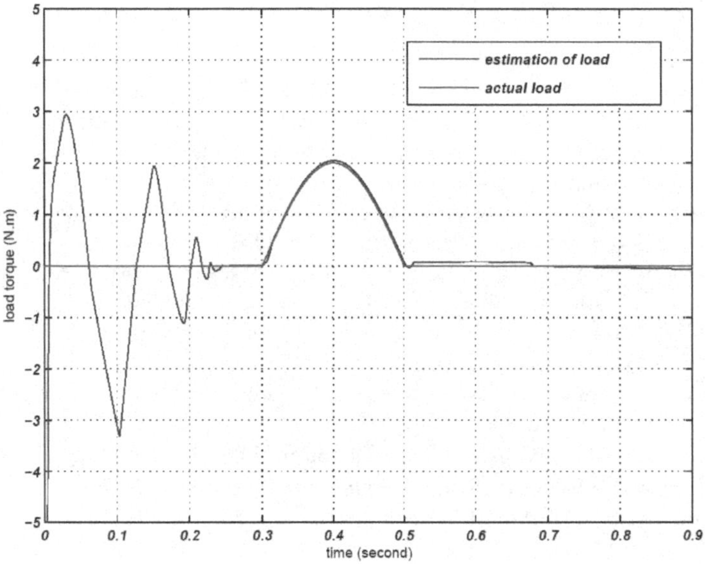

Fig. 11. External disturbance load torque and its estimation of motor. Available into the equation (62).

$$\tilde{T}_l = p[(L_d - L_q)x_3 + \psi_f]x_4 - B(z_{12} + \dot{x}_{1ref}) - J(z_{22} + \ddot{x}_{1ref}) \tag{66}$$

Through calculation online, the estimation of disturbance load is obtained. Take the estimated value into the control system so that the uncertain disturbance load become the determine input. In this case, the system performance is improved effectively.

From the figure 11 we can see that, taking use of high order sliding mode with differentiator, disturbance load torque get a better estimation. Disturbance torque is estimated online successfully so that it is no longer unknown uncertainties factor. It also improves the performance of the system. The maximum torque value is $2N \cdot m$ in the figure. The sliding mode variable converges into origin at the 0.25s.

The figure 12 shows that the actual angular position track reference of PMSM with the disturbance load. From the figure we can see that the maximum error of the angular position is not more than 0.12 rad. The system gets a better control performance.

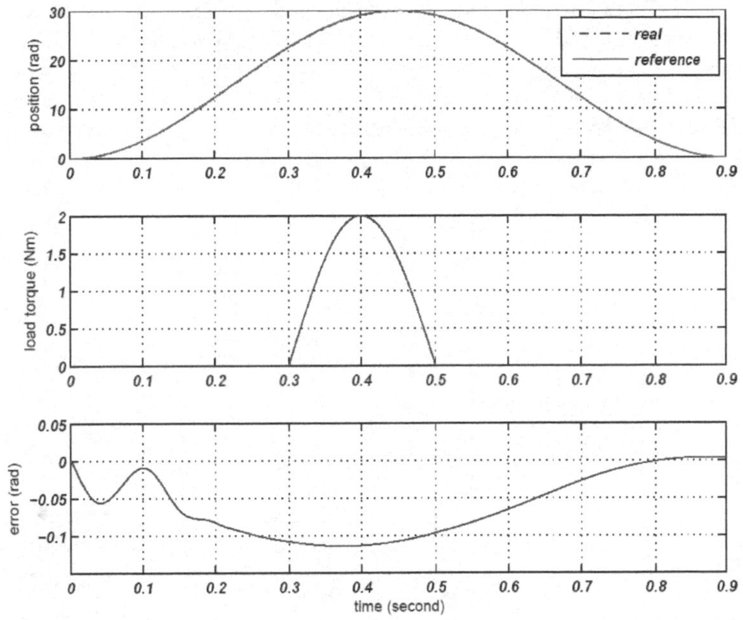

Fig. 12. Position tracking curve with load torque disturbance.

2.4 Experimental results and analysis

The dSPACE is a equipment of control exploitation and test system based on MATLAB/Simulink that is from Germany. It implements seamless link with the MATLAB/Simulink completely. It can complete the control algorithm design, test and implementation, overcoming the shortage of the traditional control system, for example, the difficult to achieve the complex algorithm and the long development cycle. It has advantages of high speed, ease to use and user-friendly.

Taking DS1005PPC control board as the core, with DS2001AD acquisition board, DS2002/2003 multi-channel AD acquisition board, CP4002 Multi-I/O board, DS2102DA output board, DS3002 incremental encoder interface board, we constitute a standard component hardware parts of dSPACE DS1005 system, which is used in this experiment.

After the completion of the experimental platform, the development steps of control system for PMSM based on the dSPACE include the following points:

1. MATLAB/Simulink modeling and off-line simulation. Take use of MATLAB/Simulink to establish a mathematical model for the simulation object, and design control programs. At the same time, complete the system off-line simulation.
2. Input/output interface (I/O) experimental model. In the MATLAB/Simulink environment, we need to retain module that is downloaded to the dSPACE. Select the real-time control required for I/O modules from the RTI library. Replace the original connection relationship with the hardware interface, and configure I/O parameters. In some special cases, we also need to set up hardware and software interrupt priority levels.

3. The dSPACE/RTW provides tools to automatically generate code and download. Since MATLAB and dSPACE with seamless connectivity features, a simple operation can complete real-time C code generation, compile, link and download for the target system. In other word, model is downloaded into target board DS1005PPC as running program.
4. The dSPACE integrated experiment and debugging. The dSPACE provides real-time ControlDesk software as well, which changes the parameters and real-time control.

The figure 13 is a control system in MATLAB/Simulink environment with the dSPACE/RTI module.

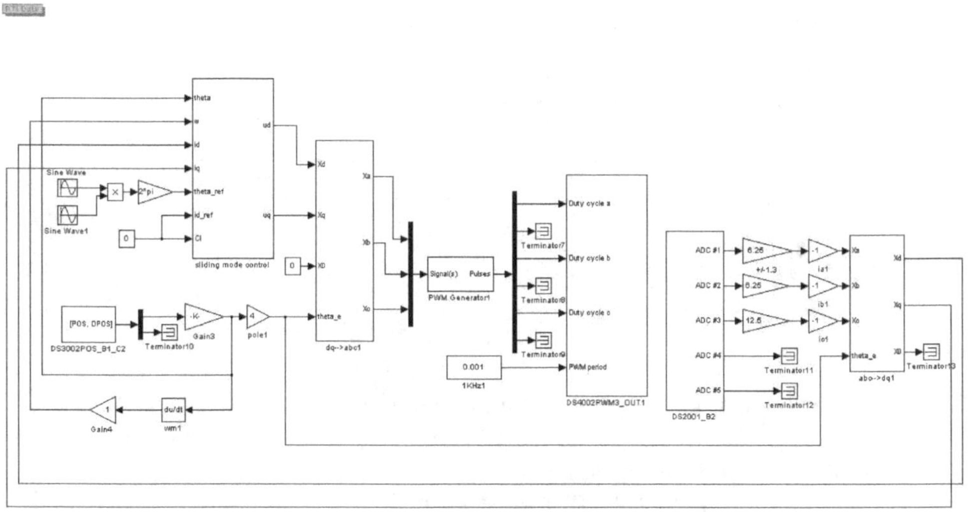

Fig. 13. MATLAB/Simulink environment based on dSPACE/RTI control system.

i. Content and intention:
1. Validate feasibility of high order sliding mode control in PMSM;
2. Test system using high sliding mode control whether it can release chattering phenomenon;
3. Test system using high sliding mode control whether it has robustness.

ii. Equipments:

Name	Type	Unit	Amount
dSPACE controller	DS1005	Dais	1
DC regulated power	WYK-303B2	Dais	1
Slide-wire rheostat	BX8D-3/7	Dais	3
Switch regulated power	S-100-24	Dais	1
Universal meter	LINI-T/UT58A	Dais	1
Ondoscope	Tektronix/TDS2024	Dais	1
Industrial computer	ADLINK	Dais	1

Table 1. The list of experimental equipments.

iii. Experimental procession:

Step 1: Off-line simulation. According to the principle of high order sliding mode control and differentiator, combining with chapter 5 of the application for permanent magnet synchronous motor, the theoretical simulation is researched in the MATLAB/Simulink firstly. In detail, set the sampling frequency and differential equation solution, and save the .mdl model file;

Step 2: After the control algorithm verification, remove the inverter model and motor model replaced by the physical prototypes of actual system. And then complete all of the system interface, including the A /D, D/A, I/O, PWM and other interfaces of the dSPACE. Afterwards, compile on-line to generate. cof configuration file;

Step 3: Check all connections are correct. After that, start the dSPACE. Compile and download files real-time (RTI) in the environment of MATLAB/Simulink. At this moment, algorithm program code is downloaded to the DSP core program area of dSPACE controller;

Step 4: Start the dSPACE/ControlDesk. Create an experimental file .prj in the interface, and design the required .lay layer file. Observe compiler-generated variable file .sdf in order to facilitate observe the real-time dynamic performance of the system;

Step 5: After the completion of the above, check the status of external devices is good or not. Finally, start bus power, while start system operation in dSPACE/ControlDesk interface.

iv. Controlled device:

The controlled object in experiments uses non-salient pole permanent magnet synchronous motor of Delta's ASMT series, whose main parameters are as follows table 2:

Name	Value	Unit
Resistance	$R = 3.052$	Ω
Inductance	$L_d = 8.4$	mH
Rating Power	$P = 1.0$	kW
Torque	$T = 3.3$	$N \cdot m$
Pole-pairs	$N_p = 4$	---
Voltage	$U = 300$	V
Speed	$n_N = 3000$	$r / \min$
Rotary inertia	$J = 0.00026$	$kg \cdot m^2$

Table 2. Parameters of PMSM in experiment d.

Host-computer control surface adopts visual man-machine surface the dSPACE/ControDesk to realize data acquisition and display. Figure 14 is pictorial diagram based on the dSPACE control system. The system consists of inverter, isolation circuit, detection circuit, power circuit and etc.

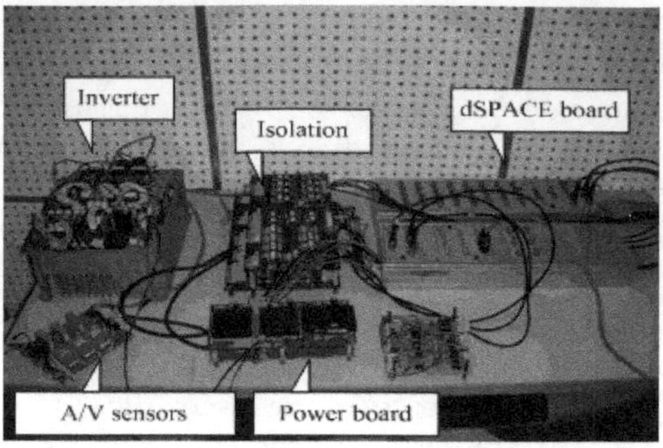

Fig. 14. Control system hardware circuit with dSPACE interface.

v. Waveform:

Because the research of nonlinear system high order sliding mode control theory still is in primary stage, it is face with much challenge. For example, it strictly requires all of the system functions are smooth, and norm-bounded. Otherwise, there is the higher derivative of reference value in control law. In our experiment, 60V DC regulated power is supplied. Experiment is tested under the conditions above. The main test results are following.

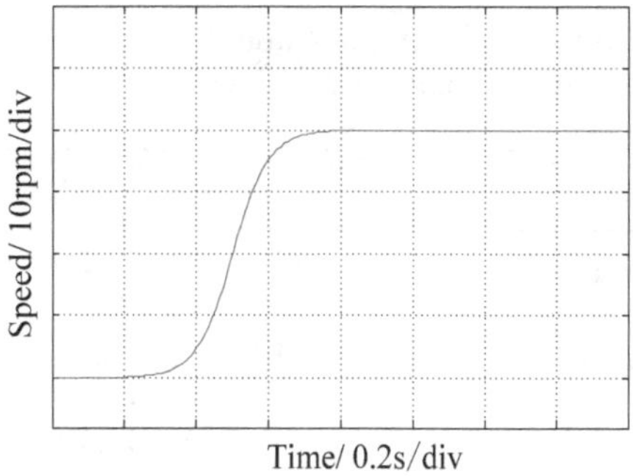

Fig. 15. Speed reference curve of PMSM.

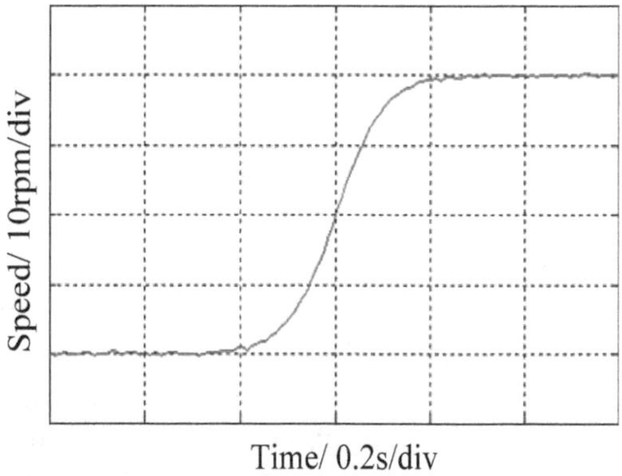

Fig. 16 Dynamic speed feedback curve.

High order sliding mode control law has high derivative of reference signal, so the reference signal must be smooth and continues enough function. For testing speed dynamic response of PMSM in the experiment, the reference signal is set as Fig. 15. Actual measurement of speed dynamic response is shown in Fig. 16.

By comparing Fig. 15 and Fig 16, nonlinear PMSM holds good dynamic tracking character with high order sliding mode control.

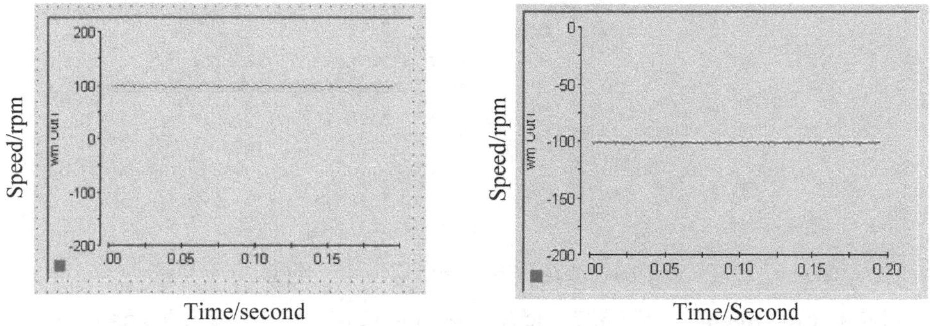

Fig. 17. Steady speed of clockwise/ Anti-clockwize displayed in dSPACE/ControlDesk.

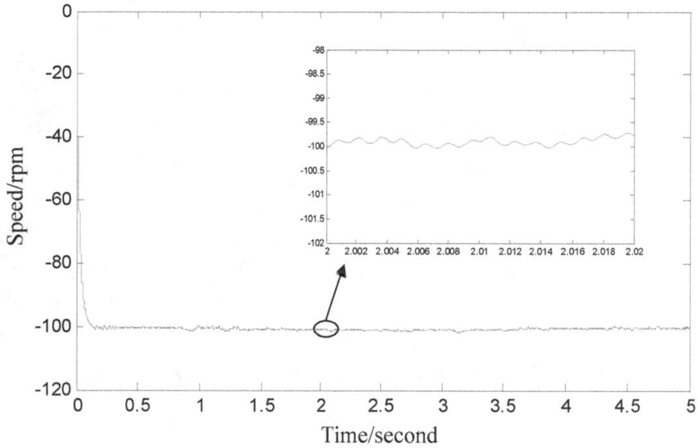

Fig. 18. Speed curve of PMSM in MATLAB/Simulink using traditional sliding mode control.

Fig. 17 is steady speed clockwise/anti-clockwise curve of PMSM. It is can be seen that the PMSM also takes on good steady performance.

The Fig. 18 is outline simulation speed waveform of PMSM using traditional sliding mode control. It displays anti-clockwise speed waveform of PMSM. And the Fig. 19 is outline simulation speed curve of PMSM using high order sliding mode. After partial amplification, comparing with Fig. 18, high order sliding mode control is provided with the ability of avoidance chattering. But, its algorithm is more complicated than tradition. The adjusting time is longer, too.

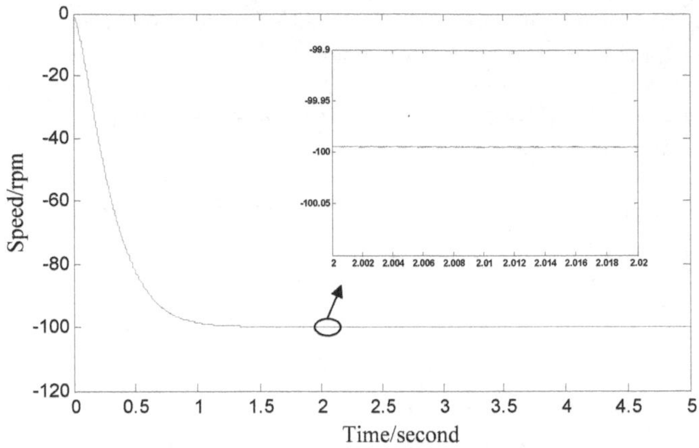

Fig. 19. Speed curve of PMSM in MATLAB/Simulink using high order sliding mode control.

To validate experiment intention 2 and 3, show high order sliding mode control with free chattering and robustness, the experiment designs traditional sliding mode controller, too. Simulation and actual measurement are recorded in order to compare with high order sliding mode.

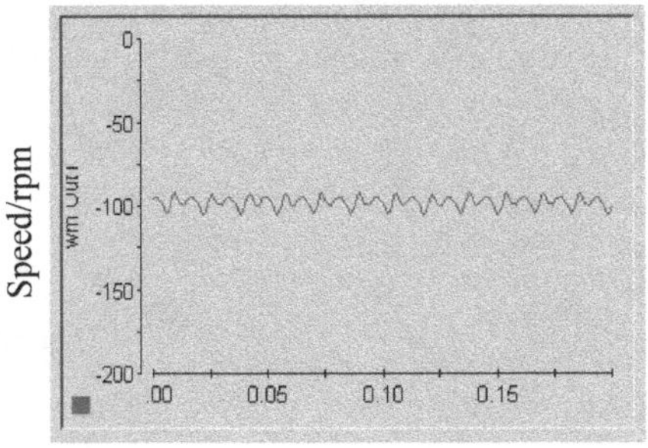

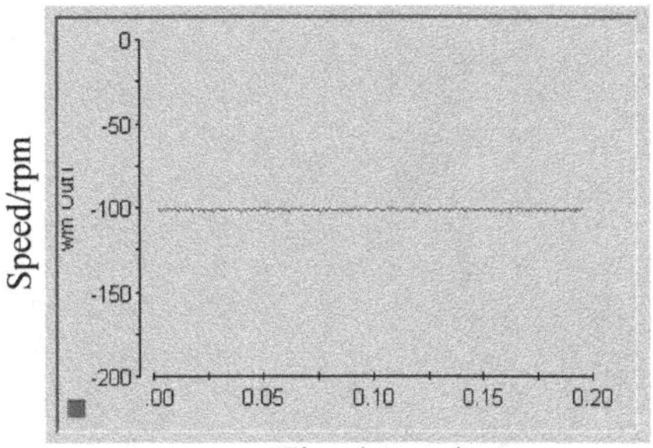

Fig. 20. Speed curve in dSPACE/ControlDesk using traditional/high order sliding mode control.

Due to the traditional sliding mode control uses discontinues control law acting on sliding mode manifold surface, chattering problem is caused. The great of the coefficient in sliding mode control law, the faster of convergence, when the system enter into sliding mode, chattering phenomenon is more obvious. The left figure of Fig. 20 is actual measurement speed curve of PMSM, which adopts conventional sliding mode control. The control law is $u = -K_i \operatorname{sgn} s$, in current loop $K_1 = 5$, in speed loop $K_2 = 8.2$. From the comparison of Fig. 20, we can obtain a conclusion that chattering is released in high order sliding mode.

Hereto, both of simulation and experiment results prove that high order sliding mode control can reduce the chattering phenomenon which exists in conventional. Following experiment will test the robustness of high order sliding mode control.

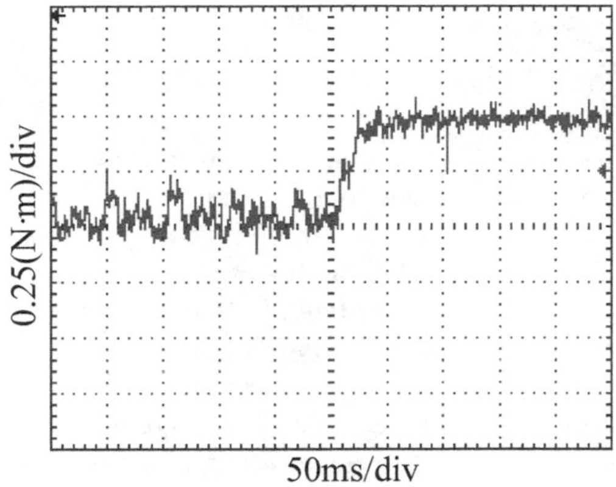

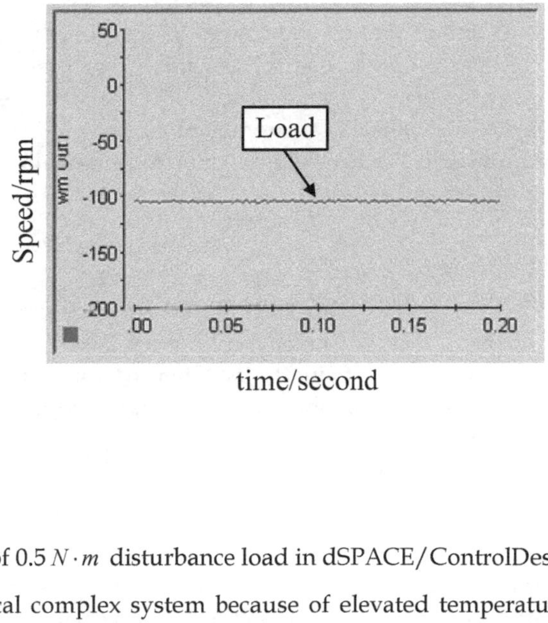

Fig. 21. Speed curve of 0.5 $N \cdot m$ disturbance load in dSPACE/ControlDesk.

The PMSM is a typical complex system because of elevated temperature, saturation, time delay and a good many elements. These reasons lead to the synchronous motor is nonlinear, variation parameter, close coupled system. For the sake of testing high order sliding control, which is insensitive to the parameter uncertainness and disturbance, experiment is injected about 0.5 $N \cdot m$ external load disturbance at the 0.01 second. The speed actual measurement waveform is shown in Fig. 21. From this figure, speed curve is smooth without flutter. The

experiment result illuminates high order sliding mode control reserves robustness of conventional sliding mode.
Experimentally verified, high order sliding mode control provides an effective method to improve accuracy and robustness further for nonlinear systems

3. Conclusion

This chapter applies the research of nonlinear control and high order sliding mode control theory in PMSM control, and achieves robust control for a PMSM in spit of the internal parameter uncertainties and unknown external disturbance load torque. The simulation results show good performance; in addition, the estimation online of system state variables is also one of the hot issues in the control field. In this chapter, a new design based on high order sliding mode with differentiator for PMSM, access to the state variable estimation; Besides, unknown uncertain load impacts the performance of motor control. In order to improve system performance, this chapter also achieves external disturbance load estimation online. It makes sure the load can be accurately estimated.
This chapter described dSPACE physics experiment control platform the build and development process in detail. Through the dSPACE real-time control platform, the nonlinear high order sliding mode control theory research is applied to the control of permanent magnet synchronous motor. The experimental results and simulation results are consistently indicate that synchronous motor has better dynamic performance and steady accuracy, proves the feasibility of this technology in practical application systems; It is also verified by high order sliding mode control technique that preserves the robustness of traditional sliding mode control. The high order sliding mode essentially eliminates the chattering caused by discrete control law. From another point of view, the simulation and physical experiment provide a certain reference value for the nonlinear systems high order sliding mode control further application.

4. Acknowledgment

I would like to express my gratitude to all those who helped me during the writing. A special acknowledgement should be shown to Professor Salah Laghrouche, from whose lectures I benefited greatly. I am particularly indebted to Prof. Liu Weiguo, who gave me kind encouragement and useful instructions all through my writing. Finally I wish to extend my thanks to my university. This chapter is supported by the Basic Research Foundation of Northwestern Polytechnical University.

5. References

Emelyanov, S.V.; Korovin, S.K. & Levantovskiy, A. (1990). New class of second order sliding algorithm. *Mathematical modeling*, Vol.2, No.3, pp. 85-100

Emelyanov, S.V.; Korovin, S.K., & Levant, A. (1996). High-order sliding modes in control systems. *Computational mathematics and modeling*, Vol.7, No.3, pp.294-318, ISSN: 1046-283X

Levant A. (1993). Sliding order and sliding accuracy in sliding mode control. *International Journal of Control*, Vol. 58, No.6, pp.1247-1263, ISSN: 0020-7179

Levant A. (1998). Robust exact differentiation via sliding mode technique. *Automatica*, Vol.34, No.3, pp.379-384, ISSN: 0005-1098

Levant A., Pridor A., Ben-Asher J.Z., Gitizadeh R. & Yaesh I. (2000). 2-sliding mode implementation in aircraft pitch control. *Journal of Guidance Control and Dynamics*, Vol.23, No.4, pp.586-594, ISSN 0731-5090

Levant A. (2003). Higher-order sliding modes, differentiation and output feedback control. *International Journal of Control*, Vol.76, No.9, pp.924-941, ISSN: 0020-7179

Bartolini G.; Ferrara A. & Usai E. (1997). Application of a sub-optimal discontinuous control algorithm for uncertain second order systems. *International Journal of Robust and Nonlinear Control*, Vol. 7, No.4, pp.299-319, ISSN: 1049-8923

Bartolini G., Ferrara A. & Giacomini. (1999). A robust control design for a class of uncertain nonlinear systems featuring a second order sliding mode. *International Journal of Control*, Vol. 72, No.4, pp.321-331, ISSN: 0020-7179

Bartolini G., Ferrara A. & Punta E. (2000). Multi-input second order sliding mode hybrid control of constrained manipulators. *Dynamics and Control*, Vol. 10, pp.277-296, ISSN: 0925-4668

Fridman L. & Levant A. (2002). High order sliding mode. In: *Sliding Mode Control in Engineering*, W. Perruquetti and J.P. Barbot, editors, pp.53-102. Marcel Dekker, ISBN: 0824706714, New York

Utkin V.I. (1992). *Sliding modes in control and optimization*. Springer-Verlag, ISBN: 3540535 160

Glumineau A., Hamy M., Lanier C. & Moog C. (1993). Robust control of a brushless servo motor via sliding mode. *International Journal of Control*, vol.58, pp.979–990, ISSN: 0020-7179.

Ziribi M., Ramirez Sira H. & Ngai A. (2001). Static and dynamic sliding mode control schemes for a permanent magnet stepper motor. *International Journal of Control*, vol.74, No.2, pp.103-117, ISSN: 0020-7179.

Caravani P. & Gennaro S. D. (1998). Robust control of synchronous motor with non-linear and parameter uncertainties. *Automatica*, vol.34, pp.445-450, ISSN: 0005-1098.

Yan Y., Zhu J., Guo Y., & Lu H. (2006). Modeling and simulation of direct torque controlled pmsm drive system incorporating structural and saturation saliencies. *Industry Applications Conference. 41st IAS Annual Meeting.*, vol.1, pp. 76–83, Oct. 2006

Poznyak A. S. & Medel J. (1999). Matrix forgetting with adaptation. *International Journal of Systems Science*, vol.30, No.(8), pp. 865–878, ISSN :0020-7721.

Poznyak, A. S. (1999) Matrix forgetting factor. *International Journal of Systems Science*, vol.30, No.2, pp.165-174, ISSN :0020-7721.

Floret-Pontet F. & Lamnabhi-Lagarrigue F. (2001). Parameter identification methodology using sliding mode observers. *International Journal of Control*, vol.74, pp.1743-1753, ISSN: 0020-7179.

Koshkouei A. & Zinober A. (2002). Sliding mode observers for a class of nonlinear systems. *Proceedings of American Control Conference*, vol. 8, pp. 2106 - 2111, Anchorage, Alaska, USA, 2002.

14

Robust Control of Sensorless AC Drives Based on Adaptive Identification

Birou M.T. Iulian
Technical University of Cluj-Napcoa, Department of Electrical Drives and Robots
Romania

1. Introduction

In most of the modern drive systems with alternating current (AC) machines which require rotor speed control, the main task is to design and develop different controllers, able to achieve high dynamic performance and to maintain the system response within specified tolerances, for a wide range of speed and torque values, for parameter variations and for external perturbations like: total inertia moment, friction coefficient, etc. (Leonhard, 1985). Various concepts for controlled AC drives without speed sensor (sensorless control) have been developed in the past few years (Holtz, 2002; Rajashekara et al., 1996; Vas, 1998). Ongoing research has focused on providing sustained operation at high dynamic performance at very low speed, including zero speed and zero stator frequency (Akatsu & Kawamura, 2000; Holtz & Quan, 2002; Hurst et al., 1998; Lascu et al., 2005). In speed sensorless control, motor parameter sensitivity is an important and large discussed and analyzed problem (Akpolat et al., 2000; Toliyat et al., 2003). In many existing speed identification algorithms, the rotor speed is estimated based on the rotor flux observer. Therefore, these algorithms are, to a certain degree, machine parameter dependent. The solution proposed in this chapter is to apply robust control to sensorless AC drive systems.
The designing procedure of the speed controllers can be very difficult, if a complex mathematical model of the plant (here of the AC machine) is used. But robust controllers keep the dynamic and stability performance of the controlled system even if structured or unstructured uncertainties appear. That's why, robust speed controllers can be designed by using simplified models of the AC machines, and have to be used in a complex structure based on the field-oriented control (FOC) principle (Birou & Pavel, 2008). Thus, the requirements of a digital control application are: a flexible control structure, reduced hardware configuration and a good dynamic behavior of the controlled process. The last two aspects can be realized by finding a compromise between the reducing of the control cycle times and the increasing of controller complexity. For industrial applications the hardware costs are also important.
Two different algorithms will be presented to estimate the rotor speed in this chapter, one based on the model reference adaptive system (MRAS) and the other on a full order observer (FOO). The speed identification algorithms, the designing procedure of the optimal H_∞ controller and the robust control of the sensorless driving system will be accomplished by simulated and experimental results. Based on the results obtained, advantages and disadvantages of the proposed control structures will be discussed.

2. Control of AC machines

Electrical machines are the major and most efficient source to generate motion for a large number of applications in a wide range of power (from μW to several hundred of MW). Among all types of electromechanical converters, the AC machines are now, from fare, the most produced and used in variable speed applications, because of their high performance/cost ratio. If for low power applications (i.e. servo drives), generally permanent magnet synchronous machines (PM-SM) and for very high powers electrical excited synchronous machines (SM) are used, the largest number of applications use rotor cage induction machines (IM) because of their higher mechanical robustness and lower cost (Birou et al., 2010; Holtz, 2002; Kelemen & Imecs, 1991; Leonhard, 1985; Moreira et al., 1991; Wieser, 1998; Trzynadlowski, 1994). The main disadvantage of using in the past the IM as motion source in variable speed applications, namely the difficulty to precisely control speed and/or torque, is now compensate by using:

- power electronics in wide power range (voltage-source or current-source converters), to fed AC machines with variable amplitude/frequency power signals (voltage or current);
- modern control methods, like field oriented based vector control (VC) or direct torque control (DTC) strategies of AC drive systems;
- high frequency, real-time, digital computing systems, based on microcontrollers (μC) or digital signal processors (DSP), able to implement an perform the designed strategies and control methods.

Depending on the dynamic performances, energy efficiency demands and final cost of the electrical drive system, following control strategies can be used:

- scalar control (SC) of AC machines, considering the two torque producing components of the electrical machine (the current and the electromagnetic flux) only as scalar variables, without information about their phasorial positions. The current, speed or position control loops are able to impose good enough dynamic performances for a large number of applications;
- vector control (VC) of AC machines, based on the field-oriented control (FOC) principle, where the motion control loop (position, speed or torque loop) and the magnetizing control loop (flux loop) are decoupled by using the flux phasor (vector) as reference system and splitting the current phasor into an active and a reactive component. This control strategy is the most computer time and effort demanding (revealed also in the costs of the system) but ensure the best dynamic performances and energy efficiency in variable speed control;
- direct torque control (DTC) of AC machines, used widely in variable torque applications like electric traction systems, based on the direct control of the torque producing current, considering the limited number of possible topologic configurations of one of the power converter components, namely the pulse width modulated (PWM) inverter.

In the designing procedure of the controllers, it is important to know the transfer function of the process. A transfer function which describes exactly the behavior of the AC machine is almost impossible to obtain, because of the nonlinearities of the mathematical model of the machine. Consequently a simplified transfer function of the process is used to design the speed controller. Then, the control law is introduced in the not simplified and nonlinear "original" control structure, in order to simulate and analyze the dynamic behavior of the mechanical and electrical variables (speed, torque, currents, voltages, etc.). In our drive system, the simplified transfer function describes the linear model of the AC machine corresponding to a steady state working point and is presented in Fig. 1. A vector control strategy will be applied to control the variable speed electrical drive systems discussed in this chapter. For the proposed FOC of the AC machine, the rotor flux vector is considered to be the reference system. In this case the speed controller has as input the speed error Δn_r and computes the control variable as the active component of the stator current $i^*_{Active}=i_{sq\lambda r}$, as described by Equation 1.

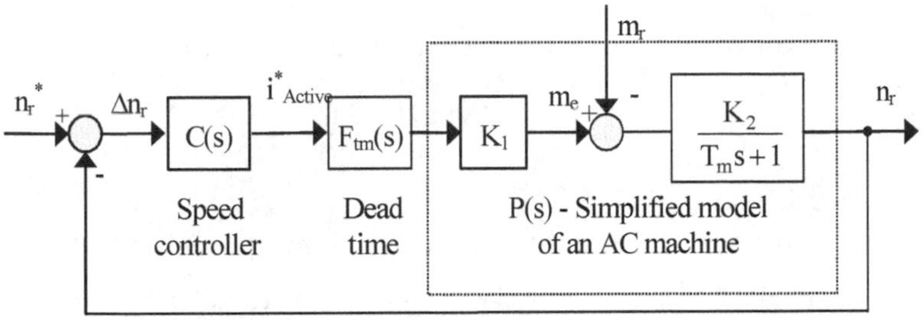

Fig. 1. Simplified speed close-loop control structure of an ac machine.

Using the torque producing expression:

$$m_e = \frac{3}{2} z_p \frac{L_m}{L_r} \Im m\left(\underline{i}_s \underline{\Psi}_r^*\right) = \frac{3}{2} z_p \frac{L_m}{L_r} \Psi_r i_{sq\lambda_r}, \tag{1}$$

with L_m and L_r the magnetic (mutual) and rotor inductance respectively, z_p the number of pole pairs and the motion equation

$$m_e = Js\omega_r + B\omega_r + m_r, \tag{2}$$

where J is the total moment of inertia, B the friction coefficient, s the derivate symbol and ω_r the rotor angular velocity

$$\omega_r = \frac{\omega}{z_p} = n_r \frac{2\pi}{60}, \tag{3}$$

with ω the electrical angular velocity and n_r the rotor speed. The simplified transfer function of the rotor-flux oriented AC machine can be written:

$$P(s) = \frac{n_r}{i_{sq\lambda r}^*} = K_1 \frac{K_2}{T_m s+1} = \frac{K_m}{T_m s+1}. \tag{4}$$

If we apply to the speed control loop presented in Fig. 1 the module criteria and consider the non compensable component described by the dead-time transfer function:

$$F_{t.m}(s) = e^{-\tau_m s}, \tag{5}$$

the speed controller will have a transfer function as follows:

$$C_{PI}(s) = K_P \cdot \left(1 + \frac{1}{T_i s}\right). \tag{6}$$

It results a classical PI controller, having K_p - the proportional coefficient and $K_i = K_p / T_i$ - the integrator coefficient. Considering the two first-order integrator type transfer functions of the direct loop having constant times of different ranges, with $\tau_m << T_m$,

$$K_m e^{-(\tau_m + T_m)s} \cong K_m e^{-T_m s}, \tag{7}$$

the equivalent closed-loop transfer function of Fig.1 becomes:

$$H_o(s) = \frac{K_P K_m (1 + T_i s)}{T_i s (T_m s + 1) + K_P K_m (1 + T_i s)} \tag{8}$$

3. Sensorless control of AC machines based on adaptive identification

The common accepted definition of sensorless control for electrical drives means the need of speed and/or torque control of an electrical machine without using any mechanical speed or position measuring device placed on the rotor ax. Recently, sensorless control of AC drives is a prolific research area and many viable solutions have been proposed and implemented. It combines favorably the cost advantage with increased reliability due to the absence of the mechanical sensor and its communication cable. Speed sensorless AC drives are today well established in industrial applications where no persistent operation at lower speed occurs.

The main philosophy in sensorless control is to use the electrical machine itself as a "sensor" by offering the necessary information able to estimate its position or speed (Consoli et al., 2003; Lorenz 2010). Several techniques have been developed and published in application with both FOC and DTC of AC drives. A first category comprises signal injection techniques, based on spectral analysis which use either the natural (if it exists), or an artificial created, anisotropy of the magnetic field of the AC machine (Briz et al., 2004; Degner & Lorenz, 2000; Holtz 2006; Kim & Lorenz, 2004). By injecting appropriate voltage signals in the stator (mainly high frequency signals) and analyzing the obtained current or voltage harmonics, valuable information can be extracted to determine the rotor position. A second category comprises techniques which estimate the rotor position/speed starting from the real process (drive system) and from the mathematical model of the machine by using different identification algorithms, like:

- open-loop state estimation using simple models and improved schemes with compensation of nonlinearities and disturbances (Holtz & Quan, 2002);
- model reference adaptive system based techniques (Birou & Pavel, 2008; Cirrincione & Pucci, 2005; Landau, 1979; Lascu et al., 2005);
- adaptive and robust observer (mainly Kalman filter or Lueneberger observers) based on fundamental excitation and advanced models (Caruana et al., 2003; Hinkkanen, 2004; Jansen et al., 1994);
- estimators using artificial intelligence, in particular fuzzy-logic systems, neural networks and genetic algorithms (Zadeh, 1996) .

The proposed solution is based on a FOC structure with AC machine, using for speed estimation a model reference adaptive system (MRAS) algorithm and a full order observer (FOO) respectively, like presented in Fig. 2.

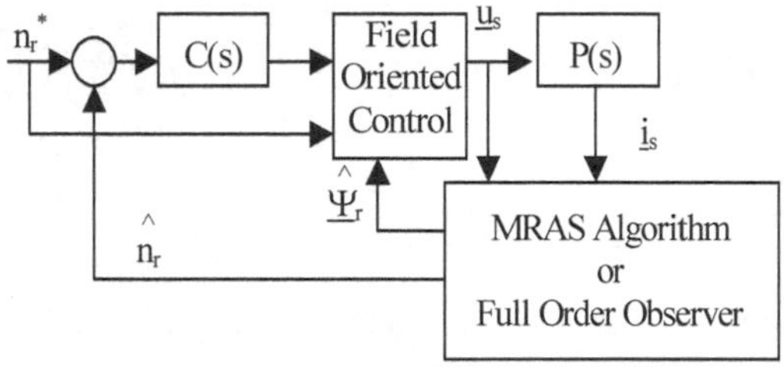

Fig. 2. Block diagram of the speed sensorless vector control of the induction machine

3.1 Model reference adaptive system algorithm for speed identification

In order to achieve sensorless control, the rotor speed estimation has to be indirectly derived based on the measured stator voltages and currents. Therefore, a mathematical model of the induction machine is needed. The model is described in the stationary (stator) reference frame. The block diagram of the MRAS speed identification is shown in Fig. 3. It contains a reference model, an adjustable model and an adaptive algorithm. Both models have as inputs the stator voltages and currents. The reference model outputs a performance index p and the adjustable model a performance index $\hat{p}$. The difference between the two values is used by the adaptive algorithm to converge the estimated speed $\hat{\omega}$ to its real value.

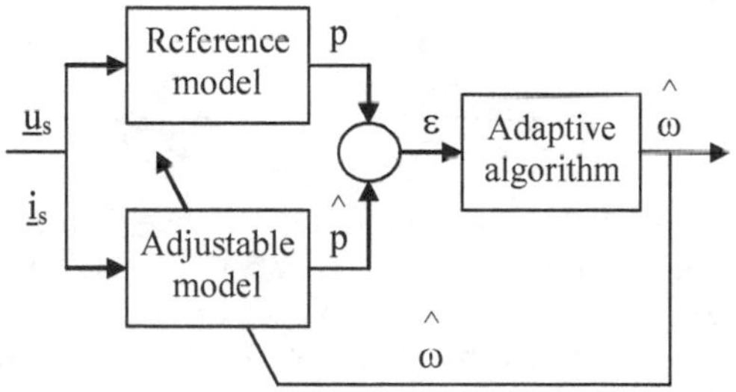

Fig. 3. Model reference adaptive system algorithm (MRAS) for speed identification.

In order to estimate the rotor speed accurately, the performance index of the reference model has to be robust over the entire speed range and insensitive to the machine parameters. According to the equations of the induction machine, we can obtain the value of the rotor flux phasor based on stator equations:

$$\frac{d\underline{\Psi}_r}{dt} = \frac{L_r}{L_m}\left(\underline{u}_s - R_s\underline{i}_s - L_\sigma \frac{d\underline{i}_s}{dt}\right), \tag{9}$$

where L_σ is the equivalent inductance and R_s is the stator resistance. The same rotor flux phasor based on the rotor equations:

$$\frac{d\underline{\Psi}_r}{dt} = -\frac{1}{\tau_r}\underline{\Psi}_r + j\omega\underline{\Psi}_r + \frac{L_m}{\tau_r}\underline{i}_s, \tag{10}$$

where $\tau_r = L_r/R_r$ is the rotor time constant. Considering the electromotive induced voltage (back EMF) being:

$$\underline{e} = \frac{L_m}{L_r}\frac{d\underline{\Psi}_r}{dt} \tag{11}$$

and decoupling Equation 9 on the stationary (stator-fixed) reference frame d-q, we obtain:

$$e_d = u_{sd} - R_s i_{sd} - L_\sigma \frac{di_{sd}}{dt}, \tag{12}$$

$$e_q = u_{sq} - R_s i_{sq} - L_\sigma \frac{di_{sq}}{dt}. \tag{13}$$

Considering a formal magnetizing current

$$\underline{i}_m = \frac{1}{L_m}\underline{\Psi}_r \tag{14}$$

and decupling Equation 10 on the fix reference frame d-q, we have:

$$e_{md} = -\frac{L_m^{\,2}}{L_r}\left(\frac{1}{\tau_r}i_{md} + \omega i_{mq} - \frac{1}{\tau_r}i_{sd}\right), \tag{15}$$

$$e_{mq} = -\frac{L_m^{\,2}}{L_r}\left(\frac{1}{\tau_r}i_{mq} - \omega i_{md} - \frac{1}{\tau_r}i_{sq}\right). \tag{16}$$

The reference model is described based on Equations 12 and 13 and is parameter dependent, namely with the stator resistance R_s and the equivalent inductance L_σ. In the reference model there are no integral operations, so the model can be used also for low speed estimation. To improve the robustness of the reference model, one of the two machine parameters can be avoided by choosing an optimal way to define the reference model performance index p. To eliminate the effect of the inductance L_σ, Equations 12 and 13 are cross multiplied by the derivates of the two stator current components and we obtain:

$$p = u_{sd}\frac{di_{sq}}{dt} - u_{sq}\frac{di_{sd}}{dt} - R_s\left(i_{sd}\frac{di_{sq}}{dt} - i_{sq}\frac{di_{sd}}{dt}\right). \tag{17}$$

Equation 17 describes the performance index of the reference model. To obtain the performance index of the adjustable model, same mathematical operations applied to Equations 15 and 16 give:

$$\hat{p} = \frac{L_m^{\ 2}}{L_r}\frac{1}{\tau_r}\left(i_{sd}\frac{di_{sq}}{dt} - i_{sq}\frac{di_{sd}}{dt}\right) - \frac{L_m^{\ 2}}{L_r}\frac{1}{\tau_r}\left(i_{md}\frac{di_{sq}}{dt} - i_{mq}\frac{di_{sd}}{dt}\right) - \frac{L_m^{\ 2}}{L_r}\hat{\omega}\left(i_{mq}\frac{di_{sq}}{dt} - i_{md}\frac{di_{sd}}{dt}\right) \tag{18}$$

having the two formal magnetizing current components described by:

$$\frac{di_{md}}{dt} = -\frac{1}{\tau_r}i_{md} - \hat{\omega} i_{mq} + \frac{1}{\tau_r}i_{sd}\,, \tag{19}$$

$$\frac{di_{mq}}{dt} = -\frac{1}{\tau_r}i_{mq} + \hat{\omega} i_{md} + \frac{1}{\tau_r}i_{sq}\,. \tag{20}$$

Equation 17 is used for the reference model and Equation 18 for the adjustable model. The error between the two performance indexes

$$\varepsilon = p - \hat{p} \tag{21}$$

is the input for the adaptive algorithm, see Fig. 3. This algorithm estimates the $\hat{\omega}$ rotor speed in order to converge the performance index of the adjustable model to the performance index of the reference model (converge the error ε to zero). In designing the adaptive mechanism of the presented MRAS structure, it is necessary to ensure the stability of the control system and the convergence of the estimated speed to the real one. Based on the hyper-stability theory (Landau, 1979), following adaptive mechanism is used in order to guarantee the system stability:

$$\hat{\omega} = K_p\varepsilon + K_i\int \varepsilon dt\,, \tag{22}$$

where, K_p and K_i are the gain parameters of the adaptive algorithm, limited only by noise considerations and having for our control structure the particular values K_p=3 and K_i=10. The MRAS algorithm presented above can also be used for on-line identification of some parameter of the induction machine, namely the stator resistance, the equivalent inductance or the rotor time constant.

3.2 Speed and rotor flux estimator based on a full order observer

The speed estimation strategy with full order observer (FOO) is based on the fundamental excitation variables as information source, like presented in Fig. 4. The rotor speed estimator is based on comparing the stator current estimate value $\hat{i}_s$ to the actual stator current i_s and updating the estimated speed $\hat{\omega}$ such that the error i_s- $\hat{i}_s$ is minimized in some sense. This will be done by using a full-order observer for the estimated stator current, rotor flux and rotor speed, described by equations:

$$L_\sigma \frac{d\hat{\underline{i}}_s}{dt} = \underline{u}_s - \left(R_s + R_r + j\omega_\lambda L_\sigma\right)\hat{\underline{i}}_s + \left(\frac{R_r}{L_m} - j\omega^\wedge\right)\hat{\underline{\Psi}}_r + k_1\left(\underline{i}_s - \hat{\underline{i}}_s\right), \tag{23}$$

$$\frac{d\hat{\underline{\Psi}}_r}{dt} = R_r \hat{\underline{i}}_s - \left[\frac{R_r}{L_m} + j\left(\omega_\lambda - \hat{\omega}\right) \right] \hat{\underline{\Psi}}_r + k_2 \left(\underline{i}_s - \hat{\underline{i}}_s \right), \tag{24}$$

$$\frac{d\hat{\omega}}{dt} = \Re e \left\{ k_3 \left(\underline{i}_s - \hat{\underline{i}}_s \right) \right\}, \tag{25}$$

where ω_λ is the speed of the reference frame and k_1, k_2 and k_3 are the gain parameters of the algorithm, calculated from the Ricatti equation.

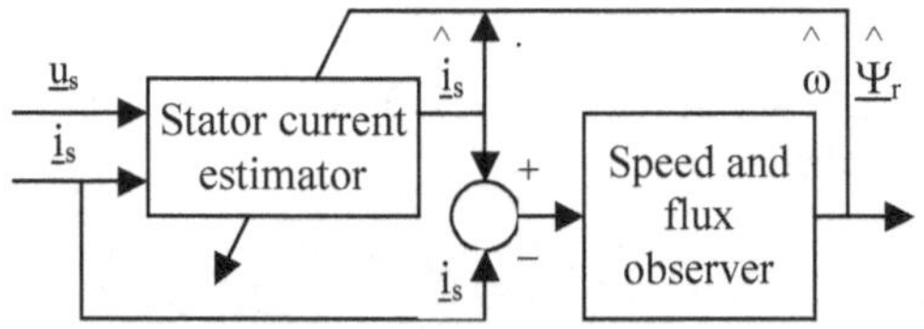

Fig. 4. Full order observer (FOO), for speed and rotor flux estimation

The speed estimator must converge significantly faster than the mechanical speed control loop in order to ensure good tracking. So, the dynamics of the speed estimator can be neglected as seen from the much slower flux and speed dynamics and thus it can be considered only that value of estimated speed and stator current which have converged to quasi steady-state values. The control structure based on the MRAS algorithm presented in 3.1 will be implemented on a driving system, composed of an induction machine with the following main catalog values:

- rated power P_N 2,2 *kW*,
- rated speed n_N 1435 rpm.,
- nominal stator current I_{sN} 4,9 *A*,
- rated stator voltage U_{sN} 400*V*,
- nominal load torque M_N 14,7 *Nm*.

Simulated results of the MRAS algorithm are presented in Fig. 5, where the reference model performance index p, the adjustable model performance index $\hat{p}$ (Equations 17 and 18), and error ε (Equation 21) are for a starting process to the rated speed with rated load torque.

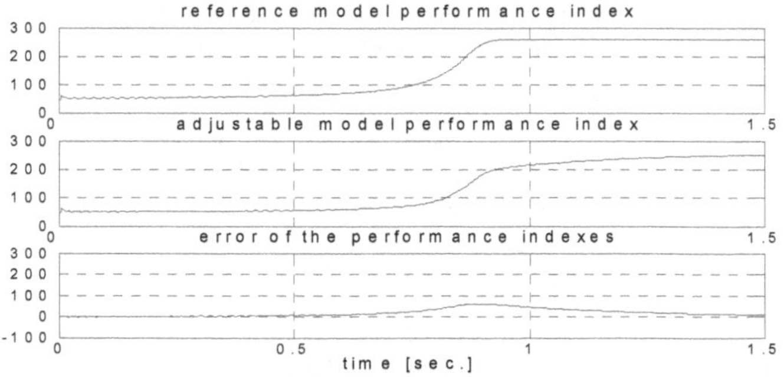

Fig. 5. The performance index of reference model p, adjustable model $\hat{p}$ and error index ε.

The simulated speed of this process, the estimated speed based on the MRAS algorithm and the speed error estimation are presented in Fig. 6. Problems that may occur by derivation of the measured stator currents can be avoided using specific digital algorithms.

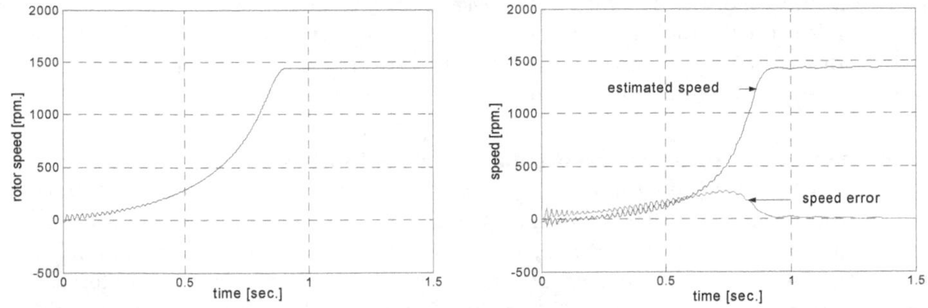

Fig. 6. Rotor speed, estimated speed based on the MRAS algorithm and speed error for a starting process at rated speed with rated torque.

Simulated results confirm that the advantage of using the MRAS algorithm, for the control of a sensorless driving system, is a high dynamic performance at speed and torque steps. The error of the estimated speed in the starting process is relative big, because of the sensitivity of the control structure with speed estimators to parameter variations (rotor time constant) and external perturbations (moment of inertia, friction coefficient). By modifying the gain parameters from Equation 22 we can avoid this, but we disturb the control performance parameters (overshooting, stationary error). So, increasing robustness of the sensorless control is needed. The proposed solution is to apply the robust control theory to the AC drive, by designing an optimal H_∞ controller, to ensure the stability and robustness performances of the driving system.

4. Robust control of AC drives

A control system is considered to be robust if it is insensitive to internal process parameter variations or external perturbations (McFarlene & Glover, 1990; Safonov, 1980). In driving systems with AC machines, the most sensible elements are:

- rotor resistance or rotor time constant because of their strong variation due to the inner temperature of the machine and because of their influence in the machine model;
- mutual inductance (magnetic inductance) because of his nonlinearity (saturation effect);
- total inertia moment of the system with possible nonlinear or even random variations (especially by robot arms);
- load torque for a wide range of applications.

The main goal of a robust controller is to compensate the effects introduced by the variations of the sensitive elements described above to the dynamic process of the controlled system

The designing process of a robust controller may follow different methods, applying various robust control system synthesis techniques (Ball & Helton, 1993; Chiang & Safonov, 1992; Doyle et al., 1989; Morari & Zafiriou, 1990; Zames, 1996). The main methods are based on geometric-analytical, frequency domain or steady-state approaches like: Hardy space based, optimal H_2 and H_∞ techniques (Green & Limebeer, 1995; Ionescu et al., 1998; Kwakernaak, 1993; Mita et al., 1998), linear quadratic optimal LQG (Kucera, 1993), LQG/LTR (Doyle et al., 1989) or LQR (Chiang & Safonov, 1992) techniques and square root based μ synthesis techniques (Apkarian & Morris, 1993). An optimal H_∞ technique will be used in this chapter for the robust control of the driving system because of the relative simple designing process of the controller and the high robust performances obtained (Bryson, 1996). The designing procedure for the optimal controller will start by describing the driving system with AC machine in steady state equations as a linear multivariable system.

4.1 Mathematical model of the real driving system with AC machine

Fig. 1 presents the closed loop control system of an AC drive. The controlled process is described by a simplified model $P(s)$ of the AC machine (valuable for both the induction and the synchronous machine). The robust control problem is to design an optimal speed controller $C(s)$ able to satisfy the robust-stability and robust-performance criteria of the controlled system. The difference between the real physical system (in our case the AC driving system) and his mathematical model, difference defined as mathematical uncertainty may have several causes, namely:

- the AC driving system (like most of the real systems) is nonlinear, while the mathematical model is linear around a static working point, so the model exactly describes the process only around this working point;
- simplification constrains in modeling the process (AC machine in our case) based on high number of variables and parameter involved;
- process parameter variations and external perturbations are difficult to be exactly modeled;
- dynamic behavior of the driving system can not be exactly modeled.

The mathematical uncertainties can be structural uncertainties, based on parameter variations of the dynamic process like rotor time constant and nonstructural uncertainties, frequency dependent like magnetic saturation or external perturbations (moment of inertia, load torque). The study of system robustness based on the H_∞ control theory is based on describing the model uncertainty as transfer function (matrix) different from the nominal one. The most used methods to describe them are like additive uncertainties, multiplicative uncertainties or a superposition of both uncertainties, like presented in Fig. 7. Using them, the real process can be written based on the modeled one (nominal plant) as:

$$P(s) = P_N(s) + \Delta_A(s) \tag{26}$$

in the case of additive uncertainties, and :

$$P(s) = (I + \Delta_M(s))P_N(s) \tag{27}$$

in the case of multiplicative uncertainties, where $P_N(s)$ is the nominal (rated) plant, $P(s)$ is the real plant (perturbed process), $\Delta_A(s)$ is the additive uncertainty and $\Delta_M(s)$ is the multiplicative uncertainty. Analyzing the dynamic behavior of the process in frequency domain by using additive or multiplicative uncertainties, the model will describe better the real system in stationary frame or at lower frequencies and the uncertainties will increase at higher frequencies.

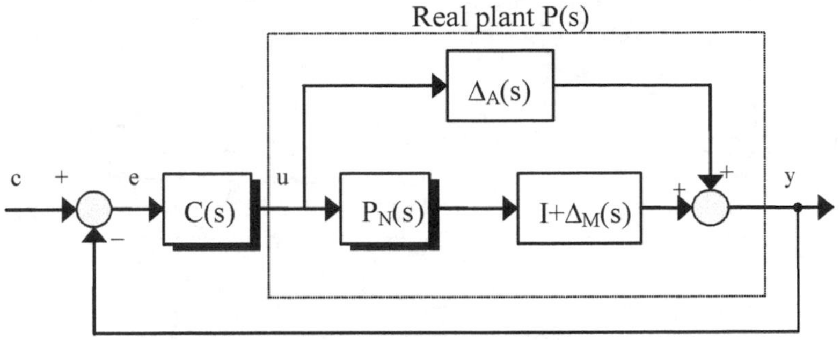

Fig. 7. Diagram of the controlled process using the additive and multiplicative uncertainty.

4.2 Optimal H$_\infty$ controller design for the driving system

The extended H$_\infty$ control theory is used to design a robust speed-control solution for AC driving systems. It has to satisfy the robust stability characteristics of the control structure as well as the dynamic performances of the driving system. Considering a Laplace transform matrix $G(s) \in C^{mxn}$ of a multivariable system with n inputs and m outputs and $\overline{\sigma}$(G) the greatest singular value of matrix G, the H$_\infty$ norm of $G(s)$ can be defined as:

$$\|G\|_\infty \overset{\Delta}{=} \sup_{\omega \in \Re} \overline{\sigma}[G(j\omega)] . \tag{28}$$

For a single input-single output system the H$_\infty$ norm of a transfer function can be defined as:

$$\|G\|_\infty = \max_{\omega} \|G(j\omega)\| . \tag{29}$$

The H$_\infty$ optimal control designing problem in the particular case of applying the small gain problem is to form an augmented plant of the process, $P(s)$ like in Fig. 8, with the weighting functions $W_1(s)$, $W_2(s)$, $W_3(s)$ applied to the signals: error e, command u and output y respectively, so that the weighted (y_{11}, y_{12}, y_{13}) and not weighted y_2 system outputs can be defined as:

$$\begin{cases} y_{11} = W_1 e = W_1(u_1 - P_N x_2) = W_1 u_1 - W_1 P_N u_2 \\ y_{12} = W_2 u = W_2 u_2 \\ y_{13} = W_3 y = W_3 P_N u_2 \\ y_2 = e = u_1 - P_N u_2 \end{cases} \tag{30}$$

and the real, perturbed process $P(s)$ can be described as:

$$P(s) = \begin{bmatrix} W_1(s) & -W_1(s)P_N(s) \\ 0 & W_2(s) \\ 0 & W_3(s)P_N(s) \\ I & -P_N(s) \end{bmatrix} . \tag{31}$$

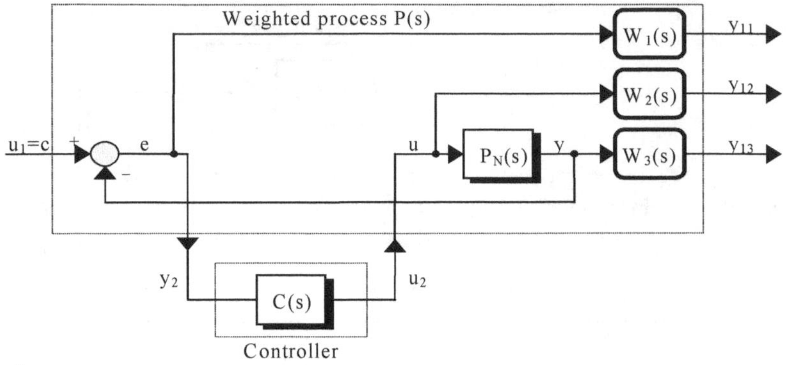

Fig. 8. Structure of speed control system with weighted process.

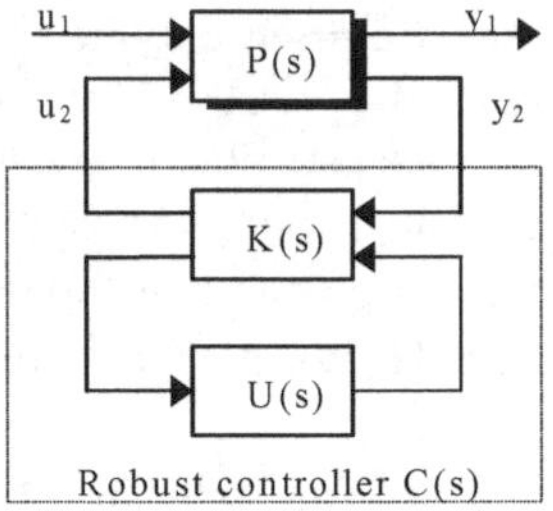

Fig. 9. Robust H_∞ controller

The second step of the robust control designing problem is to find an optimal stabilizing H_∞ controller having the structure presented in Fig. 9. The optimal stabilizing H_∞ controller is described by the control law:

$$u_2(s) = C(s)y_2(s) \tag{32}$$

so that the infinity norm of the cost function T_{y1u1}, defined as:

$$T_{y1u1}(s) \overset{\Delta}{=} \begin{bmatrix} W_1(s)S(s) \\ W_2(s)R(s) \\ W_3(s)T(s) \end{bmatrix} \tag{33}$$

is minimized and is less then one (Doyle et al., 1989; Kwakernaak, 1993):

$$\left\| T_{y1u1} \right\|_\infty < 1 , \tag{34}$$

where

$$\begin{cases} S(s) = [I + P(s)C(s)]^{-1} \\ R(s) = C(s) \cdot [I + P(s)C(s)]^{-1} = C(s) \cdot S(s) \\ T(s) = P(s)C(s) \cdot [I + P(s)C(s)]^{-1} = I - S(s) \end{cases} . \tag{35}$$

Considering the robust stability and robust performance criteria, the weighting functions for the optimal H_∞ controller are chosen and then the iterative computing process continues, until the norm condition is full fit. The performance design specifications of the speed control loop with the H_∞ controller are imposed in frequency domain (Ionescu et al., 1998; Morari & Zafiriou, 1990):

- robust performance specifications: minimizing the sensitivity function S (reducing it at least 100 times to approximate 0.3333 rad/sec).
- robust stability specifications: -40 dB/decade roll-off and at least -20dB at a crossover band of 100 rad/sec.

According to them, following weighting functions have been considered to describe the perturbed AC drive system with variable moment of inertia and friction coefficient:

$$\begin{cases} \dfrac{1}{W_1(s)} = W_1^{-1}(s) = \dfrac{1}{\gamma} \cdot \dfrac{(3s+1)^2}{100} \\ \dfrac{1}{W_3(s)} = W_3^{-1}(s) = \dfrac{150}{s+145} \end{cases}, \tag{36}$$

where γ represents the actual step value. The iterative process continues, until the graphic representation in Bode diagram of cost function T_{y1u1} reach its maximum value in the proximity of 0 dB axis. In our case, for γ=39,75 we obtain the infinite norm

$$\left\| T_{y1u1} \right\|_\infty = 0{,}9999 . \tag{37}$$

Respecting condition imposed by Equation 34 the corresponding H_∞ speed controller is:

$$H_\infty(s) = \frac{2327s^2 + 22211s + 16495}{s^3 + 822951s^2 + 548632s + 91442} . \tag{38}$$

The inverse weighting functions $W_1^{-1}(s)$ and $W_3^{-1}(s)$ and the sensitivity functions $S(s)$ and $T(s)$ are presented in Fig. 10. From the diagram results the influence of the weighting function $W_3^{-1}(s)$ to limit the peak value of $T(s)$ function. The output of the speed controller, i.e. the active current component, was limited.

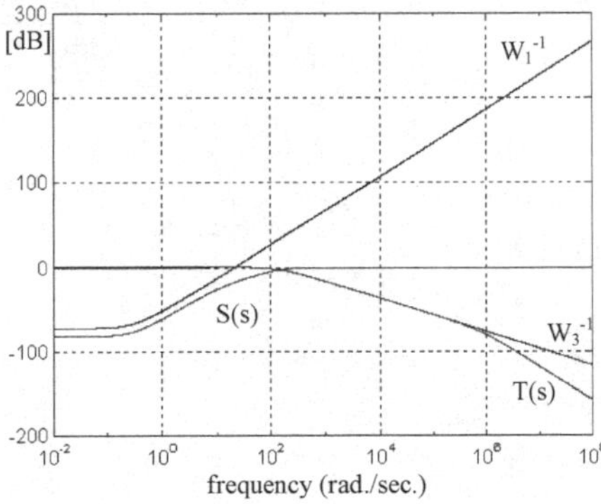

Fig. 10. Weighting functions $W_1^{-1}(s)$, $W_3^{-1}(s)$ and sensitivity functions $S(s)$ and $T(s)$.

The logarithmic Bode diagram and the Nyquist diagram of the direct-loop transfer function of the weighted process are presented in Fig. 11. According to them we establish the following stability parameters: crossover band $\Delta\omega_B$ = 153,7 rad./sec., stability margins: gain margin = 130,3 dB, phase margin = 86,8°. For the same performance and robust stability specifications, a great number of weighting functions described by Equation 36 can be chosen, so the solution of designing an optimal H_∞ controller is not unique (Chiang & Safonov, 1992; Zames, 1996). To analyze if the speed control structure with the H_∞ controller presented in Equation 38 is robust stable, we apply the stability theorem for a perturbation in the drive system, namely a highest variation of total inertia moment from J_{mot} to $10J_{mot}$ and of the friction coefficient B_{mot} to $100*B_{mot}$. The condition

$$\left\| \overline{\Delta_M}(s)T(s) \right\|_\infty < 1 \tag{39}$$

must be tested, where $\overline{\Delta_M}(s)$ represents the greatest multiplicative uncertainty for the nominal plant.

4.2.1 Stability analyze for a variation from J_{mot} to $10J_{mot}$

Considering the calculus way of the transfer function of the process, a ten times growing of the inertial moment, practically means a ten time growing of the time constant of the fixed part. The transfer functions of the nominal process and of the disturbed process are:

$$\begin{cases} P_N(s) = \dfrac{K_m}{T_m s + 1} \\ P(s) = \dfrac{K_m}{10T_m s + 1} \end{cases}, \tag{40}$$

Using Equation 27 and considering T_m=1,232 sec., the maximum multiplicative uncertainty in the case of ten times growing the inertial moment J, can be modeled:

$$\overline{\Delta_M}(s) = \frac{-9T_m s}{10T_m s + 1} = \frac{-11,097s}{12,33s + 1} \tag{41}$$

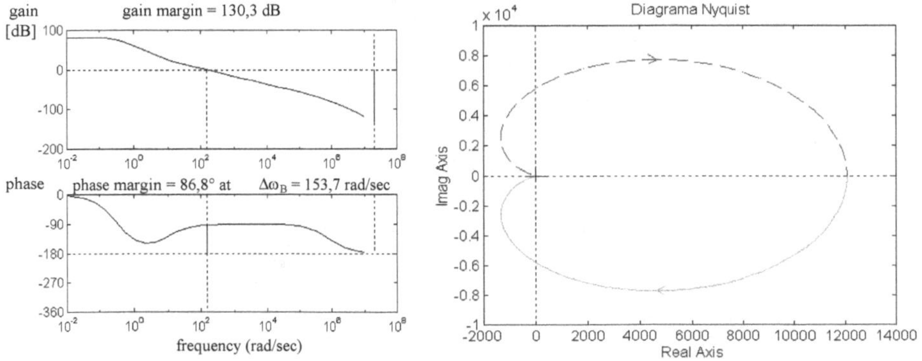

Fig. 11. Direct-loop transfer function of the weighted process in Bode and Nyquist diagram.

Knowing the expression of the complementary sensibility function T(s), the condition of robust stability can be determined, and is:

$$\left\| \overline{\Delta_M}(s)T(s) \right\|_\infty = 0{,}9359 . \tag{42}$$

Concluding, the control system with H_∞ controller remains robust stable for a variation of 10 times of the total inertial moment of the system, related to the catalogue one. Fig. 12 shows the direct-loop transfer function $H_d(s)$ family curves for the PI controller and for the optimal H_∞, controller, at variations of the inertial moment of the synchronous motor, starting at J_{mot} value, from 3, 5, 7 and 10 times of this value. As we can see from the presented graphs, at the variations of J, though the PI controller doesn't go in instability, thus it is more sensitive at the parameter variations than the H_∞ controller. This shows a better robustness of the H_∞ optimal regulator.

4.2.2 Stability analyze for a variation from B_{mot} to $100B_{mot}$

Considering that the largest variation of the friction coefficient of the mechanical system is $100{*}B_{mot}$ catalogue value. A greater friction coefficient practically means a smaller value of the time constant as like of the amplification factor of the fixed part. Considering the above mentioned, the transfer functions of the nominal process and of the disturbed processes are:

$$\begin{cases} P_N(s) = \dfrac{K_m}{T_m s + 1} \\ P(s) = \dfrac{K_m / 100}{(T_m / 100)s + 1} \end{cases} . \tag{43}$$

Using Equation 27 and the time constant of the nominal process, the maximal multiplicative uncertainty, in the case of $100{*}B_{mot}$ friction coefficient, can be written as:

$$\overline{\Delta_M}(s) = \frac{-99}{T_m s + 100} = \frac{-99}{1{,}232s + 100} . \tag{44}$$

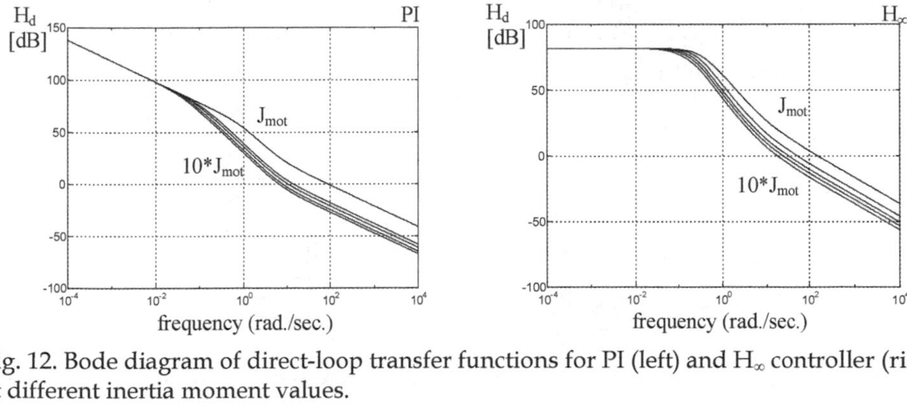

Fig. 12. Bode diagram of direct-loop transfer functions for PI (left) and H_∞ controller (right), at different inertia moment values.

The robust stability condition will be expressed as:

$$\left\| \overline{\Delta_M}(s)T(s) \right\|_\infty = 0,9999 . \tag{45}$$

We can find that the control system with the H_∞ controller remains robust stable for a 100 times variation of the friction coefficient.

5. Simulated and experimental results

Some results of the sensorless control of AC machines based on adaptive identification are presented in main paragraph 3. Because of its sensitivity to parameter variations and external perturbations, a robust solution for the speed controller was proposed and discussed in paragraph 4. Simulated results of an AC drive system controlled by a robust optimal H_∞ controller (chapter 5.1) will demonstrate the advantage of using robust control in applications with permanent variation of system parameter or external perturbations, (i.e. robot arms, traction systems, etc.). Finally, some experimental results of a robust control system, with sensorless AC drive, based on adaptive identification, will be presented.

5.1 Simulated results of robust controlled driving system with permanent magnet synchronous machine

A variable speed, FOC structure, of the PM-SM with cancelled longitudinal reaction, fed by a PWM voltage source inverter is presented in Fig.13. The stator current vector split into components leads to the characteristic loops of a FOC system. Rotor position information is obtained from the encoder and rotor speed is computed. The control system was simulated in Matlab/Simulink. The speed controller was designed and simulated using more optimizations criteria, to be compared with. The designed optimal robust H_∞ controller was implemented (see Equation 33), a PI controller (see Equation 6) and an optimal H_2 controller based on the same performance design specifications like the optimal robust H_∞ controller.

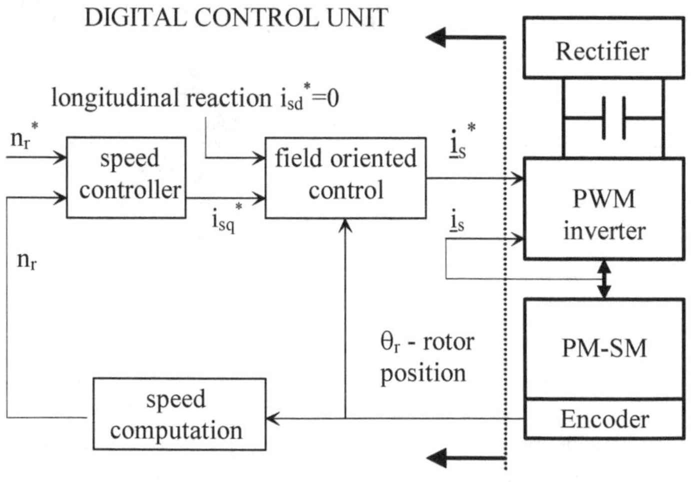

Fig. 13. Variable speed VC structure of PM-SM with different types of speed controller.

The power converter is a 1kW voltage source converter, composed by a diode rectifier and a PWM inverter. The PM-SM is a three phase machine, having following catalog values:

- rated speed	n_N	3000 rev/min,
- rated torque	M_N	1,7 Nm,
- electromotive constant	k_E	110 V/(1000 rpm.),
- rated power	P_N	530 W,
- motor constant	k_M	1,05 Nm/A,
- magnetic induction	B	1,3 T,
- rated stator current	I_N	1,6 A,
- pole pairs	z_p	3,
- PM flux	Ψ_{PM}	0,2334 Wb,
- *d* ax stator inductance	L_{sd}	0,049 H,
- *q* ax stator inductance	L_{sq}	0,046 H,
- stator resistence	R_s	10 Ω,
- inertia moment	J_{mot}	$1{,}85 \cdot 10^{-4}$ kgm^2,
- friction coefficient	B_{mot}	$5 \cdot 10^{-5}$ Nm(rad/sec)$^{-1}$.

Fig. 14 presents the simulated results for a speed control of the synchronous machine with the designed PI, H_2, and H_∞ controller, having all parameters at the nominal value, for a starting process to the rated rotor speed with no load torque (left diagram) and with rated load torque (right diagram). In Fig. 15 the speed response is for a perturbed plant with total friction coefficient $B_{tot}=50B_{mot}$ for the same imposed speed step without (left) and with nominal load torque (right). The speed response for a similar simulation of a perturbed plant with total moment of inertia variation $J_{tot}=11J_{mot}$ is presented in Fig. 16 for a no load start (left) and a rated load start (right).

For the nominal plant the dynamic performances at a speed step are similar for all three controllers. It is normal to be so, because the controllers have been designed using a simplified model of the machine, working in the steady-state nominal point. The advantage of using optimal H_∞ robust controller is evident in the presented simulations when the nominal plant is perturbed, by changing the load torque, the total moment of inertia or the friction coefficient.

Fig. 17 presents the speed response for a speed control of the synchronous machine with the designed PI, H_2, and H_∞ controllers for a starting process at rated speed with no load followed at 0.3 sec. by a rated load step (1.7 Nm). Fig. 18 details the imposed torque step m_r and the obtained electromagnetic torque m_e and dynamic torque m_j. A starting process at rated speed, followed by a stopping process for the PM-SM without load and with rated load is presented in Fig. 19. A simulation of the starting process with low speed step is also presented in Fig. 20 for all three types of designed controllers.

In conclusion, we consider that the H_∞ optimal robust controller ensures good dynamical performances and stability for a domain of variation large enough of the parameters that can be modified in the process. In applications, where electromechanical parameter variations or load perturbations appear (such as robot control), performant drive systems with AC machines can be considered, by using robust speed (or position) controllers.

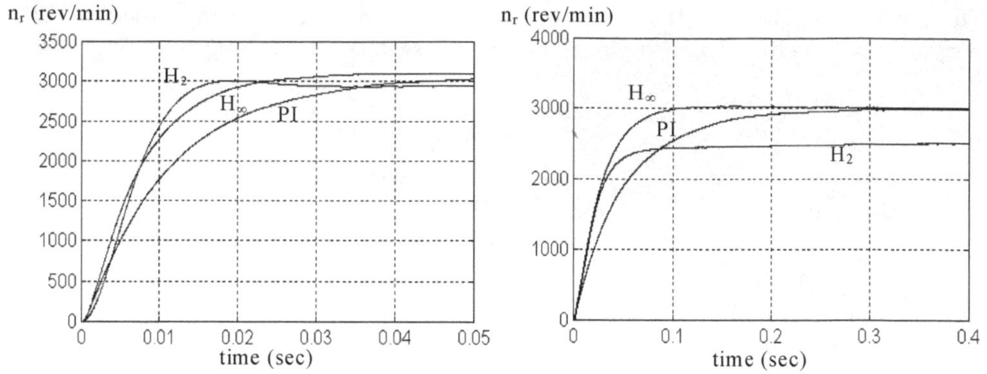

Fig. 14. Starting process with PI, H_2 and H_∞ controller for a nominal plant without load torque (left) and with rated torque (right).

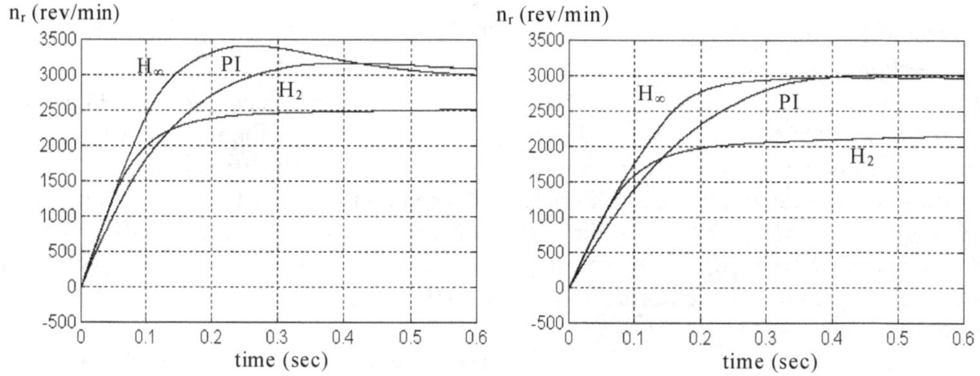

Fig. 15. Starting process with PI, H_2 and H_∞ controller for a perturbed plant (moment of inertia $J_{tot}=11J_{mot}$) without load torque (left) and with rated torque (right).

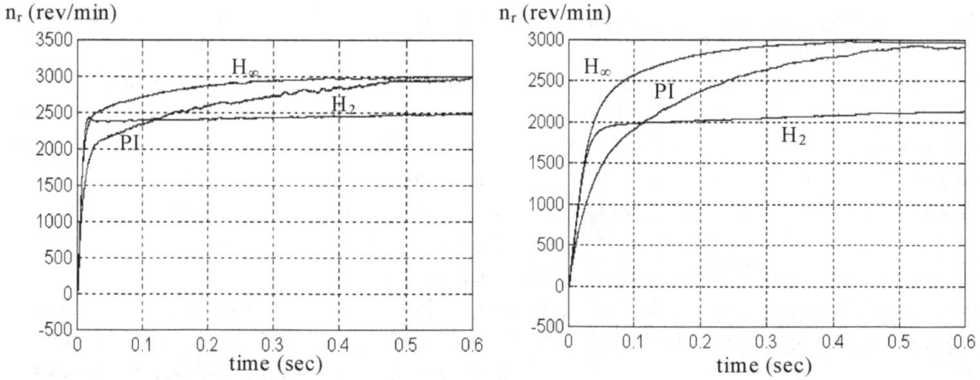

Fig. 16. Starting process with PI, H_2 and H_∞ controller for a perturbed plant (friction coefficient $B=50B_{mot}$) without load torque (left) and with rated torque (right).

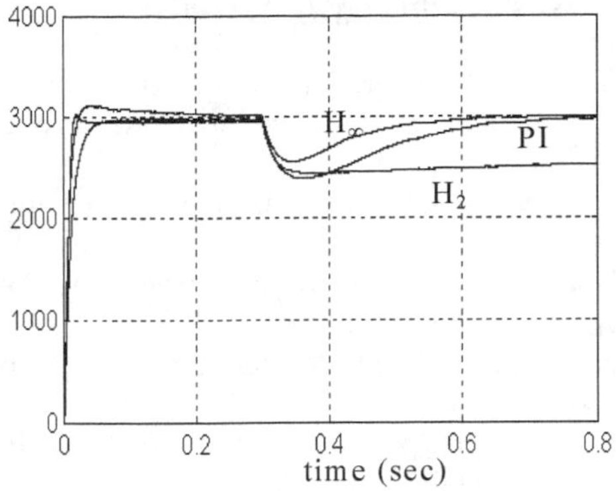

Fig. 17. Speed response for speed and torque steps

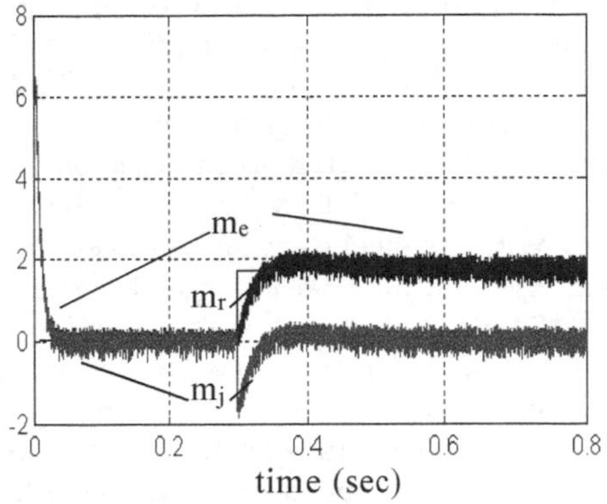

Fig. 18. Torque diagrams.

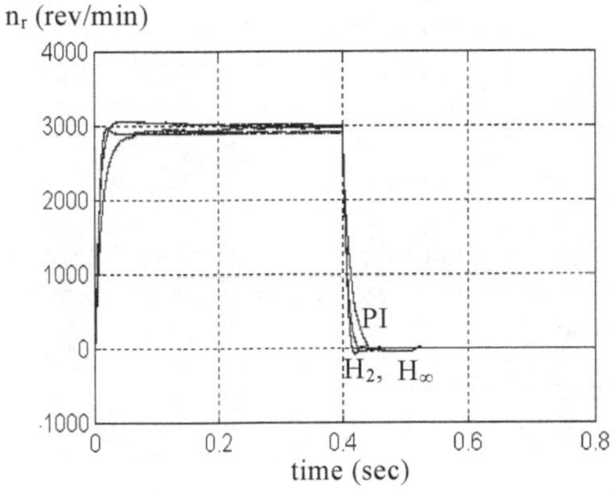

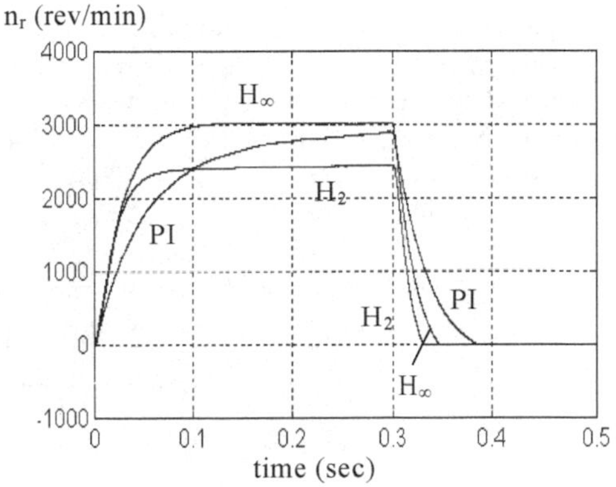

Fig. 19. Starting and fast stopping process with PI, H_2 and H_∞ controllers for a nominal plant with no load (left) and with rated load (right).

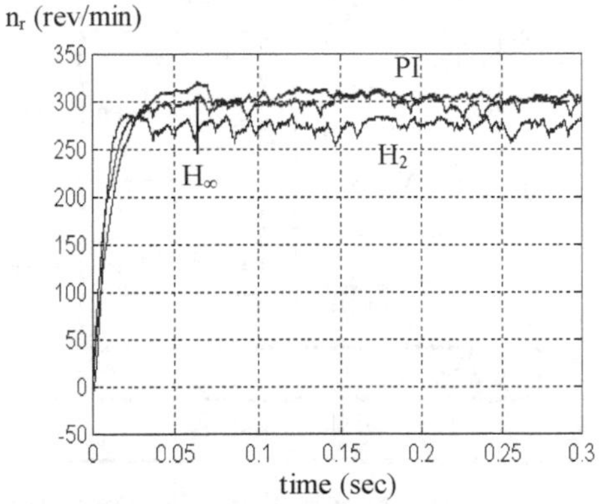

Fig. 20. Speed response at low speed step (300 rev/min) with PI, H_2 and H_∞ controllers.

5.2 Experimental results of robust controlled sensorless driving system with induction machine and adaptive speed estimation

The control unit is based on the fixed-point TMS320C50 Digital Motor Control Board developed by Texas Instruments. The complete schematic of the control architecture is presented in Fig. 21. It is composed of:

- a high speed TDM type serial bus for interconnection with the master processor and with the other dedicated processors.
- the control board (target hardware) consisting in a microcomputer, based on the TMS320C5x signal processor and the following dedicated modules:
  - a PWM unit controlled by the processor and realized in FPGA technologies, which generates the three output signals for the power converter;
  - a interfacing unit to the incremental encoder giving the position of the rotor (used to confirm the speed estimation algorithm), also implemented in FPGA technologies;
  - an analogic signal acquisition unit consisting in a A/D converter and an analogic multiplexer for 8 channels, used for the input of the stator currents and voltages.
- the AC drive system composed by a frequency voltage source PWM converter with current reaction and a induction machine having following main parameters:
  - rated power P_N 2,2 *kW*,
  - rated speed n_N 1435 rpm.,
  - nominal stator current I_{sN} 4,9 *A*,
  - rated stator voltage U_{sN} 400*V*,
  - nominal load torque M_N 14,7 *Nm*.
- a debugging computer interfaced to the target hardware through a serial RS232 driver and an emulation and debugging module XDS510. This computer will be used only in the software developing and debugging phase.

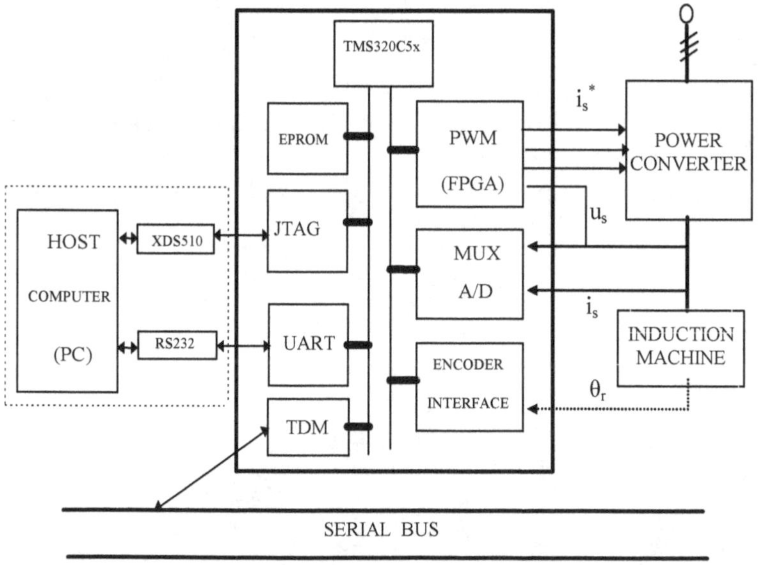

Fig. 21. Hardware structure of the robust controlled sensorless driving system with induction machine and adaptive speed estimation.

The three control loops (presented also in Fig. 13), namely: speed control loop, implemented with a robust controller; minor loop, necessary for the field-orientation based on the rotor flux and the stator current control loop of the PWM generator are software implemented. In order to obtain the best approach speed and accuracy a fixed point, fractional arithmetic was used. The program modules are: *main*( ) the main loop realizing the hardware initialization and the communication functions with the main processor and the other dedicated processors; *tint*( ) interrupt handling routine executing the current control loop and minor control loop and *int_4*( ) interrupt handling routine executing the PWM current control loop. The TMS320C5x assembler language was used to achieve an effective software implementation for the *main* routine and ANSI-C language was used for the control routines *tint* and *int_4*. Library functions (in C or assembly language) are used for handling the incremental encoder, the A/D converter, the PWM control signal generator and the communication through the serial interface with the screen terminal. The interrupts are generated by programmable counters. So *tint* interrupt is generated by processor internal programmable counter and has a 100μs period. *Int_4* interrupt is generated by the PWM module and has a 10μs period.
The dynamic evolution of rotor speed, estimated speed based on the MRAS algorithm and speed error for a robust controlled (using the optimal H_∞ controller) starting process of the sensorless driving system with induction machine at rated speed step with no load torque is presented in Fig. 22. It can be observed, that the maximum speed error in the dynamic process (starting process) is less then 9 rpm, that means a relative error (speed error/real speed) of around 0,6%, which is a considerable better value then the results obtained for the same sensorless drive system, without a robust speed controller. The relative sped error of the sensorless robust control, after the transitory dynamic process is ended and the drive system works at stabilized speed, is less then 0.05%, which means a really performant estimation (less then 0,7 rpm.). The differences between the two sensorless control structures, the one without a robust control (speed control results presented in Fig.6) and the one with robust control (speed control results presented in Fig. 22), can be explained by the increased robustness imposed by the optimal H_∞ controller, to a process (the AC drive system) which is sensitive to parameter variations (rotor time constant) and external perturbations (moment of inertia, friction coefficient), because of the adaptive estimation algorithm used to determine the rotor speed.

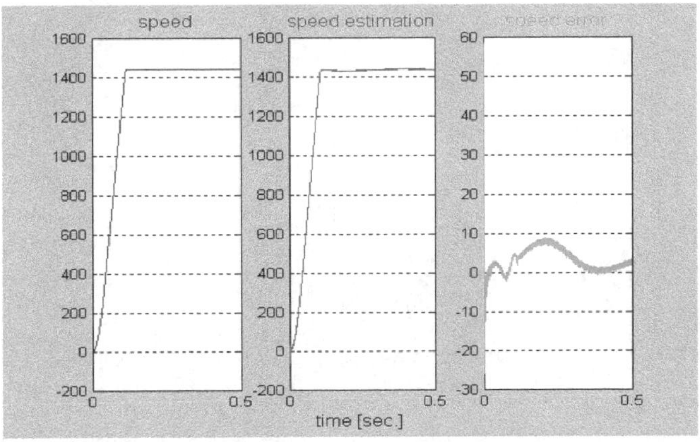

Fig. 22. Speed, estimated speed and speed error for a robust controlled starting process.

The speed and estimation speed error for the same control structure at a full loaded starting process (with nominal imposed torque) are presented in Fig. 23. The time constant of the transitory starting process is as expected a few times bigger than in the starting process with no load (Fig.22.) and the relative speed error is around 0,3%, that means less then at no-load start. That can be explained, due to the fact that the speed estimator itself is less sensitive to parameter variations when it works with nominal inputs. The dynamic evolution of the different currents of the induction machine for the same process are presented in Fig. 24, namely the stator current, the active (torque producing) and reactive (flux producing) components of the stator current and the estimated magnetizing current.

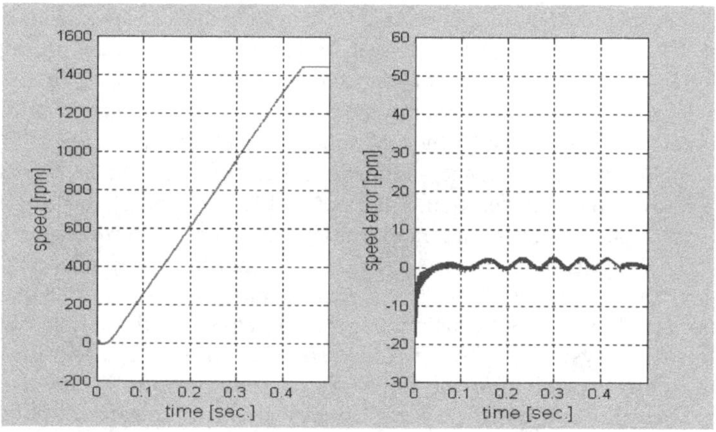

Fig. 23. Rotor speed and speed error at rated load starting process.

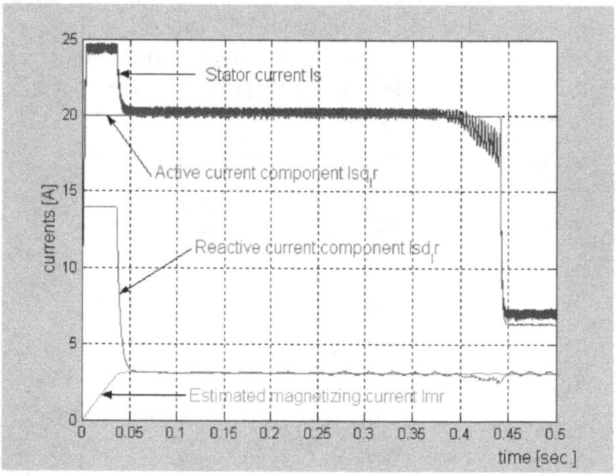

Fig. 24. Different currents of the IM at a starting process with rated load.

The dynamic behavior of the AC drive, if a rated load step is imposed to the system running at a stable rotor speed (rated speed), is tested. Fig. 25 presents the performance indexes of the MRAS based speed identification algorithm (the reference model performance index p, the adjustable model performance index $\hat{p}$, and the error ε), the imposed load torque step at 0,31 sec. and the developed electromagnetic torque of the AC machine. The stator current was limited in the starting process to a 3,5 times value of the rated current ($I_{s,max}$=17A). The estimated speed, the rotor speed and the speed error are presented in Fig. 26. The maximum relative speed error in the transitory process (around 1,4%), is significantly greater as for a rated speed step and the zero convergence time of the speed error is significantly longer. It is an expected result because in all presented FOC structures, by using a speed controller in the active control loop of the AC drive (Fig. 2 and Fig. 13), the rotor speed is directly controlled while the electromagnetic torque is indirectly controlled. In applications where a direct torque control is needed, the dynamic performances of torque response can be improved.

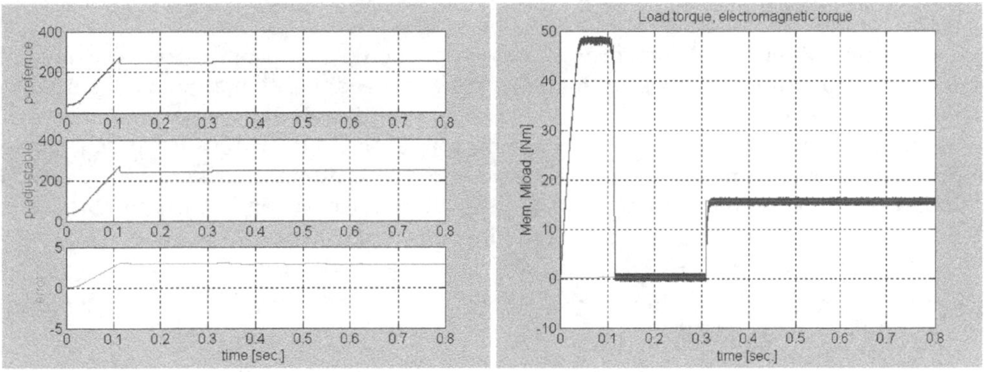

Fig. 25. Performance indexes of MRAS algorithm (left diagram), imposed load torque step and developed electromagnetic torque (right diagram).

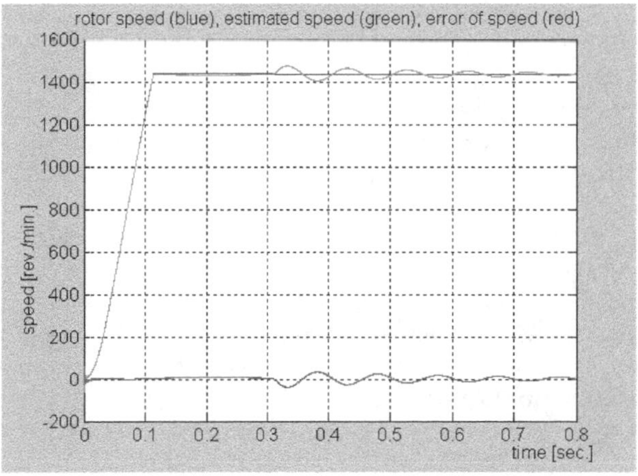

Fig. 26. Speed evolution for a starting process and a rated load step at t=0.3 sec.

The results confirm, that the robust control, using an optimal H_∞ speed controller, of the sensorless AC drives, based on adaptive identification with MRAS algorithm for speed estimation, assure:

- good estimation in steady state and transient operations;
- robustness to electrical parameter variations as stator resistance and mutual inductance (reference model) or rotor time constant (adjustable model);
- robustness to external perturbations (moment of inertia, friction coefficient),

but needs greater computing time for the control loop, that means more powerful real time computing systems (with high frequency digital signal processors) and increasing costs.

6. Conclusion

Sensorless control of AC drive systems became in the last years a challenge for intelligent motion control. To estimate rotor speed or position, by using adaptive identification algorithms based on model reference, is a relative easy task and became therefore a valuable solution for applications where not high precision of speed/position estimation is needed. The main disadvantage of the MRAS identification algorithms is the relative high sensitivity to machine parameter variations (i.e. rotor time constant) and to external perturbations (i.e. moment of inertia, friction coefficient). Using the robust control theory seams to be a good solution to increase the speed/position estimation accuracy and to apply the same estimation method for a large number of motion control applications. The optimal H_∞ speed controller makes the AC drive system stable to a large scale of parameter variations and perturbations and provides high dynamic performance as well as accurate speed estimation to the sensorless control structure.

7. Acknowledgment

The author would like to acknowledge the Alexander von Humboldt Foundation for their support in the research activity, which made possible an important part of the presented results.

8. References

Akatsu, K. & Kawamura, A. (2000). Sensorless Very Low-Speed and Zero-Speed Estimation with Online Rotor Resistance Estimation of Induction Motor Without Signal Injection. In *IEEE Transactions on Industry Applications*, Vol.36, No.3, pp.764-771, ISSN: 0093-9994

Akpolat, H., Asher, G. & Clare, J. (2000). A Practical Approach to the Design of Robust Speed Controllers for Machine Drives. In *IEEE Transactions on Industrial Electronics*, Vol.47, No.2, pp. 315-324, ISSN: 0278-0046

Apkarian, P., Morris, J. (1993). Robust modal controllers. New H_∞/μ synthesis structures. In *Proceedings of the European Control Conference ECC'93*, Groningen, Netherlands, March 1-4, 2003, pp. 1819-1825

Ball, J., Helton, J. (1993). Nonlinear H_∞ Control Theory: A Literature Survey. In *Automatica*, Vol. 29, No. 2, Great Britain, pp. 1-12, ISSN: 0005-1098

Birou, I. & Pavel, S. (2008). Sensorless AC Driving Systems Based on Adaptive Identification Algorithms and Robust Control Strategies. In *Proceedings of the 9th International Conference DAS'2008*, May 22-24, Suceava, Romania, pp. 93-96, ISSN 1844-5038

Birou, I., Maier, V., Pavel, S. & Rusu, C. (2010). Control of AC Drives; a Balance Between Dynamic Performance, Energy Efficiency and Cost Constrains. In: *Anals of University of Craiova, Electrical Engineering series,* No. 34, Vol. II, Craiova, Romania, 7-8 oct. 2010, pp. 42-47, ISSN 1842-4805

Briz, F., Degner, M., Garcia, P. & Lorenz, R (2004). Comparison of Saliency-Based Sensorless Control for AC Machines. In *IEEE Transactions on Industry Applications*, Vol.40, No.4, pp. 1107-1115, ISSN: 0093-9994

Bryson, A. (1996). Optimal control. In *IEEE Control Systems*, Vol. 16, No.3, pp. 26-33

Caruana, C., Asher, G., Bradley, K. & Woolfson, M. (2003). Flux Positon Estimation in Cage Induction Machines Using Synchronous HF injection and Kalman Filtering. In *IEEE Transactions on Industry Applications*, Vol.39, No.5, pp. 1372-1378, ISSN: 0093-9994

Chiang, R. & Safonov, M. (1992). *Robust Control Toolbox. User's Guide*. The Math Works Inc., Massachusetts, 1992

Cirrincione, M. & Pucci, M. (2005). An MRAS-Based Sensorless High-Performance Induction Motor Drive With a Predictive Adaptive Model. In *IEEE Transactions on Industrial Electronics*, Vol.52, No.2, pp. 532-551, ISSN: 0278-0046

Consoli, A., Scarcella, G., Testa, A. (2003). Using the Induction Motor as Flux Sensor: New Control Perspectives for Zero-Speed Operation of Standard Drives. In *IEEE Transactions on Industry Electronics*, Vol.50, No.5, pp.1052-1061, ISSN: 0278-0046

Degner, M. & Lorentz, R. (2000). Position Estimation in Induction Machines Utiliying Rotor Bar Slot Harmonics and Carrier-Frequency Signal Injection. In *IEEE Transactions on Industry Applications*, Vol.36, No.3, pp.736-742, ISSN: 0093-9994

Doyle, J., Glover, K., Khargonekar, P. & Francis, B. (1989). State space solutions to standard H_2 and H_∞ control problems. In *IEEE Transaction on Automatic Control*, Vol.34, pp. 831-847

Green, M. & Limebeer, D. (1995) *Linear Robust Control*. Prentice-Hall, Englewood Cliffs, 1995

Hinkkanen, M. (2004) Analysis and Design of Full-Order Flux Observers for Sensorless Induction Motors. In *IEEE Transactions on Industrial Electronics,* Vol.51, No.5, pp. 1033-1040, ISSN: 0278-0046

Holtz, J. & Quan, J. (2002). Sensorless Vector Control of Induction Motors at Very Low Speed Using a Nonlinear Inverter Model and Parameter Identification. In *IEEE Transaction on Industry Applications,* Vol.38, No.4, pp.1087-1095, ISSN: 0093-9994

Holtz, J. (2002). Sensorless control of induction motor drives. In *Proceedings of the IEEE,* vol. 90, No. 8, August 2002, pp. 1359-1368, ISSN: 0018-9219

Holtz J. (2006). Sensorless Control of Induction Machines – with or without Signal Injection?. In *IEEE Transactions on Industrial Electronics,* Vol.53, No.1, pp. 7-30, ISSN: 0278-0046

Hurst, K., Habetler, T., Griva, G. & Profumo, F. (1998). Zero-speed tacholess induction machine torque control: simply a meter of stator voltage integration. In *IEEE Transactions on Industrial Applications*, Vol. 34, No.4, pp. 790-795, ISSN: 0093-9994

Ionescu, V., Oara, C. & Weiss, M. (1998). *Generalized Ricatti Theory and Robust Control: A Popov Function Approach*, John Wiley & Sons Ltd., Chichester, New York, 1998

Jansen, P., Lorenz, R. & Novotny, D. (1994). Observer-Based Direct Field Orientation: Analysis and comparison of alternative methods. In *IEEE Transactions on Industrial Applications*, Vol. 30, No.4, pp. 945-953, ISSN: 0093-9994

Kelemen, A. & Imecs, M. (1991) *Vector Control of AC Drives. Vol.1: Vector Control of Induction Machine Drives.* Omikk Publisher, Budapest, 1991

Kim, H., Lorenz, R. (2004). Carrier Signal Injection based Sensorless Control Methods for IPM Synchronous Machine Drives. In *Proceedings of the 39th IEEE-IAS Annual Meeting.* Vol. 2, pp. 977-984, ISBN: 0-7803-8486-5

Kucera, V. (1993). The LQG and H_2 Designs: Two Different Pproblems?. In *Proceedings of the European Control Conference*, Groningen, Netherlands, March 1-4, 2003, pp. 334-337.

Kwakernaak, H. (1993). Robust Control and H_∞ - Optimization. Tutorial Paper. In *Automatica*, Vol. 29, No. 2, pp. 255-273, ISSN: 0005-1098

Landau, I. (1979). *Adaptive Control-The Model Reference Approach*, Marcel Dekker, New York

Lascu, C., Boldea, I., Blaabjerg, F. (2005). Very-Low-Speed Variable-Structure Control of Sensorless Induction Machine Drives Without Signal Injection. In *IEEE Transactions on Industrial Applications*, Vol. 41, No.2, pp. 591-598, ISSN: 0093-9994

Leonhard, W. (1985). *Control of Electrical Drives.* Springer-Verlag, Berlin, 1985

Lorenz, R., (2010). Core Sensor Integration Technologies for Advanced Electrical Drives and Power Converters-Keynote Speaker, In *Proc. of Int. Conference on Development and Application Systems DAS'2010*, May 27-29, 2010, Suceava, Romania, ISSN 1844-5020

McFarlane, D., Glover, K. (1990). Robust Controller Design Using Normalized Coprime Factor Plant Descriptions. In *Lecture Notes in Control and Information Sciences.* Springer-Verlag, Berlin, Heidelberg, New York, 1990

Mita, T., Hirata, M., Murata, K. & Zhang, H. (1998). H_∞ Control Versus Disturbance-Observer-Based Control. In *IEEE Transactions on Industrial Electronics*, Vol.45, No.3, pp. 488-495, ISSN: 0278-0046

Morari, M., Zafiriou, E. (1990). *Robust Process Control*, Prentice Hall, Englewood Cliffs, 1990

Moreira, J., Hung, K., Lipo, T. & Lorenz, R. (1991). A simple and robust adaptive controller for detuning correction in field oriented induction machines. In *Proceedings of IEEE-IAS Annual Meeting*, pp.397-403, ISBN: 0-7803-0453-5

Rajashekara, K., Kawamura, A. & Matsuse, K. (1996). *Sensorless Control of AC Motor Drives.* IEEE Press, Piscataway, New Jersey, 1996

Safonov, M. (1980). *Stability and Robustness of Multivariable Feedback Systems*. MIT Press, 1980

Toliyat, H., Levi, E. & Raina, M. (2003). A Review of RFO Induction Motor Parameter Estimation Techniques. In *IEEE Transactions on Energy Conversion*, Vol. 18., No.2, pp. 271-283, ISSN: 0885-8969

Trzynadlowski, A. (1994). *The Field Orientation Principle in Control of Induction Motors.* Kluwer Academic Publishers, Boston, 1994

Vas, P. (1998). *Sensorless Vector and Direct Torque Control*, Oxford University Press, 1998

Wieser, R. (1998). Optimal rotor flux regulation for fast-accelerating induction machines in the field-weakening region. *IEEE Transactions on Industry Applications*, Vol.34, No.5, pp. 1081-1087, ISSN: 0093-9994

Zadeh, L. (1996). The evolution of systems analysis and control: a personal perspective. In *IEEE Control Systems*, Vol. 16, No.3, June 1996, pp. 95-98

Zames, G. (1996). Input-output feedback stability and robustness. In *IEEE Control Systems*, Vol. 16, No.3, June 1996, pp. 61-66

15

A Robust Decoupling Estimator to Identify Electrical Parameters for Three-Phase Permanent Magnet Synchronous Motors

Paolo Mercorelli
Faculty of Automotive Engineering, Ostfalia University of Applied Sciences
Germany

1. Introduction

As the high field strength neodymium-iron-boron (NdFeB) magnets become commercially available and affordable, the sinusoidal back electromagnetic force (emf) permanent magnet synchronous motors (PMSMs) are receiving increasing attention due to their high speed, high power density and high efficiency. These characteristics are very favourable for high performance applications, e.g., robotics, aerospace, and electric ship propulsion systems Rahman et al. (1996), Ooshima et al. (2004). PMSMs as traction motors are common in electric or hybrid road vehicles, but not yet widely used for rail vehicles. Although the traction PMSM has many advantages, just a few prototypes of vehicles were built and tested. The following two new prototypes of rail vehicles with traction PMSMs, which were presented at the InnoTrans fair in Berlin 2008, were the Alstom AGV high speed train and the Skoda Transportation low floor tram 15T ForCity. The greatest advantage of the PMSM is its low volume in contrast to other types of motors, which makes a direct drive of wheels possible. However, the traction drive with PMSM must meet special requirements typical for overhead-line-fed vehicles. The drives and especially their control should be robust to a wide range of overhead line voltage tolerance (typically from -30% to $+20\%$), voltage surges and input filter oscillations. These features may cause problems during flux weakening operation, which must be used for several reasons. The typical reason is to obtain constant power operation in a wide speed range and to reach nominal power during low speed (commonly 1/3 of the maximum speed). In the case of common traction motors such as asynchronous or DC motors, it is possible to reach the constant power region using flux weakening. This is also possible for traction PMSM, however, a problem with high back emf arises. In the report by Dolecek (2009), the usage of a flux weakening control strategy for PMSM as a prediction control structure is shown to improve the dynamic performance of traditional feedback control strategies. This is obtained in terms, for instance, of overshoot and rising time. It is known that, an accurate knowledge of the model and its parameters is necessary for realizing an effective prediction control. To achieve desired system performance, advanced control systems are usually required to provide fast and accurate response, quick disturbance recovery and parameter variations insensitivity Rahman et al. (2003). Acquiring accurate models for systems under investigation is usually the fundamental part in advanced control system designs. For instance, proper implementation of flux weakening control requires the knowledge of synchronous machine parameters. The most common parameters required for the implementation of such advanced control algorithms are the classical simplified model parameters: L_d - the direct axis self-inductance, L_q - the quadrature axis self-inductance, and Φ - the permanent magnet flux linkage. Prior knowledge of the previously mentioned parameters and the number of pole pairs p allows for the implementation of torque control through the use of current vector control. Techniques have been proposed for the parameters' identification of PMSM from different perspectives, such as offline Kilthau et al. (2002), Weisgerber et al. (1997) and online identification of PMSM electrical parameters Mobarakeh et al. (2001), Khaburi et al. (2003). These technique are based on the decoupled control of linear systems when the motor's mechanical dynamics are ignored. Using a decoupling control strategy, internal dynamics may be almost obscured, but it is useful to remember that there are no limitations in the controllability and observability of the system. In the report by Mercorelli et al. (2003) a decoupling technique is used to control a permanent magnets machine more efficiently in a sensorless way using an observer. The work described by Liu et al. (2008) investigates the possibility of using a numerical approach Particle Swarm Optimization (PSO) as a promising alternative. PSO approach uses a system with a known model structure but unknown parameters. The parameter identification problem can be treated as an optimisation problem, involving comparison of the system output with the model output. The discrepancy between the system and model outputs is minimised by optimisation based on a fitness function, which is defined as a measure of how well the model output fits the measured system output. This approach utilises numerical techniques for the optimisation, and it can incur in difficult non-convex optimisation problems because of the nonlinearity of the motor model. Despite limitation on the frequency range of identification, this paper proposes a dynamic observer based on an optimised decoupling technique to estimate L_{dq} and R_s parameters. The proposed optimisation technique, similar to that presented by Mercorelli (2009) applies a procedure based on minimum variance error to minimise the effects of non-exact cancelation due to the decoupling controller. In the meantime, the paper proposes a particular observer that identifies the permanent magnet flux using the estimated L_{dq} and R_s parameters. The whole structure of the observer is totally new. The limit of this observer for the estimation of the permanent magnet flux is given by the range of work frequency. In fact, examining the theoretical structure of the observer, these limits appear evident and are validated with simulated data, as the estimation becomes inaccurate for low and high velocity of the motor. Because of the coupled nonlinear system structure, a general expression of limits is not easy to find. The paper is organised in the following way: a sketch of the model of the synchronous motor and its behaviour are given in Section 2, Section 3 is devoted to deriving, proposing and discussing the dynamic estimator, and Section 4 shows the simulation results using real data for a three-phase PMSM.

2. Model and behavior of a synchronous motor

To aid advanced controller design for PMSM, it is very important to obtain an appropriate model of the motor. A good model should not only be an accurate representation of system dynamics but should also facilitate the application of existing control techniques. Among a variety of models presented in the literature since the introduction of PMSM, the two-axis dq-model obtained using Park's transformation is the most widely used in variable speed PMSM drive control applications Rahman et al. (2003) and Khaburi et al. (2003). The Park's dq-transformation is a coordinate transformation that converts the three-phase stationary variables into variables in a rotating coordinate system. In dq-transformation, the rotating coordinate is defined relative to a stationary reference angle as illustrated in Fig. 1. The dq-model is considered in this work.

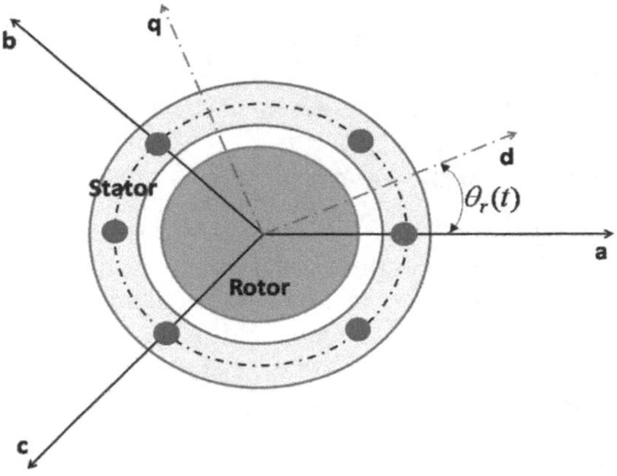

Fig. 1. Park's transformation for the motor

$$\begin{bmatrix} u_d(t) \\ u_q(t) \\ u_0(t) \end{bmatrix} = \begin{bmatrix} \frac{2\sin(\omega_{el}t)}{3} & \frac{2\sin(\omega_{el}-2\pi/3)}{3} & \frac{2\sin(\omega_{el}+2\pi/3)}{3} \\ \frac{2\cos(\omega_{el}t)}{3} & \frac{2\cos(\omega_{el}-2\pi/3)}{3} & \frac{2\cos(\omega_{el}+2\pi/3)}{3} \\ \frac{1}{3} & \frac{1}{3} & \frac{1}{3} \end{bmatrix} \begin{bmatrix} u_a(t) \\ u_b(t) \\ u_c(t) \end{bmatrix}, \tag{1}$$

$$\begin{bmatrix} i_d(t) \\ i_q(t) \\ i_0(t) \end{bmatrix} = \begin{bmatrix} \frac{2\cos(\omega_{el}t)}{3} & \frac{2\cos(\omega_{el}-2\pi/3)}{3} & \frac{2\cos(\omega_{el}+2\pi/3)}{3} \\ \frac{-2\sin(\omega_{el}t)}{3} & \frac{-2\sin(\omega_{el}-2\pi/3)}{3} & \frac{-2\sin(\omega_{el}+2\pi/3)}{3} \\ \frac{1}{3} & \frac{1}{3} & \frac{1}{3} \end{bmatrix} \begin{bmatrix} i_a(t) \\ i_b(t) \\ i_c(t) \end{bmatrix}. \tag{2}$$

The dynamic model of the synchronous motor in d-q-coordinates can be represented as follows:

$$\begin{bmatrix} \frac{di_d(t)}{dt} \\ \frac{di_q(t)}{dt} \end{bmatrix} = \begin{bmatrix} -\frac{R_s}{L_d} & \frac{L_q}{L_d}\omega_{el}(t) \\ -\frac{R_s}{L_q} & -\frac{L_d}{L_q}\omega_{el}(t) \end{bmatrix} \begin{bmatrix} i_d(t) \\ i_q(t) \end{bmatrix} + \begin{bmatrix} \frac{1}{L_d} & 0 \\ 0 & \frac{1}{L_q} \end{bmatrix} \begin{bmatrix} u_d(t) \\ u_q(t) \end{bmatrix} - \begin{bmatrix} 0 \\ \Phi\omega_{el}(t) \end{bmatrix}, \tag{3}$$

and

$$M_m = \frac{3}{2}p\{\Phi i_q(t) + (L_d - L_q)i_d(t)i_q(t)\}. \tag{4}$$

In (3) and (4), $i_d(t)$, $i_q(t)$, $u_d(t)$ and $u_q(t)$ are the dq-components of the stator currents and voltages in synchronously rotating rotor reference frame, $\omega_{el}(t)$ is the rotor electrical angular speed, the parameters R_s, L_d, L_q, Φ and p are the stator resistance, d-axis and q-axis inductance, the amplitude of the permanent magnet flux linkage, and p the number of couples of permanent magnets, respectively. At the end, M_m indicates the motor torque. Considering an isotropic motor with $L_d \simeq L_q = L_{dq}$, it follows:

$$\begin{bmatrix} \frac{di_d(t)}{dt} \\ \frac{di_q(t)}{dt} \end{bmatrix} = \begin{bmatrix} -\frac{R_s}{L_{dq}} & \omega_{el}(t) \\ -\frac{R_s}{L_{dq}} & \omega_{el}(t) \end{bmatrix} \begin{bmatrix} i_d(t) \\ i_q(t) \end{bmatrix} + \begin{bmatrix} \frac{1}{L_{dq}} & 0 \\ 0 & \frac{1}{L_{dq}} \end{bmatrix} \begin{bmatrix} u_d(t) \\ u_q(t) \end{bmatrix} - \begin{bmatrix} 0 \\ \Phi\omega_{el}(t) \end{bmatrix}, \tag{5}$$

and

$$M_m = \frac{3}{2}p\Phi i_q(t), \tag{6}$$

with the following movement equation:

$$M_m - M_w = J\frac{d\omega_{mec}(t)}{dt}, \tag{7}$$

where $p\omega_{mech}(t) = \omega_{el}(t)$ and M_w is an unknown mechanical load.

3. Structure of the decoupling dynamic estimator

The present estimator uses the measurements of input voltages, currents and angular velocity of the motor to estimate the "d-q" winding inductance, the rotor resistance and amplitude of the linkage flux. The structure of the estimator is described in Fig. 2. This diagram shows how the estimator works. In particular, after having decoupled the system described in (5), the stator resistance R_s and the inductance L_{dq} are estimated through a minimum error variance approach. The estimated values $\hat{R}_s$ and L_{dq} are used for to estimate of the amplitude of the linkage flux ($\hat{\Phi}$).

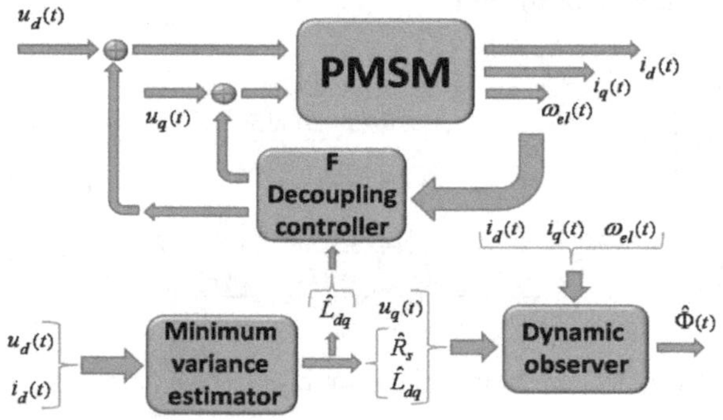

Fig. 2. Conceptual structure of the whole estimator

3.1 Decoupling structure and minimum error variance algorithm

To achieve a decoupled structure of the system described in Eq. (5), a matrix $\mathbf{F}$ is to be calculated such that,

$$(\mathbf{A} + \mathbf{BF})\mathcal{V} \subseteq \mathcal{V}, \tag{8}$$

where $\mathbf{u}(t) = \mathbf{Fx}(t)$ is a state feedback with $\mathbf{u}(t) = [u_d(t), u_q(t)]^T$ and $\mathbf{x}(t) = [i_d(t), i_q(t)]^T$,

$$\mathbf{A} = \begin{bmatrix} -\frac{R_s}{L_{dq}} & \omega_{el}(t) \\ -\frac{R_s}{L_{dq}} & \omega_{el}(t) \end{bmatrix}, \mathbf{B} = \begin{bmatrix} \frac{1}{L_{dq}} & 0 \\ 0 & \frac{1}{L_{dq}} \end{bmatrix}, \tag{9}$$

and $\mathcal{V} = im([0,1]^T)$ of Eq. (8), according to Basile et al. (1992), is a controlled invariant subspace. More explicitly it follows:

$$\mathbf{F} = \begin{bmatrix} F_{11} & F_{12} \\ F_{21} & F_{22} \end{bmatrix}, \text{and} \begin{bmatrix} u_d(t) \\ u_q(t) \end{bmatrix} = \mathbf{F} \begin{bmatrix} i_d(t) \\ i_q(t) \end{bmatrix},$$

then the decoupling of the dynamics is obtained via the following relationship:

$$\mathrm{im}\left(\begin{bmatrix} -\frac{R_s}{L_{dq}}\ \omega_{el}(t) \\ -\frac{R_s}{L_{dq}}\ \omega_{el}(t) \end{bmatrix}\right) + \mathrm{im}\left(\begin{bmatrix} \frac{1}{L_{dq}} & 0 \\ 0 & \frac{1}{L_{dq}} \end{bmatrix}\begin{bmatrix} F_{11} & F_{12} \\ F_{21} & F_{22} \end{bmatrix}\begin{bmatrix} 0 \\ 1 \end{bmatrix}\right) \subseteq \mathrm{im}\begin{bmatrix} 0 \\ 1 \end{bmatrix}, \tag{10}$$

where the parameters F_{11}, F_{12}, F_{21}, and F_{22} are to be calculated in order to guarantee condition (10) and a suitable dynamics for sake of estimation. Condition (10) is guaranteed if

$$F_{12} = -\omega_{el}(t)L_{dq}. \tag{11}$$

$$\frac{di_d(t)}{dt} = -\frac{R_s}{L_{dq}}i_d(t) + \frac{u_d(t)}{L_{dq}}, \tag{12}$$

Because of the possible inexact decoupling, it follows that:

$$\frac{d\hat{i}_d(t)}{dt} = -\frac{R_s}{L_{dq}}\hat{i}_d(t) + \frac{u_d(t)}{L_{dq}} + n(\Delta(\omega_{el}(t)(L_{dq} - \hat{L}_{dq}))), \tag{13}$$

where $n(\Delta(L_{dq} - \hat{L}_{dq}))$ is the disturbance due to the inexact cancelation.

Proposition 1. *Considering the disturbance $n(\Delta(L_{dq} - \hat{L}_{dq}))$ of Eq. (12) as a white noise, then the current minimum variance error $\sigma(e_{i_d}(t)) = \sigma(i_d(t) - \hat{i}_d(t))$ is obtained by minimising the estimation error of the parameters L_{dq} and R_s.*

Proof 1. *If Eqs. (12) and (13) are discretised using Implicit Euler with a sampling frequency equal to t_s, then it follows that:*

$$\hat{i}_d(k) = \frac{\hat{i}_d(k-1)}{(1 + t_s\frac{R_s}{L_{dq}})} + \frac{t_s}{L_{dq}(1 + t_s\frac{R_s}{L_{dq}})}u_d(k), \tag{14}$$

$$\hat{i}_d(k) = \frac{\hat{i}_d(k-1)}{(1 + t_s\frac{R_s}{L_{dq}})} + \frac{t_s}{L_{dq}(1 + t_s\frac{R_s}{L_{dq}})}u_d(k) + n(k). \tag{15}$$

It is possible to assume an ARMAX model for the system represented by (15) and thus

$$i_d(k) = \hat{i}_d(k) + a_1\hat{i}_d(k-1) + a_2\hat{i}_d(k-2) + b_1u_d(k-1) + b_2u_d(k-2) + n(k) + c_{1u}n(k-1) + c_{2u}n(k-2). \tag{16}$$

Letting $e_{i_d}(k) = i_d(k) - \hat{i}_d(k)$ as mentioned above, it follows that:

$$e_{i_d}(k) = a_1\hat{i}_d(k-1) + a_2\hat{i}_d(k-2) + b_1u_d(k-1) + b_2u_d(k-2) + n(k) + c_1n(k-1) + c_2n(k-2), \tag{17}$$

where the coefficients a, b, c_1, c_2, are to be estimated, and $n(k)$ is assumed as white noises. The next sample is:

$$e_{i_d}(k+1) = a_1\hat{i}_d(k) + a_2\hat{i}_d(k-1) + b_1u_d(k) + b_2u_d(k-1) + n(k+1) + c_1n(k) + c_2n(k-1). \tag{18}$$

The prediction at time "k" is:

$$\hat{e}_{i_d}(k+1/k) = a_1\hat{i}_d(k) + a_2\hat{i}_d(k-1) + b_1u_d(k) + b_2u_d(k-1) + c_1n(k) + c_2n(k-1). \quad (19)$$

Considering that:

$$J = E\{e^2_{\hat{i}_d}(k+1/k)\} = E\{[\hat{e}_{i_d}(k+1/k) + n(k+1)]^2\},$$

and assuming that the noise is not correlated to the signal $e_{i_d}(k)$, it follows:

$$E\{[\hat{e}_{i_d}(k+1/k) + n(k+1)]^2\} = E\{[\hat{e}_{i_d}(k+1/k)]^2\} + E\{[n(k+1)]^2\} = E\{[\hat{e}_{i_d}(k+1/k)]^2\} + \sigma_n^2, \quad (20)$$

where σ_n is defined as the variance of the white noises. The goal is to find $\hat{i}_d(k)$ such that:

$$\hat{e}_{i_d}(k+1/k) = 0. \quad (21)$$

It is possible to write (17) as

$$n(k) = e_{i_d}(k) - a_1\hat{i}_d(k-1) - a_2\hat{i}_d(k-2) - b_1u_d(k-1) - b_2u_d(k-2) - c_1n(k-1) - c_2n(k-2). \quad (22)$$

Considering the effect of the noise on the system as follows:

$$c_1n(k-1) + c_2n(k-2) \approx c_1n(k-1), \quad (23)$$

and using the Z-transform, then:

$$N(z) = \hat{I}_d(z) - a_1z^{-1}\hat{I}_d(z) - a_2z^{-2}\hat{I}_u(z) - b_1z^{-1}U_d(z) - b_2z^{-2}U_d(z) - c_1z^{-1}N(z) \quad (24)$$

and

$$N(z) = \frac{(1 - a_1z^{-1} - a_2z^{-2})}{1 + c_1z^{-1}}\hat{I}_d(z) - \frac{(b_1z^{-1} + b_2z^{-2})}{1 + c_1z^{-1}}U_d(z). \quad (25)$$

Inserting Eq. (25) into Eq. (19) after its Z-transform, and considering the approximation stated in (23) and Eq. (21), the following expression is obtained:

$$\hat{I}_d(z) = -\frac{(a_1 + c_1 + b_1z^{-1})}{b_1(1 + c_1z^{-1}) + b_2(1 + c_1z^{-1})}U_d(z). \quad (26)$$

Using the Z-transform for Eq. (14) it follows:

$$I_d(z) = \frac{t_s}{L_{dq} + t_sR_s - L_{dq}z^{-1}}U_d(z). \quad (27)$$

Comparing (26) with (27), we are left with a straightforward diophantine equation to solve. The diophantine equation gives the relationship between the parameters $\Theta = [a_1, b_1, b_2, c_1]$ as follows:

$$-b_1 = 0 \quad (28)$$

$$a_1 + c_1 = t_s \quad (29)$$

$$b_1 + b_2 = L_{dq} + t_sR_s \quad (30)$$

$$b_1c_1 + b_2c_1 = -L_{dq}. \quad (31)$$

Guessed initial values for parameters L_{dq}, R_s are given. This yields initial values for the parameters $\Theta = [a_1, b_1, b_2, c_1]$. New values for the vector Θ are calculated using the recursive least squares method. □

Remark 1. *The approximation in equation (23) is equivalent to considering* $\|c_2\| << \|c_1\|$. *In other words, this means that a noise model of the first order is assumed. An indirect validation of this assumption is given by the results. In fact, the final measurements show in general good results with the proposed method.* □

Remark 2. *At the end, the recursive least-squares method gives an estimation of the parameters* L_{dq} *and* R_s. *These calculated parameters* L_{dq} *and* R_s *minimize the current minimum variance error* $\sigma(e_{i_d}(t)) = \sigma(i_d(t) - \hat{i}_d(t))$. □

3.2 The dynamic estimator of Φ

If the electrical part of the system "q" and "d" axes is considered, then, assuming that $\omega_{el}(t) \neq 0$, $i_q(t) \neq 0$, and $i_d(t) \neq 0$, the following equation can be considered:

$$\Phi(t) = -\frac{L_{dq}\frac{di_q(t)}{dt} + R_s i_d(t) + L_{dq}\omega_{el}(t) i_q(t) + u_q(t)}{\omega_{el}(t)}. \tag{32}$$

Consider the following dynamic system:

$$\frac{d\hat{\Phi}(t)}{dt} = -\mathcal{K}\hat{\Phi}(t) - \mathcal{K}\Big(\frac{\hat{L}_{dq}\frac{di_q(t)}{dt} + \hat{R}_s i_d(t)}{\omega_{el}(t)} + \frac{\hat{L}_{dq}\omega_{el}(t) i_q(t) + u_q(t)}{\omega_{el}(t)}\Big), \tag{33}$$

where $\mathcal{K}$ is a function to be calculated. Eq. (33) represents the estimators of Φ. If the error functions are defined as the differences between the true and the observed values, then:

$$e_\Phi(t) = \Phi(t) - \hat{\Phi}(t), \tag{34}$$

and

$$\frac{de_\Phi(t)}{dt} = \frac{d\Phi(t)}{dt} - \frac{d\hat{\Phi}(t)}{dt}. \tag{35}$$

If the following assumption is given:

$$\|\frac{d\Phi(t)}{dt}\| << \|\frac{d\hat{\Phi}(t)}{dt}\|, \tag{36}$$

then in Eq. (35), the term $\frac{d\Phi(t)}{dt}$ is negligible. Using equation (33), Eq. (35) becomes

$$\frac{de_\Phi(t)}{dt} = \mathcal{K}\hat{\Phi}(t) + \mathcal{K}_3\Big(\frac{\hat{L}_{dq}\frac{di_q(t)}{dt} + \hat{R}_s i_d(t)}{\omega_{el}(t)} + \frac{\hat{L}_{dq}\omega_{el}(t) i_q(t) + u_q(t)}{\omega_{el}(t)}\Big). \tag{37}$$

Because of Eq. (32), (37) can be written as follows:

$$\frac{de_{\Phi(t)}}{dt} = \mathcal{K}\hat{\Phi}(t) - \mathcal{K}\Phi(t), \tag{38}$$

and considering (34), then

$$\frac{de_\Phi(t)}{dt} + \mathcal{K}\Phi(t) = 0. \tag{39}$$

$\mathcal{K}$ can be chosen to make Eq. (39) exponentially stable. To guarantee exponential stability, $\mathcal{K}$ must be

$$\mathcal{K} > 0.$$

To guarantee $\| \frac{d\Phi(t)}{dt} \| << \| \frac{d\hat{\Phi}(t)}{dt} \|$, then $\mathcal{K} >> 0$. The observer defined in (33) suffers from the presence of the derivative of the measured current. In fact, if measurement noise is present in the measured current, then undesirable spikes are generated by the differentiation. The proposed algorithm must cancel the contribution from the measured current derivative. This is possible by correcting the observed velocity with a function of the measured current, using a supplementary variable defined as

$$\eta(t) = \hat{\Phi}(t) + \mathcal{N}(i_q(t)), \tag{40}$$

where $\mathcal{N}(i_q(t))$ is the function to be designed.
Consider

$$\frac{d\eta(t)}{dt} = \frac{d\Phi(t)}{dt} + \frac{d\mathcal{N}(i_q(t))}{dt} \tag{41}$$

and let

$$\frac{d\mathcal{N}(i_q(t))}{dt} = \frac{d\mathcal{N}(i_q)}{di_q(t)}\frac{di_q(t)}{dt} = \frac{\mathcal{K}\hat{L}_{dq}}{\omega_{el}(t)}\frac{di_q(t)}{dt}. \tag{42}$$

The purpose of (42) is to cancel the differential contribution from (33). In fact, (40) and (41) yield, respectively,

$$\hat{\Phi}(t) = \eta(t) - \mathcal{N}(i_q(t)) \quad \text{and} \tag{43}$$

$$\frac{d\hat{\Phi}(t)}{dt} = \frac{d\eta(t)}{dt} - \frac{d\mathcal{N}(i_q(t))}{dt}. \tag{44}$$

Substituting (42) in (44) results in

$$\frac{d\hat{\Phi}(t)}{dt} = \frac{d\eta(t)}{dt} - \frac{\mathcal{K}\hat{L}_{dq}}{\omega_{el}(t)}\frac{di_q(t)}{dt}. \tag{45}$$

Inserting Eq. (45) into Eq. (33), the following expression is obtained[1]:

$$\frac{d\eta(t)}{dt} - \frac{\mathcal{K}\hat{L}_{dq}}{\omega_{el}(t)}\frac{di_q(t)}{dt} = -\mathcal{K}\hat{\Phi}(t) - \mathcal{K}\Big(\frac{\hat{L}_{dq}\frac{di_q(t)}{dt} + \hat{R}_s i_d(t)}{\omega_{el}(t)} + \frac{\hat{L}_{dq}\omega_{el}(t)i_q(t) + u_q(t)}{\omega_{el}(t)}\Big), \tag{46}$$

then

$$\frac{d\eta(t)}{dt} = -\mathcal{K}\hat{\Phi}(t) - \mathcal{K}\frac{\Big(\hat{R}_s i_d(t) + \hat{L}_{dq}\omega_{el}(t)i_q(t) + u_q(t)\Big)}{\omega_{el}(t)}. \tag{47}$$

Letting $\mathcal{N}(i_q(t)) = k_{app}i_q(t)$, where a parameter has been indicated with k_{app}, then from (42) $\Rightarrow \mathcal{K} = \frac{k_{app}\omega_{el}(t)}{\hat{L}_{dq}}$, and Eq. (43) becomes:

$$\hat{\Phi}(t) = \eta(t) - k_{app}i_q(t). \tag{48}$$

Finally, substituting (48) into (47) results in the following equation:

$$\frac{d\eta(t)}{dt} = -\frac{k_{app}\omega_{el}(t)}{\hat{L}_{dq}}(\eta(t) - k_{app}i_q(t)) + \frac{k_{app}}{\hat{L}_{dq}}\Big(\hat{R}_s i_d(t) + \hat{L}_{dq}\omega_{el}(t)i_q(t) + u_q(t)\Big),$$

$$\hat{\Phi}(t) = \eta(t) - k_{app}i_q(t). \tag{49}$$

[1] Expression (33) works under the assumption (36): fast observer dynamics.

Using the implicit Euler method, the following velocity observer structure is obtained:

$$\eta(k) = \frac{\eta(k-1)}{1 + t_s \frac{k_{app}\omega_{el}(k)}{\hat{L}_{dq}}} + \frac{t_s \frac{k_{app}^2 \omega_{el}(k) i_q(k)}{\hat{L}_{dq}} + k_{app}\omega_{el}(k) i_q(k) + \frac{t_s \hat{R}_s k_{app} i_d(k)}{\hat{L}_{dq}}}{1 + t_s \frac{k_{app}\omega_{el}(k)}{\hat{L}_{dq}}} i_q(k) + \frac{t_s \frac{k_{app}}{\hat{L}_{dq}}}{1 + t_s \frac{k_{app}\omega_{el}(k)}{\hat{L}_{dq}}} u_q(k),$$

$$\hat{\Phi}(k) = \eta(k) - k_{app} i_q(k), \tag{50}$$

where t_s is the sampling period.

Remark 3. *Assumption (36) states that the dynamics of the approximating observer should be faster than the dynamics of the physical system. This assumption is typical for the design of observers.* □

Remark 4. *The estimator of Eq. (50) presents the following limitations: for low velocity of the motor ($\omega_{mec.}(t) << \omega_{mec_n}(t)$), where $\omega_{mec_n}(t)$ represents the nominal velocity of the motor), the estimation of Φ becomes inaccurate. Because $\omega_{el}(t)$ divides the state variable η, the observer described by (50) becomes hyperdynamic. Critical phases of the estimation are the starting and ending of the movement. Another critical phase is represented by high velocity regime. In fact, it has been proven through simulations that if $\omega_{mec}(t) >> \omega_{mec_n}(t)$, then the observer described by (50) becomes hypodynamic. According to the simulation results, within some range of frequency, this hypo-dynamicity can be compensated by a suitable choice of k_{app}.* □

Remark 5. *The Implicit Euler method guarantees the finite time convergence of the observer for any choice of k_{app}. Nevertheless, any other method can demonstrate the validity of the presented results. Implicit Euler method is a straightforward one.* □

4. Simulation results

Simulations have been performed using a special stand with a 58-kW traction PMSM. The stand consists of a PMSM, a tram wheel and a continuous rail. The PMSM is a prototype for low floor trams. The PMSM parameters are: nominal power 58 kW, nominal torque 852 Nm, nominal speed 650 rpm, nominal phase current 122 A and number of poles 44. The model parameters are: $R = 0.08723$ Ohm, $L_{dq} = Ld = Lq = 0.8$ mH, $\Phi = 0.167$ Wb. Surface mounted NdBFe magnets are used in PMSM. The advantage of these magnets is their inductance, which is as great as 1.2 T, but theirs disadvantage is corrosion. The PMSM was designed to meet B curve requirements. The stand was loaded by an asynchronous motor. The engine has a nominal power 55 kW, a nominal voltage 380 V and nominal speed 589 rpm. Figures 3, 4, and 5 show the estimation of R_s stator resistance, L_{dq} inductance, and Φ magnet flux, respectively. These simulation results are obtained using values of k_{app} equal to 2 and 20 respectively. From these results, in particular from flux estimation, an improvement, passing from values of $k_{app} = 2$ $k_{app} = 20$, is visible. From these figures, the effect of the limit of the procedure discussed in remark 4 is visible at the beginning of the estimation. Figure 6 shows the angular velocity of the motor. In the present simulations, $t = 0$ corresponds to $\omega_{el}(t) = 0$.

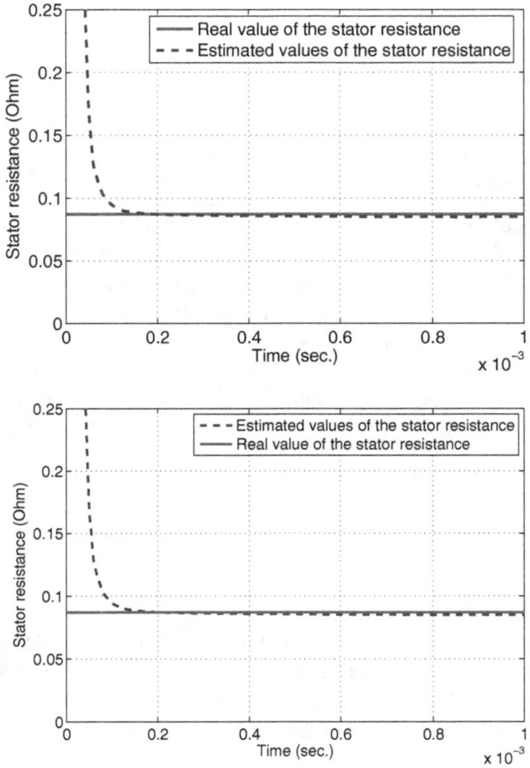

Fig. 3. Estimated and real values of R_s stator resistance for $k_{app} = 2$ (on the top) and $k_{app} = 20$ (on the bottom)

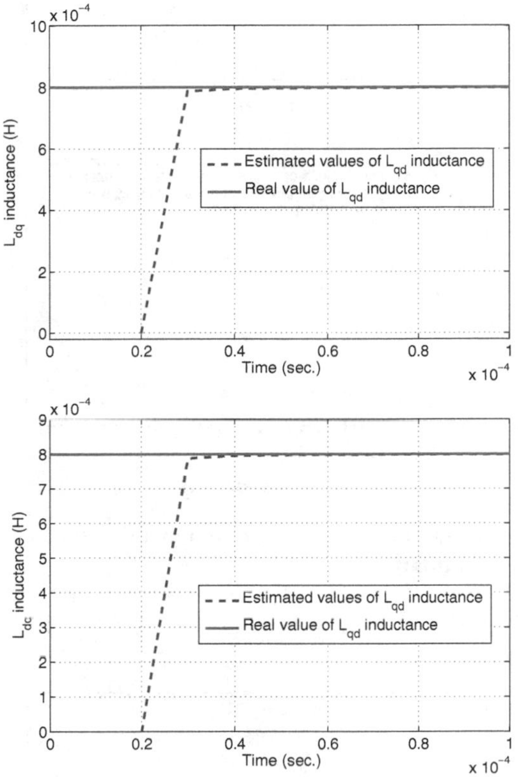

Fig. 4. Estimated and real values of L_{dq} inductance for $k_{app} = 2$ (on the top) and $k_{app} = 20$ (on the bottom)

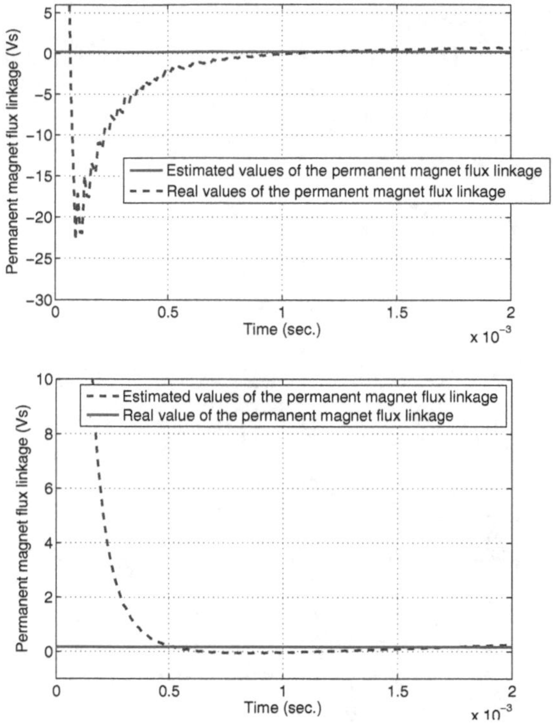

Fig. 5. Estimated and real values of the permanent magnet flux linkage for $k_{app} = 2$ (on the top) and $k_{app} = 20$ (on the bottom)

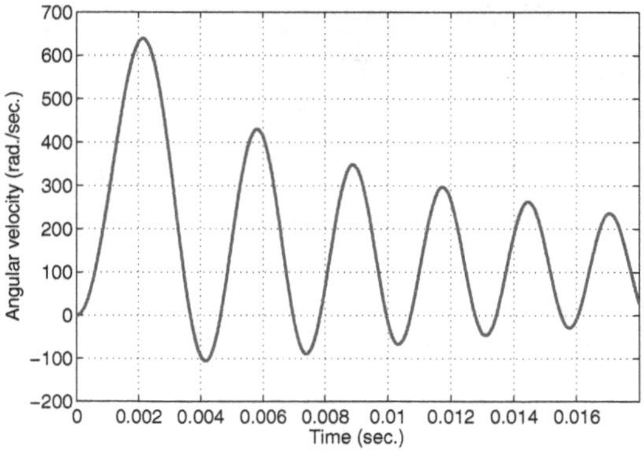

Fig. 6. Angular velocity

5. Conclusions and future work

This paper considers a dynamic estimator for fully automated parameters identification for three-phase synchronous motors. The technique uses a decoupling procedure optimised by a minimum variance error to estimate the inductance and resistance of the motor. Moreover, a dynamic estimator is shown to identify the amplitude of the linkage flux using the estimated inductance and resistance. It is generally applicable and could also be used for the estimation of mechanical load and other types of electrical motors, as well as for dynamic systems with similar nonlinear model structure. Through simulations of a synchronous motor used in automotive applications, this paper verifies the effectiveness of the proposed method in identification of PMSM model parameters and discusses the limits of the found theoretical and the simulation results. Future work includes the estimation of a mechanical load and the general test of the present algorithm using a real motor.

6. References

G. Basile and G. Marro. "Controlled and conditioned invariants in linear system theory", New Jersey-USA, Prentice Hall, 1992.

R. Dolecek, J. Novak, and O. Cerny. "Traction Permanent Magnet Synchronous Motor Torque Control with Flux Weakening", Radioengineering, Vol. 18, No. 4, December 2009

D.A. Khaburi and M. Shahnazari. "Parameters Identification of Permanent Magnet Synchronous Machine in Vector Control", in Proc. of the 10th European Conference on Power Electronics and Applications, EPE 2003, Toulouse, France, 2-4 Sep. 2003.

A. Kilthau, and J. Pacas. "Appropriate models for the controls of the synchronous reluctance machine", in Proc. IEEE IAS Annu. Meeting, 2002, pages 2289-2295.

Li Liu, Wenxin Liu and David A. Cartes. "Permanent Magnet Synchronous Motor Parameter Identification using Particle Swarm Optimization", International Journal of Computational Intelligence Research Vol.4, No.2 (2008), pages 211-218

P. Mercorelli. "Robust Feedback Linearization Using an Adaptive PD Regulator for a Sensorless Control of a Throttle Valve", Mechatronics, a Journal of IFAC, Elsevier Science publishing. DOI: 10.1016/j.mechatronics.2009.08.008, Volume 19, Issue 8, pages 1334-1345, December 2009.

P. Mercorelli, K. Lehmann and S. Liu. "On Robustness Properties in Permanent Magnet Machine Control Using Decoupling Controller", in Proc. of the 4th IFAC International Symposium on Robust Control Design, 25th-27th June 2003, Milan (Italy).

B.N. Mobarakeh, F. Meibody-Tabar, and F. M. Sargos. "On-line identification of PMSM electrical parameters based on decoupling control", in Proc. of the Conf. Rec. IEEE-IAS Annu. Meeting, vol. 1, Chicago, IL, 2001, pages 266-273.

M. Ooshima, A. Chiba, A. Rahman and T. Fukao. "An improved control method of buried-type IPM bearingless motors considering magnetic saturation and magnetic pull variation", IEEE Transactions on Energy Conversion, vol. 19, no. 3, Sept. 2004, pages 569-575.

M.A. Rahman and P. Zhou. "Analysis of brushless permanent magnet synchronous motors", IEEE Trans. Industrial Electronics, vol. 43, no. 2, 1996, pages 256-267.

M.A. Rahman, D.M. Vilathgamuwa, M.N. Uddin and T. King-Jet. "Nonlinear control of interior permanent magnet synchronous motor", IEEE Trans. Industry Applications, vol. 39, no. 2, 2003, pages 408-416.

S. Weisgerber, A. Proca, and A. Keyhani. "Estimation of permanent magnet motor parameters", in Proc. of the IEEE Ind. Appl. Soc. Annu. Meeting, New Orleans, LA, Oct. 1997, pp. 29Ű34.

16

Sliding Controller of Switched Reluctance Motor

Ahmed Tahour[1] and Abdel Ghani Aissaoui[2]
[1]*University of Mascara,*
[2]*IRECOM Laboratory, University of Sidi Bel Abbes,*
Algeria

1. Introduction

Switched reluctance motors (SRMs) can be applied in many industrial applications due to their cost advantages and ruggedness. The switched reluctance motor is simple to construct. It is not only features a salient pole stator with concentrated coils, which allows earlier winding and shorter end turns than other types of motors, but also features a salient pole rotor, which has no conductors or magnets and is thus the simplest of all electric machine rotors. Simplicity makes the SRM inexpensive and reliable, and together with its high speed capacity and high torque to inertia ratio, makes it a superior choice in different applications.

The dynamics of these systems are highly nonlinear and their models inevitable contain parametric uncertainties and unmodeled dynamics. The application of non linear robust control techniques is a necessity for successful operation electrical system. The industrial applications necessitate speed/position variators having high dynamic performances, a good precision in permanent regime, a high capacity of overload and robustness to the different perturbations. Thus, the recourse to robust control algorithms is desirable in stabilization and in tracking trajectories [1, 2].

Variable structure control with sliding mode, is one of the effective non linear robust control approaches. Sliding Mode Control (SMC) has attracted considerable attention because it provides a systematic approach to the problem of maintaining stability. It has been studied extensively to tackle problems of the nonlinear dynamic control systems. The sliding mode control can offer many good properties such as good performance against unmodelled dynamics systems, insensitivity to parameter variation, external disturbance rejection and fast dynamic [5, 9].

Sliding mode control has long proved its interests. Among them, relative simplicity of design, control of independent motion (as long as sliding conditions are maintained), invariance to process dynamics characteristics and external perturbations, wide variety of operational modes such as regulation, trajectory control [1], model following [2] and observation [3].

However, the motor is highly nonlinear and operates in saturation to maximize the output torque. Moreover, the motor torque is a nonlinear function of current and rotor position. This highly coupled nonlinear and complex structure of the SRM make the design of the controller difficult [4].

Section 2, investigates a case study of sliding mode control. In a more general study, the third section develops sliding mode controllers for switched reluctance motor drive; the proposed controller is described, and used to control the speed of the switched reluctance motor. Simulation results are given to show the effectiveness of this controller. Conclusions are summarized in the last section.

2. SRM model

2.1 Description of the system

In a switched reluctance machine, only the stator presents windings, while the rotor is made of steel laminations without conductors or permanent magnets. This very simple structure reduces greatly its cost. Motivated by this mechanical simplicity together with the recent advances in the power electronics components, much research has being developed in the last decade. The SRM, when compared with the AC and DC machines, shows two main advantages:

- It is a very reliable machine since each phase is largely independent physically, magnetically, and electrically from the other machine phases;
- It can achieve very high speeds (20000 - 50000 r.p.m.) because of the lack of conductors or magnets on the rotor;

The switched reluctance machine motion is produced because of the variable reluctance in the air gap between the rotor and the stator. When a stator winding is energized, producing a single magnetic field, reluctance torque is produced by the tendency of the rotor to move to its minimum reluctance position [5].

A cross-sectional view is presented in figure 1.

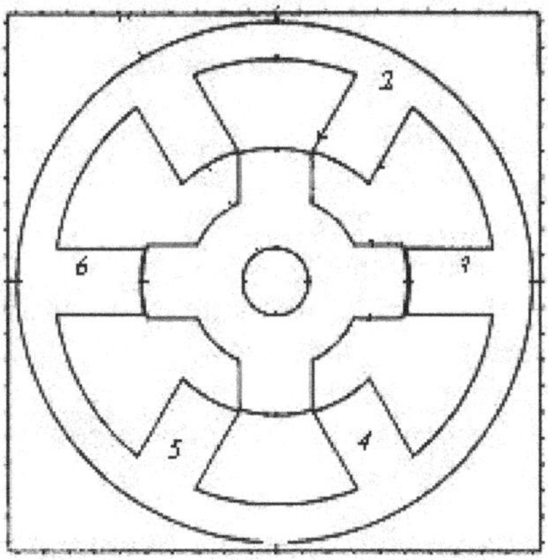

Fig. 1. Switched reluctance motor.

The schematic diagram of the speed control system under study is shown in figure 2. The power circuit consists with the *H*-bridge asymmetric type converter whose output is connected to the stator of the switched reluctance machine. Each phase has two IGBTS and two diodes. The parameters of the switched reluctance motor are given in the Appendix [5, 6].

The SMC inputs are obtained by manipulating the speed reference and feedback, while the SMC output is integrated to produce the current reference.

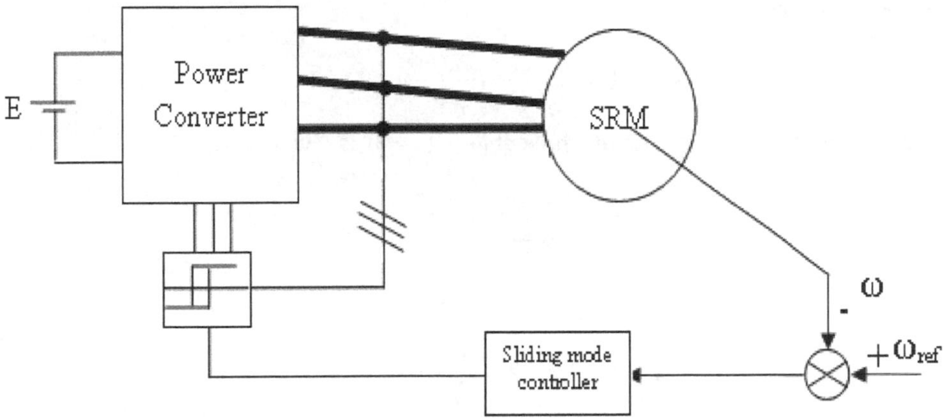

Fig. 2. Control of SRM.

2.2 Machine equation

The switched reluctance motor has a simple construction, but the solution of its mathematical models is relatively difficult due to its dominant non-linear behaviour. The flux linkage is a function of two variables, the current I and the rotor position (angle θ).
The instantaneous voltage across the terminals of a phase of an SR motor winding is related to the flux linked in the winding by Faraday's law as:

$$V_j = RI_j + \frac{\partial \Psi_j(i,\theta)}{\partial t} \tag{1}$$

With $j = 1,....3$
Because of the double salience construction of the SR motor and the magnetic saturation effects, the flux linked in an SRM phase varies as a function of rotor position θ and the phase current. Equation (1) can be expanded as

$$V_j = RI_j + \frac{\partial \Psi_j(i,\theta)}{\partial i}\frac{di}{dt} + \frac{\partial \Psi_j(i,\theta)}{\partial \theta}\omega \qquad j = 1,....3 \tag{2}$$

In which:

$$\omega = \frac{\partial \theta}{\partial t}$$

where $\frac{\partial \Psi_j}{\partial i}$ is defined as $L(\theta,i)$, the instantaneous inductance, and term $\frac{\partial \Psi}{\partial \theta}\frac{\partial \theta}{\partial t}$ is the instantaneous back e.m.f.
While excluding saturation and mutual inductance effects, the flux in each phase is given by the linear equation

$$\Psi_j(\theta,i_j) = L(\theta)i_j \tag{3}$$

It can be written as

$$V_j = RI_j + L(\theta)\frac{\partial i}{\partial t} + i\frac{\partial L(\theta)}{\partial \theta}\omega \qquad j = 1,....3 \tag{4}$$

The total energy associated with the three phases $(n = 3)$ is given by

$$W_{total} = \frac{1}{2}\sum_{j=1}^{3} L(\theta + (n - j - 1)\theta_s)I_j^{\;2}$$

with

$$\theta_s = 2\pi(\frac{1}{N_r} - \frac{1}{N_s}) \tag{5}$$

Each phase inductance displaced by an angle θ_s.
The average torque can be written as the superposition of the torque of the individual motor phases:

$$T_e = \sum_{phase=1}^{n} T_{phase} \tag{6}$$

and the motor total torque by

$$T_e = \frac{\partial W_{total}}{d\theta} = \frac{1}{2}\sum_{j=1}^{3} \frac{\partial L(\theta + (n - j - 1)\theta_s)}{\partial \theta} I_j^2 \tag{7}$$

The mechanical equations are

$$J\frac{\partial \omega}{\partial t} = T_e - T_l - f\omega \tag{8}$$

Where V - the terminal voltage, I - the phase current, R - the phase winding resistance, Ψ - the flux linked by the winding, J - the moment of inertia, f - the friction coefficient, $L(\theta)$ - the instantaneous inductance, N_r number of rotor poles, N_s number of stator poles, T_l is the torque load and T_e is the total torque.

3. SRM sliding mode speed controller

3.1 Sliding mode principle

Sliding modes is phenomenon may appear in a dynamic system governed by ordinary differential equations with discontinuous right-hand sides. It may happen that the control as a function of the system state switches at high frequency, this motion is called sliding mode. It may be enforced in the simplest tracking relay system with the state variable x(t) [7, 8]:

$$\frac{\partial x}{\partial t} = f(x) + u \tag{9}$$

With the bounded function $f(x)$ $|f(x)| < f_0$ f_0 $constant$ and the control as a relay function (figure(3)) of the tracking error $e = r(t) - \frac{\partial x}{\partial t}$ $r(t)$ is the reference input and u is given by:

$$u = \begin{cases} u_0 & if\ e > 0 \\ -u_0 & if\ e < 0 \end{cases} \text{ or } u = u_0 sign(e) \qquad u_0 = constant$$

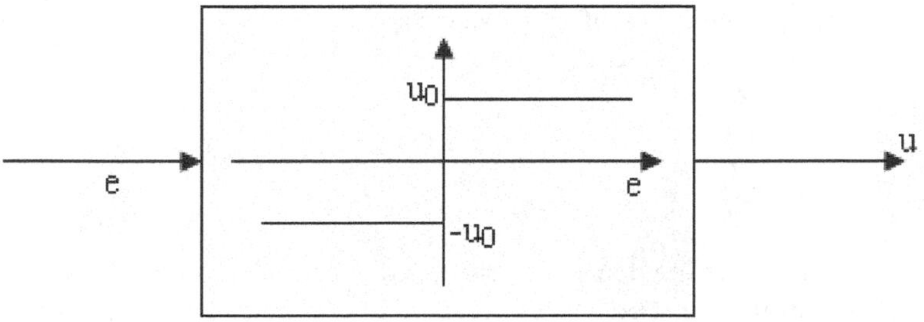

Fig. 3. Relay control.

The values of e and $\frac{\partial e}{\partial t} = \frac{\partial r}{\partial t} - f(x) - u_0 sign(e)$ have different signs if $u_0 > f_0 + \left|\frac{\partial r}{\partial t}\right|$.

3.2 Sliding mode controller

The equivalent total phase power becomes [9, 10]

$$P_{eq}(t) = I_c^2(t)(\omega \frac{\partial L(\theta)}{\partial \theta} = V_{dc} I_c(t) \tag{10}$$

The electromagnetic torque over the switching period is then

$$T_e = (\frac{V_{dc}}{\omega}) I_c(t) \tag{11}$$

If $I_c(t) = K_t(\frac{\omega}{V_{dc}}) I_t(t)$ then electromagnetic torque can be further simplified as

$$T_e = K_t I_t(t) \tag{12}$$

Where K_t is a proportional torque constant and $I_t(t)$ is the equivalent dc-link current providing electromagnetic torque.

The electromagnetic dynamic model of a switched reluctance motor and loads can be expressed as follows [11,12, 13]:

$$\frac{\partial \omega}{\partial t} = \frac{(T_e - T_l - f\omega)}{J} \tag{13}$$

From (11) and (12), (13) can be obtained:

$$\frac{\partial \omega}{\partial t} = \frac{(K_t I_t(t) - T_l - f\omega)}{J} \tag{14}$$

Speed control can be implemented by a sliding-mode variable structure controller, but a discontinuous torque control signal would cause chattering of the speed response. In order to enable smooth torque control and reduce the chattering problem $I_t(t)$ must be smoothed according to (11). The phase variable state representation of Fig. 4 can be used to develop the required control scheme. It can be simplified as:

$$\begin{bmatrix} \frac{\partial x_1}{\partial t} \\ \frac{\partial x_2}{\partial t} \end{bmatrix} = \begin{bmatrix} \frac{-f}{J} & \frac{K_t}{J} \\ 0 & -\frac{R}{L(\theta)} \end{bmatrix} \cdot \begin{bmatrix} x_1 \\ x_2 \end{bmatrix} + \begin{bmatrix} 0 \\ \frac{1}{L(\theta)} \end{bmatrix} . U + \begin{bmatrix} 1 \\ 0 \end{bmatrix} . (\frac{T_l}{J}) \tag{15}$$

Where $x_1 = \omega - \omega_{ref}$, ω_{ref} is the demand rotor speed, $x_2 = I - I_{ref}$, and U is a control signal which is used to control the current error, irrespective of drive system parameter variations. The sliding line in the phase plane diagram [Fig. 4] can be described as follows:

$$S = \omega - \omega_{ref} \tag{16}$$

from the equation (13) and (15) , we can be obtains

$$\frac{\partial S}{\partial t} = \frac{K_t}{J} I - \frac{f}{J}\omega - \frac{T_l}{J} - \frac{\partial \omega_{ref}}{\partial t} \tag{17}$$

the current of control is given by

$$I_c = I_c^{eq} + I_c^n$$

With

$$I_c^{eq} = \frac{1}{K_t}(J\frac{\partial \omega_{ref}}{\partial t} + f\omega + T_l) \tag{18}$$

$$I_c^n = K_w \operatorname{sgn}(S(\omega))$$

To satisfy the existence condition of the sliding-mode speed controller, the following must be satisfied:

$$\lim_{S \to 0} S\frac{dS}{dt} <= 0 \tag{19}$$

The controller can be designed as follows:

$$U = ax_1 + b\frac{\partial x_1}{\partial t}$$

Where:

$$a = \begin{cases} \alpha_1 & if\ Sx_1 > 0 \\ \beta_1 & if\ Sx_1 < 0 \end{cases}$$

$$b = \begin{cases} \alpha_2 & if\ S\dfrac{\partial x_1}{\partial t} > 0 \\ \beta_2 & if\ S\dfrac{\partial x_1}{\partial t} < 0 \end{cases} \qquad (20)$$

a and b are proportional and derivative gain constant respectively, and $\alpha_1, \alpha_2, \beta_1\ and\ \beta_2$ are real constants.

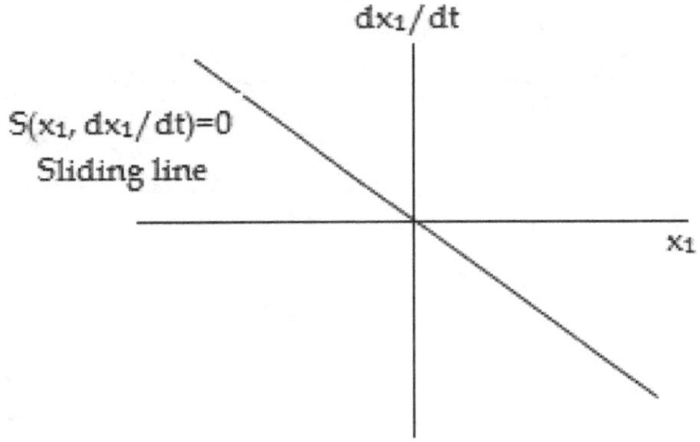

Fig. 4. A prescribed sliding line in phase plane.

4. Simulation result

The speed regulation of the SRM, despite its mechanical simplicity, is not simple to achieve. In the previous sections, we saw the importance that the values of the commutation angles have to torque oscillations. A linear controller as the PI regulator presents good results for the SRM speed control [8]. However, the controller will be only valid for a given operating point. Therefore, some authors have investigated recently non-linear controllers based on the sliding mode [11,12,16] applied to SRM speed control. In this section, we discuss and illustrate the advantages and drawbacks of the SRM speed control by using a PI regulator and a sliding mode controller.

To show the sliding mode controller performances we have simulated the system described in figure 2. The simulation of the starting mode without load is done. The simulation is realized using the SIMULINK software in MATLAB environment. Figure 5 shows the performances of the sliding mode controller.

The saturating function in the PI block diagram is necessary since during the transient, if the current demanded is high and if the speed reference is also high, then the f.e.m. produced will prevent the current to grow. Hence, the maximum current value of the block *saturation* has been fixed in 25A.

Fig. 5.b shows the speed regulation for a reference of 120rad/s, with $\theta_{on} = 0°$ and $\theta_{off} = 38°$. Values of PI parameters K_p and K_i have been optimized in order to have the best compromise between response time and overshoot. Fig. 5.b shows good results for the speed regulation with weak speed oscillations in the permanent regime. Using a PI controller, a good compromise for K_p and K_i parameters has been found in order to have weak speed oscillations. The values found were: $K_p = 0{,}18$ and $K_i = 2{,}85$.However, if a load is applied, the speed oscillations will increase, as illustrated in Fig. 5.b. These results have been obtained with a load of $T_l = 1{,}5\text{Nm}$ applied at $t = 0{,}6\text{s}$.
Fig. 5 shows the very good performance reached by the sliding mode controller. Indeed, one notes that the overshoot is less important in the case of the sliding mode regulator, with a best response time without increasing the overshoot. Follow, we show the robustness of the PI and the sliding mode controller for the same operating condition.

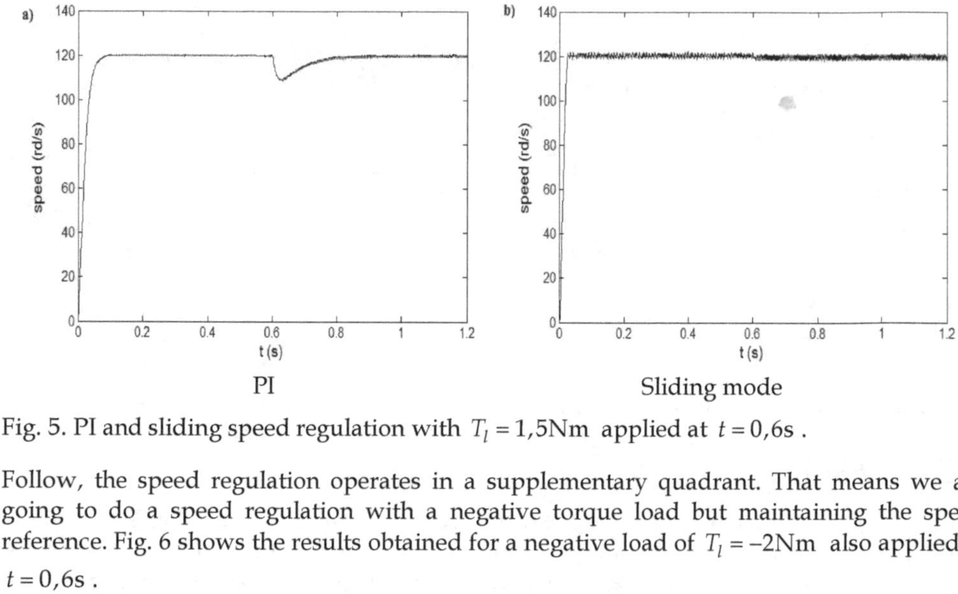

PI Sliding mode

Fig. 5. PI and sliding speed regulation with $T_l = 1{,}5\text{Nm}$ applied at $t = 0{,}6\text{s}$.

Follow, the speed regulation operates in a supplementary quadrant. That means we are going to do a speed regulation with a negative torque load but maintaining the speed reference. Fig. 6 shows the results obtained for a negative load of $T_l = -2\text{Nm}$ also applied at $t = 0{,}6\text{s}$.

Fig. 6 shows that the speed regulation is not assured anymore after $t = 0{,}6\text{s}$. From (8), the motor speed is given by

$$\omega = \frac{(T_e - T_l)}{f} \tag{21}$$

Therefore, the minimum speed for a possible regulation without producing a braking torque, meaning that the regulator will have its reference current to zero, will be

$$\omega_{min} = \frac{-T_l}{f} \tag{22}$$

In our case, the minimum speed stays $\omega_{min} = 96{,}3rd/s$, as shown in Fig. 6. Now, if one wants to continue the speed regulation at 90 rd / s, it will be necessary to produce a braking torque when the speed error is negative. The controller by sliding mode gives good result compared to that of regulator PI. The increase speed is reduced during the application of a negative torque. However, when the negative torque load is applied at $t = 0{,}5s$, the speed oscillations become significant. Previous results in Fig. 6 showed significant oscillations in the speed signal due to an initial bad choice of the θ_{on} value.

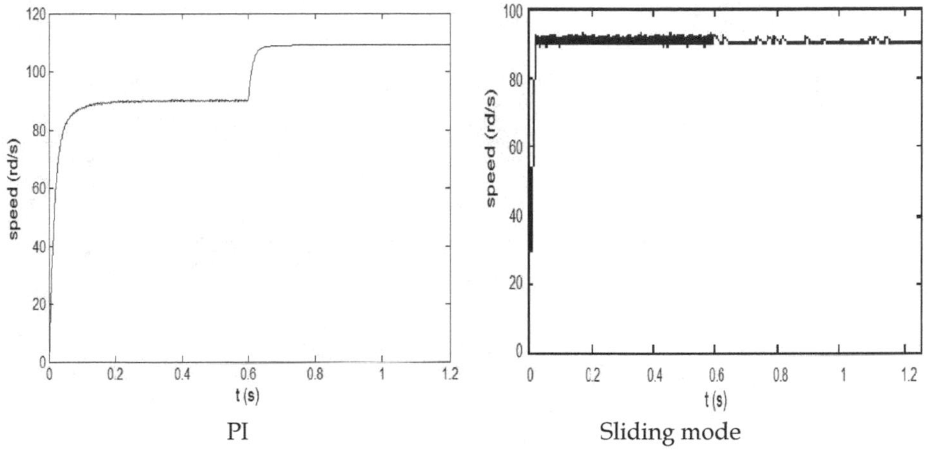

Fig. 6. PI and sliding speed regulation with $T_l = -2\text{Nm}$ applied at $t = 0{,}6s$.

Figure 7 shows the very good performances reached by the sliding mode controller. Indeed, one notes that the overshoot is less important in the case of the sliding regulator, with a best response time without increasing the overshoot.

For this test, the sliding controller proves to be well more robust because the speed curve is hardly of its reference. On the other hand, the speed signal evolution obtained with the PI controller deviates about 10% from its reference value (figure 7). The speed tracking is satisfactory, and the torque ripple is low. These results demonstrate the robustness of the drive under unpredictable load conditions. The decreasing speed oscillations with the PI controller are owed to a slower reaction of the current, as shown in figure 7.

4.1 Robustness

In order to test the robustness of the proposed control, we have studied the speed performances. Two cases are considered:

1. Inertia variation,
2. Stator resistance variation.

The figure 8 shows the tests of the robustness: a) The robustness tests concerning the variation of the resistances, b) the robustness tests in relation to inertia variations.

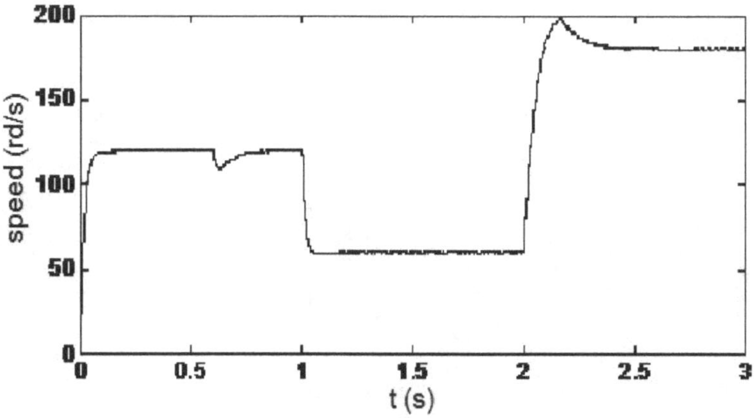

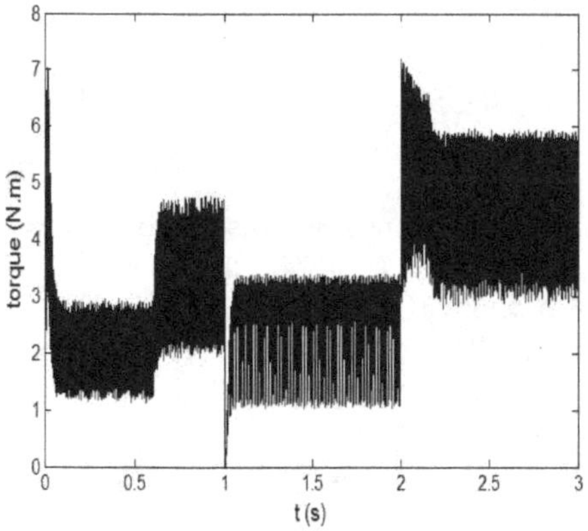

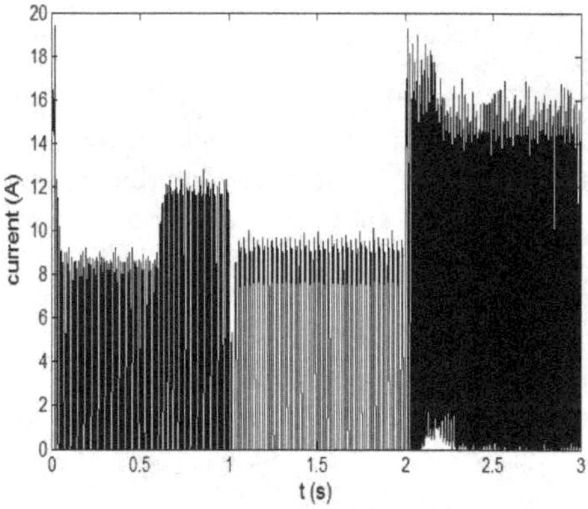

PI controller

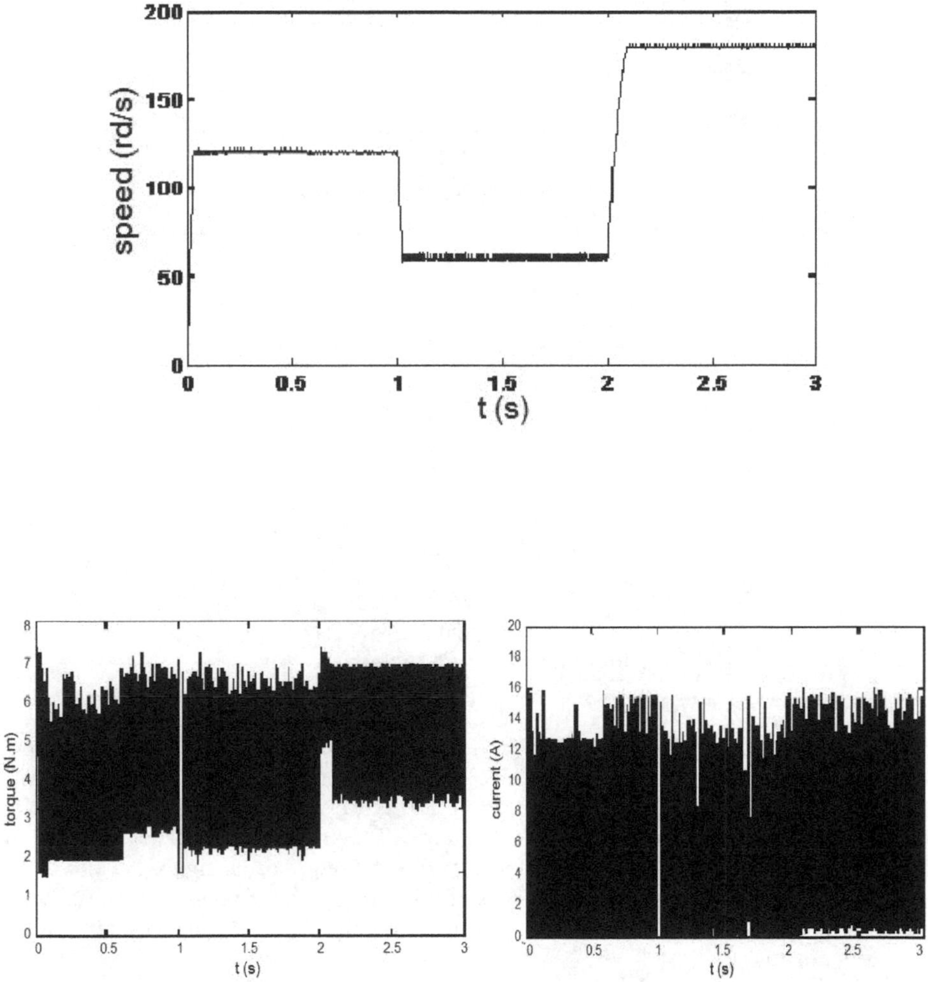

Sliding controller

Fig. 7. Simulation results of speed control.

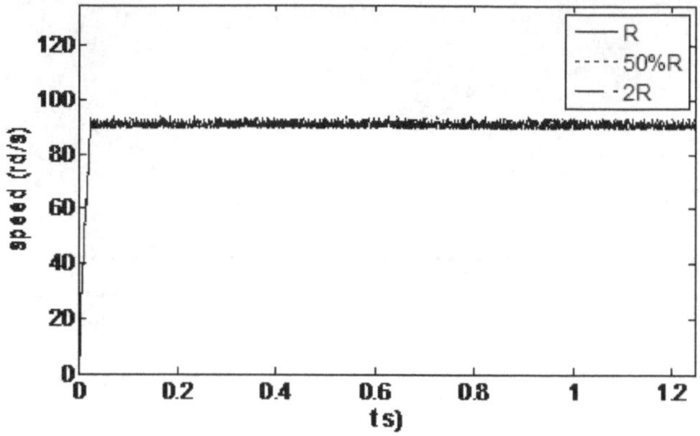

a) Different values of resistance of stator

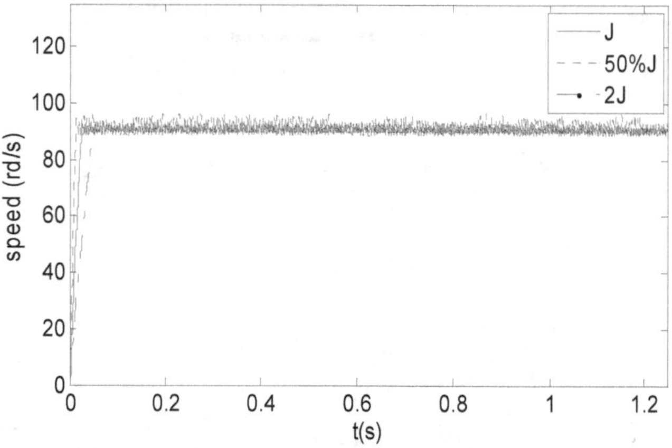

b) Different values of moment of inertia

Fig. 8. Test of robustness.

Figure 8-b shows the parameter variation does not allocate performances of proposed control. The speed response is insensitive to parameter variations of the machine, without overshoot and without static error. The other performances are maintained.

For the robustness of control, a decrease or increase of the moment of inertia, the resistances doesn't have any effects on the performances of the technique used (figure 8.a and 8.b). An increase of the moment of inertia gives best performances, but it presents a slow dynamic response (figure 8.b). The controller suggested gives good performances although the parameters are unknown.

5. Conclusion

This chapter presents a new approach to robust speed control for switched reluctance motor. It develops a simple robust controller to deal with parameters uncertain and external disturbances and takes full account of system noise, digital implementation and integral control. The control strategy is based on SMC approaches.

The simulation results show that the proposed controller is superior to conventional controller in robustness and in tracking precision. The simulation study clearly indicates the superior performance of sliding control, because it is inherently adaptive in nature. It appears from the response properties that it has a high performance in presence of the plant parameters uncertain and load disturbances. It is used to control system with unknown model. The control of speed by SMC gives fast dynamic response without overshoot and zero steady-state error. The controller contains only two structures and the only way of changing them is by switching. A major drawback of this system is chattering, which is caused by a fast switching of the controller structure

6. Appendix

Throughout this section the motor parameters used to verify the design principles are:
Number of phase 3, Number of stator poles 6, Pole arc 30°, Number of rotor poles 4, Pole arc 30°, Maximum inductance 60mH, Minimum inductance 8mH, resistance 1,3Ω, Moment of inertia 0,0013Kg;m^2, friction 0,0183Nm/s, Inverter voltage 150v.

7. References

V.Utkin, J.Guldner, J.Shi "Sliding mode control in electromechanical systems" Ed Taylor and Francis 1999.

V. I. Utkin, "Sliding mode control design principles and applications to electric drives", *IEEE Trans.* Industrial Electronics, Vol. 40, No. 1, February 1993

S. K. Panda and P. K. Dash, "Application of nonlinear control to switched reluctance motors: A feedback linearization approach," *Proc.Inst. Elect. Eng.*, vol. 143, pt. B, no. 5, pp. 371-379,1996.

W. Perruquetti, J.P.Barbot "Sliding Mode Control In Engineering" Ed Marcel Dekker, 2002

Ahmed TAHOUR, Hamza ABID2, Abdel Ghani AISSAOUI " Speed Control of Switched Reluctance Motor Using Fuzzy Sliding Mode" Advances in Electrical and Computer Engineering Volume 8 (15), Number 1 (29), 2008.

F. Soares and P.J. "Costa Branco Simulation of a 6/4 Switched Reluctance Motor Based on Matlab/Simulink Environment "aerospace and electronic system. IEEE transactions, Vol 37 pp989-1009, July 2001.

R. A. De Carlo, S. H. Zak and G. P. Matthews, "Variable structure control of nonlinear multivariable systems: a tutorial", Proceedings IEEE, Vol. 76, No. 3, March 1988, pp. 212-232.

J. Y. Hung, W. Gao, and J. C. Hung, "Variable structure control : a survey", *IEEE Trans. Industrial Electronics,* Vol.40, No. 1, February 1993, pp. 2-22.

D. G. Taylor, "Nonlinear control of electric machines: An overview", *IEEE Control Systems magazine,* Vol. 14, No. 6, December 1994, pp. 41-51.

J.J.E. Slotine, J.K. Hedrick and E.A. Misawa, "On sliding observers for nonlinear systems", Transactions of the ASME: Journal of Dynamic Systems Measurement and Control, Vol. 109, pp. 245-252, 1987.

E. Y. Y. Ho and P. C. Sen, "Control dynamics of speed drive systems using sliding mode controllers with integral compensation" IEEE Trans.Ind. Applicat., vol. 27, pp. 883–892, Sept./Oct. 1991.

B. K. Bose, "Sliding mode control of induction motor," in Proc. IEEEIAS Annu. Meeting, 1985, pp. 479–486.

Tzu-Shien Chuang and Charles Pollock "Robust Speed Control of a Switched Reluctance Vector Drive Using Variable Structure Approach" IEEE Transactions On Industrial Electronics, Vol. 44, No. 6, DECEMBER 1997 pp.800.808

Roy A. McCann, Mohammad S. Islam,, I.Husain," Application of a Sliding-Mode Observer for Position and Speed Estimation in Switched Reluctance Motor Drives" IEEE Transactions On Industrial On Industry Applications, Vol. 37, NO. 1, JANUARY/FEBRUARY 2001 pp.51.58

Zheng Hongtao, Qiao Bin, Guo Zhijiang, and Jiang Jingping. (2001) "Modeling of Switched Reluctance Drive Based on Variable Structure Fuzzy-Neural Networks" Fifth International Conference on Electrical Machines and Systems, (ICEMS 2001), Vol. 2, pp.1250-1253

Gobbi, K. Ramar and N.C. Sahoo."Fuzzy Iterative Technique for Torque Ripple Minimization in Switched Reluctance Motors" Electric Power Components and Systems. Vol. 37, Issue. 9, July 2009. pp. 982 - 1004.

Gobbi. R and K. Ramar, "Optimization Techniques for a Hysteresis Current Controller to Minimize Torque Ripple in SR Motors", IET Electric Power Applications, 2009. Vol.3, Issues 5, pp 453-460

17

LMI Robust Control of PWM Converters: An Output-Feedback Approach

Carlos Olalla[1], Abdelali El Aroudi[1], Ramon Leyva[1] and Isabelle Queinnec[2]
[1]*Universitat Rovira i Virgili, 43007 Tarragona*
[2]*CNRS ; LAAS ; 7 avenue du colonel Roche, F-31077 Toulouse Cedex 4*
Université de Toulouse ; UPS, INSA, INP, ISAE, UT1, UTM ;
LAAS ; F-31077 Toulouse Cedex 4
[1]*Spain*
[2]*France*

1. Introduction

This chapter proposes a systematic approach for the synthesis of robust controllers for dc-dc converters. The approach is based on the Linear Matrix Inequalities (LMIs) framework and the associated optimization algorithms. The aim of this approach is to allow the designer to describe the uncertainty of the converter and to deal with the requirements of the application beforehand.

The aforementioned dc-dc converters (see Figure 1) are devices that deliver a dc output voltage, with different properties from those in the input voltage (Erickson & Maksimovic, 1999). They are usually employed to adapt energy sources to the load requirements (or vice versa). These devices present several challenges regarding their robust control. First, the converter must maintain a tight regulation or tracking of the output. Moreover, the controller design is focused on maximizing the bandwidth of the closed-loop response in order to reject the usual disturbances that appear in these systems. Finally, the response of the converter must satisfy desirable transient characteristics, as for example, the shortest possible output settling time or the minimum overshoot. Besides of these common requirements, the converter can be affected by uncertainty in its components or by input or output disturbances that may appear.

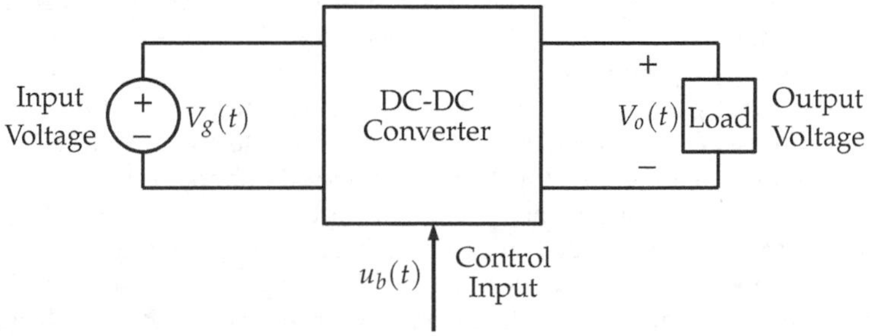

Fig. 1. General scheme of a dc-dc converter.

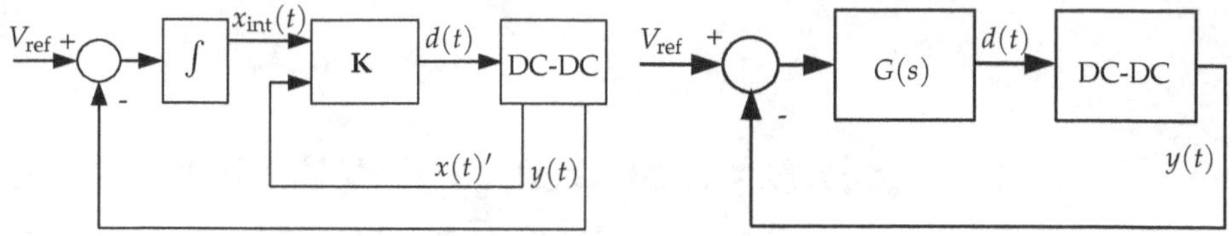

(a) Block diagram of a state-feedback system with controller **K** and error integration.

(b) Block diagram of an output-feedback system with controller $G(s)$.

Fig. 2. State-feedback and output-feedback block diagrams.

Nevertheless, most of the modeling approaches in the literature disregard these uncertainties. Moreover, due to the switching nature of the system, pulse-width modulation (PWM) is commonly used in the industry applications, while the models that are usually employed disregard that part of the dynamics (i.e. the high frequency dynamics) and other inherent nonlinearities, such as saturations and bilinear terms.

The chapter proposes a systematic approach to deal with these challenges, using the concepts of LMI control (Ben-Tal et al., 2009; Bernussou, 1996; Boyd et al., 1994; El Ghaoui & Niculescu, 2000; Pyatnitskii & Skorodinskii, 1982). Linear matrix inequalities have become an important topic in the field of Automatic Control due to the following facts. First of all, LMIs can be solved numerically by efficient computer algorithms (Gahinet et al., 1995; Löfberg, 2004; Sturm, 1999). Secondly, more and more methods have been developed to describe control problems in terms of LMI constraints. Finally, these methods are able to include descriptions of the uncertainty.

Some of the previous literature on LMI control of dc-dc converters are (Montagner et al., 2005; Olalla et al., 2009a; 2010a). In these papers, the uncertainty of the converter is taken into account and the control synthesis deals with different operating points. Nevertheless, they do not consider the stability of the system trajectories when the system changes from one operating point to another, nor they include other nonlinearities such as saturations. The versatility of LMI control has allowed to deal with some of these nonlinearities (Olalla et al., 2009b), (Olalla et al., 2011).

These approaches share the same feedback scheme, which is based upon state-feedback with error integration (Figure 2(a)). The main advantage of this approach is that the synthesis optimization problem can be posed as a convex semidefinite programming and that the implementation of the controller is simple. On the other hand, state-feedback requires sensing of the state variables, which may not be easily measurable or may require estimation in some cases. In practice, most of the designs that can be found in the power electronics literature employ output-feedback approaches since they usually rely on frequency-based concepts which are well-known by electrical engineers. This is the reason why this chapter focuses on LMI-based synthesis methods which may be applicable to the output-feedback scheme (Figure 2(b)), with the aim to derive robust controllers for dc-dc converters.

In order to introduce such synthesis methods, the chapter is organized as follows. The first section deals with modeling of dc-dc converters, the averaging method, the sampling effect of the pulse-width modulator and the uncertainty. Section II reviews some of the results of previous works on LMI synthesis for state-feedback approaches. Section III puts forward the problem of output-feedback and some of the strategies that can be employed to pose such problem in terms of semidefinite programming. Concretely, Section III proposes the

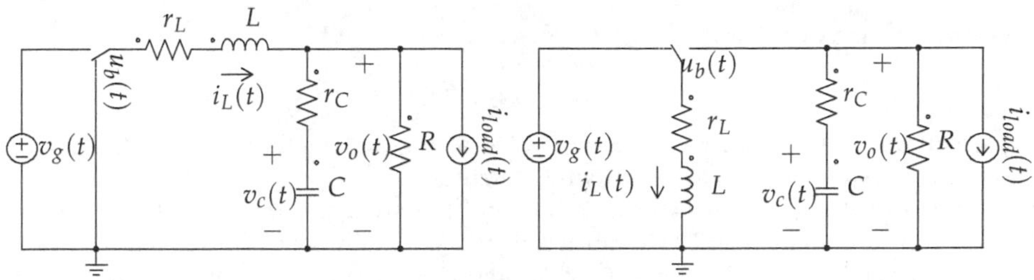

(a) Buck converter with stray resistances. (b) Buck-boost converter with stray resistances.

Fig. 3. Schematic of the buck and the buck-boost converter.

following strategies. First, the classic dynamic output-feedback control problem is treated. This approach can be carried out with a change of variables as in (Scherer et al., 1997). However, with such an approach the uncertainty must be modeled with elaborated models, as for example, weighting functions Wallis & Tymerski (2000). Therefore, the chapter also proposes the synthesis of output-feedback controllers based on the static case. Both the static output-feedback and a parametrization (Peaucelle & Arzelier, 2001b) to deal with dynamic output-feedback are considered. The advantages and drawbacks of the three approaches shown in the chapter will be discussed and the results will be compared.

Notation

For symmetric matrices A and B, $A > B$ means that $A - B$ is positive definite. $\mathbf{A}$ denotes that the matrix A is an unknown variable. A' denotes the transpose of A. $\text{Co}\left\{v_j,\ j = 1, \ldots, N\right\}$ denotes the convex hull defined by N vertices $v_j \in \mathbb{R}^n$. The identity matrix of order n is noted as $\mathbb{1}_n$ and the null $n \times m$ matrix is noted as $\mathbf{0}_{\ n,m}$. The symbol $\star$ denotes symmetric blocks in partitioned matrices.

2. Modeling of uncertain dc-dc converters

This subsection shows the state-space averaged models of the buck and the buck-boost converters of Figures 3(a) and 3(b). The models are assumed to operate in Continuous Conduction Mode (CCM), i.e. the inductor current is always larger than zero. Besides of the averaged models, this section also introduces a model of the sampling effect caused by the PWM. Finally, at the end of the section, the uncertainty modeling of dc-dc converters is discussed and a simple example is shown.

2.1 Model of the buck converter

The first model that is introduced considers a buck converter, which is characterized by linear averaged control-to-output dynamics. As stated in (Olalla et al., 2010b), the transfer functions of dc-dc converters can strongly depend on the stray resistances of the converter. Since the chapter considers different output-feedback synthesis approaches, these stray resistances are considered in the models.

Figure 3(a) shows the circuit diagram of a dc-dc buck converter where $v_o(t)$ is the output voltage, $v_g(t)$ is the line voltage and $i_{load}(t)$ is the load disturbance. The output voltage must be kept at a given reference V_{ref}. The converter load is modeled as a linear resistor R. The stray resistances of the switch during the on and the off position are combined with the resistance of the inductor and noted as:

$$\begin{aligned} r_{on} &= r_{d_{on}} + r_L \\ r_{off} &= r_{d_{off}} + r_L \end{aligned} \tag{1}$$

The measurable states of the converter are noted as $x_a(t)$. Note that the time dependence of the variables may be omitted to simplify the notation.
The binary signal $u_{\mathrm{b}}(t)$, which turns on and off the switches, is genereated by means of a Pulse Width Modulation (PWM) subcircuit, working at a constant frequency $1/T_{\mathrm{s}}$. The switching period T_{s} is equal to the sum of t_{on} and t_{off}. For a unit-amplitude sawtooth PWM, the duty-cycle $d(t) = t_{\mathrm{on}}/(t_{\mathrm{on}} + t_{\mathrm{off}})$ is the control input of the converter.
As shown in (Erickson & Maksimovic, 1999) and (Leyva et al., 2006), considering that the state-space matrices of the converter are [A_{on}, B_{on}] during t_{on} and [A_{off}, B_{off}] during t_{off}, the general state-space averaged model of a dc-dc converter can be written as:

$$\begin{aligned} \dot{x}(t) = &(A_{\mathrm{off}} + (A_{\mathrm{on}} - A_{\mathrm{off}})U)X + (B_{\mathrm{off}} + (B_{\mathrm{on}} - B_{\mathrm{off}})D) \left[\begin{smallmatrix}1\\0\end{smallmatrix}\right] W \\ &+ (A_{\mathrm{off}} + (A_{\mathrm{on}} - A_{\mathrm{off}})U)\tilde{x}(t) + (B_{\mathrm{off}} + (B_{\mathrm{on}} - B_{\mathrm{off}})D) \left[\begin{smallmatrix}0\\1\end{smallmatrix}\right] \tilde{w}(t) \\ &+ ((A_{\mathrm{on}} - A_{\mathrm{off}})X + (B_{\mathrm{on}} - B_{\mathrm{off}}) \left[\begin{smallmatrix}1\\0\end{smallmatrix}\right] W)\tilde{d}(t) \\ &+ ((A_{\mathrm{on}} - A_{\mathrm{off}})\tilde{x}(t) + (B_{\mathrm{on}} - B_{\mathrm{off}}) \left[\begin{smallmatrix}0\\1\end{smallmatrix}\right] \tilde{w}(t))\tilde{d}(t), \end{aligned} \tag{2}$$

where the equilibrium (noted with capital letters) and the incremental vectors (noted with tildes) are as follows. X and $\tilde{x} \in \mathbb{R}^n$ correspond to the state vectors, D and $\tilde{d} \in \mathbb{R}^m$ are the control inputs, while W and $\tilde{w} \in \mathbb{R}^l$ stand for the disturbance inputs.
In the buck converter, $A_{\mathrm{on}} = A_{\mathrm{off}}$, and the averaged model (2) can be rewritten as:

$$\frac{d\tilde{x}(t)}{dt} = (AX + B_{\mathrm{w}}W) + A\tilde{x}(t) + B_{\mathrm{w}}\tilde{w}(t) + B_{\mathrm{u}}\tilde{d}(t) + B_{\mathrm{n}_w}\tilde{w}(t)\tilde{d}(t) \tag{3}$$

where:

$$A = \begin{bmatrix} -\frac{r_{eq}}{L} - \frac{Rr_C}{(R+r_C)L} & -\frac{R}{(R+r_C)L} \\ \frac{R}{(R+r_C)C} & -\frac{1}{(R+r_C)C} \end{bmatrix}, \; B_{\mathrm{w}} = \begin{bmatrix} \frac{D}{L} & \frac{Rr_C}{(R+r_C)L} \\ 0 & -\frac{R}{(R+r_C)C} \end{bmatrix},$$

$$B_{\mathrm{u}} = \begin{bmatrix} \frac{V_g}{L} \\ 0 \end{bmatrix}, \; B_{\mathrm{n}_w} = \begin{bmatrix} \frac{1}{L} \\ 0 \end{bmatrix}, \tag{4}$$

$$X = \begin{bmatrix} \frac{V_g D}{1 + r_{eq}/R} \\ \frac{R}{\frac{V_g D}{1 + r_{eq}/R}} \end{bmatrix}, \; W = \begin{bmatrix} V_g \\ 0 \end{bmatrix}, \; \tilde{x}(t) = \begin{bmatrix} \tilde{i}_L(t) \\ \tilde{v}_{\mathrm{o}}(t) \end{bmatrix}, \; \tilde{w}(t) = \begin{bmatrix} \tilde{v}_g(t) \\ i_{\mathrm{load}}(t) \end{bmatrix},$$

being $r_{eq} = Dr_{on} + D'r_{off}$ and $D' = 1 - D$. The dimensions of the system matrices are defined as $A \in \mathbb{R}^{n\times n}$, B_{u}, $B_{\mathrm{n}_w} \in \mathbb{R}^{n\times m}$, $B_{\mathrm{w}} \in \mathbb{R}^{n\times l}$.
Similarly, the averaged outputs of the buck converter can be written as:

$$Y + \tilde{y}(t) = (C_y X + E_{\mathrm{yw}} W) + C_y \tilde{x}(t) + E_{\mathrm{yw}} \tilde{w}(t) \tag{5}$$

where in a general case $C_y \in \mathbb{R}^{q\times n}$, $E_{yw} \in \mathbb{R}^{q\times m}$. Considering the load voltage $v_o(t)$ as the only output, these matrices are written as:

$$C_y = \begin{bmatrix} \frac{Rr_C}{R+r_C} & \frac{R}{R+r_C} \end{bmatrix}, \ E_{yw} = \begin{bmatrix} 0 & -\frac{Rr_C}{R+r_C} \end{bmatrix}. \tag{6}$$

2.2 Model of the buck-boost converter

In the buck-boost converter, matrices A_{on} and A_{off} are not equal, and therefore, the averaged model contains bilinear terms concerning the control input, the states and the disturbance inputs. According to those nonlinear terms, the linearized transfer function depends on the operating point, hence making the control subsystem design more difficult. In order to derive accurate transfer functions of the buck-boost converter for output-feedback approaches, the stray resistances are also taken into account.

For the buck-boost converter, the averaged model in the form of (3) contains bilinear terms, and can be expressed as follows:

$$\frac{d\tilde{x}(t)}{dt} = (AX + B_w W) + A\tilde{x}(t) + B_w\tilde{w}(t) + B_u\tilde{d}(t) + B_{n_x}\tilde{x}(t)\tilde{d}(t) + B_{n_w}\tilde{w}(t)\tilde{d}(t) \tag{7}$$

where:

$$A = \begin{bmatrix} -\frac{r_{eq}}{L} - D'\frac{Rr_C}{(R+r_C)L} & D'\frac{R}{(R+r_C)L} \\ -D'\frac{R}{(R+r_C)C} & -\frac{1}{(R+r_C)C} \end{bmatrix}, \ B_w = \begin{bmatrix} D\frac{1}{L} & -D'\frac{Rr_C}{(R+r_C)L} \\ 0 & -\frac{R}{(R+r_C)C} \end{bmatrix},$$

$$B_u = \begin{bmatrix} \frac{V_g}{L}\left(1 + \frac{Dr_C}{D'^2(R+r_C)} + \frac{D'DR^2}{D'R(D'R+r_C)+(R+r_C)r_{eq}}\right) \\ \frac{DV_g}{CD'^2(R+r_C)} \end{bmatrix},$$

$$B_{n_w} = \begin{bmatrix} \frac{1}{L} & -\frac{Rr_C}{(R+r_C)L} \\ 0 & 0 \end{bmatrix}, \tag{8}$$

$$X = \begin{bmatrix} \frac{V_g D'DR(R+r_C)}{(-D'R(-D'R-r_C)+(R+r_C)r_{eq})D'R} \\ \frac{-V_g D'DR(R+r_C)}{-D'R(-D'R-r_C)+(R+r_C)r_{eq}} \end{bmatrix}, \ B_{n_x} = \begin{bmatrix} \frac{Rr_C}{L(R+r_C)} & -\frac{R}{(R+r_C)L} \\ \frac{R}{(R+r_C)C} & 0 \end{bmatrix}.$$

being $r_{eq} = Dr_{on} + D'r_{off}$. The dimensions of the system matrices are defined as A, B_{n_x}, $B_{n_w} \in \mathbb{R}^{n\times n}$, $B_u \in \mathbb{R}^{n\times m}$, $B_w \in \mathbb{R}^{n\times l}$.

The averaged output $v_o(t)$ of the buck-boost converter can be written as:

$$Y + \tilde{y}(t) = (C_y X + E_{yw}W) + C_y\tilde{x}(t) + E_{yw}\tilde{w}(t) + C_{yu}X\tilde{d}(t) + C_{yu}\tilde{x}(t)\tilde{d}(t) \tag{9}$$

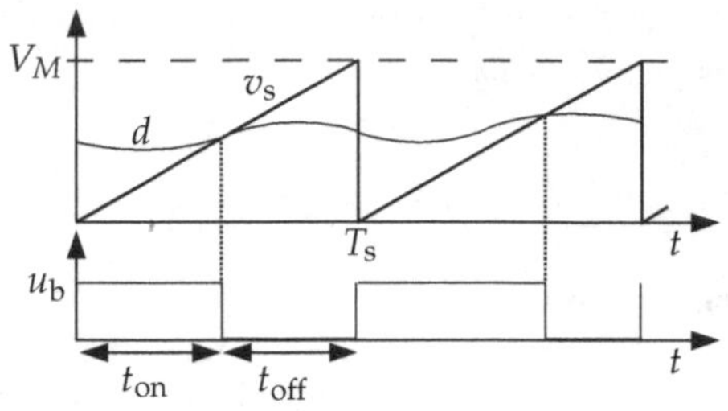

Fig. 4. Waveforms of the PWM process.

where:

$$C_y = \left[-D'\frac{Rr_C}{R+r_C}\ \frac{R}{R+r_C}\right],\ C_{yu} = \left[\frac{Rr_C}{R+r_C}\ 0\right],\ E_{yw} = \left[0\ -\frac{Rr_C}{R+r_C}\right]. \tag{10}$$

These models are employed in Section 3 to derive robust controllers for the buck and the buck-boost converters.

2.3 Delay model for the PWM actuator

The models presented above do not take into account the sampling effect of the modulation (Brown & Middlebrook, 1981; Erickson & Maksimovic, 1999) (see Figure 4).

Usually, the sampling effect is not considered, and only the linear gain of the modulator is taken into account. In a voltage-mode modulator, the duty-cycle input is usually constrained between zero and the amplitude of the sawtooth signal V_M, and therefore the linear gain of this modulator is $1/V_M$ (Erickson & Maksimovic, 1999). For simplicity the amplitude V_M can be considered equal to one, such that the linear model shown previously is valid for a duty-cycle input $d \in [0,1]$.

However, the sampling effect can be taken into account in order to limit the control-loop bandwidth in the automatic control synthesis algorithms. Such an effect can be incorporated to the power stage model as a sampling at the switching frequency $1/T_s$ and a zero-order hold block, assuming that the switch is fired once every switching cycle T_s (Maksimovic, 2000). The equivalent transfer function for this sampling model is then:

$$G_{ZOH}(s) = \frac{1-e^{-sT_s}}{sT_s} \tag{11}$$

The exponential factor e^{-sT_s} can be approximated by a Padé function:

$$e^{-sT_s} \approx \frac{\sum_{k=0}^{n} -1^k c_k T_s s^k}{\sum_{k=0}^{n} c_k T_s s^k},$$
$$c_k = \frac{(2n-k)!n!}{2n!k!(n-k)!},\qquad k = 0,1,\cdot,n. \tag{12}$$

Taking the first order approximation $n = 1$ we obtain

$$e^{-sT_s} \approx \frac{1-(T_s/2)s}{1+(T_s/2)s} \tag{13}$$

The equivalent hold transfer function with the Padé approximation writes

$$G_{ZOH}(s) = \frac{1}{1 + s\frac{T_s}{2}} \tag{14}$$

which is a strictly proper transfer function whose representation in state-space form could be:

$$\begin{cases} \dot{\tilde{x}}_p(t) = -(2/T_s)\tilde{x}_p(t) + (2/T_s)\tilde{d}(t) \\ \tilde{d}_2(t) = \tilde{x}_p(t) \end{cases} \tag{15}$$

where $\tilde{x}_p(t)$ is the state variable of the $G_{ZOH}(s)$, $\tilde{d}(t)$ is its input and $\tilde{d}_2(t)$ is its output.

2.4 Modeling of uncertainty

As stated in (Gahinet et al., 1995), the notion of system uncertainty is of major importance in the field of robust control theory. First of all, one of the key features of feedback is that it reduces the effects of uncertainty. However, when designing a control system, the model used to represent the behavior of the plant is often approximated. The difference between the approximated model and the true model is called model uncertainty. Also the changes due to operating conditions, aging effects, etc... are sources of uncertainty.

The two main approaches shown in (Gahinet et al., 1995) when dealing with system uncertainties and LMI control are:

- Uncertain state-space models, relevant for systems described by dynamical equations with uncertain and/or time-varying coefficients.
- Linear-fractional representation (LFR) of uncertainty, in which the uncertain system is described as an interconnection of known LTI systems.

While LFR models have had a main role in modern robust control synthesis methods such as in μ-synthesis (Zhou et al., 1996), state-space models have been used in convex optimization approaches (Boyd et al., 1994). Since this chapter presents approaches that do not employ the concept of structured singular value on which the μ-synthesis method is based, the following subsection is focused on uncertain state-space models.

If some of the physical parameters are approximated or unknown, or if there exists nonlinear or non-modeled dynamic effects, then the system can be described by an uncertain state-space model:

$$\begin{cases} \dot{x} = Ax + Bu \\ y = Cx + Du \end{cases} \tag{16}$$

where the state-space matrices A, B, C, D depend on uncertain and/or time-varying parameters or vary in some bounded sets of the space of matrices. One of the state-space representations of relevance in LMI control problems is the class of polytopic models:

Definition 2.1. *A polytopic system is a linear time-varying system*

$$\begin{cases} \dot{x} = A(t)x + B(t)u \\ y = C(t)x + D(t)u \end{cases} \tag{17}$$

in which the matrix $G(t) = \begin{bmatrix} A(t) & B(t) \\ C(t) & D(t) \end{bmatrix}$ *varies within a fixed polytope of matrices*

$$G(t) \in \mathrm{Co}\{G_1, \ldots, G_N\} := \left\{ \sum_{j=1}^{N} \delta_j G_j : \delta_j \geq 0, \sum_{j=1}^{N} \delta_j = 1 \right\} \tag{18}$$

where $G_1, \ldots, G_N$ *are the vertices of the polytope.*

In other words, $G(t)$ is a convex combination of the matrices $G_1, \ldots, G_N$. Polytopics models are also called *linear differential inclusions* LDI in (Boyd et al., 1994).

2.4.1 Example: Buck converter polytopic model

Consider the buck converter model introduced in subsection 2.1, with $\tilde{w}(t) = 0$. For simplicity, the stray resistances are disregarded. If we take R and V_g as uncertain parameters of the converter, the uncertain system is described as follows

$$\begin{cases} \dfrac{d\tilde{x}(t)}{dt} = \left(\sum\limits_{j=1}^{N} A_j \delta_j \right) \tilde{x}(t) + \left(\sum\limits_{j=1}^{N} B_{uj} \delta_j \right) \tilde{d}(t) \\ \tilde{y}(t) = C_y \tilde{x}(t) + E_{yw} \tilde{w}(t) \end{cases} \tag{19}$$

with $\delta_j \geq 0$, $\sum\limits_{j=1}^{N} \delta_j = 1$. The uncertain matrices A_j and B_{uj} are

$$A_j = \begin{bmatrix} 0 & -\dfrac{1}{L} \\ \dfrac{1}{C} & -\dfrac{1}{R_j C} \end{bmatrix}, \quad B_{uj} = \begin{bmatrix} \dfrac{V_{g_j}}{L} \\ 0 \end{bmatrix}, \tag{20}$$

where $R_j = \{R_{min}\ R_{max}\ R_{min}\ R_{max}\}$, and $V_{g_j} = \{V_{g_{min}}\ V_{g_{min}}\ V_{g_{max}}\ V_{g_{max}}\}$, which represents a uncertain polytope of four vertices (2 power the number of uncertain parameters, that are R_j and V_{g_j} in this example).

3. Robust control of dc-dc converters

Consider a general LTI model with states $x(t)$, controlled outputs $y(t)$ and performance outputs $z(t)$:

$$\Sigma : \begin{cases} \dot{x}(t) = Ax(t) + B_w w(t) + B_u u(t) \\ y(t) = C_y x(t) + E_{yw} w(t) + E_{yu} u(t) \\ z(t) = C_z x(t) + E_{zw} w(t) + E_{zu} u(t) \end{cases}. \tag{21}$$

It is possible to assume that some elements involved in the system matrices are uncertain or time-varying. For the sake of simplicity, the performance and measurable outputs are discarded, hence these uncertain elements are concentrated in matrices A, B_w and B_u and they are grouped in a vector p. Thus, matrices A, B_w and B_u depend on such uncertainty vector, and we can express (21) as function of these parameters:

$$\dot{x}(t) = A(p)x(t) + B_w(p)w(t) + B_u(p)u(t). \tag{22}$$

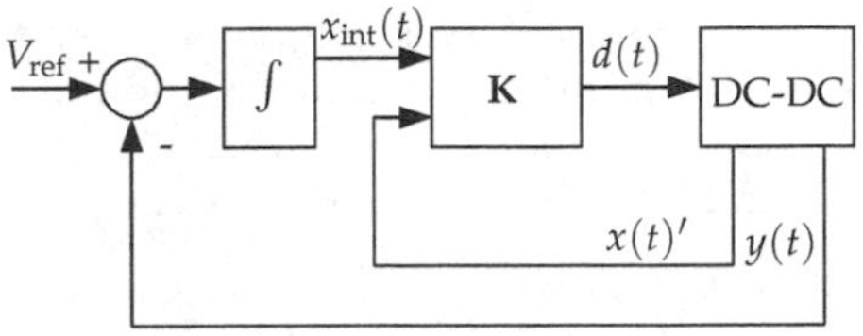

Fig. 5. Block diagram of a state-feedback system with controller **K** and error integration.

This state-space representation has been previously used to derive robust control synthesis methods for dc-dc converters, which generally result in a state-feedback law that stabilizes the system for a certain range of uncertainty: parameter-dependent approaches for the linear dynamics of the converters are presented in (Montagner et al., 2005) and (Torres-Pinzon & Leyva, 2009) while (Hu, 2011) introduces a representation of the nonlinear dynamics. Consistent experimental results with tight performances are presented in (Olalla et al., 2009a; 2010a; 2011). The small-signal stabilization of nonlinear dc-dc converters is considered in (Olalla et al., 2009a; 2010a), where the converter is ensured to be stable in a range of operating points, but its trajectory between those points is not ensured to be stable due to the disregard of the nonlinear dynamics. These nonlinearities are taken into account in (Olalla et al., 2011) where also a less conservative polytopic uncertainty model is introduced. The state-feedback formulation of the control problem is of interest since (i) it may deliver better performance than some output-feedback approaches, (ii) it can be posed as a convex optimization problem with no conservatism or iterations and (iii) it is very simple to implement. However, the main disadvantage of state-feedback is that the full state vector must be available for measure, which is not always true. Therefore, it may require additional components and sensors to obtain the state or to implement estimators of the unaccessible states. Robust output-feedback approaches are then an alternative to derive robust controllers with known performances.

Robust control via output-feedback has been the subject of extensive research in the field of automatic control (de Oliveira & Geromel, 1997; Garcia et al., 2004; Peaucelle & Arzelier, 2001a;b; Scherer et al., 1997; Skogestad & Postlethwaite, 1996), but it has been hardly employed in dc-dc converters (Rodriguez et al., 1999). Power electronics engineers tend to use current-mode approaches (Erickson & Maksimovic, 1999) that employ an inner current loop before applying the output-feedback loop and, in that way, ease the control of the dc-dc converter. However, current-mode approaches require current sensing, as state-feedback control, and they suffer from noise, since in some cases, as in peak-current control, the current waveform must be sensed accurately. Therefore, a plain output-feedback approach can be of interest in certain cases in which a simple control is required and the sensing of all the states of the converter is not possible.

3.1 State-feedback control

The most simple control problem in terms of an LMI formulation is the one in which all the system states are measurable. The state-feedback problem considers the stabilization of (22) with a simple controller $u = \mathbf{K}x$, where $\mathbf{K} \in \mathbb{R}^{m \times n}$, as follows

$$\dot{x}(t) = \big(A(p) + B_{\mathrm{u}}(p)\mathbf{K}\big)x(t) + B_w(p)w(t)\,. \tag{23}$$

Since the state-feedback approach does not allow to eliminate steady-state error, an additional integral state can be introduced for the regulated output of the system, as shown in Figure 5. Once the augmented system has been rewritten in the form of (23), the following result, adapted from (Bernussou et al., 1989), points out a synthesis method to obtain a state-feedback controller that stabilizes quadratically the closed-loop system.

Theorem 3.1. *The system* (23) *is stabilizable by state-feedback* $u = \mathbf{K}x$ *if and only if there exist a symmetric matrix* $\mathbf{W} \in \mathbb{R}^{n \times n}$ *and a matrix* $\mathbf{Y} \in \mathbb{R}^{m \times n}$ *such that*

$$\begin{cases} \mathbf{W} > \mathbf{0} \\ A\mathbf{W} + \mathbf{W}A' + B_u\mathbf{Y} + \mathbf{Y}'B_u' < \mathbf{0} \end{cases} \tag{24}$$

then, the state-feedback is given by $\mathbf{K} = \mathbf{Y}\mathbf{W}^{-1}$.

Proof. *The proof uses a quadratic Lyapunov function* $V(x) = x'\mathbf{P}x$, $\mathbf{P} = \mathbf{P}' > 0$, *whose time-derivative along the trajectories of the closed-loop system* $\dot{x} = (A + B_u)\mathbf{K}x$ *must be definite negative (Boyd et al., 1994). It follows that the following condition*

$$A'\mathbf{P} + \mathbf{P}A + \mathbf{K}'B_u'\mathbf{P} + \mathbf{P}B_u\mathbf{K} < \mathbf{0} \tag{25}$$

has to be satisfied. Finally, considering the left and right-hand multiplication of the previous condition by $\mathbf{W} = \mathbf{P}^{-1}$, *and the substitution of* $\mathbf{KW} = \mathbf{Y}$, *LMI condition* (24) *follows.*

A single Lyapunov function can be used to guarantee the stability of an uncertain system. The following theorem yields the state-feedback condition in the case of a polytopic representation.

Theorem 3.2. *The uncertain system defined by a convex polytope* $\mathrm{Co}\{G_1, \ldots, G_N\}$ *is quadratically stabilizable by state-feedback* $u = \mathbf{K}x$ *if and only if there exist a symmetric positive definite matrix* $\mathbf{W}$ *and a matrix* $\mathbf{Y}$ *such that*

$$A_j\mathbf{W} + \mathbf{W}A_j' + B_{uj}\mathbf{Y} + \mathbf{Y}'B_{uj}' < \mathbf{0} \quad \forall j = 1, \ldots, N, \tag{26}$$

then $\mathbf{K} = \mathbf{Y}\mathbf{W}^{-1}$ *is a state-feedback matrix.*

The proof of this theorem is given in (Bernussou et al., 1989). It is worth to point out that there exist more recent works which have been concerned with the stability of polytopic uncertain systems considering in particular multiple Lyapunov functions instead of a single one (Apkarian et al., 2001; Bernussou & Oustaloup, 2002; Peaucelle & Arzelier, 2001c), in order to reduce the conservatism of the quadratic approach.

Example 1. *Buck-Boost Converter*
In this example, an uncertain polytopic model of the buck-boost converter is presented and a robust state-feedback controller is derived.
Consider the buck-boost converter model introduced in Section 2.2. Since for state-feedback control, the capacitor voltage is considered measurable, the stray resistance r_C *is neglected. Also the stray resistances of the inductor and the semiconductor devices are disregarded. In order to obtain zero steady-state error between the voltage reference* V_{ref} *and the output voltage* $v_o(t)$, *the model is augmented with an additional state variable* $x_{\mathrm{int}}(t)$, *which stands for the integral of the output voltage error, i.e.* $x_{\mathrm{int}}(t) = -\int (V_{ref} - v_o(t))dt$. *The state vector of the new model is then written as*

$x(t) = \begin{bmatrix} i_L(t) \\ v_o(t) \\ x_{\text{int}}(t) \end{bmatrix}$. *Considering*

$$AX + B_w W + \begin{bmatrix} 0 \\ 1 \\ 0 \end{bmatrix} V_{ref} = 0, \tag{27}$$

the linear dynamics of the buck-boost converter are then written as:

$$\dot{\tilde{x}}(t) = A\tilde{x}(t) + B_w\tilde{w}(t) + B_u\tilde{u}(t) \tag{28}$$

$$A = \begin{bmatrix} 0 & \frac{D'}{L} & 0 \\ -\frac{D'}{C} & -\frac{1}{RC} & 0 \\ 0 & 1 & 0 \end{bmatrix}, \; B_w = \begin{bmatrix} \frac{D}{L} & 0 \\ 0 & -\frac{1}{C} \\ 0 & 0 \end{bmatrix}, \; B_u = \begin{bmatrix} \frac{V_g}{D'L} \\ \frac{DV_g}{D'^2RC} \\ 0 \end{bmatrix}. \tag{29}$$

Uncertainty:

Polytopic uncertainty (19) is introduced in the model of the converter to cope with the variations of D and R. The parameters of this example take the values shown in Table 1. Note that the transient performance requirements are only fulfilled when the trajectory starts from an equilibrium point. Consequently, the variations of D and R must be slow enough to allow the system states to return to the equilibrium.

Parameter	Value
$R \in$	$[10, 50]\ \Omega$
V_g	$12\ V$
D	$[0, 0.7]$
C	$200\ \mu$ F
L	$100\ \mu$ H
T_s	$5\ \mu$ s

Table 1. Buck-boost: converter parameters

As in (Olalla et al., 2009a), additional variables are introduced, in order to remove the non affine dependence of the system matrices on the uncertain terms. The uncertainty parameter vector is defined as $p = [R\ D'\ \delta_1\ \delta_2]$, *where:*

$$\begin{aligned} R &\in [R_{min},\ R_{max}], \\ D' &\in [D'_{min},\ D'_{max}], \\ \delta_1 &\in [1/D'_{max},\ 1/D'_{min}], \\ \delta_2 &\in [D_{min}/D'^2_{max},\ D_{max}/D'^2_{min}]. \end{aligned} \tag{30}$$

Note that the uncertain model is inside a polytopic domain formed by $N = 2^4$ *vertices. Also note that the multiplication between* δ_2 *and* $1/R$ *in the second row of* B_u *does not imply a new variable because both functions are strictly decreasing.*

Sampling effect:

In this example the sampling effect has not been included in the converter, as the state variables of the modulator model can not be measured.

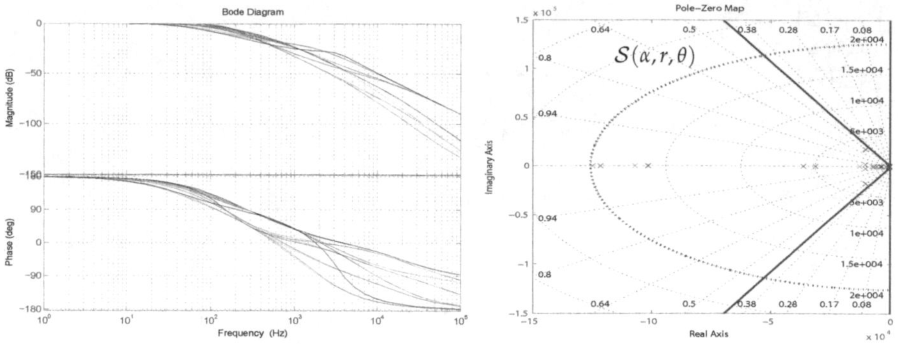

(a) Bode plot of closed loop transfer function from reference to output

(b) Pole location map of the closed loop system

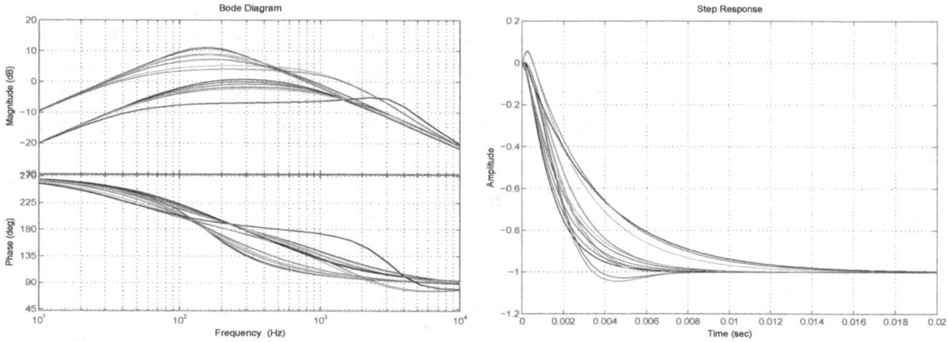

(c) Bode plot of closed loop transfer function from output disturbance to output.

(d) Output voltage transient response to a step reference.

Fig. 6. Simulation results of Example 1, with controller $\mathbf{K}_1$, for the sixteen vertices of the uncertainty set.

Performance Specifications:

Following the synthesis method shown in (Olalla et al., 2010a), the objective function to be minimized is the H_∞ *norm of the transfer function between the output disturbance* $\tilde{i}_{load}(t)$ *and the output voltage* $\tilde{v}_o(t)$.

In order to assure robust transient performances, the closed loop poles are constrained in an LMI region $\mathcal{S}(\alpha, r, \theta)$*, where the desired minimum damping ratio is set to* $\theta = \frac{1}{\sqrt{2}}$*, the required maximum damped frequency is* $r = \frac{1}{10}\frac{2\pi}{T_s}$*, and the minimum decay rate, for a settling time lower than 20 ms, is set to* $\alpha = 200$.

Results:

The robust control synthesis algorithm yields a controller $\mathbf{K}_1$*:*

$$\mathbf{K}_1 = [-0.31 \quad -0.25 \quad 194.70] \tag{31}$$

that ensures an H_∞ *norm from output disturbance to output voltage of 3.80 (11.6 dB). Figure 6 shows*

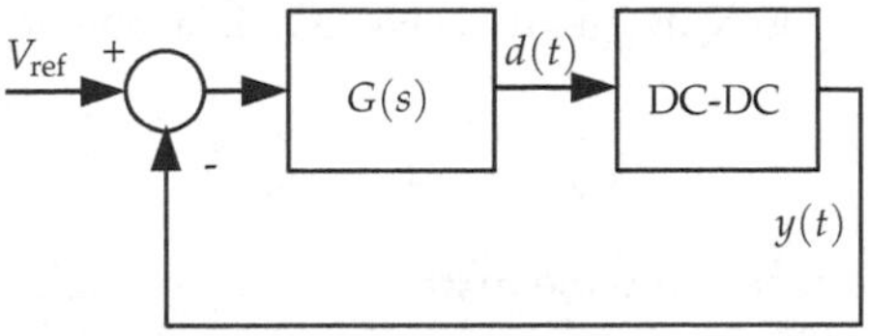

Fig. 7. Block diagram of an output-feedback system with controller $G(s)$.

the simulation results of the controller over the sixteen vertices of the set of matrices. Since the nonlinear terms are disregarded, the robust stability and performance of the converter is guaranteed while the converter remains in the considered operating points, assuming that the change between these operation points is sufficiently slow. In order to account for the neglected dynamics, see (Hu, 2011; Olalla et al., 2009b; 2011).

3.2 Output-feedback control

Figure 7 shows the general diagram of an output-feedback control system. Depending on the structure of the controller $G(s)$, two main approaches can be differentiated for the synthesis of output-feedback controllers: static and dynamic controllers.

Given the system Σ as described in (21), for the buck and the buck-boost converter $E_{yu} = 0$ can be considered. Then, in the case of a dynamic controller of order k with the following structure

$$\Sigma_K \quad : \quad \begin{cases} \dot{x}_c = \mathbf{A_c} x_c + \mathbf{B_c} y \\ u = \mathbf{C_c} x_c + \mathbf{D_c} y \end{cases}, \tag{32}$$

the closed loop system has the form

$$T_{\Sigma_K} \quad : \quad \begin{cases} \dot{x}_{cl} = \mathcal{A} x_{cl} + \mathcal{B} w \\ z = \mathcal{C} x_c + \mathcal{D} w \end{cases} \tag{33}$$

where

$$\left[\begin{array}{c|c} \mathcal{A} & \mathcal{B} \\ \hline \mathcal{C} & \mathcal{D} \end{array}\right] = \left[\begin{array}{cc|c} A + B_u \mathbf{D_c} C_y & B_u \mathbf{C_c} & B_w + B_u \mathbf{D_c} E_{yw} \\ \mathbf{B_c} C_y & \mathbf{A_c} & \mathbf{B_c} E_{yw} \\ \hline C_z + E_{zu} \mathbf{D_c} C_y & E_{zu} \mathbf{C_c} & E_{zw} + E_{zu} \mathbf{D_c} D_{yw} \end{array}\right] \tag{34}$$

In the case of a static controller, $\mathbf{K} \in \mathbb{R}^{m \times q}$

$$u = \mathbf{K} y = \mathbf{K}(C_y x + E_{yw} w) \tag{35}$$

and the closed loop system has the following structure

$$T_K \quad : \quad \begin{cases} \dot{x} = \mathcal{A} x + \mathcal{B} w \\ z = \mathcal{C} x + \mathcal{E} w \end{cases} \tag{36}$$

where

$$\left[\begin{array}{c|c} \mathcal{A} & \mathcal{B} \\ \hline \mathcal{C} & \mathcal{E} \end{array}\right] = \left[\begin{array}{c|c} (A + B_u \mathbf{K} C_y) & (B_w + B_u \mathbf{K} E_{yw}) \\ \hline (C_z + E_{zu} \mathbf{K} C_y) & (E_{zw} + E_{zu} \mathbf{K} E_{yw}) \end{array}\right] \tag{37}$$

For both problems the Lyapunov inequality is written, in a generic form:

$$\begin{cases} \mathbf{P} > \mathbf{0} \\ \mathcal{A}'\mathbf{P} + \mathbf{P}\mathcal{A} < \mathbf{0} \end{cases}, \tag{38}$$

which depends non-linearly on $\mathbf{P}$ and the matrices of the controller ($\mathbf{K}$ in the static case or $\mathbf{A_c}$, $\mathbf{B_c}$, $\mathbf{C_c}$, $\mathbf{D_c}$ in the dynamic case).

There exist several methods to linearize the output-feedback synthesis problem. For the dynamic output-feedback case, the results of reference (Scherer et al., 1997) are summarized. In the case of static output-feedback, the methods shown in (de Oliveira & Geromel, 1997) and (Peaucelle & Arzelier, 2001a) are employed.

3.2.1 Dynamic output-feedback

The dynamic output-feedback synthesis method shown in (Scherer et al., 1997) employs the following transfer function parametrization defined from the exogenous input $w = w_j R_j$ to the cost output $z_j = L_j z$ as follows:

$$T_j(s) = \frac{z_j(s)}{w_j(s)} := \left[\begin{array}{c|c} \mathcal{A} & \mathcal{B}_j \\ \hline \mathcal{C}_j & \mathcal{D}_j \end{array}\right] = \left[\begin{array}{c|c} \mathcal{A} & \mathcal{B}R_j \\ \hline L_j\mathcal{C} & L_j\mathcal{D}R_j \end{array}\right] = \left[\begin{array}{cc|c} A + B_u\mathbf{D_c}C_y & B_u\mathbf{C_c} & B_j + B_u\mathbf{D_c}F_j \\ \mathbf{B_c}C_y & \mathbf{A_c} & \mathbf{B_c}F_j \\ \hline C_j + E_j\mathbf{D_c}C_y & E_j\mathbf{C_c} & D_j + E_j\mathbf{D_c}F_j \end{array}\right] \tag{39}$$

where

$$B_j := B_w R_j, \quad C_j := L_j C_z, \quad D_j := L_j E_{zw} R_j, \quad E_j := L_j E_{zu}, \quad F_j := E_{yw} R_j. \tag{40}$$

To find a controller which stabilizes the closed-loop system, there must exist a quadratic Lyapunov function

$$V(x_{cl}) = x_{cl}'\mathbf{P}x_{cl}, \tag{41}$$

such that

$$\begin{cases} \mathbf{P} > \mathbf{0} \\ \mathcal{A}'\mathbf{P} + \mathbf{P}\mathcal{A} < \mathbf{0} \end{cases} \tag{42}$$

The LMI constraints are formulated for a transfer function $T_j(s) = L_j T(s) R_j$, in terms of the state-space matrices $\mathcal{A}, \mathcal{B}_j, \mathcal{C}_j, \mathcal{D}_j$. The goal is to synthesize an LTI controller Σ_K that:

- internally stabilizes the system
- meets certain specifications (H_2, H_∞ , pole placement,...) on a particular set of channels.

Generally, each transfer function T_j will satisfy each specification S_j, if there exists a Lyapunov matrix $\mathbf{P}_j > 0$ that satisfies some LMI constraints in $\mathbf{P}_j$. The control problem usually includes a number i of specifications. Therefore, the synthesis problem involves a set of matrix inequalities whose variables are:

- the controller matrices $\mathbf{A_c}$, $\mathbf{B_c}$,$\mathbf{C_c}$, $\mathbf{D_c}$.
- the i Lyapunov matrices $\mathbf{P}_1, \ldots, \mathbf{P}_i$, one per specification.
- additional auxiliary variables to minimize, for example, the norm cost H_∞.

Since this problem is nonlinear and hardly tractable numerically, the method shown in (Scherer et al., 1997) requires that all the specifications are satisfied with a single Lyapunov function, that is:

$$\mathbf{P}_1 = \ldots = \mathbf{P}_i = \mathbf{P}. \tag{43}$$

This restriction involves conservatism in the design, but it leads to a numerically tractable LMI problem, it produces controllers of reasonable order and it exploits all degrees of freedom in $\mathbf{P}$ (Scherer et al., 1997). Actually, if a single Lyapunov function $\mathbf{P}$ is considered, the following change of variable linearizes the control problem and makes it solvable with LMIs.
Let n be the number of states of the plant, and let k be the order of the controller. Partition $\mathbf{P}$ and $\mathbf{P}^{-1}$ as

$$\mathbf{P} = \begin{bmatrix} \mathbf{Y} & N \\ N' & * \end{bmatrix}, \quad \mathbf{P}^{-1} = \begin{bmatrix} \mathbf{X} & M \\ M' & \star \end{bmatrix} \tag{44}$$

where $\mathbf{X}$ and $\mathbf{Y}$ are $\in \mathbb{S}^n$, and $\star$ is a symmetric positive definite matrix such that $\mathbf{P}\mathbf{P}^{-1} = \mathbb{1}$ holds.
From $\mathbf{P}\mathbf{P}^{-1} = \mathbb{1}$ we infer $\mathbf{P}\begin{pmatrix} \mathbf{X} \\ M' \end{pmatrix} = \begin{pmatrix} \mathbb{1} \\ \mathbf{0} \end{pmatrix}$, which leads to

$$\mathbf{P}\Pi_1 = \Pi_2, \quad \Pi_1 = \begin{bmatrix} \mathbf{X} & \mathbb{1} \\ M' & \mathbf{0} \end{bmatrix}, \quad \Pi_2 = \begin{bmatrix} \mathbb{1} & \mathbf{Y} \\ \mathbf{0} & N' \end{bmatrix} \tag{45}$$

The change of variables is as follows

$$\begin{cases} \hat{\mathbf{A}} := N\mathbf{A_c}M' + N\mathbf{B_c}C_y\mathbf{X} + \mathbf{Y}B_u\mathbf{C_c}M' + \mathbf{Y}(A + B_u\mathbf{D_c}C_y)\mathbf{X} \\ \hat{\mathbf{B}} := N\mathbf{B_c} + \mathbf{Y}B_u\mathbf{D_c} \\ \hat{\mathbf{C}} := \mathbf{C_c}M' + \mathbf{D_c}C_y\mathbf{X} \\ \hat{\mathbf{D}} := \mathbf{D_c} \end{cases} \tag{46}$$

where $\hat{\mathbf{A}}, \hat{\mathbf{B}}, \hat{\mathbf{C}}$ have dimensions $n \times n, n \times m, q \times n$ respectively. If M and N have full row rank, and $\hat{\mathbf{A}}, \hat{\mathbf{B}}, \hat{\mathbf{C}}, \hat{\mathbf{D}}, \mathbf{X}, \mathbf{Y}$ are given, the matrices $\mathbf{A_c}, \mathbf{B_c}\mathbf{C_c}, \mathbf{D_c}$ can be computed. If M and N are square $n = k$ and invertible, then $\mathbf{A_c}, \mathbf{B_c}, \mathbf{C_c}, \mathbf{D_c}$ are unique.
The motivation for this change of variables lies in the following identities

$$\begin{aligned} \Pi_1'\mathbf{P}\mathcal{A}\Pi_1 = \Pi_2'\mathcal{A}\Pi_1 &= \begin{bmatrix} A\mathbf{X} + B\hat{\mathbf{C}} & A + B_u\mathbf{D}C_y \\ \hat{\mathbf{A}} & \mathbf{Y}A + \hat{\mathbf{B}}C_y \end{bmatrix} \\ \Pi_1'\mathbf{P}\mathcal{B}_j = \Pi_2'\mathcal{B}_j &= \begin{bmatrix} B_j + B_u\mathbf{D}F_j \\ \mathbf{Y}B_j + \hat{\mathbf{B}}F_j \end{bmatrix} \\ \mathcal{C}_j\Pi_1 &= \begin{bmatrix} C_j\mathbf{X} + E_j\hat{\mathbf{C}} & C_j + E_j\hat{\mathbf{D}}C_y \end{bmatrix} \\ \Pi_1'\mathbf{P}\Pi_1 = \Pi_1'\Pi_2 &= \begin{bmatrix} \mathbf{X} & \mathbb{1} \\ \mathbb{1} & \mathbf{Y} \end{bmatrix} \end{aligned} \tag{47}$$

which can be used in a congruence transformation to derive the LMI constraints. A detailed proof is given in (Scherer et al., 1997).
Once the variables $\hat{\mathbf{A}}, \hat{\mathbf{B}}, \hat{\mathbf{C}}, \hat{\mathbf{D}}, \mathbf{X}, \mathbf{Y}$ have been found, let us recover the original system by following this procedure. First we need to construct M, N and $\mathbf{P}$ that satisfy (45). M and N should be chosen such that $NM' = \mathbb{1} - \mathbf{YX}$. With the following LMI:

$$\begin{bmatrix} \mathbf{X} & \mathbb{1} \\ \mathbb{1} & \mathbf{Y} \end{bmatrix} > \mathbf{0} \tag{48}$$

we assure $\mathbf{Y} > \mathbf{0}$ and $\mathbf{X} - \mathbf{Y}^{-1} > \mathbf{0}$ such that $\mathbb{1} - \mathbf{YX}$ is nonsingular. Hence, M and N can always be found. After that, Π_1 and Π_2 are also nonsingular, and $\mathbf{P} = \Pi_2\Pi_1^{-1}$ can be found.

Then $\mathbf{D_c}, \mathbf{C_c}, \mathbf{B_c}$ and $\mathbf{A_c}$ can be solved, in this order:

$$\begin{cases} \mathbf{D_c} := \hat{\mathbf{D}} \\ \mathbf{C_c} := \left(\hat{\mathbf{C}} - \mathbf{D_c} C_y \mathbf{X}\right) M'^{-1} \\ \mathbf{B_c} := N^{-1}\left(\hat{\mathbf{B}} - \mathbf{Y} B_u \mathbf{D_c}\right) \\ \mathbf{A_c} := N^{-1}\left(\hat{\mathbf{A}} - N\mathbf{B_c} C_y \mathbf{X} - \mathbf{Y} B_u \mathbf{C_c} M' - \mathbf{Y}\left(A + B_u \mathbf{D_c} C_y\right)\mathbf{X}\right) M'^{-1} \end{cases} \tag{49}$$

For a list of LMI constraints which respond to several specifications with this change of variables, it is recommended to read (Scherer et al., 1997).

Example 2. *Buck Converter*
In this example, the synthesis of an output-feedback controller for a buck converter is carried out. The objective of the synthesis algorithm is, again, to minimize the H_∞ norm of the output disturbance to output voltage transfer function.
In this case the stray resistances of the converter are taken into account, since only the output signals are used. This design considers a unique output signal $v_o(t)$ to set-up a voltage-regulation operation.

Sampling effect:

The sampling effect could be included in the converter model, in order to prevent the optimization algorithm to yield unrealistic results due to the switching action. However, in this case, a weighting function on the complementary sensitivity response can be used for this purpose.

Uncertainty:

Polytopic uncertainty (19) can be introduced in the model of the converter to cope with the variations of the uncertain parameters, as the load or the input voltage. However, in the case of output-feedback the polytopic representation of uncertainty introduces nonlinear relationship between the variables of the inequalities. This problem is treated in (Courties, 1997; 1999) where a cross-decomposition algorithm is described to obtain a local optimum controller giving an initial feasible solution. The solution proposed in this example exploits the weighting transfer functions to obtain the expected sensitivity and complementary sensitivity responses. The parameters of this example take the values shown in Table 2. The synthesis algorithm closely follows the linearizing change of variables of (Scherer et al.,

Parameter	Value
R	$1000\ \Omega$
V_g	$55\ V$
C	$1000\ \mu$ F
L	$100\ \mu$ H
r_{eq}	$150\ m\Omega$
r_C	$30\ m\Omega$
T_s	$5\ \mu$ s

Table 2. Buck: converter parameters

1997) and the methodology explained in chapters 5 and 6 of (Gahinet et al., 1995):

1. *First, the design specifications are expressed in terms of loop shapes and their corresponding shaping filters.*
2. *Then, the original plant is augmented with such filters to obtain a weighted plant.*
3. *Finally, the augmented plant is used in the optimization algorithm to derive a controller that meets certain LMIs.*

The algorithm yields a controller of the same order as the augmented plant, that is, the order of the original plant plus the order of the shaping filters.

Performance Specifications:

The objective of the design procedure is to minimize the H_∞ norm of the disturbance to output transfer function. For such objective, a weighting function $W_1(s)$ for the error signal (i.e. for the sensitivity function) and a weighting function $W_2(s)$ for the output signal (i.e. for the complementary sensitivity function) are considered. Both weighting functions are depicted in Figure 8(b). In order to obtain small steady-state error, $W_1(s)$ is very large at low frequencies.
Other performance requirements could have been included (pole placement, H_2, ...) in the optimization problem, but they have not been used to maintain all the degrees of freedom in the research of the minimum H_∞ norm.

Results:

The minimization algorithm yields the following controller transfer function (1 input, 1 output):

$$\mathbf{K}_2(s) = -3.00\frac{(s+z_1)(s+z_2)(s+z_{3,4})(s+z_{5,6})}{(s+p_1)(s+p_2)(s+p_{3,4})(s+p_{5,6})} \tag{50}$$

where

$$\begin{array}{l|l} p_1 = -1.05\cdot 10^{-2} & z_1 = -4.39\cdot 10^2 + j6.04\cdot 10^2 \\ p_2 = -4.90\cdot 10^3 & z_2 = -4.39\cdot 10^2 - j6.04\cdot 10^2 \\ p_3 = -6.66\cdot 10^4 & z_3 = -1.89\cdot 10^3 \\ p_4 = -1.36\cdot 10^9 & z_4 = -3.50\cdot 10^9 \end{array} \tag{51}$$

The maximum guaranteed gain peak from disturbance to output is $\gamma = 0.045$ (-26.93 dB). Figure 8 depicts the simulation results for the nominal frequency and time-domain response of the buck converter.

3.2.2 Static output-feedback

An alternative to the use of weighting functions and frequency dependent uncertainty models is to consider the static output-feedback case. Static output-feedback considers a gain $\mathbf{K}$ to set up the feedback loop as $u = \mathbf{K}y$.
The survey on output-feedback design methods (de Oliveira & Geromel, 1997) differentiates between several approaches to solve the synthesis of a static output gain as follows:

1. Nonlinear programming methods. They work on the parametric space defined by $\mathbf{K}$ and $\mathbf{P}$ to find an optimal value of a cost variable, if any. The search is done by means of classical optimization methods as, for example, a gradient algorithm, primal or dual Levine-Athans' method, etc. The solution of the algorithm, which converges to a local optimum, strongly depends on an initial stabilizing gain, which must be found beforehand.
2. Parametric optimization methods. These methods optimize the objective function for the parametric space defined by $\mathbf{P}$, for some matrix $\mathbf{K}$. The determination of the controller, if it exists, is decomposed in independent steps. These methods can be easily implemented using LMI solvers.
3. Convex programming methods. They solve a sufficient version of the Lyapunov inequality (38) obtained by the addition of constraints which lead to a convex feasibility set.

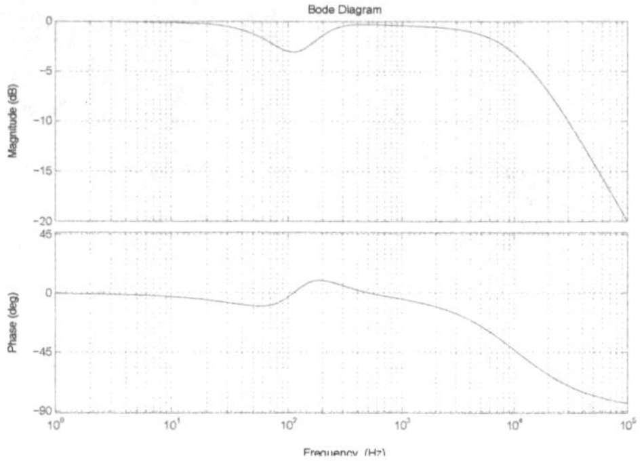

(a) Bode plot of closed loop transfer function from reference to output.

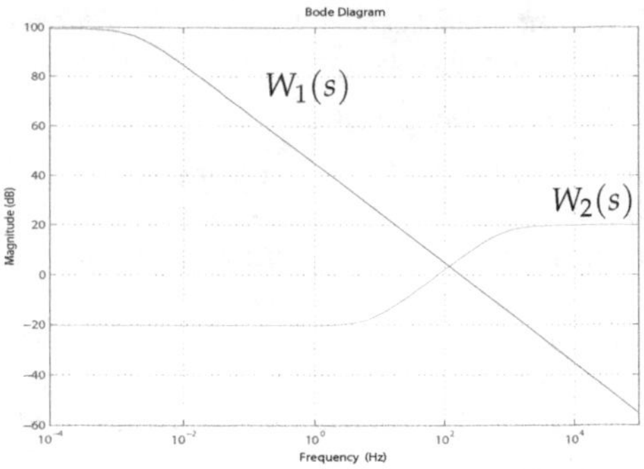

(b) Weighting functions for dynamic output-feedback synthesis.

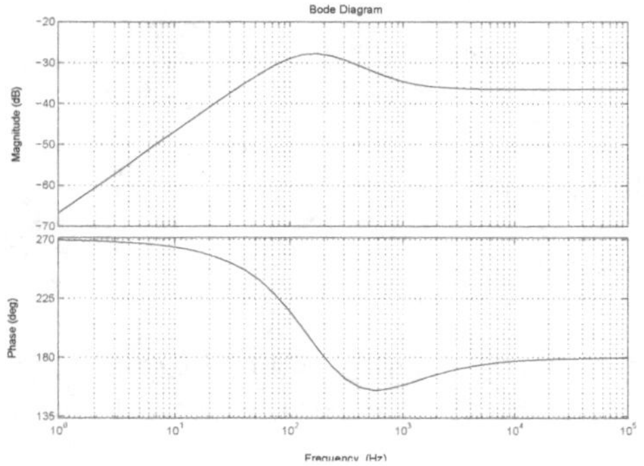

(c) Bode plot of closed loop transfer function from output disturbance to output.

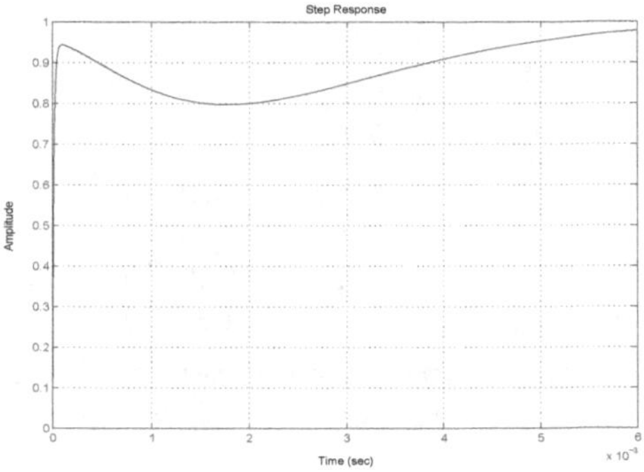

(d) Output voltage transient response to a step reference.

Fig. 8. Simulation results of Example 2 with controller $\mathbf{K}_2(s)$.

The proposed parametrization is based on the elimination lemma (Boyd et al., 1994) and the introduction of additional variables to obtain an iterative algorithm. It has been extracted from (Peaucelle & Arzelier, 2001a).

Theorem 3.3. *The Lyapunov inequality (38) can be rewritten as follows*

$$\begin{cases} \mathbf{P} > \mathbf{0} \\ \begin{bmatrix} A'\mathbf{P} + \mathbf{P}A & \mathbf{P}B_2 \\ B_2'\mathbf{P} & \mathbf{0} \end{bmatrix} + \begin{bmatrix} \mathbf{K}_s' \\ \mathbb{1} \end{bmatrix} \begin{bmatrix} \mathbf{R}C_y & -\mathbf{F} \end{bmatrix} + \begin{bmatrix} C_y'\mathbf{R}' \\ -\mathbf{F}' \end{bmatrix} \begin{bmatrix} \mathbf{K}_s & -\mathbb{1} \end{bmatrix} < \mathbf{0} \end{cases} \tag{52}$$

where $\mathbf{K}_s$ is a state-feedback gain that stabilizes the system. At the optimum point, which depends on the objective function, the output-feedback controller is given by $\mathbf{K} = \mathbf{F}^{-1}\mathbf{R}$.

Proof. *The equation* (38) *can be written as the following product of matrices:*

$$\begin{bmatrix} \mathbb{1} & C_y'\mathbf{K}' \end{bmatrix} \begin{bmatrix} A'\mathbf{P} + \mathbf{P}A & \mathbf{P}B_2 \\ B_2'\mathbf{P} & \mathbf{0} \end{bmatrix} \begin{bmatrix} \mathbb{1} \\ \mathbf{K}C_y \end{bmatrix} < \mathbf{0} \tag{53}$$

Applying the elimination lemma with

$$Q = \begin{bmatrix} A'\mathbf{P} + \mathbf{P}A & \mathbf{P}B_2 \\ B_2'\mathbf{P} & \mathbf{0} \end{bmatrix} \quad N = \mathbf{K}C_y \tag{54}$$

we obtain

$$\begin{bmatrix} A'\mathbf{P} + \mathbf{P}A & \mathbf{P}B_2 \\ B_2'\mathbf{P} & \mathbf{0} \end{bmatrix} + \begin{bmatrix} C_y'\mathbf{K}' \\ \mathbb{1} \end{bmatrix} \mathbf{G}' + \mathbf{G} \begin{bmatrix} \mathbf{K}C_y & -\mathbb{1} \end{bmatrix} < \mathbf{0} \tag{55}$$

With $\mathbf{G} = \begin{bmatrix} \mathbf{F}_s \\ -\mathbf{F} \end{bmatrix}$*, the previous inequality is written as*

$$\begin{bmatrix} A'\mathbf{P} + \mathbf{P}A & \mathbf{P}B_2 \\ B_2'\mathbf{P} & \mathbf{0} \end{bmatrix} + \begin{bmatrix} C_y'\mathbf{K}' \\ \mathbb{1} \end{bmatrix} \begin{bmatrix} \mathbf{F}_s' & -\mathbf{F}' \end{bmatrix} + \begin{bmatrix} \mathbf{F}_s \\ -\mathbf{F} \end{bmatrix} \begin{bmatrix} \mathbf{K}C_y & -\mathbb{1} \end{bmatrix} < \mathbf{0} \tag{56}$$

With the following change of variables

$$\mathbf{K}_s' = \mathbf{F}_s\mathbf{F}^{-1}, \qquad \mathbf{R} = \mathbf{F}\mathbf{K}, \tag{57}$$

it is verified that $\mathbf{K} = \mathbf{F}^{-1}\mathbf{R} = \mathbf{F}^{-1}\mathbf{F}\mathbf{K}$*, and we obtain the result of (52).*

This parametrization has been adapted to the minimization of the performance indexes H_2 and H_∞ (Peaucelle & Arzelier, 2001a;b).

With the new introduced variables we can split the optimization problem into two linear steps; in the first step, $\mathbf{K}_s$ is kept constant, and the problem is solved for $\mathbf{P}, \mathbf{R}$ and $\mathbf{F}$. Then, in the next step, $\mathbf{R}$ and $\mathbf{F}$ are kept constant and the problem is solved for $\mathbf{P}$ and $\mathbf{K}_s$. With this iterative process, a stabilizing gain that satisfies a given cost function can be obtained.

A key point of this approach is however related to the initialization step, for which and admissible stabilizing state-feedback has to be selected. On the other hand, this algorithm presents the advantage that the Lyapunov matrix $\mathbf{P}$ is set as a free variable in both steps.

Algorithm 3.1.

1. *Initialization. Step* $k = 1$*. Choose a stabilizing state-feedback gain.*
2. *Iterative step k first part. Solve the LMI* (52) *in which* $\mathbf{K}_s$ *is constant.*
3. *Iterative step k second part. Solve the LMI* (52) *in which* $\mathbf{F}$ *and* $\mathbf{R}$ *are constant.*
4. *Final step. If the objective function satisfies the requirements, then stop* $\mathbf{K} = \mathbf{F}^{-1}\mathbf{R}$*, else* $k = k + 1$ *and return to step 2.*

Example 3. *Buck Converter*

In this example, the previous output-feedback parametrization is employed to derive a static controller for a buck converter, whose model was introduced in Section 2.2. The stray resistances of the model are taken into account in this case. Also, note that the augmented model contains an integrator of the error between the output and the reference.

Uncertainty:

The output-feedback parametrization allows to consider the polytopic uncertainty model shown in Section 2.4. In this case, the uncertain model is formed by $N = 2^2$ *vertices. The values of the converter are shown in Table 3.*

Parameter	Value
R	$\in [10, 1000]\ \Omega$
V_g	$\in [33, 55]\ V$
C	$1000\ \mu$ F
L	$100\ \mu$ H
r_{eq}	150 mΩ
r_C	50 mΩ
T_s	$5\ \mu$ s

Table 3. Buck: converter parameters

Sampling effect:

Since only the output signal is used, the sampling effect is included in the converter model in order to obtain an accurate model up to half the switching frequency. This addition also prevents the optimization algorithms to yield unrealistic results due to the switching action.

Performance Specifications:

Following the synthesis method shown in (Olalla et al., 2010a), the objective function to be minimized is the H_∞ norm of the transfer function between the output disturbance $\tilde{i}_{load}(t)$ and the output voltage. As in the state-feedback case, the closed loop poles are constrained in an LMI region $\mathcal{S}(\alpha, r, \theta)$, in order to assure robust transient performances. Again, the desired minimum damping ratio is set to $\theta = \frac{1}{\sqrt{2}}$, the required maximum damped frequency is $r = \frac{1}{10}\frac{2\pi}{T_s}$, and the minimum decay rate, for a settling time lower than 40 ms, is set to $\alpha = 100$.

Results:

The robust control synthesis algorithm yields a controller $\mathbf{K}_3$:

$$\mathbf{K}_3 = 4.472 \tag{58}$$

that assures an H_∞ norm from output disturbance to output voltage of 0.656 (-3.66 dB). The waveforms of a numerical simulation and corresponding Bode plots of the converter with controller $\mathbf{K}_3$ over the four vertices of the set of matrices are depicted in Figure 9. It can be observed that the static output-feedback controller does not achieve the performance of the dynamic output-feedback controller $\mathbf{K}_2(s)$.

3.2.3 Dynamic output-feedback with static parametrization

The parametrization method shown in the previous subsection for the static case can be adapted to the synthesis of a dynamic output-feedback controller. The following theorem can be found in (Martenson, 1985; Nett et al., 1989).

Theorem 3.4. *The synthesis of a dynamic controller Σ_K for the system Σ (for simplicity, in absence of perturbations ($w = 0$)) can be expressed as the synthesis of a static controller for the augmented system Σ_{aug}:*

$$\Sigma_{aug} \quad : \quad \begin{cases} \dot{x}_{aug} = \begin{bmatrix} A & \mathbf{0} \\ \mathbf{0} & \mathbf{0} \end{bmatrix} x_{aug} + \begin{bmatrix} \mathbf{0} & B \\ \mathbb{1} & \mathbf{0} \end{bmatrix} u_{aug} \\ \\ y_{aug} = \begin{bmatrix} \mathbf{0} & \mathbb{1} \\ C & \mathbf{0} \end{bmatrix} x_{aug} + \begin{bmatrix} \mathbf{0} & \mathbf{0} \\ \mathbf{0} & D \end{bmatrix} u_{aug} \end{cases} \tag{59}$$

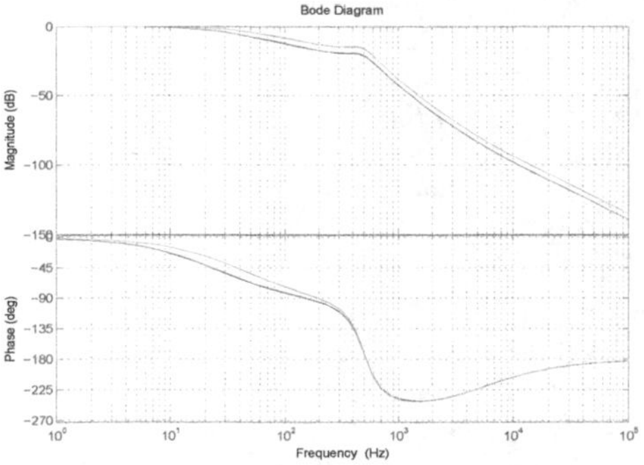

(a) Bode plot of closed loop transfer function from reference to output.

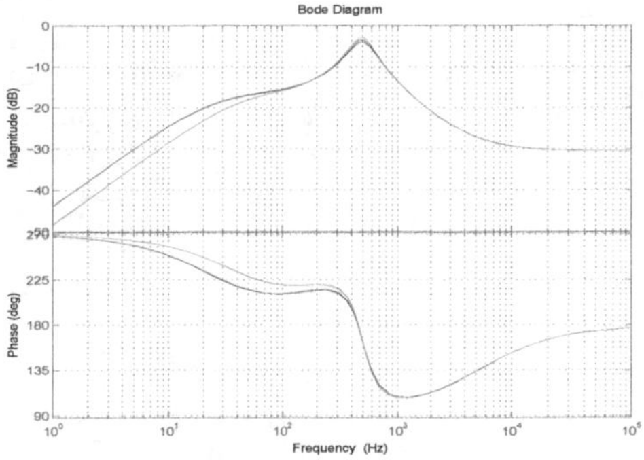

(b) Bode plot of closed loop transfer function from output disturbance to output.

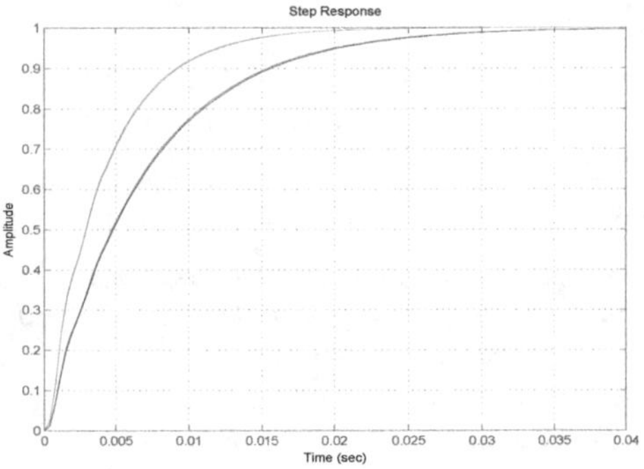

(c) Output voltage transient response to a step reference.

Fig. 9. Simulation results of Example 3 with controller $\mathbf{K}_3$.

where

$$x_{aug} = \begin{bmatrix} x \\ x_c \end{bmatrix} \qquad u_{aug} = \begin{bmatrix} \dot{x}_c \\ u \end{bmatrix} \qquad y_{aug} = \begin{bmatrix} x_c \\ y \end{bmatrix} \tag{60}$$

and

$$\mathbf{K} = \begin{bmatrix} \mathbf{A_c} & \mathbf{B_c} \\ \mathbf{C_c} & \mathbf{D_c} \end{bmatrix} \tag{61}$$

Example 4. *Buck Converter*
A dynamic controller using the static output-feedback parametrization is derived in this subsection. As in the static case, the stray resistances and a pure integrator are considered. The system is augmented with an integrator and with the controller states to obtain a dynamic controller. For this case a simple first-order controller is considered.

$$\mathbf{K}(s) = k\frac{(s+z)}{(s+p)} \tag{62}$$

Uncertainty:

As in the previous subsection, the synthesis considers a polytopic model. A new LMI is introduced for every vertex of the uncertain model. The polytopic model used in this subsection considers the same uncertain load R and input voltage V_g, as shown in Table 4.

Parameter	Value
R	$\in [10, 1000]\ \Omega$
V_g	$\in [33, 55]\ V$
C	$1000\ \mu$ F
L	$100\ \mu$ H
r_{eq}	150 mΩ
r_c	50 mΩ
T_s	$5\ \mu$ s

Table 4. Buck: converter parameters

Sampling effect:

Again, the sampling effect is included in the converter model in order to obtain an accurate model up to half the switching frequency.

Performance Specifications:

As in the previous case, the objective is to minimize the H_∞ norm of the transfer function between the disturbance and the output. Also, the closed loop poles are constrained in the same LMI region $\mathcal{S}(\alpha, r, \theta)$, in order to assure robust transient performances.
The initialization step is constrained with the corresponding pole placement inequalities and its objective function tries to enforce the states of the dynamic controller, using a weight β on $\mathbf{R} = \mathbf{FK}$.

$$\begin{array}{l} \max f(\beta \mathbf{R}) \text{ subject to} \\ \mathbf{W} > \mathbf{0} \\ \mathbf{W}A' + A\mathbf{W} + \mathbf{Y}'B_u' + B_u\mathbf{Y} < \mathbf{0} \end{array} \tag{63}$$

where for this case of one input and one state of the dynamic controller can be considered $\beta = \begin{bmatrix} \beta_1 & 0 \\ 0 & \beta_2 \end{bmatrix}$, $\beta_1 > \beta_2$. If an initial state-feedback is found then the iterative step minimizes the H_∞ norm γ.

Results:

For the present case the algorithm yields the following controller:

$$\mathbf{K}_4 = \left[\begin{array}{c|c} \mathbf{A_c} & \mathbf{B_c} \\ \hline \mathbf{C_c} & \mathbf{D_c} \end{array}\right] = \left[\begin{array}{c|c} -7475.4 & -97.9 \\ \hline 851.3 & 10.3 \end{array}\right] \tag{64}$$

Note that the integrator is not included in the previous expression. The Bode plot of the controller with the integrator is depicted in Figure 10(b).
The guaranteed H_∞ norm with the controller $\mathbf{K}_4$ achieves the value $\gamma = 0.571$. The simulation results are shown in Figure 10. It can be observed that the lag-lead compensation of the controller slightly changes the gain peak of the transfer function of interest, yielding slightly better output disturbance attenuation, but longer settling time with respect to the constant output feedback gain. Consequently, this method can be seen as an intermediate solution between dynamic and static output feedback,

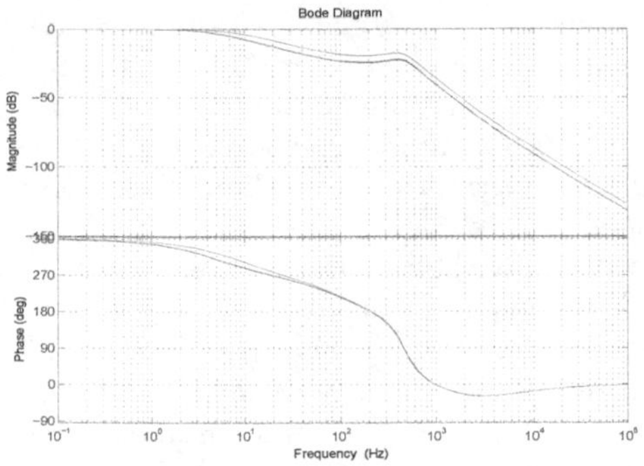

(a) Bode plot of closed loop transfer function from reference to output.

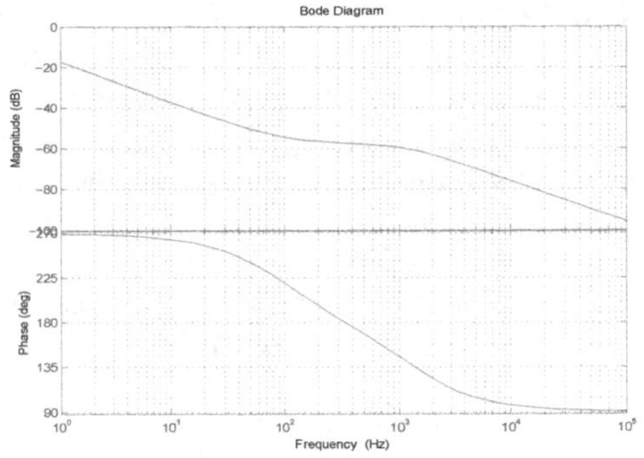

(b) Bode plot of controller $\mathbf{K}_4$.

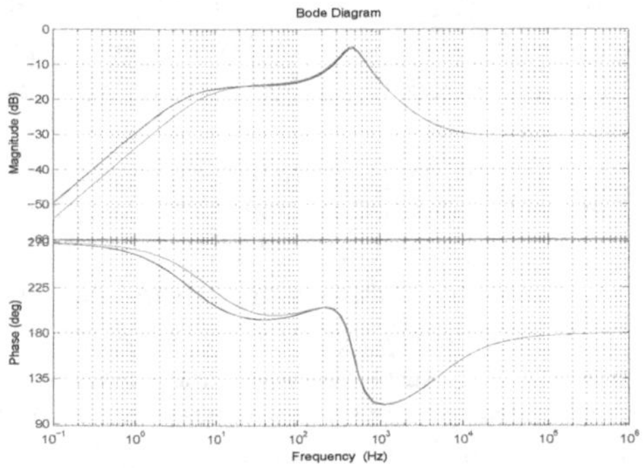

(c) Bode plot of closed loop transfer function from output disturbance to output.

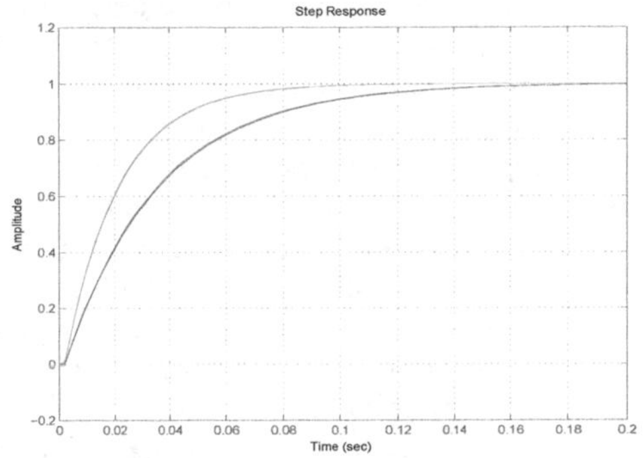

(d) Output voltage transient response to a step reference.

Fig. 10. Simulation results of Example 4 with controller $\mathbf{K}_4$.

with the main drawback that the solution of the iterative algorithm may depend on the chosen initial state-feedback gain.

4. Conclusions

In the chapter, it has been shown how a control formulation based on linear matrix inequalities can cope not only with academic optimization problems, but also with large real-life complex problems, since the numerical solution can be found by efficient computer algorithms.
The synthesis (or analysis) of the control system can be made by solving an optimization problem, using the concepts of Lyapunov stability and positive definiteness. Besides, frequency-based and time domain performance requirements can also be posed in form of LMIs, as H_∞, H_2 or pole placement.
LMI-based state-feedback synthesis methods have been already applied successfully in the field of power conversion, since they can be applied directly with no additional conservatism. However, output-feedback approaches require the linearization of the synthesis variables in order to be solvable with LMIs. Such linearization methods often impose changes in the matrix variables or require an initial feasible result.

The results presented in this chapter with LMI control of a buck and a buck-boost converter demonstrates the feasibility of this approach, but also shows some of the limitations.
The buck-boost converter presents nonlinear dynamics; such control problem has been tackled with a state-feedback approach, so that the information about the converter states allows to consider the uncertainty coming from the disregarded dynamics, but also limits the achievable performance. Such limitation also allows to neglect the sampling effect of the modulation, since the effective feedback bandwidth of the control is well below the switching frequency.
On the other hand, the control of the buck converter, whose averaged dynamics are basically linear, has been dealt with an output-feedback realization. In this case, the closed-loop performance and its associated bandwidth can reach high frequencies, and it is advisable to take into account the sampling effect of the modulator. From the comparison between the three output-feedback approaches, the best results have been achieved with the H_∞-based dynamic controller, but this approach also presents some limitations, as the impossibility to deal with easy-to-derive uncertainty models. Another drawback of this technique is that the choice of appropriate weighting functions must be made by trial and error and therefore this task requires good knowledge of the plant limits. Nevertheless, such limitations also appear in the dynamic output-feedback approach by static parametrization, since the results strongly depend on the initial feasible solution for the iterative algorithm.
Depending on the application of the dc-dc converter, it may be easier to implement a state-feedback controller or an output-feedback controller. For instance, the inductor current may not be accessible or the capacitor stray resistance cannot be assumed small enough.
Future research on LMI control of power converters could focus on the improvement of the output-feedback synthesis algorithms, which still require the tedious task of selecting weighting functions, even for the initial controller of the static feedback parametrization. Besides of the inherent limitations of output-feedback, the synthesis algorithms are still very conservative and do not lead to tight performances, when compared with state-feedback approaches.

5. References

Apkarian, P., Tuan, H. D. & Bernussou, J. (2001). Continuous-time analysis, eigenstructure assignment, and H2 synthesis with enhaced linear matrix inequalities (LMI) characterizations, *IEEE Transactions on Automatic Control* 46(12): 1941–1946.

Ben-Tal, A., El Ghaoui, L. & Nemirovski, A. (2009). *Robust Optimization*, Princeton Series in Applied Mathematics, Princeton University Press.

Bernussou, J. (1996). *Commande Robuste*, Hermès, Paris (in French).

Bernussou, J. & Oustaloup, A. (2002). *Conception des Commandes Robustes*, Systèmes Automatisés I2C, Lavoisier, Paris (in French).

Bernussou, J., Peres, P. L. D. & Geromel, J. (1989). A linear programming oriented procedure for quadratic stabilization of uncertain systems, *Systems and Control Letters* 13: 65–72.

Boyd, S., El Ghaoui, L., Feron, E. & Balakrishnan, V. (1994). *Linear Matrix Inequalities in Systems and Control Theory*, Vol. 15 of *Studies in Applied and Numerical Mathematics*, SIAM, Philadelphia.

Brown, A. R. & Middlebrook, R. D. (1981). Sampled-data modeling of switching regulators, *IEEE PESC '81; Power Electronics Specialists Conference, Boulder, CO*, pp. 349–369.

Courties, C. (1997). H_∞ robust control for polytopic uncertain systems, *Technical Report LAAS 97344*, Laboratoire d'Analyse et d'Architecture des Systèmes du CNRS.

Courties, C. (1999). *Sur la commande robuste et LPV de systemes a parametres lentement variables*, PhD thesis, Institut National des Sciences Appliquées de Toulouse (in French).

de Oliveira, M. C. & Geromel, J. C. (1997). Numerical comparison of output feedback design methods, *Proceedings of the American Control Conference, ACC'97*, Vol. 1, pp. 72–76.

El Ghaoui, L. & Niculescu, S. (2000). *Advances in linear matrix inequality methods in control: advances in design and control*, Society for Industrial and Applied Mathematics, Philadelphia, PA, USA.

Erickson, R. W. & Maksimovic, D. (1999). *Fundamentals of Power Electronics*, Kluwer Academic, Norwell, Massachusetts.

Gahinet, P., Nemirovski, A., Laub, A. J. & Chilali, M. (1995). *LMI Control Toolbox for use with Matlab*, The MathWorks, Inc.

Garcia, G., Tarbouriech, S., Gomes da Silva, J. M., J. & Castelan, E. B. (2004). Pole assignment in a disk for linear systems by static output feedback, *IEE Proceedings on Control Theory and Applications* 151(6): 706–712.

Hu, T. (2011). A nonlinear-system approach to analysis and design of power-electronic converters with saturation and bilinear terms, *IEEE Transactions on Power Electronics* 26(2): 399–410.

Leyva, R., Cid-Pastor, A., Alonso, C., Queinnec, I., Tarbouriech, S. & Martinez-Salamero, L. (2006). Passivity-based integral control of a boost converter for large-signal stability, *IEE Proceedings Control Theory and Applications* 153(2): 139–146.

Löfberg, J. (2004). YALMIP : A toolbox for modeling and optimization in MATLAB, *Proceedings of the CACSD Conference*, Taipei, Taiwan, pp. 284–289. [Online] `http://control.ee.ethz.ch/~joloef/yalmip.php`.

Maksimovic, D. (2000). Computer-aided small-signal analysis based on impulse response of dc/dc switching power converters, *IEEE Transactions on Power Electronics* 15(6): 1183–1191.

Martenson, B. (1985). The order of any stabilizing regulator is sufficient a priori information for adaptive stabilization, *Systems and Control Letters* 6: 87–91.

Montagner, V. F., Oliveira, R. C. L. F., Leite, V. J. S. & Peres, P. L. D. (2005). LMI approach for H_∞ linear parameter-varying state feedback control, *IEE Proceedings on Control Theory and Applications* 152(2): 195–201.

Nett, C., Bernstein, D. & Haddad, W. (1989). Minimal complexity control law synthesis, part I: Problem formulation and reduction to optimal static feedback, *Proceedings of the American Control Conference, ACC'89.*, Pittsburgh, pp. 2056–2064.

Olalla, C., Leyva, R., El Aroudi, A. & Queinnec, I. (2009a). Robust LQR control for PWM converters: an LMI approach, *IEEE Transactions on Industrial Electronics* 56(7): 2548–2558.

Olalla, C., Leyva, R., El Aroudi, A. & Queinnec, I. (2010a). LMI robust control design for boost PWM converters, *IET Power Electronics* 3(1): 75–85.

Olalla, C., Leyva, R., El Aroudi, A., Queinnec, I. & Tarbouriech, S. (2009b). Hinf control of DC-DC converters with saturated inputs, *Proceedings of the IEEE Annual Conference on Industrial Electronics, IECON'09*, Porto.

Olalla, C., Queinnec, I. & Leyva, R. (2010b). *Robust linear control of DC-DC converters: A practical approach to the synthesis of robust controllers*, VDM Verlag.

Olalla, C., Queinnec, I., Leyva, R. & El Aroudi, A. (2011). Robust optimal control of bilinear dc-dc converters, *Control Engineering Practice* 19(7): 688–699.

Peaucelle, D. & Arzelier, D. (2001a). An efficient numerical solution for H_2 static output feedback synthesis., *European Control Conference*, Porto, pp. 3800–3805.

Peaucelle, D. & Arzelier, D. (2001b). An iterative method for mixed H_2/H_∞ synthesis via static output-feedback., *IEEE Conference on Decision and Control*, Las Vegas, pp. 3464–3469.

Peaucelle, D. & Arzelier, D. (2001c). Robust performance analysis using LMI-based methods for real parametric uncertainty via parameter-dependent lyapunov functions, *IEEE Transactions on Automatic Control* 46(4): 624–630.

Pyatnitskii, E. S. & Skorodinskii, V. I. (1982). Numerical methods of Lyapunov function construction and their application to the absolute stability problem, *Systems and Control Letters* 2(2): 130–135.

Rodriguez, H., Ortega, R. & Escobar, G. (1999). A robustly stable output feedback saturated controller for the boost dc-to-dc converter, *Proceedings of the IEEE Conference on Decision and Control, CDC'99.*, Vol. 3, pp. 2100–2105.

Scherer, C., Gahinet, P. & Chilali, M. (1997). Multiobjective output-feedback control via LMI optimization, *IEEE Transactions on Automatic Control* 42(7): 896–911.

Skogestad, S. & Postlethwaite, I. (1996). *Multivariable Feedback Control: Analysis and Design*, John Wiley and Sons, New York.

Sturm, J. (1999). Using SeDuMi 1.02, a MATLAB toolbox for optimization over symmetric cones, *Optimization Methods and Software* 11-12: 625–653. [Online] `http://fewcal.kub.nl/sturm`.

Torres-Pinzon, C. A. & Leyva, R. (2009). Fuzzy control in DC-DC converters: an LMI approach, *Proceedings of the IEEE Annual Conference on Industrial Electronics, IECON'09*, Porto, pp. 510–515.

Wallis, G. F. & Tymerski, R. (2000). Generalized approach for μ synthesis of robust switching regulators, *IEEE Transactions on Aerospace and Electronic Systems* 36(2): 422–431.

Zhou, K., Doyle, J. & Glover, K. (1996). *Robust and Optimal Control*, Prentice-Hall, New Jersey.

18

Analysis, Dimensioning and Robust Control of Shunt Active Filter for Harmonic Currents Compensation in Electrical Mains

Andrea Tilli, Lorenzo Marconi and Christian Conficoni
Center for Complex Automated Systems (CASY) Dept. of Electronics, Computer Engineering and Systems (DEIS), University of Bologna, Viale Risorgimento n.2, 40136 Bologna Italy

1. Introduction

Harmonic pollution in the AC mains determines additional power losses and may cause malfunctioning or even damage to connected equipments. Distortion of the currents circulating on electric mains is mainly originated by non linear loads, as AC/DC uncontrolled rectifiers used for motor drives, that absorb undesired current harmonics. Therefore, local countermeasures have to be taken in order to keep the portion of grid affected by distortion as small as possible, hence preventing relevant power losses and "saving" other equipments, connected to the rest of the grid.
Traditionally, passive filtering components have been adopted to cope with harmonic compensations, however they are affected by several drawbacks; they are very sensitive to network impedance variation and environmental conditions, moreover they need to be tuned on fixed frequencies. In order to overcome those limitations, in the last decades, thanks also to the fast growth in power electronics and control processor technologies, a remarkable research attempt has been devoted to the study of the so-called Active Power Filters (APFs), both from a theoretical and technological point of view (see Gyugyi & Strycula (1976), Akagi (1996), Singh & Al-Haddad (1999)). These devices are able to properly work in a wide range of operating conditions, providing better performance and overtaking intrinsic limitations of passive devices, they are far more insensitive to network impedance, they can be tuned onto different frequencies just varying some software parameters. Furthermore, the system reliability is improved, resonance phenomena are avoided and a diagnosis system can be implemented on the control processor to monitor the system variables and adopt some recovery strategy in case of faulty conditions.
In this chapter, the general issues related to analysis, dimensioning and control of a particular class of APFs, the so-called Shunt Active Filters (SAFs), are addressed; the main purpose of this kind of power system is to inject into mains a proper current, in order to cancel out, partially or totally, the power distortions generated by nonlinear loads. The SAFs considered in this work are based on a three-phases three-wires AC/DC boost converter topology (see Fig. 1) connected in parallel to the distorting loads.

The first step to properly design a SAF is the selection of suitable hardware components; as it will become clear in the next section, owing to the structural properties of the system, the sizing procedure cannot be considered apart from the canonical control aspects, hence a correct dimensioning algorithm (Ronchi & Tilli, 2002) is proposed to ensure feasibility of the desired control objectives and to minimize costs. In addition, according to such method, it is shown how a time-scale separation between different dynamics of SAF usually takes place "for free". This point is very useful for control design and stability analysis.

Once a correct hardware sizing has been carried out, the first control issues to deal with are: the current/power control algorithm and the load current analysis method adopted to define the filter current reference. Various solutions have been proposed in literature. As regards current/power harmonic tracking, in (Chandra et al., 2000) an hysteresis current control (Kazmierkowski & Malesani, 1998) is proposed, while in (Jeong & Woo, 1997) predictive current control is adopted. For what concerns the generation of the filter currents reference, beside Fast Fourier Transform Techniques, instantaneous power theory (Akagi et al., 1984), time domain correlation techniques (Van Harmelen & Enselin, 1993), notch filter theory (Rastogi et al., 1995) and other methods have been proposed. Solution based on state observer have been proposed, too, as in (Bhattacharya et al., 1995) and (Tilli et al., 2002).

However, what renders the SAF control problem challenging and different from other conventional tracking problems is the presence of peculiar and unstable internal dynamics, given by the voltage dynamics of the DC-link capacitor bank. This capacitor bank is the main energy storage element, which provides the voltage, modulated by the control, to steer the filter currents and, at the same time, is required to oscillate to exchange energy with the line and the load to compensate for current harmonics. Actually, this element needs to be carefully considered also in the previously-mentioned dimensioning stage; a correct capacitor sizing is crucial for control objective feasibility, whatever control technique is adopted. Moreover, it can be shown that, if perfect harmonic compensation is achieved, the DC-link voltage dynamics are unstable, due to the system parasitic resistances that lead to a slow discharge of the capacitor. Hence, a suitable stabilizing action for DC-link voltage dynamics needs to be provided. Since no additional circuit is used to feed the DC-link capacitor independently of the three-phase port used to inject currents, (see Fig. 1), the voltage stabilization would need to be integrated with the controller devoted to harmonic compensation (the AC/DC boost-based SAF is an underactuated system). This is a crucial point and it has to be tackled preserving harmonic compensation performances as far as possible.

In this work a power/current controller, based on Internal Model Principle, (see Marconi et al. (2003), Marconi et al. (2004), Marconi et al. (2007)) is designed in order to cancel current harmonics, ensuring robustness with respect to SAF parameter uncertainties. By exploiting the internal model approach, the proposed solution also allows to merge and solve at the same time the two above-mentioned problems of current harmonics isolation and current reference tracking. As regards the robust stabilization of the DC-link voltage internal dynamics, a cascade control structure is proposed. An additional voltage controller, acting on the references of the power/current controller, is introduced. This controller is designed taking into account the structural voltage oscillations required for harmonic compensation and minimizing the impact on harmonic compensation. In particular, by exploiting a proper averaging (Sanders et al., 1991) of the capacitor voltage dynamics, the average value of the capacitor voltage is chosen as output variable to be controlled (Hanschke et al., 2006).

As far as the overall stability is concerned, the previously mentioned time-scale separation between portions of SAF dynamics can be effectively exploited to decouple power/current

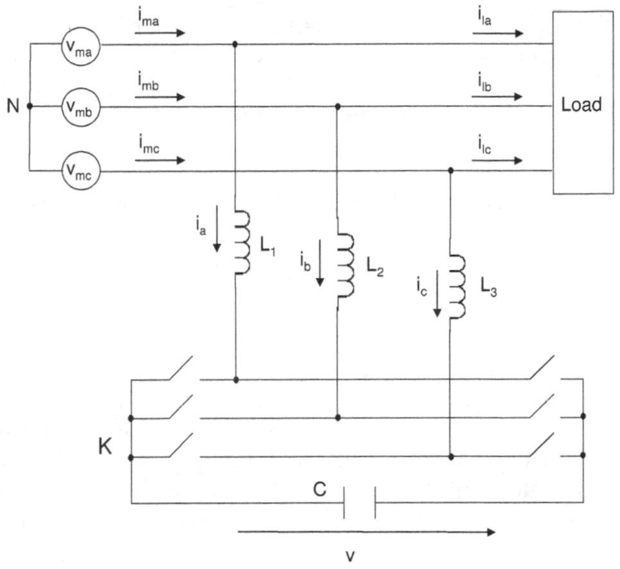

Fig. 1. Shunt Active Filter scheme.

tracking and voltage stabilization control problems, using *averaging* and *singular perturbation theory* techniques (Khalil, 1996).

This chapter is organized as follows. In Section 2, the general framework is described, the SAF model is derived and the control objectives are formally defined. In Section 3, two methodological approaches are presented for the SAF components sizing. The first one is based on the knowledge of the load currents harmonic spectrum, the values selected for the hardware components are the minimums allowing the SAF to deal with the considered load distortion. Differently, the second approach is related to the maximum current of the AC/DC boost switching devices. In this case the selected components values are the minimums which enable the SAF to compensate for all possible loads giving distorted currents smaller or equal to the switches peak value. In Section 4 both the internal model-based power/current controller and the averaging voltage controller design are presented, stability analysis is carried out relying upon the time-scale separation imposed by the design algorithm; both the power and the voltage subsystem are proven to be asymptotically stable, then practical stability of the overall system is claimed exploiting general results on two time-scale averaged systems (Teel et al., 2003). The effectiveness of the proposed control solution is tested in Section 5 through simulations.

2. Shunt active filter model and control problem statement

The scheme of the shunt active filter considered in this chapter is reported in Fig. 1, as mentioned in the introduction it is based on a three-phase three-wire AC/DC boost converter, where the main energy storage element is a DC-bus capacitor, while the inductances are exploited to steer the filter currents by means of the converter voltages. The switching devices of the three-leg bridge (also called "'inverter"') are usually realized by IGBTs (Insulated Gate Bipolar Transistors) and free-wheeling diodes.

In this work the following notation is used to denote the SAF variables; $v_{mabc}=(v_{ma}, v_{mb}, v_{mc})^T$ is the mains voltage sinusoidal balanced and equilibrated tern, $i_m=(i_{ma}, i_{mb}, i_{mc})^T$ are the mains currents, $i_l=(i_{la}, i_{lb}, i_{lc})^T$ are the load currents, while $i=(i_a, i_b, i_c)^T$ are the filter currents. L indicates the value of the inductances, and C the DC-link bus capacitor value.

2.1 Mathematical model

Considering the inductors dynamics, the filter model can be expressed as

$$\begin{bmatrix} v_{ma}(t) \\ v_{mb}(t) \\ v_{mc}(t) \end{bmatrix} - L\frac{d}{dt}\begin{bmatrix} i_a(t) \\ i_b(t) \\ i_c(t) \end{bmatrix} - R\begin{bmatrix} i_a(t) \\ i_b(t) \\ i_c(t) \end{bmatrix} = \begin{bmatrix} u_x(t) \\ u_y(t) \\ u_z(t) \end{bmatrix} v(t) - v_{NK}\begin{bmatrix} 1 \\ 1 \\ 1 \end{bmatrix} \tag{1}$$

where R is the parasitic resistance related to the inductance L and to the cables, v_{NK} is the voltage between the nodes N and K reported in Fig. 1, $v(t)$ is the voltage on the DC-link capacitor, and $u_1 = (u_x, u_y, u_z)^T$ is the switch command vector for the legs of the converter. Since a PWM (Pulse Width Modulation) strategy is assumed to control the inverter, the above-mentioned control inputs can be considered such that $u_{1i} \in [0, 1]$, $i = x, y, z$. According to the three-wire topology for any generic voltage/current vector x it holds

$$\sum_{i=a,b,c} x_i = 0 \tag{2}$$

hence, from the sum of the scalar equations in (1) it follows that

$$v_{NK} = \frac{u_x(t) + u_y(t) + u_z(t)}{3} v(t) \tag{3}$$

defining

$$u_{abc} = [u_a(t),\ u_b(t),\ u_c(t)]^T = \begin{bmatrix} u_x(t) \\ u_y(t) \\ u_z(t) \end{bmatrix} - \frac{u_x(t) + u_y(t) + u_z(t)}{3}\begin{bmatrix} 1 \\ 1 \\ 1 \end{bmatrix} \tag{4}$$

it can be verified by direct computations that

$$[1\,1\,1]u_{abc}(t) = 0 \ \forall t \geq 0. \tag{5}$$

For what concerns the state equation relative to the capacitor voltage dynamics, it can be derived considering an ideal inverter and applying a power balance condition between the input and the output of the filter, then replacing (3) into (1), the complete filter model results

$$\begin{aligned} \frac{di}{dt} &= -\frac{R}{L}I_3 i(t) - \frac{v(t)}{L}u_{abc}(t) + \frac{1}{L}v_{mabc} \\ \frac{dv}{dt} &= \frac{1}{C}u_{abc}^T(t)i(t) \end{aligned} \tag{6}$$

where the filter currents dynamics have been written in a more compact form with respect to (1), multiplying the current vector by the identity matrix of suitable dimension I_3. Exploiting equations (3), (5), the system model can be reduced to the standard *two-phase planar representation* of a three-phase balanced systems (Krause et al., 1995), which can be obtained

u_x u_y u_z	u_a	u_b	u_c	u_α	u_β
0 0 0	0	0	0	0	0
1 0 0	2/3	-1/3	-1/3	2/3	0
1 1 0	1/3	1/3	-2/3	1/3	$1/\sqrt{3}$
0 1 0	-1/3	2/3	-1/3	-1/3	$1/\sqrt{3}$
0 1 1	-2/3	1/3	1/3	-2/3	0
0 0 1	-1/3	-1/3	2/3	-1/3	$-1/\sqrt{3}$
1 0 1	1/3	-2/3	1/3	1/3	$-1/\sqrt{3}$
1 1 1	0	0	0	0	0

Table 1. Control function table.

applying the following coordinates transformation

$$\begin{aligned} i_{\alpha\beta}(t) &= [i_\alpha\, i_\beta]^T =^{\alpha\beta} T_{abc} i(t) \\ u_{\alpha\beta}(t) &= [u_\alpha\, u_\beta]^T =^{\alpha\beta} T_{abc} u_{abc}(t) \\ v_{m\alpha\beta} &= [v_{m\alpha} v_{m\beta}]^T =^{\alpha\beta} T_{abc} v_m \\ {}^{\alpha\beta}T_{abc} &= \frac{2}{3}\begin{bmatrix} 1 & -\frac{1}{2} & -\frac{1}{2} \\ 0 & \frac{\sqrt{3}}{2} & -\frac{\sqrt{3}}{2} \end{bmatrix} \end{aligned} \tag{7}$$

the SAF dynamics expressed in this $\alpha - \beta$ reference frame become

$$\begin{aligned} \frac{di_{\alpha\beta}}{dt} &= -\frac{R}{L} I_2 i_{\alpha\beta}(t) - \frac{v(t)}{L} u_{\alpha\beta}(t) + \frac{1}{L} v_{m\alpha\beta} \\ \frac{dv}{dt} &= \frac{3}{2C} u_{\alpha\beta}^T(t) i_{\alpha\beta}(t) \end{aligned} \tag{8}$$

according to the hypothesis of three-phase balanced sinusoidal line, the ideal main voltage tern can be expressed in the above-defined bi-dimensional reference frame as follows

$$[v_{m\alpha}\ v_{m\beta}]^T = V_m [cos(\omega_m)\ sin(\omega_m)]^T$$

where V_m is the voltage amplitude and ω_m the grid angular frequency. For what concerns the control vector u_{abc}, in this reference frame the eight possible configurations of the switching network (reported in Tab. 1) can be mapped in the $\alpha - \beta$ plane, obtaining the vertexes and the origin of the feasibility space illustrated in Fig.2, while each point in the hexagon can be obtained as mean value in a PWM period. As it will become clear in the next sections, in order to simplify the control objectives definition and the controller design, it is very useful to adopt a further transformation from the two-phase current variables $[i_\alpha\ i_\beta]^T$ to a two-phase real-virtual (imaginary) power variables defined as

$$x = [x_d\ x_q]^T =^{dq} T_{\alpha\beta} i_{\alpha\beta} \tag{9}$$

where

$${}^{dq}T_{\alpha\beta} = V_m \begin{bmatrix} cos(\omega_m t) & sin(\omega_m t) \\ -sin(\omega_m t) & cos(\omega_m t) \end{bmatrix}.$$

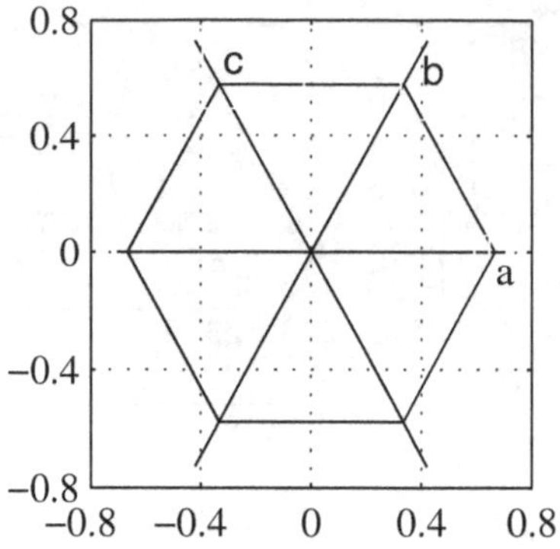

Fig. 2. Hexagon of feasible u_{abc}.

In this so-called *synchronous* coordinate setting, aligned with the mains voltage vector, the model of the SAF is expressed as

$$\begin{aligned} \dot{x} &= M(R,L)x - \frac{v}{L}u_{dq} + d_0 \\ \dot{v} &= \frac{\epsilon}{2}u_{dq}^T x \end{aligned} \tag{10}$$

where

$$d_0 = \begin{bmatrix} E_{md}/L \\ 0 \end{bmatrix},\ M(R,L) = \begin{bmatrix} -R/L & \omega_m \\ -\omega_m & -R/L \end{bmatrix},\ \epsilon = \frac{3}{CE_{md}},\ E_{md} = V_m^2,\ u_{dq} = ^{dq}T_{\alpha\beta}u_{\alpha\beta} \tag{11}$$

it is further to notice that, since the filter currents, the mains voltage and the DC-link voltage are measurable, the full state (x,v) is available for feedback, moreover the actual control action $u = [u_x\ u_y\ u_z]$ can be determined from u_{abc}, which in turn can be derived from u_{dq}.
As regards the load description, the same two-phase real-virtual power representation can be used, in particular following (Akagi et al., 1984), the load currents can be approximated as periodic signals given by the sum of a finite number N of harmonics, with frequencies multiple of $f_m = \omega_m/2\pi$. Hence the load currents can be expressed in power variables as

$$x_{lj} = X_{lj0} + \sum_{n=1}^{N+1} X_{ljn}cos(n\omega_m t + \psi_{jn}),\ \ j = d,q \tag{12}$$

where the harmonics amplitudes $X_{ld0}, X_{lq0}, X_{ldn}, X_{lqn}$ and phases ψ_{dn}, ψ_{qn} are constants. Since the load currents and the mains voltages are measurable, also the variables $(x_{ld},\ x_{lq})$ will be considered known and available for control purpose.

2.2 Problem statement and control objectives

Roughly speaking the main control objective of the considered SAF is to steer the variables x_d, x_q, injecting power into the line to compensate for the load harmonics. However the ability of tracking current references relies upon the energy stored in the DC-link capacitor, which is the main power source of the filter, therefore another general objective is to keep the DC-link voltage confined in a suitable region, to avoid overcharge and, at the same time, to ensure the capability to steer the filter currents. On the other hand the ability of maintaining DC-link voltage into a suitable region is strictly related to the power exchanged with the mains, which in turn is affected by the current harmonics to be compensated for. The general control objective is then two-folds; one related to the tracking of current disturbances, the other concerns the voltage internal dynamics stabilization. In this paragraph a precise and feasible control problem is formally defined, recalling the considerations made above, and assuming that a suitable dimensioning, that will be deeply discussed in the next section, has been carried out.

Bearing in mind the power variables representation of a generic nonlinear load expressed in (12), it turns out that the only desired load component is X_{ld0}, since it represents first-order harmonics aligned with the mains voltages, while the remaining part of the real component $x_{ld} - X_{ld0}$ is an oscillatory signal with null balance over a line period, and the imaginary component x_{lq} represent a measure of the misalignment between mains ideal voltage and load currents (see Mohan et al. (1989)) and do not contribute to the power flow. In this respect, the terms $x_{ld} - X_{ld0}$, x_{lq} are undesired components which should be canceled by the injected filter currents, hence ideally the control problem can be formulated as a state tracking problem, for system (10), of the following reference

$$x^*(t) = [x_d^* \ x_q^*]^T = \left[X_{ld0} - x_{ld} \quad -x_{lq}\right]^T \tag{13}$$

a prefect tracking of this reference would ensure pure sinusoidal mains currents perfectly aligned with the mains voltages. However, this ideal objective is in contrast with the requirement to have a DC-link voltage bounded behavior. In order to formally motivate this claim, consider the steady state voltage dynamics in case perfect tracking of the power reference $x^*(t)$ is achieved, after some computations it results

$$\frac{dv^2}{dt} = \epsilon L\left(d_0 + M(R,L)x^*(t) - \dot{x}^*(t)\right)^T x^* := \epsilon \Upsilon(x^*(t)) \tag{14}$$

the signal $\epsilon\Upsilon(x^*(t))$ which drives the integrator is periodic with period $T = 1/f_m$, and it is composed by the sum of a zero mean value signal $\epsilon L(d_0 - \dot{x}^*)^T x^*$, and the signal $\epsilon L(M(R,L)x^*)^T x^*$ which has negative mean value as long as parasitic resistance R or reference x^* are not zero. By this, no matter the starting voltage value of the DC-link, the capacitor will be discharged and the voltage will drop, providing a loss of controllability of the system.

To avoid this phenomenon, the reference must be revised, taking into account an additional power term, which should be drained from the line grid by the active filter, in order to compensate for its power losses. Following this motivation, and recalling that the unique useful component for the energy exchange is the real part of the power variables, the ideal reference signal (13) is modified as

$$x^*_{\varphi_0} = x^* + (\varphi_0 \ 0)^T \tag{15}$$

in which φ_0 is a solution of the following equation

$$R\varphi_0^2 - E_{md}\varphi_0 + Rf_m \int_0^{1/f_m} (x_d^{*2}(\tau) + x_q^{*2}(\tau))d\tau = 0 \tag{16}$$

this represents the power balancing condition which guarantees that the internal voltage dynamics in case of perfect tracking of the modified reference $x^*_{\varphi_0}$ is

$$\frac{dv^2(t)}{dt} = \epsilon\Psi(x^*_{\varphi_0}(t)) \tag{17}$$

and the right hand side $\epsilon\Psi(x^*_{\varphi_0})$ is periodic with period $1/f_m$ with zero mean value. A brief discussion is needed for the solutions of equation (16), it has two real positive solutions if the following condition is verified

$$E^2_{md} \geq 4R^2 f_m \int_0^{1/f_m} (x^{*2}_d(\tau) + x^{*2}_q(\tau))d\tau \tag{18}$$

from a physical viewpoint relation (18) set an upper bound on the admissible undesired components which can be compensated and on the parasitic resistance R, however, as typically $E_{md} >> R$, this condition is not limitative at all. The two solutions of (16) under condition (18) are

$$\begin{aligned} \varphi_0 &\approx \frac{R}{E_{md}} f_m \int_0^{1/f_m} (x^{*2}_d(\tau) + x^{*2}_q(\tau))d\tau \approx 0 \\ \varphi_0 &\approx \frac{E_{md}}{R} \end{aligned} \tag{19}$$

the first solution, minimizing the power drained from the line grid to compensate the power losses, is the physically most plausible, because the power consumed by parasitic resistances in the filter is usually quite small, hence it will be considered throughout the chapter.
The control problem which will be faced in this work can now be precisely stated; the issue is to design the control vector u_{abc} in a way such that the following objectives are fulfilled:
A) Given the reference signal $x^*_{\varphi_0}$ defined in (15), asymptotic tracking must be achieved, that is

$$\lim_{t\to\infty} (x(t) - x^*_{\varphi_0}) = 0; \tag{20}$$

B) Given a safe voltage range $[v_m, v_M]$, with $v_M > v_m > 0$, and assuming $v(t_0) \in [v_m, v_M]$, it is required that

$$v(t) \in [v_m, v_M], \forall t > t_0; \tag{21}$$

it can be verified that the tracking of the modified power reference is potentially achievable keeping the voltage dynamics inside the safe region, only if the zero mean value oscillating component of $\epsilon\Psi(x^*_{\varphi_0})$ is properly bounded, this can be ensured by a suitable capacitor design. In the regulator design, saturation of the actual input u_1, imposed by PWM strategy, will not be taken explicitly into account, also this approximation takes advantage of a correct sizing methodology; as it will become clear in Section 3, a suitable choice of the DC-link voltage lower bound v_m, depending on the currents to be compensated for, has to be made to meet the constraint $u_1 \in [0, 1]$, at least when the power tracking error is reasonably small.
A further consideration needs to be made on the requirement $v(t_0) \in [v_m, v_M]$; according to the AC/DC boost converter theory (Mohan et al., 1989), the natural response of the system would lead the DC-link voltage at twice the line voltage peak value, due to the resonant behavior of the LC pair and the free-wheeling diodes of the switching bridge. If a proper design has been performed, this value is expected to be greater than the voltage range lower

bound v_m; hence, after a transient period, the controller can be switched on having the initial voltage value inside the admissible region as required by objective B.
Finally it is further to remark that $x^*_{\varphi_0}$ depends on parasitic resistance R through (16), hence it has to be considered as an unknown variable, to be reconstructed by estimating the power losses by means of a proper elaboration of the DC-link voltage signal.

3. Shunt active filter sizing methodology

The aim of this section is to present a precise algorithm to properly select the SAF hardware components, two different design objectives are considered, the first is to select the minimal component values dependent on the level of current distortion imposed by the load, while the second is to find the minimum capacitor value necessary to compensate all the possible loads compatible with the maximum current rating of the inverter switching devices. Both the methods are control-oriented, that is they ensure the feasibility of control objectives stated in 2.2 and that control input saturation is avoided under nominal load and line voltage conditions.
The proposed design method is based on the model derived in Section 2, a further approximation is considered with respect to equation (6); the inductors are modeled as pure inductance, that is the parasitic resistance R is neglected, while ideal mains voltage tern and converter switches are considered as in the previous section.

3.1 Inductance value selection

The inductance value can be selected regardless the loads, hence this part of the design procedure is the same for both the design objectives previously defined.
The design criterion is based on the maximum current ripple ΔI_{Mpp} allowed for the filter currents; current ripple is a consequence of the PWM technique applied to obtain the reference command value u^*_{abc}, it has to be bounded in order to limit high frequency distortion. The actual command vector $u_{abc}(t)$ and filter current $i(t)$ are affected by a ripple component

$$\begin{aligned} i(t) &= i^*(t) + \Delta i(t) \\ u_{abc}(t) &= u^*_{abc}(t) + \Delta u_{abc}(t) \end{aligned} \tag{22}$$

substituting these expressions in the state equation (6) it turns out

$$L\frac{\Delta i(t)}{dt} = -\Delta u_{abc}(t)v(t) \tag{23}$$

by simple computation it can be showed that the worst ripple case occurs when the desired command value u^*_{abc} is in the middle of a feasibility hexagon side (see Fig. 3). In this condition, assuming that the DC-link voltage has constant value V in a PWM period, the peak to peak current ripple is

$$\Delta I_{pp} = \int_t^{t+T_s/2} \frac{d\Delta i(t)}{dt}dt = \frac{V}{6f_{PWM}L} \tag{24}$$

where the sampling period T_s and the PWM frequency f_{PWM} are assumed already set before starting the sizing procedure. If the peak to peak ripple must be bounded by the desired

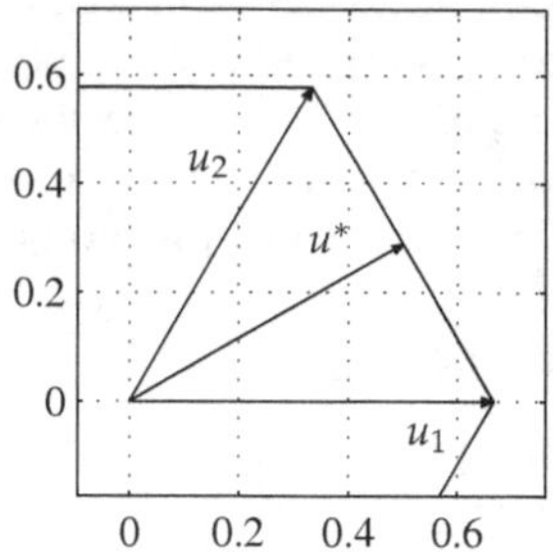

Fig. 3. Current ripple worst case.

maximum value ΔI_{Mpp}, the following inequality needs to be fulfilled

$$L \geq \frac{v_M}{6 f_{PWM} \Delta I_{Mpp}} \Rightarrow L_{min} = \frac{v_M}{6 f_{PWM} \Delta I_{Mpp}} \tag{25}$$

the upper bound of the voltage range v_M depends only on the kind of capacitor and it can be supposed already chosen before starting the design procedure, hence the minimum inductance value L_{min} compatible with the desired maximum current ripple can be selected applying equation (25).

3.2 Load-based approach

Let us now consider the first design algorithm based on the knowledge of the load to be compensated for. The load distortion will be modeled as in equation (12), taking into account the constraint on the maximum current I_{max} of the device implementing the bridge switches. The switching devices sizing depends on the total amount of power (distorted and reactive) $P = 3V_{mRMS} I_{SAFRMS}$ that the filter has to compensate for (if the load is known then P is known), hence by the route mean square value I_{SAFRMS}, the maximum current that the switches need to drain can be readily obtained as $I_{max} = \sqrt{2} I_{SAFRMS}$.
The desired filter currents (denoted with *) necessary to fulfill the tracking objective A defined in 2.2 can be effectively imposed by the converter if each component is less than the maximum allowed value, i.e

$$i^*(t) = [i_a^*(t)\ i_b^*(t)\ i_c^*(t)]^T \leq I_{max}[1\ 1\ 1]^T,\ \forall t \tag{26}$$

this feasibility condition can be graphically represented considering that each projection of the filter currents vector must be less then I_{max}, hence the feasibility space is an hexagon similar to that reported in Fig. 4 (obtained taking $P = 45kVAR$ as filter size, $V_{mRMS} = 220V$ and then $I_{max} = 70A$). Therefore condition (26) can be readily checked considering the inscribed circle in the feasibility hexagon. If the load currents do not satisfy constraint (26) the number of current harmonics to be compensated for has to be reduced, differently, when the filter performance cannot be decreased, the opportunity to connect two shunt active filters to the same load can be considered.
Assuming that an inductance value such that $L \geq L_{min}$ has been selected, the voltages at the input of the six switches bridge can be calculated as

$$v_{dq}^*(t) = v(t) u_{dq}^*(t) = \begin{bmatrix} V_m \\ 0 \end{bmatrix} - L \frac{di_{dq}^*}{dt} + \begin{bmatrix} 0 & \omega_m \\ -\omega_m & 0 \end{bmatrix} i_{dq}^* \tag{27}$$

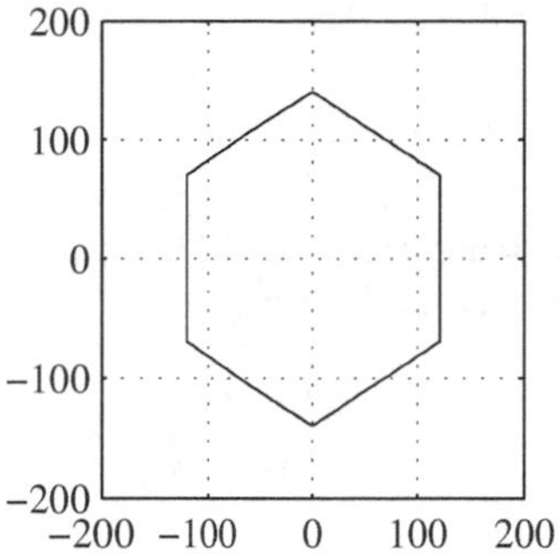

Fig. 4. Hexagon of feasible filter current.

the above equation is obtained by inversion of equation (10) with $R = 0$ and expressing the model in the *synchronous* reference frame in current rather than in power variables, in order to directly consider the load currents in the design approach.
The constraints on the command inputs need to be considered too, by (27) the inductance value must be as low as possible in order to make u^*_{dq} feasible, taking into account also the current ripple limitation we select $L = L_{min}$. As mentioned, the choice of the of the capacitor voltage lower bound value plays a key role to avoid saturation issues on command inputs, this can be easily verified approximating the hexagon in Fig. 2 with the inscribed circle. In order to avoid control action saturation (assuming perfect power tracking) it must be imposed that

$$||u^*_{abc}|| = \frac{||v^*_{abc}(t)||}{v(t)} \leq \frac{||v^*_{abc}(t)||}{v_m} \leq r_{in} = \frac{1}{\sqrt{3}}, \ \forall t \tag{28}$$

with r_{in} the radius of the inscribed circle and $v^*_{abc} = v(t)u^*_{abc}$. From (28) design equation for v_m can be obtained

$$v_M \geq v_m \geq \frac{||v^*_{abc}(t)||}{r_{in}}, \forall t \in \left[\frac{n}{f_m}, \frac{n+1}{f_m}\right], \ n = 0, 1, \ldots \tag{29}$$

usually v_m is oversized with respect the value given by the inequality above, in order to avoid saturation even if non-zero tracking errors are present. If condition (29) cannot be satisfied, some alternatives need to be considered; the capacitor can be changed in order to adopt an higher upper bound v_M, when the costs of the project have to be limited and the kind of capacitor cannot be substituted, the number of harmonics considered must be reduced until (29) is satisfied. To preserve the number of harmonics to compensate, the inductance value can be reduced, penalizing the current ripple and then tolerating a greater high frequency distortion.
The capacitor value can then be selected assuming an ideal converter and writing the balance equation between the instantaneous reference power at the input of the six switches bridge and the power of the DC-link capacitor, hence

$$p_{filt}(t) = [v_{dq}(t)]^T i^*_{dq}(t) = \frac{d}{dt}\left(\frac{1}{2}Cv^2(t)\right) \tag{30}$$

the corresponding energy can be calculated as

$$E_{filt}(t) = \int_{t_0}^{t} p_{filt}(\tau)d\tau \tag{31}$$

by the hypothesis of sinusoidal load currents and ideal mains voltages $E_{filt}(t)$ is periodic of frequency f_m and its mean value is zero. Defining

$$\begin{aligned} E_{max} &= max|E_{filt}(t)| \\ v_{ref} &= \frac{v_M + v_m}{2} \end{aligned} \tag{32}$$

and imposing that the voltage variation corresponding to E_{max} is $v_{ref} - v_m$, the capacitor value design equation can be written as

$$C = \frac{2E_{max}}{v_{ref}^2 - v_m^2} \tag{33}$$

3.3 Switches-based approach

As stated at the beginning of this section, a different design method aims to find the capacitor value that makes the filter able to compensate for the worst load compatible with the switches maximum current. If the resulting capacitor value is not too expensive, this method allows to design the filter only knowing the amount of current that has to be compensated.

During the optimization procedure the load currents need to be the only varying parameters while all the other values must be fixed. The inductance value is chosen equal to the minimum compatible with the allowed ripple, while the minimum capacitor voltage v_m is supposed sufficiently low to make simple the voltage control, and, at the same time, the resulting capacitor value feasible. Writing the filter currents spectrum in the $d-q$ synchronous reference frame, an expression similar to (12) can be obtained

$$i_j(t) = I_{j0} + \sum_{n=1}^{N+1} I_{jn} cos(2\pi n f_m t + \psi_{jn}), \quad j = d, q \tag{34}$$

the parameters to be varied in order to calculate the worst E_{max} are the $(2N+1)+1$ magnitudes and the $2N+1$ phases, so the following optimization problem

$$E_{max}^{worst} = \max_{z} \max_{t} \left| \int_{t_0}^{t} [v_{dq}(\tau)]^T i_{dq}(\tau)d\tau \right| \tag{35}$$

has to be solved with respect to the array z of $4(N+1)+1$ variables, taking into account the following constraints

- switches currents must be less than the maximum allowed, that is the current vector must be inside an hexagon similar to that reported in Fig. 4. This can be easily checked approximating the hexagon with its inscribed circle;
- the control output must be feasible, that is the vector u_{abc} must be inside the hexagon reported in Fig. 2. This can be easily checked approximating the hexagon with its inscribed circle;
- harmonics components phases have to be greater than $-\pi$ and less than π.

Once E_{max}^{worst} has been determined, substituting its value in (33), the capacitor value relative to the switches-based design approach can be selected.
In the discussion above, ideal mains voltages have been assumed, if also the grid line voltages are distorted, the capacitor has to provide more energy to the load, hence its value must be higher than the one calculated under ideal conditions.
In case of ideal mains voltages the load instant power is the one calculated in (12) and the only power term that the filter must deliver is $x_{ldn} = \sum_{n=1}^{N+1} X_{ldn} cos(n\omega_m t + \psi_{dn}) = V_m i_{ldn}$ having zero mean value. If the mains voltages are distorted, their representation in the synchronous reference frame is

$$v_{mdq}(t) = [V_m + v_{mdn}, \ v_{mq}]^T \tag{36}$$

line voltages harmonic perturbation produces additive terms in the load instantaneous power expression, that by direct computation can be written as

$$p_{ladd} = v_{mdn}(t) i_{ldn}(t) + v_{mq} i_{lq}(t) \tag{37}$$

the above equation shows that the filter has to provide more power to the load, furthermore the power mean value in a PWM period can be different from zero. Hence also assuming that the mean value becomes zero in a finite time, the capacitor must be oversized with respect to the ideal situation, in order to accumulate more energy.

4. Robust controller design

In this section the control problem defined in 2.2 is addressed, relying upon a suitable capacitor value given by the procedure described in the previous section, the two interlaced objectives A and B defined in 2.2 can be approached individually by exploiting the principle of singular perturbation. Two independent controllers (reported in the block diagram of Fig. 5) will be designed. An internal model-based controller (IMC) is proposed in order to deal with the problem of robust reference tracking (defined in objective A) for the fast subsystems composed by the power variables dynamics, while an independent voltage controller for the slow DC-link voltage subsystem is designed to produce a reference modification η which compensate the unknown power losses term φ_0, allowing to achieve objective B. The averaged voltage value is chosen as the controlled variable, and a phasor variables representation is exploited to design the regulator, this choice allows for the necessary voltage oscillation during nominal operation, and improves the voltage dynamics behavior with respect to other proposed solutions (Marconi et al., 2007). Stability analysis is carried out in two steps; the *reduced averaged dynamics*, obtained replacing the steady state of the fast subsystem into the slow voltage dynamics and carrying out the average value to obtain a phasor variables representation, and the *boundary layer system*, obtained considering the SAF currents dynamics and an ideal energy storage element, are proved to be asymptotically stabilized by the proposed controllers. Then practical stability for the overall closed-loop error system is stated exploiting well-established singular perturbation and two time-scale systems theory results.
Before detailing the proposed control structure, consider the first preliminary control law

$$\bar{u}(t) = v(t) u_{dq}(t) \tag{38}$$

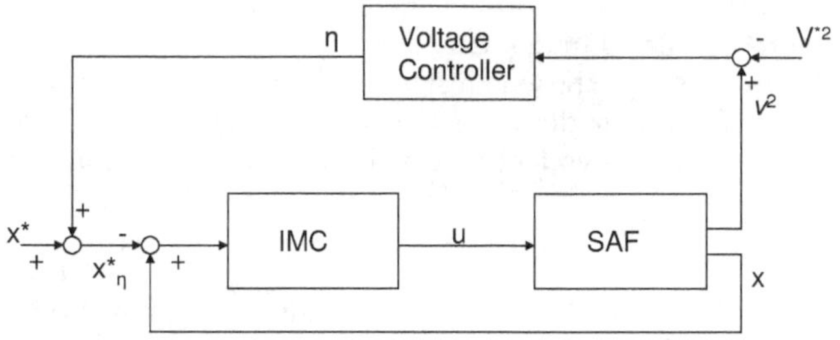

Fig. 5. Controller structure.

which is always well defined provided that $v(t) \geq v_m > 0$ for all $t \geq 0$ according to objective B. Replacing (38) into (10) yields

$$\begin{aligned} \dot{x} &= M(R,L)x + \frac{1}{L}\bar{u} + d_0 \\ \frac{dv^2}{dt} &= \epsilon \bar{u}^T x \end{aligned} \tag{39}$$

now consider the modified power reference

$$x_\eta^* = x^* + (\eta \;\; 0)^T \tag{40}$$

and define the change of variables

$$\tilde{x} = x - x_\eta^*, \quad \tilde{z} = v^2 - V^{*2} \tag{41}$$

where $V^{*2} = (v_m^2 + v_M^2)/(2)$ is the reference value for the square DC-link voltage. Note that the requirement B of having $v(t) \in [v_m \;\; v_M]$ for all $t \geq t_0$ can be equivalently formulated in the error variable $\tilde{z}$ requiring $\tilde{z}(t) \in [-l^* \;\; l^*]$ for all $t \geq t_0$, with $l^* = (v_M^2 - v_m^2)/2$. The complete system (39) can be then expressed in the error variables defined in (41), the transformed model results

$$\begin{aligned} \dot{\tilde{x}} &= M(R,L)\tilde{x} - \frac{1}{L}\bar{u} + d_0 - \dot{x}_\eta^* + Mx_\eta^* \\ \dot{\tilde{z}} &= \epsilon \bar{u}^T[\tilde{x} + x_\eta^*]. \end{aligned} \tag{42}$$

The controller design will be carried out considering the error dynamics in (42), in summary the idea is to steer the closed loop dynamics toward a steady state in which $\tilde{z}$ is free to oscillate within the admissible region, but its mean value is steered to zero (i.e the DC-link voltage mean value is steered to V^*), and $\tilde{x}$ is steered to zero, i.e the power x follows a reference which is the sum of the term x^*, which takes into account the undesired harmonic load components, and a constant bias η which is needed in order to compensate the power losses and to make the range $[v_m \ v_M]$ an invariant subspace for the voltage dynamics.

4.1 Averaging voltage controller

In order to fulfill objective B the voltage dynamics need to be stabilized, in this respect the subsystem composed by the capacitor voltage dynamics will be considered, a suitable *reduced averaged system* will be sought, and then a controller for the capacitor voltage DC component will be designed.

The first step is to average the voltage differential equation to obtain the dynamics in the so-called *phasor-variables*, then, a control law, itself expressed on phasor representation, can be designed following an approach similar to that proposed in (Valderrama et. al, 2001), however in this work the only voltage subsystem is controlled using phasor variables, while the power subsystem is controlled in the real time domain.

The controlled variable is chosen to be the time-window averaged value $\tilde{z}_a$ of the square voltage error $\tilde{z}$, and the averaging is performed over the time interval $[t-T, t]$. In terms of (Sanders et al., 1991) this average value is a zero-order phasor defined as

$$\tilde{z}_a(t) = \int_{t-T}^{t} \tilde{z}(\tau) d\tau \tag{43}$$

the fact that $\tilde{z}_a$ is a zero-order phasor allows to obtain its derivative by simply applying the same averaging procedure to its differential equation in (42)

$$\dot{\tilde{z}}_a = \frac{1}{T}\int_{t-T}^{t} \dot{\tilde{z}}(\tau) d\tau = \epsilon \int_{t-T}^{t} \bar{u}^T[\tilde{x} + x_\eta^*] d\tau \tag{44}$$

note that the average voltage derivative can also be expressed as the difference over one period of the actual voltage, hence

$$\frac{d}{dt}(\tilde{z}_a) = \frac{d}{dt}\int_{t-T}^{t} \tilde{z}(\tau) d\tau = \frac{\tilde{z}(t) - \tilde{z}(t-T)}{T} \tag{45}$$

this insight connotes the availability of $\tilde{z}_a$ for measurement in real time, and, as it will later clarified, it is of crucial importance for an actual implementation of the controller.

All further elaborations will focus on the integral-differential equation (44) representing the averaged error voltage dynamics. This equation depends on $\bar{u}$ which is actually provided by the power tracking controller, to eliminate $\bar{u}$ consider that the differential equation for $\tilde{x}$ in (42) can be rewritten as

$$\bar{u} = L(M(R, L)x_\eta^* - \dot{x}_\eta^* + M(R, L)\tilde{x} + d_0 - \dot{\tilde{x}}) \tag{46}$$

replacing (46) into (44) the following equation is obtained

$$\dot{\tilde{z}}_a = \frac{\epsilon L}{T}\int_{t-T}^{t} (M(R, L)x_\eta^* - \dot{x}_\eta^* + d_0)^T x_\eta^* d\tau + \epsilon L\tilde{D}(\tilde{x}) \tag{47}$$

where $\tilde{D}(\tilde{x})$ collects all the terms depending on the power tracking error $\tilde{x}$. The next step is to exploit the fact that the reference term x^* is T-periodic ($T = 1/f_m$), hence it results in a constant value when averaged over this period, this is a key advantage of the averaging approach for the voltage system. The T-periodic terms in (47) can be summarized to

$$D^* = \frac{1}{T}\int_{t-T}^{t}[(M(R,L)x^* - \dot{x}^* + d_0)^T x^*]d\tau \tag{48}$$

since x^* is periodic in T, D^* is a constant disturbance, and, due to power losses induced by the parasitic resistance R, it also follows that $D^* < 0$. For further simplification the integral operator can be applied to the occurring derivative terms. Using definitions (11), (40), after some computations the averaged error voltage dynamics can be expressed completely in phasor variables

$$\dot{\tilde{z}}_a = \epsilon[E_{md}\eta_a - 2R\nu_a - L\dot{\nu}_a + LD^* + L\tilde{D}] \tag{49}$$

where the following nonlinear term has been defined

$$\nu(t) = \eta(t)\left(\frac{1}{2}\eta(t) + x_d^*\right) \tag{50}$$

which enters (49) with its average and its averaged derivative

$$\begin{aligned} \nu_a(t) &= \frac{1}{T}\int_{t-T}^{t}\nu(\tau)d\tau \\ \dot{\nu}_a(t) &= \frac{\nu_a(t) - \nu_a(t-T)}{T} \end{aligned} \tag{51}$$

the averaged error voltage system is thus controlled by means of the averaged control input

$$\eta_a(t) = \frac{1}{T}\int_{t-T}^{t}\eta(\tau)d\tau. \tag{52}$$

According to singular perturbation theory, the voltage controller design can be carried out considering only the *reduced dynamics*, obtained confusing the value of $\tilde{x}$ with its steady state value $\tilde{x} = 0$.

As previously remarked, this approximation can be introduced thanks to the small value of ϵ which, multiplying the voltage dynamics in the second of (42), makes the voltage subsystem much slower with respect to the power dynamics in the first of (42) (this phenomenon is usually referred as two time-scale system behavior) that will approach the steady state much faster then $\tilde{z}$. Thus reduced voltage dynamics can be obtained by (49) simply dropping the coupling term $\tilde{D}$, because by definition $\tilde{D}(0) = 0$.

The nonlinear terms ν_a, and $\dot{\nu}_a$ cannot be managed easily, beside non-linearity they contain an integral, a time delay and a time-varying term x_d^*. In order to simplify the mathematical treatment, a sort of linearized version of system (49) will be considered. This linear approximation is motivated by several facts; since the parasitic resistance R and the filter inductance value L are usually very small with respect to the term E_{md} in every realistic setup, nonlinear term are much smaller than the linear ones. Furthermore the component x_d^* has no influence at all in averaging terms if η is constant, thanks to the fact that it is T-periodic with zero mean value. Hence it will influence the averaged system only while η is varying, and also in this case its oscillatory part will be filtered by the averaging procedure. As a result of the previous steps and considerations, the linearized averaged model for the reduced dynamics can be written as

$$\dot{\tilde{z}}_a = \epsilon E_{md}[\eta_a - \varphi_0] \tag{53}$$

where, as mentioned, φ_0 is the smallest solution of equation (16).
Now it is possible to design the control input η_a in order to stabilize the origin of system (53), a standard PI regulator in the averaged variables is proposed

$$\begin{aligned} \eta_a &= -K_P\tilde{z}_a + \theta \\ \dot{\theta} &= -\epsilon K_I \tilde{z}_a \end{aligned} \tag{54}$$

it is further to notice that the ϵ factor in the integral action of the controller is introduced to keep the voltage controller speed in scale with the voltage subsystem to control, thus maintaining the two-time scale behavior of the overall system.
In order to prove the asymptotic stability of the closed-loop system resulting by the interconnection of (54) and (53) consider the change of coordinates $\tilde{\theta} = \theta - \varphi_0$, which results in the closed-loop error dynamics

$$\frac{d}{dt}\begin{bmatrix}\tilde{z}_a \\ \tilde{\theta}\end{bmatrix} = \epsilon \begin{bmatrix} -E_{md}K_P & E_{md} \\ -K_I & 0 \end{bmatrix} \begin{bmatrix}\tilde{z}_a \\ \tilde{\theta}\end{bmatrix} \tag{55}$$

since ϵ, E_{md} are positive, the matrix in (55) is Hurwitz for all $K_P > 0$, $K_I > 0$, and system (55) result asymptotically stable despite the unknown disturbance φ_0.
The problem with implementing the regulator (55) is that the resulting control signal is the average value of the actual control input η, thus some procedure is required to synthesize a real-world control signal whose mean value satisfies the above conditions. In the SAF specific case this problem can be solved, consider the derivative of signal η_a

$$\frac{d}{dt}\eta_a = \frac{d}{dt}\frac{1}{T}\int_{t-T}^{t}\eta(\tau)d\tau \tag{56}$$

it can be rewritten on the left side as the difference over one period, while the right side is replaced with the derivative of η_a expressed in (54);

$$\frac{1}{T}[\eta(t) - \eta(t-T)] = -K_P\dot{\tilde{z}}_a + \dot{\tilde{\theta}} = -K_P\dot{\tilde{z}}_a - \epsilon K_I \tilde{z}_a \tag{57}$$

solving for $\eta(t)$ yields

$$\eta(t) = -TK_P\dot{\tilde{z}}_a(t) - \epsilon T K_I \tilde{z}_a(t) + \eta(t-T) \tag{58}$$

using (45), the derivative of the averaged square voltage error is actually measurable, thus the above formula is implementable. However, while the interconnection between voltage subsystem and controller is stable in sense of the averaged value, a further step is required. In the incremental implementation (58) there is no more an integral action, the control input history is kept in memory for one period, still the controller provides stability for the averaged voltage error $\tilde{z}_a$. Consider now that for the phasor variables system, a stable steady-state guarantees that all the variables have a constant average value, while being allowed to oscillate freely. This property is desired for what concern the capacitor voltage and it is the main motivation for applying the averaging procedure, however implementation according to (58) can introduce undesired periodic oscillation in the control input η, moreover oscillation

will persist being remembered through the time delay term. In summary, while η_a will approach the constant power loss value φ_0, the actual input η might be any periodic signal with average value equal to φ_0. Recalling that η modifies the real power reference value x_d^*, any oscillation will result in a non-zero error for the power tracking controller.
In order to avoid this situation the following term can be added to (58)

$$d_\eta(t) = \eta(t-T) - \eta_a(t-T/2) \tag{59}$$

the reason of this modification is to cancel the oscillations stored in memory, by correcting the stored signal towards its own mean value $\eta_a(t-T/2)$. It is important to remark that the averaged value is not the actual mean value of its corresponding signal, the mean value s_m of a signal $s(t)$ is defined as

$$s_m = \frac{1}{T}\int_{t-T/2}^{t+T/2} s(\tau)d\tau \tag{60}$$

the above equation is identical to the zero-order phasor definition, except for a time shift of $T/2$. For this reason the mean value of the stored signal $\eta(t-T)$ has been expressed as its time shifted average value, note that the mean value of this stored signal can be computed because also its "future" values are available. The additive term d_η is a zero mean value signal, because it is obtained removing its DC-value to a periodic signal. Since the control input η enters the averaged system (55) after being averaged itself, any modification having zero mean value will not affect the behavior of the averaged system dynamics. Hence the final implementation of control input together with (59) is

$$\eta(t) = -TK_P\dot{\tilde{z}}_a - \epsilon TK_I\tilde{z}_a + \eta_a(t-T/2) \tag{61}$$

this controller will not introduce undesired oscillation because it depends solely on averaged signals, whose simplified dynamics (55) cannot give oscillations.

4.2 Power tracking controller

The voltage controller output reported in (61) can be replaced into the filter error power dynamics in (42), recalling also equation (54), it turns out

$$\dot{\tilde{x}} = M(R,L)\tilde{x} - \frac{1}{L}\tilde{u} + d(t) + f(\epsilon, \tilde{z}_a, \tilde{\theta}, \dot{\tilde{z}}_a, \dot{\tilde{\theta}}) \tag{62}$$

where

$$d(t) = d_0 + M(R,L)x^* - \dot{x}^* + M(R,L)\varphi_0 \tag{63}$$

is a T-periodic term composed by the sum of a constant term and sinusoids having known frequency, while

$$\begin{aligned} f(\tilde{z}_a, \tilde{\theta}, \dot{\tilde{z}}_a, \dot{\tilde{\theta}}, \epsilon) &= TK_p\ddot{\tilde{z}}_a + \epsilon K_I\dot{\tilde{z}}_a + K_p\dot{\tilde{z}}_a(t-T/2) - \dot{\tilde{\theta}}(t-T/2) \\ &+ M(R,L)[-TK_p\dot{\tilde{z}}_a - \epsilon K_I\tilde{z}_a - K_p\tilde{z}_a(t-T/2) + \tilde{\theta}(t-T/2)]. \end{aligned} \tag{64}$$

The problem of forcing $\tilde{x}$ in (62) clearly requires the ability of the control law to compensate for the signal $d(t)$, perfect tracking cannot be achieved by a feedforward action since SAF parameters and $d(t)$ are not fully known. To comply with uncertainties and provide robustness we propose an internal model-based controller. Each component of the vector

$d(t)$ can be seen as the output of the following linear system

$$\begin{aligned} \dot{w}_i(t) &= \Omega w_i(t), \;\; w_i \in \mathbb{R}^{2N+1} \\ d_{im}(t) &= \Gamma_i w_i(t), \;\; i = d, q \end{aligned} \tag{65}$$

where $\Gamma_i \in \mathbb{R}^{(1\times 2N+1)}$ are suitably defined vectors and matrix $\Omega \in \mathbb{R}^{(2N+1)\times(2N+1)}$ is defined as $\Omega = blkdiag(\Omega_j)$ with $\Omega_0 = 0$ and

$$\Omega_j = \begin{bmatrix} 0 & j\omega_m \\ -j\omega_m & 0 \end{bmatrix}, \;\; j = 1, \ldots, N \tag{66}$$

with the pairs (Γ_i,Ω) observable. Defining $\Phi = blkdiag(\Omega, \Omega)$ and $\Gamma = blkdiag(\Gamma_d, \Gamma_q)$, the following internal model-based controller can be designed

$$\begin{aligned} \dot{\xi} &= \Phi\xi + Q\tilde{x} \\ \bar{u} &= \Gamma\xi + K\tilde{x} \end{aligned} \tag{67}$$

where matrices Q and K need to be properly assigned. Once chosen $\bar{u}$ as in (67) and defined the internal model error variables as $\tilde{\xi} = \xi - Lw$, where $w := [w_d^T, w_q^T]^T$, the power subsystem closed-loop error dynamics can be rewritten as

$$\begin{aligned} \dot{\tilde{x}} &= (M(R,L) - \frac{1}{L}K)\tilde{x} - \frac{1}{L}\Gamma\tilde{\xi} + f(\tilde{z}_a, \tilde{\theta}, \dot{\tilde{z}}_a, \dot{\tilde{\theta}}, \epsilon) \\ \dot{\tilde{\xi}} &= \Phi\tilde{\xi} + Q\tilde{x}. \end{aligned} \tag{68}$$

According to the general two time-scale averaging theory, the power tracking problem can be studied focusing on the *boundary layer system*, obtained by putting $\epsilon = 0$ into the overall error dynamics, hence by (47), (54) and $\dot{\tilde{z}}_a = 0, \dot{\tilde{\theta}} = 0$, thus system (68) becomes

$$\begin{aligned} \dot{\tilde{x}} &= (M(R,L) - \frac{1}{L}K)\tilde{x} - \frac{1}{L}\Gamma\tilde{\xi} + f(\tilde{z}_a, \tilde{\theta}, 0, 0, 0) \\ \dot{\tilde{\xi}} &= \Phi\tilde{\xi} + Q\tilde{x}. \end{aligned} \tag{69}$$

Now matrices K, Q need to be selected such that asymptotic stability is provided for the boundary layer system. Define two arbitrary Hurwitz matrices F_d, $F_q \in \mathbb{R}(2N+1) \times (2N+1)$, and two arbitrary vectors G_d, G_q such that the pairs (F_d, G_d), (F_q, G_q) are controllable, taking the controller matrices as

$$K = k\begin{bmatrix} k_d & 0 \\ 0 & k_q \end{bmatrix}, \; Q = \begin{bmatrix} E_d^{-1} & 0 \\ 0 & E_q^{-1} \end{bmatrix} \begin{bmatrix} G_d & 0 \\ 0 & G_q \end{bmatrix} K \tag{70}$$

with k_d, k_q two arbitrary positive scalars, k a positive design parameter, and E_d, E_q defined as non-singular solutions of the following Sylvester equations:

$$\begin{aligned} F_d E_d - E_d \Omega_d &= -G_d \Gamma_d \\ F_q E_q - E_q \Omega_q &= -G_q \Gamma_q \end{aligned} \tag{71}$$

asymptotic stability of the boundary layer system can be stated. In order to prove this claim let us define the vector

$$R_{\xi} = \begin{bmatrix} -\frac{R}{\Gamma_{d1}} & 0_{2N} & -\frac{\omega_m L}{\Gamma_{q1}} & 0_{2N} \end{bmatrix}^T \tag{72}$$

where Γ_{d1}, Γ_{q1} denote the first element of vectors Γ_d, Γ_q respectively and 0_{2N} is a zero raw vector having dimension $2N$. Consider now the change of variables

$$\tilde{\chi} = E\tilde{\xi} - ER_{\xi}(\tilde{\theta}(t - T/2) - K_p\tilde{z}_a(t - T/2)) + LG\tilde{x} \tag{73}$$

where $E = blkdiag(E_d, E_q)$, $G = blkdiag(G_d, G_q)$, in this coordinates system (69) results

$$\begin{aligned} \dot{\tilde{x}} &= (M(R,L) - \frac{1}{L}K + \Gamma L^{-1}G)\tilde{x} - \frac{1}{L}\Gamma E^{-1}\tilde{\chi} \\ \dot{\tilde{\chi}} &= F\tilde{\chi} - L(FG - GM(R,L))\tilde{x} \end{aligned} \tag{74}$$

where $F = blkdiag(F_d, F_q)$. Using standard linear system tools it can be verified that a value $\bar{k}$ exists, such that $\forall\ k \geq \bar{k}$ the state matrix of the system in the new coordinates is Hurwitz, hence asymptotic stability of the boundary layer system can be stated.

4.3 Overall system stability

Asymptotic stability has been stated for the boundary layer system and a linearized version of the averaged reduced voltage dynamics. Exploiting the main results of the two time-scale averaged systems theory, it can be proved that the two separately designed controllers are able to provide practical stability for the complete system (42), i.e it is possible to claim that the set

$$\{(\tilde{x}, \tilde{\xi}) : \tilde{x} = 0,\ \tilde{\xi} = 0\} \times \mathcal{A}_z,\ \ with\ \ \mathcal{A}_z = \{(\tilde{z}, \tilde{\theta}) : |\tilde{z}| \leq l^*, \tilde{\theta} = 0\}$$

is *practically stable* (Khalil, 1996) for the closed-loop trajectories of the complete error system. More precisely we can define the positive values ϵ^*, $\bar{k}$, l_s^*, such that for all positive $l_s \leq l_s^*$, $k \geq \bar{k}$, $\epsilon \leq \epsilon^*$, the trajectories of the overall closed loop system with initial condition $(\tilde{x}(0), \tilde{\xi}(0))$ belonging to an arbitrary compact set, and $(\tilde{z}(0), \tilde{\theta}(0))$, such that $dist((\tilde{z}(0), \tilde{\theta}(0)), \mathcal{A}_z) \leq l_s$ (*dist* denotes the distance of the initial state vector from the set $\mathcal{A}_z$), are bounded. Moreover there exist positive M, λ, and a class $\mathcal{KL}$ function (Khalil, 1996) β such that

$$\begin{aligned} |\tilde{x}(t)| &\leq Me^{-\lambda t}|\tilde{x}(0)| + \nu \\ dist((\tilde{z}, \tilde{\theta}), \mathcal{A}_z) &\leq \beta(dist((\tilde{z}(0), \tilde{\theta}(0)), \mathcal{A}_z), \epsilon t) + \nu \end{aligned} \tag{75}$$

for all $\nu > 0$. Proof of this result is omitted owing to space limitation, it relies upon the results for two-time scale averaged systems given in (Teel et al., 2003) (see in particular Theorem 1). Analyzing the previous result, it can be clarified how the proposed controller satisfies the objectives in a practical way; by the second of (75) we deduce that $\tilde{\theta}$ tends arbitrary close to the power loss term φ_0, while by the first of (75), it can be seen that the power vector x is steered arbitrary close to the reference value $x^*_{\varphi_0}$. In particular the asymptotic tracking error can be arbitrary reduced by taking a smaller value for ϵ, namely by increasing the capacitor value C.

It's further to notice that the practical stability result is semi-global for what concerns the power variables, i.e the initial state $(\tilde{x}(0), \tilde{\xi}(0))$ can belong to an arbitrary compact set, while

it is only local with respect to the set $\mathcal{A}_z$ for the voltage initial condition $(\tilde{z}(0), \tilde{\theta}(0))$. However, as remarked in 2.2, this is not a constraint for $\tilde{z}(0)$, since it is always possible to switch on the control when the capacitor voltage is inside the admissible range, as regards $\tilde{\theta}$, since typical values of φ_0 are usually very small, the restriction on the initial state $\tilde{\theta}(0)$ is always in practice fulfilled taking $\tilde{\theta}(0) = 0$.
In summary, even if asymptotic stability of the complete system has not been stated, and formally the tracking error is not asymptotically null, in practice the two control objectives defined in 2.2 can be considered achieved, in fact, by properly tuning the control parameters and dimensioning the hardware components, we can ideally (assuming no cost or technology limitations) improve the filter tracking performance keeping the capacitor voltage value in a safe range.

5. Simulation results

Simulation tests have been performed in order to validate the proposed control solution. Two different scenarios have been adopted; first model (6) has been implemented in MATLAB/Simulink and a load scenario with two harmonics at $7\omega_m$ and $13\omega_m$ has been chosen. Then, in order to validate the controller performance in a situation closer to a real setup, the proposed continuous-time regulator has been discretized adopting a sampling frequency $f_s = 7KHz$, then the SAF converter components have been modeled by using Simulink/SimPowerSystems toolbox, and a suitable PWM technique with a carrier frequency equal to f_s has been implemented. Finally a three-phase diode bridge has been selected as nonlinear load scenario.
The following system parameters have been set, according to the procedure illustrated in Section 3; $C = 4400\mu F$, $L = 3.3mH$, $R = 0.12\Omega$, while the DC-link voltage limits have been set to $v_m = 700V$, $v_M = 900V$. Ideal three-phase mains voltages with amplitude $V_m = 310V$ and frequency $f_m = 50Hz$ have been modeled.
For what concern the simulations in time continuous domain, the internal-model based controller has been tuned to the load disturbances, according to the procedure described in 4.2. As regards the diode rectifier load scenario, the most relevant power disturbances, that is the 6th and the 12th load current harmonics expressed in the *synchronous* $d - q$ reference frame (corresponding respectively to the 5th and the 7th, and to the 11th and the 13th in the fixed reference frame), have been considered. Then the IMC controller has been discretized according to the procedure reported in (Ronchi et al., 2003), thus the following matrices have been selected; $\Omega = blkdiag(\Omega_0, \Omega_6, \Omega_{12})$, $\Gamma_d = \Gamma_q = (1, 1, 0, 1, 0)^T$, $K = diag(200, 200)$ and $Q = 10^3 diag(Q_d, Q_q)$, where $Q_d = Q_q = (40.6, 80.7, 7.15, 78.7, 17.6)^T$. For what concerns the voltage stabilizer described in 4.1, the following parameters have been selected $K_P = 0.3$, $K_I = 3.7$.
Consider now the performance obtained on the first simulation scenario, with ideal SAF model and the 7th, 13th disturbance harmonics; in Fig. 6 the tracking error on both real and imaginary power variables is reported, as expected, asymptotic tracking is achieved and the vector $\tilde{x}$ is steered arbitrary close to the origin. This ideal behavior is confirmed by Fig. 7, 8; the two harmonics currents are totally canceled out by the filter currents, while a small current component oscillating at the first-order harmonic frequency and aligned to the corresponding voltage, arises on the line side due to the voltage controller action. In table 2 the harmonics compensation performance are summarized.
For what concerns the voltage controller, in order to validate the stability properties, a value

Harmonic frequency (Hz)	i_{ma} (A)	i_{la} (A)	Compensation percentage
350	0.0039	10	99.96%
650	0.0038	10	99.96%

Table 2. Compensation performance for the two harmonics disturbance scenario.

quite far from the mean voltage reference value $(v_m^2 + v_M^2)/2 = 800V$ has been chosen as initial condition for the capacitor voltage. As showed in Fig. 9, even though the average value is initialized at zero and needs one period before representing the actual voltage, the controller reacts immediately, thanks to its dependence on the averaged derivative $\dot{\tilde{z}}_a$. Hence the voltage averaged error is successfully steered to zero, and the capacitor voltage is brought back to the middle of the safe interval, without exceeding the upper and lower bounds. The initial nonlinear behavior of the voltage error trajectories is originated by the neglected nonlinearities and also by the coupling term $\tilde{D}(\tilde{x})$, although it has been discarded due to two time-scale behavior hypothesis, it is excited by the internal model controller transient when harmonics compensation starts.

As regards the second simulation scenario, carried out in discrete time domain and with a more detailed filter physical model, the power tracking performance are reported in Fig. 10, 11, 12. In this case the power error variables $\tilde{x}_d$, $\tilde{x}_q$ are higher with respect to the previous situation, due to the fact that the AC/DC rectifier high order harmonics are not compensated by the internal model, furthermore the discretization effects have to be taken into account. However the load currents harmonics for which the controller has been tuned are strongly reduced at the line side, as the currents magnitude spectrum reported in Fig. 12 shows. Analyzing the currents waveform in the time domain (Fig. 11), it can be verified that the mains currents are almost sinusoidal and perfectly aligned with the corresponding phase voltages, hence also the load imaginary power is almost totally compensated. The ripple introduced by the pulse with modulation can be noted on the filter current, it affects also the mains currents, however thanks to a correct inductance sizing, the high frequency distortion is properly bounded. Quantitative performance of the power-tracking controller obtained with this scenario are summarized in Tab. 3.

The current component corresponding to the line frequency oscillation is slightly larger at the line side than at the load side, due to the additional active power drained to compensate for the filter losses.

As regards the averaging voltage controller, a discrete time version has been implemented, while the same initial conditions of the first scenario have been reproduced. In Fig. 13 the squared voltage error, its averaged value and the actual capacitor voltage are reported, also in this case the objective relative to the voltage dynamics behavior is accomplished, similar considerations to those made for the previous scenario can be made.

Harmonic frequency (Hz)	i_{ma}(A)	i_{la}(A)	Compensation percentage
250	0.03	3.88	99.2%
350	0.04	1.91	97.9%
550	0.03	1.57	98.1%
650	0.02	1.08	98.1%

Table 3. Compensation performance for the diode bridge load scenario.

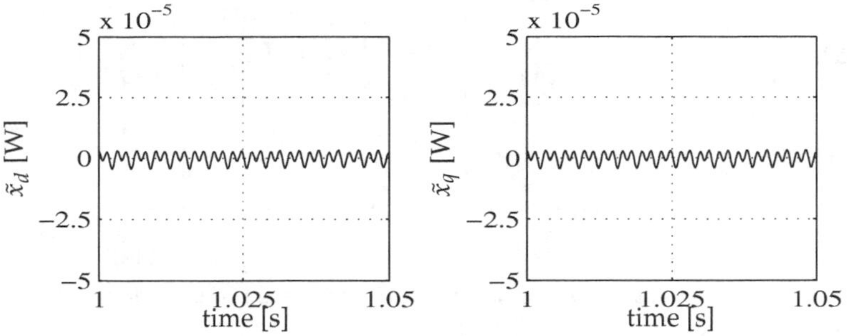

(a) Real power component tracking error.

(b) Virtual power component tracking error.

Fig. 6. Error variables $\tilde{x}_d$, $\tilde{x}_q$: two harmonics load scenario.

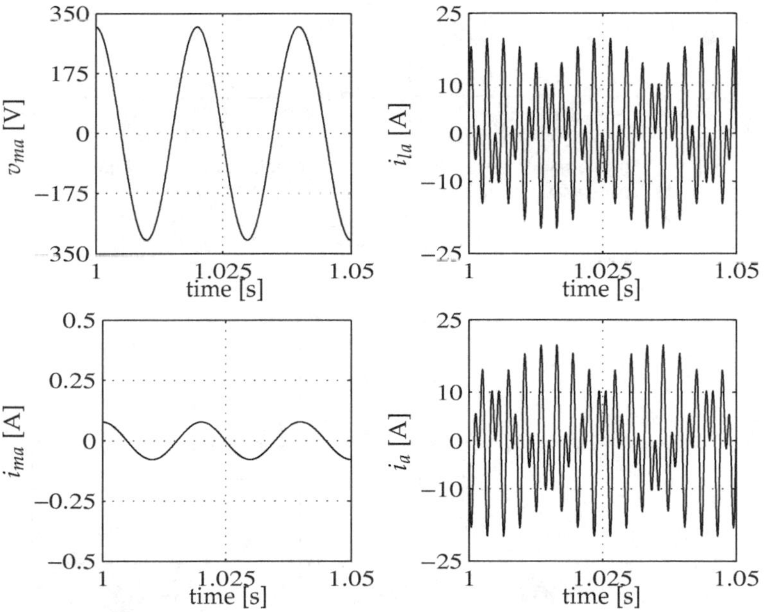

Fig. 7. Current and line voltage waveforms on phase a: two harmonics load scenario.

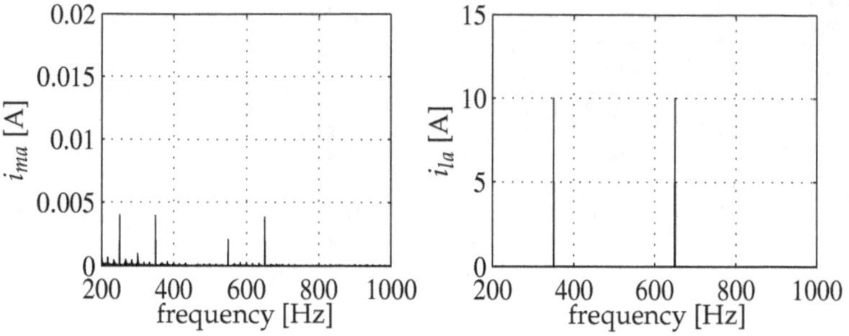

(a) Main current magnitude spectrum. (b) Load current magnitude spectrum.

Fig. 8. FFT of the a-phase main current and of the corresponding load current: two harmonics load scenario.

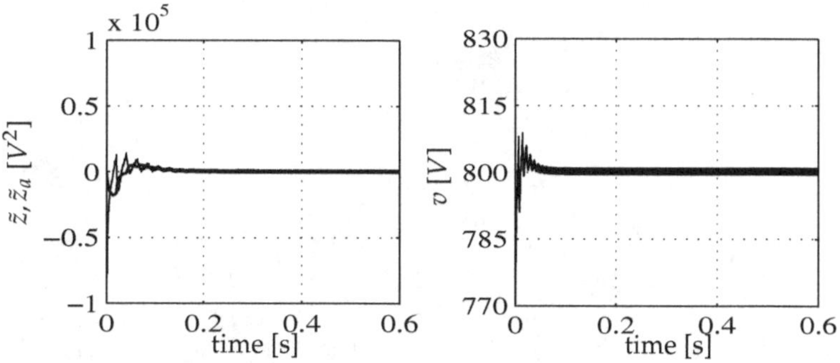

(a) Square capacitor voltage error and computed average value (bold). (b) Actual capacitor voltage value.

Fig. 9. Voltage controller performance: two harmonics load scenario.

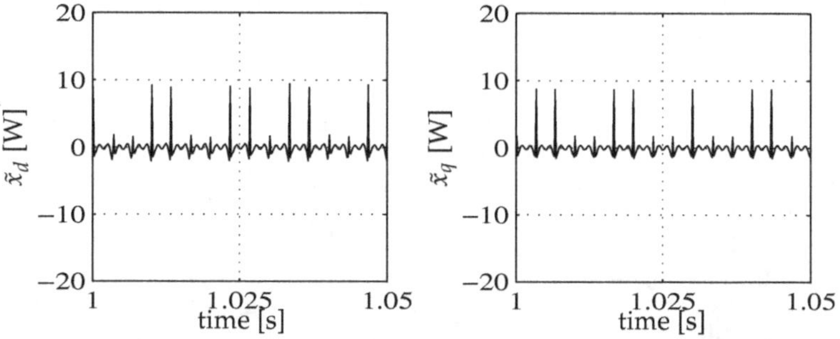

(a) Real power component tracking error. (b) Virtual power component tracking error.

Fig. 10. Error variables $\tilde{x}_d$, $\tilde{x}_q$: diode bridge load scenario.

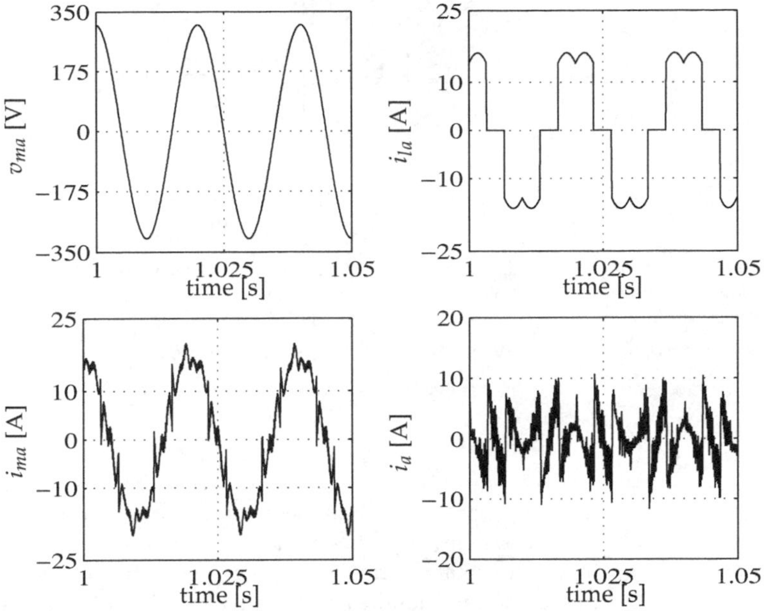

Fig. 11. Current and line voltage waveforms on phase *a*: diode bridge load scenario.

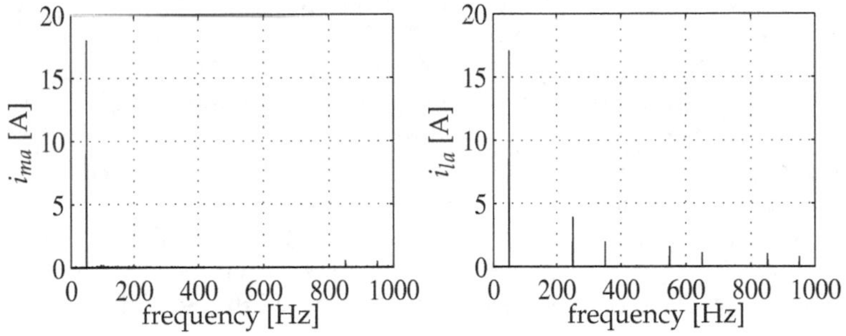

(a) Main current magnitude spectrum. (b) Load current magnitude spectrum.

Fig. 12. FFT of the a-phase main current and of the corresponding load current: diode bridge load scenario.

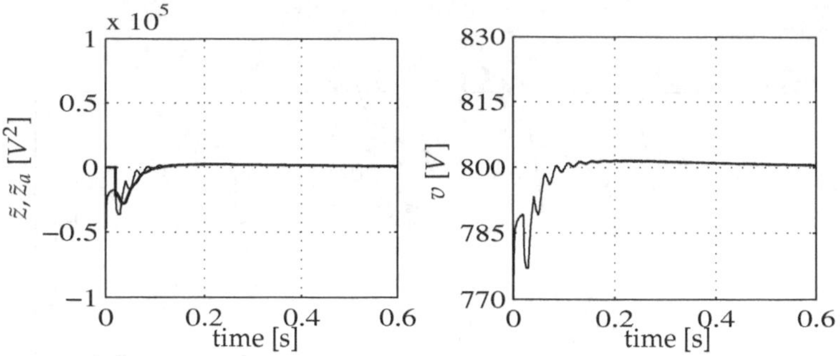

(a) Square capacitor voltage error and computed average value (bold).

(b) Actual capacitor voltage value.

Fig. 13. Voltage controller performance: diode bridge load scenario.

6. Conclusions

In this chapter a nonlinear robust control solution for a shunt active filter has been proposed, the focus has been firstly put on the hardware components design issue, providing a suitable algorithm, based on the structural system properties, which gives guarantees on the feasibility of the control problem and allows to obtain a crucial time-scale separation between the power and voltage dynamics. Then exploiting nonlinear systems analysis well established tools, such as averaging and singular perturbation theory, an averaging capacitor voltage controller and a power tracking controller based on the internal model principle, have been presented. The former exploits the insight that, regulating the averaged voltage value, makes it possible to ignore the necessary oscillations for a proper filter operation, and improves the voltage dynamics behavior. The second is chosen in order to ensure asymptotic tracking of undesired load current components, providing also robustness with respect to disturbances and model uncertainties.

Saturation issues have not been explicitly addressed in this work, owing to space limitation, however it is of utmost importance to deal with these phenomena for an actual industrial implementation with stability and performance guarantees. Some solutions, for the SAF specific case, have been proposed (see Cavini et al. (2004), Cavini et al. (2004)), however this is still an open research topic. Future effort will thus be devoted to improve the filter performance under control input saturation, analyzing the problem in the context of modern anti-windup approaches, hence providing a rigorous characterization of the system under saturation constraints. Moreover discretization issues relative to the nonlinear controller here discussed will be further analyzed, in order to improve the discrete-time controller performance with respect to that obtained applying standard discretization techniques.

7. References

Akagi, H., Kanagawa, Y. & Nabae, A. (1984). "Instantaneous reactive power compensator comprising switching devices without energy storage components", *IEEE Transactions on Industry Application*,20, 1984.

Akagi, H. (1996). "New trends in active filters for power conditioning",*IEEE Transactions on Industrial Applications*,vol. 32, pp. 1312-1332, 1996.

Bhattacharya, S., Veltman, A., Divan, D. M. & Lorentz, R. D. (1995). "Flux based active filter controller, *IEEE-IAS Annual Meeting*, pp. 2483-2491, Orlando, Florida, USA, 1995.

Cavini, A., Rossi, C., & Tilli, A. (2004). "Digital implementation of decoupled nonlinear control strategies for shunt active filters", *IEEE International Conference on Industrial Technology*, pp. 364-369, Hammamet, Tunisia, 2004.

Cavini, A., Rossi, C. & Tilli, A. (2004). "Shunt Active Filters controller with new saturation strategy", *Annual Conference of the IEEE Industrial Electronics Society*, pp. 546-551, Busan, Korea, 2004.

Chandra, A., Singh, B. & Al.Haddad, K. (2000). "An improved control algorithm of shunt active filter for voltage regulation, harmonic elimination, power-factor correction, and balancing of nonlinear loads", *IEEE Transactions on Power Electronics*,vol. 15, pp 495-507, 2000.

Gyugy, L. & Strycula, E. (1976). "Active ac power filters",*IEEE-IAS Annual Meeting*, pp. 529-535, Cincinnati, Ohio, USA, 1976.

Hanschke, J., Marconi, L. & Tilli, A. (2006). "Averaging control of the DC-link voltage in shunt active filters", *IEEE Conference on Decision and Control*, pp 6211-6216, San Diego, CA, USA, 2006.

Jeong,S. G. & Woo, M. H (1997). "Dsp-based active power filter with predictive current control", *IEEE Transactions on Industrial Electronics*,vol. 44, pp 329-336, 1997.

Kazmierkowski, M. & Malesani, L.(1998). "Current control techniques for three-phase voltage-source pwm converters: a survey", *IEEE Transactions on Industrial Electronics*,vol. 45, pp 691-703, 1998.

Khalil, H. (1996). *Nonlinear Systems*, McMillan, 2nd Edition, New York (USA), 1996.

Krause, P., Wasynczuk, O. & Sudhoff, S.D. (1995). *Analysis of Electric Machinery*, IEEE Press, Piscataway, NY (USA), 1995.

Marconi, L., Ronchi, F. & Tilli, A. (2004). "Robust control of shunt active filter based on the internal model principle", *American Control Conference*,vol. 5, pp. 3943-3948, Denver, Colorado, USA, 2003.

Marconi, L., Ronchi, F. & Tilli, A. (2004). "Robust perfect compensation of load harmonics in shunt active filters", *IEEE Conference on Decision and Control*, pp. 2978-2983, Paradise Island, Bahamas, 2004.

Marconi, L., Ronchi, F. & Tilli, A. (2007). "Robust nonlinear control of shunt active filters for harmonic current compensation", *Automatica 2007*, vol. 43, pp. 252-263, 2007.

Mohan, N., Undeland, T. M. & Robbins, W. P. (1989). *Power Electronics.Converters, applications and design*, Wiley, 2nd Edition, New York, NY (USA), 1989.

Rastogi, M., Mohan, N. & Edris, A. A. (1995). "Hybrid-active filtering of harmonic currents in power systems", *IEEE Transactions on Power Delivery*, vol. 10, pp 1994-2000, 1995.

Ronchi, F. & Tilli, A. (2002). "Design methodology for shunt active filters",*EPE-PEMC, 10th International power electronics and motion control conference*,2002.

Ronchi, F., Tilli, A. & Marconi, L. (2003). "Control of an active filter based on the internal model principle: tuning procedure and experimental results",*European control conference*, 2003.

Sanders, S, Novorolsky, M., Liu, X. & Verghese, G. (1991). "Generalized averaging method for power conversion circuits", *IEEE Transactions on Power Electronics*, vol. 6, no.2, pp 251-259, 1991.

Singh, B. & Al-Haddad, K. (1999). "A review of active filters for power quality improvement" *IEEE Trans. Ind. Electron.*, vol. 46, pp. 960-971, 1999.

Teel, A. R., Moreau, L. & Nesic, D. (2003). "A unified framework for input-to-state stability in systems with two time scales", *IEEE Transactions on Automatic Control*, vol. 48, pp. 1526ï£¡1544, 2003.

Tilli, A., Ronchi, F. & Tonielli, A. (2002). "Shunt active filters: selective compensation of current harmonics via state observer", *IEEE-IECON, 28th Annual Conference of the Industrial Electronics Society*, vol. 2, pp. 874-879, 2002.

Valderrama, G., Mattavelli, P. & Stankovic, A. (2001). "Reactive power and unbalance compensation using STATCOM with dissipativity-based control", *IEEE Transactions on Control Systems Technology*, vol.9, no.5, pp. 718-727, 2001.

Van Harmelen, G. L. & Enslin, J. H. R. (1993). "Real-time dynamic control of dynamic power filters in supplies with high contamination", *IEEE Transactions on Power Electronics*, vol. 8, pp. 301-308, 1993.

19

Passivity Based Control for Permanent-Magnet Synchronous Motors

Achour Abdelyazid
*Department of Electrical Engineering,
A. Mira University, Bejaia,
Algeria*

1. Introduction

The Passivity based control (PBC) is a well established technique which has proved very powerful to design robust control for physical system, especially electrical machinery. The PBC have clear physical interpretation in terms of interconnection system with its environment, and are robust overlooked non dissipative effects modelled. These features are extremely valuable in practical implementations of controllers. In this chapter, we show how the PBC can be used to control the speed of permanents magnets synchronous motor (PMSM). In first part, we consider the Euler-Lagrange model in the $\alpha\beta$-referential to design the Passivity Based Voltage Controller. The dq-model of the PMSM is considered to design the Passivity Based current Controller in the second part.

The idea of Passivity Based Control (PBC) design is to reshape the natural energy of the system and inject the required damping in such a way that the control objective is achieved. Expected advantages of this approach are the enhanced robustness properties, which stem from the fact that conciliation of system nonlinearities is avoided.

The technique has its roots in classical mechanics (Arnold, 1989) and was introduced in the control theory in the seminal paper (Takegaki & Arimoto, 1981). This method has been instrumented as the solution of several robot manipulator (Ailon & Ortega, 1993; Ortega & Spong; Takegaki & Arimoto, 1981) induction motor (Gökder & Simaan, 1997; Kim et al., 1997; Ortega et al., 1996, 1997; Ortega & Loria), and power electronics (Sira-Ramirez et al., 1995), which were intractable with other stabilization techniques.

PBC was also combined with other techniques (Achour & Mendil, 2007; Ortega & García-Canseco 2004a, 2004b; Qiu & Zhao, 2006; Petrović et al., 2001; Travieso-Torres et al., 2006, 2008). The design of two single-input single-output controllers for induction motors based on adaptive passivity is presented in (Travieso-Torres et al., 2008). Given their nature, the two controllers work together with field orientation block. In ((Travieso-Torres et al., 2006), a cascade passivity-based control scheme for speed tracking purposes is proposed. The scheme is valid for a certain class of nonlinear system even with unstable zero dynamic, and it is also useful for regulation and stabilization purposes. A methodology based on energy shaping and passivation principles has been applied to a PMSM in (Petrović et al., 2001). The interconnection and damping structures of the system were assigned using the Port-Controlled Hamiltonian (PCH) structure. The resulting scheme consists of a steady state feedback to which a nonlinear observer is added to estimate the unknown load torque. The authors in (Qiu & Zhao, 2006) developed a PMSM speed control law based on PCH that achieves stabilization via system passivity. In particular, the PCH interconnection and damping matrices were shaped so that the physical (Hamiltonian) system structure is preserved at the closed-loop level. The difference between the physical energy of the system and the energy supplied by the controller forms the closed-loop energy function. A review of the fundamental theory of the Interconnection and Damping Assignment Passivity Based Control technique (IDA-PBC) can be found in (Ortega & García-Canseco 2004a, 2004b). In the concerned papers it was showed the role played by the three matrices (i.e. interconnection, damping, Kernel of system input) of the PCH model in the IDA-PBC design.

The permanent-magnet synchronous motor (PMSM) has numerous advantages over other machines that are conventionally used for ac servo drives. It has a higher torque to inertia ratio and power density when compared to the Induction Motion or the wound-rotor Synchronous Motor, which makes it preferable for certain high-performance applications like robotics and aerospace actuators. However, it presents a difficult control problem. This is due to the following reasons: first, the dynamical model of PMSM is nonlinear. Second, the motor parameters (e.g., stator resistance) can vary considerably from the nominal values. Also, the state variable (velocity and current) measurements are often contaminated with a considerable amount of noise. Generally, velocity and current sensors are omitted due to the considerable saving in cost, and volume.

In Section 2, we propose a design strategy that utilizes the passivity concept in order to develop a combined controller-observer system for Permanent-Magnet Synchronous Motors (PMSM) speed control using only rotor position measurement and voltages applied to the stator windings. To this end, first a desired energy function for the closed loop system is introduced, and then a combined controller-observer system is constructed such that the closed loop system matches this energy function. A damping term is included to ensure asymptotic stability of the closed loop system. The interesting feature of this approach is the fact that it establishes a duality concept between the controller and observer design strategy. Such a duality feature is unique for nonlinear systems. Simulation tests on the combined controller-observer design are provided to show the feasibility and the performances of this method.

The work of Section 3 is related with previous work concerning the voltage control of PMSM (Achour & Mendil, 2007). The PBC has been combined with a variable structure compensator (VSC) in order to deal with important parameter uncertainties plant, without raising the damping values of the controller. The dynamics of the PMSM were represented as feedback interconnection of a passive electrical and mechanical subsystem. The PBC is applied only to the electrical subsystem while the mechanical subsystem has been treated as a passive perturbation. A new passivity based current controller (PBCC) designed using the dq-model of PMSM is proposed in this Section 3.

2. Passivity based controller-observer design for permanent magnet synchronous motors

In this part, we develop a control algorithm based on the passivity concept that forces the PMSM to track desired velocity and torque vectors without the need for velocity and stator current measurements, but using only rotor position and stator voltage measurements.

The passivity-based controller design proceeds as follows. First, we carry out a decomposition of the system dynamics as a feedback interconnection of passive subsystems,

where the outputs of the forward subsystem are the regulated outputs. Second, we design an inner feedback loop that, via the injection of a nonlinear damping term, ensures the controlled subsystem defines a strictly passive map from control signals to regulated outputs. Third, the passivity-based technique is applied to this subsystem leaving the feedback subsystem as a "passive perturbation". This last step involves the definition of the desired closed loop energy function whose associated "target" dynamics evolves on a subspace of the state space ensuring zero error tracking.
The main contribution is in the design of an observer that utilizes the high quality position information and voltage for reconstructing the velocity and current signals. The proposed observer is inspired from the passivity based controller design concept. The problem is tackled by constructing an observer that forces the estimated error to match a desired energy function, thereby preserving the passivity property. In addition, for asymptotic stabilization, damping has to be included in the loop. The main feature of this approach is in the fact that it establishes a concept duality between the controller and observer design strategy. Using passivity concept solves stability of the combined controller-observer design. We will introduce a desired energy function that consists of two parts, one for the closed loop controller dynamic and the other for the closed loop observer dynamic.
The organization of this Section is as follows: In Subsection. 1.2 we present the two phases αβ model of PMSM described by Euler-Lagrange (EL) equations, and his properties. The design procedure and the stability problem of the combined controller-observer are given in Subsection. 1.3. Simulation results are presented in Subsection. 1.4. Finally, concluding remarks are given in Subsection. 1.5.

2.1 Permanent-magnet synchronous motor model

2.1.1 Model

The PMSM uses surface mounted rare earth magnets. We consider the following assumptions: -No significant saliency effects; -negligible damping effects in the rotor; -negligible saturation effects; -ideal symmetrical phases and sinusoidal distributed phase windings; -negligible capacity effects in stator windings, considering rigid shaft and not magnetic material in stator. Under the assumptions above, the standard two phases αβ model of PMSM obtained in (Ortega et al., 1997) via direct application of EL equation is given by:

$$D_e \ddot{q}_e + W_2(q_m)\dot{q}_m + R_e \dot{q}_e = U \tag{1}$$

$$D_m \ddot{q}_m + R_m \dot{q}_m = \tau(\dot{q}_e, q_m) - \tau_L \tag{2}$$

$$\tau(\dot{q}_e, q_m) = W_2^T(q_m)\dot{q}_e \tag{3}$$

where

$$D_e = diag\{L_d, L_q\}; R_e = diag\{R_a, R_a\}$$

$$W_2(q_m) = \frac{d\,\mu(q_m)}{dq_m}.$$

$\dot{q}_e = \left[\dot{q}_{e\alpha}, \dot{q}_{e\beta}\right]^T \in \Re^2$ is stator current vector; $(q_m, \dot{q}_m) \in \Re^2$ are the rotor angular position and velocity respectively; μ (q_m) is the flux linkages due to permanent magnets; L_d, L_q are the direct and quadrate stator inductance respectively; D_m is the rotor inertia; $R_m \geq 0$ is the mechanical friction; $U = \left[u_\alpha, u_\beta\right]^T$ is stator voltage vector; and τ, τ_L are the generated and load torque respectively. The subscripts $(.)_e$, $(.)_m$, $(.)^T$ denotes the electrical, mechanical and vector transposition respectively.

2.1.2 Properties

In this subsection, we present three properties of the PMSM model, which are useful for the methodology of control design.

2.1.2.1 Passivity property of permanent-magnet synchronous motor

Lemma 1

The PMSM represents a passive system, if $v = \left[U^T, -\tau_L\right]^T$ and $\dot{q} = \left[\dot{q}_e^T, \dot{q}_m\right]^T$ are considered as inputs and outputs respectively.

Proof

The total energy H of the PMSM is:

$$H(\dot{q}_e, \dot{q}_m, q_m) = \frac{1}{2}\dot{q}_e^T D_e \dot{q}_e + \mu^T(q_m)\dot{q}_e + \frac{1}{2}D_m \dot{q}_m^2 \tag{4}$$

Taking the time derivative of H along the trajectory (1)-(3), we get:

$$\dot{H}(\dot{q}_e, \dot{q}_m, q_m) = -\dot{q}^T R \dot{q} + \dot{q}^T v + \frac{d}{dt}\left(\mu^T(q_m)\dot{q}_e\right) \tag{5}$$

Integrating $\dot{H}$ from zero to $\gamma > 0$, and setting $\beta = -\left(H(0) + \left[\mu^T(q_m)\dot{q}_e\right]_0^\gamma\right)$, proves the passivity of the PMSM.

2.1.2.2 Passive Feedback Decomposition

Lemma 2

The PMSM can be represented as the negative feedback interconnection of the electrical and mechanical passive subsystems.

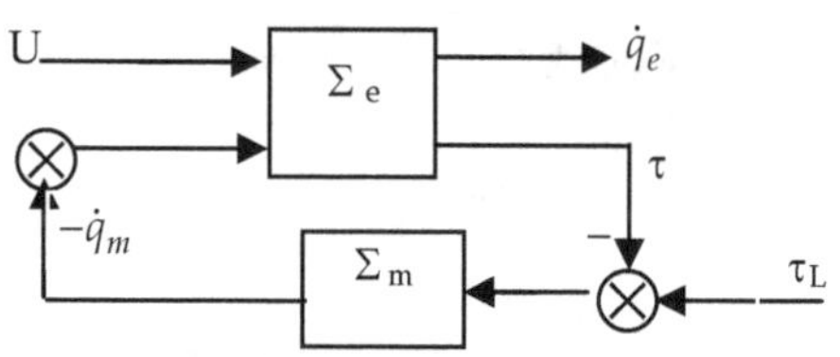

Fig. 1. Passive subsystem decomposition.

$$\Sigma_e: \quad L_{2e}^3 \rightarrow L_{2e}^3$$

$$\begin{bmatrix} U \\ -\dot{q}_m \end{bmatrix} \mapsto \begin{bmatrix} \dot{q}_e \\ \tau \end{bmatrix}$$

$$\Sigma_m : \quad L_{2e} \rightarrow \quad L_{2e}$$
$$(\tau - \tau_L) \mapsto \dot{q}_m$$

where L^3_{2e} , L_{2e} are the spaces of 3 and 1 dimension respectively of square integral, essentially bounded functions and their extensions.

Proof

Considering the total energy H_e of the electric subsystem Σ_e, that is:

$$H_e(\dot{q}_e, q_m) = \frac{1}{2}\dot{q}_e^T D_e \dot{q}_e + \mu^T (q_m)\dot{q}_e \tag{6}$$

A similar procedure used above to prove the passivity of PMSM can be used to establish the passivity of Σ_e, and for mechanical Σ_m we consider the energy function $H_m (\dot{q}_m) = \frac{1}{2} D_m \dot{q}_m^2$ to prove the passivity property.

2.1.2.3 Workless forces

In order to introduce the third property, we note that the model (1)-(3) can be written under the following compact form:

$$D \ddot{q} + W(q)\dot{q} + R\dot{q} = MU + \xi \tag{7}$$

Where, $D = diag\{D_e, D_m\}$; $R = diag\{R_e, R_m\}$

$$M = [I_2, 0_{1\times2}]^T ; \dot{q} = [\dot{q}_e^T, \dot{q}_m]^T ; \xi = [0_{2\times1}, -\tau_L]^T$$

$$W(q_m) = [W_2^T(q_m)\, \dot{q}_m \ , -\dot{q}_e^T W_2(q_m)]^T \tag{8}$$

Based on the passivity property of the PMSM and the relations (1)-(3), we deduce that the "workless forces" are given by:

$$C(q_m) = \begin{pmatrix} 0_{2\times2} & W_2(q_m) \\ -W_2^T(q_m) & 0_{1\times1} \end{pmatrix} \tag{9}$$

as C (q_m) verifies:

$$C(q_m) = -C^T(q_m) \tag{10}$$

(i.e., C (q_m) is a skew symmetric matrix.)

Remark

In the present of the saliency effects, the "workless forces" are given by:

$$C(q_m, \dot{q}) = \begin{pmatrix} C_{11} & C_{12} \\ C_{21} & C_{22} \end{pmatrix} \tag{11}$$

Where

$$C_{11} = \frac{1}{2} W_1 (q_m)\dot{q}_m$$

$$C_{12} = (\frac{1}{2} W_1\ (q_m)\dot{q}_e + W_2\ (q_m))$$

$$C_{21} = -(\frac{1}{2}\dot{q}_e^T W_1\ (q_m) + W_2^T\ (q_m))$$

$$C_{22} = 0$$

as $C\ (q_m, \dot{q})$ verifies: $\dot{D}\ (q) = C\ (q_m, \dot{q}) + C^T\ (q_m, \dot{q})$

(i.e., $(\dot{D}\ (q) - 2C\ (q_m, \dot{q}))$ is a skew symmetric matrix).

The previous identification of the workless forces permitted us to write the relation (7) under the following form:

$$D\ddot{q} + C(q_m)\dot{q} + R\dot{q} = MU + \xi \tag{12}$$

It is with noting that, these properties have been already derived for Induction machine in (Ortega et al., 1996).

2.2 Problem formulation and design procedure

2.2.1 Problem formulation

The control problem can be formulated as follows: Consider the PMSM model (1)-(3) with state vector $\dot{q} = \left[\dot{q}_e^T, q_m, \dot{q}_m\right]^T$; inputs $U \in \Re^2$; regulated outputs $(\tau, \dot{q}_m)$; measurable output q_m; immeasurable outputs $(\dot{q}_e^T, \dot{q}_m)^T$. The problem consists of constructing an observer-based controller such that for all smooth desired output function $\tau^*(t) \in L_\infty$, with known derivative $\dot{\tau}^*(t) \in L_\infty$, global torque tracking with internal stability is achieved

2.2.2 Design procedure

The steps to follow are mentioned in section 1. We consider the ideal case to simplify the procedure, where all outputs are supposed available from measurement, then we design an observer to reconstruct the states that we not available.

2.2.2.1 Passivity approach to controller design

The desired dynamics must be compatible with the bounded constraints of the PMSM. From equations (1)-(3), we deduce the following desired dynamics:

$$D_e\ddot{q}_e^* + W_2(q_m)\dot{q}_m + R_e\dot{q}_e^* = U^* \tag{13}$$

$$D_m\ddot{q}_m^* - W_2^T(q_m)\dot{q}_e^* + R_m\dot{q}_m^* = -\tau_L \tag{14}$$

Where $\dot{q}_e^*, \dot{q}_m^*$ is the desired current and desired rotor velocity respectively.

The error dynamic are described by:

$$D_e\dot{e}_e + R_e e_e = U - U^* \tag{15}$$

$$D_m\ \dot{e}_m - W_2^T(q_m)\ e_e + R_m\ e_m = 0 \tag{16}$$

Where $e_e = \dot{q}_e - \dot{q}_e^*$, $e_m = \dot{q}_m - \dot{q}_m^*$ are the current error and rotor speed error respectively.

The problem is to find a control law U, which ensures $Lim_{t\to\infty} e(t) = 0$, where $e = \left[e_e^T, e_m\right]^T$.

To this end, we shape the energy of the closed loop to match a desired energy function, as:

$$H_e^*(e_e) = \frac{1}{2} e_e^T \ D_e \ \mathrm{e_e} \tag{17}$$

Taking the time derivative of H_e^*, along the trajectory (15), we get:

$$\dot{H}_e^*(e_e) = -e_e^T \ (R_e + (\mathrm{U} - \mathrm{U}^*)) \ \mathrm{e_e} \tag{18}$$

In order to ensure the convergence of the e_e to zero, we take:

$$U = U^* \tag{19}$$

Since $R_e = R_e^T \rangle 0$, we has

$$\dot{H}_e^*(e_e) = -e_e^T \ R_e \ \mathrm{e_e} \le -\lambda_{\min}\{R_e\}\|e_e(t)\|^2 \ , \forall \ \mathrm{t} \tag{20}$$

we conclude that:

$$\|e_e(t)\| \ \le \ \mathrm{m_e} \ \|e_e(0)\| \ e^{-\rho_e \, t} \tag{21}$$

Where,

$$m_e = \sqrt{\frac{\lambda_{\max}\{D_e\}}{\lambda_{\min}\{D_e\}}} \rangle 0 \ , \ \rho_e = \frac{\lambda_{\min}\{R_e\}}{\lambda_{\max}\{D_e\}} \rangle 0 \, .$$

$\lambda_{\min}\{\cdot\}, \lambda_{\max}\{\cdot\}$ are the minimum and maximum eigenvalues respectively.

Hence the desired current $\dot{q}_e^*$ is asymptotically attainable. We have the following result:

Proposition 1

Let,

$$U = U^* - K_1 \ e_e \tag{22}$$

where $K_1 = k_e I_2$, $k_e \rangle 0$, I_2 identity matrix 2x2.

Then the convergence to the desired state trajectory is faster.

Proof

Considering the quadratic function (17), and using the same procedure, we get:

$$\|e_e(t)\| \ \le \ \mathrm{m_e} \ \|e_e(0)\| \ e^{-\rho_{e1} \, t} \tag{23}$$

Where,

$$\rho_{e1} = \frac{\lambda_{\min}\{R_e + K_1\}}{\lambda_{\max}\{D_e\}} \rangle 0 \tag{24}$$

The control law is:

$$U = D_e \ddot{q}_e^* + W_2(q_m)\dot{q}_m + R_e \dot{q}_e^* - K_1 e_e \tag{25}$$

Remarks

1. Since, we can not control the magnetic fields from the permanent magnets; it is reasonable to expect that we must eliminate the effect on electric subsystem Σ_e of the flux linkages due

to the permanent magnets. Which is seen from (25), the term from the permanent magnets must be concealed out a drawback of the scheme. However, this term is a vector in a measurable quantity (position).
2. In the closed loop system, the positive definite matrix K_1 increases the convergence of the tracking error and overcome the imprecise knowledge of system parameters, if we choose high gain k_e.

2.2.2.2 Desired current and desired torque

The PMSM operating under maximum torque if the direct current i_d in the general reference frame d-q (direct-quadrate) equals to zero.
Under the above condition, the desired current in $\alpha\beta$ reference frame is chosen as:

$$\dot{q}_e^* = \frac{2\,\tau^*}{3\,n_p \lambda_m} \begin{pmatrix} -\sin(q_m) \\ \cos(q_m) \end{pmatrix} \tag{26}$$

where $\tau^\bullet$ is the desired torque; n_p is the number of pole pairs, and λ_m is the amplitude of the flux linkage established by the permanent magnet.
The desired torque is deduced from the desired mechanical dynamic (14), we have:

$$\tau^* = D_m \ddot{q}_m^* + R_m \dot{q}_m^* + \tau_L \tag{27}$$

It has been proved in (Kim et al., 1997), that this scheme has two drawbacks, it is an open loop scheme (in the speed tracking error), and its convergence rate is limited by the mechanical constant time (D_m / R_m). In (14) $\tau^\bullet$ is defined as:

$$\tau^* = D_m \ddot{q}_m^* - z + \tau_L \tag{28}$$

$$\dot{z} = -a\,z + b\,e_m, \quad \text{and } a, b \rangle 0 . \tag{29}$$

With this choice, the convergence rate of the speed error $\omega_m - \omega_m^*$ does not depend only on the natural mechanical damping. This rate can be adjusted by means of the positives gains b and a have the same role of proportional-derivative (PD) control law.

Remark

If, v and $\dot{q}_e$ are considered as input and output, then it is easy to prove the strict passivity of the closed loop system.

$$v = D_e \ddot{q}_e^* + R_e \dot{q}_e^* \tag{30}$$

2.2.2.3 A passivity Approach to observer design

The problem is to construct an auxiliary dynamic system that asymptotically reconstructs the current and velocity signals from input-output measurements, i.e., stator voltage U and rotor position q_m, respectively. To this end we will use a passivity approach. An interesting feature of this approach is that it establishes a conceptual duality, between the strategies of PMSM controller and observer design. Such a duality feature is rather unique for nonlinear systems.
Based on the physical structure of the PMSM model (1)-(3) and the controller structure (25), we introduce the current and velocity observer systems as follows:

$$D_e\ddot{\hat{q}}_e + W_2(q_m)\dot{\hat{q}}_m + R_e\dot{\hat{q}}_e = U - L_e\dot{\tilde{q}}_e \tag{31}$$

$$D_m\ddot{\hat{q}}_m - W_2^T(q_m)\dot{\hat{q}}_e + R_m\dot{\hat{q}}_m = -\tau_L - L_v\dot{\tilde{q}}_m \tag{32}$$

where $\dot{\hat{q}} = \left[\dot{\hat{q}}_e^T, \dot{\hat{q}}_m\right]^T$ is the observer state; $\dot{\hat{q}}_e$, $\dot{\hat{q}}_m$ represents the estimated current and estimated velocity respectively; $\dot{\tilde{q}}_e = \dot{\hat{q}}_e - \dot{q}_e$, $\dot{\tilde{q}}_m = \dot{\hat{q}}_m - \dot{q}_m$ are the estimated current error and estimated velocity error; where:

$$L_e = L_e^T \rangle 0, \quad L_v \rangle 0 \tag{33}$$

The model (31), (32) can be written under the following form:

$$D\ddot{\hat{q}} + C(q_m)\dot{\hat{q}} + R\dot{\hat{q}} = MU + \xi - L\dot{\tilde{q}} \tag{34}$$

Where $\dot{\tilde{q}} = \left[\dot{\tilde{q}}_e^T, \dot{\tilde{q}}_m\right]^T$ and $L = diag\{L_e, L_v\}$

From the equation (12) and (34), we deduce the observer error dynamic:

$$D\ddot{\tilde{q}} + C(q_m)\dot{\tilde{q}} + (R+L)\dot{\tilde{q}} = 0_{3\times 1} \tag{35}$$

In order to prove the asymptotic stability of the observer estimated error; we choose the following desired energy error function:

$$H_o^*(\dot{\tilde{q}}) = \frac{1}{2}\dot{\tilde{q}}^T D\,\dot{\tilde{q}} \tag{36}$$

Taking the time derivative of H_o^*, along the trajectory (35), we get:

$$\dot{H}_o^*(\dot{\tilde{q}}) = -\dot{\tilde{q}}^T (R+L)\,\dot{\tilde{q}} \tag{37}$$

Since $L = L^T \rangle 0$, $\dot{\tilde{q}} = 0$ is asymptotically stable.

Following the same procedure used in section II.2.1, we conclude that:

$$\left\|\dot{\tilde{q}}(t)\right\| \le m_o \left\|\dot{\tilde{q}}(0)\right\| e^{-\rho_o t}, \forall\, t. \tag{38}$$

where $m_o = \sqrt{\dfrac{\lambda_{\max}\{D\}}{\lambda_{\min}\{D\}}} \rangle 0$, $\rho_o = \dfrac{\lambda_{\min}\{R+L\}}{\lambda_{\max}\{D\}} \rangle 0$

We conclude that, the observer (34) reconstructs asymptotically the current and velocity signals.

Remark

We can notice that the gain matrix L has the same effect than that of matrix K_1 in (25), i. e; L is the damping that is injected in the observer system to ensure the asymptotic stability of the observation error.

2.2.2.4 Combined Controller-Observer Design

The desired dynamics, when only rotor position is measurable are:

$$D_e\ddot{q}_e^* + W_2(q_m)\dot{\hat{q}}_m + R_e\dot{q}_e^* = U^* \tag{39}$$

$$D_m\ddot{q}_m^* - W_2^T(q_m)\dot{q}_e^* + R_m\dot{q}_m^* = -\tau_L - k_m e_m \tag{40}$$

Where, km > 0.

We have the following result: The controller law becomes:

$$U = D_e\ddot{q}_e^* + W_2(q_m)\dot{\hat{q}}_m + R_e\dot{q}_e^* - K_2 e_e \tag{41}$$

In order to establish the stability of the closed loop system with presence of the observer, we consider equation of state error (35). We get from (25), (16), (40) and (41):

$$D\dot{e} + G(q_m)e + N(q_m)\dot{\tilde{q}} = 0 \tag{42}$$

Where,

$$G(q_m) = \begin{pmatrix} (R_e + K_2) & 0_{2\times1} \\ -W_2^T(q_m) & (R_m + k_{m2}) \end{pmatrix}$$

$$N(q_m) = \begin{pmatrix} L_{e2} & -W_2(q_m) \\ 0_{1\times2} & (R_m + l_{m2}) \end{pmatrix}$$

Proposition 2

Consider the PMSM model (1)-(3) in closed loop with the observer-controller (32)-(33) and (41)-(43). Then, the closed loop system is asymptotically stable provided that:

$$\begin{aligned} k_{e2} &> \frac{1_{e2}}{4} - R_a^2 \\ k_m &> \frac{1_{v2}}{4} - R_m^2 \\ 1_{v2} &> 41_{e2} + 4R \end{aligned} \tag{43}$$

Proof

To prove the convergence of the vector error $z_o = \left[e^T, \dot{\tilde{q}}^T\right]^T$, let consider the desired energy function error as:

$$H_{co}^{cl}(e, \dot{\tilde{q}}) = \frac{1}{2}e^T D e + \frac{1}{2}\dot{\tilde{q}}^T D \dot{\tilde{q}} \tag{44}$$

The time derivative of H_{co}^{cl} along the trajectory (35), (42), gives:

$$\dot{H}_{co}^{cl} = -e^T G(q_m) e - e^T N(q_m) \dot{\tilde{q}} - \dot{\tilde{q}}^T (R+L) \dot{\tilde{q}} \tag{45}$$

Which can be written as,

$$\dot{H}_{co}^{cl} = -z_o^T Q z_o \tag{46}$$

Where,

$$Q = \begin{pmatrix} G(q_m) & \frac{1}{2}N(q_m) \\ \frac{1}{2}N^T(q_m) & (R+L) \end{pmatrix}$$

Then, if matrix Q is positive, we can conclude that the closed loop system is asymptotically stable.
Matrix Q is positive if and only if the following inequality is satisfied:

$$G\,(q_m)\,(\mathrm{R}+\mathrm{L})\text{-}\frac{1}{4}N(q_m)N^T(q_m) > 0 \tag{47}$$

which can be written after calculations;

$$G\,(q_m)\,(\mathrm{R}+\mathrm{L})\text{-}\frac{1}{4}N(q_m)N^T(q_m) = \begin{pmatrix} F_{11} & F_{12} \\ F_{21} & F_{22} \end{pmatrix}$$

Where,

$$F_{11} = (\mathrm{R_e}+K_2)(\mathrm{R_e}+L_{e2}) - \frac{1}{4}(L_{e2}L_{e2}+W_2W_2^T)\mathrm{R_e} + K_2(\mathrm{R_e}+L_{e2}) - \frac{1}{4}(L_{e2}L_{e2}+W_2W_2^T)$$

$$F_{12} = \frac{l_{v2}}{4}W_2$$

$$F_{21} = \frac{l_{v2}}{4}W_2^T - W_2^T(\mathrm{R_e}+L_{e2})$$

$$F_{22} = (\mathrm{R_m}+k_{m2})(\mathrm{R_m}+l_{v2}) - \frac{l_{v2}^2}{4}$$

for simplicity, we have chosen:

$$L_{e2} = l_{e2}\,I_2\,,\ K_2 = k_2\,I_2, \text{where } \mathrm{k}_2 > 0;\ \mathrm{l}_{e2} > 0\,.$$

We note that if conditions see that the matrix Q is positive definite if conditions (43) are satisfied.
A block diagram representing the passivity-based method is show in Fig. 2.

2.3 Simulation results

The performance of the controller-observer system was investigated by simulation. We used a PMSM model, whose parameters are given in the Appendix 1.
The filter and damping parameters taken in the simulation are; a=100; b=87.5; k_{e2}=100; l_{e2}=1000 and l_{v2}=1500. We have limited the desired stator current and chosen the initial observer conditions equal to zero.
Fig. 3 shows the time response, of the motor, where a load torque τ_L of 1.35 Nm is applied to the PMSM at the starting phase and we take a speed reference of 150 rad/s. The rotor speed converges with of setting time of 0.4s. The estimated observer current and speed errors converge to zero.
Fig. 4 illustrate the time response of the closed loop system without load torque, and speed reference of (150 rad/s if t<=0.65 and -150 rad/s if t>0.65). We can see that the rotor velocity tracks its reference, and the estimation error converges.
In Fig. 5, we show the robustness of the combined controller-observer system. We take these uncertainties in the parameters of PMSM ($3R_a$, $2R_m$, $2L_d$, $2L_q$, $1.5D_m$, $0.75\lambda_m$,). We note that, the rotor speed converges, but the setting time is increased lightly.

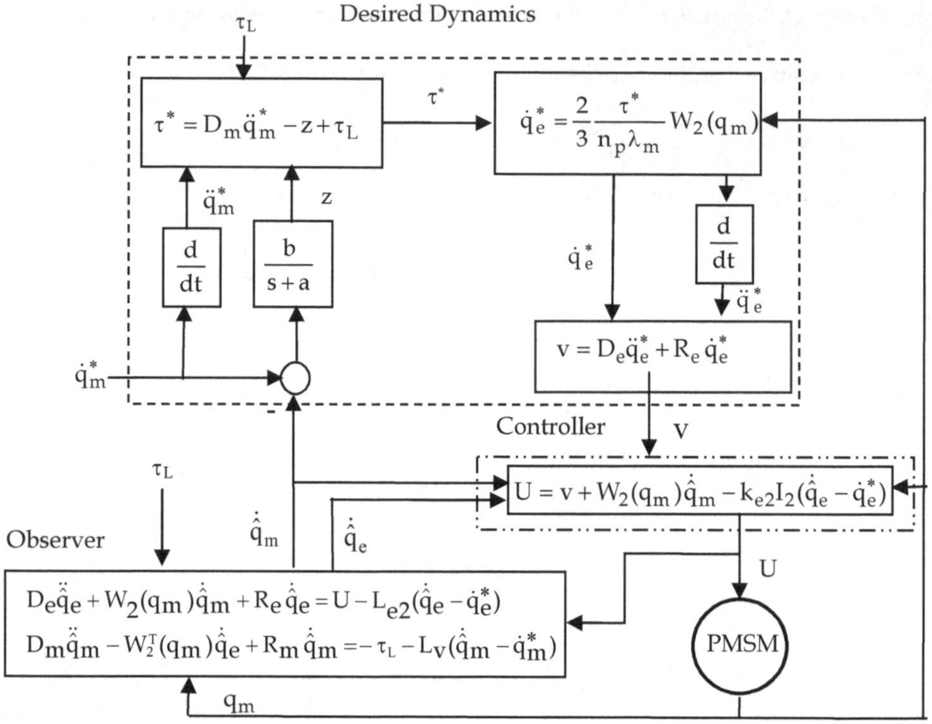

Fig. 2. Block diagrams for the passivity-based method.

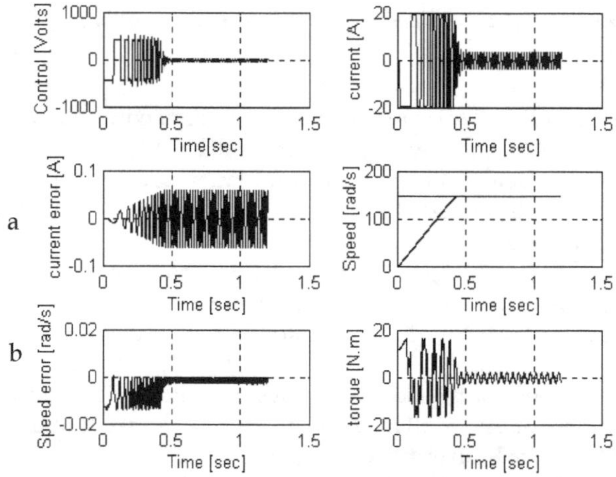

Fig. 3. Control of speed with reference 150 rd/s; a) Estimated current error; b) Estimated velocity error.

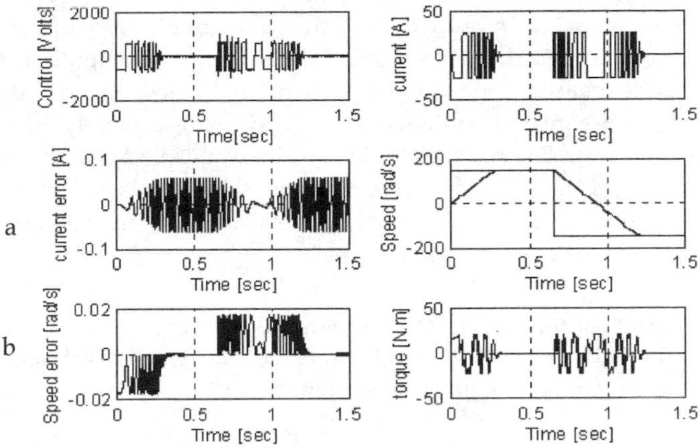

Fig. 4. Control of speed with reference (150 rd/s if t<=0.65 and -150 rd/s if t>0.65), a) Estimated current error ; b) Estimated velocity error.

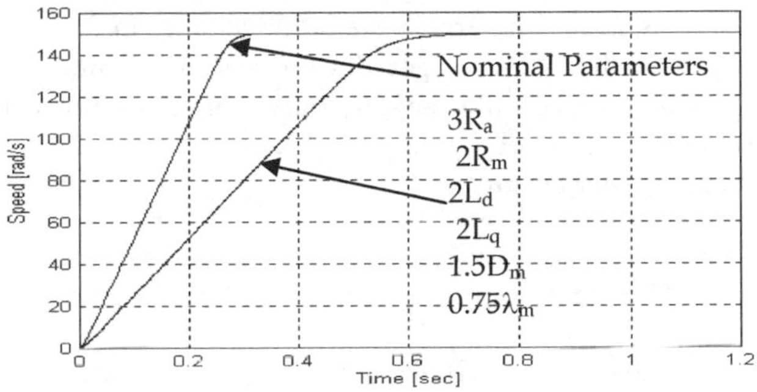

Fig. 5. Robustness test.

3. Passivity based controller design for a permanent magnet synchronous motor in dq-frame

Within this Section, a new passivity-based controller designed to force the motor to track time-varying speed and torque trajectories is presented. Its design avoids the using of the Euler-Lagrange model and destructuring since it uses a flux-based dq-modelling, independent of the rotor angular position. This dq-model is obtained through the three phase abc-model of the motor, using Park transform. The proposed control law does not compensate the model workless force terms which appear in the machine dq-model, as they have no effect on the system energy balance and they do not influence the system stability properties. Another feature is that the cancellation of the plant primary dynamics and nonlinearities is not done by exact zeroing, but by imposing a desired damped transient. The effectiveness of the proposed control is illustrated by numerical simulation results.

The Section 2 is organized as follows. The PMSM dq-model and the inner current loop design are presented at Subsection 2.2. In Subsection 3, the passivity property of the PMSM in the dq-reference frame is introduced. Subsection 2.4 deals with the computation of the current, flux and the torque references. The passivity property of the closed loop system and the resulting control structure are given in Subsections 2.5 and 2.6, respectively. Simulation results are presented in Subsection 2.7. Subsection 2.8 concludes this Section. The proof of the passivity property of the PMSM in the dq frame is given. The analysis and proof of the exponential stability of the flux tracking error is introduced. Subsections 2.5 contain the proof of the passivity property of the closed loop system.

3.1 Permanent-magnet synchronous motor model in dq frame

The PMSM uses buried rare earth magnets. Its electrical behaviour is described here by the well known dq model (Krause et al., 2002), given by Equation (48):

$$L_{dq}\dot{i}_{dq} + R_{dq}i_{dq} + n_p\omega_m \Im L_{dq}i_{dq} + n_p\omega_m \Im \psi_f = v_{dq} \tag{48}$$

In this equation the following notations have been employed:

$$L_{dq} = \begin{bmatrix} L_d & 0 \\ 0 & L_q \end{bmatrix};\ i_{dq} = \begin{bmatrix} i_d \\ i_q \end{bmatrix};\ R_{dq} = \begin{bmatrix} R_S & 0 \\ 0 & R_S \end{bmatrix};\ \psi_f = \begin{bmatrix} \phi_f \\ 0 \end{bmatrix};\ \Im = \begin{bmatrix} 0 & -1 \\ 1 & 0 \end{bmatrix};\ v_{dq} = \begin{bmatrix} v_d \\ v_q \end{bmatrix}$$

In the above-presented relations, L_d and L_q: are the stator inductances in dq frame, R_S: is the stator winding resistance, ϕ_f: is the flux linkages due to permanent magnets, n_p: is the number of pole-pairs, ω_m: is the mechanical speed, v_d and v_q: are the stator voltages in dq frame, i_d and i_q: are the stator currents in dq frame.

The mechanical equation of the PMSM is given by:

$$J\dot{\omega}_m + f_{VF}\omega_m = \tau_e - \tau_L \tag{49}$$

where J is the rotor moment of inertia, f_{VF} is the viscous friction coefficient, and τ_L is the load torque.

The electromagnetic torque τ_e can be expressed in the dq frame as follows:

$$\tau_e = \frac{3}{2}n_p\left(\left(L_d - L_q\right)i_d i_q + \phi_f i_q\right) \tag{50}$$

The rotor position θ_m is given by Equation (51):

$$\dot{\theta}_m = \omega_m \tag{51}$$

where ψ_d and ψ_q are the flux linkages in dq frame.

The interdependence between the flux linkage motor ψ_{dq} and the current vector i_{dq} can be expressed as follow (Krause et al., 2002):

$$\begin{bmatrix} \psi_d \\ \psi_q \end{bmatrix} = L_{dq}i_{dq} + \psi_f \tag{52}$$

where ψ_d and ψ_q are the flux linkages in dq frame.

Substituting i_{dq} value obtained by Relation (52) in Equations (48) and (50), yields:

$$\dot{\psi}_{dq} + n_p \omega_m \Im \psi_{dq} = v_{dq} - R_{dq} i_{dq} \tag{53}$$

$$\tau_e = -\frac{3}{2} n_p \psi_{dq} \Im i_{dq} \tag{54}$$

Current controlled dq-model of PMSM

Let us define the state model of the PMSM using the state vector $\begin{bmatrix} \psi_d & \psi_q & \omega_m & \theta_m \end{bmatrix}^T$ and Equations (49), (51), (53) and (54). The reference value of the current vector i_{dq} is denoted by:

$$i_{dq}^* = \begin{bmatrix} i_d^* \\ i_q^* \end{bmatrix}$$

The proportional-integral (PI) current loops, used to force $\begin{bmatrix} i_d & i_q \end{bmatrix}^T$ to track the reference $\begin{bmatrix} i_d^* & i_q^* \end{bmatrix}^T$, are of the form of equations below:

$$v_d = k_{dp}\left(i_d^* - i_d\right) + k_{di} \int_0^t \left(i_d^* - i_d\right) \mathrm{d}t, \quad k_{dp}, k_{di} > 0 \tag{55}$$

$$v_q = k_{qp}\left(i_q^* - i_q\right) + k_{qi} \int_0^t \left(i_q^* - i_q\right) \mathrm{d}t, \quad k_{qp}, k_{qi} > 0 \tag{56}$$

Assuming that by the proper choice of positive gains k_{dp}, k_{di}, k_{qp}, k_{qi}, these loops work satisfactory. Then, the reference vector i_{dq}^* can be considered as control input for the PMSM model. This result on the simplified dynamic dq-model of the PMSM given below:

$$\dot{\psi}_{dq} + n_p \omega_m \Im \psi_{dq} = -R_{dq} i_{dq}^* \tag{57}$$

$$J\dot{\omega}_m + f_{VF} \omega_m = \tau_e - \tau_L \tag{58}$$

$$\dot{\theta}_m = \omega_m \tag{59}$$

$$\tau_e = -\frac{3}{2} n_p \psi_{dq}^T \Im i_{dq}^* \tag{60}$$

This simplified form of the PMSM model is further used to design the control input i_{dq}^* using the passivity approach.

3.2 Passivity property of dq-model

Lemma 3

The PMSM represents a strictly passive system if the reference vector, of the stator currents, i_{dq}^* and the flux linkage vector, ψ_{dq} are considered as the input and the output vectors, respectively.

Proof

First, multiply both sides of Equation (57) by $\frac{\psi_{dq}^T}{R_s}$, yields

$$\psi_{dq}^T i_{dq}^* = -\frac{1}{2R_s}\frac{\mathrm{d}\left(\psi_{dq}^T \psi_{dq}\right)}{\mathrm{d}t} \tag{61}$$

where ψ_{dq}^T is the transposed of vector ψ_{dq}.

Note that the term $\frac{n_p \omega_m}{R_s}\psi_{dq}^T \Im \psi_{dq}$ does not appear on the right-hand side of (61), since $\psi_{dq}^T \Im \psi_{dq} = 0$ due to skew-symmetric property of the matrix $\Im$. Integrating both sides of Equation (61), yields

$$\int_0^t \left(\psi_{dq}^T i_{dq}^*\right)\mathrm{d}t = -\frac{1}{2R_s}\left(\psi_{dq}^T \psi_{dq}\right)(t) + \frac{1}{2R_s}\left(\psi_{dq}^T \psi_{dq}\right)(0) \tag{62}$$

Consider that the i_{dq}^* is the input vector and ψ_{dq} is the output vector. Then, with positive definite function

$$V_f = \frac{1}{2}\psi_{dq}^T \psi_{dq} \tag{63}$$

the energy balance Equation (62) of the PMSM becomes

$$\int_0^t \left(\psi_{dq}^T i_{dq}^*\right)\mathrm{d}t = -\frac{1}{R_s}V_f(t) + \frac{1}{R_s}V_f(0) \tag{64}$$

This means that the PMSM is a strictly passive system (Ortega et al., 1997). Thus, the term $n_p \omega_m R_{dq}^{-1} \psi_{dq}^T \Im \psi_{dq}$ has no influence on the energy balance and on the asymptotic stability of the PMSM also; it is identified as the workless forces term.

3.3 Analysis of tracking errors convergence using passivity-based method

The desired value of the flux linkage vector ψ_{dq} is:

$$\psi_{dq}^* = \begin{bmatrix} \psi_d^* \\ \psi_d^* \end{bmatrix} \tag{65}$$

and the difference between ψ_{dq} and ψ_{dq}^* representing flux tracking error, as:

$$e_f = \begin{bmatrix} e_{fd} \\ e_{fq} \end{bmatrix} = \psi_{dq} - \psi_{dq}^* \tag{66}$$

Rearranging Equation (66)

$$\psi_{dq} = e_f + \psi_{dq}^* \tag{67}$$

Substituting Equation (16) in Equation (68), yields

$$\dot{e}_f + n_p\omega_m\Im e_f = -R_{dq}i^*_{dq} - \left(\dot{\psi}^*_{dq} + n_p\omega_m\Im\psi^*_{dq}\right) \quad (68)$$

The aim is to find the control input i^*_{dq} which ensures the convergence of error vector e_f to zero. The energy function of the closed-loop system is defined as

$$V(e_f) = \frac{1}{2}e_f^T e_f \quad (69)$$

Taking the time derivative of $V\left(e_f\right)$ along the Trajectory (17), gives

$$\dot{V}\left(e_f\right) = -e_f^T\left(R_{dq}i^*_{dq} + \dot{\psi}^*_{dq}n_p\omega_m\Im\psi^*_{dq}\right) \quad (70)$$

Note that the term $n_p\omega_m e_f^T\Im e_f = 0$ due to the skew-symmetric property of the matrix $\Im$.
The convergence to zero of the error vector e_f is ensured by taking

$$i^*_{dq} = -R_{dq}^{-1}\left(\dot{\psi}^*_{dq} + n_p\omega_m\Im\psi^*_{dq}\right) + R_{dq}^{-1}K_f e_f \quad (71)$$

where $K_f = \begin{bmatrix} k_{fd} & 0 \\ 0 & k_{fq} \end{bmatrix}$ with $k_{fd} > 0$ and $k_{fq} > 0$.

The control input signal, i^*_{dq} consists of two parts: the term which encloses the reference dynamics and the damping term injected to make the closed-loop system strictly passive.
The PBCC ensures the exponential stability of the flux tracking error.

3.3.1 Proof of the exponential stability of the flux tracking error

Consider the quadratic Function (69) and its time derivative in Equation (70). Substituting i^*_{dq} of (71) in (70), yields

$$\dot{V}\left(e_f\right) = -e_f^T K_f e_f \le -\lambda_{\min}\left\{K_f\right\}\left\|e_f(t)\right\|^2, \ \forall\ t \ge 0 \quad (72)$$

where $\lambda_{\min}\left\{K_f\right\} > 0$ is the minimum eigenvalue of the matrix K_f and $\|.\|$ is the standard euclidian vector norm.
The square of the standard Euclidian norm of the vector e_f is given as:

$$\left\|e_f\right\|^2 = e_{fd}^2 + e_{fq}^2 = e_f^T e_f \quad (73)$$

Which combined with Relation (69), gives

$$V(e_f) = \frac{1}{2}e_f^T e_f \le \left\|e_f\right\|^2, \ \forall\ t \ge 0 \quad (74)$$

Multiplying both sides of (74) by $(-\lambda_{\min}\left\{K_f\right\})$, leads to

$$\left(-\lambda_{\min}\left\{K_f\right\}\right)V(e_f) \ge \left(-\lambda_{\min}\left\{K_f\right\}\right)\left\|e_f\right\|^2, \ \forall\ t \ge 0 \quad (75)$$

which combined with Relation (72), gives

$$\dot{V}\left(e_f\right) \leq -\lambda_{\min}\left\{K_f\right\} V(e_f),\ \forall\ t \geq 0 \tag{76}$$

Integrating both sides of the Inequality (76), yields

$$V(e_f) \leq V(0)e^{-\rho_f t},\ \forall\ t \geq 0 \tag{77}$$

where $\rho_f = \lambda_{\min}\left\{K_f\right\} > 0$. Considering the Relation (74) at t=0, and multiplying it by $e^{-\rho_f t}$, gives

$$V(0)e^{-\rho_f t} \leq \left\|e_f(0)\right\|^2 e^{-\rho_f t} \tag{78}$$

which combined with Relation (77), leads to the following inequality:

$$V(e_f) \leq \left\|e_f(0)\right\|^2 e^{-\rho_f t},\ \forall\ t \geq 0 \tag{79}$$

The Inequalities (74) and (79) give that:

$$\left\|e_f(t)\right\| = \left\|e_f(0)\right\| e^{-\frac{\rho_f}{2}t} \tag{80}$$

The Equation (80) shows that, the flux tracking error e_f is exponentially decreasing with a rate of convergence of $\rho_f/2$.

3.3.2 Flux reference computation

The computation of the control signal i_{dq}^* requires the desired flux vector ψ_{dq}^*. If the direct current i_d in the dq frame is maintained equal to zero, then the PMSM operates under maximum torque. Under this condition and using Equation (52), results in

$$\psi_d^* = \varphi_f \tag{81}$$

$$\psi_q^* = L_q i_q^* \tag{82}$$

The torque set-point value τ_e^* corresponding to ψ_{dq}^* is given by Equation (54). Substituting ψ_d^* from (81) and i_q^* from (82) in (54), it results that:

$$\tau_e^* = \frac{3}{2}\frac{n_p \varphi_f}{L_q}\psi_q^* \tag{83}$$

Therefore the value of the flux reference is deduced as

$$\psi_q^* = \frac{2}{3}\frac{L_q}{n_p \varphi_f}\tau_e^* \tag{84}$$

3.3.3 Torque reference and load torque computation

The desired torque τ_e^* is computed by the expressions (28)-(29).

In practical applications, the load torque is unknown, therefore it must be estimated. For that purpose, an adaptive law (Kim et al., 1997) has been used:

$$\dot{\hat{\tau}}_L = -k_L(\omega_m - \omega_m^*), \quad \mathrm{k_L} > 0 \tag{85}$$

3.4 Passivity property of the closed loop system in the general dq reference frame

Lemma 4

The closed loop system represents a strictly passive system if the desired dynamic output vector given by

$$\vartheta = -R_{dq}^{-1}\left(\dot{\psi}_{dq}^* + n_p\omega_m \Im \psi_{dq}^*\right) \tag{86}$$

and the flux linkage vector ψ_{dq} are considered as input and output, respectively.

Proof

Substituting the control input vector i_{dq}^* from (71) in Equation (57), gives

$$\dot{\psi}_{dq} + n_p\omega_m \Im \psi_{dq} = -R_{dq}\vartheta - K_f e_f \tag{87}$$

where ϑ is given by Relation (86).

Multiplying both sides of Equation (87) by $\frac{\psi_{dq}^T}{R_s}$

$$\psi_{dq}^T\vartheta = -\frac{1}{2R_s}\frac{\mathrm{d}\left(\psi_{dq}^T\psi_{dq}\right)}{\mathrm{d}t} - \psi_{dq}^T K_f e_f \tag{88}$$

The term $\frac{n_p\omega_m}{R_s}\psi_{dq}^T \Im \psi_{dq}$ disappears from (88), since $\psi_{dq}^T \Im \psi_{dq} = 0$ due to skew-

-symmetric property of the matrix $\Im$. According to Relation (80), the flux tracking error e_f is exponentially decreasing. Thus, the term $\psi_{dq}^T K_f e_f$ becomes insignificant. And Equation (88) is writes as

$$\psi_{dq}^T\vartheta = -\frac{1}{2R_s}\frac{\mathrm{d}\left(\psi_{dq}^T\psi_{dq}\right)}{\mathrm{d}t} \tag{89}$$

Integrating both sides of Equation (45), yields

$$\int_0^t \left(\psi_{dq}^T\vartheta\right)\mathrm{d}t = -\frac{1}{2R_s}\left(\psi_{dq}^T\psi_{dq}\right)(t) + \frac{1}{2R_s}\left(\psi_{dq}^T\psi_{dq}\right)(0) \tag{90}$$

Let us consider the positive definite function V_f from Relation (67). The Energy Balance (90) of the closed loop system becomes

$$\int_0^t \left(\psi_{dq}^T\vartheta\right)\mathrm{d}t = -\frac{1}{R_s}V_f(t) + \frac{1}{R_s}V_f(0) \tag{91}$$

The previous relation shows that, the closed-loop system is a strictly passive (Ortega et al., 1997). Thus, the term $\frac{n_p \omega_m}{R_s} \psi_{dq}^T \Im \psi_{dq}$ has no influence on the energy balance and the asymptotic stability of the closed-loop system; it is identified as the workless forces term.

3.5 Passivity based current controller structure for PMSM

The design procedure of the passivity-based current controller for PMSM leads to control structure described by the block diagram in Fig. 6. It consists of three main parts: the load torque estimator given by Equation (85), the desired dynamics expressed by the Relations (28)-(29), (81)-(85), and the controller given by Equations (55), (56) and (71). In this design the imposed flux vector, ψ_{dq}^*, is determined from maximum torque operation conditions allowing the computation of the desired currents i_{dq}^*. Furthermore, the load torque is estimated through speed error, and directly taken into account in the desired dynamics.
The inner loops of the PMSM control are based on well known proportional-integral controllers. Park transform is used for passing electrical variables between the three-phase and dq frame.
The actuator used in the control application is based on a PWM voltage source inverter. Voltage, currents, rotational speed and PMSM angular position are considered measurable variables.

3.6 Simulation results

The parameters of the PMSM used for testing the previously exposed control structure are given in Appendix. 2.
The plant and its corresponding control structure of Fig.6 are implemented using Matlab and Simulink software environment. It employs the PMSM model represented by the Equations (48)-(51) whose parameters are given in appendix 2. The chosen solver is based on Runge-Kutta algorithm (ODE4) and employs an integration time step of 10^{-4} s. The parameter values of the control system are determined using the procedures detailed in Subsections 2.2 and 2.4 as follows. From the imposed pole locations, the gains of the current PI controller are computed as: k_{dp}=95, k_{di}=0.85, k_{qp}=95, and k_{di}=0.8. The gains concerning the desired torque are set at a=75 and b=400 using pole placement method also. The damping parameters values have been obtained by using a trial-and-error procedure starting from guess values based on the stability Condition (71); their final values are k_{fd} = k_{fq} = 650. The gain of the load torque adaptive law is set to k_L=6, value which ensures the best asymptotic convergence of the speed error.
In all tests performed in this study, the following signals have been considered as representative for performance analysis: rotational speed (Fig. 7(a)), line current (Fig. 7(b)), electromagnetic torque (Fig. 7(c)), the stator voltages in dq frame (Fig. 7(d)), zoom of voltage at the output of the inverter (Fig. 7(e)), and zoom of line current (Fig. 7(f)). Fig. 7 shows the motor response to square speed reference signal with magnitude ±150 rad/s. This study concerns the robustness test of the designed control system to disturbances. To this end, a load torque step of τ_L=10 N·m has been applied at time 0.5 second and has been removed at time 4.5 seconds (see Fig. 7). The results of Fig. 7 show that the response of the rotor speed to the disturbance is quite and the electromagnetic torque, τ_e, have been increased to a value corresponding to the load applied. The rotational speed and line current tracks quickly the

reference, without overshoot and all other signals are well shaped. The peaks visible on the electromagnetic torque evolution are due to high gradients imposed to the rotational speed. In practice, these peaks can be easily reduced by limiting the speed reference changing rate and by limiting the imposed current i_q^* value. However, such situation has been chosen for a better presentation of the control law capabilities and performances.

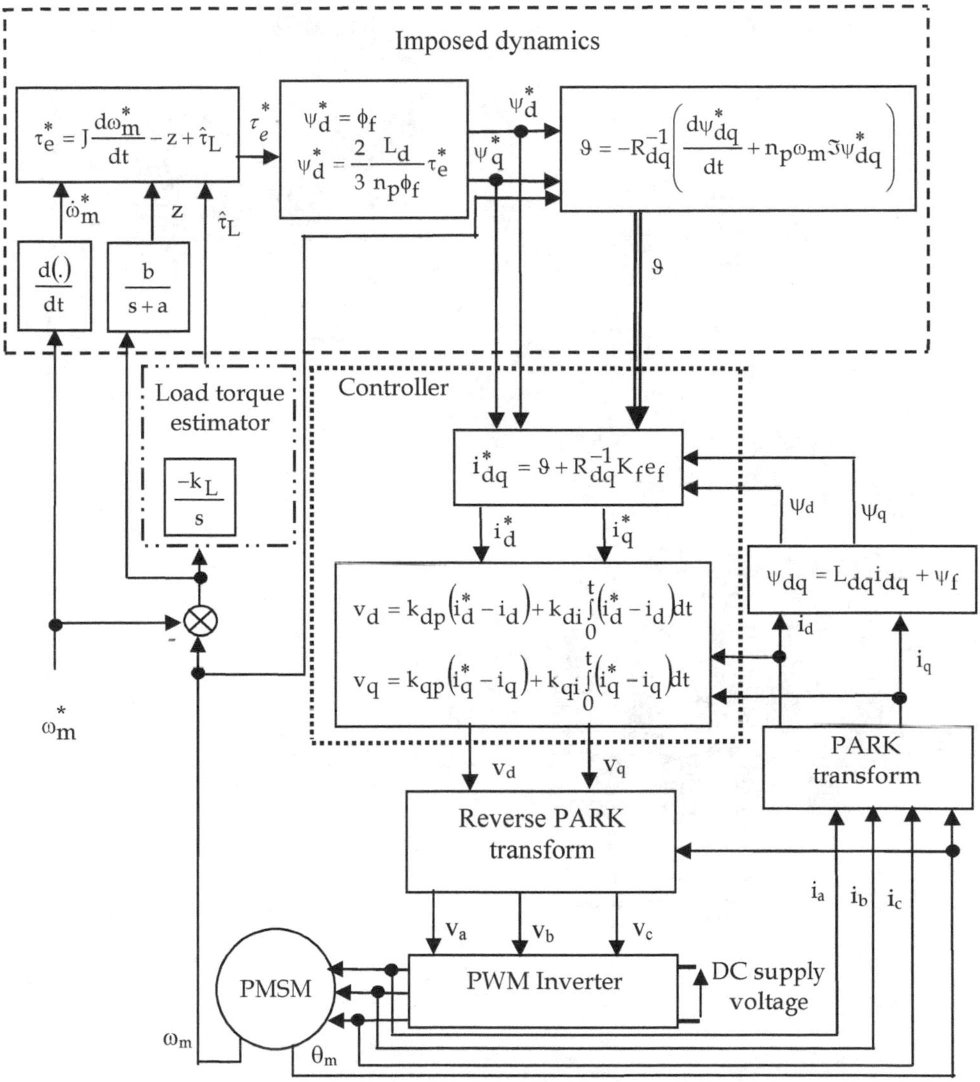

Fig. 6. The block diagram for the passivity-based current controller.

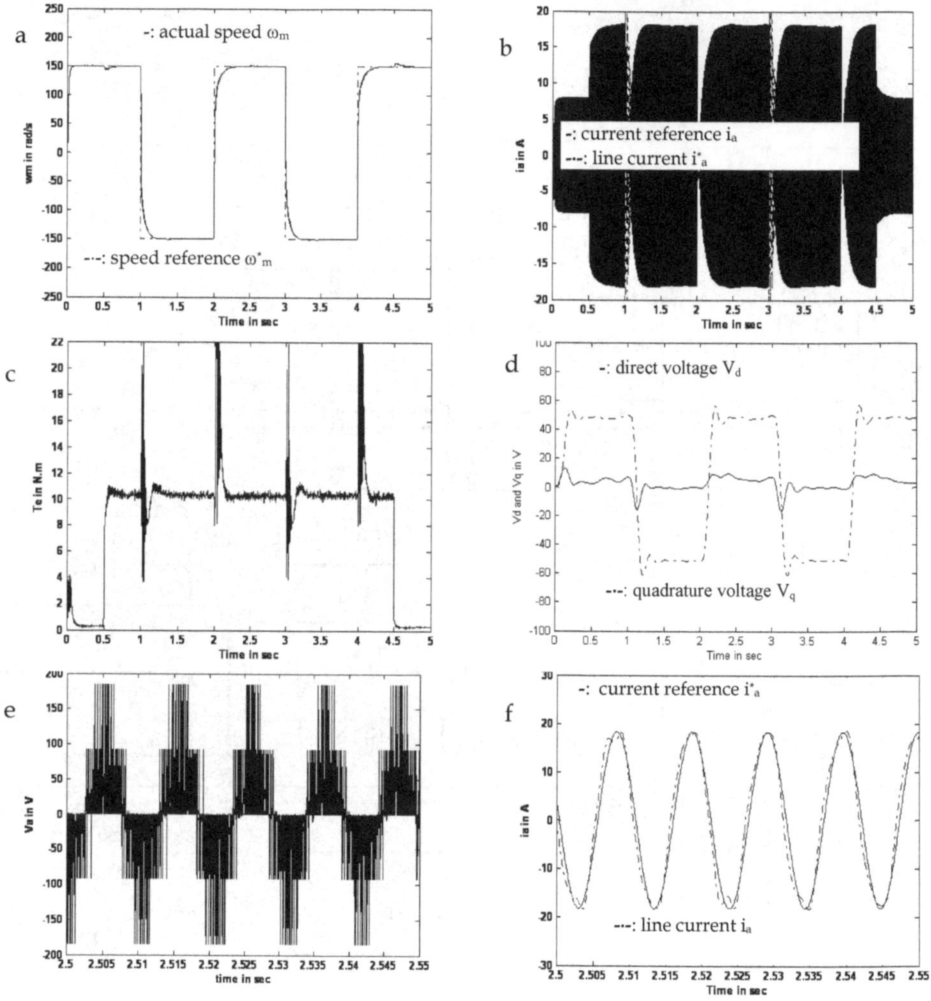

Fig. 7. Motor response to square speed reference signal with a load torque step of 10 Nm from t=0.5s to t=4.5s.

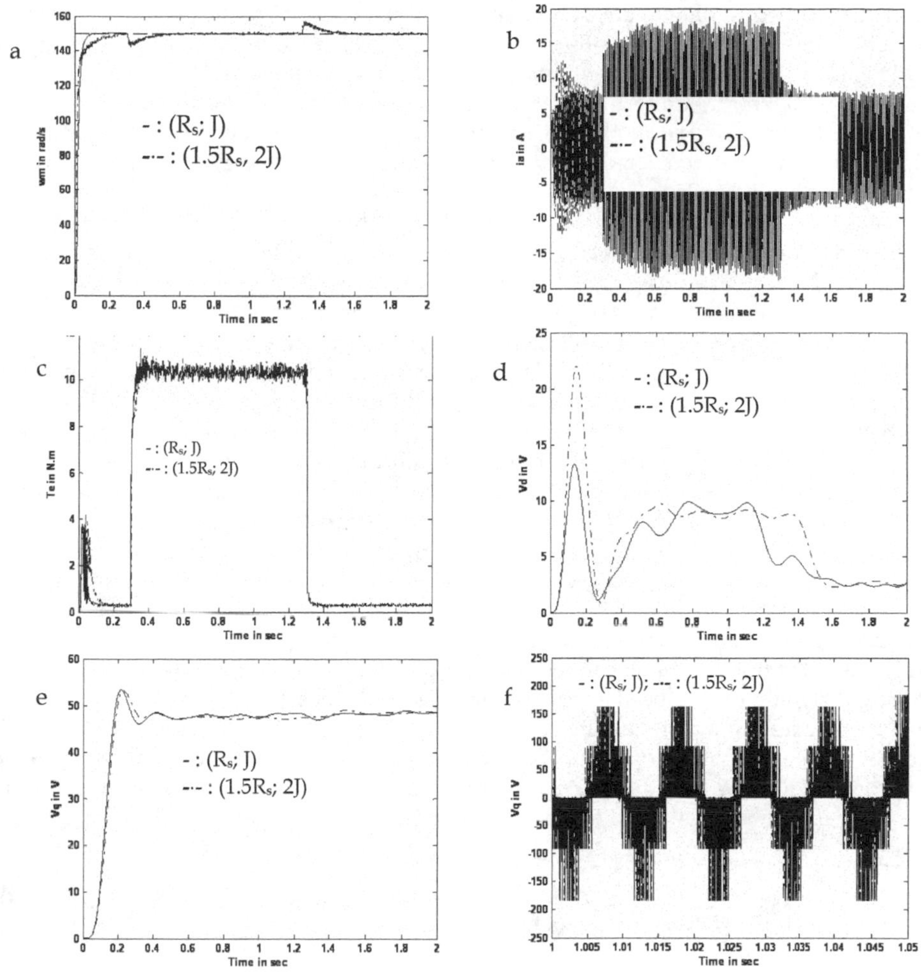

Fig. 8. Motor response to step reference with a change of +50% of the stator winding resistance R_s and a change of +100% of the inertia moment J.

A test of robustness at parameter changes has been performed. As presented in Fig. 8, a simultaneous change of +50% of the stator winding resistance R_s and +100% of the moment inertia J. The change of the stator winding resistance, R_s, affects slightly the dynamic motor response. This is due to the fact that the electrical time constant ρ_f of closed-loop system appearing in Equation (80) is compensated by the imposed damping gain, K_f, from Equation (71). However, a change of +100% inertia moment J increases the mechanical time constant and hence the rotor speed settling time (see Fig. 2.5). The designed PBCC is based only on the electrical part of the PMSM and has no direct compensation effect on the mechanical part.

4. Conclusion

In the section 2, a strategy for designing PMSM control system that requires only rotor position and stator voltage measurements was presented. To this end, the passivity approach to design a controller-observer is adopted. It was shown that this strategy can provide asymptotically stabilizing solutions to the output feedback motor tracking problem. It is shown from simulation results that the robustness of the combined controller-observer with respect to the load and model uncertainties. This is mainly due to the fact that both of the controller and observer exploit the physical structure of the PMSM system and the injection of the high damping.

A new passivity-based speed control law for a PMSM has been developed in the section 3. The proposed control law does not compensate the model workless force terms as they have no effect on the system energy balance. Therefore, the identification of these terms is a key issue in the associated control design. Another feature is that the cancellation of the plant primary dynamics is not done by exact zeroing but by imposing a desired damped transient. The design avoids the using of the Euler-Lagrange model and destructuring (singularities effect) since it uses a flux-based dq-modelling, independent of the rotor angular position. The inner current control loops which have been built using classical PI controllers preserve the passivity property of the current-controlled synchronous machine.

Unlike the majority of the nonlinear control methods used in the PMSM field, this control loop compensates the nonlinearities by means of a damped transient. Its computation aims at imposing the currents set-points based on the flux references in the dq-frame. These latter variables are computed based on the load torque estimation by imposing maximum torque operation conditions.

The speed control law contains a damping term ensuring the system stability and the adjustment of the tracking error convergence speed. The obtained closed-loop system allows exponential zeroing of the speed error, also preserving the passivity property.

Simulation studies show the feasibility and the efficiency of the proposed controller. This controller can be easily included into control structures developed for current-fed induction motor commonly used in industrial applications. Its relatively simple structure should not involve significant hardware and software implementation constraints.

Appendix 1

R_a= 2 Ω; R_m ; 0.00019 Nm/rd/s; λ_m =0.2 Wb ; n_p=2 ; L_d=3.1 mH; L_q= 3.1 mH; D_m=0.024 Kgm2; I_n=15 A; V_n=250 V; P_n=3.75 KW; N=4000 r n/mn.

Appendix 2

Rated power = 6 Kw; Rated speed = 3000 rpm; Stator winding resistance = 173.77 e-3 Ω ; Stator winding direct inductance = 0.8524 e-3 H; Stator winding quadrate inductance = 0.9515 e-3 H; Rotor flux = 0.1112 Wb; Viscous friction = 0.0085 Nm/rad/s; Inertia = 48 e-4 kg.m^2; Pairs pole number = 4; Nominal current line = 31 A; Nominal voltage line = 310 V and the machine type is Siemens 1FT6084-8SK71-1TGO.

5. References

Achour, AY.; Mendil, B. (2007). Commande basée sur la passivité associée aux modes de glissements d'un moteur synchrone à aimants permanents. *JESA*, vol.41, No3-4, April 2007), pp 311-332, ISBN 978-2-7462-1854-3

Ailon, A.; Ortega, R. (1993). An observer-based set-point controller for robot manipulators with flexible joints. *System Control Literature* 1993, vol.21, No.4, (October 1993), pp 329-335

Arnold, V I. (1989). *Mathematical Methods of Classical mechanics*, Springer, ISBN 0-387-96890-3, New York, USA, 1989

Berghis, H.; Nijmeijer, H. (1993). A passivity approach to controller-observer design for robots. *IEEE Transaction on robotic and automatic,* vol.9, No.6, (December 1993), pp-754, ISSN 1042-296X

Gökder, LU.; Simaan, MA. (1997). A passivity-based control method for Induction motor control. *IEEE Transactions on Industrial Electrical.* Vol.44, No.5, (October 1997), pp 688-695, ISSN 0278-0046

Kim, KC.; Ortega, R.; Charara, A.; Vilain, JP. (1997). Theoretical and experimental Comparison of two nonlinear controllers for current-fed induction motors. *IEEE Transactions on Control System Techniques*, vol.5, No.5, (May 1997), pp 338-348, ISSN 1063-6536

Ortega, R.; Spong, M. (1989). Adaptive motion control of rigid robots: A tutorial, *Automatica,* vol.25, No.6, (November 1989), pp 877-888

Ortega, R.; Nicklasson, PJ.; Espinoza–Pérez, G. (1996). On speed control of induction motors, *Automatica,* vol.3, No.3, (March 1996), pp 455-466

Ortega, R.; Nicklasson, PJ.; Espinoza–Pérez, G. (1997). Passivity-based controller of a Class of Blondel-Park transformable electric machines, *IEEE Transactions on Automatic Control,* vol.42, No.5, (May 1997), pp 629-647, ISSN 0018-9286

Ortega, R.; Loria, A.; Nicklasson, PJ. (1998). *Passivity-based control of Euler-Lagrange systems*, , ISBN 1-85233-016-3, New York, USA, 1998

Ortega, R.; García-Canseco, E. (2004). Interconnection and damping assignment passivity-Based control: Towards a constructive procedure-Part I, *Proceedings of 43rd IEEE conference on Decision and Control,* pp 3412-3417, ISBN 0-7803-8682-5, Atlantis, Island, Bahamas, December 14-17, 2004

Ortega, R.; García-Canseco, E. (2004). Interconnection and damping assignment passivity-Based control: Towards a constructive procedure-Part II, *Proceedings of 43rd IEEE conference on Decision and Control,* pp 3418-3423, ISBN 0-7803-8682-5, Atlantis, Paradise Island, Bahamas, December 14-17, 2004

Petrović, V.; Ortega, R.; Stanković, AM. (2001). Interconnection and damping assignment approach to control of Pm synchronous motors, *IEEE Transactions on Control System Techniques,* vol.9, No.6, (November 2001), pp 811-820, ISSN 1063-6536

Qiu, J.; Zhao, G. (2006). PMSM control with port-controlled Hamiltonian theory, *Proceedings of 1st International Conference on Innovative Computing, Information and Control (ICICIC'06),* pp 275-278, ISBN 0-7695-2616-0, Ville, Pay, August 30-31, 2006

Sira-Ramirez, H.; Ortega, R.; Perez-Moreno, R. ; Garcia-Esteban, M. (1995). A sliding mode controller-observer for DC-to-DC power converters: a passivity approach, *Proceedings* 34th IEEE conference on Decision and Control, pp 3379-3384, ISBN 0-7803-2685-7, New Orleans, LA, 13-15 December, 1995

Sudhoff, S.; Wasynczuk, O.; SD Krause, PC. (2002). *Analysis of electric machinery and drive Systems*, Wiley-IEEE Press, ISBN 9780470544167, New York, USA, 2002.

Takegaki, M.; Arimoto, S. (1981). A new feedback for dynamic control of manipulators, *Transaction of the ASME, Journal of Dynamic Systems Measurements Control*, vol. 103,.2, (June 1981), pp 119-125

Travieso-Torres, JC.; Duarte Mermoud, MA. ; Estrada, JL. (2006). Tracking control of cascade Systems based on passivity: The non-adaptive and adaptive cases, *ISA Transactions*, Vol.45, No.3, (July 2006), pp 435-445

Travieso-Torres, JC.; Duarte Mermoud, MA. (2008). Two simple and novel SISO controllers for induction motors based on adaptive passivity, *ISA Transactions*, vol.47, No.1, (January 2008), pp 60-79

Van der Schaft, A. (2000). *L_2-Gain and Passivity Techniques in Nonlinear Control*, Springer, ISBN 1-85233-073-2, London, King Doom, 2000

Permissions

The contributors of this book come from diverse backgrounds, making this book a truly international effort. This book will bring forth new frontiers with its revolutionizing research information and detailed analysis of the nascent developments around the world.

We would like to thank Andreas Mueller, for lending his expertise to make the book truly unique. He has played a crucial role in the development of this book. Without his invaluable contribution this book wouldn't have been possible. He has made vital efforts to compile up to date information on the varied aspects of this subject to make this book a valuable addition to the collection of many professionals and students.

This book was conceptualized with the vision of imparting up-to-date information and advanced data in this field. To ensure the same, a matchless editorial board was set up. Every individual on the board went through rigorous rounds of assessment to prove their worth. After which they invested a large part of their time researching and compiling the most relevant data for our readers. Conferences and sessions were held from time to time between the editorial board and the contributing authors to present the data in the most comprehensible form. The editorial team has worked tirelessly to provide valuable and valid information to help people across the globe.

Every chapter published in this book has been scrutinized by our experts. Their significance has been extensively debated. The topics covered herein carry significant findings which will fuel the growth of the discipline. They may even be implemented as practical applications or may be referred to as a beginning point for another development. Chapters in this book were first published by InTech; hereby published with permission under the Creative Commons Attribution License or equivalent.

The editorial board has been involved in producing this book since its inception. They have spent rigorous hours researching and exploring the diverse topics which have resulted in the successful publishing of this book. They have passed on their knowledge of decades through this book. To expedite this challenging task, the publisher supported the team at every step. A small team of assistant editors was also appointed to further simplify the editing procedure and attain best results for the readers.

Our editorial team has been hand-picked from every corner of the world. Their multi-ethnicity adds dynamic inputs to the discussions which result in innovative outcomes. These outcomes are then further discussed with the researchers and contributors who give their valuable feedback and opinion regarding the same. The feedback is then collaborated with the researches and they are edited in a comprehensive manner to aid the understanding of the subject.

Apart from the editorial board, the designing team has also invested a significant amount of their time in understanding the subject and creating the most relevant covers. They scrutinized every image to scout for the most suitable representation of the subject and create an appropriate cover for the book.

The publishing team has been involved in this book since its early stages. They were actively engaged in every process, be it collecting the data, connecting with the contributors or procuring relevant information. The team has been an ardent support to the editorial, designing and production team. Their endless efforts to recruit the best for this project, has resulted in the accomplishment of this book. They are a veteran in the field of academics and their pool of knowledge is as vast as their experience in printing. Their expertise and guidance has proved useful at every step. Their uncompromising quality standards have made this book an exceptional effort. Their encouragement from time to time has been an inspiration for everyone.

The publisher and the editorial board hope that this book will prove to be a valuable piece of knowledge for researchers, students, practitioners and scholars across the globe.

List of Contributors

Seddik M. Djouadi
Electrical Engineering & Computer Science Department, University of Tennessee, Knoxville, TN 37996-2100, USA

César Elizondo-González
Facultad de Ingeniería Mecánica y Eléctrica, Universidad Autónoma de Nuevo León, México

Eitaku Nobuyama and Takahiko Aoyagi
Kyushu Institute of Technology, Japan

Yasushi Kami
Akashi National College of Technology, Japan

Cheng-Lun Chen
National Chung Hsing University, Taiwan, R.O.C.

George T.-C. Chiu
Purdue University, West Lafayette, USA

Hossein Oloomi
Department of Electrical & Computer Engineering, Purdue University at Fort Wayne, USA

Bahram Shafai
Department of Electrical & Computer Engineering, Northeastern University, USA

Yasushi Kami and Eitaku Nobuyama
Akashi National College of Technology and Kyushu Institute of Technology, Japan

Tatsuo Narikiyo and Michihiro Kawanishi
Toyota Technological Institute, Japan

A. Luis Rodríguez and Yu Tang
National University of Mexico, Mexico

Andreas Mueller
University Duisburg-Essen, Chair of Mechanics and Robotics, Germany

Takayuki Kuwashima, Jun Imai and Masami Konishi
Okayama University, Japan

Recep Burkan
Istanbul University, Faculty of Engineering, Mechanical Engineering Department, Istanbul, Turkey

Changzhu Wei, Yi Shen, Naigang Cui and Jifeng Guo
Harbin Institute of Technology, Harbin, China

Changzhu Wei
Yonsei University Observatory, Seoul, Republic of Korea

Xiaoxiao Ma
Xuzhou Air Force College, Xuzhou, China

Huangfu Yigeng and Liu Weiguo
Northwestern Polytechnical University, China

S. Laghrouche and A. Miraoui
University of Technology of Belfort-Montbéliard, France

Birou M.T. Iulian
Technical University of Cluj-Napcoa, Department of Electrical Drives and Robots, Romania

Paolo Mercorelli
Faculty of Automotive Engineering, Ostfalia University of Applied Sciences, Germany

Ahmed Tahour
University of Mascara, Algeria

Abdel Ghani Aissaoui
IRECOM Laboratory, University of Sidi Bel Abbes, Algeria

Carlos Olalla, Abdelali El Aroudi and Ramon Leyva
Universitat Rovira i Virgili, 43007 Tarragona, Spain

Isabelle Queinnec
CNRS ; LAAS ; 7 avenue du colonel Roche, F-31077 Toulouse Cedex 4, Université de Toulouse ; UPS, INSA, INP, ISAE, UT1, UTM, LAAS, F-31077 Toulouse Cedex 4, France

Andrea Tilli, Lorenzo Marconi and Christian Conficoni
Center for Complex Automated Systems (CASY) Dept. of Electronics, Computer Engineering and Systems (DEIS), University of Bologna, Viale Risorgimento n.2, 40136 Bologna, Italy

CPSIA information can be obtained
at www.ICGtesting.com
Printed in the USA
LVHW081000041020
667873LV00002B/11

9 781632 402004